MINOT-SLEEPER LIBRARY
Bristol
New Hampshire

Open Monday and Wednesday
1 to 8 p.m.
Friday, 3 to 8 p.m.
Saturday, 9 a.m. to 3 p.m.

Time. Books may be kept 14 days.

Renewals. A book may be renewed for another 14 days on application, unless it is reserved for another borrower.

Fines. Two cents a day for each book kept overtime. If kept two weeks overtime, a book may be sent for at the borrower's expense.

If a person loses or materially injures a book, he shall make good the loss or damage in such way as the Librarian or Trustees may direct. Failure to pay fines of assessments for loss or damage shall debar from use of the Library.

FOOTPRINTS OF THE PAST:

IMAGES OF
CORNISH, NEW HAMPSHIRE
&
THE CORNISH COLONY

by

Virginia Reed Colby

&

James B. Atkinson

Virginia H. Colby

Jim Atkinson

New Hampshire Historical Society
Concord, New Hampshire

Published by the New Hampshire Historical Society and George Reed, II.

ISBN 0-915916-22-3

Library of Congress Catalog Card Number: 96-71064

Dust jacket photographs: *Augusta Saint-Gaudens* by Thomas Wilmer Dewing; *Gnome Costume Design* by Maxfield Parrish; *Cornish-Windsor Bridge* by Edward Seager, 1848; *Saint-Gaudens's Garden* by Edith Prellwitz; *Landscape, Cornish, New Hampshire,* painted by John White Alexander.

Frontispiece: Eric Pape's painting of *A Masque of "Ours": The Gods and the Golden Bowl.* In creating this scene, Pape used individual photographs of the actors in costume and in these poses. We have used some of these individual photographs to illustrate the appropriate chapters in the Cornish Colony section of this book.

TABLE OF CONTENTS

Dedicated to the memory of

Herbert P. Reed

&

Stanley W. Colby

and in honor of my son,

George Morton Reed, II

who has encouraged me all the way.

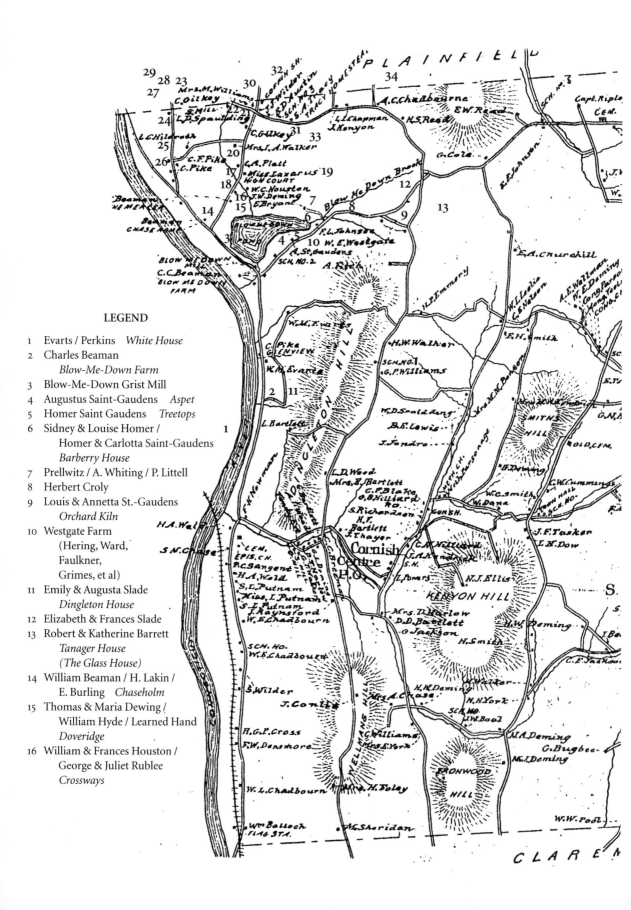

LEGEND

1. Evarts / Perkins *White House*
2. Charles Beaman
     Blow-Me-Down Farm
3. Blow-Me-Down Grist Mill
4. Augustus Saint-Gaudens *Aspet*
5. Homer Saint Gaudens *Treetops*
6. Sidney & Louise Homer /
     Homer & Carlotta Saint-Gaudens
     Barberry House
7. Prellwitz / A. Whiting / P. Littell
8. Herbert Croly
9. Louis & Annetta St.-Gaudens
     Orchard Kiln
10. Westgate Farm
     (Hering, Ward,
     Faulkner,
     Grimes, et al)
11. Emily & Augusta Slade
     Dingleton House
12. Elizabeth & Frances Slade
13. Robert & Katherine Barrett
     Tanager House
     (The Glass House)
14. William Beaman / H. Lakin /
     E. Burling *Chaseholm*
15. Thomas & Maria Dewing /
     William Hyde / Learned Hand
     Doveridge
16. William & Frances Houston /
     George & Juliet Rublee
     Crossways

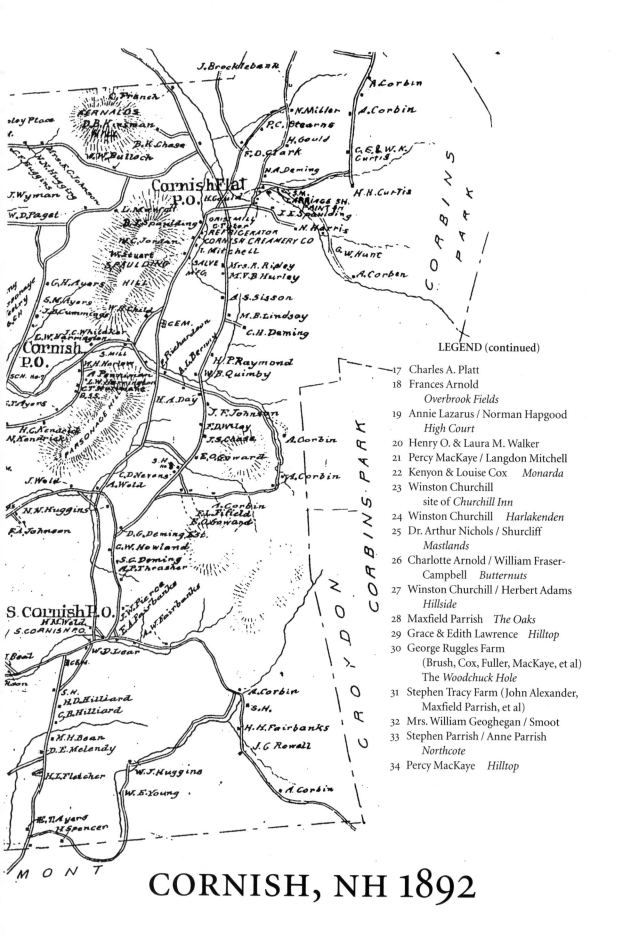

LEGEND (continued)

17 Charles A. Platt
18 Frances Arnold
    Overbrook Fields
19 Annie Lazarus / Norman Hapgood
    High Court
20 Henry O. & Laura M. Walker
21 Percy MacKaye / Langdon Mitchell
22 Kenyon & Louise Cox   *Monarda*
23 Winston Churchill
    site of *Churchill Inn*
24 Winston Churchill   *Harlakenden*
25 Dr. Arthur Nichols / Shurcliff
    Mastlands
26 Charlotte Arnold / William Fraser-
    Campbell   *Butternuts*
27 Winston Churchill / Herbert Adams
    Hillside
28 Maxfield Parrish   *The Oaks*
29 Grace & Edith Lawrence   *Hilltop*
30 George Ruggles Farm
    (Brush, Cox, Fuller, MacKaye, et al)
    The *Woodchuck Hole*
31 Stephen Tracy Farm (John Alexander,
    Maxfield Parrish, et al)
32 Mrs. William Geoghegan / Smoot
33 Stephen Parrish / Anne Parrish
    Northcote
34 Percy MacKaye   *Hilltop*

CORNISH, NH 1892

PREFACE

FOOTPRINTS OF THE PAST is the culmination of my mother's passion, over the past twenty-three years, for Cornish and its multifaceted history. Fortunately for all of us, she completed her manuscript prior to her sudden passing in April of 1995; we are confident this passion accounted for her vitality, determination, and enthusiasm to the end. Thanks to the dedication of her publishing "team"—Dr. Carrie Brown, John Dryfhout, Barbara Homeyer, Frank Lather, and Nancy Norwalk, to name a few—there was never a doubt that these efforts would go to print.

My mother was especially grateful to Dr. James B. Atkinson for his dedication to the Cornish Historical Society (taking over the reins as president in 1993) and for his essential contributions to this work, first as editor of what was initially conceived as a collection of Cornish profiles and ultimately as co-author of this more ambitious reference document. Jim has integrated his own thoughtful perspective on Cornish and the Cornish Colony, all the while being sensitive to preserve Virginia's style and spirit—no small feat for an accomplished author, yet no surprise to those who know him. (To plagiarize his metaphor, herein you will find the "footprints" of both Virginia Colby and Jim Atkinson.)

I continue to learn lessons from my mother that reach beyond Cornish history: an ever-growing appreciation for her years of inquisitiveness and detective work; her tenacity in combing old records and source material; her careful attention to the details of events long passed; her insistence on accuracy and thoroughness, balanced by a respect for the privacy of residents and Colony members; her years of dedication to the Cornish Historical Society and other organizations; her respect for and appreciation of the town of Cornish (its participatory government traditions, as well as its beautiful landscape); her selfless enthusiasm in assisting the many historians who sought information and her generosity in sharing with others what she had learned; and, most of all, her modesty and unassuming nature. Virginia Hunt Colby proves quite a role model!

It is important to acknowledge others who lent vital support and inspiration to my mother, and to her memory, including Anna, Bea, Betsy, Hannah, Gerry, Gordon, Marion, Orville, and Yvonne.

George M. Reed
White Swan Farm
Cornish, New Hampshire

Summer 1996

ACKNOWLEDGEMENTS

THIS BOOK IS THE RESULT of my long and pleasant association with the Cornish, New Hampshire Historical Society. In 1973, while on a trip west with my husband, Herbert Reed, I was elected president (in absentia) of the newly formed historical society. Herb had just been diagnosed with leukemia and I was still in shock, not knowing what lay before me; Herb was delighted at my election, believing it would offer a preoccupation and fill a void. He offered me much encouragement and support.

One evening, not long after my election, a Dr. Stearns telephoned me in my capacity as "historian," asking me what I knew about a Dr. Nathan Smith, as he was writing a book on doctors in Sullivan County. I had to admit, at that time, I had never heard of Nathan Smith. Upon researching Dr. Smith, I found a fascinating character, a strong leader, a man with the stuff of which our early settlers were made. This exercise really whetted my appetite for learning as much as I could about early Cornish.

In the 1980s I started writing a weekly column for the *Windsor Chronicle* under the title "Footprints of the Past" based on topics related to Cornish history. My second husband, Stan Colby, raised in neighboring Plainfield, gave me lots of encouragement, not to mention suggestions for topics. The column proved fun and challenging; those research efforts serve as a foundation for much of this book. (As an aside, little of the original source material from that research has been edited; many quotations retain their contemporary spellings and punctuation, which may appear odd to today's reader but are historically accurate.)

I am indebted to James B. Atkinson, Ph.D., for his very thoughtful and painstaking work on this book, which made it what it is; to Gretchen Holm, Judith Nyhus, John Dryfhout, and Greg Schwartz for proofreading, editing, and research assistance; Nancy Norwalk for typing, proofreading, and advice; Barbara Homeyer for her layout and publishing expertise; and Jeffrey Nintzel for photography.

At the risk of overlooking someone, I would also like to acknowledge the contributions and support of Christy MacKaye Barnes, Virginia Lopez Begg, Lucy Ruggles Bishop, Walter Breckenridge, Dr. Gregory G. Brunk, Mary Cassedy, William Chadbourne, Beatrice Bishop Clark, William S. Clark, Katherine Conlin, Allyn Cox, Dr. Philip Cronenwett, Anne Curfman, Elizabeth deVeer, Frances Eastman, Rosamond Taylor Edmondson, Lee Fenner, Elisabeth Donaghy Garrett, Deborah VanBuren Gourevitch, Susan Hobbs, Laird Klinger, Susan Littell, Whittemore Littell, John Manship, Bonnie McAdam, Wayne McCutcheon, Polly Monette, H. Wayne Morgan, Jill Nooney, Carol Odell, Alan Penfold, Kathleen Pyne, Marguerite Lewin Quimby, Albert K. Read, III, Kathleen Philbrick Read, Patricia Ronan, Dolly Thrasher Russell, Rona Schneider, Jacqueline W. Smith, Major Eric Steinbaugh, Pringle Hart Symonds, Anthony Bacon Venti, Ruth Wood, Virginia Wood, and Claudia Yatsevitch.

Virginia Hunt Colby
White Swan Farm
Cornish, New Hampshire

April 1995

FOREWORD

THE NEW HAMPSHIRE HISTORICAL SOCIETY takes great pleasure in publishing this wonderful book on Cornish, New Hampshire, and the Cornish Colony. Simply put, *Footprints of the Past* is a beautiful book about a time and a place that nurtured the creative spirit in many significant American artists. Many of us know and enjoy the art done by Maxfield Parrish, Augustus Saint-Gaudens, and Kenyon Cox as well as the commentary and humor from the likes of Herbert Croly and Finley Peter Dunne. This book brings together for the first time the biographies and stories about hundreds of Cornish Colony artists, writers, musicians, and philosophers whose creative impulses have shaped American art and culture since the mid-nineteenth century. Not only do we learn about these artists and their families, we also learn about the relationships they had with one another during their time in Cornish and elsewhere.

This book's appearance is the result of Virginia Reed Colby's work of nearly twenty years, of the tenacity of a group of people brought together by her son, George Reed, to see the work completed, and of the ability of the New Hampshire Historical Society to serve as publisher of this important new work in New Hampshire history. *Footprints of the Past* is local history at its best. After examining Cornish history, the book shifts its focus to the Cornish Colony. Thus we are able to imagine, from story to story, the incredible impact that the New Hampshire landscape has had upon the artistic spirit; we can also sense the nurturing effect that this "circle of friends" has had on one another. As James B. Atkinson so aptly points out, this book reminds us "that greatness has passed through Cornish and left its imprint on the town." We are all fortunate to have *Footprints* to help us visit Cornish and the Cornish Colony many more times in the future.

Michael P. Chaney, Editor
Historical New Hampshire

September 1996

INTRODUCTION

BECAUSE THE ORIENTATION OF *Footprints of the Past* is primarily biographic, its intention can easily be summarized in a quatrain from Longfellow's "A Psalm of Life":

> Lives of great men all remind us
> We can make our lives sublime.
> And, departing, leave behind us
> Footprints on the sands of time.

The brief vignettes in this book are not meant to be read as formal history; they are reminders that greatness has passed through Cornish and left its imprint on the town. In addition to jogging our memories with some idea of where we have been, the notion of footprints also provides some idea of the direction in which we are headed. A footprint, after all, is an impression, a trace, a track—shadowy evidence of someone's presence. As such, a footprint has often served as a clue to solving a mystery. Footprints can provocatively suggest that there is a story in need of reconstruction.

The metaphorical footprints of Cornish's past appear in two tantalizing sets. Instead of these being parallel, however, we discover a double image: one set lies nested within another. That they were made at different times suggests the very plot threads that this book sets out to delineate. Late eighteenth-century and most of nineteenth-century Cornish thrived as an agricultural and light-industrial community; it defines the first plot line. The suggestive evidence of footprints that this group left is first apparent in the pioneering spirit of the original settlers. Members of the Chase family, beginning with Judge Samuel Chase and descending through Jonathan, Philander, and Salmon P. Chase, set a high standard. In the next century a varied group of grateful followers, with activities ranging from Nathan Smith's contributions to medicine to James Tasker's innovations in bridge construction, took that initial legacy of fearlessness and developed a forward-looking sense of what the land and its people could achieve. A similar sense of progress characterized some of the local footprints that imprinted places in Cornish (its bridges and buildings) and things associated with Cornish (its celebrations and its turnpikes). With the series of economic depressions that paradoxically characterized the Gilded Age of late nineteenth-century America, however, came the depletion of the original financial supports for the town. This community, with its indomitable spirit, thus left the first set of footprints for us to examine.

The second plot line begins when a second set of footprints can be discerned within those that this battered community left. Taking their cue from the resoluteness of early Cornish residents, a group of artists and writers made their way to the area because houses and land were readily available. Their story, an integral part of Cornish's past, also needs to be told. Searching for a quiet, beautiful place in which to nurture their creative spirits, they were delighted to leave their set of prints. Similar to the birds from which they took their nicknames, "chickadees" like the MacKayes and Fullers and Shipmans left footprints that were visible all year long; other couples like the Adamses and Coxes were content to leave theirs only during the summer months. Yet the footprints of the Colony collectively help us to recollect that this artistic community was rooted in a conviction perfectly consonant with the Cornish past that nourished it, namely, that the nobility of its artistic creations was a merited, not an inherited, achievement.

These two separate plot lines define the narrative threads this book relates. Its various vignettes tell the story of what happened when two ostensibly disparate groups came together at what turned out to be a crucial juncture for them both. With a modicum of friction and fuss, artists and writers with similar interests and concerns, and many with a significant national reputation, found themselves easily and gracefully able to connect with a locality rich in the virtues—both human and natural—that both groups mutually admired. The narrative recounts how the former, in effect, superimposed their footprints on already existing ones. Throughout its rich history, partly enforced by a geographic division between activities carried out in the hills and those done in valleys, the town of Cornish has possessed its own unique sense of unity. Thus the two divisions of *Footprints of the Past*—one describing the people, places, and things of Cornish and the other detailing the second group of Cornish Colonists—mirror and actually encapsulate the narrative of the town's history.

This book will have fulfilled its aim if its readers are able to discern the footprints that evoke the two-fold story of the town's past. For the evidence of these footprints to be useful in any meaningful way, it needs to be augmented by solid facts so that its readers will build on this reconstruction of the past. And in so doing, they will create not only a greater understanding of their heritage but also a more concrete sense of where that heritage might lead them.

Invaluable contributions to this effort already exist in William H. Child's two-volume *History of the Town of Cornish* (1911) and Hugh Mason Wade's, *A Brief History of Cornish 1763-1974* (1976; reprinted in 1991). The former book is essential for the facts about the people, places, and things in Cornish's past; the latter skillfully sets the Cornish colony in context and provides helpful interpretations of Child's material. A useful example of each historian's method, and how it differs from the one followed in this book, can be seen in the treatment of the visit of President Theodore Roosevelt to Cornish Flat in August of 1902. Child and Wade both cite a speech he delivered before the Soldiers' Monument in Cornish Flat to a crowd including children from the local schools and veterans of the Civil War:

> I cannot think of anything that augurs better for the country than in just such a typical old American town as this to have the school children drawn up before a monument like that (pointing to the Soldiers' Monument) in the town which was the birthplace of Salmon P. Chase, and to have them look towards *you*, the veterans of the great Civil War, *you* who have proved your truth by your endeavor, and to see in *you* an example of what they are to be when they grow up. . . . I think there is but one class of people who deserve as well as the soldiers, and these are they who teach their children of the present how to be the masters of our country in the future.

Child quotes the brief speech in its entirety and Wade quotes judiciously from it. However, this book's chapter about Roosevelt's visit to Cornish and Windsor excludes this quotation even though there is much in it to comment upon—what it says, how it says it, and why both historians refer to it. Despite its intrinsic interest, it is absent from the chapter below precisely because this book aims to point out "footprints" that have escaped previous scrutiny. So, President Roosevelt's visit is described by quoting extensively from a contemporary newspaper account that is not readily available. Perforce, there are references in what follows to both historians as well as to Barbara Eastman Rawson's third volume of the Cornish history published in 1963, but this examination of Cornish's people, places, and things does not seek to reexamine the content of these earlier works. Generally speaking, this book follows the procedure established in the example of President Roosevelt's visit to Cornish. It seeks to remind its readers about less familiar aspects of the past, not to reiterate them. There are occasions when Child's prose offers its own pleasure, even sly humor; for example, it has been worked into the chapter about the background of the town office buildings. The book's method will have succeeded if it whets the reader's appetite to explore further Cornish's many historical crannies. The numerous mills that once dotted the Cornish landscape are a case in point. Their imprints, in the form of visible cellar holes, should prompt our collective memories. These footprints still bear witness, still have much to teach.

Finally, the footprints left by people, places, and things in Cornish provide a needed background for the second section of the book focused on the Cornish Colony. They set the tone and defined the landscape—both natural and human—that fostered the Colony. Artist colonies have sprouted all over America for a variety of reasons—some fortuitous, some financial. But surely the traditions symbolized in the footprints of Cornish's people, places, and things were what secured Beaman's promise to Saint-Gaudens that the sculptor would find "plenty of Lincoln-shaped men" in this particular human and natural landscape.

James B. Atkinson

Defining the Landscape:

Cornish, New Hampshire

People, Places & Things

Figure 1 (reverse): *Workmen at the sawmill of the Blue Mountain Forest Association, Corbin's Park, early twentieth century.*

ELMER WOOD
BARTLETT

1874 – 1965

Figure 2.

ALTHOUGH ELMER WOOD BARTLETT was not an artist associated with the Cornish Colony, he made significant contributions to the local art scene. He was born August 11, 1874, in the brick house on Dingleton Hill in Cornish where he would remain for the rest of his life. His father, Edwin, was a farmer and a music teacher, and his mother was Emeline Wood Bartlett. Elmer attended Kimball Union Academy and Windsor High School.

His interest in art began with photography; he became expert in the art of taking and developing pictures. His photographs provide vital details of country life in Cornish. But Elmer Bartlett is most widely known for his reverse painting on glass which he did on clock faces, mirrors, and lamp shades. He also painted many local scenes and was adept at wood carving. A sample of his wood carving may be seen at the George H. Stowell Library in Cornish Flat.

He was also an active member of the community. He taught school at several of the one-room schools in Cornish: Dingleton Hill, Beaman District, Tracy, City, and Goward. Activities concerned with music, however, were his favorites. He served as organist at the Methodist Church in Windsor for nearly thirty years, he played the flute in the Cornish Drum Corps, and he sang in a local quartet. For many years this quartet, comprising his brother Arthur and the Quimby twins, Elwin and Erwin, was featured at the annual Old Home Day programs.

On the event of his ninetieth birthday, Elmer Bartlett was the honored senior citizen chosen by the Cornish Grange No. 25.[1] He held the Boston Post Cane for several years. He died in 1965 at the age of ninety-one and is buried in Comings Cemetery on Root Hill Road.[2]

ENDNOTES

1. Virginia Colby, telephone interview with Ginny and Ruth Wood, May 25, 1992.
2. Virginia Colby, telephone interview with Polly Monette, May 25, 1992.

Figure 3. *Painting of the Bartlett homestead on Dingleton Hill by Elmer Bartlett; oil on birch bark.*

JONATHAN CHASE
1732 – 1800

Figure 4. *General Jonathan Chase (1732–1800). Nineteenth-century copy of an eighteenth-century portrait attributed to Joseph Steward.*

JONATHAN CHASE was born in Sutton, Massachusetts, in 1732 and migrated to Cornish, New Hampshire, in 1765 at the time the town was settled. He devoted himself actively to the interests of the new community; he became a land proprietor, farmer, and surveyor. Chase was responsible for the first store, the first inn, as well as the first sawmill and gristmill in the area.

The unrest of the colonial times—among the settlers themselves and with the skirmishes of the 1750s and 1760s between the French and the Native American population—prompted Chase to organize and lead a militia drawn from Cornish and its vicinity. On August 30, 1775, his outstanding leadership qualities led the Assembly to confer upon him the commission of colonel of the territorial regiment that included the towns of Hanover, Lebanon, Lyme, Orford, Cornish, and Plainfield, NH.[1]

By orders of Major General Horatio Gates, then commander of Fort Ticonderoga, Chase marched with his regiment from Cheshire County to reinforce the troops at Ticonderoga in October of 1776. He again marched to reinforce the northern Continental Army at Saratoga in 1777, a distance of 110 miles that they covered on foot in only three days. Judge Samuel Chase served in his son's regiment.[2] A letter to his wife Sarah (Hall) Chase dated June 1777 gives a good account of his life at the front:

There is Nothing Remarkable with us as to News I Expect to be Discharged in a few Days have this Day obtain a Discharg for 27 men: Dresser & Whiden are got home I sopose thay Desarted and are REturned as such it is a helthy time in the Army: my Regement are chefely well save some who has got the meezels But None as yet Dangeros: the Enemy Came down ye other Day as far as Split Rock whar thay understood by the Inhabetance the meleshe was arived in Grate Numbers five New 100 Canon and Returnd By the Best Acompts we can git: thare is Now 4 or 5 Scouts out Some of which Bound to Canada one Came in hesterday from Beyond Split Rock mad no Discoverys of the Enemy we Expect General Sant Clare Every our tis thoat we shall be Relesd when He arives—

I am as Harty as the Day is long Have Not had an Day sence I left Home for which I

Desire & Have abondence cawse to Bless God: I hope you & all frined are well may the good Lord presarve our Lives & Helth & Grante in Due time we may se oneanother in Pese I am in grate Hast can ad no more am yours &C - &C - &C

Jon[th] Chase

June 8th 1777
To Mis Sale Chase etc - etc - etc[3]

After the war, Chase was appointed brigadier-general on Governor John Langdon's staff. John Langdon was instrumental in getting New Hampshire to be the ninth—and crucial—state to ratify the Constitution of the United States, June 21, 1788. In 1789, under the same rank and title, Chase was appointed to the staff of Governor Pickering.[4] By virtue of these appointments, and supported by a splendid military record, his claim to the title of "general" was undisputed; this title he ever afterwards bore.[5]

Turning to town affairs, Chase served as selectman for nine years, as treasurer for three years, and as representative in the General Assembly in 1788. The general fought for the opening of new highways in town and established the first ferry across the Connecticut River between Cornish and Windsor, Vermont. The ferry operated from 1784 until 1795.

The ferry worked fine in the summer months; but when the river froze in the winter, problems ensued. Chase decided that a toll bridge was needed and went to Concord to appear before the General Court. The trip to Concord took several days by horseback. His account book says he stopped at Adkin's Tavern in Claremont; in Newport, he stayed at Readington and Fisher's; in Sutton, at a tavern run by Kimball; in Warner, at two taverns: Peatte's and Currier's; in Hopkinton, he stopped at Wiggins; and in Concord, his

Figure 5. *Mrs. Jonathan (Sarah Hall) Chase (1742-1806). Nineteenth-century copy of an eighteenth-century portrait attributed to Joseph Steward.*

log listed several—among them was Stickney's Tavern. Chase's trip to Concord was successful.[6] He established the Proprietors of the Cornish Bridge and became the corporation's first president. He held on to control of the corporation through his retention of forty shares; the other eighty shares were sold in various allotments to investors. The shares initially sold for $16.67 each.[7]

Jonathan Chase was married twice and had eleven children. He died January 12, 1800, and is buried in the Trinity Church Cemetery.

ENDNOTES

1. Preface, *General Jonathan Chase (1732-1800) of Cornish, New Hampshire, His Papers,* published by the Cornish Bicentennial Commission (Cornish, NH, 1977); see also William H. Child, *History of the Town of Cornish with Genealogical Record: 1763-1910,* (Concord, NH: The Rumford Press, 1911?; reprinted edition, Spartenburg, SC: The Reprint Company, 1975), Vol. 1, p. 288.

2. John Carroll Chase and George Walter Chamberlain, *Seven Generations of the Descendants of Aquila and Thomas Chase,* reprinted (Somersworth, NH: The New England History Press, 1983), p. 176.

3. *Chase Papers,* p. 159.

4. Hugh Mason Wade, *A Brief History of Cornish 1763-1974* (Hanover, NH: University Press of New England, 1976; reprinted edition, 1991), p. 18; hereinafter cited as Wade, *A Brief History.*

5. *Chase Papers,* p. 188, correspondence dated June 1786.

6. From a talk on "Highways, Turnpikes, and Taverns" given by John Dryfhout to the Cornish and Plainfield Historical Societies at the Plainfield School, February 24, 1987.

7. *A History of the Proprietors of Cornish Bridge and the Cornish, NH-Windsor, VT Covered Toll Bridge (1796-1943),* prepared by the New Hampshire Department of Public Works and Highways, Concord, NH, 1984, p. 4.

Figure 6.

PHILANDER CHASE
1775 – 1852

PHILANDER CHASE, whose name means "lover of mankind," was the youngest son of Dudley and Alice (Corbett) Chase; he was born in Cornish on December 14, 1775. He graduated from Dartmouth College in 1795. While he was there, he came across an Episcopal Book of Common Prayer in the chapel and his study of it resulted in his conversion.

Philander Chase then convinced his family and neighbors to conform to the doctrine and practices of the Episcopal Church. In 1793 they cooperated in drawing up an "Instrument of Association." The first wardens of the parish were Ithamar Chase, father of Salmon P. Chase, and General Jonathan Chase, uncle of Philander. In 1795 the church was incorporated as Trinity Church in the Diocese of New Hampshire. The present church building was erected in 1808 by a local carpenter and builder, Philip Tabor. It was purchased and restored in 1984 by Peter Burling.

Chase served the Episcopal Church in various capacities in New York state, Louisiana, and Connecticut. The first person Philander Chase baptized after he became a minister was James Fenimore Cooper's sister. Since the Protestant Episcopal Church had barely established itself in America, Chase decided to devote his energies to missionary work. He saw a need for organizing new parishes. So, in 1817 he headed out for the wilds of Ohio; on February 11, 1819, he was consecrated as the first bishop of Ohio. Chase saw a need for a college to educate men for the priesthood in the Episcopal Church. Realizing the need for funds, he thought of soliciting help from the mother church in England. Few people on either side of the Atlantic thought this was a good idea. Nevertheless, he obtained a letter of introduction from his friend Henry Clay, the statesman and orator, to Lord Gambier in England. Eventually Bishop Chase persuaded the English Church officials to support his cause. Chase raised $30,000 on this trip to England. It was even said that "England had not seen such a bishop in a thousand years."[1]

Eight thousand acres of land was then purchased in Knox County, Ohio. Land was cleared and buildings were constructed. The hill on which the college was located was called "Gambier Hill" in honor of Lord Gambier of England who had made large gifts. The college was named "Kenyon College" in honor of Lord Kenyon, who was the largest donor. It was formally opened in 1828. At first there were twenty-five students. Board cost $1.25 a week and tuition was $10 a year for grammar school and $20 a year for college. By 1829 there were seventy-five pupils. Chase undertook to direct operations of the college along with the entire 8,000 acres. George Franklin Smythe wrote the following poem in his honor:

The first of Kenyon's goodly race
Was that great man, Philander Chase;
He climbed the Hill and said a prayer,
and founded Kenyon College there.

He dug up stones, he chopped down trees,
He sailed across the stormy seas,
And begged at every noble's door,
And also that of Hannah More.

The king, the queen, the lords, the earls,
They gave their crowns, they gave their pearls,
Until Philander had enough,
And hurried homeward with the stuff.

He built the College, built the dam,
He milked the cow, he smoked the ham,
He taught the classes, rang the bell,
And spanked the naughty freshmen well.

And thus he worked with all his might,
For Kenyon College day and night;
And Kenyon's heart still holds a place
Of love for old Philander Chase.

Chase wanted to establish the college as a religious institution for the education of clergy and lay members of the Protestant Episcopal Church. The trustees, on the other hand, wanted it established as a college for general education. This caused a split and Chase resigned as president in 1832. Needless to say, Kenyon College is still going strong.

Chase moved to Michigan but was soon called to be Bishop of Illinois. His dreams were of another college. He again journeyed to England and raised money, this time only $9,480. Once he had purchased 3,160 acres of land in Peoria County, he built and named "Jubilee College." After Bishop Chase died in 1852, the college fell into inefficient hands; with the approach of the Civil War, no more funds came from the South. Contrary to the will of Philander Chase, college land was sold from time to time; eventually only ninety-eight acres remained. In due time the land was given to the state of Illinois for a state park. Only the chapel has been restored.

An interesting sidelight to Chase's personality is a way he found to stretch his budget. Whether he was serving in Gambier, Ohio, or in Robin's Nest, Illinois, where Jubilee College was located, he applied to be postmaster of both towns. He acted as these towns' postmaster and, as such, according to the *Postal Laws and Instructions of 1825,* had a franking privilege; it was a part of a postmaster's compensation. As bishop and college president, he must have had many letters to send; if they could be sent free of charge, so much the better. He may well have been the only U.S. bishop to have served simultaneously as college president and postmaster while administering his see.[2]

Bishop Chase is buried in the cemetery in back of the church at Jubilee. His gravestone is surrounded by an iron fence.

SUGGESTIONS FOR FURTHER READING

Virginius H. Chase, "Jubilee College and its Founder," *Journal of the Illinois State Historical Society,* 40 (1947): 154-167.

Jill Henry, "Father of Two Colleges," *Illinois History,* 18, #1 (October 1964): 15-16.

Douglas F. Mayer, "In the Footsteps of Bishop Chase," *Kenyon Alumni Bulletin* (Jan.-Mar. 1971).

Laura Chase Smith, *The Life of Philander Chase* (New York: E. P. Dutton, 1903).

ENDNOTES

1. Child, William H. *History of the Town of Cornish with Genealogical Record: 1763-1910,* (Concord, NH: The Rumford Press, 1911?; reprinted edition, Spartenburg, SC: The Reprint Company, 1975), Vol. 1, p. 288 1:295.

2. Richard B. Graham, "Postal History—Philander Chase: Bishop, Educator, Postmaster," *Linn's Stamp News* (May 11, 1992), p. 19.

Figure 7. *Trinity Episcopal Church, Cornish, New Hampshire.*

SALMON PORTLAND CHASE

1808 – 1873

CORNISH NATIVE SALMON PORTLAND CHASE served as Secretary of the Treasury and Chief Justice of the United States Supreme Court. His portrait appears on the $10,000 bill, the highest existing denomination of currency.

Chase, a descendant of some of the first settlers of Cornish, was born January 13, 1808, in Cornish, son of Ithamar and Janette (Ralston) Chase. When he was eight years old, his family moved to Keene, New Hampshire. The following year Salmon's father died, and his mother sent him to live with his uncle, Philander Chase, the first Episcopal Bishop of Ohio. Salmon attended the bishop's school at Worthington and enrolled at Cincinnati College, where his uncle was president. He subsequently enrolled at Dartmouth College, graduating in 1826.[1] He came back to Cincinnati to settle and turned his energies to the compilation of the *Statutes of Ohio,* which appeared in three volumes from 1833 to 1835. It became a standard work and required heavy labor to prepare. These volumes also served to establish Chase's legal reputation.

On the slavery question, an issue that was eventually to affect his interest in the law, Chase's position was an anti-slavery one. Since he frequently spoke at anti-slavery meetings, he earned the nickname of "attorney general for runaway Negroes." Chase continued to be active in politics, serving as one of

Figure 8. Salmon Portland Chase *by Ulysses Dow Tenney, after Henry Ulke.*

Ohio's United States senators from 1849 to 1855. Then, in 1855, he was elected governor of Ohio, an office which he held four years.

In 1846 he was an unsuccessful candidate for the Republican nomination for president of the United States. He endeavored to obtain the presidential nomination again in 1860, but, since he received only forty-nine votes on the first ballot, his supporters later threw their votes to Abraham Lincoln. In 1861, Lincoln invited Chase, whom Lincoln

Figure 9. *$10,000 bill with Salmon Portland Chase's portrait.*

thought to be "about one-and-a-half times bigger than any other man I ever knew," to become Secretary of the Treasury.[2] Relinquishing his Ohio senatorship, he accepted and took office in March. Hardly had Chase become Secretary of the Treasury when, in April of 1861, the Civil War began.

Chase is considered one of the greatest secretaries because of his work during the war. The national banking system, first established by law on February 25, 1863, was originated by Chase, who formally submitted his proposal in December of 1862. His aim was to increase the sale of government bonds, to improve the currency by providing reliable bank notes backed by government security, and to suppress the "evils" of state bank notes. This innovation may well have been his most important piece of statesmanship. But he is better known for what he did in 1864 when the two-cent piece, the first United States coin to bear the motto "In God We Trust," was struck. Salmon P. Chase, Secretary of the Treasury, authorized this motto to be placed on the coin.[3]

Chase resigned in 1864 because of a policy dispute; Lincoln, who disliked him personally, named him Chief Justice in recognition of his ability. Chase presided over the impeachment trial of President Andrew Johnson. As our country's fifth Chief Justice, Chase held the office until 1873. During this period Chase paid his last visit to Cornish in July of 1866 to attend a reception given in his honor by Chester Pike, a prominent farmer and local politician (see below pp. 35-37). Later, Chase aspired to the 1872 Republican presidential nomination but failing health prevented his acceptance. He died of a stroke on May 7, 1873.[4]

A New Hampshire historic highway marker on Route 12A now designates the site in Cornish where he was born.

SUGGESTION FOR FURTHER READING

Donn Haven Lathrop, "Salmon P. Chase: The New Hampshire Boy Who Almost Made It," *Upper Valley Magazine,* September-October 1994, pp. 32-40.

ENDNOTES

1. Child, William H. *History of the Town of Cornish with Genealogical Record: 1763-1910,* (Concord, NH: The Rumford Press, 1911?; reprinted edition, Spartenburg, SC: The Reprint Company, 1975), Vol. 1, pp. 300-303.
2. Lincoln also let Chase write the last paragraph of "The Emancipation Proclamation" (1862), the paragraph calling upon "the considerate judgment of mankind" to view the proclamation as "an act of justice, warranted by the Constitution"; see William Least Heat-Moon, *PrairyErth (a deep map)* (Boston: Houghton Mifflin, 1991), p. 134.
3. George Stimpson, *A Book About the Bible* (New York: Harper, 1945), p. 8. Chase modified a line from the fourth stanza of "The Star-Spangled Banner" by Francis Scott Key, "And this be our motto, 'In God is our trust' "; see Heat-Moon, p. 144.
4. Allen Johnson and Dumas Malone, eds., *Dictionary of American Biography* (New York: Scribner's, 1930), pp. 27-34.

JUDGE SAMUEL CHASE
1707 – 1800

Figure 10. *Judge Samuel Chase painted by Joseph Steward.*

SAMUEL CHASE, whom everyone referred to as "Judge Chase," inspired the first band of men determined to settle what is now Cornish. The group, which also included his son Dudley, his son-in-law Daniel Putnam, and Dyer Spalding, ventured up the Connecticut River in 1765. Judge Samuel Chase, however, decided to stay in the settlement of Walpole until the following year. Judge Chase had meanwhile made extensive purchases of land in Cornish. At this point he was nearly sixty years of age.

Judge Samuel Chase's activities in Cornish were both political and military. He was the first justice of the peace in town, and, as such, called the first town meeting in 1767.[1] He was the first moderator and also the town's first selectman. Later, he joined the regiment of his son Colonel Jonathan Chase and marched to Saratoga and Bennington on September 26, 1777, a total of 110 miles.[2] Finally, during the "New Hampshire Grants" controversy, which continued through most of the second half of the eighteenth century, Judge Chase figured conspicuously. His name appears on all the reports of public gatherings.

Before they left Sutton, Massachusetts, Judge Chase married Mary Dudley in May of 1728; they had ten children, all of whom were born before they came to Cornish.

Judge Chase's portrait now hangs in the Cornish library. It was painted by Joseph Steward, probably in 1793 when Steward was commissioned by Dartmouth College to paint portraits of Eleazer Wheelock and John Phillips (see below pp. 49-51).[3]

Chase died in Cornish on August 12, 1800; he was almost ninety-three years old. He is buried in the Trinity Church Cemetery.

ENDNOTES

1. Child, William H. *History of the Town of Cornish with Genealogical Record: 1763-1910,* (Concord, NH: The Rumford Press, 1911?; reprinted edition, Spartenburg, SC: The Reprint Company, 1975), Vol. 2, p. 59.

2. *New Hampshire Revolutionary War Rolls,* 2:373-276; *General Jonathan Chase (1732-1800) of Cornish, New Hampshire, His Papers,* published by the Cornish Bicentennial Commission (Cornish, NH, 1977), p. 616.

3. Chase portrait files, collection Cornish Historical Society.

DR. ALBERT PARKER FITCH

1877 – 1944

DR. ALBERT PARKER FITCH, a lovingly remembered member of the Cornish community, was graduated from Union Theological Seminary in 1903. The following summer he served as a supply minister at the Presbyterian Church of the Covenant in Washington. Following the death of the pastor of the church, though he had had no previous pastoral experience, he was paid the unusual honor of a call to this church. Dr. Fitch declined and, after a brief pastorate in a small church on Long Island, accepted one at the Mt. Vernon Church in Boston, from which he was called to the Andover Seminary, an unusual honor for a young man of only thirty-two.[1]

Dr. Fitch married Flora May Draper of England in 1903 and in 1908 they bought a lot on Dingleton Hill in Cornish from his cousin for $300. Dr. Fitch then hired Italian stone craftsmen to build the house which was to be constructed of native stone. Frank Jones, a neighbor, along with Ernest Plummer and Morris French, helped with the building. It is said not only that Dr. Fitch even fired two workmen who swore too much, but also that he brought soil in from the south pasture to make the lawn.[2]

The Fitches became involved in community activities: they opened their home to concerts and Dr. Fitch read aloud to the boys at the Cornish library.[3] When Dr. Fitch was in Cornish, he was frequently a guest preacher at the Congregational Church on Center Road, now the United Church of Cornish, where there was always a full congregation. It was even swelled by President Woodrow Wilson, who had his summer home in Cornish from 1913 to 1915. Although he was a Presbyterian, he attended the Congregational Church whenever he was in town. There is a story that President Wilson was on his way to church one Sunday in his "horseless carriage" when he overtook Dr. Fitch in his horse-drawn buggy. Thinking it improper to pass the minister, President Wilson ordered his chauffeur to slow down and to follow the minister at the horse's slow pace to the church.[4] It was said that Dr. Fitch seemed glad of the opportunity that the pulpit provided him for advising the President. The President's first wife, Ellen Axson Wilson, described Dr. Fitch as "delightfully human and simple." The Wilsons enjoyed a visit at the Fitches' and Mrs. Wilson commented that she hoped that the following summer they might become "intimate friends."[5] Edith Bolling Galt, Wilson's second wife, thought the Fitches were "very stimulating."[6]

During this period young Arthur Quimby of Cornish was the organist at the Congregational Church. The Fitches took Arthur under their wing, paid his tuition at Harvard,[7] and frequently entertained him at dinner at their Boston home.[8] Another local connection was with Dr. Fitch's cousin, James Fitch. While the Fitches were in Cornish, Dr. Fitch often had to make trips to Boston. James Fitch transported him to and from the Windsor Railroad Station.

Dr. Fitch later went on to become pastor of the Park Avenue Presbyterian Church in New York City and associated with Amherst College in Massachusetts and Carleton College in Minnesota. He also was the author of several books.[9]

On August 5, 1940, the Fitches sold their stone house on Dingleton Hill to Betsy P. C. Purves of Philadelphia.[10]

Dr. Fitch died in Englewood, New Jersey, on May 22, 1944; he left no children.[11] His ashes were spread by his widow, Flora, in the pasture east of the stone house in 1945. Flora died April 17, 1962. Her ashes were spread in the same location as her husband's on May 13, 1962, by Reverend Roswell Barnes.[12]

Figure 11. *Stone house (c. 1908) on Dingleton Hill built by Dr. Albert Parker Fitch.*

ENDNOTES

1. Cornish Historical Society files, Cornish, NH.

2. Interview: Virginia Colby with James B. Fitch (age 102), July 2, 1986. For J.C. Leyendecker's visit to Dr. Fitch, see below pp. 484-485.

3. George H. Stowell Library, scrapbook.

4. Pat Youden, "President's Romance in a Cornish White House," *Valley News,* July 3, 1981.

5. Arthur S. Link, ed. *The Papers of Woodrow Wilson* (Princeton: Princeton University Press, 1978), 28, July 20, 1913; see below p. 429 for context and p. 437 for more on Fitch.

6. Edwin Tribble, ed., *A President in Love* (Boston: Houghton Mifflin, 1981), p. 95.

7. Per conversation with Arthur Quimby's son, Conrad, 1986.

8. Letters from Arthur W. Quimby to Marguerite Lewin in the possession of Carol Quimby Heath, New Haven, CT.

9. Year Book, Congregational Churches, 1944.

10. Sullivan County Hall of Records, Newport, NH, War. Vol. 272, p. 11.

11. Year Book, Congregational Churches, 1944.

12. Cornish Gravestone Records, Ashes.

Figure 12.

SARAH JOSEPHA HALE
1788 – 1879

THE CAREER OF SARAH JOSEPHA (BUELL) HALE has a tenuous connection with the history of Cornish through her youngest daughter, Sarah Josepha Hale, born in 1820. We know that the latter attended Miss Seton's school in Cornish because of a box the girl painted while there.[1] It is possible that she was in Cornish after 1828 because her mother sent her two girls to be with their Uncle Selma in Keene and the two were put into a boarding school then.[2] The actual location of Miss Seton's school, however, remains a puzzle; but there is a record of Dr. Erastus Torrey (see below pp. 55-56) selling his lot on the Connecticut River to a Penelope Seton on March 7, 1812.[3] We also know that the school existed as early as 1811 because of this notice: "Mrs. Seton respectfully informs her friends that her school recommences on Monday the 2nd September."[4]

Although these are the few facts we have about the daughter, her mother is quite a bit more famous. She is most popularly remembered as the author of "Mary Had a Little Lamb." Its second verse is less familiar, yet it could well serve as a motto for Sarah's life: "And you each gentle animal/In confidence man bind/And make them answer to your call/If you are always *kind*."

Her parents, Gordon and Martha (Whittlesay) Buell, arrived in New Hampshire by wagon from Connecticut in 1783 to establish a homestead on 400 acres in the East Mountain section of Newport. Sarah was born on October 24, 1788, one of four children. When her two older brothers went off to school, Sarah was bitterly disappointed she could not go too. It was then that she discovered that formal education was practically nonexistent for girls. At an early age her parents thought Sarah would become more mature by reading Shakespeare, Milton, Cowper, and Burns.

Sarah's brother, Horatio, attended Dartmouth College. During school vacations he tutored Sarah in his subjects; when he graduated in 1809 with top honors, Sarah had received the equivalent of a college education.

Figure 13. *Inside lid of box painted by Sarah Josepha Hale, daughter of Sarah Josepha (Buell) Hale, at Miss Seton's school in Cornish, New Hampshire.*

To help her father supplement his income, Sarah began teaching boys and girls in a school near her home. When her father could no longer cope with farming, the family sold the farm and built an inn in the center of Newport. It was here that Sarah met her future husband, David Hale, a promising young lawyer; they were married on October 23, 1813.

Sarah enjoyed writing and David encouraged her by having some of her poems and stories printed in the local newspaper, *The New Hampshire Spectator*. Her ability and reputation as a writer grew. Meanwhile, Sarah and David had five children, three boys and two girls. The last girl was her mother's namesake, Sarah Josepha Hale. After David's early and tragic death in 1822, Sarah was left with five young children to support. So, she turned from her chosen profession of teaching to a joint venture with her sister as milliners since it paid more than teaching. During the evenings, she worked on her poetry and her first book of poems was published in 1823, *The Genius of Oblivion*

Figure 14. *Outside of box.*

and Other Original Poems, "by a lady of New Hampshire." *Northwood, A Tale of New England,* her first novel, was published in 1827 and became an instant success. It was responsible for her move to Boston where, because of it, she was offered an editorial position with the *Ladies' Magazine*. Taking this job would mean that her children could go to college. Sarah edited the new magazine and wrote much of it herself.

One of Sarah's early projects was to use the power of her magazine and its subscribers to effect the completion of the Bunker Hill Monument. This granite obelisk had run out of funds and lain unfinished for five years. Sarah asked for a contribution of one dollar from each female reader, with the husband's consent, of course, of the *Ladies' Magazine*. This was the first time such a solicitation had ever been made in a periodical; they eventually raised enough money to complete the monument in 1843—much to Sarah's credit.

Her next major interest was the Seamen's Aid Society of Boston. Its purpose was to alleviate the very poor living conditions of sailors and their families. The Seamen's Aid Society was "the first organization of American women" and "the first to promote better working conditions and higher wages for women—and the first to *begin* the fight for the retention of property rights for married women."[5]

Her social concern for women went hand-in-glove with her passionate desire for what the title of one of her early articles called the "Advancement of Female Education." The dominant theme on this topic was announced in the last book of Jean-Jacques Rousseau's *Emile* (1762):

> The education of women should always be relative to men. To please, to be useful to us, to make us love and esteem them, to educate when young and to take care of us when grown up, to advise us, to console us, to render our lives easy and agreeable; these are the duties of women at all times.[6]

At a time when over 50 percent of women were illiterate,[7] Sarah Hale succinctly expressed her contrary view in the August 1837 issue of *Godey's Lady's Book:* "We cannot learn, neither can we teach, by a sort of magic peculiar to ourselves: give us the facilities for education enjoyed by the other sex, and we shall at least be able to try what are the capabilities of women."[8] Equality of education was a consistent theme of her editorials.

The year before Louis Godey of Philadelphia had bought what was then the *American Ladies' Magazine* and merged it with *Godey's Lady's Book.* Sarah Josepha Hale was its new editor, and Sarah was required to move from Boston to Philadelphia. From her monthly column "The Lady's Mentor" in *Godey's Lady's Book,* its new editor defined her "final goal": "to carry onward and upward the spirit of moral and intellectual excellence in our sex, till their influence shall bless as well as beautify civil society."[9]

Another cause Sarah Hale tackled was the preservation of George Washington's home, Mount Vernon, and its buildings. They were in a dilapidated, decaying state. In 1860, with great effort on Sarah's part, and on the part of many others, Mount Vernon became the property of the American people. Her editorials in aid of this task helped to bring the North and South together shortly before the Civil War erupted.

Her final crusade, Thanksgiving Day, was indebted to George Washington and his proclamation in 1789 to dedicate the last Thursday in November to a "Day of Thanksgiving and prayer." The idea of having a specific American holiday had not originated with Sarah. It took many years of her hard work before Abraham Lincoln signed a proclamation for a national observance of Thanksgiving in 1863. But it took seventy-eight more years until the fourth Thursday in November was declared a national legal holiday; a joint resolution of Congress did so in 1941.

Sarah Josepha Hale died on April 30, 1879, after a very long and illustrious career: fighting for the cause of women.

ENDNOTES

1. It currently is in the Abbey Aldrich Rockefeller Folk Art Center in Williamsburg, VA. An inscription on it reads "Painted by Sarah Josepha Hale at Miss Seton's School, Cornish, N.H." Locally the school teacher was referred to interchangeably as "Miss" and "Mrs."

2. Sherbrooke Rogers, *Sarah Josepha Hale: A New England Pioneer, 1788-1879* (Grantham, NH: Thompson and Rutter, Inc., 1985), p. 27.

3. Deed, March 7, 1812, Cheshire County Records, Vol. 3, p. 42; Vol. 9, p. 144 for January 19, 1833. She later sold this property to Dr. Caleb Chase, March 18, 1833.

4. A local newspaper, the *Washingtonian*, August 21, 1811; this information was generously provided by Katherine Conlin of Windsor, VT. Child, *History of Cornish* 1:366 lists the death of a seventy-five-year-old man, Christopher Seton, June 15, 1830.

5. Rogers, p. 58.

6. As quoted in Ibid., p. 39.

7. Ibid., p. 121.

8. Ibid., p. 8. Perhaps Sarah would have admired a novel written by her Cornish neighbor Anna Levina Lear (1842-1893). *One Little Woman* describes what a plucky, educated woman can accomplish. Child says of Lear that "she manifested a gift as an authoress and wrote several books, among them one entitled 'One Little Woman,' which has won much commendation." (*History of Cornish,* Vol. 2, p. 253). The following quotation from a chapter entitled "The Model School-Teacher" could well be based on Lear's immediate observation of life in late nineteenth-century Cornish:

   > After this small excitement—though it did not seem small to them—life went on in the ordinary tranquil way at the mountain farm. The usual round of indoor and out-door work was regularly performed; and little do the careless dwellers of the town understand what a ceaseless routine this work is, from early spring till latest autumn; the latter season is, perhaps, the busiest of all; since then must all the fruits of the pre-vious months' labors be gathered and stored, and that with small delay. . . . The apples were gathered, and bushels and bushels of them cut and dried; and many a "yellow-mated" pumpkin, ditto; then there was "the gypsy-fire" and "kettle over-hung" out of doors, where, amid smoke and much discomfort the cider was boiled down—"to 'lasses". . . —in which the "pound-sweets" were cooked until trans-formed into the most appetizing of sauces; the corn was husked and stored—a long pile of "farmer's gold"; the sheep and young cattle were called down from the moun-tain pasture; the chickens and the troublesome "quiting" turkeys were fattened and dressed for market; the "banking" was put around the house, the outside windows put on, the storm-door hung, and all made snug for Winter. (*One Little Woman* [Boston: James H. Earle, 1893], pp. 74-75)

9. Ibid., p. 66.

SAMUEL HARDY

1804 – 1879

IF YOU HAVE NEVER HAD AN OCCASION to sample "Hardy's Genuine Salve," so much the better. But just in case you ever have any of these symptoms, you might like to know that:

Hardy's Genuine Salve is recommended for Lame Backs, also for Chilblains, Cracked Hands, Splinters, Cuts, Bruises, Minor Burns (not blisters). For lame fingers and toes, apply with a bandage. For Corns and Calluses apply every day or two and it will soften it so that it will come out easily. Also recommended by many for removing warts. Directions for use: Warm end of roll, spread from roll on sterile band aid or sterile cloth; warm the plaster and apply to parts affected. It will adhere wherever applied.

Samuel Hardy was born in Grantham (in the area that was later annexed to Cornish in 1844) in 1804; from his earliest days he was frail and sickly. During his youth and early manhood he learned the chairmaker's trade, since that occupation required less physical stamina than did farming. When he was about twenty-one, he moved to western New York where he remained about ten years. In 1827 he married an estimable, but sickly woman; throughout their eleven-year marriage her health remained delicate. At the age of thirty-two he found himself in extremely poor health and unable to work, with a sick wife and four small children, and with a cash capital of $2.40. His condition was desperate. But since he was a devoted Christian and was buoyed up by the conviction that if he did his best his Heavenly Father would provide for him, he turned his attention to the one enterprise in which it seemed possible for him to earn an honest living: namely, the manufacture of Hardy's Salve, which for years was very popular.[1]

The composition of this salve was the result of a long series of experiments Dr. Hardy conducted while he was unable to work. At first the sale was small, but it was sufficient to keep the wolf from the door of the sick family and was, therefore, satisfactory. His success with the salve, which established its own reputation wherever it was introduced, induced him to extend his research and experiments with the curative properties of various herbs and roots. Subsequently, he offered the public several remedies, all of which were tested on his own family. While in New York, he became acquainted with an old

Indian doctor of the Cayuga tribe who was credited with performing marvelous cures. From him he obtained a formula from which he compounded a medicine from roots and herbs that, with almost miraculous suddenness, restored his wife's good health.

His final line of products consisted of: HARDY'S ROOT and HERB TONIC BIT-TERS; HARDY'S ELECTUARY or TONIC BITTERS; HARDY'S MAGICAL PAIN DESTROYER; HARDY'S INDIAN VEGETABLE WORM POWDER; and HARDY'S EXTERNAL ANODYNE to invigorate and procure quiet sleep. One of the best sellers was "WOMAN'S FRIEND, or NATURE'S GRAND ASSISTANT" which guarded against and cured:

> Falling of the Womb, Wasting Profusion, Leucorrhea, or Whites, Bearing Down, Hys-terical Trouble, Heart, Spinal, Paralytic, Hectic and Pulmonary Diseases, Scrofula, Can-cerous and Tumorous Affections, and all diseases having their origin in the one leading and fatal cause—derangement of female constitutional law. By its use the *critical periods* of life are passed in safety. It is peculiarly adapted to the wants of operatives in factories, whose symptoms are overworked by standing.[2]

Dr. Hardy began selling these products in 1836 and continued until his retirement in 1869 when he turned the business over to his two sons, Philemon C. and Charles Torrey, who had purchased their father's interest. This partnership continued until the death of Charles in 1885; the older brother then carried on alone.

The Hardy brothers used to travel throughout New England by horse and wagon selling the products. Dr. Hardy's son, Follansbe Carroll, worked as a traveling salesman, living in Worcester, Massachusetts. He was so successful with the Hardy products that he added other medicines and goods.

In 1874 wholesale prices were:

Doz. Hardy's Salve	$2.00
Doz. Hardy's Cathartic Elect'y or Tonic Bitters	2.00
Doz. Hardy's Worm Powder	2.00
Doz. Hardy's Bottle Bitters	5.00
Doz. Woman's Friend	9.00
Doz. External Anodyne	4.00

By the early 1880s, however, business was very poor; the Hardy brothers were anxiously soliciting testimonials to be published in an advertising circular.

So, by the time Philemon C. Hardy sold the business to George Hunt of Cornish in 1886 or 1887, all their products had been dropped from production except the salve. Hunt's wife, Kate Thrasher Hunt, operated the concern until her two sons, Harry and Kenneth, took it over. During the time the Hunt brothers owned the salve company, Lena Read sold them beef tallow, which she "tried out" on the kitchen stove. Her hus-band, Palmer Read, delivered the tallow; when he returned with the money, he would often ask his wife if the money smelled as bad as the fat. Nevertheless, son Albert Read points out that they always kept a stick on hand. The salve company remained in the Hunt family until about the mid-1950s when they sold it to Milton Sklar of Claremont. However, Sklar, although he lived in Claremont, contracted with Kenneth Hunt to con-tinue the manufacture of the salve.[3] In 1965 Robert LaClair of Cornish Flat purchased

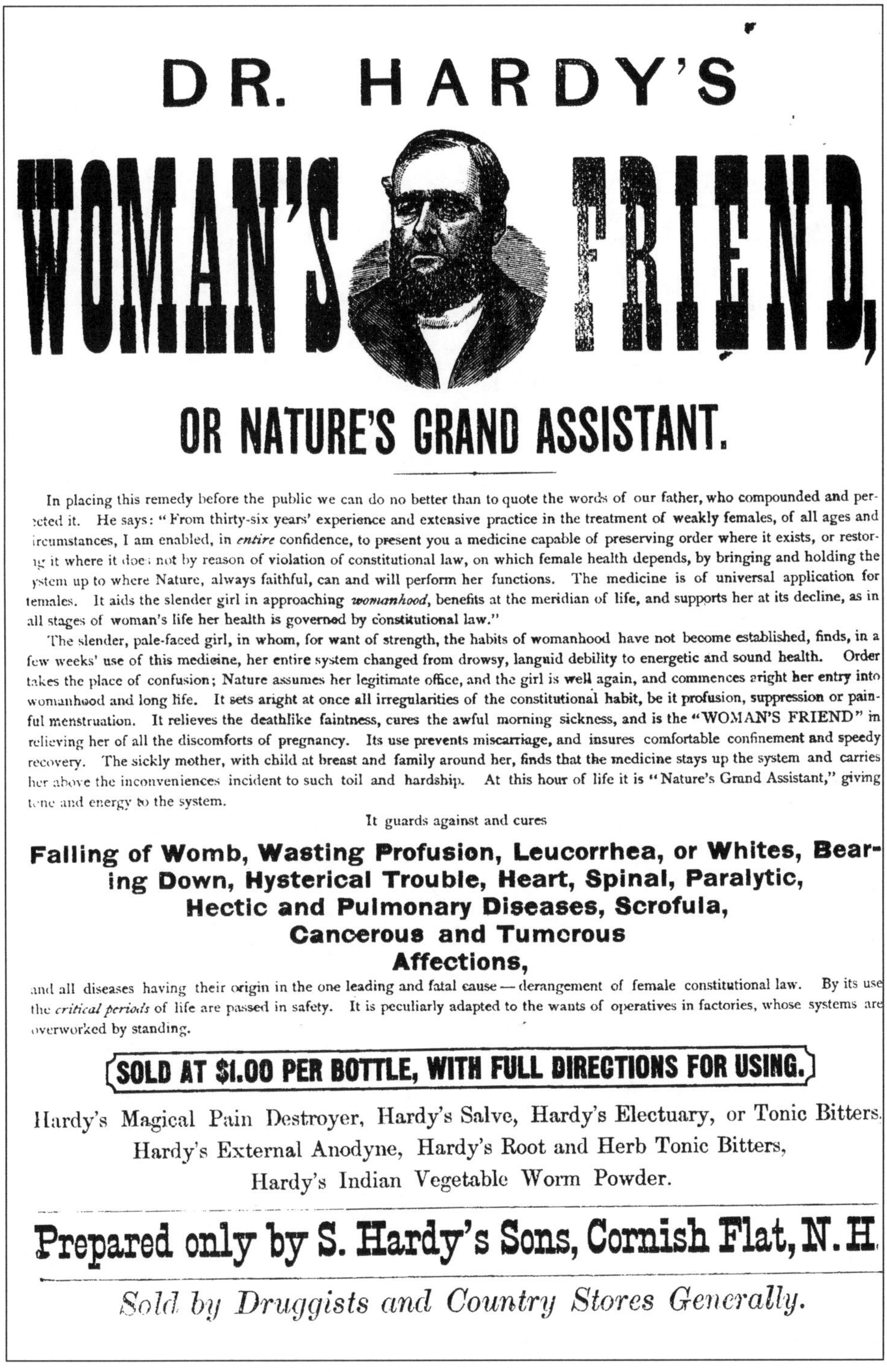

DR. HARDY'S
WOMAN'S FRIEND,
OR NATURE'S GRAND ASSISTANT.

In placing this remedy before the public we can do no better than to quote the words of our father, who compounded and perfected it. He says: "From thirty-six years' experience and extensive practice in the treatment of weakly females, of all ages and circumstances, I am enabled, in *entire* confidence, to present you a medicine capable of preserving order where it exists, or restoring it where it does not by reason of violation of constitutional law, on which female health depends, by bringing and holding the system up to where Nature, always faithful, can and will perform her functions. The medicine is of universal application for females. It aids the slender girl in approaching *womanhood*, benefits at the meridian of life, and supports her at its decline, as in all stages of woman's life her health is governed by constitutional law."

The slender, pale-faced girl, in whom, for want of strength, the habits of womanhood have not become established, finds, in a few weeks' use of this medicine, her entire system changed from drowsy, languid debility to energetic and sound health. Order takes the place of confusion; Nature assumes her legitimate office, and the girl is well again, and commences aright her entry into womanhood and long life. It sets aright at once all irregularities of the constitutional habit, be it profusion, suppression or painful menstruation. It relieves the deathlike faintness, cures the awful morning sickness, and is the "WOMAN'S FRIEND" in relieving her of all the discomforts of pregnancy. Its use prevents miscarriage, and insures comfortable confinement and speedy recovery. The sickly mother, with child at breast and family around her, finds that the medicine stays up the system and carries her above the inconveniences incident to such toil and hardship. At this hour of life it is "Nature's Grand Assistant," giving tone and energy to the system.

It guards against and cures

Falling of Womb, Wasting Profusion, Leucorrhea, or Whites, Bearing Down, Hysterical Trouble, Heart, Spinal, Paralytic, Hectic and Pulmonary Diseases, Scrofula, Cancerous and Tumorous Affections,

and all diseases having their origin in the one leading and fatal cause — derangement of female constitutional law. By its use the *critical periods* of life are passed in safety. It is peculiarly adapted to the wants of operatives in factories, whose systems are overworked by standing.

SOLD AT $1.00 PER BOTTLE, WITH FULL DIRECTIONS FOR USING.

Hardy's Magical Pain Destroyer, Hardy's Salve, Hardy's Electuary, or Tonic Bitters.
Hardy's External Anodyne, Hardy's Root and Herb Tonic Bitters,
Hardy's Indian Vegetable Worm Powder.

Prepared only by S. Hardy's Sons, Cornish Flat, N.H.

Sold by Druggists and Country Stores Generally.

Figure 15. *One of Dr. Hardy's advertising flyers.*

the Hardy Salve Company. In 1989 it was sold to Robert Weaver who still makes and sells Hardy Salve.

The salve continues to be made in the old original way. The resin, tallow, and beeswax are heated in a big kettle until they are melted; then the "essential oils," part of the secret formula, are added. When the mixture is cooled to the proper temperature, it is poured into 612 molds which have been lined with paper wrappers containing the instructions for use. When it is cold, the sticks of molded salve are removed from the molds and packaged. New molds were made in 1933 in the pattern shop of the old Sullivan Machine Company in Claremont.

ENDNOTES

1. Hardy Papers; gift to the Cornish Historical Society from Mrs. Robert Thompson, Brockton, MA.
2. Hardy Papers; various advertisements for Hardy Salve.
3. Hardy Papers; gift to the Cornish Historical Society from Milton E. Sklar, Claremont. NH, in memory of Mildred Sklar.

Figure 16.

DAVID HALL HILLIARD
1805 – 1877

A NINETEENTH-CENTURY CORNISH GUNSHOP, owned by David Hall Hilliard, turned out material in such great demand that even the town's historians seem surprised. Hilliard's "reputation [stretched] far and wide, and orders came from the Far West . . . even Siberia."[1] This esteem for his craftsmanship resulted in part from his insistence on testing every one of his products himself. Hilliard made all types of guns: bench rifles, target guns, hunting rifles, and target pistols. Hilliard was born December 3, 1805, the eldest son of Benjamin and Roxana (Hall) Hilliard of Cornish. But the son did not start out as a gunsmith; rather, he followed in his father's footsteps as a carpenter and cabinetmaker. Hilliard also learned the trade of blacksmith at the shop of Mr. Watrous on Mill Brook in Windsor. This is where he made his first gun. Furthermore, Hilliard worked for Thomas Woolson of Claremont for whom he designed stove patterns which were in turn cast at Tyson, Vermont. He invented the "Yankee Cook Stove," the first with an elevated oven. In November of 1840 he obtained a patent for this stove and he describes his invention as "a new and useful furnace or apparatus, which I denominate the air-tight furnace, and which may either be used alone as a distinct furnace or may be appended to various kinds of cooking-stoves now in use."[2]

Hilliard seems to have had quite a nest egg early in his life. The Sullivan County Registry of Deeds records his many land transactions from 1830 to 1871. In 1837 N. Waldo,

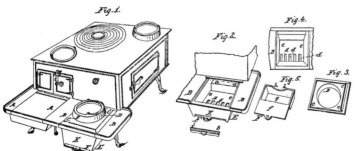

Figure 17. Cooking Stove, an illustration accompanying David H. Hilliard's request to the U.S. Patent Office for a patent governing his invention. Patent #1858 was issued to him November 26, 1840.

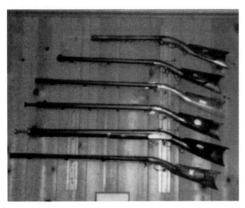

Figure 18. *An array of Hilliard rifles.*

cabinetmaker, sold property to David H. Hilliard, who is identified as a "pattern maker."

David Hilliard found his vocation when he went to work for Nicanor Kendall and the latter's father-in-law, Asahel Hubbard. They, along with Asa Story, had a thriving gunshop in Windsor, Vermont, where they were producing underhammer guns. The simplicity of the underhammer action on firearms was just beginning to catch on. One is described as "a unique-looking piece having a long octagonal barrel and a heavy black walnut stock mounted with polished brass. The lock differed in the extreme from anything ever produced before, being what would generally be called upside down, with the trigger in the rear."[3]

Hilliard eventually negotiated for the patent and manufacturing rights to these underhammer rifles. Armed with this authority, he soon established his own gun manufacturing shop in Cornish around 1842. Hilliard took along with him two of the gunmakers from the Kendall plant: W. B. Smith and his brother-in-law, Chase Smith. Hilliard married Sarah Smith on September 10, 1835.

Hilliard's gunshop was located on Town House Road near the junction of Center Road, and his house was just across the road from the shop. At peak production he employed fifteen men. He paid $5.50 per week for a highly skilled machinist, whereas an apprentice received room and board plus $30 for the first year and $50 for the second year. Hilliard kept a daily record of business accounts (down to the very penny) and of other activities. His entry for Monday, February 25, 1856, is typical:

Rather cold and windy today. Chase and William in the shop today until evening when they went away to a meeting. Charles worked in the shop in the forenoon and in the afternoon on the hill. George worked on the hill all day. I worked in the shop all day until about two in the afternoon when I went to Windsor and carried letters to the post office. One letter to John Hudson of Lynn, Mass., with $22 enclosed for parts and had the letter registered. Another letter posted to Hitchcock and Muzzy & Co. of Worcester, Mass. Also sent letters to Chas. Trull of Lawrence, Mass., and to Wm. Read and Sons of Boston with $6 enclosed to order powder and caps. Also sent letters to Ira W. Merrill of Sutton, N.H. acknowledging receipt of $18 in payment of the rifle which has since been sent out to him. Letters also sent to the following in regard to orders. A. Parker of Ludlow, Vt., and another to Sanford Rowe of Braggersville, Mass., and one to a Mr. John C. Bartlett of Columbus, Columbia County, Wisconsin. I paid $1 for postage and for registering of the letters. At the Union Store I bought the following, one gallon of molasses 50 cents, ½ lb. of paper 8 cents, ¼ lb. Cassia [coarse, cinnamon bark] 11 cents for which I paid. At Stockers and Whites I bought 1½ bushel of corn which came to $1.50 and also got from them .08 worth of buttons and 25 cents tidy yarn. I went to the Armory and got six gun barrels which were bought of Mr. Maynard for $7.50, said Mr. Maynard owed me $6.50 and I paid him the difference of $1. I paid Stevens 7 cents for grinding the corn. Sold a rifle to Mr. Kingsley of Plainfield at $16.50 later in evening, he also took a screw driver at

50 cents and a ladle and patching cloth at 60 cents and he also bought ½ lb. powder at 33 cents. Leonard Gilson visited us this evening. Also Abby Harlan paid us a visit later.

At the onset of the Civil War, one of the first military companies from New Hampshire was equipped with the Hilliard telescope rifle by order of Governor Barry. Men who lived in the area were allowed the privilege of selecting their own guns.

Hilliard obtained shotgun barrels from Robbins and Lawrence and also barrels from Remington as well as from Hitchcock and Muzzy. He did his own rifling. Two of his rifling machines still exist and are displayed in Windsor, Vermont, at the American Precision Museum which is the former Robbins and Lawrence Company (often referred to as the "armory").

Hilliard made single barreled shotguns, buggy pistols, and over- and underhammer action guns. The buggy pistol was made to be carried in a special holder on the front of the buggy. It was about halfway in size between a pistol and a rifle. The buggy rifle shown at the top of Figure 18, illustrated on p. 26, has a barrel length of 17⅛ inches with a tiger maple stock. It was a gift from the late James B. Rogers of California to the Cornish Historical Society, which was also willed his entire Hilliard gun collection consisting of six long guns and a pistol. They, too, may be viewed at the American Precision Museum during their regular visiting hours from May to October.

There the visitor can observe Hilliard's frequent use of birdseye, tiger, and curly maple to fashion his stocks; he coated them with a very hard and protective finish. The secret of this "piano finish" has not survived, though some people believe it may have had some beeswax embedded in it that hardened and mellowed with age.

David Hall Hilliard died in Cornish on June 10, 1877; he is buried in Comings Cemetery on Root Hill Road. He was prominent in the affairs of the town, serving on the School Board and as a Justice of the Peace for twenty-five years.

Upon his death his son, George, took over the gun shop. He did mostly repairs and worked on his own patents until the turn of the century when the shop closed. Hilliard's older son, Charles, moved to Ilion, New York, where he worked at the Remington Arms Company.

ENDNOTES

1. Child, William H. *History of the Town of Cornish with Genealogical Record: 1763-1910*, (Concord, NH: The Rumford Press, 1911?; reprinted edition, Spartenburg, SC: The Reprint Company, 1975), Vol. 1, p. 183; Wade, *A Brief History*, p. 35.
2. Specifications of Letters patent No. 1858, dated November 26, 1840.
3. Unidentified clipping from a scrapbook belonging to Wallace Williams, Virginia Colby's files.

GENERAL MARQUIS DE LAFAYETTE
1757 – 1834

Figure 19.

GENERAL MARQUIS DE LAFAYETTE'S affection and love for America and its causes is manifested in his devotion to this country and to its leaders. Lafayette gave up personal wealth and status in his own country when he helped us in our fight against England during the Revolutionary War. He even attained the rank of major general in the American army. Lafayette so admired George Washington that he named his only son George Washington Lafayette.

America eventually returned this affection. In 1824, at the age of sixty-seven, Lafayette was invited to visit the United States as a guest of the government. The Congress appropriated $200,000 to finance the trip. The tour lasted fifteen months, and he visited all twenty-four states. His local visit caused quite a stir. On June 6, 1825, the local newspaper, the *Vermont Republican and American Yeoman,* carried the following account:

> We regret to hear that the beloved guest of the nation has met with a serious accident. I have just received a letter from the postmaster at Wheeling, stating that two or three steamboats had just arrived from the fall of Ohio, bringing the unpleasant news of the loss of the steamboat "Mechanick," which had nearly proved fatal to the nation's friend and guest, General Lafayette. The account says that at about 150 miles below Louisville, the "Mechanick" ran foul of a snag, which caused her to sink in about 15 minutes and that some of the passengers saved themselves only by swimming. The general has lost all his papers and baggage, together with his private carriage. He saved nothing but one or two trunks. Among other articles lost was the cane which belonged to his early friend, the immortal Washington, and which General Lafayette had received as a present. The disaster must have occurred about the 10th [June 6, 1825].

This newspaper also covered Lafayette's trip through New Hampshire; locally he visited Newport and Claremont in mid-July. "As it was not known till the evening before, that the general would pass through Claremont, there was no attempt at military parade, the reception being entirely in the 'civic style.'" He was expected on June 26, and Leonard Jarvis, Esquire, was chosen to greet the general. School children were waiting with baskets of flowers and sixty gentlemen, handsomely mounted, along with great numbers of citizens, were all on hand to receive him. But there was a failure in his carriage spring, so he did not enter Claremont until half past nine. He was greeted with a thirteen-gun salute, bells were rung, and a "band of musick played the nation airs." The general stayed at W. Steven's Hotel.[1]

After ceremonies, speeches, and responses, Lafayette spent the night in Claremont. The following morning his party left for Windsor, Vermont; they stopped for refreshments at the tavern owned by Godfrey Cooke on the Turnpike going from Claremont to Windsor. (The site on today's Route 12A is noted by a marker which reads, "Site of the old tavern house, Lafayette stopped here, 1825." It was erected by the Samuel Ashley Chapter of the Daughters of the American Revolution in 1911.) The procession continued toward Vermont. A regal carriage drawn by six white horses and carrying General Marquis de Lafayette, his son, George Washington Lafayette, and the general's personal aide, crossed the Cornish-Windsor toll bridge on Tuesday, June 28, 1825, amid great fanfare. His arrival at the toll bridge was announced by the firing of cannon.[2]

General Mower and his staff from Woodstock, Vermont, met the Lafayette entourage at Claremont as part of the escort into Vermont.[3] Daniel Kellogg, secretary to the governor, along with the governor's aides, Colonels Cushman and Austin, and the Committee of Arrangements from Windsor, which included A. Forbes, J. Lull, H. Everett, J. H. Hubbard, and Erastus Torrey, accompanied the Marquis. A man who called himself Colonel Brown collected tolls for the Proprietors of the Cornish Bridge from 1825 to 1836. He noted in his daily journal for Tuesday, June 28, 1825, that "Marquis Fayette passed with his suit."[4]

Ceremonies for Lafayette in Windsor included a military escort in uniform, the Jefferson Artillery, a rifle company from Hartland, Vermont, a light infantry company from Weathersfield, Vermont, the Springfield, Vermont Brass Band, the governor with his aides, and other state and local officials. They all escorted the general in open carriages. There were also Revolutionary soldiers and officers from the army and navy along with members of the Masonic Fraternity, clergy, and students. The affair was held at Pettes' Coffee House with a speech by the Honorable Horace Everett with a response from General Lafayette.[5]

Some of the expenses F. Pette incurred for the celebrations in Windsor included, "Horse and Coach to Claremont and toles—$6.00; 10 horsekeeping and grain for band of music—$4.50; 273 meals of vituals for solgers (25 cts)—$68.75."[6] Eight horses and trimmings were used along with two coaches and eight changes, making sixty-four horses from Windsor to Burlington, Vermont, with attendance, expenses, etc. $20. Mrs. Norman Williams of Woodstock, Vermont, making a trip at this time, reported the difficulty in obtaining any good horses because they were all in use for Lafayette's trip. Incidentally, the horses during the New Hampshire and Vermont part of the trip had to be changed about every ten miles because of the pace and the rough roads.

Since Lafayette had been expected to enter Vermont at some point farther south than Windsor, the citizens of Weathersfield planned to make a road to the summit of Mt. Ascutney so that Lafayette might have a more impressive view of the entire surrounding area from that vantage point. This undertaking had to be abandoned, though, because of Lafayette's late arrival and tight schedule.

Upon leaving Windsor, the general continued on to Montpelier and Burlington, where he lay a cornerstone of the South College Building at the University of Vermont.

LAFAYETTE'S BASKET WAGON

"The body of this basket wagon is made of yellow-painted willow. The curved canvas-covered top, supported by slender wooden pillars, is lined with a patterned blue silk. The branched steps are made of wrought iron; the handles, dash rail, loops and nuts are silver-plated.

The seat and fall curtain are trimmed in red velvet, edged with a two-inch needlepoint border in a Greek key pattern. A red and yellow patterned silk and linen decorative drapery, edged in twisted silk fringe, is attached to the lower edge of the top. Made of a continuous piece of fabric, the shallow drapery was drawn up into swags by leather strips. Beige linsey-woolsey roll-up curtains, originally lined with blue silk, are fitted at the sides and rear of the body.

The wagon belonged to the United States diplomat Dr. Leonard Jarvis of Claremont who drove the general in this carriage to Windsor, Vermont, some ten miles northwest of Claremont, across the Connecticut River."[7]

Figure 20. *The basket wagon in which General Lafayette rode to Windsor, Vermont; it was owned by Dr. Leonard Jarvis of Claremont, New Hampshire.*

ENDNOTES

1. *Vermont Republican and American Yeoman,* July 18, 1825.

2. A. A. Parker, *Recollections of General Lafayette on his visit to the United States, in 1824 and 1825* (Keene, NH: Sentinel Printing Company, 1879). See also The Queens Museum Catalogue, *Lafayette, Hero of Two Worlds,* essays by Stanley J. Idzerda, Anne C. Loveland, and Marc H. Miller (Hanover, NH: University Press of New England, 1989).

3. Walter Newman Dooley, *Lafayette in New Hampshire,* a thesis submitted to the University of New Hampshire in partial fulfillment of the requirements for the degree of Master of Arts (Durham, NH, 1941), p. 99.

4. *A History of the Proprietors of Cornish Bridge and the Cornish, NH-Windsor, VT, Covered Toll Bridge (1796-1943),* prepared by the New Hampshire Department of Public Works and Highways, Concord, NH (1984), p. 13.

5. Jay Read Pember, *A Day with Lafayette in Vermont* (Woodstock, VT: The Elm Tree Press, 1912), p. 6.

6. For this and the following information, see Mary Grace Canfield, *Lafayette in Vermont,* privately printed (1934), pp. 10-11.

7. Otis F. R. Waite, *History of the Town of Claremont, New Hampshire* (Manchester, NH: Clarke, 1895), p. 380.

Figure 21. Self-portrait, *1812-13,*
by Samuel Finley Breese Morse.

SAMUEL F. B. MORSE
1791 – 1872

SAMUEL FINLEY BREESE MORSE, famous first as a painter then as an inventor, had a close connection with Cornish and New Hampshire during his early years. At that time his focus was primarily on art.

His greatest desire was to paint a picture in the great rotunda of the United States Capitol which was being built in the early 1830s. He said, "I have too long lived in the hope of doing something for the capitol. I have studied and travelled to prepare myself. I have made sacrifices of feeling and of pecuniary interest buoyed up with this phantom of hope which is daily growing dimmer and will soon vanish . . . I see year after year of the vigor of my life wasted in this vain expectation; Raphael had accomplished all his wonders and had died some years before my present age; a few more years and my fate in art is decided." Perhaps now was the time to decide it, and he resigned himself to portraiture, "that department of art which will leave bread to my children." Not long afterward a dilatory congress engaged John Vanderlyn to paint a likeness of George Washington and hired Horatio Greenough to model a statue; but no commission was awarded to Morse or to any other contender for the rotunda walls. Morse had in mind what he considered to be two appropriate subjects: the departure and the return of Christopher Columbus.[1]

Morse began his artistic career as a student of Washington Allston. In 1811 Morse accompanied Allston and his wife to England and studied in Benjamin West's London studio. In 1813 the first attempt at sculpture, his *Dying Hercules,* won for him the gold medal of the Adelphi Society. His later portrait of Lafayette (1825) is in the New York City Hall. However, the Cornhill Exhibition, held in the spring of 1816, was a financial failure for Morse as he did not even meet his expenses. Even though he considered portraiture a lower form of art, he closed his "painting rooms," his studio, and took to the road to seek patrons in the back country of the United States.

By August he was roaming the streets of Concord, New Hampshire, looking for patrons in the large old-fashioned homes there. Morse secured a painting room in the home of Reverend Asa McFarland and found lodging in the rambling Stickney Tavern, where the stagecoaches stopped. Morse soon reported that he had taken five likenesses in eight days at fifteen dollars each. Adapting himself to the purses of his sitters, he made these half lengths of Sparhawk and other Concord people on small slabs of millboard, ten inches wide and a foot high; he could complete one in a few hours' work. The backgrounds were dark and the figures rather stiffly posed against the scrolling backs of their chairs. Morse could not render these Yankee faces with fluency, but his sharply observant eye and his small careful brush deftly brought each one to life.

By autumn of that year Morse had completed seven panels at Windsor, Vermont, four at Hanover, New Hampshire, and several in Portsmouth, New Hampshire. He moved quickly from town to town in 1816 and 1817. At Hanover he painted Judge Woodward and his wife, as well as the Reverend Francis Brown, president of Dartmouth College. The latter painting subsequently became the basis for an engraving. While he had been at Windsor, Morse used a 25x30-inch canvas for a portrait of Jeremiah Evarts, a prominent lawyer who edited *The Panoplist*. During his stop in Cornish he painted a local doctor, Erastus Torrey (1780-1828), who graduated from Dartmouth's Medical School in 1805. Sometimes Morse crowded as many as four sitters in one day and worked as much as eleven hours a day.[2]

In 1824 Morse began to put the finishing touches on his painting career by organizing an association which later became the National Academy of Design, of which he was the founder and first president (1826-1842). Yet, his interests were gradually shifting to another direction.

When he became interested in the electric telegraph in 1832, he had virtually given up painting. He was on his way home from Europe in the ship "Sulley" when, during a dinner conversation at sea, he learned that men had found they could send electricity instantly over any known length of wire. From that moment he was fired with the idea of an electric telegraph. On his return from Europe the University of the City of New York offered him a position as teacher of painting and sculpturing. Every cent he earned, however, went into work on his invention.

Morse could not buy insulated wire on reels. Rather, he had to buy wire by the piece, solder the pieces together, then wrap the wire inch by inch, foot by foot, mile by mile, with cotton thread. After he had worked on the project for five years, he demonstrated the telegraph in 1837. He had hoped that the men who saw it would invest money to help him complete the project. They found it interesting and amusing—but not enough to invest in it.

Alfred Vail, a university student who watched the demonstration and whose father owned an iron and brass works, offered to help build a sturdier model of the telegraph. Morse made him a partner with a one-fourth interest in the telegraph. Finally, after several unsuccessful attempts, Congress appropriated $30,000 to test the telegraph. Morse strung a line from the Supreme Court room in the Capitol to Baltimore, Maryland. On May 24, 1844, Morse stood among a large group of spectators and tapped out his famous message: "What hath God wrought!"

Morse won wealth and fame. He was showered with gifts of money, medals, and, finally, a statue in his honor was unveiled in 1871 in New York City's Central Park. He died the following year in New York City.

ENDNOTES

1. Oliver Larkin, *Samuel F. B. Morse and American Democratic Art,* Oscar Handlin, ed. (Boston-Toronto: Little, Brown & Co., 1954).

2. See below pp. 55-56 and also the article on Dr. Erastus Torrey by Arthur R. Blumenthal, *Portraits at Dartmouth* (Hanover, NH: Dartmouth College Museum and Galleries, 1978), p. 47. Around 1825 Morse also painted a portrait of Dr. Nathan Smith (formerly of Cornish); see below pp. 40-44.

CHESTER PIKE

1829 – 1897

Figure 22.

CHESTER PIKE was one of the leading citizens of Cornish during the last half of the nineteenth century. In fact, his reputation was statewide: he is listed among the "names of leading citizens who have aided in the publication of the Town and City Atlas of New Hampshire."[1] He was born in Cornish on July 30, 1829, son of Eben Pike and his wife, Mary. Mrs. Pike was a descendant of the Bryants and Chases of Cornish, some of the town's earliest settlers.

Chester attended Cornish schools along with a term at the academy in Hartland, Vermont. He proceeded to Kimball Union Academy in Meriden, whose principal was then the Reverend Cyrus Richards. Following school, Pike became a teacher during the winter and a farmer during the summer. He was also a cattle trader.

A leading paper stated in 1893:

> Capt. Chester Pike of Cornish has one of the largest, if not the largest, farms in the state. It contains about 1,000 acres of land, divided into wood, mowing, tillage, and pasture land; 40 acres in corn, and 70 acres in wheat, rye, oats, barley, and potatoes. Last season he raised 6,800 baskets of corn.
>
> He has 130 head of cattle, 300 sheep, 37 horses, and 40 hogs, and raises hay enough to keep his stock through the season, or about 300 tons.
>
> Capt. Pike's farm lies in the town of Cornish, on the east bank of the Connecticut River, immediately opposite the farm of the Hon. William M. Evarts, late secretary of state, situated in Windsor, Vt., which is of about equal dimensions, and, in fact, the largest farm in Vermont.
>
> Mr. Evarts raises about the same amount of stock, hay and produce as Captain Pike. On both of these farms may be found all the modern appliances, such as mowing and reaping machines, seeders for sowing grain, two-horse cultivators for hoeing corn, most of the work being done by machinery, the same as the largest farms of the West.

Pike was a member of the firm of Lamson, Dudley, and Pike of Boston, for which he would frequently purchase as much as 75 to 125 tons of poultry, and between 200,000 and 300,000 pounds of wool, all for resale. He also purchased large numbers of cattle and sheep. All this activity was in addition to the cultivation and stock growing on his own farm.

Chester Pike was a selectmen in Cornish from 1857 to 1859. From 1859 to 1861 he served as county commissioner for Sullivan County and as representative to the general court for 1862 and 1863. The first year he served on the committee on manufacturers and in his second year he was made chairman of the committee on banks, a very responsible position in the house.

In 1863, Pike was appointed district Provost Marshal of the third New Hampshire Military District: in that capacity he recruited thirty-seven men between the ages of eighteen and forty-five from Cornish. Pike had a finely crafted walnut lottery box that was used in the Civil War draft lottery run out of the third district's headquarters in West Lebanon; it is now owned by the New Hampshire Historical Society in Concord.[2]

Figure 23. *Civil War Lottery Box originally belonged to Chester Pike of Cornish, who was the district Provost Marshal during the Civil War.*

Because of his success as Provost Marshal, Pike was appointed United States collector of internal revenue in 1866. He served until the districts of the state were consolidated. In 1876 he received a unanimous vote as Cornish's delegate to the Constitutional Convention. It is not surprising that his political activities continued on the state level. He served in the state senate in 1883 and 1884 and became its president in 1885 and 1886. He was a member of the legislature in 1887 and 1888. More locally, Pike acted as a director of the Claremont National Bank for twenty-five years as well as being involved in Sullivan County and local agricultural activities.

During Salmon Portland Chase's last visit to Cornish in 1866, Pike held a reception for him. Captain Chester Pike's house burned in 1875 and its site later became the home of Charles Beaman. The Cornish Colony muralist and portrait painter Henry Oliver Walker purchased part of the Pike farm in 1889. "The Turnpike House," a place where quite a few members of the Cornish Colony stayed when they first came to visit, was located at the northern end of the long river meadow north of the Cornish-Windsor Covered Bridge; it too was acquired by Beaman.

Dr. A.H. Nichols, a physician from Boston whose wife was a sister of Mrs. Augustus Saint-Gaudens, acquired part of the Chester Pike farm on Route 12A in 1890; after considerable renovations, the Nicholses became permanent summer residents in 1892. Chester Pike died on November 29, 1897.

SUGGESTIONS FOR FURTHER READING

Biographical Review Containing Life Sketches of Leading Citizens, Sullivan and Merrimack Counties, New Hampshire, Vol. 22 (1897), pp. 361-363.

"Chester Pike," *Granite Monthly* (July 1893), pp. 291-294.

Child, *History of Cornish,* Vol. 2, p. 285-286.

ENDNOTES

1. An atlas published in Boston, MA, by D.H. Burd in 1892 (p. 336).
2. Edwin A. Battison of Windsor, VT, donated the box to the society in 1945. In 1975 the Smithsonian's National Museum of American History borrowed the box for its Bicentennial Exhibition, "A Nation of Nations." This exhibit was in such demand that it and the box were on view for sixteen years. Pike's lottery box finally returned to New Hampshire in 1992.

PRESIDENT THEODORE ROOSEVELT
VISITS CORNISH AND WINDSOR

Figure 24. *President Theodore Roosevelt in Windsor, Vermont.*

AT THE FORMER PRESIDENT'S HOME, Sagamore Hill—now a National Historic Site—in Oyster Bay, Long Island, New York, there hangs a boar's head that President Theodore Roosevelt shot in Cornish, on Friday, August 29, 1902. The President was taking a swing through New England as a guest of Windsor, Vermont resident, Maxwell Evarts. At the urging of Senator Proctor of Vermont, who was a member of the Blue Mountain Forest Game Club, Roosevelt found himself unable to resist the invitation to hunt wild boar in Corbin's Park. President Roosevelt's own account of the incident is quoted from the September 6, 1902, issue of the *Vermont Journal:*

> We had no luck at first, but just about dusk a wild boar bolted out of the brush, fifty yards ahead of us. Bill Morrison, the guide, saw him first, Senator Proctor and I last of all. The boar took a slanting course to the right through the thick brush, with us after him. A second later we lost him in the gloom. But we kept up the chase, and suddenly I spotted him. "There he is!" I shouted. "Wrong!" yelled the senator, squinting ahead. "That's a deer." "It's a boar, I tell you," said I, bringing my rifle to my shoulder. But I knew better and blazed away. It looked like a miss at first. Like a frightened rabbit the big boar plunged straight ahead, going faster than before the shot. But just as I took sight for

a second try he pitched forward and rolled over dead.

"Now, that's the story of the hunt, gentlemen. And as to that shot of mine, all I have to say is that it was a mighty lucky one."[1]

That night, following the shoot, the President slept in one of the plainly furnished rooms of the clubhouse at Corbin's Park, far from the crowds and the pressures of the presidential office, and unaware of his impact on Cornish the following day.

A profusion of flags and buntings decorated the houses and stores at Cornish Flat in anticipation of President Roosevelt's visit that Saturday morning. Nearly a thousand adults turned out to greet him along with about fifty children—the boys carrying flags and the girls bearing bouquets of garden flowers. Roosevelt made a brief speech to the crowd lauding the veterans for their support in the Civil War and urging the young people to follow in their elders' footsteps.

The children were lined in front of the Soldiers' Monument with the veterans of the Grand Army of the Republic on their right. The President was driven in front of the line and was saluted by the veterans. The children followed with the Salute to the Flag. They then marched by the carriage so that the President could take the flowers from the girls. At the President's urgent request, the veterans marched by the carriage so that the President might shake each veteran's hand.

Saying goodbye to the New Hampshire delegation, which had accompanied him through the state, the President mounted Winston Churchill's tally-ho (a pleasure coach drawn by four horses) and joined Mr. and Mrs. Churchill, Senator Proctor, Secretary Cortelyou, and others for the ride to Windsor. Mr. Churchill drove his handsome four-in-hand, taking the President on a drive through Cornish and past his home, Harlakenden. The Presidential party crossed the Cornish-Windsor Covered Toll Bridge and went on to the mansion of Mr. and Mrs. William M. Evarts for a reception. President Roosevelt paid his respects to Mrs. Evarts, and in commemoration of the fifty-ninth anniversary of the day of her marriage, partook with her of a piece of the wedding cake that had been preserved from her wedding day.

Following his visit to Mrs. Evarts, the President and his party attended the horse show at the Windsor County Fair; they were driven there in the Woodstock Inn coach. Mr. Maxwell Evarts introduced the President to the crowd. Charles Taylor, a veteran sulky driver, won the race and was asked to step up into the President's stand whereupon he was congratulated by the President.

It was a day not soon to be forgotten by the residents of Cornish and Windsor.

ENDNOTE

1. Charles R. Cummings, "The President in the Connecticut Valley," *Inter-State Journal*, 5, No. 6-7 (Sept.-Oct. 1902). For more on what President Roosevelt said in Cornish Flat, see the Introduction, p. xii. The "Programme" for the "Windsor Horse and Cattle Show, Saturday, August 30, 1902—President's Day" indicates that at 1:20 that afternoon, President Roosevelt spoke to those present; a copy exists in the Cornish Historical Society Files, Lagercrantz Collection.

DR. NATHAN SMITH

1762 – 1829

DESPITE HIS SIGNIFICANT CONTRIBUTIONS to medicine, Nathan Smith was a farmer; his interest in medicine was sparked when a country doctor ministered to a sick member of his family. Smith, then twenty-eight years old, decided to study medicine; he went on to found medical schools at Dartmouth (1797), Yale (1813), Bowdoin (1821), and the University of Vermont (1822).

Nathan Smith was born in Rehoboth, Massachusetts, on September 30, 1762. His family subsequently moved to Chester, Vermont, in 1770 where his father was an early pioneer and farmer. Young Smith served in the Vermont militia and at the age of eighteen was promoted from the ranks to a captain in his regiment. Later he served as a teacher in a local school.

Nathan Smith's first brush with medicine occurred in 1784 when Dr. Josiah Goodhue of Putney, Vermont, came to Chester to amputate a man's leg. Dr. Goodhue asked, of those who had come to watch the operation, if one of them would be willing to assist by holding the leg. Nathan boldly volunteered; he even went so far as to tie the arteries. This episode so aroused his desire to study medicine that, after certain educational requirements were met, Dr. Goodhue offered him a home and medical tuition in return for some work required in the household of a country doctor. This arrangement lasted for three years.[1] Following his apprenticeship, Nathan Smith began the practice of medicine in Cornish, New Hampshire.

One result of Smith's Cornish connection was the establishment of a life-long friendship with Lyman Spalding (1775-1821) with whose family Smith boarded while in Cornish.[2] This connection, in time, spawned another important medical contribution. Lyman Spalding, son of Colonel Dyer Spalding, frequently accompanied Dr. Nathan Smith on his medical rounds through the countryside. Through Smith's influence Lyman Spalding became a doctor and the principal founder of *The United States Pharmacopeia* (USP) an authoritative guide for all registered pharmacists and physicians.

After two or three years of medical practice in Cornish, Nathan Smith realized that he clearly needed more knowledge in medicine and surgery. So, he gave up his practice in Cornish and went to Cambridge, Massachusetts, where he attended lectures on anatomy, surgery, chemistry, the theory and practice of medicine, and natural philosophy. In 1790

Figure 25. *The Nathan Smith house, built in 1791.*

he was awarded the degree of M.B. (Bachelor of Medicine) at Harvard; he was the only one in a class of four. His "Inaugural Dissertation on the Circulation of the Blood" was published at the request of the faculty.[3]

Upon graduation Dr. Smith returned to Cornish and married, January 16, 1791, Elizabeth, daughter of General Jonathan Chase and Mrs. Thankful Sherman Chase. Elizabeth died two years later leaving no children. Subsequently Dr. Smith married the half-sister of Elizabeth, the daughter of General Jonathan Chase and his second wife, Sarah Hall Chase. Meanwhile, Dr. Smith was acquiring a large practice in Cornish—usually making his rounds by horseback. Their first child, a son, was born in 1795.[4]

In August of 1796, Dr. Smith presented a plan to the trustees of Dartmouth College for establishing a Professorship of the Theory and Practice of Medicine. The trustees voted in favor of the plan, but they postponed action for one year. At this time there were only three schools in the United States where medicine was taught: the University of Pennsylvania, Columbia College, and Harvard College.

To wait out the delay, Dr. Smith decided to spend the following year in acquiring for himself the best medical education he could obtain by enrolling in the University of Edinburgh, then considered to be the finest medical school in the world. He incurred great sacrifices since he had to borrow money for the trip and to be separated from his family. He sailed on the ship "Hope" December 18, 1796. He attended classes, purchased books and supplies, and spent three months in a London hospital working with eminent physicians.

With communications not as we know them today, and with death striking so swiftly, it was not uncommon for one to return home from a trip only to find a loved one had died. Nathan Smith wrote the following letter, in part, to his wife, ". . . yet my thoughts continually turn on you and our dear little son, whose name I cannot write without shedding tears on it. I imagine a thousand evils ready to befall him. . . . Do my dear, if he still be living, and I dare not think otherwise, do I say, watch over him with maternal care, kiss him for me a thousand times each day and tell him that his papa is coming soon."[5] Nathan Smith returned to Boston in September of 1797.

That fall he delivered the first full course of medical lectures at Dartmouth. Dr. Smith was appointed a professor in August of 1798 "whose duty it shall be to deliver public lectures upon Anatomy, Surgery, Chemistry, and the Theory and Practice of Physic."[6] Thus, the fourth medical school in the country was begun.

In 1801 Dr. Smith had so many students in his Dartmouth classes that he employed, at his own expense, Dr. Lyman Spalding to give three courses in chemistry and to help him with his medical practice. Also in 1801 Dartmouth College conferred the degree of M.D. upon Dr. Smith.[7] It was with great difficulty and personal sacrifice, however, that Nathan Smith taught at Dartmouth. His family still lived in Cornish, and he received from the college neither salary—only small pay from the medical students—nor adequate accommodations for the medical department. He still had to maintain his local medical practice by horseback and over bad roads in all kinds of weather to support his family in Cornish. Finally, the New Hampshire state legislature granted Smith $600 in 1803 for chemical apparatus. And in 1804 the trustees of Dartmouth voted Dr. Smith a salary of $200 per year on condition that he move his family to Hanover.

Another hardship he endured proves that missing library books is not a new problem. In those days books were expensive and scarce. Dr. Smith had been very generous with his own library; he placed it in the school for the students' use. In 1806, during an inventory he conducted while school was in recess, he found a total of forty-two books missing. He promptly removed the remainder to his house with instructions that no one was to take a book without his knowledge.

Figure 26. Professor Nathan Smith, M.D. *by S.F.B. Morse.*

Money for a medical building, though, was very slow in coming. During Smith's time at Dartmouth he spent hours trying to persuade the legislature to appropriate money for a medical building. At that time many people were vehemently opposed to the "cutting up of dead bodies"[8] or dissection. Now it is a common procedure. Pressure was brought to bear on many legislators not to grant money for a building which would be used to promote such activity. Finally, in 1809, the legislature did appropriate $3,450 for a building which was, by then, woefully inadequate despite the fact that Smith had offered to give the land on which the building would stand and to furnish it with his own apparatus.

During the school term, Dr. Smith was busy with classes and lecturing. But during the school recess he traveled all through the area from Boston to the south to upper Coos County in northern New Hampshire, eighty miles above Hanover, performing various kinds of operations. All this, of course, he accomplished by horseback or stage. Not until 1810 did the trustees of Dartmouth employ an assistant for Dr. Smith; he had literally carried out all his work alone.

In the following years Dr. Smith expanded his career considerably. By 1811 he was president of the state medical society and Dr. Lyman Spalding was its secretary. A successful cataract operation on Governor Lincoln at Worcester, Massachusetts that year brought Dr. Smith much joy and praise. In 1812 Yale College decided to establish a medical school and appealed to Dr. Smith to become professor of the Theory and Practice of Physic, Surgery and Obstetrics in the new institution. So, Dr. Smith left Hanover for New Haven, Connecticut, in the autumn of 1813 with his two sons, David Solon and Nathan Ryno, who were enrolled as students at Yale. The rest of the family remained in Hanover.

New Haven was now to be the focus of Smith's attention, though it was a while before he severed his connections with Hanover completely. In 1814 President Wheelock and the trustees of Dartmouth accepted Dr. Smith's resignation. But he was delayed in moving his family to New Haven because of an epidemic of typhoid fever; there were nearly sixty cases, including students and members of his own family. Smith lost only one patient to this dread disease due to an original treatment which he had devised in 1798 and practiced in Cornish.[9] In addition to Dr. Smith there were four other professors teaching in the medical school at Yale; thus he had an opportunity to establish a medical practice immediately. For a visit with prescription he charged fifty cents; surgery seldom reached five dollars. One of Smith's first patients in New Haven was a young woman with white swelling of the knee. She told the doctor that she had had it set five times by "bone-setters" but, instead of getting better, it grew worse each time. At that time it was common practice to seek "bone-setters" for a broken bone instead of a doctor.

A sadness befell Dr. Smith in the spring of 1815 when he was called from New Haven to his home in Hanover by the severe illness of his daughter, Sally Malvina, whose life he could not save. Hanover continued to be peripheral to his activity. During the school recess at Yale, Dr. Smith would lecture at Dartmouth; this practice lasted until the spring of 1817 when he moved his entire family to New Haven.

Smith's son, David Solon, graduated with an M.D. degree in 1816 and in 1817 Nathan Ryno received the degree of A.B. Later Nathan Ryno returned to Yale to work for an M.D. degree. David Solon, or Solon as he was called, established a thriving medical practice in Sutton, Massachusetts, the home of many of his ancestors. In 1819 the tenth and last child was born to the Smiths.

Nathan Smith's medical activities, however, were going far afield. The medical school at Bowdoin in Maine was opened in the spring of 1821 and he delivered various lectures. The first course had twenty-one students enrolled; in the second year there were forty-nine. The great increase in enrollment was directly attributed to his reputation and popularity. He continued teaching at Bowdoin during the summer when Yale was not in session.

Soon after Nathan Ryno graduated from Yale with his M.D. degree, he moved to Burlington, Vermont, where he established a medical practice and also a medical department at the University of Vermont. He was aided by his father who traveled to Burlington to give a series of lectures. The elder Smith kept in close and constant correspondence giving his son the benefit of his wisdom and experience. Thus, a fourth medical school was established under both his supervision and his guidance.[10]

In addition to performing hundreds of operations, Dr. Nathan Smith wrote many medical papers which are considered years ahead of their time. When he reached the age of sixty-five, he decided to quit traveling such distances to give lectures and to work in the New Haven area only. Thus his medical practice rapidly increased. Nevertheless, from his early writings two interesting facts emerge. There is evidence in the correspondence with his devoted student, Dr. Lyman Spalding, that he had been experimenting with smallpox vaccination as early as 1800. Also, in the ledger of students that Smith kept of his classes at Dartmouth for the year 1800, the name of Daniel Webster can be found.

Dr. Smith died in 1829 at the age of sixty-seven in New Haven. He left a legacy to the medical profession not soon to be repeated. He also left four sons dedicated to carrying on his work: healing the sick. A portrait of him done around 1825 by Samuel F. B. Morse (see above pp. 32-34) now hangs in the Yale Medical School in New Haven, Connecticut.

SUGGESTION FOR FURTHER READING

Oliver S. Hayward, M.D. and Constance Putnam, *Improve, Perfect, and Perpetuate: Dr. Nathan Smith and Early American Medical Education* forthcoming in 1999 under the auspices of the Dartmouth Medical School.

ENDNOTES

1. Jerold Wikoff, "The Medical Genius of Nathan Smith," *Valley News,* September 22, 1981, p. 13; reprinted in Jerold Wikoff, *The Upper Valley: An Illustrated Tour Along the Connecticut River Before the Twentieth Century* (Chelsea, VT: Chelsea Green Publishing Company, 1985), pp. 80-85.

2. Emily A. Smith, ed., *The Life and Letters of Nathan Smith, M.B., M.D.* (New Haven: Yale University Press, 1914), p. 9.

3. Carl M. Stearns, M.D., *The Early History of Medicine in Sullivan County, N.H.* (Springfield, VT: Hurd's Offset Printing, 1974), p. 121.

4. Child, William H. *History of the Town of Cornish with Genealogical Record: 1763-1910,* (Concord, NH: The Rumford Press, 1911?; reprinted edition, Spartenburg, SC: The Reprint Company, 1975), Vol. 2, p. 335.

5. Smith, p. 19.

6. Ibid., p. 23.

7. Oliver S. Hayward, M.D., "Nathan Smith (1762-1829), Politician," *New England Journal of Medicine,* Vol. 263 (December 15, 22, 1960), pp. 1235-43, 1288-91.

8. Quoted in a letter to George Shattuck, Hanover, May 14, 1810, in Smith, p. 51.

9. Later, while at Yale, Smith wrote an important paper on typhoid fever in which "he challenged the accepted methods of purging, sweating, and bleeding to reduce fever, and instead advocated a cold water and milk treatment. Little was added to this treatment . . . until the advent of antibiotics." Wikoff, p. 13; p. 84.

10. Smith, p. 120. Although Child in his *History of Cornish* spells the sons name "Rhino," it is usually spelled "Ryno."

DR. LYMAN SPALDING

1775 – 1821

LYMAN SPALDING was the son of Dyer Spalding, one of the first three men to settle in Cornish in 1765, two years after George III granted a charter to the town's original proprietors. Dyer Spalding was a colonel in the Revolutionary War and fought at the Battle of Saratoga in October of 1777. He also served as quartermaster in Colonel Chase's regiment. Such is the pioneering stock from which Lyman sprang.

Dyer's third child, Lyman, was born in Cornish June 5, 1775. In early adolescence he came under the influence of Dr. Nathan Smith, who boarded at the Spalding farm while he was practicing medicine in Cornish. (The house was later known as the "King Elm Farm" on Route 12A; it burned sometime in the 1960s.) Young Lyman used to accompany Dr. Smith on his housecalls. Because of this friendly association, Lyman enrolled in the medical school of Cambridge, now the Harvard Medical School, and he became the twenty-second graduate of that institution in 1797.[1] He soon returned to New Hampshire and began assisting Dr. Smith in the establishment of chemical and anatomic courses at the Dartmouth Medical School, which Smith was in the process of establishing. Both men delighted in keeping medicinal plants and herb gardens throughout their lives as a professional and a recreational activity.

Dr. Spalding started his own practice of medicine in 1799 in Portsmouth, New Hampshire, where he founded a local medical society and became active in the New Hampshire Medical Society. That same year he began compiling a *Bill of Mortality* that he continued until 1814. It brought him national recognition. From it we learn that in 1801 the list of deaths for Portsmouth were from the following complaints: Aphtha, 1; Apoplexy, 1; Atrophy, 5; Cancer, 2; Cholera Infantum, 7; Consumption, 20; Debauchery, 2; Dropsy, 2; Dropsy in the brain, 1; Epilepsy, 3; Fever—bilious, 10; Fever—pulmonic, 4; Whooping Cough, 11; Iliac Passion, 1; Mortification, 1; Nephritis, 2; Old Age, 5; Palsy, 12; Phrenitis, 1; Scrophula, 1; and Stillborn, 1. His description of casualties included: Burnt, 1; Drowned, 3; Fall, 1; Frozen, 1; and Paregoric, 1.[2]

Dr. Spalding also introduced the widespread use of the smallpox vaccination in 1801. The process was relatively new and many people were still afraid that being vacci-

BILL OF MORTALITY,

For Portsmouth, Newhampshire, for A.D. 1801.

BY LYMAN SPALDING, M.B. &c.

COMPLAINT.	AGE.	Jan	Feb	Mil	Ap.	My	Jun	Jul	Au	Sep	Oct	Nov	Dec	Total.
Aphtha.	3 weeks.							1						1
Apoplexy	39 years											1		1
Atrophy	3 weeks, to 3 years, 4 months 55 years.	1				2			1			1		5
Cancer	65 76 years									1	1			2
CholeraInfantum	6 to 18 months							1	1	2	3			7
Consumption	54.50.56.75.44.35.17.83.65.69. 56.50.60.44.31.55.26.40.48.52.	4	1		1	3		1	3	1	2	2	2	20
Debauchery	25, 29 years					1								2
Dropsy	28, 41 years						1	1						2
Dropsy in the brain	12 months			1										1
Epilepsy	4 w. 10 y. 8 w.	1		1					1					3
Fever, billious	16. 30-45-18. 28-18. 14-64-8. 33.			2		1	2		2	1		2		10
Fever, pulmonic	12 d. 15.21.84 y		1		1					1	1			4
Hooping cough	3 m. to 4 years									4	7			11
Illiac passion	95 years									1				1
Mortification	60 years	1												1
Nephritis	74. 66 years						1			1				2
Old age	82.99.75.76.80	2						1		1		1		5
Palsy	54.41-65.L.,-17.46.64-64.43-60,19,80,			2	2	3			2			3		12
Phrenitis	31 years			1										1
Scrophula	8 years					1								1
Still born		1												1
CASUALTIES { Burnt	71 years	1												1
Drowned	60. 18. 45 years											1		1
Fall	17 years							1			1	1		3
Frozen	38 years	1									1			1
Paregoric	6 months												1	1
Total.		11	3	6	6	4	10	4	8	9	15	12	12	100

Portsmouth, situated 43d. 5m. north, 70d. 41m. west from London, contains 5511 inhabitants. The town has been very healthful, not one in fifty five having died. A billious remitting fever prevailed the whole year, which in several instances, in september and october, manifested the malignant type.—From june to october, the cholera infantum was prevalent. From september to the end of the year, the hooping cough was endemic, very few children escaped it. A fifth part have died of phthisis pulmonalis!!! "Is there no balm in Gilead? Is there no physician there?"

Figure 27. *Dr. Spalding's "Bill of Mortality."*

nated might make them sicker. Spalding, however, introduced public tests to demonstrate the vaccine's effectiveness. He published a notice in the local newspaper seeking volunteers. Four brave souls responded, but they had to wait until a smallpox patient entered the hospital. Then these four volunteers, plus Dr. Spalding, received the smallpox vaccination inoculation, entered the hospital, and lived in close proximity with the patient for an entire week. None of the five contracted the dread disease. Thus, he proved to the public that the process was safe and effective.[3]

Figure 28. *Home of Dyer (sometimes spelled Dier) Spalding who was one of the first settlers in Cornish. The brick house, which was located on Route 12A, burned in 1968.*

His annual summary for the town's medical situation for the year 1801 reads:

> Portsmouth, situated 43d. 6m. north. 70d. 41m. west from London, contains 5511 inhabitants. The town has been very healthful, not one in fifty-five having died. A bilious remitting fever prevailed the whole year, which in several instances, in september and october, manifested the malignant type—From june to october, the cholera infantum was prevalent. From september to the end of the year, the hooping cough was endemic, very few children escaped it. A fifth part have died of pluthisis pnumonalia!! IS THERE NO BALM IN GILEAD? IS THERE NO PHYSICIAN THERE?[4]

Dr. Spalding attended the College of Physicians at Philadelphia from 1809 to 1810. He was appointed professor of Anatomy and Surgery at Fairfield Academy in Herkimer County, New York, and subsequently became the president of the academy. He resigned in 1816 and moved to New York City where he opened a private practice.[5]

At this stage of medical history there was no organized system for designating the names and recommended dosages of various medicines. In fact, some plants and medicines were known by different names in different geographical regions. Therefore, they were compounded differently and they were not dispensed in uniform dosages. Furthermore, precise and uniform standards for medicines were hard to come by because many doctors learned their trade simply by following an established doctor on his rounds—usually in small country towns.

Since it was obvious that a uniform standard should be adopted, Dr. Lyman Spalding presented a paper to the New York Medical Society pointing out the need for a national pharmacopoeia and proceeded to call for a group of doctors to prepare such a guide. For three years doctors from across the country collected data. On January 1, 1820, the first pharmaceutical convention was held in Washington, DC. And in December of that year, the first volume of *The Pharmacopoeia of the United States of America* was published as a result of this convention; Dr. Lyman Spalding was the chairman of the Committee of Publication.[6]

Dr. Spalding died a curious death at the young age of forty-six. He was struck on the head by a box of garbage thrown out of a window of a New York apartment. He suffered many months and finally died October 30, 1821.[7]

ENDNOTES

1. Child, William H. *History of the Town of Cornish with Genealogical Record: 1763-1910,* (Concord, NH: The Rumford Press, 1911?; reprinted edition, Spartenburg, SC: The Reprint Company, 1975), Vol. 2, p. 338.

2. Lyman Spalding, M.B., etc., *Bill of Mortality for Portsmouth, New Hampshire for A.D. 1801,* Dartmouth College, Archives Department. Dr. Spalding spells his name without a "u," but both town historians, W. H. Child and Hugh M. Wade, spell it "Spaulding."

3. Emily A. Smith, ed, *The Life and Letters of Nathan Smith, M.B., M.D.* (New Haven: Yale University Press, 1914), p. 25.

4. Spalding, "Bill of Mortality," see Figure 26 on p. 46.

5. Rylance A. Lord, "Dr. Lyman Spalding Founder of Pharmaceutical Guide," *The Northern Light,* Vol. 5, No. 3 (June 1974), p. 9.

6. Dartmouth College, Dana Biomedical Library files.

7. Jerold Wikoff, "How a Young Doctor from Cornish Changed the World of Medicine," *The Valley News,* March 15, 1983, p. 12.

Figure 29. *Self-portrait of Joseph Steward and his daughter.*

JOSEPH
STEWARD
1753 – 1822

ARTIST JOSEPH STEWARD painted many portraits in both eastern Connecticut and Hartford, Connecticut, as well as in New Hampshire. That he "was one of New England's most competent provincial artists and many of his large canvases are rich in color and detail"[1] made him an interesting forerunner of Cornish's artistic tradition.

Steward was born in Upton, Massachusetts, on July 6, 1753, and attended Dartmouth College, graduating with the class of 1780. He studied for the ministry under the Reverend Doctor Levi Hart of Preston, Connecticut. Though he had been licensed to preach and had proved himself acceptable, he was unable to continue in the ministry because of "bodily disorders" that required constant nursing care for two-and-one-half years.

Steward must have regained his health somewhat because he next is found in Hampton, Connecticut, where there was a vacant pulpit and he did fill in at times. It belonged to Reverend Samuel Moseley, pastor of the Hampton church, who, while attending an ecclesiastical convention in Boston in 1782, was stricken with paralysis. He was carried back to Hampton in a litter fashioned between two horses. Moseley remained in a helpless condition for nine years, but he was constantly cared for by his youngest daughter Sarah. In the last wedding service her father performed, Sarah Moseley and Joseph Steward were married in 1789.

About this time Steward turned to portraiture painting in Connecticut, mainly in Pomfret, Windham, Hartford, and Preston. In 1793 the trustees of Dartmouth College commissioned Steward to paint full-length portraits of John Phillips, founder of the academies at Andover and Exeter, and of Eleazar Wheelock, the first president of the college. In order for the Dartmouth trustees to commission these works, Steward must have established a good reputation as an artist. For one thing, Wheelock had been dead since 1779, fourteen years. So Steward, who was attending Dartmouth College at the time Wheelock died, would have had to paint Wheelock from memory.[2] It was during

Figure 30. The Reverend Eleazar Wheelock (1711-1779), first President of Dartmouth College (1769-1779) *by Joseph Steward.*

this period that he probably painted the portraits of Peter and Sarah Olcott of Windsor, Vermont, as well as Jonathan and Sarah Chase and Judge Samuel Chase of Cornish.[3]

Steward customarily incorporated furnishings typical of the period into many of his paintings. For instance, in the painting of Jeremiah Halsey, who gave the state of Connecticut considerable money with which to complete the State House, he painted a vignette of the building into the background. Fortunately so, for it happens to be the only likeness of this early building that we have today.

Steward's commitment to art was fundamental to his life. He announced the opening of a painting room in the State House in Hartford in 1796, and was available for portrait painting.[4] The following year he announced the opening of his museum, also in the State House. As the museum grew and more space was needed, he moved up the street to larger quarters. Thus, in 1815 *The Connecticut Courant* published the following advertisement:

Museum

The proprietor of the Hartford Museum, having made greater additions the last year than have been made in any one year since its establishment, and from the approbation of the most intelligent strangers and others, he flatters himself the public patronage will still be continued; and that the curious who visit the Museum will be gratified. The patronage of gentlemen sailing to foreign parts is earnestly requested, and every favour will be gratefully acknowledged. Portrait Painting performed, and profile likenesses taken at the Museum.

Admittance 25 cents.[5]

The museum exhibited, along with paintings, wax figures and "natural and artificial curiosities" which consisted of stuffed animals, specimens of crystals, ores, and shells.[6] The museum collection was more extensive than any in the New England states.

Estimates of Steward's commitment to art have been many and varied. Not all art critics held the talents of Joseph Steward in high esteem. William Dunlap, in his *History of the Rise and Progress of the Arts of Design in the United States,* published in 1834, says:

"Mr. Stewart [*sic*] painted wretched portraits about and before this time (1802) in Hartford, Connecticut. This gentleman had been, (as I was informed at the time I saw him and his pictures) a clergyman. What turned him from the cure of men's souls to the caricature of their bodies, I never learned." (II, 151). Henry Willard French, in *Art and Artists in Connecticut* (1879) seconds this opinion: "He painted for a very low price, but probably received all the work was worth." These points of view are balanced, however, by the comments of Nina Fletcher Little, quoted in the first paragraph, and George T. Chapman, who believes Steward "attained a good degree of excellence in portraits."[7]

ENDNOTES

1. Nina Fletcher Little, *Paintings by New England Provincial Artists, 1775-1800* (Boston: The Museum of Fine Arts, 1976), p. 158.

2. Arthur R. Blumenthal, *Portraits at Dartmouth* (Hanover, NH: Dartmouth College Museum and Galleries, 1978), p. 45.

3. Joseph Steward painted portraits of Mrs. Sarah Hall Chase and General Jonathan Chase of Cornish. They are owned by the New Hampshire Historical Society. Steward painted the portrait of Judge Samuel Chase of Cornish which is owned by the George M. Stowell Memorial Library in Cornish. For further information see Thompson R. Harlow, "The Life and Trials of Joseph Steward," *The Connecticut Historical Society Bulletin*, Vol. 46, No. 4 (October 1981), pp. 113, 138, and Thompson R. Harlow, "The Versatile Joseph Steward, Portrait Painter and Museum Proprietor," *The Magazine Antiques*, 121, No. 1 (January 1982): 303-311.

4. *The Connecticut Historical Society Bulletin*, Numbers 1-2 (January-April 1953), 18:2.

5. April 19, as quoted in *The Connecticut Historical Society Bulletin*, 18:3.

6. *The Connecticut Historical Society Bulletin*, 46:107.

7. George T. Chapman, *Sketches of the Alumni of Dartmouth College from the First Graduation in 1771 to the Present Time, With a Brief History of the Institution* (Cambridge, MA: Riverside Press, 1867), p. 29.

JAMES F. TASKER

1826 – 1903

ALTHOUGH HE WAS BEST KNOWN as a builder of covered bridges, James F. Tasker of Cornish had the reputation of being a "jack of all trades." He also worked for the town building roads, culverts, and open bridges; many people also considered him to be an expert in moving buildings.

Described as a large strong man with a dark bushy beard, Tasker was born on September 15, 1826, in Cornish, the son of James Tasker, Jr., and Mary Huggins Tasker. His grandfather was also named James Tasker.[1] Although no photograph of him has yet been found, we can get some idea of him from entries in official town records. He first appears on them in 1851 when he was paid $50 for building a town bridge. In 1853 the town records also indicate that he owned three and a half acres, two horses, and one cow with a total valuation of $200. In 1871 Tasker was living on Parsonage Road in the same house later owned by Margaret and Randall Kenyon, who constructed lobster traps in their barn. His property, which at that time consisted of 242 acres, was valued at $7,210.[2] The records also indicate that he was first married to Mary Elizabeth Kelly, by whom he had three children, Henry, Arthur, and Delia. Soon after Mary died at the age of thirty-four in 1864, he married her younger sister, Addie, by whom he had two more children, Robert and Minnie.

A better picture of his career can be obtained from Richard Sanders Allen's book *Covered Bridges of the Northeast.* He has this to say about Tasker:

> James F. Tasker of Cornish, a black-bearded and bushy-browed man of iron build, was in charge of erecting the Cornish-Windsor Bridge. With a partner, Bela J. Fletcher of Claremont, New Hampshire, he employed an adaptation of the Town plan, using heavy squared timbers rather than plank to form the web of the lattice. The partners put up other bridges, none of which remains today, on this same timber lattice plan: these include crossings of the Connecticut at Orford-Fairlee and Hanover-Lewiston, and the Pemigewasset River at West Campton, New Hampshire.
>
> The big rivers spanned, Mr. Tasker turned his attention to the lesser streams. For these he designed a truss employing a series of multiple kingposts. Like others before him, Tasker first built a model. It was eight feet long and thirteen inches square and was made of light wood, and it gave little appearance of strength. When Tasker appeared in downtown Claremont one Saturday afternoon with his flimsy-looking model, he was laughed at by the corner loungers. The builder took the little bridge into a nearby hard-

Figure 31. *The Meriden Covered Bridge built by James F. Tasker in 1880.*

ware store and without a word beckoned the men inside. Then he began piling kegs of nails onto it, pyramid-fashion. When he had stacked up ten kegs, he climbed up and sat on the top one. Since he was a giant weighing over 200 pounds, the unbelievers' laughter turned to cheers.

It was on this same design that James Tasker built small covered spans in Cornish and Plainfield, New Hampshire, and in Weathersfield and Windsor, Vermont. He would cut the lumber on his own farm in Cornish, have it sawed and made ready at the mill in Claremont, and then haul it by wagon to the bridge site. There it was a simple matter for a trained gang of men under his direction to frame and set up a bridge in a matter of days, using previously prepared abutments. A couple of specialists were left to side and shingle the structure while Tasker's dayworkers went on to the next job. Here truly was rural construction genius at work. Several of the bridges built in this manner have survived to the present day.[3]

In addition to his work on bridges, he left his mark on Cornish in other ways. In 1893 Tasker submitted the low bid for enlarging the town's hearse house on Town House Road. The town had purchased a new hearse which was too long for the existing building. He simply sawed the structure in half, pulled the two halves apart, and promptly clapboarded the middle areas. He ingeniously completed the operation in less than half a day. Until recently, when the building was repainted, the new area in the middle could still be detected. Tasker is also credited with another contribution to Cornish. He built the large barn now on Paget Road in Cornish for Joseph B. Comings in 1864; it is now owned by the Baillargeons.

He has also left his mark locally thanks to the many stories that have circulated about Tasker's construction genius. One concerns his method for installing a new lead water pipe. He simply hitched his team to one end of the old lead pipe, fastened the new pipe to the far end of the old pipe, and pulled them both through—in jig time. Another points out that since his theory was that screwdrivers were for taking the screws out, not putting them in, he is said to have driven in all his screws with a hammer.

Some stories and accounts about Tasker assert that he could neither read nor write. The notion may have originated in a confusion of names. A copy of a deed signed May 2, 1828, shows that James Tasker of Cornish sold forty-four square rods of land to James Tasker, Jr.; it is signed with an "X" and the words "James Tasker his mark" and witnessed by Daniel C. Rowell and William Whittelsey.[4] These Taskers were, respectively, the grandfather and father of the James F. Tasker who built the bridges. Furthermore, the bridge-building James Tasker was less than two years old at the signing of that deed. Although there are no Cornish school records available for the years when Tasker would have been going to school to corroborate his ability to read and write, it is absolutely clear that he could sign his name. Proof exists in copies of several deeds, signed with his name, deposited in the Sullivan County Court House in Newport for land that he sold at various times (April 10, 1890; September 16, 1893; May 9, 1894; May 15, 1894).

The *National Eagle,* a newspaper in Claremont, New Hampshire, provided the following account on Saturday, July 25, 1903:

> Mr. James F. Tasker died, from injuries received by being thrown from his wagon, at the hospital in Claremont, Saturday, July 18. He was born and, with the exception of the last few years which he has spent at D. Moulton's, Meriden, always lived in this town. He was at one time a prosperous farmer and noted bridge builder. The present toll bridge at Windsor being of his construction. He had calls to do important work of this kind from adjoining towns. He leaves a son A.K. Tasker of this town, and a daughter, Mrs. Delia Cogswell of Haverhill, Mass., by his first marriage also a son Robert of Brooklyn, Mass., and a daughter Minnie of Derry, Mass., by a second marriage. All were present at the funeral except Robert. The funeral was held at his son's, A.K. Tasker, Tuesday at 1 p.m. Rev. Cain of Windsor officiating. Interment at Cornish Cemetery.[5]

He was buried in Comings Cemetery in Cornish and was seventy-seven years old.

Tasker left us a legacy of at least eleven covered bridges built in New Hampshire and Vermont. Six of these are still standing; for the four in Cornish, see below pp. 65-67:

(1) The Cornish-Windsor Bridge;

(2) The Blacksmith Shop Covered Bridge on Town House Road;

(3) The Dingleton Hill Covered Bridge, also on Town House Road;

(4) The Blow-Me-Down Covered Bridge, located in Squag City in the northern part of Cornish near the Plainfield town line;

(5) The covered bridge in Meriden that crosses Blood's Brook, which was built in 1880 and restored in 1963;

(6) The recently moved and restored Salmond Covered Bridge, built sometime between 1870 and 1880, which is in Amsden, Vermont, near Weathersfield, on the Henry Gould Road.

ENDNOTES

1. Child, William H. *History of the Town of Cornish with Genealogical Record: 1763-1910,* Vol. 2, pp. 363-364.
2. Cornish Town Records, Selectmen's Office, Cornish, NH.
3. Richard Sanders Allen, *Covered Bridges of the Northeast* (Brattleboro, VT: Stephen Greene Press, 1974), pp. 45-46.
4. Sullivan County Deeds, Newport, NH, Vol. 28, p. 55.
5. Cornish Historical Society Records, Cornish, NH.

Figure 32. Dr. Erastus Torrey *painted by Samuel F. B. Morse, c. 1817.*

DR. ERASTUS TORREY
1780 – 1828

ALTHOUGH A RESIDENT OF CORNISH for only a brief period while he practiced medicine, Dr. Erastus Torrey's life is of interest because it intersected with the town in several ways. First, his friend Dr. Nathan Smith, the founder of four medical colleges, and Dr. Erastus Torrey each married daughters of General Jonathan Chase. Torrey married Gratia, the youngest daughter of Jonathan Chase and his second wife, Sarah Hall.[1]

Second, Erastus Torrey studied medicine under Dr. Nathan Smith at Dartmouth College and was graduated from the Dartmouth Medical School in 1805, the same year he married Gratia Chase. Since he owned land along the Connecticut River in Cornish, Torrey was also one of Smith's neighbors. Torrey practiced medicine in Cornish until 1812[2] when, on March 7, he sold his lot on the Connecticut River to Penelope W. Seton. (Could this be where Miss Seton's School was located?)[3]

The deed records also indicate a third connection with Cornish—one that also opened up his interest in Windsor, Vermont. In 1807 Gratia and Erastus Torrey sold land Gratia had inherited from her father, General Jonathan Chase. Nathan Smith, who by then was living in Hanover, bought the land, a fifty-acre lot listed as #10 in the ninth range in the town of Windsor.[4] Torrey then moved to Windsor and purchased land on the west side of Main Street where he opened a medical office. Dr. Torrey must have had a successful practice because he owned stock in both the Windsor Bank and the Cornish Bridge Corporation. Furthermore, there are over fifteen listings for his real estate transactions.

It was while Dr. Torrey was in Windsor that he met Samuel F. B. Morse, who invented the telegraph, but who started his career as a portrait painter. While Morse was in Cornish and Windsor during 1816 and 1817, he painted several portraits including one of Dr. Torrey. It was donated to Dartmouth College by his granddaughter Ellen Cabot Torrey in 1930.

Gratia Chase Torrey died August 4, 1826, and Torrey then married a woman named Sarah; their prenuptial agreement is dated December 11, 1826. Torrey's three children were all by his first wife, Gratia.

Dr. Erastus Torrey's final connection with Cornish and Windsor involved his work on the "Committee of Arrangements" when General Lafayette visited the area in June of 1825.[5]

The final disposition of Dr. Torrey's property offers an interesting perspective on early nineteenth-century life. At his death in 1828, Torrey left to his son, Erastus Chase Torrey, all of his medical books and surgical instruments, as well as his office building on the west side of Main Street, the land on which the building stands, and two feet of land on either side of the building. To his daughter Gratia Ann he left all his miscellaneous books, the household furniture belonging to her mother, which he had carefully listed in his own handwriting on the inventory sheet, plus a lot and dwelling on the east side of Main Street in Windsor where he was then living. His son Francis P. Torrey inherited his father's entire set of encyclopedias, which were then valued at $400, the house and lot lying on the west side of Main Street, occupied in 1828 by Thomas Boynton, as well as "the buildings and lot at the corner between the Main Street and the street which leads westwardly to the state prison." All the stock in the Bank of Windsor and in the Cornish Bridge Corporation and other interests were sold and divided equally among the three children. The final accounting was recorded on December 31, 1828.[6]

ENDNOTES

1. Child, William H. *History of the Town of Cornish with Genealogical Record: 1763-1910,* (Concord, NH: The Rumford Press, 1911?; reprinted edition, Spartenburg, SC: The Reprint Company, 1975), Vol. 2, p. 63.

2. Arthur R. Blumenthal, *Portraits at Dartmouth* (Hanover, NH: Dartmouth College Museum and Galleries, 1978), p. 54.

3. Deed March 7, 1812, Cheshire County Records, Vol. 3, p. 42 and Vol. 9, p. 144, January 19, 1833. For Miss Seton's school, see above pp. 17-18.

4. Ibid., Vol. 9, p. 38.

5. *Vermont Republican and American Yeoman,* July 4, 1825, p. 3.

6. Land Records, Town Clerk's Office, Windsor, VT, Vol. 18, pp. 314-315.

REVEREND JAMES WELLMAN
1723 – 1808

Figure 33.

BEFORE HE ARRIVED IN CORNISH to be minister of the Congregational Church in 1768, Reverend James Wellman already knew many of his congregation. Wellman had been pastor of the Second Congregational Church in Sutton, Massachusetts, since 1747 and several families of the early Cornish settlers, Judge Samuel Chase, for example, came to Cornish from Sutton. Wellman had been dismissed in 1760 because of disagreements with some members of his congregation. Perhaps because he was known to have a very stiff and autocratic manner.[1]

Prior to his ordination in 1747, Wellman graduated from Harvard in 1744 with a B.A. degree. He married Sarah, daughter of Isaac and Sarah (Stearns) Barnard of Sutton, Massachusetts, on November 8, 1750. Reverend Wellman was called to the Cornish settlement on April 28, 1768.

As background for understanding the implications of that call, we need to be reminded that it was customary in colonial New Hampshire for the voters in a town to decide mutually what church denomination would be theirs. Whether or not a person belonged to that church, each citizen was taxed to support it. As Child points out: "The towns regarded it as their right to manage all the prudential concerns of the church; to raise the necessary funds for their support and employ their ministers and pay them for their services. So then a minister was pastor not only of the church, but of the town."[2]

The settlement in Windsor also proposed to unite under Wellman's ministry for a five-year period; at that point they expected to be able to support their own minister. The joint parishes offered him land and forty pounds a year; he quickly accepted. His installation took place on September 19, 1768. Under the agreement with their new pastor, he was to receive 200 acres and 40 pounds, of which Windsor was to provide one-third, some of which could be paid in grain, pork, beef, or days' labor.

Wellman proceeded to build a small house which still stands on the River Road in Cornish, about a mile south of the Cornish-Windsor Bridge. The ferry had not yet been established and there was no bridge, so, as tradition has it, Wellman had to ford the river on horseback, often entering the pulpit to preach in Windsor little short of dripping wet.[3] Reverend Wellman continued his ministry in Windsor until the expiration of his contract in 1773, holding services in various barns in the summer and different homes in the winter. In 1773 a meetinghouse was erected on the banks of the Connecticut River, near the spot where the Trinity Episcopal Church now stands.

However, all was not well in Cornish religious matters. A large number of the members were staunch Calvinists and could not accept the more liberal views of the day. Wellman's views were so considered, especially his principle that allowed "the receiving to membership those of doubtful doctrine and practice."[4] Nevertheless, Mr. Wellman continued to preach until October of 1785 when churches in Claremont and Charlestown met in council and dissolved the pastoral relation of Mr. Wellman to the church and town.[5]

Following the dismissal from the church, he and his wife moved to Cornish Center and opened a store. Since it soon became clear that it could not support a family, he took up farming. He served in the New Hampshire legislature from 1789 to 1793. Dartmouth College awarded him an M.A. in 1792 and he later was appointed a justice of the peace for Cheshire County. He died December 18, 1808.[6]

SUGGESTIONS FOR FURTHER READING

James Wellman's Diary is in the Archives of the New England Historical Genealogical Society.

"A History of the Ch[urc]h in Cornish which was in Union with Windsor the first Five Years"; also a record of 115 marriages solemnized by Reverend James Wellman from January 1769 to March 1805, published in *The New England Historical and Genealogical Register,* Vol. 72 (1918).

ENDNOTES

1. Ezra Hoyt Byington, *History of the First Congregational Church of Windsor, Vermont, 1768-1898* (Windsor, VT: The Journal Company, 1898), pp. 7-8.

2. Child, William H. *History of the Town of Cornish with Genealogical Record: 1763-1910,* (Concord, NH: The Rumford Press, 1911?; reprinted edition, Spartenburg, SC: The Reprint Company, 1975), Vol. 1, p. 110.

3. Byington, p. 8; Gladys Skinner, "Old South Church 1768-1963" in *Heritage of the Old South Church* (Windsor, VT, 1963), p. 9.

4. Child, *History of Cornish,* 1:111.

5. Alvah Spalding's article on "Cornish" in Robert Lawrence, *New Hampshire Churches; Comprising Histories of the Congregational and Presbyterian Churches in the State* (Claremont, NH: Claremont Manufacturing Company, 1856), p. 439.

6. Clifford K. Shipton, *Biographical Sketches of those who Attended Harvard College in the Classes 1741-1745,* Sibley's Harvard Graduates, Vol. 11 (Boston: Massachusetts Historical Society, 1960), pp. 487-493.

THE CONNECTICUT RIVER

THE CONNECTICUT RIVER served as the first "road" to Cornish and Windsor. Indeed, "They called this quiet river/'A highway made by God'/That pierced a mighty forest / Where never man had trod."[1] The English settlers used the Indian name for the river which was *Quinn-tukq-ut* or *Quonch-ta-cut* and means "beside the long (tidal) river." It is the longest and most important river in New England.

Before Cornish's first settlers could travel the "road," they needed protection from the Indians. It could be found at Fort Number 4, now Charlestown, New Hampshire, which was built in 1744 as a place of refuge from Indian raids. The log houses were enclosed in stockades and sheltered all the settlers as well as their cattle and horses.

Dudley Chase, Daniel Putnam, and Dyer Spalding were the first men who went up the river in a canoe beyond the fort in order to settle in Cornish. Mrs. Dudley Chase

Figure 34. *The ferry on the Connecticut River.*

(Alice) and her seven small children, however, were left at Fort Number 4 until they had cleared the land and planted crops—a period of some two years. She missed her husband so much that when Dyer Spalding returned to the fort for supplies, Mrs. Chase begged, indeed demanded, to be taken to Cornish with him. Spalding relented and they packed the canoe with the necessary provisions, along with Mrs. Chase and her seven children, for the sixteen-mile river trip north to Cornish. Dudley Chase was nearly overcome when first he saw his wife and children. The men hastily built a shelter for the night. The next day all hands were called to build a cabin for the family.[2]

In addition to travel along the "road," some means had to be found to get across it. One early solution was a ferry. Dudley Chase's son Jonathan was granted the right to operate a ferry across the Connecticut River by the New Hampshire legislature in 1784. The ferry landing was located near the easterly end of what is now known as Bridge Street in Windsor and thus a significant link between Cornish and Windsor was created. However, New England weather made ferry travel impossible during the winter months. Crossing on ice was done during very cold weather when the ice was deemed safe. Nevertheless, there are gruesome stories of horses and riders falling through the ice.[3]

Joseph Kimball, Esquire, of Plainfield was granted at town meeting on April 20, 1779, the right to establish a ferry on the Connecticut River from Plainfield to Hartland. The New Hampshire legislature granted him the exclusive privilege of keeping the ferry over the Connecticut River on February 25, 1786. Thus, no person could transport over the river within three miles in either direction of the ferry. It was located near the north end of the Earle W. Colby farm, which had been in the Colby family from 1833 until the mid-1970s when it was purchased by Lockwood Sprague. The ferry changed hands many times during the intervening years. Before 1890 Fred Smith bought the ferry and moved it in 1891 to the south end of the Colby meadow. The ferry was bought by "Doc" Melbourne of Hartland in 1906. However, he neglected to beach the boat before the river froze over, so the next spring the ice carried the boat down the river. The road across Edith Colby's meadow to the site of the old ferry was discontinued by vote at the annual town meeting in March 1912.

J. Daniel Porter gives the following account of the ferry operation:

> Two weeks ago in driving through North Hartland, I saw an old man walking along the street, Mr. Melbourne, who used to operate the upper ferry near Earle Colby's. If you wanted to cross the river, you blew a dinner horn hanging on a post. The ferryman would come over with the boat which was attached at each end to a cable across the river. Then you would drive your horse and buggy onto the boat and take a ride. My father once bought a cow in Vermont. We could not get her onto the boat. The ferryman said, "Never mind." He hitched her to the corner of the boat and let her swim.

Another means to cross the "road" was a bridge. The Cornish-Windsor Covered Bridge, though, was not the only solution to the vexing problem of getting across the obstacle. The Hart Island bridge was built across the Connecticut River also near the Cornish-Plainfield town line; it opened for travel in March of 1821. David H. Sumner initiated this project, but the bridge was swept away by a freshet in 1839 or 1840. It was rebuilt by Mr. Sumner and opened in 1841. The second bridge met the same fate in 1859, but it was never rebuilt. Instead, Mr. Sumner returned to the first solution to the crossing problem and invested in a ferry. He received a radius of two miles' protection from the New Hampshire legislature. The following toll was established by the General Court:

> Sect. 2. A toll is hereby established for the benefit of said proprieter, his heirs and assigns, as follows, to wit: for each foot passenger, three cents; for each horse and rider, six cents; for each horse and wagon, chaise, chair, sulkey, or other riding carriage drawn by one horse only, twelve cents; for each riding sleigh drawn by one horse, ten cents; for each riding sleigh drawn by more than one horse, twelve cents; for each coach, chariot, pheaton, or other four-wheeled carriage for passengers drawn by more than one horse, five cents; for each curricle, twelve cents; for each cart, wagon, or other carriage of burden, drawn by two beasts, twenty cents, and three cents for every additional beast; for each horse or neat creature, exclusive of those riden, or driven in carriages, two cents; for sheep and swine, one cent each; and to each team one person, and no more, shall be allowed as a driver, free of toll.

The ferry was controlled by a cable which kept it from being carried away by the current, and it was long enough to carry a wagon and a four-horse team. After Sumner's death in 1867, his heirs operated the ferry until 1872 when they sold it to James Wood.

The next occasion we hear of this ferry is when Charles C. Beaman of Cornish bought the house and ferry in 1895 for $500 from John Freeman, Esquire, of Plainfield. Beaman stipulated that no liquor was to be sold on the ferry or on the premises. This may be a reason why the artist Lucia Fairchild Fuller mentioned in her diary in 1903 that she took her children over on the ferry to visit friends in Windsor.

By 1893 John Freeman of Plainfield thought an alternative to a ferry was in order. He began agitating for a free iron bridge across the Connecticut River from Plainfield to Hartland to replace the Sumner's Bridge that had washed away in 1859. Freeman secured estimates from the United Construction Company bridge builders in Albany, New York. The prices ranged from $36,000 to $40,000—depending on the design selected.

Fred Moulton, on the other hand, was strongly opposed to a bridge. He argued that a bridge was not needed because there was not enough business between Plainfield and Hartland to warrant the expense and because "the settlement of New York people" would like the bridge but it would be useful only for pleasure. In the meantime Mr. Freeman asked Winston Churchill to sign a petition in favor of the bridge. Although Churchill refused to sign, saying that he did not want to look as if he was sponsoring the project, he later tried to get a bill through the legislature to have the town reimbursed for the cost of the bridge.

Meanwhile, Mr. Freeman was soliciting private funds for the bridge from the "New York people," that is, members of the Cornish Colony. Henry B. Fuller wrote that he would be glad to subscribe whatever he could. Winston Churchill offered to subscribe $500. Charles Platt offered to subscribe $100, should the project go through. Herbert Adams said that were such a bridge built, he would subscribe $50. A petition was circulated, dated September 29, 1902, in favor of building the bridge. It was signed by eighty Plainfield residents that included Maxfield Parrish, George S. Ruggles, and Henry B. Fuller, so it was not exclusively a project for "New York people." A similar petition was circulated in Hartland. Nevertheless, the bridge was never built.[4]

The "road" was useful, too, as a means of travel for something other than people: logging along the Connecticut River was an important industry. The following account of a log drive was published in the *Inter-State Journal,* published in White River Junction, for June 1901:

> The annual log drive of the Van Dyke Company passed down the river the last of this month and unless something unusual happens the time made to Turner's Falls will be the quickest on record. Fifty-five million feet comprised their run this year. The Connecticut River Lumber Co. owns the land and sells the logs and the Connecticut River Manufacturing Co. drives them. The drive starts at the uppermost waters of the river, in the vicinity of the Connecticut Lakes and along the border between New Hampshire and Canada and extends as far down as Stewartstown, a little above the White Mountains.
>
> Several hundred men start the drive but 140 men and about 40 horses handled the logs on the river this year. This is a very small crew as compared with former years and was made possible by the good water, even in height. At Fifteen Mile Falls, near Waterford, a slight rise of the river occurred and the drive went through easily instead of being delayed a month as sometimes happens. A large part of the logs are stored in a lagoon at Mt. Tom, where some are used by a mill, and the rest of the drive is let down to Holyoke as needed. The entire length of the run is about 200 miles.
>
> The Ammonoosuc River drive of the International Paper Co. went to Bellows Falls earlier in the season and the White River drive will follow later. In the last year or so some of the romance of camp life on these trips has been removed. The men sleep in tents on shore as usual but the cooking is done in a house on a scow or raft, which floats down the river and is made in sections, to be transported around the rapids and falls. Those who have often visited the camps in the neighborhood of the villages, and tasted the appetizing baked beans, cooked in a hole in the ground or have been favored with doughnuts hot from the kettle of the "cookee" will regret the change of his dominions to the raft.

The *Vermont Journal* of May 20, 1882, told of an earlier log drive of sixty-five million feet of lumber. By early July the drive had passed Windsor. That year was one of the toughest because everything to bother a riverman seemed to occur. One thing the loggers hated most was a bridge built on piers: they so readily caused a log jam that the entire drive could be stymied. The Windsor railroad bridge went out in 1897, perhaps because of the riverman's willful efforts, but the Boston and Maine rebuilt it. The last big log drive on the Connecticut River was in 1915.[5]

ENDNOTES

1. See below p. 92 for these lines from a poem by Mrs. M.W. Palmer at Cornish's sesquicentennial celebration.

2. Child, William H. *History of the Town of Cornish with Genealogical Record: 1763-1910,* (Concord, NH: The Rumford Press, 1911?; reprinted edition, Spartenburg, SC: The Reprint Company, 1975), Vol. 1, p. 140.

3. *A History of the Proprietors of Cornish Bridge and the Cornish, N.H.-Windsor, Vt. Covered Toll Bridge (1796-1943),* prepared by the New Hampshire Department of Public Works and Highways, Concord, NH [1984], p. 1.

4. John Freeman papers in possession of Mary Cassedy, Plainfield, NH.

5. Robert E. Pike, *Tall Trees, Tough Men* (New York: Norton, 1967), p. 237. The book's subtitle indicates its aim, "an anecdotal and pictorial history of logging and log-driving in New England."

THE FIRST CORNISH-WINDSOR BRIDGE
1796 – 1824

BY AN ACT PASSED by the New Hampshire legislature in 1784, Jonathan Chase of Cornish was granted the right to operate a ferry across the Connecticut River between Cornish and Windsor, Vermont. Jonathan Chase established his ferry landing at a location near the easterly end of what is now known as Bridge Street in Windsor. This ferry represented the first step in the development of an historically vital transportation link between these rural northern New England communities and the marketplace of Boston.

New England weather conditions soon demanded a more versatile and dependable means of crossing the river. By 1793 Jonathan Chase had begun to conceive of erecting a toll bridge to replace his ferry. On June 7, 1793, Chase purchased a ten-acre tract of land from Elisha Hawley in Windsor on the bank of the Connecticut River adjacent to the area where his ferry docked. During the months of December 1794 and January 1795 Chase traveled to Concord to procure a grant for the bridge. His trip to Concord was successful and in 1795 and 1796 the New Hampshire legislature passed bills permitting the construction of the toll bridge across the Connecticut River, establishment of toll rates, and the solicitation of funds to finance the venture.

Incidentally, Chase meticulously noted the expense for those trips to Concord in his records. Thus, he began a remarkable 140-year history of carefully kept financial and historical records for one of the oldest privately financed public utility enterprises in the nation. This enterprise became known as the Proprietors of Cornish Bridge and Jonathan Chase was the corporation's first president.

The bridge was opened to traffic "around the eighteenth of October," 1796. However, it was not a covered bridge. "It was an open two-span structure supported by a pair of wooden arches designed by Moody Spofford, who was also the architect of bridges at Andover and Haverhill, [New Hampshire]. It is believed to have rested 8 to 14 feet lower than the bridge that exists on the same location today." The cost was much higher than had been expected, $18,677.23. Nevertheless, the bridge "was considered a remarkable engineering accomplishment for its day."[1]

John A. Graham, during his trip to Windsor, Vermont, in 1796, gives this contemporary account of the bridge:

> In the last week of October, 1796, was completed a bridge between *Cornish (New Hampshire)* and this town, which is five hundred and twenty-one feet, from one abutment to the other, and thirty-four feet wide. With a sublime boldness its arms embrace the subjugated flood that rolls beneath; there are two arches, each one hundred and thirty-four

Figure 35. *Watercolor of the second Cornish-Windsor bridge, painted by Edward Seager, 1848.*

feet and four inches in length, with a pier in the centre forty-six feet one way, by forty-one the other, with the addition of a heater, or triangular front, extending up the river about seventy feet at the bottom, and gradually diminishing until it comes sufficiently above high water mark, to break the force of the ice, and defend the structure from danger. This bridge is universally allowed to be the best and most perfect in *America;* and it is the first of the kind thrown across the *Connecticut* River.[2]

During an early spring freshet, February 16, 1824, the bridge was partially demolished along with several other bridges in the area.

There is no known picture of this first bridge, which lasted twenty-eight years. However, artist Edward Seager (1809-1886) passed through the Connecticut River Valley during the summer of 1848 and stopped in Windsor, Vermont, long enough to draw a picture of the Cornish-Windsor Bridge, the second one built on the site; it, too, was uncovered. It did not fare as well as the first one, lasting only twenty-five years, and washed away the year following Seager's trip through New England.[3]

ENDNOTES

1. The quotation in this paragraph came from the Cheshire County Superior Court documents, *Quinquennial Report by the Proprietors of Cornish Bridge, 1802*, Keene, New Hampshire, the *Windsor, Vermont Cornish Bridge Corporation Paper 1826-1951*, and Richard T. Dana, *The Bridge at Windsor, Vermont and Its Economic Implications*, as quoted in *A History of The Proprietors of Cornish Bridge and the Cornish, N.H.-Windsor, Vt. Covered Toll Bridge (1796-1943)*, prepared by the New Hampshire Department of Public Works and Highways, Concord, NH, 1984, p. 6.

2. John A. Graham, *A Descriptive Sketch of the Present State of Vermont—One of the United States of America* (London: 1797, printed by Henry Fry at the Cicero Office, Finsburg Place), pp. 119-120.

3. Sandra K. Feldman, *The Drawings of Edward Seager 1809-1886,* Catalogue of Hirschl & Adler Galleries, New York, February 16-March 16, 1983. This pencil sketch, done from the Vermont side of the Connecticut River, depicts the bridge nestled among the Cornish hills.

COVERED BRIDGES IN CORNISH

ANTIQUE BRIDGES ABOUND IN CORNISH: there are four covered bridges; each is listed in the National Register of Historic Places.

The most famous of the covered bridges is the four-hundred-sixty-foot[1] Cornish-Windsor Covered Bridge that spans the Connecticut River and connects Cornish with Windsor, Vermont. It was built in 1866 by James F. Tasker of Cornish and Bela Fletcher of Claremont, though it is the fourth one built from Cornish to Windsor. The other three were destroyed.[2] For this bridge Tasker modified the Town lattice timber truss design, which was patented by the architect Ithiel Town of Connecticut in 1820. Although the 1866 bridge did not come under Town's scrutiny, he had the habit of sending out scouts to discover if anyone had used his patented design without his permission. If any violators were found, they received a hefty fine.[3] For seventy years, the bridge was owned by the Proprietors of the Cornish Bridge, a private company that operated it as a toll bridge until 1936 when the state of New Hampshire bought it. The Proprietors of the Cornish Bridge agreed to sell it for $22,000 ($20,000 from New Hampshire and $2,000 from Vermont).

When the New Hampshire legislature initially authorized the purchase of the bridge company in 1936, it had stipulated that tolls were to be collected for a period of ten years or until the cost of the bridge had been recovered. Local citizens appealed to the New Hampshire General Court in 1943 asking that the bridge be freed because the price of $20,000, in addition to maintenance costs of $12,000 with approximately $1,000 to spare, had been collected. A special bill was then introduced in the New Hampshire legislature in 1943 by Representative Lena Read of Plainfield. With appropriate ceremonies, the bridge was freed on June 1, 1943.

The Cornish-Windsor Covered Bridge was officially listed in the National Register of Historic Places on November 21, 1976. It became a National Historic Civil Engineering Landmark in 1970. It is now recognized as the longest covered bridge in the United States and the longest two-span covered bridge in the world. The New Hampshire Division of Economic Development lists the bridge as Number 20 and the 1989 edition of the *World Guide to Covered Bridges* lists it as Number 45-14-14. After eight years of haggling, it was repaired by Chesterfield Associates and the restoration was rededicated on December 8, 1989.

There are three more covered bridges in Cornish—thus equating the town with Swanzey as having the most covered bridges in one New Hampshire locality. The eighty-

Figure 36. *Blow-Me-Down Covered Bridge, built by James F. Tasker in 1877.*

five-foot Blow-Me-Down Covered Bridge, built in 1877, spans the Blow-Me-Down Brook in the northern part of Cornish near the Plainfield town line. It is of a multiple kingpost truss design and originally cost the town $528. This bridge had been closed to traffic for several years, but was restored by Milton Graton Associates of Ashland, New Hampshire, and re-opened to traffic on October 26, 1980. The Blow-Me-Down Covered Bridge was placed on the National Register of Historic Places April 2, 1978. It is listed as Number 23 in the New Hampshire Division of Economic Development booklet and as Number 29-10-10 in the *World Guide to Covered Bridges*.

There is also the Kenyon Hill Covered Bridge, more popularly known as the Blacksmith Shop Covered Bridge because of its proximity to Charlie Sturtevant's smithy. It is located in "Cornish City" on Town House Road and spans Mill Brook. The ninety-six-foot bridge, of multiple kingpost truss design, was built by James F. Tasker of Cornish in 1881 at a cost of $873. It is in a fine state of preservation with very few structural changes. The bridge is listed in the New Hampshire Division of Economic Development brochure as bridge Number 21 and in the *World Guide to Covered Bridges* as bridge Number 29-10-01. The bridge was named to the National Register of Historic Places on June 3, 1978. Restoration on the bridge was completed in 1983 with dedication ceremonies held on September 18. Milton S. Graton, and Associates were the restorers.

Figure 37. *Blacksmith Shop Covered Bridge (Kenyon Hill Covered Bridge), built by James F. Tasker in 1881. By a vote of the town in 1983, it was restricted to non-vehicular traffic.*

Finally, the Dingleton Hill Covered Bridge was also restored in 1983 with dedication ceremonies held on October 23. This, too, is a Tasker bridge, for which he was paid $812, of the multiple kingpost truss design; it is eighty-one feet long and was built in 1882. Spanning Mill Brook, too, it is located at Cornish Mills and connects Town House Road with Root Hill Road. The Dingleton Hill Bridge is listed in the New Hampshire Division of Economic Development brochure as bridge Number 22 and in the *World Guide to Covered Bridges* as Number 29-10-02. The bridge was named to the National Register of Historic Places on November 8, 1978. This structure was also restored by the Gratons.

It is important to note that all three restorations of Cornish's three smaller covered bridges were done under the auspices of the Cornish Historical Society.

Figure 38. *Dingleton Hill Covered Bridge, built by James F. Tasker in 1882.*

ENDNOTES

1. The standard for the length of the bridges in this chapter is taken from the *Thirty-fifth Anniversary World Guide to Covered Bridges* published June 1, 1989, by the National Society for the Preservation of Covered Bridges, pp. 51-53. Slightly different lengths can be found in Richard G. Marshall, *New Hampshire Covered Bridges*, New Hampshire Department of Transportation, Concord, NH, 1994, pp. 33-45.

2. For more on the first bridge (1796-1824), see the previous chapter. It was "an uncovered bridge 521 feet long and 34 feet wide, supported by 134-foot wooden arches which rested on piers including a massive central one"; the second bridge (1825-1849) "had a covered truss structure but no roof"; and the third bridge (1850-1866) was covered and was supported by a single, central pier; see the publication published in connection with the dedication ceremonies, "The Cornish-Windsor Covered Bridge," pp. 3-4; 6.

3. In a paper written in 1839 Ithiel Town concisely explains why people covered bridges once they had built them: "The importance and economy of covering bridges from the weather is too well understood to need recommendation, after the experience this country has already had. The objection that covering is an exposure of the bridge to wind is not correct, nor does experience show it."; quoted in W. Edward White, *Covered Bridges of New Hampshire* (Littleton, NH: Courier Printing Company, 1942), p. 3. Town also had an interesting thing to say about the dimensions of the openings of covered bridges: "The bridge opening is designed to be a load of hay wide and a load of hay high."

CREAMERIES IN CORNISH

WHEN THE DE LAVAL SEPARATOR was invented and patented in 1877, many creameries were soon established in agricultural and dairy regions. This process of separating the cream from the milk by rapid rotation had always been done by hand—usually by the housewife. So the invention of machinery to do the work was of great value, especially for wives who were usually regarded as the family's "butter-maker."

It did not take long for the Cornish Creamery, a cooperative company, to become the town's first creamery. It was established at Cornish Flat in 1888. Its records indicate that it annually distributed between ten and fifteen thousand dollars among its patrons.[1] The Cornish Creamery went on to win many important awards under the management of Edwin L. Child. Child was a Cornish native educated at the New Hampshire Agricultural College associated with Dartmouth College. Fixing his interests on butter-making, he graduated from the Vermont Dairy School at Burlington and was the superintendent of the Cornish Creamery from 1897 to 1909. He successfully competed with 972 of the leading creameries and dairies in this country and Canada; at the Pan-American Exhibition at Buffalo in 1901, he won first honors in every case except one. At the Paris World's Exhibition in 1893, his butter received the highest score of any butter made in New Hampshire and was awarded the only gold medal coming to the state. Twice he captured the state's grand sweepstakes prize, winning the silver trophy offered by the Granite State Dairymen's Association.[2] Bert Huggins was the last superintendent of the Cornish Creamery. In 1918 he left the area to become an instructor at the University of New Hampshire. The program for the "First Annual Tour" in 1915 of the "Cheshire County Farmers and Business Men Through Sullivan County, " which, incidentally was "famous for fine farms, towns, delightful climate, beautiful scenery, beautiful summer homes, [and the] prominent people who reside here," contained the following notation for the eighth stop. It was at the "Cornish Flat Creamery," B. E. Huggins, Supt." and was described as "co-operative, stock owned by farmers, operated continually for past 27 years, large number patrons, receives mostly cream instead of whole milk, makes fancy butter. Has won many prizes."[3] The creamery building was then sold and became a private dwelling.[4]

Two incidental notes help us to see a more human side of the creamery. First, Myron Quimby reports that his grandfather, a satisfied patron, used the Cornish Creamery. Later, his father made his own butter, but bought skimmed milk from the creamery for raising the calves. Second, the George H. Stowell Library in Cornish has a signboard

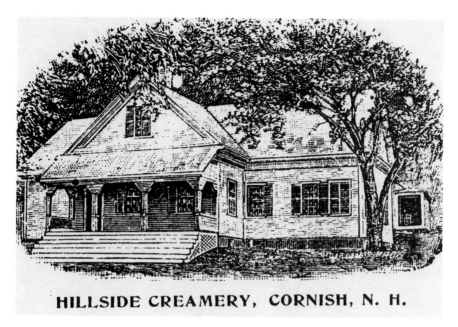

HILLSIDE CREAMERY, CORNISH, N. H.

Figure 39.

listing the Cornish Creamery expenses per day for help: E. L. Child, $1.41; B. E. Huggins, $.72; E. B. Hunt, $.41; A. H. Freeman, $.65; and R. Emerson, $.59. The daily total for five men was $3.78.[5]

The second important creamery in town was incorporated the year after the Cornish Creamery, March 30, 1899. The Hillside Creamery, located in the western section of Cornish just opposite the Cornish-Windsor Covered Bridge, was built through the efforts of Charles C. Beaman. He saw to it that the old Israel Hall house was torn down to make way for the creamery building. By May 18 of that year the new roof was on and the Hillside Creamery began to receive milk on July 1. In 1899 a new ice house was built; it was filled with ice from the Blow-Me-Down Pond.[6] Naturally enough, Beaman was interested in improving his dairy herds and breeding the best possible stock.[7] Many local farmers patronized the Hillside Creamery, including the Westgate family; it was also easily accessible for farmers from the Windsor area. A director's report to the stockholders for the first six months the creamery was in operation states that it averaged 55 patrons a month and produced 5,235 pounds of butter per month. The farmers were paid eighteen and a half cents per pound for the butter. The directors felt that this was a good beginning. The directors for the Hillside Creamery included: Chester Pike, Dwight Tuxbury, Sylvester E. Hoisington, George M. Hodgman, William E. Westgate, Erastus Reed, Samuel N. Stone, William H. Barrett, Maxwell Evarts, and William E. Chadbourne. At one time C. H. Waterhouse was superintendent, but he tendered his resignation to accept the appointment of chief of the dairy department of the Agricultural College at Durham, New Hampshire.

The year before the Hillside Creamery burned to the ground, it was the fourth stop on the 1915 "First Annual Tour" of the "Cheshire County Farmers and Business Men Through Sullivan County." Its description read "co-operative, stock owned by farmers, operated for past 26 years, about 120 patrons, receives whole milk, makes fancy butter. Has won many prizes."[8] When it burned on November 28, 1916, the newspaper headline and story read:

BIG CREAMERY AT CORNISH BURNS

Severe Set-Back to Community—Loss Estimated at $5,000.

SPECIAL TO THE UNION (MANCHESTER, N.H.).
CORNISH, NOV. 28.—The Hillside Creamery burned to the ground today, entailing a loss of nearly $5,000, it is estimated, and throwing a half-dozen hands out of employment, as well as interfering materially with the consumption of local dairy products.

The Hillside Creamery does a large business with local farmers and it ships its products considerable distances, having established a good reputation during the past years. The creamery was two and a half stories high, about 50 feet long and 30 feet wide, and was of good construction.[9]

The creamery was never rebuilt.

ENDNOTES

1. Child, William H. *History of the Town of Cornish with Genealogical Record: 1763-1910,* (Concord, NH: The Rumford Press, 1911?; reprinted edition, Spartenburg, SC: The Reprint Company, 1975), Vol. 1, p. 185.
2. Ibid., 2:87.
3. A copy of this program exists in the Cornish Historical Society files, Lagercrantz Collection.
4. Barbara Eastman Rawson, *History of the Town of Cornish, New Hampshire, with Genealogical Record, 1910-1960* (Littleton, NH: Courier Printing Co., 1963), p. 60.
5. Collection, George H. Stowell Library, Cornish, NH.
6. Windsor, VT, Library scrapbook, clippings 1889, 1897.
7. He had a prize Jersey Bull whose portrait was painted by the well-known Cornish Colony artist George de Forest Brush in 1893.
8. A copy of this program exists in the Cornish Historical Socity files, Lagercrantz Collection.
9. *Blow-Me-Down Record,* November 28, 1916, p. 248.

Figure 40. *The Cornish Town House, originally the Perfectionist Meetinghouse (c. 1840).*

THE TOWN HOUSE OF CORNISH

THE EARLY HISTORY OF THE CORNISH TOWN HOUSE is closely linked to attempts by two religious sects participating in the Second Great Awakening during the first half of the nineteenth century. The Second Great Awakening emphasized the renewal of the Christian spirit in the individual thereby subverting the weight and power of established churches. Each sinner could be saved by a direct appeal to God; no preacher's intervention was necessary.

One group to affect, if not infect, Cornish was a sect known as the Perfectionists. Their doctrine originated in the teachings of the social reformer John Humphrey Noyes, who was born in Brattleboro, Vermont, in 1811. After graduating from Dartmouth College and preparing for the ministry at Yale with Timothy Dwight, he proclaimed himself free from sin and announced that he had attained perfection. These claims were too much for the Congregationalists; they deprived him of his license to preach. Consequently, he set up his own bold community in Putney, Vermont, in 1839.

Perfectionism was pretty much a self-styled doctrine rooted in a widely held notion that Christ's Second Coming had already occurred. Thus, mankind was not locked into a life of sin. Quite the contrary, since the world was free from sin, people could attain "perfect sanctification" and the "second blessing" right here on earth—in Putney—in Cornish. Noyes wrote that "a stream of eternal love gushed through my heart and rolled back again to its source. Joy unspeakable and full of glory filled my soul. All fear and doubt and condemnation passed away. I knew that my heart was clean and that the Father and Son had come and made it their abode."[1] Just as it made it easier for the founder to renounce orthodox practices like Sunday worship, prayer, and adherence to the Ten Commandments, since he was convinced that his heart was pure and that sin was banished from his life, so it was among the grateful Perfectionists who joined his sect.

As he wrote to a friend, such perfection on earth made "marriage . . . a feast at which every dish is free to every guest . . . in a holy community there is no more reason why sexual intercourse should be restrained by law, than why eating and drinking should be—and there is as little occasion for shame in the one case as the other . . . I call a certain woman my wife—she is yours, she is Christ's, and in him she is the bride of all saints."[2] Although his intent clearly was to integrate sexual desire and spiritual desire so that the harmony of the individuals would be mirrored in the immediate community, such notions horrified the wider community beyond the confines of his group. The good people of Putney drove him out of Vermont in 1847.

George Bernard Shaw called this Putney experiment in Perfectionism "one of those chance attempts at Superman which occurs from time to time, in spite of the interference of man's blundering institutions."[3] What Shaw had in mind refers more to what Noyes accomplished at the Oneida Community that he founded in New York after he was forced out of Putney. Although written after he left Vermont, the titles of some of his books are indicative of the ideas that aroused the ire of the Putney populace: *Bible Communism* (1848), *Male Continence* (1848), and *Scientific Propagation* (1873). His experiment was mostly religious in nature, but it also contained social and economic principles. It involved "complex" or plural marriage—though some called it free love, the practice of "male continence" for those whom the leaders deemed to be inappropriate fathers, and "the purest experiment in Communism ever carried on in the United States."[4]

Another offshoot of the Second Great Awakening in Cornish was the group known as the "Millerites," named after their founder William Miller (1782-1849), who grew up in Vermont. After a long revival session made him a devout member of a Calvinist Baptist Church, Miller devoted much time to the study of the Bible—and he tended a large farm. Miller studied the King James version of the Bible with Archbishop Usher's chronology in the margins as his only guide, concentrating on the book of Daniel. Counting the days referred to in certain passages of this highly symbolic apocalypse (especially 9:24-27 and 8:14), making each "day" a year, and accepting Usher's date for these events as 457 B.C. (see Neh. 2:1), Miller discovered that the "seventy weeks" of 9:24 added up to the date of Christ's death (A.D. 33, according to Usher) while the "two thousand three hundred days" of 8:14 added up to A.D. 1843. As a result of these calculations, meetings were organized all across the country between 1840 and 1843. Miller himself lectured hundreds of times. Despite warnings and condemnation from many quarters, thousands began to prepare for the Lord's coming. Just as there had been during the Reformation, there was even a comet to heighten popular apprehension. When the great Halley's Comet appeared in 1843, coincidental with Millerite predictions of the Second Coming, thousands of believers were alerted to Christ's impending reappearance on earth. With its huge, brilliant tail overshadowing a less visible head, the comet hovered in the sky for a month. Many were convinced that it was a sign of the world's last days.[5]

Great excitement prevailed among the Cornish parishioners; it was heightened as the "Second Coming" day approached. Yet March of 1843 and even March of 1844 passed by with no definitive signs. Finally October 22, 1844, the last positive date to be set by the movement's leadership, passed with no significant event occurring. The mass movement collapsed amid a general feeling of betrayal. After the "Great Disappointment," the Cornish congregation dwindled and the church finally closed.

Nevertheless, as this religious fervor and revivalism connected with the Second Great Awakening was sweeping the country—and particularly New England—Cornish was not left out. Meetings of both sects were held in homes of local residents until Hiram C. Fletcher of Cornish deeded a tract of land to a group consisting of John Johnson, Gilbert Hilliard, Constant W. Smith, and Judah S. Deming.[6] A house of worship, known as the Perfectionist Meetinghouse, was erected on this land.

Meanwhile, it turned out that the town needed a building in which to hold its annual meeting as well as other large communal gatherings. The 1845 town meeting was held at the Perfectionist Meetinghouse. A November 1845 warrant for town meeting included an item, "To see if the town will provide a suitable place for holding their annual and other meetings and appropriate a sufficient sum of money for that purpose." The following statement resulted from that meeting:

> Voted that the providing at this time for the use of the town of a permanent and convenient place in a central situation for holding their annual and other meetings is a desirable and important object. Therefore voted that the Selectmen be a committee in behalf of the town to accomplish that object and that said committee be and hereby is authorized (if it may be done on reasonable terms) to contract and agree with the proprietors of the "Perfection Meetinghouse" so called in this town for the use of that house for the above mentioned purpose; and if said committee shall so contract with said proprietors it may for convenience be called in the warnings of the Selectmen the "Town House" (hence, the name Town House Road).[7]

Action was postponed indefinitely, but future meetings continued to be held in the Perfectionist Meetinghouse. Finally in 1849 the Honorable Eleazer Jackson, justice of the peace, was appointed a committee of one "to see upon what conditions the Perfection Meetinghouse can be purchased." It was not until October 26, 1850, however, that the Perfectionist Meetinghouse was deeded to the town of Cornish for the sum of $300.[8] Nevertheless, the few remaining members reserved the right to hold religious meetings on the Sabbath.

Years later a grateful Cornish community continues to use the building as its Town House.

ENDNOTES

1. As quoted in Ralph Nading Hill, *Contrary Country* (Brattleboro, VT: Stephen Greene Press, 1961), p. 93.
2. Ibid., p. 94.
3. As quoted in Ralph Nading Hill, *Yankee Kingdom* (New York: Harper, 1960), p. 215.
4. Ibid.
5. Information on William Miller comes from the entry written by Everett N. Dick in the *Dictionary of American Biography,* ed. Dumas Malone (New York: Scribner's, 1933), Vol. 12, pp. 641-643.
6. Warranty Deed dated August 12, 1840, Vol. 27, p. 519, Sullivan County Hall of Records.
7. Town Record Book, Vol. 22, pp. 74, 77, 78, 79, 88, 151, 158, 179, 202.
8. Vol. 50, p. 425, Sullivan County Hall of Records.

Figure 41. *An early picture (c. 1910) of the present-day Cornish Town Office Building.*

TOWN OFFICE BUILDINGS: THEIR BACKGROUND

THE STORIES THAT LIE BEHIND how the various church buildings in Cornish came to be built tell a series of tortuous tales. From Child's *History of Cornish* we can glean some idea of the pain and passion generated by the debates that led to the erection of these churches. It is a sad commentary, however, that in the closing decade of the twentieth century few of them are still serving their original function. Most of them succumbed to a process of secularization. The new town office building recently occupied by the selectmen began as one of those tales. Even the building the selectmen formerly occupied in Cornish Flat is tangentially related to those tales.

What we all used to know as the Cornish Grange building owes its existence to a dispute within the largest religious group in Cornish during its earliest days, the Congregationalists. The first meetings of the Congregationalists are described in the chapter on James Wellman, above, pp. 57-58. After some dissension among the faithful, a church was erected in 1799; it came to be known as the old Congregational Church on the hill—on the west side of North Parsonage Road near the top of the hill at the junction with Harrington Road. In 1841, however, the group felt that "the meeting house on the hill was becoming old and uncomfortable, especially for the winter season."[1] Unrest continued to roil the waters of the Congregationalists. Some members talked of moving the church building off the hill down to what is now Center Road where they did erect the "Congregational Church at the Center" (what is now the home of the United Church of Cornish). This decision increased the tension: "a large and important portion of the church in the southern and western parts of the town felt aggrieved, and decided they could no longer remain in fellowship with the other portion. The 'high hills' of separation arose between them."[2] In 1841 this group formed "The First Congregational Society of Cornish" and, as Child continues, "public-spirited men among them, at their own expense, erected a parsonage with vestry attached, during the first year. . . . On the September following they took united action about building a new meeting house (42 x 56) on ground in the rear of the new parsonage, to be completed on or before November 1, 1842." Thus the groundwork for the building that is now the Selectmen's Office at the junction of Center Road and Town House Road was laid.

But the Congregationalists continued their internal bickering. The break-away "First Congregational Society of Cornish" angered the Sullivan County Congregational Association, the body responsible for governing all the Congregational churches within its jurisdiction. It refused to recognize Cornish's new group. Hence, regarded as spiritual outlaws by the Association and itself growing deeper and deeper in debt, the doom of the new church and its new building "was now sealed. *It was compelled to die.*"[3] The last recorded meeting of Cornish's First Congregational Society was in 1853.

Help for the building, however, came from an unexpected quarter: the Methodist Episcopal church. They first organized in Cornish during 1838; its membership, though faithful, was small. They used schoolhouses and members' homes until they realized, during the early 1850s, that they might be able to use the building that the First Congregational Society had erected. They rented it for several years; then, in 1860, they appointed a committee "to negotiate for the mortgage on the church and parsonage, for the benefit of the Methodist Church."[4] By June 27, 1867, they were fully ready to take over and held their dedicatory services. Unfortunately, many Methodists were attracted to their like-minded brethren in Claremont, so the Methodists in Cornish were unable to nurture their group for very long. "Soon after the opening of the present century, it was found that the Methodist Episcopal Society of Cornish had become nearly extinct, and the church edifice was partly in ruins."[5] Just as the Methodists had been rescuers of the First Congregational Society, so the Unitarians became the rescuers of the Methodists in 1905. Calling themselves the "Independent Parish of Cornish," and affiliated with the Unitarian Church in Windsor, Vermont, this group dedicated their church, as Child puts it, "in its new order and dress," in 1906.[6]

In the meantime, however, the building had acquired another use: as the meeting place for the Cornish Grange #25. The national Grange organization, those "patrons of husbandry," was first formed in 1867 as what we would today call an agricultural lobby. Their purpose "was to arouse the farmers to a sense of their privileges and to restore dignity to their occupation by placing it at once on a level with the other callings and professions."[7] Locally, the Grange was first "organized at the Methodist vestry by Dudley T. Chase, then master of the New Hampshire State Grange" on March 25, 1874.[8] Paying an annual rent of five dollars for the vestry in the old hall, the Grange continued to expand and utilize their new building. Then, "on June 28, 1917, the church building formally became the grange hall. . . . the Grange purchased, for four hundred dollars, from the Methodist Conference all the church property: this included the church, the parsonage, the vestry and the surrounding grounds."[9] (Although the Unitarians had been holding their services in the building for over a decade, its formal control remained with the body governing local Methodist churches, the Methodist Conference.)

The Cornish Grange remained excellent stewards of the building and put it to good use for one hundred and twenty years. In 1950 they had to add a fire escape; its final secularization occurred in 1961 when the steeple was removed. As the Grange membership gradually declined toward the end of this century, the members decided to do something to preserve their building. On February 11, 1994, the "Cornish Grange #25 proposed to donate the Grange Building to the town for the purpose of establishing town office facilities on the lower floor of the Grange while retaining the upper floor as a meeting room."[10] Extensive renovations, for which the town appropriated $164,000, resulted in the town's selectmen, Stuart Hodgeman, Robert Maslan, and John M. White, Jr., holding their first meeting in their new building on February 20, 1995.

Of further interest is the fact that there is even a tinge of religious history involved in the building the selectmen vacated. As the previous chapter points out, the building we know as the Town House was once the Perfectionist Meetinghouse. It was officially deeded to the town in 1850 for the royal sum of $300. But again a problem arose with the secularization of a religious institution. Child's definition of this issue is a treat to read:

> While the town was generally well satisfied with the Town House as a place for a full meeting of the town, there existed a pressing need of a place to safely deposit the accumulating records, books, papers, etc., belonging to the town. With every change of town clerk these valuables were shifted to a new home, incurring more or less risk of damage and loss. A large safe was provided by the town for the most valuable portion of its documents; but this afforded only a partial solution of the difficulty, as its capacity was insufficient for its requirements, and this cumbrous article had to migrate to the home of the newly elected clerk, there to remain until his successor was chosen. Then, again, a convenient room for the selectmen to meet in for the transaction of the town's business was much needed.[11]

Because the Perfectionist Meetinghouse lacked all the accoutrements necessary for the Town House, the 1886 town meeting agreed to appropriate $800 to construct a Record Building. Thus the former Selectmen's Office was born. Child continues, noting that it was "a small brick building, containing all needful safety vaults, library cases, etc., with a commodious selectmen's room in front, with all necessary furnishings." The beautiful safe Child mentions is still there today. It was a Steam Fire Proof safe the town purchased in Boston for $300 from the American Steel Safe Company. It had previously been in the Boynton Brother's store, which has subsequently been "the E. P. Brown store, then A. C. Thornton's, and now the Schad building."[12]

In 1895, to the tune of $450, the town added an annex onto the Record Building "furnishing the only 'lock-up' belonging to the town. Its chief use has been to accommodate certain moneyless traveling gentry, called tramps, with cheap lodgings, crackers and cheese moistened with 'Adam's Ale,' all at the expense of the town. Sometimes this institution receives its share of patronage, but has no constant boarders."[13] Recent "boarders" in the jail have been Paul LaClair, who used it as a Civil Defense office, and Bernice Johnson, who moved the town clerk's office to it in the late 1970s. In the annex's centennial year, then, the town clerk's office moved with the selectmen to the new office building, with its rich religious and secular history.[14]

water

ENDNOTES

1. Child, William H. *History of the Town of Cornish with Genealogical Record: 1763-1910,* (Concord, NH: The Rumford Press, 1911?; reprinted edition, Spartenburg, SC: The Reprint Company, 1975), Vol. 1, p. 114.

2. Ibid., p. 116.

3. Ibid., p. 117.

4. As quoted in Child, *History of Cornish,* 1:136.

5. Ibid., p. 140.

6. Ibid., p. 141. Child also pointed out that William C. and Frances Houston as well as the Albion Langs provided "special gifts of value for furnishing the interior of the house" (p. 140).

7. Ibid., p. 174.

8. Ibid.

9. Barbara Eastman Rawson, *History of the Town of Cornish, New Hampshire,* vol. 3 (Littleton, NH, Courier Printing Co., 1963), pp. 45-46. Rawson also points out that there was another Grange, the Park Grange #249, established "in 1896 by the more eastern members of Cornish Grange." On August 29, 1906, they dedicated their new building, which had formerly been the Batchelor house, on the south side of School Street in Cornish Flat.

10. The 1994 report from Alan Penfold for the Town Office Building Committee, *The 228th Annual Report of the Selectmen and Other Town Officers (for 1994),* Cornish, New Hampshire, 1995, p. 58.

11. Child, *History of Cornish,* 1: 235.

12. From Bernice F. Johnson, "History of the Cornish Selectmen's Office, 1886-1995," in *The 228th Annual Report,* on the back cover page. Child mentions that the safe had been the object of some thieves' attention while it had been in the Boynton's store: "They drilled through the outer door of the safe and attempted blowing it open with explosives, but fortune did not favor their designs so they abandoned the job and got nothing," Vol. 1, p. 236. Some people think that the design represents Mt. Ascutney. If the records of the American Steel Safe Company were available, perhaps this question could be settled.

13. Child, loc. cit.

14. Johnson, "History of the Cornish Selectmen's Office" also contains an anecdote about the jail: "the Cornish Flat Home Ec Club sanded and painted the old jail cell; it was loaded onto a flat-bed truck and used in the Cornish Fair parade, members of the club singing 'The Jailhouse Blues' while Harriet Runnels was banging it out on the piano, 'highly' dressed with dustmop hair, lots of make-up."

Figure 42.

THE
BOSTON POST
CANE

EARLY IN THIS CENTURY Cornish was one of the many towns in New England that the *Boston Post* selected as a recipient of a special cane to honor the town's oldest living citizen. The evidence clearly states the newspaper's intention and obliquely suggests the publicity benefits it hoped to reap.

On August 18, 1909, it printed the following article:

The *Boston Post* recently forwarded to the chairmen of each of 700 New England towns a fine Gaboon ebony cane with gold head, with the request that it be presented with the compliments of the *Boston Post* to the Oldest Citizen of the town.

A great deal of interest has been aroused all over New England by this presentation. Almost without exception the Selectmen of the various towns have expressed their cordial approval of the idea, and have very willingly accepted the informal trust.

In many towns the *Post* cane has already been presented to the Oldest Citizen, the occasion in numerous instances being marked by a special gathering and the presentation being publicly made.

In a few instances there has been some doubt as to who was entitled to the cane. After a little investigation the problem has usually been solved by the Selectmen, who from their familiarity with the citizens of their town were naturally in the best position to determine the matter.

The inscription on the head of each cane is as follows:

Presented By the *Boston Post*
To The
Oldest Citizen of

....
(To be transmitted.)

The chairman of the selectmen in 431 New England towns within the newspaper's range of readers received the following letter:

Dear Sir—We take the liberty of requesting of you and other members of the Board of Selectmen of your town a little favor, which we trust you may be able to grant.

The *Boston Post* desires to present, with its compliments, to the Oldest Citizen of your town, a gold-headed cane, and as you are doubtless well informed as to the citizens of your town, we ask that you make the selection and presentation.

The cane is a fine one, manufactured especially for this purpose by J. F. Fradley & Co. of New York, who are generally recognized as the leading manufacturers of fine canes in this country. The stick is of carefully selected Gaboon ebony from the Congo, Africa, and the head is made of rolled gold of 14-karat fineness.

The head of the cane is artistically engraved as presented by the *Boston Post* to the Oldest Citizen of your town (to be transmitted). The idea is that the cane shall always be owned and carried by the Oldest Citizen of your town, and that upon the decease of the present Oldest Citizen it shall be duly transmitted to the then Oldest Citizen, remaining always in the possession of whoever is the Oldest Citizen of your town. Upon the head of the cane a blank space has been left where the name of the owner may be engraved locally, if desired.

We request that in an informal way your board act as trustee of the cane, and see that the stick is duly presented and duly transmitted when such a change of holders becomes necessary. We do not suggest any formal trust or any legal or financial responsibility of your part, but simply that you act in the matter in accordance with the plan outlined as your best judgment indicates. There is no charge whatever by the *Post* to your board or to the holder of the cane.

In case your board will undertake to act for us, as suggested, we would request that you notify us to that effect, a directed envelope being inclosed.

We also inclose a blank, leaving space for data as to the holder of the cane, and requesting that at your convenience, after the cane is presented, you will fill out and forward to Gold Cane Department, the *Boston Post,* to be filed in our archives. We would also be pleased to receive a photograph of the citizen to whom you may award the cane, with his name and address written upon the back. We are sending similar canes to various other towns, and as opportunity serves it is our purpose to publish some of these sketches and photographs.

A description of the cane is also inclosed, explaining the method of its manufacture and presentation, which we would be pleased to have you hand to your local paper for publication, if deemed worthy. It is possible that there may be sufficient interest in this matter to make the presentation of the cane an occasion for an informal meeting of the friends of the recipient. This lies of course wholly within your discretion.

We are forwarding the cane, express paid, to your address. If for any reason you are unable to act for us in this matter, kindly notify us at once and hold the cane until we may be able to make other arrangements for its presentation.

Trusting, however, that you may favor us by acting as requested, We beg to remain,

Very respectfully yours,

BOSTON POST

By E. A. Grozier

The *Boston Post* also provided a lengthy, glowing description of the cane:

The cane is a splendid specimen of such manufacture. It is made by J. F. Fradley & Co. of New York, who are widely recognized as the leading manufacturers of fine canes. The materials used in the *Boston Post* cane are the best obtainable. The sticks are of Gaboon ebony from the Congo, Africa. They are shipped to this country in logs, about seven feet long, and then cut into stick lengths. They are allowed to dry for six months, so they will be thoroughly seasoned. After this they are carefully examined, and all cracked, warped or otherwise imperfect sticks are discarded. The perfect ones are then turned to the desired sizes on a lathe, and allowed about three months for further drying. They are given a coat of shellac and rubbed down with pumice, coated with the finest quality of French varnish and then polished by hand with very fine pumice and oil. It takes about a year from the time the ebony logs are cut to produce a perfect stick.

The gold in the heads of the *Post* canes is of 14-karat fineness. It is rolled into sheets, cut to the desired size and soldered in a conical tube, then placed in a sectional steel chuck or form, which admits of its being drawn into the exact shape of the finished head. The tops are first cut into discs, and then soldered to the cane after it has been shaped. They are then filled with a hard composition and "chased," or ornamented, by hand, after which this composition filling is removed and they are sent to the polishing room for final finishing.

The *Boston Post* cane is not merely an ornamental cane. It is designed for every day usage and will last for many years.

The *Post* enclosed the following request for information:

THE BOSTON POST CANE

Town of ....

State ....

Name of oldest citizen ....

Age .... Place of birth ....

How long a citizen ....

Family . ...

Date of cane presentation ....

The newspaper had some additional requests to make:

Please state here anything in the life of the Oldest Citizen that might be of interest. Offices held, if any. Societies? G.A.R. record? Health and habits? Especially to what does he attribute his longevity?

(Please fill out and forward to Gold Cane Department, The *Boston Post,* for filing in its archives. If convenient, a photograph, with name and address of oldest citizen written upon the back, would also be appreciated.)

A large number of reports have already been received. From time to time, as opportunity serves, the *Post* proposes to publish in its daily and Sunday editions some of the photographs of the venerable men, who now possess the *Post* cane. They will present an interesting galaxy of the vigor and longevity of New England manhood.

Thus began the long tradition of the *Boston Post* cane. Passing the gold-headed cane on to the oldest citizen became a customary New England salute to its senior citizens. However, some senior citizens did not consider it an honor and refused to accept the cane. One elderly lady, who was eligible for it, said she did not want the old thing as everybody else who had been given it had died.

Originally only men were presented with the cane, probably because only they went to town meeting and voted. During the 1930s, though, that situation changed. Over time many canes have been lost, either because they were in fires or because they went away when their holders moved. It is not known how many towns still possess their canes. Since the *Boston Post* ceased publication in 1956, no replacements are available.

Following the death of Cornish resident Elmer Bartlett in the mid-1960s, the cane was due to go to Miss Frances Arnold. She, however, declined the offer. Because no provisions were made for the cane to go to the next in line, the selectmen held the cane until after Miss Arnold's death. In 1977, it was then given to James Fitch, who retained it until his death in 1987. It subsequently was awarded to W. Seymour Smith. The actual cane is preserved in the Cornish Historical Society and a replica of the original is presented to each new recipient.

SUGGESTIONS FOR FURTHER READING

Ross W. Beales, Jr., "The *Boston Post* Gold-Headed Canes: Origins of a Tradition," *The Bay State Historical League Bulletin 8* (Nos. 3-4), 1-4.

Tim Clark, "Keepers of the Cane," *Yankee Magazine* (March 1983).

New Hampshire State Library: relevant newspaper clippings.

OLD HOME DAY

OLD HOME DAY, or "Old People's Visit" as it was originally called, originated in Cornish on August 15, 1877. It is interesting to know how it was celebrated here and to discover how the concept spread to the neighboring communities of Meriden and Plainfield, New Hampshire, and Windsor, Vermont.

Reverend and Mrs. James T. Jackson, of the Congregational Church in Cornish Center, began it all by inviting eighteen elderly people to their home in the parsonage on Center Road to renew old acquaintances. It was such an enjoyable occasion that they all decided to meet again the following year. The second meeting, in 1878, was again held at the Congregational Church, Cornish Center; it was attended by seventy-five people. After the third year's meeting in 1879, attended by twice as many people, those present voted to create an organization and to elect officers. Attendance at these annual events has reached as high as 800.[1] The idea of an "Old People's Visit" gradually spread throughout all of New England. From the earliest days until now, the meetings have been of a social nature, with time for visiting, usually a picnic or a pot-luck meal, a program with speakers, and also music.

Some of the local celebrations are noteworthy. In 1915 Cornish held a combined celebration to commemorate both the town's sesquicentennial and the thirty-eighth Old Home Day meeting. The program is printed below pp. 89-110. In 1927, to celebrate the fiftieth anniversary of Old Home Day in Cornish, the New Hampshire governor, John G. Winant, gave the principal address. An open air concert was also presented by the Windsor Military Band.

During this same period there were some notable people who spoke at some of the early programs in Plainfield: Winston Churchill, Albion Lang, Norman Hapgood, and C. C. Beaman, who spoke at one celebration on "Our Three Neighbors—The Past—The Present—and The Future." Some distinguished people present were: Augustus Saint-Gaudens, Stephen Parrish, Herbert Adams, Maxfield Parrish, William Howard Hart, Mrs. Ellen Shipman, Mrs. Woodrow Wilson, and her daughters. Plainfield's Old Home Day in 1902 consisted of selections by the Meriden Cornet Band, a welcome by Daniel C. Westgate, and a song by Mrs. O. S. Bugbee. Addresses were given by Norman Hapgood and Winston Churchill. Reverend Chas. Richards, D.D., reminisced about Plainfield; he was followed by selections played by the Windsor Band.[2]

There were also some gala celebrations in Meriden. The one in 1901 had 1,200 people in attendance. Music was by the Meriden Cornet Band and a quartet consisting of

Messrs. Kenyon, Ruggles, Read and Quimby of Plainfield. Governor Jordan addressed the crowd, mentioning his school days at Kimball Union Academy; he was followed by an address by Winston Churchill.[3]

Finally, Windsor celebrated an Old Home Week in 1901. One of the days was observed with the ringing of bells followed by sports on the Common. Goldenrod was banked on the front of the stage of the town hall for a reception, while all around the room were hung portraits of the most distinguished people of Windsor. A bountiful dinner of baked beans, cold meats, pies, cakes, ice cream, and coffee was served to 1,500 guests in the high school building. Speeches were given by Honorable J. C. Enright, Honorable Marsh O. Perkins, and G. A. Davis, all of Windsor, and by Reverend Prescott Evarts and Sherman Evarts of New York. In the evening a band concert was given in the town hall.

By 1906, then, Old Home Day had become a statewide institution in New Hampshire with state officers and an official programme.[4] Because of Cornish's significance in the history of the development of this institution, a bronze plaque on a granite stone was dedicated at the Center Church in Cornish on Old Home Day in 1948 honoring the memory of Reverend and Mrs. James T. Jackson, founders of the Old Home Day movement.

ENDNOTES

1. Child, William H. *History of the Town of Cornish with Genealogical Record: 1763-1910,* (Concord, NH: The Rumford Press, 1911?; reprinted edition, Spartenburg, SC: The Reprint Company, 1975), Vol. 1, p. 260.
2. *Inter-State Journal* (September–October 1902), Vol. 5, pp. 6-7.
3. *Inter-State Journal* (August 1901), Vol. 3, p. 5.
4. *The Official Programme, Old Home Week in New Hampshire, 1906,* Cornish Historical Society files, Cornish, NH.

A REGISTER OF
REVOLUTIONARY WAR SOLDIERS
Buried in Cornish, New Hampshire

[NOTE: Virginia Colby compiled this register of the soldiers from Cornish who fought in the Revolutionary War and the year in which they died by consulting: General Jonathan Chase, *Papers*; the records both of *Connecticut Men in the Revolution* and of *Massachusetts Soldiers and Sailors in the War of the Revolution*; and finally the *New Hampshire Revolutionary War Rolls*.] To complement this list, see the *Cemetery Records of Cornish, New Hampshire, Vol. 1, 1760-1993* compiled by Teenie and Jack Rock and available at the Town Office.

CENTER CEMETERY
Isaac Wellman 1840

CHASE CEMETERY
John Bartlett 1797
Nathaniel Bartlett 1838
Elias Bingham 1829
Israel Bryant 1814
Joseph Chase 1834
Moses Chase 1799
Capt. Nahum Chase 1827
Robert Dunlap 1801
Hezekiah Fitch 1830
James Fitch 1805
Samuel Fitch 1841
Thomas Hall 1797
Jonathan Huggins 1809
Eliphalet Kimball 1805
William Paine 1812
Benjamin Smith 1834
Ichabod Smith 1814
Capt. Andrew Tracy 1819
Moses Vinson 1789
Richard Vinson 1794

COMINGS CEMETERY
Samuel Comings 1826
David Robinson 1851

CORNISH FLAT CEMETERY
John Allen 1843
Joshua Atwood 1813
Moses Barrows 1795
Daniel Chase 1841
Dea. John Chase 1844
Stephen Child 1831
Ebenezer Cobb 1846
Francis Cobb 1846
Merrill Coburn 1842
James Hall 1826
Abraham Johnson 1803
Caleb Luther 1840
Caleb Plastridge 1838
Joseph Richardson 1827
Reuben Wood 1830
Moses Wright 1856

EDMINSTER CEMETERY
Joseph Bartlett 1852
Seth Deming 1819
William Deming 1833
Luther Hillard 1850
Eleazer Jackson 1834
Aaron Smith 1824
Maj. John Vinton 1838
John Weld 1831
William York 1849

GOWARD CEMETERY
John Lothrop 1836

HUGGINS CEMETERY
Capt. Silvanus Bryant 1832
Joseph Chapman 1810
David Davis 1847
William Furnald 1816
John Huggins 1781
Nathaniel Huggins 1828
Reuben Jirauld 1800
Abel Johnson 1819
Thomas Luey 1837
William Luey 1801
James Ripley 1842
William Ripley 1818
Josiah Stone 1833
James Wellman 1841

JENCKS CEMETERY
James Cate 1802

JOHNSON FARM CEMETERY
Dea. Samuel Hilliard 1831

KENYON HILL CEMETERY
Samuel Huggins 1809

OLD TRINITY CEMETERY
Elias Cady 1826
Dudley Chase 1814

Gen. Jonathan Chase 1800
Peter Chase 1792
Samuel Chase 1800
Samuel Chase, Jr. 1790
Samuel Chase, 3rd 1838
Solomon Chase 1828
Ephraim French 1810
Nathaniel Hall 1809
John Morse 1822
Capt. Daniel Putnam 1809
John Smith 1798
Abel Spaulding 1800
Abel Spaulding, Jr. 1802
Dier Spalding 1814
Rev. James Wellman 1808
Solomon Wellman 1841
Robert Wilson 1822
Thomas Young 1832

PARSONAGE ROAD CEMETERY
Thomas Ayers 1843
Jonathan Bingham 1812
Benjamin Comings 1813
Samuel Comings 1796
Capt. Joseph Taylor 1813

WHITTEN CEMETERY
John Whitten 1826

TURNPIKES AND STAGECOACHES

TRAVEL IN EARLY NINETEENTH-CENTURY New Hampshire relied heavily on public stagecoaches. Consequently, there was some fierce competition among the early stage-coach lines. The first stagecoach line was established in 1818 between Newport, New Hampshire, and Windsor, Vermont; it made the trip each way once a week. People came from all over to witness the exciting event.

It is not surprising, therefore, that competition soon ensued. Joseph Dewey started a line which ran from his house in Hanover over the Croydon Turnpike to Newport. It lacked sufficient passengers to make it profitable, so it was soon abandoned. But in 1828 Captain John Russ revived it. The Windsor line, of course, regarded this as an infringe-ment of its right to carry all the passengers from Hanover. Competition went to such lengths that Russ decided to carry his passengers for nothing. Not to be outdone, the Windsor line followed suit and, in addition, decided to pay its passengers' grog bills at the taverns.

The roads for these stagecoach lines to travel on were another matter entirely. In the eighteenth century a few were blazed through the wilderness. Local towns, until the con-struction of larger turnpikes began, were responsible for the roads within their localities. The need for turnpikes funded both by lotteries and by private investment capital in turnpike corporations began in the 1790s. Locally, in 1768, Moses Chase of Cornish was granted a tract of land on the Connecticut River near Blow-Me-Down Brook, containing five hundred acres with the provision that he build a road through the tract within two years three rods wide, suitable for carriages (a rod is sixteen and one-half feet). The road from D. Wilmarth's corner in Newport to Cornish was built in 1804. The Cornish Turn-pike Corporation received $1,500 to extend it from Newport to the Cornish Bridge.

In addition to the quality of the roads being an issue, there were concerns about the quality of the bridges on the roads. Horses were made to walk across the bridge or the owner would be fined since if the horses galloped, they would set up a momentum which would rock the bridge. Therefore, they were obliged to break cadence. Hence, the ratio-nale for the sign posted on covered bridges, "walk your horses or pay two dollars fine."

Finally, there was the question of the people using the roads. To meet the needs of the traveler, many farmhouses were turned into taverns. The Cornish Inn and store at Cor-nish Flat was begun by Daniel Chase in the early 1800s. It burned in 1927. Also, some of the people objected to paying their way on turnpikes. Because they were constructed by private capital, they were privately owned. To protect their investment, these owners, on some of the early turnpikes, erected gates at which a traveler had to stop and pay a toll.

Naturally enough, some localities built roads that avoided the toll. Hence, the origin of the word "shunpike."

There are several brief, interesting accounts of happenings and mishappenings on our local roads. In 1886 this news item appeared in the *New Hampshire Argus and Spectator,* "Croydon Flat—Another smash-up in town, this time it being a wagon loaded with eggs, which were being transported by Seth Cole of Cornish over the celebrated mountain road which leads from Four Corners to Cornish Flat. Damage claimed, $300." Somewhat later, in 1903, this note appeared in a local newspaper: "Frank E. Corey, the popular stage driver between Meriden and Windsor, recently received a handsome present from his city friends along the route as a token of appreciation of his services." One of these city friends may well have been Maud Howe Elliott, daughter of Julia Ward Howe, who wrote the words for "The Battle Hymn of the Republic." Maud Elliott pointed out that, around 1904, "The only public conveyance was the old stage coach that jogged by on its way to Windsor every morning."[1]

SUGGESTED FOR FURTHER READING

Draft of a talk on "Highways, Turnpikes, and Taverns" given by John Dryfhout to the Cornish and Plainfield Historical Societies at the Plainfield School, February 24, 1987; copy in Cornish Historical Society files, Cornish, NH.

Donna-Belle Garvin and James L. Garvin, *On the Road North of Boston: New Hampshire Taverns and Turnpikes, 1700-1900* (Concord, NH: New Hampshire Historical Society, 1988).

ENDNOTE

1. Maud Howe Elliott, *John Elliott, the Story of an Artist* (Boston: Houghton Mifflin, 1930), p. 144.

THE SESQUICENTENNIAL BOOKLET:
Cornish's One Hundred Fiftieth Anniversary

(Cornish celebrated the sesquicentennial of its settlement at the Old Home Day festivities on August 18, 1915. The observances on this notable occasion included many speeches and exhibits of historical items. A crowd estimated to be about 800 people attended; even some members of President Woodrow Wilson's family were present. The booklet published in conjunction with this event is an interesting document, but not many copies of it have survived. That is only one of the reasons why it is printed here in its entirety; generally speaking, it retains the usage, capitalization, and punctuation of the original. More importantly, it is placed at the end of this section about Cornish's people, places, and things because it serves as a significant transition to the next section about the Cornish Colony. On the one hand, it contains a speech about "The Colony" by one of its stalwart representatives, Winston Churchill. It is thus a contemporary source for who was then considered to be a member of the Colony. On the other hand, it provides a fitting close to the earlier section of this book because its poetry and speeches are replete with feelings of pride, respect, and admiration for the past as well as optimism for the present and future of Cornish. Their sentiment and expression may strike us as old-fashioned—even quaint and complacent. Nevertheless, the booklet remains a vivid reminder, made more so by the passage of time, of the glories of Cornish.)

Proceedings and Exercises of the
One Hundred Fiftieth Anniversary of the settlement of
CORNISH, NEW HAMPSHIRE

August 18th, 1915

IN CONNECTION WITH OLD HOME DAY
OR THE ANNUAL OLD PEOPLE'S VISIT

How the 150th Anniversary Was Heralded

At the annual meeting in March [1915], the town appropriated a sum of money for the observance of the One Hundred and Fiftieth Anniversary of the Settlement of Cornish, and appointed the Selectmen, P. S. Gordon, F. A. Tifft and W. W. Balloch, to act with the Old Home Committee, F. B. Comings, W. H. Sisson and G. L. Deming, in expending the same. The Selectmen requested the Old Home Committee to arrange the program and have charge of the proceedings, being in readiness themselves to assist as occasion might require.

The Committee issued a poster, which was practically the same as in previous years.

This invitation to the sons and daughters of Cornish scattered abroad had been previously extended:

1765–1915
CORNISH, N.H. 150th ANNIVERSARY CELEBRATION
—and—
THE OLD PEOPLE'S VISIT / WEDNESDAY, AUGUST 18, 1915

THE TOWN OF CORNISH, N.H. will celebrate the 150th Anniversary of its Settlement

In connection with the "Old People's Visit" on Wednesday, August 18, 1915, at the Congregational Church, as usual.

The Committee appointed by the Town earnestly desire that all sons and daughters, former residents, and all others interested in the history of Cornish, shall on this occasion unite with its citizens in celebrating the anniversary of its settlement.

PEARL S. GORDON, Cornish Flat, N.H
FRED A. TIFFT, Cornish Flat, N.H.
WM. W. BALLOCH, Windsor, Vt., R.F.D., No. 4
Selectmen of Cornish.
FENNO B. COMINGS, Windsor, Vt., R.F.D., No. 4.
WM. H. SISSON, Cornish Flat, N.H.
GEO. L. DEMING, Cornish Flat, N.H.
Committee Old People's Association.

At the appointed hour the church was filled and many remained outside. Programs as follows were distributed, after which the President called to order.

1765–1915
Programme of THE OLD PEOPLE'S VISIT
And the Celebration of THE 150th ANNIVERSARY of the Settling of the TOWN OF CORNISH
New Hampshire
Wednesday, August 18, 1915
AT CONGREGATIONAL CHURCH, Cornish Center, N.H.

Order of Exercises
1:30 P.M.

1. MUSIC
2. INVOCATION AND SCRIPTURE READING
   By the Rev. Messrs. Skinner and Sisson
   (Joshua 24:1-3, 13-17; Hebrews 11:1, 2, 8-13, 32-40).
3. THE WELCOME   Mr. F. B. Comings
4. RESPONSE   Original Poem by Mrs. M. W. Palmer
5. MUSIC   Mr. Herbert E. Wood
6. THE BEGINNINGS
   (a) The Settling   Mr. G. L. Deming
   (b) The First Churches   Mr. W. H. Child
   (c) Our Soldiers   Mr. W. H. Sisson
7. ORIGINAL HYMN   Words by G. E. Fairbanks
              Music composed by H. E. Wood
8. LATER HAPPENINGS
   (a) The Early Ways   Dr. Fitch
   (b) The District Schools   Prof. Tracy
   (c) The Colony   Col. Churchill
9. MUSIC—Song   Mrs. Lombard
10. FINAL ADDRESS   Hon. S. L. Powers
11. SONG—"God Be With You Till We Meet Again."
12. BENEDICTION   Rev. G. Skinner

The singing was by the Bartlett and Quimby quartette, comprising Arthur and Elmer Bartlett, Erwin and Elwin Quimby, the twins that look alike. Herbert Wood was organist.

Scripture selections were read by Rev. George Sisson, D.D., and Rev. George Skinner offered prayer.

ADDRESS OF WELCOME
By Mr. F. B. Comings

Citizens of Cornish, Ladies and Gentlemen, and Invited Guests:

The event we celebrate today is the most notable and important in our history: the settlement of Cornish, one hundred and fifty years ago. We are proud of our town; we admire its natural scenery; but most of all we pay our homage to the founders of our town whose foresight and sagacity made possible the Cornish of today.

It gives me pleasure, on behalf of the town and on behalf of the "Old People's Association" to welcome you all to this festival and to offer you the program of the day.

One thing we are sure you will find quite beyond criticism,—the warmth and sincerity of your welcome.

RESPONSE
By Mrs. M. W. Palmer

The response was by Mrs. Marion Palmer, who prefaced her poem with a few well chosen words, expressing a surprise at being chosen for this task, but a willingness and pleasure to assist in any possible way.

Years that are more than thirty
Dear Friends, have passed away
Since our first invitation
Here on an August day
Then 'twas the Old Folks' Visit,
And we their names revere,
Who made that Institution
A yearly blessing here.
With Old Home Day united,
It e'er will speak the worth
Of two most faithful people,
Who gave this gathering birth.[1]
In vain I look for faces,
And Oh, I miss them so,
Who gave us cordial welcome
Here forty years ago;
Instead of these, their children
Are with us here today,
And bring their own, attesting
God's promise true alway.
Some, with the benediction
That lengthened years attain,
Still bless us with their presence;
Oh, may they long remain;
For them we ask rich blessing
Through their remaining years,
With hearts in peace abiding

And eyes unwashed by tears.
The workers God is changing
But still the work goes on,
We leave them in His keeping,
That loved and absent throng.
Today a double reason
Has brought us from our homes,
For, through the centuries sounding
A voice compulsive comes;
The Pioneers are calling—
Today they seem alive
And ask for the remembrance of 1765.
The Pioneers of Cornish!
Amid these hills so green,
They made it like a garden
Where forests wild had been.
The birth year of old Cornish!
We come, her children true,
Back to the dear Old Mother
To give her honor due.
No word or gratulation
We gave her hundredth year,
For grief for brothers fallen
Was causing many a tear;[2]
But, with another fifty
Now added to her crown,
We come, with joy and music,

To greet our own home town.
What visions come before us—
They almost bring the tears—
When we alone consider
Her first, long, fifty years.
We see a shining river,
Dark woods on either side
And boats, with men of wisdom
Breasting the rolling tide,
Into the forest coming.
Not as we come, 'tis true,
Today with "Autos" shrieking,
But paddling their own canoe,
They called this quiet river
"A highway made by God"
That pierced a mighty forest
Where never man had trod.
The work that for them waited!
Roads, houses, laws to make;
Schools for the coming children,
Churches for Christ's dear sake.
Unselfish in their planning
The fathers ever tried
Home, school and church to nurture
Close planted, side by side.
Under the trees they worship
When Summer lights the skies,
Again from humble dwellings
Their songs of praise arise.
Not saints, were all these people,
Dissensions oft' arose;
And angry words were spoken,
As the church record shows.
In this primeval forest
were trees so straight and tall
They graced the King's own Navy,
Obedient to his call.
So of her sons and daughters
Cornish most gladly gave;
Isles of the sea have blessed her,
For leaders true and brave.
Among these scenes of hardship
Women were not afraid,
One brought her children seven.
And here, her home she made.[3]

We seem to hear the grating
Of the boat upon the sand,
She waiting, 'til her husband
Should see "the freight" at hand.
Altho' the number doubled
She did not wish them less.
And thro' the halls of Dartmouth
Sent seven the world to bless.
Down through the ages coming
The story has oft' been told
Of her brave and patient living
Through storm and heat and cold.
And there were other mothers,
With needle, wheel and loom,
Busy at ceaseless labor
For comfort in the home.
A library went travelling[4]
About from door to door,
And blessings for its readers
Upon its leaves it bore.
The evening schools were many
By light of candles dim.
For spelling and to cipher
We gladly gathered in.
Ah, let no chronic croakers
Before us dare to say,
As sometimes I have heard them,
That country life is "gray."
The Fathers took the title
To hill and vale and plain
to them and theirs forever,
And so they ours remain.
Not only by the maples
That grew so fair and tall,
Nor lilies blooming fragrant
Do we those homes recall.
The sweet and tender graces
That made those houses home
Abide with us forever
Wherever we may roam.
Their faith and hope and patience
With love to crown them all,
Blossomed with sweeter fragrance
Than roses by the wall.
Bound by a tie enduring,

Which strengthens every year;
We never can forget them
Those early homes so dear.
I love those old-time houses
Built four-square, stout and strong,
As if for useful service
Thro' many years and long.
They seem to speak in silence
Of those who've passed their doors,
Who trod, in all their freshness,
Their steps and stairs and floors.
One line along the river
Tells where the Chases dwelt;
Their power to mould and guide them
Both town and College felt.
Then by the winding streamlets
We find the Comings skill
Still speaking to the ages
In houses, church and mill.
The Wymans and the Wellmans
Stood firm for truth and right;
Their homes remain—their influence
Still shineth as a light.
We all recall the Bartletts
On Dingleton so fair,
Their sons and daughters many
Made music in the air.
Then farther north the Tracys
With Stones and Rowells vie
In spreading education
From east to western sky.
Tho' time forbids the mention
Of all, whom we revere,
One other name undying
I wish to speak of here—
For one Colonial mansion
Still standing trig and pat
Today attracts attention
When we reach Cornish Flat.
Here lived a worthy couple
And here a servant dwelt
Who toiled for but a pittance,
But in her soul she felt

Desire to help the heathen,
And from her scanty hoard
The first bequest was given
To the American Board.[5]
Another dwelling pointeth
To a physician brave
Whose sons and grandsons earnest
Tried stricken souls to save.[6]
In one was early nurtured
The woman, who still stands
Beside her husband, equal,
In Kimball Union bands.[7]
Still other houses tell us
In valley and on hill
Of men, whose influence lasteth
Abiding with us still.
Amid them all the Library
Doth now our thoughts engage;
A blessing thro' the coming years.
A present to our age.[8]
What lessons do they teach us,
These builders of the past?
They say "Work for the future;
Do those things that will last;
Not for ourselves our labor,
Not for ourselves our toil,
For the children that came after
We tilled the virgin soil;
For town and state and country
We gave our very best;
When either called we answered,
Obeying her behest."
May their example help us,
Who now are in the strife,
To live a little better,
A little purer life;
So that, when comes the summons
That calls us, one by one,
The world may be the better
For what our age has done.
Let's send a hearty greeting
By who may be alive
To those who come together / In 1965.

The Orchestra then entertained the audience with several ancient musical selections, recalling the days of "Old Lang Syne."

THE SETTLING OF CORNISH

by Mr. G.L. Deming

Mr. President, Ladies and Gentlemen:

Everything which hath an ending, must of necessity, also have a beginning; and you notice that our program speaks of "The beginnings" and my remarks are but the beginning of "The beginnings." For contrary to my wishes and against my best judgment I have been selected to give a few historical facts concerning the coming of the pale face, a sort of introduction to the treat in store for you—for when I inquired what was expected of me, what to do or to say, I was told "to get them here" meaning, I suppose, the Colonists, as this would be the starting point of the gentlemen who are to address you. So if you will bear with me, I will see to it that my words shall have the merit of brevity.

I am not expected to give an address, I could not if I would.

Fifty-two years ago an attempt was made to commemorate the one hundredth anniversary of the granting of the charter which occurred in 1763. I well remember that the late David Hilliard was much interested in it, but this was in the midst of the war, the town was in mourning, greater things were taking the attention of the people and the matter was dropped. Now, we commemorate not the granting of the charter but the settlement of the town.

We understand that 150 years ago, this entire town and others around it were a wilderness; a "howling wilderness" I suppose it would be called, but what did the howling unless it were the wolves, I do not know, it certainly was not the Indians. For it was a very favorable time to found Colonies at about this time, for the French and Indian wars were nearly at an end, the conquest of Canada by the British put an end to Indian raids led on by the French, and no hostile tribes lived within striking distance.[9] White men had been here previous to the coming of the settlers, sent by the British government which reserved all pine trees suitable for masts for the Royal Navy.

The camp they erected, probably a log house, was still standing, known as the "Mast Camp." This was a short distance south-easterly from Cornish Mills. It is supposed by many that these men felled the pines and floated them down the river; but this seems well-nigh impossible. Without roads it must have taken several men and teams to have done this, and there is no record, so far as I know, of the Colonists finding roads, or other evidences of such work, only a camp. I rather suspect they were searching the forest for the trees to be reserved, and marking them with an arrow to protect them from settlers whenever they came. It is claimed that Daniel Putnam and Mr. Dyer Spaulding and others, lived in this camp during the winter of 1764–1765. Mr. Putnam had married the daughter of Judge Chase of Sutton and was probably looking for a suitable place in the wilderness to make his home. How they busied themselves during the winter is not known. It may be a portion of the time was spent in felling the trees and getting in readiness for putting in a crop, for Mr. Putnam soon left the other Colonists and returned to near where he had spent the winter, and began the homestead still remaining in the name, the only instance. They went back in the early spring and a little later returned, Judge Chase stopping at Walpole and the other members of their families at Charlestown, then called No. 4. They located near the mouth of "Blow-Me-Down" Brook on land now owned by Mrs. Beaman. This name "Blow-Me-Down" appears as early as 1772, its origin is still a mystery. The late Mr. Beaman offered a reward of $50 for its solution but the money is still unclaimed. Deacon Dudley Chase, son of Judge Chase, was of the party and his wife among those left at No. 4. Later on Mr. Spaulding returned to No. 4 for supplies and Mrs. Chase insisted on returning with him, although he told her plainly that they had no shelter even for themselves, but like the ladies of today, she had her way, for come she would and come she did. Their daughter Alice was the first white child born in town, her brilliant scholarship is mentioned by the historian. I might speak of the character of these Colonists, their sterling worth, but that is for another. I might speak of their deep religious interest, how in three years they had organized a Church and settled a Pastor, but that is still another's subject. I might speak of their independence and readiness to battle for their rights, but that is also for another. I might speak of their desire to establish schools, the struggles they made for an education. With their desire to prepare the means of education a legend which still lingers seems incredible. That the founders of Dartmouth desired to locate the college on the plain near Trinity church, but that the owners of the land refused to sell and they proceeded on to Hanover. I will, however, say this, General Chase was probably one of the greatest "all-around men" that the town of Cornish has ever produced, and Samuel Chase was "it" in much of the town's early history. I have felt a bond of sympathy with him for it was he who presided over the deliberations of the town at its first annual meeting and it has been my fortune to perform the same duties at its last. The charter was granted to Rev. Samuel McClintock of Greenfield and 69 others. The compensation demanded was one ear of corn annually at Christmas, if lawfully demanded.

The town was to be six miles square and divided into seventy-six shares, each grantee having one, Governor Wentworth two, a school lot, first minister lot, ministerial lot and propagation lot. The town received its name from Cornish, in England, some of the grantees coming from there. Each grantee was also to have one acre as near the center of the town as practical, evidently to found a village. Nothing seems to have been done with this. But few names of the grantees appear in the early town records. We find Ayers, Bartlett, Johnson, Foss, Huggins and a few others. Fortunate indeed was the town in being settled by so worthy a class of pioneers; noble men and women they were. And I am proud to be one of those who believe that Cornish continued even to the present day to produce great men and noble women, competent to fill any position to which duty called.

Ready to dare, to do, or to die, if need-be for home and country. And I further believe that the character of her citizenship as well as her beautiful scenery, has been a prominent factor in inducing others to make their homes on our hillsides; not agriculturists, but representing many of the arts, of which another will speak to you, during these exercises, a class which Cornish can and does welcome. I hold in my hand an early plot of the town giving the names of most of the purchasers of the lots.

THE FIRST CHURCHES
by Mr. W. H. Child

Ladies and Gentlemen:

I am told that the subject of the "History of the First Churches of Cornish" has been assigned me for this afternoon.

Every one can readily perceive that this is no small subject, and one that needs considerable time to do the justice it requires.

I am also told that I am limited in time to ten minutes, and in no case to exceed fifteen minutes. It cannot be expected that in so short a time I can cover but a small part of the subject. It reminds me of the story of the boy who was told to go and set a hen. So he gathered a large lot of eggs and built a large nest and then set the hen upon it. Upon being asked why he had built so large a nest and put in so many eggs, he replies: "I wanted to see the old hen spread herself." As it will be impossible for me to cover all the subject calls for, I will make brief mention of some leading facts.

The Congregationalists were the first sect on the ground in the early settlement of the town. The first inhabitants came chiefly from Sutton, Mass. They had enjoyed the services of their pastor there—Rev. James Wellman, and as a prominent portion of his congregation were leaving for Cornish, it was only a natural desire that in due time he should receive a call to settle in Cornish where a large part of his congregation had already gone. He was therefore called in April, 1768. He accepted the call, and on the following September a church was organized by the Congregational Council, with Rev. James Wellman as pastor and minister of the "Church of Cornish and Windsor."

In those years the town assumed all the provision for the preacher's needs, as salary, etc., and nearly the whole community attended church. This was the first church established in Cornish. For a time all things seemed to prosper, but gradually dissension arose in the church from various causes. These increased in intensity until the Congregational Conference saw fit to sever the connection between the pastor and church in 1785, and the church went out of existence after a period of 17 years and six months. As a church in those years was accounted a necessity, the former members thought best to organize again in another part of the town. This they did, and built a large church here on the hill, supposedly near the center of the town, calling it the "East Congregational church." Rev. Joseph Rowell was called and settled as their first pastor in 1800, and served as such for twenty-eight years. He was followed by Rev. G. W. Clary, and afterwards by the Rev. Alvah Spaulding. During the pastorate of Rev. Mr. Rowell, the attendance upon Divine worship reached the highest record that any church in Cornish ever had. The "go-to-meeting" spirit in those years generally pervaded the town, so that the congregations often numbered between six and eight hundred on each Lord's day. The old meeting house served till 1840, when it was deemed unfit for further use as a house of worship, especially in winter. The question arose whether to repair the old house or build anew. It was decided to build anew, but where? This question proved another source of contention and division in the church, a large minority desiring to build further southwest (which they afterwards did), but the majority finally decided to build here, the church we occupy today. It was built in 1841. Its history since then is known to many now living, who can testify as to its fidelity in accomplishing its mission.

From the first, the Congregational church had among their members those entertaining different beliefs regarding church policy, especially respecting baptism. In fact the belief in baptism by immersion had been slowly but steadily gaining ground. They had become sufficiently strong to organize a church of their faith and belief. This was done in July of 1789. It consisted at first, of but nine members. It was organized in a barn near Cornish Flat, and received the title of the "First Baptist Church of Cornish." They, at first, built their church, in 1803, near the Congregational church on the hill, and there worshipped until 1818, a period of fifteen years, when, for various good reasons, they took down their church, and carried it to the Flat and there reerected it on its present site.[10] The dedication sermon for the first house on the hill, was also preached at its rededication on the Flat by the same minister (Rev. Aaron Leland), from the same text: "This is none other but the house of God." (Gen. 28-17). Here, at the Flat, it enjoyed a greater degree of freedom than theretofore. Its record has been rich and varied. Good fortune had attended it much of the time, yet it has been no stranger to adversity although its doors have never been closed from lack of services or worshippers.

Time will allow me to speak of one more church prominently connected with the early history of the town. I refer to the Episcopal Church.[11] This, with the two already named, were all the early churches of Cornish. Philander Chase, afterwards Bishop, was the prime mover in the establishment of this sect in town. While a student in Dartmouth College, he came across an Episcopal prayer book. Its methods and doctrines appealed so charmingly to his convictions that it became to him an inspiration, and he became a power in convincing his friends and associates (including most of his relations) of the value and importance of this manner of worship.

A sufficient number favorable to this sect were soon obtained. They met in the Old Congregational meeting house (now vacant) on the river and organized a church and society on December 16, 1793. They used this old meeting house as a house of worship until 1806 when they built the church now standing, and on December 24, 1795, it was incorporated under the name of Trinity Church. It had settled rectors a part of the time, but it has been largely a mission church, and its pulpit has been usually supplied by clergymen from Claremont and Windsor.

It has doubtless been an important factor in the moral and religious development of the town. Other churches too have existed in town; as the Methodist, Unitarian, etc., all of which have contributed their share to the moral and religious status of the town.

The combined influence of all the churches upon the social, moral, and religious welfare of Cornish, who can estimate it? Eternity alone can disclose it. But it is my firm belief that when the final day comes—when the great white throne is set—when the voice from the throne, saying,— "Come up hither," is spoken to that great multitude whom no man can number, that many will be found among them who were once members and laborers in the churches of Cornish.

OUR SOLDIERS
by Mr. W. H. Sisson

Ladies, Gentlemen, Fellow Citizens and Visiting Friends:

It is folly for me in the short time allotted me to attempt to give a military history of Cornish which history covers over fifty pages of our town history, and is not then fully written; therefore what I may say must be but a condensed tale of what Cornish has done in military matters.

Cornish has a history in the different wars which the United States has had, of which it ought to be and is proud.

The French and Indian wars having been closed ere the settlement of the town, we must first look to the war of the revolution, although we learn from history that Cornish men went with Captain Taylor, whom both this town and Claremont claim, to Royalton at the time that town was sacked and burned by the Indians.

In the Revolution one name stands to me more prominent than any other, General Jonathan Chase, a name of which the town of Cornish is and ought to be proud and who, if any one ever did, deserves a fitting monument and whose biography, in the hand of an able writer would make a goodly sized volume. His leadership, furnishing (as shown by his account book now in the town) the men with blankets, arms, ammunition and needed supplies, his march to Ticonderoga, the many sacrifices he made, advancing money trusting Providence for his pay, show what he alone did to aid the cause which freed the Colonies from the tyrannical rule of England and shows to all the credit due him and of such men Cornish is proud and ought to be.

Of Lieutenant Dyer Spaulding, Putnam, Fitches, Ensign Jackson, the Chases, and how I wish I had the time and could name all those heroes who did their part. It is told of the Minute men, ready at a moment's warning to leave the plow in the furrow, that when the alarm was given by the firing of three shots at nightfall the rising of the sun showed fifty men in line ready for the fray.

Oh, how one's heart thrills as we read or have heard of the valiant men of that time and of the sacrifices of the brave women, of whom and their heroic deeds one could talk for an hour and then not tell one half.

In 1812 we find that Cornish was again ready with her men to fight again in battle for the rights of the states against the outrageous treatment of England. In 1846 Cornish men were again in the field as before to again battle for the right and though the records are incomplete, its men were ready and a Cornish-born man in business in Cambridge, Mass., fitted out a company and trusted to the state to repay him and in his veins Patriotism ran so high that today as the result of the legacy of him, Jacob Foss, Old Glory floats from more flag poles than other towns of our size can boast.[12]

As a lad I have sat hours and listened to two survivors of the Revolutionary war tell their stories and I played hookey from school to see the soldiers go to the Mexican war, and again in 1861 I stood and shook by the hand the boys from Cornish as they as members of the Second New Hampshire Regiment were on their way to the front and at that time I did not think that I should go from the same wharf as I did later. No full account of those who went to the Mexican war is obtainable, but our cemeteries and our history tell of many. In 1861, Cornish sent that was credited to the town 161 soldiers and we find 41 Cornish men credited to other towns making 202 Cornish men in all that took part in the Civil war and on our monument of which we are proud there are the names of twenty-eight who died in battle, prison pen or hospital who never again saw their home town.

How many towns in New Hampshire have a better record?

A full list of the men of '61 it was my good fortune to assist in looking up for the town history and I wish I could have time to read a full list and in part recount their valiant and heroic deeds, tell how Colonel Putnam, a descendant of one of the town's first settlers, was killed leading his regiment at Fort Wagner, how Colonel Rice was left, he then being a member of the Second New Hampshire Regiment, on the field of Bull Run as dead and came home to find that his funeral sermon had been preached and that a stone had been placed in the cemetery in his memory so as he said there would be nothing more to do at his decease but his patriotism had not abated and again he enlisted and was mustered out of service as a colonel, how Alvah Rawson was shot at Petersburgh, of Lieutenants Tyler, and Richardson, of Albert L. Hall, one of the first to enlist and who was taken prisoner at Bull Run and spent over a year in the prison pens of the south and of the many others; but time forbids my naming them and I would not forget the mothers, wives, daughters and sisters and children of those who went. Again in 1898 came the Spanish war and Cornish was again represented as she had always been when the country needed, and should war again threaten our beloved land, which God forbid, Cornish would again be found ready to furnish men to help sustain this union and fight for the Old Flag, the best that any country boasts and would show their love for Old Glory and to the town of Cornish (which has given to the world many renowned and heroic men and women) was still living.

We are proud of the military history of Cornish and can boast that our old town today 150 years has never shown the white feather.

ANNIVERSARY HYMN

Words by G. E. Fairbanks / Music composed by H. E. Wood

[Sung at the 150th Anniversary of Cornish, N.H.]

Nestling close to the mountain
  Like a beautiful blushing bride
While gently it's kissed by the waters
  That flow by the sun set aside.

CHORUS

Cornish, the gem of New Hampshire,
  How many joys and tears
The people have seen in thy borders
  This hundred and fifty years.

The breezes blow over thy forests
  Depleted by many a tree
Where once there was nothing but woodland,
  Now, beautiful homes we see.
Thy hilltops are kissed by the sunbeams
  All robed in the morning dew,

The flowers are waiting to welcome
  The singing of birds anew.

The records we find of thy people
  We scan them with heartfelt pride
Where there has been worthy achievement
  Due honors were not denied.

Whenever the needs of our nation
  Demanded a patriot's grave,
There never were any more ready
  Than soldiers that Cornish gave.

The future is standing before us,
  Our children are brave and true;
We ask them to honor old Cornish,
  And feel we can trust them to.

THE EARLY WAYS

by Rev. Albert Parker Fitch

(Dr. Fitch is one who always has a message of interest, and as he warms to the subject is a rapid speaker—without notes, the stenographer being unable to follow sufficiently to transcribe his remarks. Fortunately a reporter of the *Vermont Journal* was present and what the paper gave is all we have of a very interesting address. It says:)

"The early settlers of Cornish are distinguished by a naturalness and simplicity. Our forefathers here led uncrowded lives with the result that they were better thinkers than those who came after them. The daily press at that time was unknown, there was no news from over the seas except that which was three months old, there were no movies and no trains. Thus the attractions were so limited that the minds of the people took a turn toward the better pursuit of the art of agriculture. They found time to be versed in theology, a speculative science. The early settlement of Cornish was composed of a self-sufficing people. Today the community is interdependent. In the early days the farmer raised all his feed for his cattle and horses, he raised enough wool to make the garments of his family and many of the farm implements that were used by him were fashioned by his own hands. In these latter days almost everything is sold for money and if the farmer wants to buy anything he pays for it in this medium."

THE DISTRICT SCHOOLS
by Principal Charles Alden Tracy

When Dr. Fitch speaks of inability to say something of interest and value in ten minutes what should my feelings be? A few days ago I was asked to speak on a certain subject as were some of the other speakers but when the committee came to Mr. Powers they seem to have been out of subjects so they put him down for a "final address." I suggest to Mr. Powers that he take up some of the things that we others have had to leave out for lack of time.

I am glad an opportunity has been given me to speak of the District Schools of Cornish. I feel that I together with you owe to the District Schools what we are today and possibly all that we may be in time to come. It seems that the early settlers were possessed with the idea that their children should receive the best training possible for the life they must live. In the very early years of the settlement of this town the schools for the teaching of "reading, riting and rithmetic" were supported by money contributed by the parents as they were not required by the state to have schools until about 1827. Later each little district elected someone to act as the school committee, hire the teachers, etc., and this method obtained until 1885 when our present town system came into vogue.

I recently had an arithmetic published in 1823 and noticed some of the problems and one read something like this:—"Three jealous husbands with their three wives came to a stream and it was necessary to cross this stream in a boat that could carry but two. How could these people get across, each man with his own wife?"

For several years I have known very little about the schools in Cornish but at one time I was a pupil in them. Two years ago at Meriden I was introduced to an old school superintendent who said he remembered me very well as the dull one of an otherwise very bright family. Cornish has been very fortunate for a great many years in having K.U.A. so near, a school which has been largely attended by Cornish young people. The number of graduates from Cornish has been nearly 150 and a great many more have been enrolled for a shorter space of time. At the present time the pupils of the town are aided by the Mercer Fund in attending secondary schools.

I would like to point out if I may some of the ideals that have stood out in Cornish schools for 150 years. The early settlers wished for their children culture and looked to the schools to train them for the work of the college and for private life.

As Dr. Fitch has so well said the boys and girls, the men and women of 100 and 150 years ago were able to do one or two things and were able to do those one or two things well, because they had been trained in thoroughness in the schools. Today the boys and girls receive a much larger portion of their education in the school room than they did 100 years ago. Then their education was received in the school room of the farm and they were trained in the practical things of life. Today we are obliged to provide this training by manual arts courses.

(Prof. Tracy's remarks were somewhat abridged in the reporting.)

THE COLONY

by Col. Winston Churchill

I come today to speak as briefly as possible about the colony which has come here during the last thirty years, which is known all over this country. The Cornish Colony was first called "Little New York" but that name has now disappeared.

I remember once when making a speech in Plainfield and attempting to speak of Cornish and Plainfield I said Cornfield and Plainfield.

I think also when you speak of the colony of Cornish it can hardly be spoken of without naming certain members who live in Plainfield. I was asked to make this very brief and I shall try to do so and mention some of the noted men and women of this colony.

At one time when people spoke of Cornish they were asked "Where is Cornish?" That is not so now, everybody in the United States and England now knows about Cornish.

When we come to look into this colony we find represented Politics, Government, by the President himself, Religion, Journalism, the Stage, Music, Painting, Literature, Navy, Exploration. You will find the works of the people of this colony in the great libraries and museums of the United States, especially the works of Maxfield Parrish with the background known as the Cornish background. Edward Horton came up with his wife whose Italian gardens are famous.[13] I never knew that background was in Italy. I never knew anything like it until I knew where Maxfield Parrish got his. How many of you have noticed in the works of the old Italian masters that the background or the landscape out where the woods are, how like Cornish landscapes they are?

Charles C. Beaman was the first to come and it seems to me it is impossible to tell what Mr. Beaman was to this colony, to this country, a man of fine personality and who made his reputation in the law. The general public know what he was to this town, how generous he was and how interested in all concerning it. Cornish lost a very remarkable man in Mr. Beaman. I am glad to see his work is being carried on by his son in the town, county and state. I think that we may also claim Mr. Lakin, a rising New York lawyer, and Mr. Edward J. Holmes, a member of that well known intellectual family through Mr. Beaman's family.[14]

Then we have the Graydons, the Campbells, the Arnolds, Fraser-Campbell, whose loss we mourn, who was the true type of a British gentleman.[15] It was through the influence of Mr. Beaman and his interest here that brought Mr. Augustus Saint-Gaudens who represented in the world a great sculptor. I shall never forget that wonderful statue of Sherman, the impression it made on my mind, with its background of the Cornish woods. I think we ought to be very glad to know that Mrs. Saint-Gaudens has made a museum of Mr. Saint-Gaudens' works. We have also Homer Saint Gaudens whose work in respect to the theater is now well known.

We have Mr. C. A. Platt who is, first of all, one of four or five well known etchers and a landscape gardener. I remember being told a rather good story about Mr. Platt. He was called by Mr. Sprague, when he was little known, in consultation about a garden. Mr. Sprague had a very large garden. He said to Mr. Platt, "I want you to draw a plan for a garden." Mr. Platt said, "We will put the garden over where that road is." Mr. Sprague said "Put the garden over there, no, —I just spent $15,000 to put in that road." Mr. Platt took some notes and went away. A month passed and Mr. Sprague heard nothing from him so he went to Mr. Platt and asked him "What has become of my garden?" and Mr. Platt told him that the plans were all done and showed him the plan with the garden over the $15,000 road. Mr. Sprague took out the road and Mr. Platt put his garden there at the cost of $100,000.

I ought to mention also several other members of this colony as we have many more besides Mr. Platt. We have Stephen Parrish, an etcher; Maxfield Parrish of whom I have already spoken.

Mr. Parrish has done a great deal of valuable work and won international reputation and Mrs. Parrish shows great interest in the schools. Miss Lazarus, who built High Court; the Houstons; the Rublees; Arthur Whiting, a musician of the first rank; L. E. Shipman the playwright and who takes a great interest in local affairs and his wife who is a landscape architect; Miss Parker who has started the little tea house; Dr. and Mrs. Nichols who built their charming house; Miss Rose Nichols who is a landscape architect and has a great interest in all public questions which interest is shared by her sister, Miss Marion Nichols; Kenyon Cox, an artist and first art critic in the United States, and Mrs. Cox who is a painter of high rank.

Herbert Adams, a sculptor of the first rank; Howard Hart, a gardener, and William Hyde a well known portrait painter.

I think it well to mention Misses Augusta and Emily Slade. Miss Emily Slade, a wood carver who carved the stairway of her beautiful house on the hill.

When I was in Washington last year one of the first things I was taken to see was Ascutney Mountain in a beautiful painting there which had been recognized by Mr. Fuller first. His wife, Mrs. Fuller, is one of the foremost miniature painters in the United States today; Miss Frances Grimes a sculptor of high rank.

Louis Saint Gaudens also was a sculptor and built the high hipped house on the hill bought from the Shakers in Enfield and whose lions are seen in the Boston Library.

Mr. and Mrs. Albion E. Lang who take such an interest in the local affairs of Cornish and Plainfield and all public questions.

Lately Dr. Fitch has come and brought religion to the colony which he has brought in a way so that we can once in awhile be humorous about it.

I must mention Admiral Folger who has had a long and distinguished career in the Navy and has now come to Cornish to spend his days and farm.

Herbert Croly who has a literary record and we cannot say too much about the extent and soundness of his knowledge. He has written two books. "The Promise of American Life" alone would make a name for him and he is now doing a still greater work as editor of the *New Republic* which is so badly needed in the life of this country.

Another journalist, Norman Hapgood, a critic and biographer.

Philip Zotelle, a dramatist and critic of the first order.[16]

George Rublee is a lawyer of unusual ability and has won distinction in such cases as the Atchison R.R. and the Ballinger case. One thing worthy of mention—he is the only man in the colony who has ever succeeded in getting his taxes reduced.

We have another man Percy MacKaye who is a poet and playwright who is raising the standard of the American stage today and has presented the Pageants in St. Louis and New York.

Judge Learned Hand, one of the ablest and youngest justices in the United States District Courts and a man of wide intellectual interests.

Robert Barrett and his wife, who have so much interest in our school and library and everyone knows of the unusual and interesting house they are building on top of that hill.

In order to complete the lustre of such a group, the group that bears the title of the Cornish Colony, and to send the just fame of the Cornish hills and the Cornish countryside into every hamlet of the nation, it was only necessary to have the President of the United States. I speak for all residents, winter and summer, in expressing our pride that Woodrow Wilson is with us. Called to the helm in the most serious times since Lincoln, it is peculiarly appropriate that he should represent the thinker, the intellectual man in politics and statesmanship, and that he should be the "Cornish" President.

FINAL ADDRESS

by Hon. S. L. Powers

Professor Tracy has told you the title of my address. You have listened today about the greatness of the people who settled this town but it seems to me that those of you who have gathered here in the church and remained here from 1:30 to 4:30 to hear myself and others talk have a patience and virtue worthy of congratulation.

The only distinction I claim is that I was born in Cornish and that is a great distinction. I remember in the old years when I first went to Massachusetts to live someone would ask me where I was born and I would take down a map; usually the map didn't have the town on it, and I would have to explain that I was born in the town directly across the river from Windsor, Vermont. Now I don't wait for a man to ask me where I was born, now I tell him and he never asks where Cornish is. Now the name of Cornish is known in London, Paris and all parts of the world.

Something like fifty years ago I came to the decision that there was an easier way of getting a living than cultivating a Cornish farm. I have lived long enough to find out that it is not an easy matter to get a living anywhere. I come back to the old town to find the people living in comfort and luxury on the farm.

I go around and see my old friends and I find them living much easier and with more comfort than the people of the cities. I am seriously thinking of coming back and going to farming, especially since Dr. Fitch says that the farmers don't have to work any more. It is very certain that the people of today do not have the hardships of the old pioneers.

I come back and look at the old school house in District No. 11 and in connection with this school I had an experience in my young life which I consider the most tragic of my life. It happened in this way:—We were offered a prize for spelling of a medal to be given to the one who stood at the head the most times during the term. At that time I was about 12 years of age and there was a girl of about the same age by the name of Clara Blaisdell and it stood between Clara and myself as to who was to get the prize. As it happened the relations between my family and the Blaisdell family were not of the best, it was strongly impressed upon my mind at home that I must win the prize and of course Clara's family were equally as anxious that she should win the prize from me. Finally at the end of the term I had stood at the head 19 times and Clara had stood at the head 19 times and there was still one lesson to decide the question. I never experienced such agony as in trying to decide whether I should miss and let Clara win the prize or to win the prize myself and also the approval of my family and while I was thinking it over the lesson ended and I had won the prize. Clara broke down and I took the hateful medal and gave it to her. She being a girl of spirit declined to accept it and slapped me in the face. While I learned one thing I made up my mind that never again would I attempt to take anything which someone else wanted very much and I have gone along through life on that theory not trying to get anything away from anyone else. You cannot get a fortune in such a way but perhaps win a great many friends.

The story has been told me that the Englishmen came here and put their cross on the large trees and those were left to be used by the Royal Navy and I used to imagine when I saw those great stumps that the trees that stood there had perhaps been used on Admiral Nelson's ship in 1805. I was very sorry and somewhat pained that George Deming should come here today and make the claim that it was somewhat doubtful that this was done. I would recommend that Mr. Deming study his history a little more in order that this theory that I have often told of may be proven to be true.

Cornish has become famous by reason of this Colony, became famous by reason of these people coming to town. I suppose it is true that if Mr. Beaman had not come first and Mr. Churchill hadn't come probably the President wouldn't have come to the town. All these things and others have come to help build up this colony in Cornish.

I do not wish to say anything unpleasant about Mr. Churchill, for we have in him a writer of fiction, perhaps the greatest writer of fiction in the world today, but you must remember that this Colony came to Cornish after it was something of a town and feel that, if we never had had the fortune of these distinguished people that have come here representing literature and painting and art, Cornish would have stood well in the history of the country.

Cornish in its early history reared and gave to the world three men of great influence and distinction in our Country. First, the great Churchman, Bishop Philander Chase. I have read, as well as you, from that great Child's history, and I never read a better written history, in which you will find a description of Bishop Chase who did such a great work in this section and in Ohio and Kenyon College.

Another man known even in England as a great American was Dr. Nathan Smith, a man of great distinction in medical science. Dr. Nathan Smith at the age of 28 years was a farmer following the plow and later he took up the study of medicine studying at Harvard, afterwards founding medical schools at Dartmouth, University of Vermont and Bowdoin. I heard President Eliot of Harvard College speaking upon the influence of one man over another man and he spoke of a man who graduated from Harvard, the man who became a doctor and was in the same class with John Adams, the second president of the United States and later what influence this man had in the medical science. John Adams was at the head of this class. Dr. Smith went to Harvard, received his degree and settled in Cornish where he worked up an extensive practice.

The other man to whom I refer is the great statesman, a statesman and great judge, Salmon P. Chase. Salmon P. Chase must be classed as one of the, next to Marshall, greatest Chief Justices. His ability as a financier was shown as Secretary of the Treasury. He lived to become Chief Justice, and a great man.

From this town we gave to the world such men as Bishop Chase, Nathan Smith and Judge Chase.

Now we have here with us as a summer resident, the present President of the United States and I want to say here that, although he represents a different political party, not the one to which I belong, if he continues his present foreign policy and keeps us out of war his name will go down in history as one of the greatest Americans, beside the name of Washington and Lincoln.

Today we stand by the President, stand by his policy and believe in his judgment.

Of the many replies to invitations received we publish two only, these being of special interest, one from Rev. Joseph Rowell of San Francisco, 95 years of age. This was followed by a second more explicit in personal details, which we do not feel at liberty to publish; another from E. W. Barnard of Springfield, Vermont.

LETTER FROM REV. JOSEPH ROWELL
San Francisco, July 22, 1915.

Mr. Deming asks me to send a letter to the Old Home Day, in Cornish.

Now I remember a great many things about the old Cornish, but I fear the present new Cornish would class them with ancient Greek and Roman history.

The last meeting that I attended was presided over by Winston Churchill, who paid me a high compliment for the speech I then made. I wish that this might deserve the same.

I remember hearing Daniel Webster speak in the old meeting house up on the hill—the speaker very majestic, the speech to me, very dull. By the way, how many of you youngsters ever saw the foundation stones, still visible of that meeting house?

I remember old Elder Kendrick and his tremendous "ahem!" Once when he slipped on the ice, and came down with a thump in a sitting posture, he exclaimed: "That jarred my brains." His wife said, "I never knew before, where your brains were."

I remember my first school (as teacher) up on Dingleton Hill. One of my scholars, Henry Bartlett, I met on my last visit to Cornish.

I remember Chester Fitch with his remarkable tenor voice. He lived northwest of Dingleton, near the house of Eliphalet Kimball, whose son, William, was the brother of Edward Kimball whose donation to Cornish is still voted at your annual town meeting.[17] When Edward came of age, his father gave him a two dollar bill, and Edward said: "I will make it a hundred thousand," which I suppose he did, in the meat business in Boston.

I remember Mrs. Mary Comings, grandmother to Charles W. Comings, now one of your oldest citizens. She lived in what is now the wing of the Comings house. Her headstone is now in the Comings cemetery. I remember where "Ben" Comings, her son, set out the row of maples, on the east side of the road, leading up to the old meeting house, and a neighbor said to him: "Ben, why do you set out those maples? You will never get any profit from them." And he replied: "If I don't, somebody else will," and now his grandson Fenno, finds those maples a valuable asset.

I remember three families of Demings. One was the stock to which your present George L. belongs,—another, a brother, I suppose, who lived a half mile south of the school house, where I was one of one hundred scholars, called Lieut. Deming. His sons were William, Daniel and Pitt. I was a favorite with William. He was a stalwart grass mower, and when we mowed his broad meadow, he placed me next himself, helped me all he could, cutting my corners, and then called out to the rest: "This boy beats you all!"

He used every winter to take down a sledload of frozen turkeys to Boston, and I helped him pull the feathers off those turkeys. At one trip, he brought home codfish that was longer than I was tall. But did not know that codfish taste good! I had never tasted one, before.

I remember Dr. Elijah Boardman and how, when I last preached in Cornish, he sat in his chair before the pulpit, his head thrown back and his mouth wide open. The sermon did him no harm, anyhow.

I remember the bachelor, Daniel Davis, son of John, who built a stone house of one story, on a corner of my father's farm (now occupied by the second generation of Smiths, I believe). Strangely, Mr. Child, in his history of Cornish, overlooked Daniel Davis and his "stone jug," as we used to call it. Davis was noted for honey bees, and watermelons, and we boys liked to visit him. He used to mow my father's meadow, and was usually helped by us boys.

But I am tiring you out with these memories. I remember many more things and events in old Cornish. You have two races, I never saw in my youth—deer, and hedgehogs,—I wish you joy of them.

I would like much to visit you once more, but 3000 miles is a long journey for a man 95 years old.

May you all live to repeat old stories like these, to your great grandchildren, at future Old Home Days.

JOSEPH ROWELL.

In a personal letter Mr. Rowell says:

"The earthquake and fire of 1906 destroyed my church building and it has never been replaced. Another chaplain has been sent here and he has tried in vain to raise money to rebuild. There is no present prospect that it will ever be done.

"I am 95 years of age living alone in my own house, in a very poor way.

"The Yale Alumni here desiring to honor perhaps the oldest living graduate of Yale have offered to raise money to put me in an excellent Old People's Home, but I do not wish to be buried alive just yet."

Letter from E. W. Barnard

"OPEN RIDGE"

Springfield, Vermont,

August 8, 1915.

Committee on Celebration

of 150th Anniversary of Settlement of the Town of Cornish, N.H.

Gentlemen:

Accepting tentatively your kind invitation to be present at the Anniversary next week, allow me to state that we have recently been gravely informed in the editorial columns of a great metropolitan daily that there is no such place as Cornish on the map and that the name is best applied to a small rural suburb to a locality known as Windsor in the State of Vermont.

If as a native of the town of Cornish I may on this momentous occasion, I would as gravely inform and challenge this editorial stuffer of the linotype in New York that the star on his map used to designate the Summer White House covers also many other things. One hundred and fifty years of happenings that have helped to make later important things possible.

If nature's handiwork has made this locality a geographical magnet to draw within its radius many great human forces that enable literature and science and sculpture and poetry and music and play and many arts.

So also have the ideals and character of the habitant of the locality in this long period of time been a mental and moral magnet, to concentrate attention and respect.

But Cornish has a record. She has sent out a full quota of educated and able men and women for the world's great service and appreciation whose influence has been felt around the globe. Men who have reached the topmost round of human endeavor in theology and missionary effort, in law and statesmanship, in music and song. Her fair daughters have been an inspiration, a blessing and a final benediction in many homes in many lands. Her patriotic sons have ever responded to their country's call and once those who could not go to the front gave of their mechanical ingenuity to help to make munitions of war down at the Armory at Windsor in the State of Vermont.

If in a national sense the artistic nature—cultured under sunny southern skies—of the lamented late first lady of the land[18] could so quickly catch the message that Cornish has for all and interpret the whisperings of the pines, the murmurings of the brooklets, the warbling of the feathered songsters and trace the trails of her pastoral beauty and rural simplicity; if the mental monitor and chief executive of the will of a great nation, the man of the hour who like Washington and Lincoln was born for the time and place, has found mental inspiration and physical stamina among these hills and vales to help him in his great task to steer the ship of State safely among the shoals of uncharted seas of exacting diplomacy or has found here an environment suited for that sober second thought so important for an accurate judgment that must stand or fall; if the summer White House has for a time being been the diplomatic clearing house for one hundred millions of people, then Cornish and Cornish people may have a proud satisfaction as a contributing cause for our national well being in a period when a gigantic struggle for supremacy of moral over brute force is in progress and when civilization even, is at its supreme test and peril in the stress of unknown dangers of an uncommon day and time and an uncommon age.

If Cornish in N.H. is but a name then from this day on it is a name to conjure by, and as everlasting as the granite hills. A name and place and fame that will attract more and more as time rolls on. And while some of the good old family names that for generation after generation have given tone to the town may pass away to memory's page to be enshrined in characters enduring, yet the new comers will drink at the same fount and blend with the locality as those of yore.

And the Cornish of the future will add lustre to the Cornish of the past so replete with a record of high impulses and great accomplished deeds.

E. WELLMAN BARNARD.

THE DAY ITSELF

Providence or the weather man or both favored the occasion—for the day was an ideal one—neither too hot nor too cold. A rather strong wind in the morning subsided to a strong breeze which continued during the day. The inside of the church had been thoroughly trimmed under the direction of Mr. Sisson, the national emblem in different sizes being prominently displayed, while on the outside they floated from the gallery windows; also a large one waved from the nearby flag pole and another from a cord drawn from the belfry of the church to a tree on the opposite side of the road, the breeze seemed to have a pleasure in playing with these banners nearly all of the time.

The forenoon was spent socially. The Ladies' Aid had charge of the dinner arrangements which was served to elderly people and guests, many bringing their own lunch. An out-door stand furnished lunch free to such as desired. The orchestra consisting of Herbert Williams, Roy Taplin, Herbert Wood, and Arthur Quimby enjoyed the comfortable quarters of a small tent near the vestry and furnished music during the dinner hour.

On the platform in the church, a few reminders of "Ye Olden Time" were exhibited. These were in charge of Paul Davidson. Under glass were the account books of General Jonathan Chase. These books are the property of Mr. Davidson, and are of great interest historically. Also the sermon preached at the settlement of the first minister, Rev. James Wellman, donated to the Stowell Library by Colonel Churchill. George E. Fairbanks exhibited the sign board formerly doing duty on the turnpike to Newport. James Fitch brought the pulpit chair from the Old Congregational church on the hill, and a paring machine made by his grandfather in his early years.

W. H. Child exhibited the musket carried by his grandfather in the Revolution.

The number present is computed at about eight hundred. Many absent ones who had not visited home for many years were present.

The president's family was represented by Miss Margaret Wilson and Mrs. Sayres. The oldest person present was Mrs. Thrasher, 97, and Mr. C. W. Comings, 93 years, both active and remarkably well preserved.

The program was carried out as printed with the addition of the reading of one or two replies to invitations, and the closing song was by Mrs. E. D. Lombard of Windsor, Vt.

At mention of the President's name the unanimous clapping seemed to show the esteem in which he is held by one and all regardless of political preference and must have been pleasing to the members of his family present. Seldom have we seen an audience so patient and good for so long a time and apparently so interested in the remarks of the different speakers.

Space forbids the mention of many things of interest to the reader. Briefly the exercises were in the highest degree satisfactory to all and appreciated so fully by the town that at the annual meeting in March, 1916, a sum of money was appropriated to publish the proceedings and the same committee was appointed for the work. The Secretary having reluctantly consented to the work of arranging and preparing this anniversary souvenir begs to say, he has done his best to reproduce the events of the day and acknowledges the valuable assistance of the other members of the committee, and we send it forth fondly trusting it may be read with interest and found reasonably satisfactory.

GEORGE L. DEMING, Secretary.

MARY ANN (COTTON) THRASHER
[The oldest person present]

Mary Ann Cotton was born in Holderness, N.H., June 1, 1818, the oldest of the four children of Ebenezer Smith and Mary (Hawkins) Cotton. The Cotton line in this country starts with William Cotton of the family which was associated with Sir Ferdinando Gorges and John Mason in the original grants for the New Hampshire and Maine colonies and whose principal settlement was made in 1631 at Strawbery Bank (Portsmouth). Ebenezer Cotton bore arms in the War of 1812, and his father, John Cotton, served in the Revolution from Gilmanton.

On the Hawkins side, Mary Cotton is descended from Thomas Dudley who was born in Northampton, England, in 1576 and who came to Massachusetts in 1630 as deputy governor. He held this office in all, thirteen years, was four times governor and twice president of the United Colonies besides being a major general in the Colonial army. As governor he signed and granted the charter to Harvard College in 1636.

When Mary Ann Cotton was about a year old her parents decided to go "out West," making the trip with an ox team and requiring a week or more to reach their destination which was some fifty miles away in Vershire, Vt. It was in this town that Mary commenced her schooling, attending a district school from the time she was three years old. In 1826 the family moved to Fairlee, Vt., where with the exception of a short time spent in Grantham, N.H., in 1832, they continued to live until 1835 when they again moved, this time to Hartland, Vt. In this latter town Mary was married to Ithamar Thrasher, son of John and Betsey (Walker) Thrasher, the ceremony being performed at her home by Squire Ward Cotton on April 1, 1838. The Thrashers are of French Huguenot stock and appear in Massachusetts and New Hampshire records as early as 1643. Ithamar Thrasher's grandmother, Olle Eastman, came from the same family that gave Abigail Eastman, the mother of Daniel Webster.

About a year after their marriage they came to Cornish to live and in 1854 bought the present homestead. When Ithamar died December 18, 1864, the outlook for the widow was not a happy one. With two of her older sons serving in the Federal forces in the South and with but the assistance of a fourteen year old boy and a girl of ten to carry on a large hill farm, she met and overcame conditions which would have been impossible to a character of less strength and calm determination. In fact, it is largely through these very qualities that she is today able to celebrate her ninetieth anniversary with the full possession of all her faculties and a keen enjoyment in living.

The above sketch was written in 1908 to which we only add: On June 30 last she entered upon her 99th year still well preserved and taking much interest in passing events, busying herself with considerable correspondence, writing and even addressing her letters, and very glad to receive others in return.

CHARLES WELLMAN COMINGS

The next oldest person present was Charles Wellman Comings, who was born April 23, 1822, on the farm which his grandfather took up and cleared, going two miles into the woods by marked trees, where he has spent the most of his life except a year spent in Michigan. On his father's side, he is the eighth from Isaac Comings, while on his mother's side he is descended from Elder Brewster of the Plymouth colony.

ENDNOTES

1. The Reverend and Mrs. James T. Jackson; see above pp. 85-86.

2. I.e., the Civil War; General Robert E. Lee surrendered to General Ulysses S. Grant at Appomattox Court House, Virginia, April 9, 1865.

3. Alice (Corbett) Chase, 1732-1813, wife of Dudley Chase.

4. This may refer to the library "book wagon," which was started by Katherine Ellis Barrett, or it may refer to an earlier, similar institution. Mrs. Barrett made sure that books were distributed to ten district schools, supplying teachers with books needed for reading classes. The book wagon also visited outlying farms.

5. Sarah Thomas (1769-1813) was employed by Daniel Chase who ran a store in Cornish Flat; see Child, *History of Cornish*, Vol. 1, p. 367, for her tombstone inscription: "She by her own labor acquired the sum of 500 dollars, which she gave wholly by her will to the support of the gospel among the heathen" (Cornish Flat Cemetery, October 1, 1813). On Daniel Chase see Child, *History of Cornish*, Vol. 2, p. 76. For a fictionalized biography see Phyllis M. Hemphill, *Sally Thomas: Servant Girl* (Nashville, TN: Winston-Derek, 1991).

6. An allusion to all the physicians among the descendants of Dr. Nathan Smith (Child, Vol. 2, pp. 334-35): his two sons, David Solon Chase Hall Smith (Child, Vol. 1, pp. 336-38) and Nathan Ryno Smith (Child, Vol. 2, p. 336), and his two grandsons, Nathan and Alan P., who also had two sons who became physicians. Child's spelling of "Rhino" is generally altered to read "Ryno."

7. Hannah Chase (1758-1847), the eldest daugher of Moses Chase, who came to Cornish around 1765, married Daniel Kimball of Meriden, New Hampshire, in 1777. She was actively involved with her husband in founding Kimball Union Academy, incorporated in 1813.

8. Construction on the "Stowell Free Library" began in 1910; the building was completed in 1912 and dedicated on October 4, 1912. It was a gift to the town from George H. Stowell; see Child, *History of Cornish*, Vol. 1, pp. 340-342.

9. The French and Indian Wars lasted from 1689 until 1765, but the Seven Year War (1756-1763) highlighted the colonial rivalry between France and England in the Colonies and Canada. The Treaty of Paris in 1763 ended French control of Canada and French influence in the western United States.

10. In researching the necessary information for the papers nominating the Meetinghouse to the National Register of Historical Places in 1975, John Dryfhout came across a reference to Col. William Abbot (Abbott), who lived from 1793 to 1837 in Boscawen, New Hampshire, in Charles C. Coffin, *The History of Boscawen and Webster from 1733 to 1878* (Concord, NH, 1878). It reveals that Abbott built churches throughout New Hampshire. It is the mention of Cornish (p. 464) that produces the hypothesis that Abbott designed and built the Baptist Church that is now the Meetinghouse. Of further interest

is the recent study by Donn Haven Lathrop and Frederick Shelley, "The Amazing Stephen Hasham" in the *NAWCE* [National Association of Watch and Clock Collectors] *Bulletin*, 293 (December, 1994), pp. 723-755. It is a thoroughly researched article on the man who designed the Meetinghouse clock, installed in 1844 and 1845, complete with illustrations. For more information, see the files of the Cornish Historical Society.

11. For more information on the restoration of the Trinity Episcopal Church by Peter Hoe Burling and its dedication on October 14, 1985, see the articles in the *Valley News*, October 15, 1985, p. 2 and the Profile in the *Valley News*, "Echoes in the Valley," December 31, 1985. Copies are in the files of the Cornish Historical Society.

12. When the Mexican War (1846-1848) broke out, Foss, who was born in Cornish on October 17, 1796, advanced the money necessary to finance a company of soldiers from Charlestown (not Cambridge), Massachusetts, before he received governmental reimbursement. At his death in 1866, Foss left "his native town" $1000, "the income to be expended for the purchase of United States flags." This fund is still drawn upon to purchase the flags used to honor soldiers' graves in Cornish cemeteries each Memorial Day; see Child, *History of Cornish*, Vol. 1, pp. 314-317.

13. The identity of Mr. Horton and his wife remains a mystery, unless it refers to a Massachusetts Unitarian clergyman, author, and editor and his wife.

14. Charles Cotesworth Beaman (1840-1900) had four children. His eldest daughter, Mary Stacy, married Edward J. Holmes, the grandson of Oliver Wendell Holmes, in 1897. His second daughter, Helen Wardner, married Herbert C. Lakin in 1902.

15. For more on the people mentioned in this sentence, see Wade, *A Brief History*, pp. 80-81.

16. This is probably an error in transcription for Philip Littell (see below pp. 253-254).

17. Edward Dorr Kimball (1825-1888) "remembered his native town by a fund of $3000 for the worthy poor"; Child, *History of Cornish*, Vol. 2, p. 248.

18. A reference to President Woodrow Wilson's first wife Ellen Axson Wilson; she was an accomplished painter and painted in Cornish during the summer of 1913. She died in 1914; see below pp. 428-439.

Landscape as Inspiration:

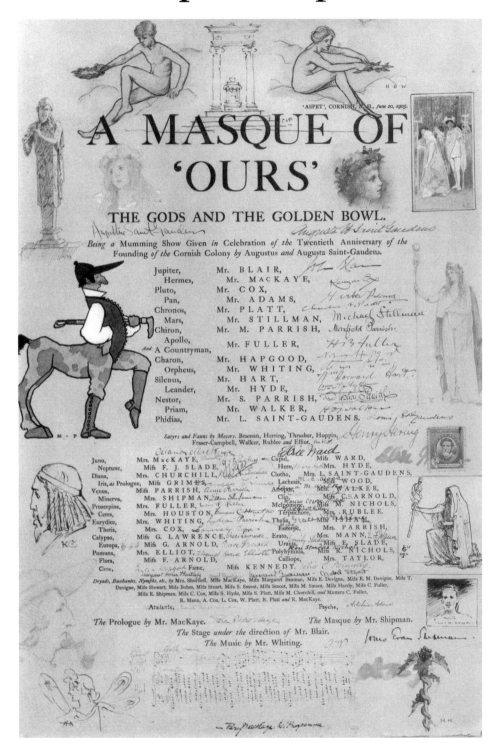

The Cornish Colony

Figure 43. *Percy MacKaye's autographed program for* A Masque of "Ours," *1905.*

INTRODUCTION TO
THE CORNISH COLONY

AT THE TURN OF THE CENTURY, Cornish was "colonized" by sculptors, painters, lawyers, poets, writers, and, eventually, a few rich admirers. Just as the first colonists of Cornish in 1765 established their "mast camp" along the banks of the Connecticut River, so their descendants clustered along the Cornish-Plainfield town line in full view of the Connecticut River and Mount Ascutney. This latter-day Colony began when Charles Cotesworth Beaman, a lawyer with a prominent New York law firm, married his senior partner's daughter, Hettie Evarts. The Evarts family, well-connected in New York legal and financial circles as well as in Washington political spheres, were large landholders in Windsor, Vermont. After the marriage in 1874, Beaman, following in his father-in-law's footsteps, started to acquire land across the Connecticut River in Cornish, New Hampshire, where he built his house called Blow-Me-Down Farm.[1] By the 1870s the population in Cornish had declined because of the failure of sheep farming and because of the migration of its people to cities and to the Midwest. Therefore, land and farms could be picked up for a song.

Beaman enjoyed surrounding himself with the company of artists and writers, so he was more than willing to sell or rent to them. Because his wife had known Augustus Saint-Gaudens in Rome, where the latter was an art student, and Beaman had known him in New York, Beaman could entice the rising artist to come to Cornish in 1885. Thus, the sculptor was the earliest Colonist. He rented "Huggin's Folly," a stark Federal brick structure that he eventually bought from Beaman for $2,500 and a bas-relief of Beaman.[2]

In Saint-Gaudens's wake came other artists: Thomas Dewing, who was famous for his atmospheric portraits of women and for being one of "The Ten" (he arrived in 1886); George de Forest Brush, who was well-known for his "modern madonna" paintings (1887); Henry Oliver Walker, who was noted for his series of murals in the Library of Congress (1888); Charles A. Platt, who was respected as an etcher and painter when he came to Cornish, who later took up landscape architecture, and finally became an esteemed architect (1889); and Stephen Parrish, who was admired as an etcher and painter (1891), and who brought in his son Maxfield, the celebrated artist and illustrator (1898).[3]

Other famous artists, exhibiting in New York, Boston, and Chicago, connected with the Colony include John White Alexander, who was also famous for his pictures of women (he came in 1890); the sculptor Herbert Adams (1894); Kenyon Cox, who was a muralist and art critic and his wife Louise, a portrait painter (1896); Henry and Lucia Fuller (1897), who later rented their house to the actress Ethel Barrymore (1906), to the sculptor Paul Manship (1915), and to William and Marguerite Zorach (1917), the former a painter and sculptor, the latter a painter and tapestry maker; the artist Everett Shinn, a member of the "Ashcan School," and his wife Florence Scovel Shinn, an illustrator (1902); the portrait painter Frances Houston (1891); the painter John Elliott and his wife Maud Howe Elliott (1903), whose mother was Julia Ward Howe, who wrote the words to "The Battle Hymn of the Republic"; Frederic Remington, who was noted for his paintings and sculptures of the West (1903); William Henry Hyde, who was a portraitist (1905); and Willard Leroy Metcalf, who was a landscape painter and also one of "The Ten" (1909).[4]

Another important wave of Colonists were writers: Winston Churchill, who was one of the most popular American novelists of his day (he arrived first in 1898); Herbert Croly, who was the founding editor of *The New Republic* and wrote *The Promise of American Life* while in Cornish (1893); Louis Evan Shipman, who was an editor and playwright (1893) and his wife Ellen, who became a famous landscape architect through Charles Platt's training; Norman Hapgood, who was an editor of *Collier's* (1903); Percy MacKaye, who was a poet and dramatist (1904); William Vaughn Moody, who was a well-loved playwright and poet (1906); Langdon Mitchell, who was a popular dramatist (1906); and Witter Bynner, a poet who was also famous for his translations of Chinese poetry (1907).

Musicians were also numbered among the Colonists: singer and pianist Grace Lawrence and her sister Edith (1891); Arthur Whiting, a composer (1893); and Otto Roth (1899), a violinist whose devotion to musical entertainments helped to establish a tradition continued by the outdoor summer concerts now held at the Saint-Gaudens National Historic Site.[5]

Following the artists and literary people, others were drawn to the area: the rich— such as Albion Lang, who made his money in streetcars (1905), and Robert Barrett, who supported many philanthropic causes in Cornish (1911)—and the powerful—such as George Rublee, a member of the Federal Trade Commission (1907); Judge Learned Hand, chief justice of the Second Circuit Court of Appeals (1908); and Alfred Nichols, a Boston physician whose wife was a sister to Mrs. Augustus Saint-Gaudens (1889).

Perhaps the most famous of the powerful visitors to the Colony was President Woodrow Wilson, who rented the novelist Winston Churchill's large brick home "Harlakenden." The President's family spent the summers of 1913 through 1914 in Cornish and brought the Summer White House here. He also established an office in the Windsor courthouse, while Secret Service men rented rooms in the Windsor House and in the Churchill Inn in Cornish.

Although these Colonists readily referred to themselves as being members of the "Cornish Colony," many of them actually lived in Plainfield. Homer Saint-Gaudens described Mrs. Davidge's old mill as being in Cornish even though it was actually on Daniels Road in Plainfield. Although her house was squarely on Main Street in Plainfield Village, Ellen Shipman's stationery was printed "Poins House, Cornish, N. H." To make matters quite clear, she even penciled "Geographically in Plainfield, Socially in Cornish" on the reverse of one of her calling cards.[6]

Geographic displacement led easily to the Colony being referred to as "Little New York." To the people who used the term, it mattered little whether the people concerned were from New York or Boston. Whatever they were called, the "city folk in Cornish" had a profound effect on the community's economy. Local people, "natives" as they were called, were hired as carpenters, chauffeurs, gardeners, and caretakers. Women did housework, laundry, and cooking; they also waited on tables for the frequent—and elaborate—dinner parties. The Colonists, in turn, did their bit by purchasing vegetables, meat, poultry, eggs, milk, and butter from local farmers.[7] The "natives" also earned a little extra income by opening their homes to boarders. Among those who did so were William Westgate, Elwin Quimby, Stephen Alden Tracy, Charles Eggleston, Ralph Jordan, and George S. Ruggles.

However glad the "natives" may have been to have the extra income, there were also occasions when they resented the Colonists' demands and their snobbery. Social contacts between the two groups were few and far between. Farmers were up at dawn and went to bed early, unlike the artists and others in the Colony whose lifestyles drew them into festive activities that lasted late into the night. The social attitudes of the day prevented employers from interacting with the "hired help." For all the buoying up of the local economy, one Cornish person would muse, "They wiped their feet on us a little."[8]

In 1890 George Ruggles, a local carpenter, helped to bridge the social gap by building a studio, later called "The Woodchuck Hole," for some of the artists and writers to use. Its three rooms, one with a large window having a northern exposure, plus a veranda on two of its sides, provided comfortable working quarters. Nestled among pine trees, it was located on his property on Thrasher Road. Among the Colony members who took advantage of this studio were Percy MacKaye, Abbott Thayer, Kenyon Cox, Thomas Dewing, Arthur Henry Prellwitz, George de Forest Brush, Barry Faulkner, and Paul Manship.

Because of its ideal location, and perhaps because assistance was readily available locally, Cornish became nationally famous for its beautiful flower gardens. Thomas and Maria Dewing are credited with introducing flower gardening to the Colony because Maria was a painter of flowers. Ellen Shipman and Rose Nichols became garden architects with a national reputation. Charles A. Platt, who had been a landscape architect before he started designing houses, exerted a definite influence on garden layout in America. Early twentieth-century issues of *Century Magazine, House and Garden, Country Life in America,* and *Suburban Life* all published articles about the gardens in Cornish. But the prize for gardening intensity among the Colonists most surely goes to Stephen Parrish. His daily journal is filled with extremely detailed descriptions of his every gardening activity.

Augustus Saint-Gaudens was the Colonists' magnet; people wanted to be associated with him for the aura he provided: he had a warm personality and loved people. Furthermore, he had established an enviable reputation in the art world. This artists' colony was different from others. It was not a planned one, it was not a teaching colony—it just happened. To celebrate the twentieth anniversary of the Saint-Gaudenses' presence in Cornish, the Colony decided in 1905 to produce a masque, an allegorical play written by

Louis Evan Shipman with a prologue by Percy MacKaye. They were deliberately harking back to a Medieval and Renaissance form of allegorical entertainment combining music and poetry with elaborate costumes, scenery, and properties that appealed to the dramatic tastes of its creators. *A Masque of "Ours": The Gods and the Golden Bowl* was presented June 22 on the grounds of "Aspet," the home of the Saint-Gaudenses, followed first by a supper and then by a ball in the new studio. The event received much national publicity. For instance, Kenyon Cox wrote in *The Nation* for July 1, 1905, "It was crammed with local allusions, many of which were more for the benefit of the chief guest and of the actors themselves than of the other guests, who could hardly be expected to understand them all, but it was meant only for agreeable nonsense and as an excuse for the spectacle."[9] The next year Saint-Gaudens designed a medallion that was reproduced in silver and inscribed with the names of the ninety participants. Although Saint-Gaudens was ill for this occasion, his wife presented the plaque to the players.

This was not the end to the pageantry. In 1913 Percy MacKaye wrote *Sanctuary: A Bird Masque* for the naturalist Ernest Harold Baynes. Baynes had started the first American bird club to encourage the feeding and protection of birds in Meriden, New Hampshire, in 1910. He had become increasingly concerned about the possible extinction of those birds whose plumage was then in favor for the stylish decoration of women's hats. This masque was produced in September at the Bird Sanctuary in Meriden; President and Mrs. Wilson attended in order to see their two daughters take part in the play— Eleanor as "Ornis," a bird spirit, and Margaret as "The Hermit Thrush" and singer of the Prelude. The stage production was directed by Joseph Lindon Smith and the dances by Juliet Barrett Rublee. The following year the masque was given at the Hotel Astor in New York City. The Redpath Chautauqua later toured the country presenting *Sanctuary* and, as a result, many bird clubs were established throughout America.[10]

The exciting potential of these masques soon piqued the interest of other Colonists. The painter William Howard Hart decided to donate the stage and lighting for the Plainfield Town Hall once the town appropriated the funds necessary to build the foundation. Maxfield Parrish, in turn, painted a scene of Mount Ascutney; his design was reproduced as a backdrop for the stage in 1916. It is still used today.[11] Hart and his friend the sculptor Herbert Adams lived near one another in Plainfield. Adams created an outdoor theater in the pine woods on his property, while Hart organized the Howard Hart Players in the late 1930s. Many Hart performances took place at the Plainfield Town Hall and at Herbert Adams's outdoor theater.

There were well over one hundred well-known people associated with the Cornish Colony, once known "to some New Yorkers as 'The Athens of America.'"[12] Some men and women stayed for merely a season while others remained for a lifetime. Devising a precise definition of what constitutes membership in the Cornish Colony is not an easy matter. Surely those who bought land and built "cottages" are to be numbered among the Colonists, but should not those who rented property—people such as Ethel Barrymore and Ernest Lawson—as well as others who left a strong impression on the Colonists—people such as Isadora Duncan, the Fuller Sisters, and Benton MacKaye—be granted membership? The main body of the discussion of the Cornish Colony yields to this elastic definition. However, to increase the flexibility of the definition and to include as wide a representation as possible, there is a "Supplemental List: People Connected with the Cornish Colony." It is a somewhat unwieldy means of separating people associated with the Colony from those who were generally thought to be its members. As a transition between the two sections, and to provide some sense of the flavor of Cornish, there is a brief chapter that focuses not on people but on "The Way It Was: Life in the Cornish Colony." It touches upon some of the customs and experiences that shaped the daily life of people in turn-of-the-century America, and especially Cornish. Nevertheless, be these people thought of as members or as associates of the Colony, they are examined here primarily for the impact Cornish had as an element in both their lives and their art. This emphasis necessarily distorts their artistic careers, but it is assumed that it is precisely that distortion that will pique the interest of this book's readers.

It is worth noting that women played a vital role as both members and associates of the Colony. Art historians need to give greater recognition to the works of Louise Howland King Cox, Maria Oakey Dewing, Lucia Fairchild Fuller, Frances Grimes, Elsie Ward Hering, Frances C. Lyons Houston, Edith Mitchell Prellwitz, Annetta Johnson St. Gaudens, Florence Scovel Shinn, and Bessie Potter Vonnoh. These women deserve a more detailed scrutiny of their contributions to American art than they have received or than they receive even here. To emphasize their autonomy as artists, they have been listed in the chapter titles of the following discussion by their full names. A fine intelligence is apparent in the writings of Adeline Pond Adams, Frances Duncan, Rose Standish Nichols, Lydia Austin Parrish, and Ellen McGowan Biddle Shipman—a first-rate landscape architect. The fact of the matter is, however, that these women were products of their time. As such, many of the married women frequently assumed that their function as wives required their artistic talents to play second fiddle to their husbands' careers. Many people today see a more clear-cut resolution of this dilemma; they can emulate the careers of Frances Duncan, Lucia Fairchild Fuller, and Ellen Shipman.

The excellent and diverse artist Marguerite Zorach is an interesting case in point. Although she pretty much belonged to a later generation of women artists and although her art was in a more modern vein than that of most Cornish artists—male or female—she still seems to have been bound by some of the assumptions tacitly governing the women of the previous artistic generation. Marguerite began her career as a painter, yet she destroyed many of her paintings at intervals throughout her life. Before her husband devoted most of his artistic energy to sculpture, William too was primarily a painter. But his decision to sculpt did not seem to liberate her so that she felt free enough to return to painting. It is difficult to know whether she was simply a perfectionist and few of her paintings met her standards, or whether the strictures against a woman competing with her husband led to her decision not to resume painting as her major activity, or whether, despite her willingness to engage in numerous efforts of creative cooperation with him, she felt some anxiety at the potential influence of William on her painting. Thus Marguerite Zorach may not have been so different from her female artistic contemporaries in the Cornish Colony. It may well be that all these women were forced to trod a traditional path—that of trying to achieve their own autonomy while not making waves.

The procedure followed in the first section of this book is retained in the following biographies of people who were either members or associates of the Cornish Colony. The material presented here is designed less to repeat elements of the earlier publication: *A Circle of Friends: Art Colonies of Cornish and Dublin,* the exhibition catalogue for the

1985 exhibition of the works of many Cornish artists, than it is to supplement it and to expand upon its coverage.

In the final analysis, the Cornish Colony—what appears to us at the end of the twentieth century as a series of vibrant threads in the fabric of American art history—gradually lost its luster and shaded off into relative obscurity. Its art and its artists were no longer in fashion. How many people who attended the exhibition of Cornish Colony artists that Dartmouth College organized in 1916 realized what they were seeing? How could they know that they were present at what was, in reality, more of a tribute to the Colony as a thing of the past rather than what the show was set up to be: a celebration of the Colony as a vital community of artists active in the present? The First World War undeniably dealt a cruel blow to the Colony. As a small token of remembrance of this famous artist colony, the Historical Committee of the state of New Hampshire has erected a roadside historical marker at the "Blow-Me-Down Mill" to commemorate the significant contributions the Cornish Colony made to the cultural life of America.

James B. Atkinson

ENDNOTES

1. Child, William H. *History of the Town of Cornish with Genealogical Record: 1763-1910,* (Concord, NH: The Rumford Press, 1911?; reprinted edition, Spartenburg, SC: The Reprint Company, 1975), Vol. 1, p. 277.

2. Now on display at the Saint-Gaudens National Historic Site; see Hugh Mason Wade, *A Brief History of Cornish: 1763-1947* (Hanover, NH: University Press of New England, 1976), p. 49.

3. According to Augustus Saint-Gaudens, these are the Colony's earliest members. He dates the Colony's actual establishment with the arrival of Thomas Dewing. In 1886, the year after Saint-Gaudens arrived, "Mr. Dewing came. He saw. He remained. And from that event the Colony developed . . .”; *The Reminiscences of Augustus Saint-Gaudens,* edited and amplified by Homer Saint-Gaudens (New York: Century Company, 1913), Vol. 1, pp. 317-318.

4. A group of American painters became known as "The Ten American Painters." They held their first exhibition in March of 1898 at the Durand-Ruel Gallery in New York. The group had been established the previous December when the ten members formally decided to hold exhibitions and to add a new member only if the group agreed on the candidate unanimously. Their members were Frank Benson (1862-1951), Joseph De Camp (1858-1923), Thomas Dewing (1851-1938), Childe Hassam (1859-1935), Willard Leroy Metcalf (1858-1925), Robert Reid (1862-1929), Edward Simmons (1852-1931), Edmund Tarbell (1862-1938), John Twachtman (1853-1902), and J. Alden Weir (1852-1919). At Twachtman's death, they elected William Merritt Chase (1849-1916). On the other hand "The Eight," or "The Áshcan School," were a disparate group of painters, adamantly opposed to any hint of the academy in their art. Their movement helped to launch the Armory Show of 1913, which introduced a shocked audience to the latest trends in modern art coming from Europe. Not held together by an allegiance to any single movement, as "The Ten" were linked by Impressionism, their group comprised Arthur B. Davies (1862-1928), William Glackens (1870-1938), Robert Henri (1865-1929), Ernest Lawson (1873-1939), George Luks (1867-1933), Maurice Prendergast (1859-1924), Everett Shinn (1876-1953), and John Sloan (1871-1951).

5. James L. Farley, "The Cornish Colony," *Dartmouth College Library Bulletin* 14 (n.s.), November 1973, pp. 6-17.

6. Virginia Colby, Cornish Colony files.

7. Christine Ermenc, "Economic Give-and-Take: Farmers and Aesthetes in Cornish and Plainfield, New Hampshire, 1885-1910," *New Hampshire Historical Quarterly,* 39, 3-4, Fall-Winter, 1984, pp. 104-119.

8. Personal interview with Virginia Colby.

9. Kenyon Cox, "An Outdoor Masque in New England," *The Nation,* July 1, 1905, p. 519. For more on masques as they relate to Saint-Gaudens, MacKaye, and the Cornish Colony, see Trudy Baltz, "Pageantry and Mural Painting: Community Rituals in Allegorical Form," *Winterthur Portfolio,* 15:3, Autumn 1980, pp. 211-228.

10. Ernest Harold Baynes Papers, Cornish Historical Society, Cornish, NH.

11. Virginia Reed Colby, "Stephen and Maxfield Parrish in New Hampshire," *The Magazine Antiques,* 115, 6, June 1979, p. 1297.

12. As quoted in Gerald Gunther, *Learned Hand: The Man and the Judge* (New York: Knopf, 1994), p. 172.

HERBERT ADAMS
1858 – 1945

and

ADELINE POND ADAMS
1859 – 1948

Figure 44. *Painting of Mrs. Herbert Adams by William Howard Hart, 1899.*

ADELINE POND ADAMS

THE SCULPTOR HERBERT ADAMS met his future wife, Adeline Valentine Pond, in Paris, and they were married in Auburndale, Massachusetts, in 1899. She inspired him to do a sculpture that would soon make him famous. His bust of Adeline, done in marble and depicting her with a beautiful smile, was shown in the Paris Salon of 1888 and won much praise. The portrait bust "is of such rare perfection of finish that . . . it 'still remains, in some sense, unsurpassed by his later achievement . . . it is of such perfect mastery that the face and neck, at least, appear plastic, as if responsive like wax to the pressure of the artist's thumb.'"[1] Adams entered this bust again, along with two other pieces, in the Columbian Exposition in Chicago of 1893. People were drawn to the new conception of feminine beauty he announced in the Adeline V. Pond bust. Although Adams was merely returning to a practice of ancient Greek and Roman sculpture, he caused quite a stir in the art world because he tinted the marble in some features of the two Exposition entries.[2]

The year after the success of the Columbian Exposition, Adeline and her husband arrived in Cornish and boarded with the Frank Johnsons (later the "Barberry House"). In 1896 they returned with their artist friend William Howard Hart in tow and boarded with Stephen Alden Tracy.[3] (Hart later built a house up behind the Adamses' house.) The Adamses also spent a summer in a little house on Freeman Road in Plainfield—the same one used by George de Forest Brush. (Unfortunately, it is no longer standing.) By 1903 the Adamses were the owners of 105 acres of the Elmer DeGoosh farm on Stage Road in Plainfield. Their house, which Charles A. Platt designed, was called "Hermitage."[4]

Adeline Adams was a biographer who specialized in artists and, not surprisingly, in sculptors. She frequently wrote for *American Art News, The American Magazine of Art,* and *The Dictionary of American Biography.* She became an authority on the history of sculpture; her book, *The Spirit of American Sculpture,* was first published in 1923 and then again in 1929 in a revised edition by the National Sculpture Society. She also provided art criticism in the form of reviews and articles for *The House Beautiful.* For it she wrote an article in 1924 entitled "Sculpture in the House, Is It Among the House-Broken Arts?" She answers her question, in part, by noting that "A portrait, marble-toned, of Mrs. Billings, by Herbert Adams, is intimate enough to be lived with comfortably in the home."[5] (The subject is Julia Parmly Billings, wife of Frederick Billings, the famous lawyer and philanthropist of Woodstock, Vermont.) The gist of her argument in the article is that "one of the paradoxical effects of democracy is this: that with its liberating impulse toward a higher life, too many of us hasten to consider ourselves fitted for doing only the highest things. But is it not true that a little medal or portrait or table-bell may unfold more of the living spirit of art than a huge, shapeless, public monument? If we really believe this truth, sculpture may without condescension declare itself among the house-broken arts."[6]

In addition to her writing on art, Mrs. Adams also wrote poetry. She published a book of poems in 1900 dedicated to their daughter Mary, who lived only about six months. (*Mary* was printed privately in Cambridge, Massachusetts.) Later, in 1912, she wrote another book, *Sylvia,* in memory of Sylvia Platt who also died young. (*Sylvia* was printed privately in Cornish, New Hampshire.) She was also adept at light verse; one of her efforts is reprinted below on pp. 147-148.

There is more serious proof that the Cornish Colony played a significant part in her social life. Mrs. Woodrow Wilson mentions the Adamses in her diary entry for August 12, 1913, in the context of a dinner party at the Kenyon Coxes': "the only other guests, Mr. and Mrs. Herbert Adams, are among the choice spirits of the Colony— both intellectually and spiritually. I could really *love* them both. He, you know, is the sculptor whom I met in Washington. They are Boston people. She also 'studies art,' but I do not hear of her doing anything now. It is pretty to see how much they are loved and honoured by the younger people here."[7]

Mrs. Adams was also active socially in local events. She played Psyche in *A Masque of "Ours": The Gods and the Golden Bowl* (1905) and Bluebird in *Sanctuary: A Bird Masque* (1913). Furthermore, she was an active member both of the Cornish Equal Suffrage League and of the Mothers' and Daughters' Club of Plainfield.[8] Finally, during the period that her husband was president of the Saint-Gaudens Memorial, she frequently furnished refreshments for their board meetings.

Mrs. Adams was a faithful companion of the sculptor for fifty-six years. She continued to make her home in Plainfield until her death on July 1, 1948, at the age of eighty-seven.

HERBERT ADAMS

IT HAS BEEN SAID of his statues that they "have a calm dignity, a repose and a studied quiet so real that they, at times, seem to move with the breath of life."[9] And his wife believed that "the wisdom, restraint, and true sense of the just and fitting, which for years have rendered all relation with his calm and balanced intellect the delight of friends and the aid of fellow workers, are mirrored in an art which so easily reflects these qualities."[10] During his lifetime Adams created more than 160 commissions. Some of his most important ones include: the McMillan Fountain in Washington, DC, (architectural setting designed by Charles A. Platt); the bronze doors representing *Writing* and a statue of Joseph Henry at the Library of Congress; a statue of William Cullen Bryant in Bryant Park behind the New York Public Library; the *Primavera* in the Corcoran Gallery of Art; *La Jeunesse* at the Metropolitan Museum of Art; the Jonathan Edwards Memorial at Northampton, Massachusetts; and the bronze statue of William Ellery Channing for the Boston Public Garden.

These commissions earned him high praise from his contemporaries. He won medals at the Philadelphia Art Club, the Louisiana Purchase Exposition in 1904, the Panama-Pacific International Exposition in 1915, the National Academy of Design, and a gold medal from the National Institute of Arts and Letters. He showed five of his works, including *La Jeunesse* at the exhibition of Cornish Artists at Dartmouth College in 1916.[11]

Given this background, it is not surprising that he served as president of the National Academy of Design, of the National Sculpture Society, and also of the Saint-Gaudens Memorial from 1933 until his death in 1945. He was a member both of the Art Commission of the City of New York and of the Federal Commission of Fine Arts; he was also a trustee of the American Academy of Arts and Letters.

For all these honors, he took advantage of the local scene while he was here. Directly traceable to his stay in Cornish are the bronze doors for the Mariners' Museum in Newport News, Virginia, which are notable because "the history of shipping and the mythology of the sea allowed freedom of fancy and freshness and variety of ornament"[12] as well as a marble bas-relief done in 1894 of the Fraser-Campbell children entitled *The Singing Boys*. The children's parents summered briefly in Cornish during the 1890s. The bas-relief, influenced by the style and technique of his friend and

Figure 45. Abe *(c. 1938) by Herbert Adams. The sitter is Albert K. Read, III of Plainfield, New Hampshire.*

Cornish neighbor Augustus Saint-Gaudens, is now in the Metropolitan Museum of Art. Adams also drew on local models for his work. A Plainfield carpenter named Charlie Hill posed for the statue of Matthias Baldwin done in 1905 and now in Philadelphia; Albert K. Read, II, a Plainfield stonemason three generations of whose family worked for Adams on his farm, posed in 1902 for a statue of General Grant, although Adams eventually lost the commission to Henry M. Shrady.[13] It seems Adams reused the form and substituted a more appropriate head and face when executing a statue of Jerome Wheelock now in Grafton, Massachusetts.[14] Kay Jordan Garey of Windsor, Vermont, posed for a fountain statue when she was a very young girl; and Albert K. Read, III posed for a head, but all that currently exists of the project is a photograph.[15] Also of note concerning his Cornish connections is the fact that he was Frances Grimes's first teacher at the Pratt Institute in Brooklyn; he was also instrumental in her coming to Cornish to work with him—and later, for Saint-Gaudens. Proof of the long-standing friendship between Adams and Grimes can be found in this tribute she wrote for him at the time of a retrospective exhibit of his work:

> Nature has revealed herself so directly to his delicate perceptions that no pose or attitude of the sculptor has interrupted her revelations. Yet without pose or attitude his character and feeling with his sense of beauty speak in his portraits as in his ideal compositions. Another contribution to art . . . is his selfless and untiring service on behalf of the art community. . . . His incorruptible sense of justice and true instinct for what is good in human conduct as well as what is beautiful to look at have made him a leader recognized and depended upon by artists young and old through all of these years.[16]

He took advantage of the local scene in other ways as well. In the woods near his house and that of his good friend William Howard Hart, Adams constructed an outdoor amphitheater which became the site of many theatrical productions such as *Robin Hood, Hansel and Gretel,* and *Folk Dance.* His model for the Grant competition, Albert K. Read II, built the stone wall which formed the outdoor stage. His interest in drama extended to playing the part of Pan, the god of forests, pastures, flocks, and shepherds, in the 1905 production at Aspet of *A Masque of "Ours": The Gods and the Golden Bowl* and playing the part of Cardinal Grosbeak in the 1913 production in Meriden of *Sanctuary: A Bird Masque.* The Plainfield town records indicate that from 1905 to 1917 Adams was taxed for possessing one cow and one horse and in 1912 for twelve neat stock. The summer of 1944 was the last summer the Adamses spent locally; he died May 23, 1945, at the age of eighty-seven.

In summarizing his career, it has been noted that the bronze statue of William Ellery Channing, finished in 1902, as well as the portrait statue of Joseph Henry and the bronze statue of William Cullen Bryant—both dating from 1911—were the highpoints of his career. "In these three monuments he approached the creative powers of Saint Gaudens (d. 1907) and J. Q. A. Ward (d. 1910), and it appeared as if he were to be their successor in the art of the portrait statue. But it was not to be . . . the battle for leadership in American sculpture that raged between the National Sculpture Society and the proponents of abstract art was . . . won by the abstractionists."[17]

ENDNOTES

1. Ernest Peixotto, "The Sculpture of Herbert Adams," *The American Magazine of Art* 9, May 1921, p. 152.

2. The bust of Adeline Pond Adams is in the collection of the Hispanic Society of America.

3. Letter from Mrs. Adams to Stephen Alden Tracy, collection of Dorothy Tracy, Cornish, NH.

4. Plainfield town tax records.

5. Adeline Pond Adams, "Sculpture in the House, Is It Among the House-Broken Arts?," *The House Beautiful: Building, Furnishing, Planting,* January 1924, p. 18. Frederick Billings was also the founder of the Billings Farm; his wife was the grandmother of Mary French Rockefeller. Mrs. Billings's daughter Laura, Mrs. Frederic Lee, lived in Cornish for a few summers before building a Platt-designed house in Woodstock, VT. This information is courtesy of Jane Curtis, letter to Virginia Colby dated February 23, 1993.

6. Ibid., p. 19.

7. Arthur S. Link, ed, *The Papers of Woodrow Wilson* (Princeton, NJ: Princeton University Press, 1978), Vol. 28, p. 146; for the context, see below p. 434.

8. *Cornish Equal Suffrage League Bulletin,* 1911, collection of Virginia Colby; see below pp. 286-289 and 443.

9. Peixotto, p. 151.

10. Adeline Pond as quoted in Beatrice Gilman Proske, *Brookgreens Gardens Sculpture* (Brookgreens Gardens, SC: Brookgreens Gardens Trustees, 1968), p. 28.

11. George Breed Zug, "Exhibition of Cornish Artists," *Art and Archaeology,* April 1916, pp. 207-211; see also *Dartmouth Alumni Magazine,* March 1916, pp. 203-205.

12. Proske, p. 27; see also the correspondence between Herbert Adams, Newport News Ship Yard, the Dry Dock Company, and the Gorham Company (Bronze Division); collection of the Mariners' Museum.

13. Interview: Virginia Colby with Albert K. Read, III, August 15, 1982, Plainfield, NH.

14. Newspaper clipping, probably from the Fitchburg, MA, *Sentinel-Enterprise,* by Adams's fourth cousin, Marilyn Gage Hyson. Virginia Colby, Cornish Colony files.

15. Katherine Derry Holler, *Herbert Adams, American Sculptor,* a thesis submitted to the faculty of the University of Delaware in partial fulfillment of the requirements for the degree of Master of Arts in the History of Art, June 1971, p. 32. The location of the statue is unknown; a photograph is on file at the New York City Public Library.

16. Frances Grimes, preface to the catalogue *Exhibition of Works by Herbert Adams* (New York: The Century Association, 1945).

17. Wayne Craven, *Sculpture in America* (New York: Thomas Y. Crowell, 1968), pp. 436-437.

JOHN WHITE ALEXANDER
1856 – 1915

JOHN WHITE ALEXANDER was one of America's most fashionable artists at the turn of the century. He spent the summer of 1890 in Cornish, probably at the invitation of his friend Charles A. Platt. Alexander, his wife, and young son James, boarded at the home of Stephen A. Tracy.[1] That summer Alexander painted three landscapes in Cornish. One of them, *Birches, Cornish, New Hampshire*,[2] was exhibited in *A Circle of Friends: Art Colonies of Cornish and Dublin* (1985). Another painting, *Landscape, Cornish, New Hampshire*, was sold by a New York dealer in 1986.

Alexander began his career working in the art department of the publisher Harper and Brothers in New York. He went to Bavaria to study and then joined Frank Duveneck and his "Duveneck Boys," painting with the group in Polling, near Munich, Florence, and Venice. This group, including Joseph De Camp, was known for its dark palette that

Figure 46. Landscape, Cornish, New Hampshire, *painted about 1890 by John White Alexander.*

strove for romantic and impressive effects. Alexander returned to New York in 1881; in 1887 he married Elizabeth Alexander, a writer whose short stories he had illustrated. Later, in 1890, he began a ten-year period of study in Paris. There he became a leading American proselytizer for the Art Nouveau movement and its aesthetic doctrines and there, too, his idealized pictures of beautiful women in lush, flowing gowns gained him prominence. His 1897 *Isabella and the Pot of Basil*, based on a poem by Keats, painted in Paris, and owned now by the Boston Museum of Fine Arts, shows just such a female figure in a dimly lit background with the picture's verticality emphasizing the Art Nouveau style. In the same vein, his *Alethea*, painted in 1895, brought a record price at a Sotheby's auction in June of 1988.[3] Commenting that "Alexander is an interesting bridge between

. . . realism and abstraction," H. Wayne Morgan points out that "Alexander was . . . noted for his elegance of line and arrangement, [he] emphasized planes, outlined forms and stripes, and mere areas of paint. His figures remained recognizable but were basically means of rearranging reality into an artistic statement that transcended visible nature."[4] He also exhibited successfully at the invitation of Secessionist groups in both Munich and Vienna. Some of his other more famous paintings, not of women, included portraits of Walt Whitman (a sophisticatedly-designed work done in 1889 that Whitman said he "never liked"[5]), Grover Cleveland, Thomas Hardy, Oliver Wendell Holmes, and Robert Louis Stevenson.

Returning to America in 1901, he was immediately elected to the National Academy of Design and eventually became its president from 1909 to 1915. As its leader, he wrote a scathing attack in a letter to *The Nation* about "the American attitude towards art." It was occasioned by the death of Gaston La Touche, because it was not properly lamented by American newspapers, and by the debate then raging over a tariff law revision, because it proposed a duty on imported art that he believed harmed art in America:

Figure 47. Isabella and the Pot of Basil, *inspired by a poem by Keats.*

> Is there anything in the world more discouraging than the attitude of the American public towards art? . . . Again and again our papers report the unveiling of a picture, or statue, giving long accounts of the ceremonies, the speeches, the music, and the people who attend the function, and never a mention of the artist who created the work. In no other country do we find such self-satisfaction and complacency in regard to art as we do over here, and nowhere else such a lack of real intelligent appreciation, although we hear a great deal about art and profess to feel deeply interested in all that concerns it. . . . We, the artists of this country, do not want [the protection of the proposed tariff]; we have not asked for it. . . . The more we can see of what is being accomplished by artists all over the world, the better it will be for our young art. New, strong work stimulates, invigorates and helps us in our efforts to produce something that each sincere worker cannot help hoping may some time stand as worthy and representative examples of American art.[6]

Even while he was abroad, he received a commission to execute a series of murals for lunettes in the Library of Congress called *The Evolution of the Book*. The panels were entitled *The Cairn, Oral Tradition, The Hieroglyphic, The Pictograph, Painting on Skins, The Manuscript,* and *The Printing Press*. Upon his return he received a commission from the Carnegie Institute in 1905 to paint a series of murals representing the *Apotheosis of Pittsburgh*—a series of panels, which he called *The Crowning of Labor*, that depicted aspects of the steel industry. For these panels he used canvas woven especially for the task; for his convenience he ordered his colors to be prepared in especially large tubes. Since he was a frail man, this commission proved to be very taxing for him; he completed fifteen panels surrounding the entrance floor; a series of very large panels at the top of the main staircase—twelve panels grouped about the second-story stairwell, and a group of panels at either side of the second-story gallery; he died, however, before the twenty-one third-floor panels were done.[7] He worked directly on the canvas and left no studies from which someone else could have completed his project. But he did live long enough to be "delighted [by] the effect of the murals upon the mill people who came to see them. As a child he played about the manufacturing districts of his native town and had a first-hand knowledge of the somber side of the great iron and steel works. The object of his decorations was to illustrate how all the toil and fatigue of the workers produces, in the end, the beauty and inspiration of life."[8] For someone who in his younger days was a friend of both Henry James and James Abbott McNeill Whistler and an artist who was influenced both by Whistler and by Japanese prints, it may seem odd for Alexander to choose this kind of subject for his art. His choice does indicate his ability to attune his art to a new direction in American art. One that "was a rejection of bucolic, idyllic subjects in favor of urban ones"[9] though he could never be mistaken for a member of "The Ashcan School."

A year after his death in 1915, the Department of Fine Arts at Dartmouth College held the first representative exhibition of original sculpture, painting, and illustration by artists of the summer colony at Cornish. Two of Alexander's paintings were shown. G. B. Zug commented, "John W. Alexander's landscape of supreme simplicity and idyllic beauty found a very large group of ardent admirers."[10]

ENDNOTES

1. Correspondence, collection of Dorothy Tracy, Cornish, NH.

2. Collection of his granddaughter Irina A. Reed. In 1884 Alexander, who was more famous for his sensuous portraits of women than for his landscapes, would write a friend that he would like to "be a sort of Thoreau in art—I have a great admiration for that man," as quoted in Sandra Leff's essay in *John White Alexander, 1856-1915: Fin-de-Siècle American*, exhibition catalogue (New York: Graham Gallery, 1980), p. 12.

3. *Antiques and The Arts Weekly*, June 10, 1988, p. 101, reported that it sold for $517,000. In connection both with these idealized, *fin de siècle* women and with current ideas about the role of women in our society, *The Weekly Enterprise* (Meriden, New Hampshire) for January 5, 1911, after his return to America, picked up an interesting interview with Alexander, dateline, New York: "If the American woman persists in her undue athletic sports, there will soon be little difference between the masculine and the feminine figure." Quoting Alexander, the paper reports: "Just where the beauty of such unnatural development comes in, I don't see. . . . If she continues her violent exercises and outdoor life, in a few years she will be so manlike in figure that she will look ridiculous in woman's attire. Up to a certain point this outdoor life and development is excellent. It gives the girl all that women of this country have been distinguished for abroad—a free, easy carriage, and an independence in movement and action that at once inspires confidence in her ability to meet a crisis. But this point has been overstepped and she is becoming anything but interesting." He continues by bewailing the fact that this tendency "is one reason why many artists doing work along classical lines find it difficult to secure a model." What we would call "aesthetic" lines, he terms "classical."

4. H. Wayne Morgan, *New Muses: Art in American Culture, 1865-1920* (Norman, Oklahoma: University of Oklahoma Press, 1978) p. 149.

5. Doreen Bolger Burke, *American Paintings in the Metropolitan Museum of Art* (New York: The Metropolitan Museum of Art and Princeton University Press, 1980), Vol. 3, p. 208.

6. *The Nation* 97, No. 2509, July 31, 1913, pp. 98-99. For more on the question of art and the tariff, see below, pp. 432-433.

7. *"The Crowning of Labor," The John W. Alexander Mural Paintings in the Carnegie Institute, Pittsburgh, With Descriptive Text by Mrs. John W. Alexander*, (The Detroit Publishing Company, March 1916), p. 28.

8. Ibid., p. 32.

9. Leff, Graham Gallery exhibition catalogue, p. 17.

10. George Breed Zug, "Exhibition of Cornish Artists," *Art and Archaeology*, April 1916, p. 208.

ROBERT L. BARRETT

1871 – 1969

ALTHOUGH THE SIGNIFICANT PROOFS of his devotion to Cornish exist throughout the town, the early career of Robert LeMoyne Barrett began far afield. Some Americans may know him as a founding member of the Association of American Geographers, but Cornish remembers his legacy to the town in his contributions to education and to the growth and development of the young.

He was born in Chicago where his father had established a profitable business in road surface materials and roofing paper. He attended Phillips Academy in Andover, Massachusetts, and entered Harvard. Because he found life after one semester there "too stuffy," he headed out to British Columbia where he lived among the Indians. "Months later he visited New Hampshire, erected a tepee on a hill in Cornish, and

Figure 48. *Robert Barrett's glass house, c. 1930.*

considered that, or a nearby cave, his residence."[1] Eventually he returned to Harvard and earned a BA degree. In the summer of 1897 he went to Norway for practical experience in the field of geography and returned again in 1898. His experience resulted in "The Sundal Drainage System in Central Norway" and the later "Features of Norway and its People." Both articles were published in professional geographic journals.

Upon his return from Norway, he entered his father's business but he was drawn to traveling: to London, to Russia, and—via the Volga River and the Caspian Sea—to unexplored areas of Asia and the Tien Shan mountain range. From the evidence of his diaries and photographs, we know later travels took him to the American Southwest and Baja California. W. M. Davis, an eminent geographer and geologist who proposed the geological concept of the erosion cycle and one of Barrett's Harvard professors, capitalized on Barrett's yen for distant lands. Davis persuaded Barrett to finance what became known as the Barrett Expedition to Inner Asia; he took with him Ellsworth Huntington, who later became a distinguished explorer and author. The two men, with an extensive retinue, journeyed through the Himalayas but parted company in 1905. Barrett, however, remained south of the Tarim Basin taking measurements of the Himalayan slopes with his theodolite. He later journeyed through Chinese Turkestan to the Gobi Desert. Shortly thereafter, while on a trip to India, his father fell ill; Barrett hurried to his side and spent nearly a year taking care of him there. Barrett's Asian expeditions were subsequently reported in *The Bulletin of the American Geographical Society* and the *Geographic Journal*. Several of his informal accounts of his trips include *The Himalayan Letter of Gypsy Davy and Lady Ba: Written on Pilgrimage to the High Quiet Places Among the Simple People of an Old Folk Tale* (1927), *A Yankee in Patagonia—Edward Chace, His Thirty Years There* (1931), and *Cloudtop Mosaics* (1932).[2]

With such an exciting life behind him, it is easy to understand why he might turn to Cornish for tranquility, but it can hardly be said that he settled down while he was here. Be that as it may, the period in Cornish is not documented in the same scholarly fashion. Robert Barrett first appears on the Cornish tax records for a poll tax in 1911. The records for 1915 show that he owned 171 acres, 3 horses, 2 mules, 3 cows, and 9 sheep.[3] The diary of Marion MacKaye provides a delightful description of him:

> He is one of the loveliest of simple souls; he looks like the god Jove, like an Arab, or Bedouin. He goes barefoot and barelegged, lives on curds and wears the most unique clothes. The children adore him, so I hear from his brother-in-law. He has a beautiful curly golden brown beard, curly hair, bald on top like a monk's, heavy eyebrows over kind blue eyes, a nose like Christ's, quite perfect, and bronze skin like an Arab's. He wears wool clothing in tan shades, sleeps under the stars and lives in a small tent, which when walking, he wears as a cape. He is a perfect-natured man, complete mentally and physically, and the children . . . who call him "Brown Beard"—love him passionately and he them. Percy and George Barnard went up to spend the night with him. . . . They sat up, so they told me, around the campfire till after three in the morning and then rolled themselves up in their wraps and slept till ten in the morning, when Barrett cooked them a most delectable breakfast of hot cakes, with honey and curds.[4]

His philanthropic concern for Cornish began officially on April 4, 1913, when he offered the trustees of the Stowell Free Library $1,000 a year for library expenses. The majority of this sum was to go toward a salary for a librarian so that the library could be kept open every weekday. As it turned out, Barrett himself hired someone to fill that position: Katherine Ruth Ellis from Charles City, Iowa, a Vassar graduate and a brilliant woman who spoke seven languages. He then turned around and married her on June 29, 1913. Katherine continued working as librarian and together they established a Library Book Wagon, the Cornish Library Club, and the Cornish Girl War Workers of World War I. Mrs. Barrett also continued her literary interests by writing several books, among which were *The Wide-Awake Book for Girls* (1908), *The Strength of the Hills,* about Cornish, and several volumes of poetry—for example, *Red Shores* (1930) and *The Trenchant Wind, Poems of Patagonia* (1932). As part of their philanthropic and pedagogic commitment to Cornish, the Barretts were also responsible for bringing the three Fuller Sisters to Cornish from England to teach singing games and folk songs to Cornish children.[5]

The Fuller Sisters, obviously captivated by the couple, provide us with descriptions of them that complement those of Marion MacKaye.

> [Mr. Barrett] is aged about forty-five, and is very tall and big and lithe. He always wears brown, with a low collar, and an art shade of green tie. He has black hair, though the top of his head is rather bald—like a monk—and his eyebrows are dark, bushy, and striking. He is very sweet and kind and quite fatherly and courteous through and through—a real gypsy. He looks a picture as he strides along with a cloak blowing out behind, a slouch hat, and, in his arms, a little green harp—which he has just bought! He carries it everywhere and, when he sits down, he plays over and over the exercise I wrote out for him!
>
> I am afraid that won't give you a very good idea of him—but the reason I am trying to describe him to you is because he is so much like a story in a book—the sort of person one never really meets. He's travelled everywhere and has had many adventures— such as getting lost in the Assyrian Desert, dining with Prussian Dukes, visiting Chinese Emperors, and staying with English Duchesses! He has also been a medicine-man in Africa. Of course, he is very, *very* wealthy, so he can do all these things. The village of Cornish love him, though they don't quite know what to make of him. Before he was married—about two years ago—he used to live alone in the woods—and be always alone—so that he was called "the crazy man."
>
> But he has always been interested in the village schools and would often come to see what they needed—and then, at night, he would go round and leave the longed-for things on the steps. Did you ever?
>
> Now he's married to a very nice woman from the Middle West—and they are very happy together. Both seem to love the gypsy life and agree in everything.[6]

The sisters also referred to Robert Barrett as "Gypsy Davy" and "The Wild One," but they are equally fond of Katherine: "Japanese workers were still putting the finishing touches to the house as Katherine Barrett, a tall, thin, angular woman with a brown face, untidy hair, and wearing a Liberty dress, came forward to greet the girls warmly. She then handed everyone sandals to wear and they went into the house and had lunch sitting on large cushions on the floor and eating from wooden plates. The girls thought that Katherine looked as unusual, and as decorative, as her husband."[7]

Furthering his pedagogic interests, Barrett established the Pasture School in Cornish designed to stimulate the interests of outstanding students. It existed from 1917 until 1919 under the tutelage of Alice Jesseman and was held in a small portable building with open decking in a pasture high on Spaulding Hill near Cornish Flat. William Chadbourne was fortunate enough to have been invited to attend in the year 1918-19, along with Jack Dinkle, Donald Emery, Lewis Elmer Fitch, Lawrence Hunt, Dayton Johnson, and Stub Weld. They were instructed in mathematics, English, woodworking, literature, and music appreciation. The school provided a two-year curriculum in one academic year. The Barretts' final contribution to the youth of Cornish was leading a group of students on two camping trips, one in 1919 and another in 1922, in the High Sierras; William Chadbourne, Lewis Fitch, and Alice Jesseman were among the group. The three-month excursion required the use of twenty-six burros.[8] Katherine Barrett drew on these trips for another of her books, *Girls in the High Sierras: A Tale of the Sierra Nevada with Himalayan Echoes* (1924).

As may well be imagined, Robert Barrett's initial living arrangements in Cornish proved to be unsatisfactory. Katherine Ellis Barrett was not interested in setting up house in a tent, but still she did not want to keep an ordinary house. They built one situated on the highest part of Dingleton Hill with a pagoda atop it designed and constructed by workers brought over from Japan. Since all the construction materials were brought up to the top of the hill by cable from the farm below, a cable way first had to be set up. Although originally Barrett had not wanted a road up to his house, a new one had to be built to the bottom of the hill so that the teams of horses and oxen from Windsor might carry up the large steam engine used for the cable way. A V-shaped tower, about forty feet high, was built at the bottom of Barrett's hill and a smaller but similar one was built on the top to support a single cable used to hoist the building material up to the site.

Locally the house was most frequently referred to as the "Glass House" because the outside walls were sliding glass panels that could be opened up, thus giving the owners an open, unobstructed view of the outdoors. There was a central fireplace and every partition was on tracks that could slide back to make one large room or close off sections at will. There was a deep cellar with a large trapdoor in the floor near the fireplace so that a dumb waiter could bring heavy items up from below. On the ridge pole for the roof, there was a small platform large enough to accommodate several people sitting on comfortable cushions or to arrange a bed so that the Barretts could sleep under the stars.

Another description of the unorthodox house describes the side walls as being made of moveable glass panels. Teak, a wood strongly resistant to insects, was imported from Florida. The roof was a Japanese-styled one, curved up at the ends. There was a special platform on the roof that provided a broad view of Mount Ascutney and the surrounding terrain. After the house was finished, the Barretts often ate their meals on the roof and Robert slept there using special hooks that were installed for his hammock. Of note were the closet spaces and cupboards constructed so that they could be lowered down into the cellar below that had been blasted out of solid rock. The closets, hidden by trapdoors in the floor, could be brought up to the main floor by pressing a button that engaged a gravity-powered pulley system.[9]

These uncommon living arrangements naturally raise the question of what kind of kitchen did the Barretts have. Since they did very little cooking for themselves, Mr. and Mrs. Ernest French, who were living in the old Oscar Johnson house, helped the

Barretts out in their splendid, hilltop isolation. Mr. French ran the farm and Mrs. French cooked their meals and packed them on two mules named Jack and Jenny; they then transported the meals up the hill to the Barretts's house.[10] Could this be the forerunner of meals on wheels?

The Barretts had several family members as neighbors. Robert Barrett's sister, the sculptress Adela, lived at the foot of the hill upon which the "Glass House" was built. Another sister, Juliet Barrett Rublee, lived on Platt Road and was married to George Rublee, a member of the Federal Trade Commission (see below pp. 342-348). The Barretts eventually moved away from the little neighborhood they had fashioned and made their home in California. After repeated vandalism, their glass house was dismantled.

ENDNOTES

1. Material in this paragraph comes from Geoffrey J. Martin, "Robert LeMoyne Barrett, 1871-1969, Last of the Founding Members of the Association of American Geographers," *The Professional Geographer* 24, No. 1, February 1972, p. 29.

2. Martin, p. 30.

3. Cornish town records; Mrs. Barrett was on the Cornish voting list from 1922 to 1935.

4. Arvia MacKaye Ege, *The Power of the Impossible: The Life Story of Percy and Marion MacKaye* (Falmouth, ME: The Kennebec River Press, 1992), p. 134. George Grey Barnard was a well-known sculptor and a lifelong friend of Percy's; when Augustus Saint-Gaudens left the Art Students League in 1897 to study in Paris, he left the teaching of his modeling class in the hands of Barnard and Mary Lawrence.

5. George Stowell Library files, Cornish, New Hampshire; see below pp. 211-215.

6. Cynthia Fuller to Riss Fuller, September 28, 1915, collection of Virginia Colby, courtesy of Carol Odell.

7. Carol Odell, "The Fuller Sisters: Fourth Tour of America, part 2, October 1914-May 20, 1916," p. 33, unpublished manuscript, collection of Virginia Colby.

8. William Chadbourne, "Notes" (Inglewood, California, 1980), p. 15; gift to the Cornish Historical Society.

9. Michele McDonald, "Who Was This Free-Spirited Man Who Built a Glass House in Cornish Seventy Years Ago?," *Eagle-Times, Impact,* Claremont, NH, October 8, 1978, pp. 3C-4C. "Steve" (Stephen Parrish, Maxfield Parrish, Jr.'s younger brother), wrote Maxfield Parrish, Jr., a more unorthodox description of this unorthodox house:

    > As a kid I used to see quite a bit of the guy [Rob Barrett] on my frequent visits to Cousin Anne's. She would drive the T model to the foot of the hill and we would walk up the hill to the Jap house. Once inside, off came the shoes so we wouldn't bugger up the fancy battleship linoleum floor. That house made a very lasting impression on me probably because it was so damned un-orthodox. The double bed crow's nest on the roof ridge pole, the floor hatch with the dumb waiter for storing the food in a deep hole in the rock below, and the fact that the crapper could only be entered by climbing a rope up the wall to the rafters and then dropping down inside via same rope. Only advantage, you didn't have to lock the door but what a predicament if you had the trots or green apple quick step. (Collection of Virginia Colby.)

10. Edith Hunter., "The Cornish-Weathersfield Connection," *The Weathersfield, Vermont, Weekly* 30, No. 7, August 25, 1979, p. 8.

Figure 49. *Portrait of Ethel Barrymore by Henry Fuller.*

ETHEL BARRYMORE
1879 – 1959

THE FAMOUS ACTRESS ETHEL BARRYMORE came to Cornish on June 2, 1906. According to poet William Vaughn Moody, "The Barrymore arrived this morning, with a full complement of sensations, including a railroad wreck." The complete passage is too rich in amusing detail not to quote in its entirety:

> My afternoon walk has intersected at various points her triumphal progress from villa to villa, as she takes a preliminary survey of her dominions. I am invited to meet her at dinner this evening, together with doubtless the entire male summer population. She is not expected to stay, by reason of Cornish's "dulness"; accordingly all work has been suspended, and the amusement of Ethel is to be the one great communistic aim. Maxfield Parrish has laid aside his Dinky Birds, Norman Hapgood his reforming of the national morals and manners, MacKaye his dreams, and I my contracts, to swim as goldfish in Ethel's parlor jar. This is more than a metaphor. Her premises include a marble swimming pool, under a vine-covered pergola, with Greek pillars from which she is said to rejoice to dive. Bathing suits are furnished by rotation of pegs, and the fit shall be as God wills.[1]

Miss Barrymore rented the Fuller house on Route 12A (now owned by the Dowd family and rented out) in Plainfield across the road from the house where Moody was staying. Despite the "dulness" of Cornish, she did stay through the fall foliage season. In fact, just as she seemed to warm to the area, so Moody softened his descriptions of her: she "install[ed] herself across the road, painting, polishing, and upholstering with her own fair hands and those of the volunteer corps, of which I am a humble but most efficient member. She is the best fun in the world, quite unspoiled, and a first-rate fellow."[2] We get some idea of the actress in a more relaxed state from Moody's letters. He notes how he and Barrymore attended a large dinner party and musical on July 7 at the home of Arthur Whiting, the composer and musician, "with music galore afterwards in a big dark room looking out on moonlit river and mountain."[3] At the party's close, Miss Barrymore graciously gave the poet a lift home in her trap. At one of her tennis parties:

> Will Moody, Richard Harding Davis and his wife, Harry Fuller [were] playing doubles, while Mr. and Mrs. Herbert Adams, Howard Hart, and Ethel herself were looking on. The next night we were invited to dine with her and we found the Davises most attractive . . . Fred Parrish was also there casting enraptured gazes at Ethel, and Kenyon Cox was more agreeable than usual. That made up the dinner party with the exception of Mr. Hart, who was made to blossom into speech under the light of La Barrymore! Mr. Hart is an abnormally quiet man who gardens and paints some and plays the part of a fastidious bachelorhood.[4]

From Ethel Barrymore's *Memories* we can get a glimpse of life in Cornish, "a place of beautiful gardens where many artists and authors lived. To me the most exciting of them was Saint-Gaudens. He was then doing his wonderful Lincoln, and he used to let me watch him work. The head was finished, and I never could look at it without wanting to cry . . . I always felt it a great privilege to have known him."[5] She saw "much of Maxfield Parrish and his father Stephen Parrish" and was fascinated by the latter's elaborate flower gardens; she thought they were "even more beautiful than the Charles Platts' and the Norman Hapgoods', which is saying a great deal."[6] She was involved in several of the Colony's social events. She relates how Mrs. Winston Churchill, "the wife of the American Winston Churchill, the novelist," asked Ethel to put her "beautiful horses" through their paces in a horse show. "I had never driven at all, but I had seen a lot of horse shows and driven with good drivers . . . I knew how to hold the reins, so without thinking, I said yes and won the blue ribbon. How extraordinarily cheeky I must have been!"[7] And she also participated in a theatrical production that was decidedly not a Broadway one. The children of the Colony performed Thackeray's comedy, *The Rose and the Ring* in Henry O. Walker's studio followed by a tea served on the lawn. Miss Barrymore coached the children, Mrs. Kenyon Cox arranged the costumes, and Mrs. Lucia Fuller painted the scenery.[8]

Ethel Barrymore also played a starring role in at least three local artistic activities. "Harry Fuller did a charming drawing" of her during her stay and Frances Houston, "Charlotte Fairchild's mother," painted her portrait.[9] It was her last work; Frances Houston died in October of 1906. The third project has a more complicated history connected with it. Kenyon Cox was busy that summer painting a mural for the new Essex County Courthouse in Newark, New Jersey. He persuaded Miss Barrymore to sit for the head of *Justice*, "a figure of a woman floating in air . . . Cass Gilbert, architect of the building," forced Cox to alter the features so that they would look like nobody in particular; Gilbert declared the only intent was to prevent any portraiture in a work which was meant to be purely decorative, and that no criticism of the artist or of the actress was involved.[10] For her part, Miss Barrymore was impressed by Cox's "enormous studio, and by his climbing up on ladders to do his huge canvasses. I had never seen anyone doing a big mural before."[11]

ENDNOTES

1. William Vaughn Moody, *Letters to Harriet,* edited with Introduction and Conclusion by Percy MacKaye (Boston and New York: Houghton Mifflin, 1935), pp. 278-279; see below p. 283 for more of Moody's remarks on Ethel Barrymore and Ege, *The Power of the Impossible: The Life Story of Percy and Marion MacKaye* (Falmouth, ME: The Kennebec River Press, 1992), p. 141. Frances Duncan described the Fuller's pool at length in "A Swimming Pool at Cornish," *Country Life in America,* July 1906, pp. 302-304.

2. Moody, p. 282.

3. Ibid., p. 288.

4. Ibid., p. 425; the passage beginning "The next night . . ." is found in Ege, pp. 142-143.

5. Ethel Barrymore, *Memories* (New York: Harper Brothers, 1955), p. 153; the statue was the *Seated Lincoln* now in Chicago's Grant Park.

6. Ibid., p. 154.

7. Ibid., p. 155.

8. Ibid., p. 154.

9. Ibid. The portrait was reproduced in *The Century Magazine* 75, April 1908, p. 933, and Thomas Dewing noted, "Mrs. Houston's canvasses have great technical value, as this charming portrait shows."; ibid., p. 957.

10. News clipping, 1907, Windsor, VT, Library scrapbook.

11. Barrymore, p. 154.

Figure 50. *Ernest Harold Baynes with "Jimmie."*

ERNEST HAROLD
BAYNES
1868 – 1925

ERNEST HAROLD BAYNES, although not noted for his contributions to art, was a naturalist who was much loved and respected by the members of the Cornish Colony. He was born May 1, 1868, in Calcutta, India, the son of John and Helen (Nowhill) Baynes. His father was engaged in foreign shipping, but returned to England with his family and eventually emigrated to the United States and settled in Westchester County, New York, where he believed he could find greater scope for his talents. He had a very inventive mind and perfected many photographic processes. His photographic knowledge and experience would later prove to be of great assistance in his son's career.

As a child Baynes was fascinated by animals. Upon leaving the College of the City of New York, he worked as a reporter for *The New York Times* while continuing his interest in nature. By 1900 Baynes was lecturing and writing magazine articles on wildlife. He wrote nature articles, frequently illustrating them with his own photographs, for *The New York Herald, Country Life in America, Nature Magazine, Scribner's Magazine,* and *Century Magazine.* In 1901 Baynes married Louise Birt O'Connell of Boston. They moved to Stoneham, Massachusetts, where he continued observing and writing about wildlife.[1]

It was during this period that he came to the attention of Austin Corbin, Jr., who in 1890 had established the Blue Mountain Forest Reservation in Sullivan County, New Hampshire. It comprised 24,000 acres surrounded by a fence 8½ feet high and 36 miles long. The park contained herds of deer, elk, wild boar, buffalo, and a large variety of birds. Once Corbin learned of Baynes's desire to settle near precisely such a reservation, Corbin offered him a house and the use of the park. The house was situated in the northwestern section of the park, about two miles from Meriden Village. The couple occupied the house, which they called "Sunset Ridge," in 1904.[2] As soon as they were settled, Baynes became acquainted with the park's animals and made friends

Figure 51. *Actaeon, the white tail deer eating with Jimmie, the black bear cub, as Dauntless, the timber wolf, looks on. They all are being fed by Mrs. Mack, the housekeeper.*

with a wild boar, fox, and other animals; he used their antics as subjects for magazine articles and books. His widely syndicated newspaper columns appeared throughout the country, entertaining and educating the public in the ways of nature. His magazine articles were illustrated with his remarkable photographs, most of which were taken in Meriden and Corbin's Park. He also wrote a number of books about these experiences: *Wild Bird Guests; Jimmie,* about a black bear cub; *Polaris,* about an Eskimo dog sired by the dogs that carried Admiral Peary to the North Pole on April 6, 1909; *The Sprite,* the story of a red fox; *Animal Heroes of the Great War; My Wild Animal Guests; Three Young Crows and Other Bird Stories; Wild Life in the Blue Mountain Forest;* and *War Hoop and Tomahawk,* about two buffalo calves that were broken to yoke and trained to pull carts. Baynes drove them in the 1905 county fair in Claremont.[3]

Buffalo were dear to his heart. He championed the national campaign to save the then virtually extinct animal, eliciting help from President Theodore Roosevelt, who had visited Corbin's Park in August of 1902 on a trip to Cornish and Windsor, Vermont.[4] Three years later Baynes was instrumental in the formation of the American Bison Society, which got Congress to provide refuges and ranges for herds whose origins were often in Corbin's Park. Baynes had help from writers and publicists who supported the cause; among them was Norman Hapgood, who, at the time, was the editor of *Collier's Weekly* and a resident of Cornish.[5]

As advocates for another issue in Cornish, Baynes and the poet Percy MacKaye had become fast friends during the time the two lived near one another.[6] The naturalist had asked MacKaye to write a poem to celebrate the dedication of the Meriden Bird

Figure 52. *A postcard with the caption "Ernest Harold Baynes driving the only team of buffaloes in the world."*

Club, which Baynes had established in 1910. At a time when caring for birds was a new concept and activity for most people, Baynes had organized a group of bird enthusiasts from Plainfield and Cornish into the Cornfield Bird Club. MacKaye's response was writing *Sanctuary: A Bird Masque,* dramatically underscoring the loss and the threat of extinction of birds for the sole purpose of using their colorful plumage in the trimming of women's hats and other domestic products.

The influence both of Baynes as the birds' knight errant and of *Sanctuary* as mobilizer of public opinion has never really been given its full due. The masque was performed in Meriden at the outdoor bird sanctuary in September 1913 with a number of the members of the artists' colony involved either as participants or patrons; they included: Herbert Adams, Witter Bynner, Kenyon Cox, William Howard Hart, Stephen Parrish, George Rublee, Juliet Barrett Rublee, Annetta St. Gaudens, and Ellen Shipman.[7] The production was attended by President and Mrs. Woodrow Wilson since their daughters Margaret and Eleanor played important roles in it. The play was a great success; it received national, as well as local, press coverage.[8] It also resulted in two local artistic creations. On the one hand, to commemorate it, Annetta St. Gaudens, the wife of Louis St. Gaudens, modeled a bronze urn birdbath depicting the play's characters;[9] on the other hand, the architect Charles A. Platt designed a purple martin birdhouse.[10] And the play was not merely a local production; it was also performed in New York City with the original cast in 1914.[11] Nor did it have merely local significance. During the next several years the Redpath Chautauqua toured the country giving performances of the play. And by 1933, when the Meriden Bird Club marked the play's twentieth anniversary, it had been performed hundreds of times across the country and spawned more than 125 bird clubs throughout America.[12]

Baynes, meanwhile, embarked on a three-year campaign on behalf of the birds. When he returned to the area in the fall of 1916, he decided to move out of Corbin's Park and to rent the house that the artist Everett Shinn had built in 1902 on Daniels Road in Plainfield. In the immediate neighborhood were some of his good friends: Percy MacKaye, Herbert Adams, William Howard Hart, and Louis Evan Shipman. Nearby in Plainfield also was the Lewin Farm on Prospect Mountain that Baynes had bought in order to realize his dreams of creating his own sanctuary.[13] Eventually, he dug a cellar, which can still be seen, and planned to fence the entire acreage;[14] he died of stomach cancer, however, before his projects could be completed.

During these final years he became embroiled in the vivisection controversy. It consumed much of his time and energy. When he read about the cruelties of vivisection, he was determined to oppose the practice. He wisely studied all sides of the matter so that he could argue effectively against these unnecessary and cruel procedures. In pursuing this study, he discovered that the anti-vivisectionist literature was distorted, untruthful, and outdated. Furthermore, he realized that, with the knowledge later obtained by means of animal experimentation, his own younger brother's life might have been saved. Consequently, Baynes shifted his position and took up the cause of animal experimentation. For a while he had difficulty in getting publishers to print his articles. Finally, *The Woman's Home Companion* had the courage to print his articles and exposés of the untruths promoted by the anti-vivisectionist societies. He carried his notions even further. He was instrumental in organizing, in the fall of 1923, the "Friends of Medical Progress." His final position was that animals could, in fact, be used for medical research in a humane way, one that would not cause them undue pain and suffering; animals could thus do something of consequence for the benefit of mankind.[15]

Baynes died in Meriden on January 21, 1925, after living in the Plainfield-Meriden area for twenty-one years. The following spring his ashes were sprinkled over his favorite spot in Blue Mountain Park.[16]

ERNEST HAROLD BAYNES AND *SANCTUARY: A BIRD MASQUE*

A major event in the history of the Cornish Colony occurred on Friday, September 12, 1913, at the Meriden Bird Club. Ernest Harold Baynes, the naturalist and Meriden resident, had recently been making headlines with his writing and lectures on natural history and especially with his national crusade to "save the bison." Part of his commitment to these concerns had taken the form of establishing the Meriden Bird Club in 1910, the first of many such organizations to be founded across the country. But part of the distinction of the September occasion was that Percy MacKaye had composed a masque entitled *Sanctuary: A Bird Masque* for the opening dedication of the Meriden Bird Sanctuary. An added feature to the opening-night performance was the attendance of the President of the United States and his wife. This was the first of three years that Woodrow Wilson would choose Winston Churchill's "Harlakenden House" as his summer White House. Moreover, both of his daughters were playing prominent roles in the masque: his daughter Margaret sang the opening Prelude, "The Hermit Thrush," and Eleanor played a leading role, the Bird Spirit. Part of the evening's excitement could be recaptured by those who saw the stunning, pearlescent images of *Sanctuary*. They were rephotographed from color screen plates (Autochromes) made by Arnold Genthe and exhibited at the Saint-Gaudens National Historic Site in the fall of 1995.[17] Another part of the evening's excitement can be captured from this contemporary account as part of a page-one story in *The Vermont Journal:*

> More than 400 people comprising the Cornish summer colony, many residents of Meriden, members of the Meriden Bird Club, and President Wilson's family saw Miss Eleanor, the President's youngest daughter in the star role of Percy MacKaye's new pastoral masque, entitled *Sanctuary*, at Meriden, New Hampshire, last Friday evening.
>
> Miss Wilson, in the part of Ornis, the bird-spirit, displayed unusual dramatic skill and was a surprise even to her closest friends. It was her first attempt before the footlights, which in this case happened to be a semi-circle of Japanese lanterns, and the artistic expression which she put into the lines of her part and the appealing tones with which she voiced the plea of the bird-spirit, brought hearty applause from the enthusiastic audience.
>
> President Wilson arrived at the summer capitol on Friday afternoon in time to witness his daughter in the role of an amateur thespian.
>
> The play, which was in the nature of a protest against the needless slaughter of birds for commercial purposes, was staged in a pine grove of the Meriden Bird Sanctuary. The bird club was sponsor of the play.
>
> A few of the more prominent people dressed as birds and acting in pantomime included Herbert Adams, Kenyon Cox, Mrs. A. Conger Goodyear, William Howard Hart, Stephen Parrish, Mrs. Maxwell Perkins, George Rublee, Mrs. Louis Saint-Gaudens, and Ellen Shipman. Others included Eleanor Wilson, Witter Bynner, and Juliette Barrett Rublee. Miss Margaret Wilson sang the opening song entitled "The Hermit Thrush."[18]

More than twenty years after the event, the Bird Spirit herself, now Eleanor Wilson McAdoo, gave the following account of the event:

> Ernest Harold Baynes, the naturalist, was trying to establish a sanctuary for birds in a lovely grove in the hills, and Percy MacKaye conceived the idea of writing a masque and presenting it there to raise money and awaken the interest of the community. For weeks we were absorbed in preparations and rehearsals. I was the Bird Spirit, Witter Bynner, the Hunter, Harold Baynes and MacKaye himself had important parts, and Margaret was a spirit voice, singing from a bush.
>
> Father came up from Washington the night of the performance, and people drove in from all over the state—more, I think, to see him than the Bird Masque.
>
> I had a headdress of white wings, and twenty minutes before the play was to begin, found that I had left it behind at Harlakenden. I was in despair, for I thought the wings very becoming and was certain that I couldn't possibly speak my lines without them. White, the swiftest of the chauffeurs, was called in, and promised that he could make the ten miles and back in time. He was as good as his word; complaining, however, that he had had a hard time getting back because he "came all the way in his own dust."
>
> After the performance, the cast, feeling very gay, drove home together. Passing through a tiny New England village [Plainfield], we saw that there was a country dance in progress in the small town hall. We had the same idea simultaneously. Stopping the car a little way off, we approached stealthily and, without warning appeared on the floor

among the startled natives. Percy MacKaye, in his long blue hooded gown, leaned with folded arms against the wall, gazing at the scene like a necromancer who had himself created it. Witter Bynner, in his leopard-skin mantle and tall feather headdress; I, in my white robe, Ruth Hall and three others dressed as birds, in brief, bright costumes, we glided and swooped three times around the hall while the village people stood against the wall in a daze. Then we disappeared as silently as we had come. I have never known whether they thought us a dream, or a visitation from an insane asylum.[19]

The play was again produced, given by the same cast, in the grand ballroom of the Hotel Astor in New York City on February 24, 1914, in conjunction with a series of lectures and conferences on wildlife and conservation. In "The Drama and Conservation," written for this occasion, Percy MacKaye concisely stated the goals of the play and the conferences: "Naturalists, museum directors, scientists, conservationists convened—for perhaps the first time—together with artists of the theatre for a common purpose: to discuss the civic uses of dramatic art as a means for giving expression and publicity to important public causes related to the conservation of wildlife and natural resources. This theme was discussed from many viewpoints by men and women notable in both fields, with enthusiasm and insight."[20]

SUGGESTION FOR FURTHER READING

Percy MacKaye, *Sanctuary: A Bird Masque* (New York: Frederick A. Stokes, 1914).

ENDNOTES

1. Raymond Gorges, *Ernest Harold Baynes* (Boston and New York: Houghton Mifflin, 1928), pp. 1-8.
2. Tom McCarthy, "Birds, Beasts, and Baynes," *New Hampshire Profiles,* September 1974, p. 24.
3. "Ernest Harold Baynes, War Hoop, and Tomahawk," picture file (No. 120) of the Claremont Historical Society, Claremont, NH.
4. See above pp. 38-39.
5. Ernest Harold Baynes, "The Fight to Save the Buffalo," *Country Life in America* 13, January 1908, pp. 295-298.
6. Interview: Virginia Colby with Mrs. Christy MacKaye Barnes, August 4, 1980.
7. "Programme" for the masque, Virginia Colby, Cornish Colony files.
8. The Ernest Harold Baynes Papers, collection of the Cornish Historical Society, gift of Barbara Yeomans, 1984, contains the following press notices: "'Sanctuary' Presented in Glade at Night as Protest Against Slaying Feathered Singers," *San Francisco Chronicle,* September 13, 1913; "Percy MacKaye's New Masque," *Boston Evening Transcript,* September 13, 1913; "President's Daughter as Bird Spirit," *Journal,* Springfield, MA, September 13, 1913; "President's Daughter in Star Role," *Argus,* Albany, NY, September 13, 1913; "Summer Colony Saw a Bird Play," *Vermont Journal,* September 19, 1913; "President Wilson a Guest of Meriden Bird Club," unidentified source; and Sara A. Dunn, "A Bird Masque to Dedicate a Bird Sanctuary," unidentified source.
9. See Linda Rose McCabe, "A Bird Masque in Bas Relief," *House Beautiful,* December 1915, and Alice Van Leer Carrick, "The Orchard Potteries," *Country Life,* January 1926.

10. Ernest Harold Baynes, *Wild Bird Guests* (New York: E. P. Dutton, 1915), pp. 209-211; the birdhouse is illustrated opposite p. 270.

11. "The President's Daughter Acts in a Bird Play," *The Saturday Evening Mail,* New York, March 7, 1914.

12. Virginia Colby, "Masques for Saint-Gaudens and the Birds," *Valley News,* February 4, 1981.

13. Gorges, p. 162.

14. Interview: Virginia Colby with Albert K. Read, III, February 18, 1982, Plainfield, NH.

15. Gorges, pp. 195-223.

16. Obituary, *Vermont Journal,* January 30, 1925, p. 2, col. 3.

17. See "Photographs and Historical Processes," exhibition catalogue, (Cornish, NH: Saint-Gaudens National Historic Site, 1 September 31 - October 1995), unpaginated. For more in Genthe, see below pp. 476-478.

18. September 19, 1913; see below pp. 432 and 436. For more on President Wilson's attendance, see below pp. 502-503, n. 3.

19. Eleanor Wilson McAdoo, "The Wilson's White House Romance," *Saturday Evening Post,* January 9, 1937, p. 32.

20. Arvia MacKaye Ege, *The Power of the Impossible: The Life Story of Percy and Marion MacKaye* (Falmouth, ME: The Kennebec River Press, 1992), p. 242.

CHARLES COTESWORTH BEAMAN
1840 – 1900

CHARLES COTESWORTH BEAMAN is chiefly responsible for the settlement of the art colony in Cornish at the turn of the twentieth century. Beaman was born in Houlton, Maine, the son of a prominent Congregational minister from Boston. Beaman graduated from Harvard, entered Harvard Law School, and eventually entered the New York City law firm of William M. Evarts.[1] Evarts had a summer home in Windsor, Vermont, and Beaman saw the beauty in the land across the Connecticut River. He also saw the beauty of Hettie Sherman Evarts; he married her August 19, 1874. Beaman began his career as a gentleman farmer by purchasing what he later called the "Blow-Me-Down Farm." In 1892 he defended the use of this name on the basis of three pieces of evidence. First, there was the charter for the town of Windsor, Vermont, dated July 6, 1761; it shows "a brook on the New Hampshire side of the Connecticut River under the name of Blow-me-down brook." Second, there was the charter for the town of Cornish, New Hampshire, dated October 1, 1763. Finally, there was the original patent granting land to Moses Chase, dated January

24, 1772—both it and the Cornish town charter show a similarly named brook.[2] Beaman continues: "It is thus evident that the name Blow-me-down was given to this brook earlier than 1761, before there was either a town of Windsor or of Cornish, and before Moses Chase settled on the land which I now own. In view of these facts, it does not seem to me probable that this

Figure 53. *Charles Beaman (holding plans) on the steps of Blow-Me-Down.*

145

name came from the word Blomidon [Nova Scotia], as one of your correspondents suggested, or from the word Bloomington, as mentioned by the other correspondent."

His activity in Cornish was extensive; his commitment to the town began early. He was important enough that by 1883 he had one of the thirty-six telephones listed in the Windsor exchange—six or seven years after Alexander Graham Bell was originally granted patents for his invention. Beaman's was one of the largest farms in the area.[3] George Hodgman, who died in 1913, acted for twenty-five years as the foreman for this farm. Beaman specialized in a good dairy herd. He had a prize Jersey bull, as we know from its portrait by George de Forest Brush, painted in 1893. Beaman was instrumental in establishing the Hillside Creamery on the west side of town, which was available to other farmers for their benefit (see above pp. 68-70).

Another agricultural activity that local farmers were able to utilize was the beautiful gristmill Beaman built on Blow-Me-Down Pond. The design for the mill was begun by Joseph Wells of the famous architectural firm of McKim, Mead, and White. Upon the death of Wells, George Fletcher Babb assumed responsibility for the project under the direction of McKim, Mead, and White themselves. The mill was completed in 1891.

Much of Beaman's other activity on the local scene was social. The event of the 1898 social season was the wedding of his daughter, Mary, to Edward Jackson Holmes, a grandson of Oliver Wendell Holmes. It took place in St. Paul's Church in Windsor and forty teams of horses were required to transport all the guests back to Blow-Me-Down Farm. There a wedding breakfast was served in a huge tent; a reception and a dance in the evening capped off the day.[4] Beaman especially enjoyed the company of artists and sculptors—so much so that he bought up many vacant houses and farms that he then sold or rented quite reasonably to them. At the height of his ambition he owned twenty-three properties, which stretched over a thousand acres, that he was prepared to "colonize" by renting to the proper people to establish "Little New York."[5] For example, he rented and later sold the property "Huggin's Folly" (or "Blow-Me-Up") to Augustus Saint-Gaudens thereby setting the stage for the development of the Cornish Art Colony. The Beamans entertained large groups frequently and eventually installed two bowling alleys in the casino on their property.[6]

Beaman died in 1900, and in his will, he left the town of Cornish $1000, the interest of which was to be used "for the erection and maintenance of guide-boards in town." Other legacies to the town include the Soldiers' Monument in Cornish Flat honoring those who died in the Civil War and "the schoolhouse in Division 10."[7]

Hettie Evarts and Charles C. Beaman were noted for their generous hospitality that was lavishly displayed at huge social functions: large dinner parties and fancy balls (they danced the Virginia Reel accompanied by fiddlers)—with "all of Cornish" invited. "All of Cornish," of course, generally meant the Cornish Colony, with perhaps some Evarts family members from Windsor. The site of many of these social affairs was the Beaman Casino, rebuilt from an early colonial structure during the summer of 1888 and furnished with a piano, a billiard table, and bowling alleys. The first party in the casino was held on September 3, 1892. That it was lighted with electricity impressed all the invited guests. On a later occasion the following song was written by Adeline Adams:

"The Big Beaman Ball"

Song and Chorus
(The words are dedicated to Mr.
Harry Arnold.)

I.

The painters, and their name is legion,
    The sculptors, and their name is mud,
Society, beauty, and fashion,
    and many a bird and a bud,
Oh, Cornish at large was invited,
    The art set, the smart set, and all,
Not even the Duffers were slighted
    That night at the big Beaman Ball.

CHORUS:—
    Walkers, dancers,—and a kicker or two
beside,
    Sayings, Dewings, Saint-Gaudens and
Brush and the bride,
    Harris, from Paris, Harvard and Yale
and all.
    O the glides and the whirls
    with the fine large girls.
    That night at the big Beaman Ball!

II.

Some went for the sake of the dancing,
    And some for the music; indeed.
It speaks to the credit of Cornish
    That none of us went for the feed.
But you should have seen the donations,
    From pantry and ice-house and hall.
Delmonico's chef wasn't in it
    That night at the big Beaman Ball!
CHORUS:—Walkers, etc.

III.

The Houstons they came in their carriage,
    The Nichols drove round by the mill,
While some, like the boarders at Johnson's,

Were first forced to take Beaman's Spill.
And many a buggy, containing
    A lady, a gent and a shawl,
Dashed up to the cordial casino
    That night of the big Beaman Ball!
CHORUS:—Walkers, etc.

IV.

The social eclat was so splendid
    That just in the midst of the rout,
The electrical lights were offended,
    And suddenly seemed quite put out.
Mrs. B. cried: "The mill!" in a flurry,
    But none added "dam,"—not at all!
You only heard giggling and scurry
    That night at the big Beaman Ball!
CHORUS:—Walkers, etc.

V.

Then the band all struck up "Where was
Moses?"
    The couples were quiet and sage;
And nothing occurred that need ever
    Bring a blush to the cheek of old age.
O the speech of our host was right merry,
    And held our rapt spirits in thrall,
Not to mention the sherbet and sherry,
    That night at the big Beaman Ball!
CHORUS:—Walkers, etc.

VI.

Next morn, when the family gathered
    To view the remains of the feast,
They found but some corks and a ham-
bone,
    O spectacle funeste and triste!
Some vertebrae, once of a salmon,
    Gloves at sixes and sevens were all,
With a powder-puff and a pawn-ticket,
    That was left from the big Beaman Ball!

CHORUS:—Walkers, etc.

VII.

Now when we ascend unto Heaven
　And pass in our checks for a seat,
And Gabriel ushers us forward,

Expecting we'll find it a treat;—
He'll be quite surprised, never doubt it,
　When we his descriptions forestall,
By remarking, "We know all about it,
　For we went to the big Beaman Ball!"
CHORUS:—Walkers, etc.

ENDNOTES

1. Evarts had a distinguished national and international career; see below pp. 471-472. During the Civil War he was a legal adviser to the legation in London from the United States; then he was the counsel during the arbitration of the *Alabama* claims (a suit concerned with a Confederate cruiser, built in an English shipyard, that had done considerable damage to the Union's shipping); later he was one of President Andrew Johnson's lawyers during his impeachment proceedings in 1868; from 1877 to 1881, he was secretary of state under Rutherford B. Hayes; and, finally, he was a senator from New York from 1895 to 1891.

2. Letter from Beaman dated New York, February 27, 1892, *The Vermont Journal,* March 16, 1892, Windsor Library scrapbook. Beaman was in part responding to a letter signed "Filologos," dated Windsor, March 27, 1884, that quoted lines about Blomidon from Longfellow's poem "Evangeline."

3. At a later date, the program for the "First Annual Tour" of the "Cheshire County Farmers and Business Men Through Sullivan County" in 1915 contained the following notation for the fifth stop, "Blow-Me-Down Farm," then in the hands of "H. S. Beaman, Prop. [and] C. E. Bryant Supt.": "Entertained here at luncheon, photographs taken. Farm contains 1700 acres, raises large crops, hay, corn, oats; also sheep and other stock. Place noted for hospitality, scenery and progressiveness." In addition to the creameries visited on the tour, the group stopped at the Cornish farm of W[illiam] L[ucius] Chadbourne ("See fine thoroughbred Holsteins, fine farm, one of the most practical and progressive farmers in county.") and the Plainfield farms of the Austin brothers ("See noted herd of thoroughbred Holsteins, one of most progressive farms in county. Raises sweet clover, alfalfa, hay and other crops. Markets cream by parcel post in winter time.") and of E. C. Daniels' Famous Sheep Farm ("Daniels family practical sheep raisers for many years. Note flocks sheep, pasture conditions, type of sheep, method of finishing off in fall, marketing, etc."); a copy exists in the Cornish Historical Society files, Lagercrantz Collection.

4. Albert K. Read, III's scrapbook, Plainfield, NH.

5. Ned Perrin, "Touring the Saint-Gaudens Sculpture Park," *New York Times,* July 24, 1983.

6. Virginia Colby, Cornish Colony files.

7. Child, William H. *History of the Town of Cornish with Genealogical Record: 1763-1910,* (Concord, NH: The Rumford Press, 1911?; reprinted edition, Spartanburg, SC: The Reprint Company, 1975), Vol. 1, pp. 277-278.

GEORGE DE FOREST BRUSH

1855 – 1941

CORNISH PLAYED AN IMPORTANT ROLE in the life of this "Master of the American Renaissance."[1] George de Forest Brush, who was born in Tennessee and spent his childhood in Connecticut, is well-known for his depictions of Native Americans, but he is better known for his "modern madonnas," paintings of mother and child (or children) inspired by Italian Renaissance compositions. He also painted many canvasses that ranged from scenes based on classical myths to portraits of society figures.

During his lifetime Brush was considered an elusive person to describe and the qualities of his art perplexing to define. Yet critics today agree that his command of line was exceptional, that his use of color was radiant, and that his ability to capture a pensive mood was unique. One of his recurrent themes was that of impermanence.

Brush's preoccupation with change is one that he shared with his friends, an educated and socially privileged class which both welcomed the progress of the age and yet was made uneasy by its pace and breadth. . . . Because of his experiences among and understanding of Native Americans, he was saddened by their mistreatment and the seemingly inevitable disappearance of their systems of belief which, on the evidence of the artist's own interpretations, placed the Indian in a seamless interdependence with nature.[2]

He studied art from 1870 to 1873 at the National Academy of Design in New York. In 1874 an

Figure 54. *Brush's* Onatoga in the Forest *done* en grisaille.

149

anonymous benefactor gave him a scholarship to study in Paris under Jean-Léon Gérôme. Thought by many of his contemporaries to be the greatest artist alive, Gérôme painted in a vein that was the antithesis of the Impressionists. In 1881, back in this country, Brush traveled to Wyoming to study Native Americans. In 1892, following a second trip to Paris, Brush turned away from his Indian subjects and toward idealized compositions of his wife and children based on Renaissance models.

Brush, however, knew the life of the American Indians intimately. During his earlier visit to the West he had camped with the Shoshone and their rivals, the Arapaho. This association produced a number of paintings that were acclaimed for their powerful and poetic interpretation of Native American life.[3] He also spent several years with his brother Alf living and painting on the Crow reservation in Montana. While with them, he painted and gathered the material for a remarkable series of pictures of Indian life and customs. He describes some of his thoughts and feelings in "An Artist Among the Indians":

All that Rembrandt asked of the human figure was that it might exhibit light and shade; he never looked for pretty people, but found in this aspect of things a life work. It is not necessary that an Indian learn to spell and make changes before we see that his long locks are beautiful as he rides against the winds. It is also a mistake to suppose that Indians are all homely. A really handsome squaw is rare, but there are more superb and symmetrical men among then than I have ever seen elsewhere, their beardless faces reminding one always of the antique; these are not rare, but are to be seen at every dance, where they are mostly naked, decorated in feathers and light fineries. Their constant light exercise, frequent steam-baths, and freedom from overwork develop the body in a manner only equaled, I must believe, by the Greeks, in choosing Indians as subjects for art, I do not paint from the historian's or the antiquary's point of view; I do not care to represent them in any curious habits which could not be comprehended by us; I am interested in those habits and deeds in which we have feelings in common.[4]

Despite the "feelings in common," Brush by and large renounced painting Native American themes in the 1890s. Various explanations have been offered for this change because both Brush's contemporaries and subsequent critics believed that his paintings were "the most poetical and the most successful renderings artistically of the red Indians" and that he "presented the Indian from a viewpoint quite different from any of his predecessors. His paintings were not directly concerned with warfare, ceremonial display or the more sensational aspects of primitive life, but rather they were interpretations of the philosophy of the Indian. He was the poet of our Indian painters."[5] But, as McCracken continues, there were not enough people interested in buying these "Indian paintings [so] that about 1890 Brush was compelled to give up the Western theme and seek some other field of art as a means of supporting his growing family."[6] But Brush's youngest daughter, Thea Cabot, believes that his renunciation resulted from his being "heartbroken about how the Indians were treated by the government, how they had been cheated of everything and forced to become drunkards."[7]

Brush and his wife Mary Taylor (Whelpley) Brush, better known as "Mittie," came to Cornish in 1887 and lived, as one might expect, in a tepee that he pitched on Saint-Gaudens's field near Blow-Me-Down Brook. The following years they rented houses from Charles Beaman in Cornish and Plainfield. They were in three houses: one on Freeman Road, one on River Road, and a third on Mill Road.[8] Since there were those in the Colony, Ernest Harold Baynes, for example, who believed that intimate interaction with nature ("in a seamless interdependence with nature") was an antidote to the unnerving progress of civilization, Brush must have felt at home here. He used George Ruggles' studio, called "The Woodchuck Hole." During the summers of 1892 and 1893 Brush painted quite a few works based on his Cornish connections: a view of Saint-Gaudens's house, a Cornish landscape, a landscape with Mount Ascutney in the background, and a portrait of Charles *Beaman's Prize Jersey Bull.*

Eventually Brush visited the Dublin, New Hampshire, colony and decided to buy a house and settle his family there. Brush went on to win prizes for his paintings and to hold many exhibitions. He died in Hanover, New Hampshire, in 1941.[9] His friend Barry Faulkner, commenting on a remark from the younger William James about "how many good and beautiful things we owe to George Brush," praises "his matchless faculty for imparting enthusiasm; for getting across to us—the younger painters—so that it became our own, his own unquenchable love of beauty and life. He was to us a warm house on a frosty night, an Arabian Nights Entertainment, a deep well of inspiration."[10]

ENDNOTES

1. This was the title of a major retrospective exhibition of his work in 1985 and 1986. It was organized by the Berry-Hill Galleries in New York City and traveled to the Currier Gallery of Art in Manchester, NH, to the Butler Institute of American Art in Youngstown, OH, and to the Fine Arts Center at Cheekwood in Nashville, TN.

2. The catalogue for the above exhibition: *George de Forest Brush, 1855-1941: Master of the American Renaissance* (New York: Berry-Hill Galleries, Inc., 1985), p. 10.

3. Barry Faulkner, "George de Forest Brush," Faulkner Papers, Manuscript Division, Library of Congress, p. 5.

4. George de Forest Brush, "An Artist Among the Indians," T*he Century Illustrated Monthly Magazine* 30, 8, May 1885 to October 1885, pp. 54-57.

5. Sadakichi Hartmann, *A History of American Art (New York, 1934)*, Vol. I, pp. 261-262 and Harold McCracken, *Portrait of the Old West* (New York, 1952), p. 173 as quoted in Joan B. Morgan, "The Indian Paintings of George de Forest Brush," *The American Art Journal* 15: 2 (Spring, 1983), p. 62.

6. McCracken, p. 175, as quoted in Morgan, p. 62.

7. As quoted in Morgan. p. 63; Morgan goes on to describe a conversation with Thea Cabot. Brush's daughter "remembered that he had taken Geronimo, chief of the Apaches, and another chief out of jail and home for dinner. . . . 'These Indians were his friends and after seeing what had happened to them, he couldn't paint them any more.'"

8. *A Circle of Friends: Art Colonies of Cornish and Dublin* (Durham, NH: University Art Galleries, University of New Hampshire, 1985), p. 77; see also p. 132, notes 1 and 2 of the Brush section.

9. Nancy Douglas Bowditch, *George de Forest Brush: Recollections of a Joyous Painter* (Peterborough, NH: William L. Bauhan, 1970), p. 240.

10. Barry Faulkner, *Sketches from an Artist's Life* (Dublin, NH: William L. Bauhan, 1973), p. 176.

Figure 55. *Witter Bynner as Stark in Percy MacKaye's* Sanctuary: A Bird Masque, *1913.*

WITTER BYNNER
1881 – 1968

THE CONNECTION WITH CORNISH for Witter Bynner—a famous writer, editor, and poet—was rooted in his friendship with Homer Saint-Gaudens and Barry Faulkner whom he met while attending Harvard University. Following his graduation in 1902, Bynner became assistant editor, and later the literary editor, of *McClure's Magazine*, famous for publishing the articles of the leading "muckrakers" of the period such as Lincoln Steffens and Ida Tarbell. Throughout his life he published poems, plays, and stories. He gave the Phi Beta Kappa lecture at Harvard in 1911 and was accorded the similar honor in 1919 by the University of California where he read part of his poem, "The New World," which had been published in 1915. He lectured and taught English at the University of California, Santa Cruz, from 1918 to 1919. From 1920 to 1922, he was president of the Poetry Society of America.

He is famous for his numerous volumes of poetry and especially for his translations of verse from the Chinese poets of the T'ang Dynasty (a period of expanding contact with other cultures, widespread printing, and a thriving of poetry and art lasting from AD 618 to 907).[1] Even earlier in his career a reviewer, slightly put off by Bynner's practice of "word-jugglery," although it was "always dexterous and sensitive to sound and color," praised highly his "delicate imitation of Chinese lyric, which happily reproduces the Oriental practice of presenting a fugitive analogy between a natural phenomenon and a human mood."[2] Perhaps his greatest fame among his contemporaries was for pulling off one of the most successful literary hoaxes in the history of American literature. Disguised under the pseudonym of Emanuel Morgan, and with the aid of Arthur Davison Ficke, a fellow poet and Harvard chum who wrote as Anne Knish, Bynner produced a volume called *Spectra* in 1916 and thereby founded a spurious school of poetry called the "spectrist school." They were "disgusted with the imagist, expressionistic, and futuristic schools of poetry" that were then gaining widespread approval among admirers of poetry. It was also assumed by many of their friends that a bottle of Scotch a day enabled the two wags to complete the volume in ten days.[3]

Bynner's association with Cornish began in 1907 when Homer Saint-Gaudens and his wife Carlota invited him to stay with them in Cornish at "Barberry House." Taking over a section of the studio belonging to Augustus Saint-Gaudens, Bynner wrote many poems there, including "Diana Captive." His ten-year stay in New England inspired him to write a volume entitled *Grenstone Poems;* it provided a portrait of a fictional New England town based on "a composite of two New Hampshire towns . . . Cornish . . . and Chesham."[4]

But Bynner's most intense commitment to local affairs was to the Cornish Equal Suffrage League, which was formed in November of 1911; he served as the organizations first vice-president.[5] Furthermore he traveled all over the state to organize the league in New Hampshire in preparation for the vote. All this was so stimulating that it acted as the catalyst to focus his thinking and his writing. He records the process in his journal for 1911 in what is an unusually revealing statement.

> Abolition of all that oppresses and estranges is the aim which has for its constructive work the establishment of unity. Every artifice of inequality and privilege must be broken down. At last explanation came of my belief in Equal Suffrage, in trusting people with their own affairs. Responsibility means eventual understanding. . . . There is a thrill in finding one's scattered ardors related to the creative vision. At college and in New York I cared more than was suspected for democratic matters. Equal Suffrage, as a matter of justice, always stirred and summoned me. Lately I have learned why. Discovering my God to be finally evolved and conjoined beauty of life, I have seen that we are ourselves God in process. As long as I believed in an absolute Power above and beyond life, I could not feel the necessity for human endeavor. . . . Friends complain that, giving so much time to Suffrage I am neglecting my work. I only wish I could give more time to it until a breach has been made among the Eastern States. To live poetry is the best way to write it. My inner assurance that the more I live by my faith the better I shall write by it reassures me as to my friends' eventual satisfaction.[6]

Continuing his active participation in local endeavors, he also played Stark, the plume hunter, in Percy MacKaye's *Sanctuary: A Bird Masque* when it was performed in Meriden in 1913. His costume was a tall feather headdress and a leopard skin mantle.[7] Finally, he was frequently listed in the Cornish Library *Notes* as having donated books to it—not only those he had written but also books written by other people.[8]

In addition to being a friend of Isadora Duncan, Bynner had some good friends among Colony members. In a diary entry for January 22, 1908, Stephen Parrish notes "evening to Fred's to dinner (Homer Saint-Gaudens and Mr. Binner, poet and playwright). He entertained us with stories of the southern Negroes, he had just come from Georgia"; Bynner's name comes up often in Parrish's diaries for 1909.[9] The death in 1913 of Homer and Carlota's son Hal, so named because "Hal" was how Bynner was affectionately known to his friends, inspired Bynner to write a play, *The Little King,* which was published in 1914 and dedicated to both Saint-Gaudenses. His 1920 collection of poems, *A Canticle of Pan,* contains "Saint-Gaudens." By conjuring up the figure of the *Adams Memorial,* Bynner composes a tribute to both the sculptor and the sculpture:

He called: and forth there came
Not wholly veiled,
Forth from the earth
Silence made visible.
Touching no finite answer on that mouth,
Yet his fine fingers found reply
And from the light upon his soul
He drew the light of the unlighted tomb,
From man and woman both
The image of the imagined face,
And left here in the Rock Creek burial-place
The arm of life,
The veil of time,
The uncorrupted presence of the dead.[9]

The Hanover Inn provided the locale for the resolution of a rift in Bynner's friendship with Robert Frost. "They had been friends from the early twenties, and at one point Frost had agreed to write an introduction to a volume of Bynner's verse, something he finally did not do." In 1935 Frost visited Santa Fe, New Mexico, where Bynner was living. As part of a joke that never really came off, "without any apparent provocation, Bynner poured his glass of beer on Frost's head. . . . Many years later Bynner was at the Hanover Inn in New Hampshire and saw Frost in the dining room. He went over to him and said, 'Robert, do you remember me? I apologize for pouring that beer on you.' Frost looked at him in silence for a brief moment . . . and then recited two of Bynner's poems." Because Bynner had felt resentment at Frost's success as a poet—success Bynner never achieved—Bynner regarded Frost's gesture as a "great compliment."[11]

Bynner moved to Santa Fe, New Mexico, in 1922, where he befriended D. H. Lawrence; indeed, Lawrence is said to have spent his first night in New Mexico at Bynner's house.[12] Bynner died in Santa Fe in 1968. The American Academy and Institute of Arts and Letters annually awards the Witter Bynner Prize to an outstanding younger poet. The award was established by the Witter Bynner Foundation for poetry in 1979.

ENDNOTES

1. This translation was published as *The Jade Mountain* (1929). Other well-known poetry titles include: *The New World* (1915); a translation of Euripedes' *Iphigenia in Tauris* (1915) that is now reprinted in the famous *The Complete Greek Tragedies*, ed. David Grene and Richard Lattimore (Chicago: University of Chicago Press, 1956); *The Beloved Stranger* (1919); *A Canticle of Pan* (1920); *Caravan* (1925); *Indian Earth* (1929); *Eden Tree* (1931); *Against the Cold* (1940); *Take Away the Darkness* (1947); *Book of Lyrics* (1955); and *New Poems* (1960).

2. A review of *The Beloved Stranger, The Nation* 109, No. 2830, September 27, 1919, p. 440.

3. Milestone column, *Time,* June 14, 1968; see also Claudia Slack, "Advancing Poetry," *The Santa Fe Reporter,* January 19, 1981, p. 25. The review in *The Nation,* quoted above, found too much "word-jugglery" in *Spectra.*

4. Witter Bynner to James Farley, June 5, 1957; Saint-Gaudens Papers, Baker Library, Dartmouth College, Hanover, NH. Bynner is writing about a book that first appeared in 1917 published by Stokes; see also Witter Bynner, *Grenstone Poems: A Sequence,* with an introduction and notes by Edgar Lee Masters (New York: Alfred A. Knopf, 1926).

5. He noted in his diary that farmers "have fewer distractions from fair thought and are free from the city panorama of sex which confuses the question. Women, I believe, vote in their Granges, as well as have their share of the work, which puts the question on its right basis," Bynner Papers, Houghton Library, Harvard University.

6. James Kraft, *Who Is Witter Bynner?* (Albuquerque, NM: University of New Mexico Press, 1995), p. 24.

7. Programme for the production: Virginia Colby, Cornish Colony files. For discussion of a photograph of him in his role and a portrait of him, see below pp. 477-478.

8. George Stowell Library scrapbooks, Cornish Flat, NH.

9. Baker Library, Dartmouth College, Hanover, NH, gift of Marian and Roy Garrand.

10. Witter Bynner, *A Canticle of Pan* (New York: Knopf, 1920), p. 153. The advertisement for this book run in the April 10, 1920, issue of *The Nation* reads: "The title poem is a chant of communion between the pagan god Pan and the Christ Child, cast in a striking original verse form. The rest of the volume is a collection—the most complete and important yet prepared—of Mr. Bynner's best recent lyrics."

11. The quotations in this paragraph come from James Kraft, *Who Is Witter Bynner?,* pp. 86-87. Bynner wrote a brief, beautiful poem at Frost's death: it can be found among his uncollected poems in *The Works of Witter Bynner: Selected Poems,* ed. Richard Wilbur (New York: Farrar, Straus, Giroux, 1978), p. 254.

12. Kay Bird, *New Mexican,* July 29, 1988, A, p. 1. In 1951 Bynner published a book about his friendship with D.H. Lawrence and his wife Frieda, *Journey with Genius: Recollections and Reflections Concerning the D.H. Lawrences.*

Figure 56. *Winston Churchill's watercolor of the original Blow-Me-Down Mill.*

WINSTON CHURCHILL
1871 – 1947

UPON HEARING THE NAME WINSTON CHURCHILL today, most people would not identify him as an important, popular early twentieth century novelist and link him with Cornish, New Hampshire. Rather, they would most likely connect the name with a host of associations related to the prime minister of Great Britain during World War II. In fact, at the turn of the century both men found their names confusingly scrambled—to such an extent that on September 23, 1899, the Englishman wrote the American from 35A Great Cumberland Place West, London:

> Dear Mr. Winston Churchill, I owe you an apology, which I gladly offer, for having left your letter so long without an answer. I have read the books you have kindly sent me with great interest. "The Celebrity" was not much appreciated in England but "Richard Carvel" is praised by everyone and I receive so many compliments because of it, that I am not so anxious as I was to distinguish between our respective works. I daresay, however, that your desire has been proportionately increased; and I therefore recommend you to adopt your own suggestion of adding ("The American") to your title page. I am afraid I cannot promise to add "The Britisher" to mine, but I will sign whatever I may write Winston *Spencer* Churchill and that will, no doubt, free me from the lion's skin which has fallen upon me, and which, however imposing, I am impelled to discard.
>
> I hope that we shall meet in the near future, and since we have been introduced to each other by Fate herself, I shall expect a pleasant acquaintanceship.
>
> Yours very truly, Winston Spencer Churchill.[1]

Praise for Churchill's writing was widespread on this side of the Atlantic as well. In 1925 *Publisher's Weekly* hailed Cornish's Winston Churchill as "the most popular author of fiction in America between 1900 and 1925."[2] His popularity rested on his ability to write a good love story, to incorporate accurate historical information in a highly readable form, and to deal with current ideas clearly. "Churchill had a keen sense of the appetites of the American reading public and an almost uncanny ability to provide the very books that appealed most to those appetites." Eventually his detractors, who seemed to speak for the general public, complained that his "novels were too long, structurally unsound, melodramatic, ineptly plotted and . . . suffered from a lack of distinctive style and lapses in grammar, diction, and syntax."[3]

Churchill was born November 10, 1871, in St. Louis, Missouri, and graduated from the United States Naval Academy in 1894. On October 22, 1895, he married Mabel Harlakenden Hall, who was also from St. Louis. After leaving the navy, he worked on the editorial staff of the *Army and Navy Journal* before becoming editor of *Cosmopolitan.* His first novel, *The Celebrity,* written in 1898, attracted much attention because the public saw it as a satire of the popular contemporary novelist, Richard Harding Davis. *Richard Carvel,* his next novel, written in 1899, enjoyed unprecedented success and sold over a million copies; it made him independently wealthy.

Winston Churchill's connection with Cornish began in 1899 when his name appears on the Cornish tax records after he purchased ninety-five acres of the Leonard Spaulding farm. Churchill soon commissioned Charles A. Platt, the famous Cornish architect, to design his house—the most elaborate of the Cornish Colony houses.[4] His home was destined to become the Summer White House. During the summers of 1913, 1914, and 1915, while the Churchills were visiting in California, the house was rented to President Woodrow Wilson.

Shortly after moving to Cornish, Churchill became quite involved in New Hampshire politics. He was elected representative in November 1902; he served two terms in the legislature where he wrote numerous reform bills, although only a few of them were ever enacted. An advocate of his friend Theodore Roosevelt's Progressive principles, Churchill proposed measures to improve the state's forests, to reform election procedures, and to enact various other progressive programs. In 1906 he was urged to seek the Republican nomination for governor, but he was defeated for the nomination largely because of his opposition to the powerful railroad monopoly. In 1912 he ran for governor on the Progressive Party ticket, but was defeated.[5]

Several sources provide glimpses into Churchill's domestic life while he lived in Cornish. During his early days here Churchill was famous for his beautiful "four-in-hand." As the sales of his novels reached unheard of heights, his local fame centered on his big automobiles. Tax records show he owned several horses, carriages, cows, and sheep. The 1908 inventory also listed one auto. He acquired more land in Plainfield until his holdings totaled nearly 500 acres.[6] Needless to say, he was a very sought-after guest on the local social scene. The Maxfield Parrishes frequently entertained the Churchills at dinners and parties. Stephen Parrish jotted in his diary a number of evenings spent at Harlakenden—noting, incidentally, that he was none too fond of political talk.[7]

His involvement in the area's immediate issues and concerns are indicative of his commitment to the region. He was a financial supporter of the Meriden Bird Sanctuary. He and Mrs. Churchill were also members of the Cornish Equal Suffrage League; Mrs. Churchill served as the organization's treasurer. Earlier, in 1902 and 1903, John Freeman was campaigning to have a bridge constructed over Sumner's Falls. It would have crossed the Connecticut River between Plainfield, New Hampshire, and Hartland, Vermont, and replaced the one that had washed out during the mid-1800s. Churchill did his best to get the proposal expedited in Concord. He also pledged $500 once the project went through.[8] Furthermore, Churchill was greatly in demand as a speaker. Meriden's Old

Home Day in 1901 was a great success, the attendance was estimated at 1200 people. The triumph was in no small measure a result of Churchill as the featured morning speaker. He also spoke at many other Old Home Day celebrations as well as numerous local functions while he lived here. For example, he was a featured speaker at the dedication ceremonies for the George W. Stowell Free Public Library in Cornish Flat on September 28, 1912 and at Cornish's Sesquicentennial Celebration in 1915 (see above pp. 101-102).

A tragic fire struck Harlakenden on October 6, 1923; the great house burned to the ground, though many of the furnishings were saved. The Churchills temporarily moved to the Churchill Inn in Plainfield until their house off New Hampshire Route 12A and Freeman Road could be made ready. (It is now occupied by the De Wald family.) Here Winston Churchill installed beautiful paneling in the living room and the dining room. He did most of the work himself. The year of the fire marked a major turning point in his life. He renounced writing for money, took up both carpentry— an avocation that deprived him of three fingers on his left hand—and painting. In later years he frequently could be seen in a field working at his easel. His writing was directed at a small circle of friends in order to "show others the serenity he had achieved." Eventually in 1940 he resolved to break his vow of silence by bringing out *The Uncharted Way,* a book that embodied his reinterpretation of the Gospels.[9] His wife died four years later and Winston died in 1947. Both are buried in a private plot on their Plainfield property.

ENDNOTES

1. As quoted in James L. Farley, "The Cornish Colony," *Dartmouth College Library Bulletin,* n.s., 14, 1, November 1973, p. 13.

2. Eric Steinbaugh, *Winston Churchill: A Reference Guide* (Boston: G. K. Hall, 1985), p. xv.

3. Ibid., pp. xv-xvi.

4. Royal Cortissoz, *Monograph of the Work of Charles A. Platt* (New York: The Architectural Book Publishing Company, 1913), pp. 12-14. This house is sometimes referred to as "Harlakenden Hall," thereby honoring his wife by way of calling attention to her maiden name; such was not Churchill's intention. He was quick to correct Mr. Porter E. Sargent, 50 Congress Street, Boston, MA, who had incorrectly referred to Harlakenden "Hall"; it "should be Harlakenden House, not Harlakenden Hall," letter dated October 12, 1915, from King's Grant, P.O. Windsor, VT; see personal correspondence in the Winston Churchill Papers, Baker Library, Dartmouth College, Hanover, NH.

5. Warren I. Titus, *Winston Churchill* (New York: Twayne Publishers, 1963), Chap. 3.

6. Virginia Colby, Cornish Colony files.

7. Stephen Parrish, diary, Baker Library, Dartmouth College, Hanover, NH, gift of Marian and Roy Garrand.

8. Mary Cassedy Collection, Plainfield, NH.

9. Steinbaugh, p. xiv; see also Robert W. Schneider, *Novelist to a Generation: The Life and Thought of Winston Churchill* (Bowling Green, OH: Bowling Green University Popular Press, 1976), Chs. 22, 23.

ALLYN COX
1896 – 1982

IN ADDITION TO HAVING PARENTS who were both noted artists (see the next chapter), Allyn Cox became a celebrated artist in his own right: "like other master muralists throughout the centuries, Cox has met [his] challenge[s] with studiousness, steady hands, and brushes. Often, the challenges left him with stooped shoulders and the goose-egg trophy of a head-on collision."[1]

The Cox family lived in Cornish from 1897 to 1923 when, following Kenyon Cox's death, they sold their house to Sophia Arnold. It was Allyn's belief that his mother had built the house from her own earnings as an artist.[2] It was during this early period, and at the age of twenty, that Cox painted his first mural at an unlikely site: the overmantle panel above the fireplace on the west wall of the Windsor, Vermont, Public Library in 1916. Recalling the commission, Cox observed: "I had just won the fellowship in the American Academy in Rome, in those days a three-year affair, in the spring . . . and looked forward to a long summer in Cornish before leaving for Rome in October. It seemed to me that, fresh from the art schools of New York, and about to start my three years' work in Rome, it might be a good idea to try to get some experience in actual wall painting."[3]

Cox proposed to Sherman Evarts, a family friend who was on the library board, to "decorate the panel free of charge." The mural depicts a man holding a scale and reading a book and a female figure holding a lyre or a musical instrument. Working on a text Evarts suggested, *lectio certa prodest varia delectat* (accurate reading profits, varied [reading] delights), Cox finished the mural by the end of the summer of 1916. For his labors he was given a copy of *The Hundred Best Pictures* for his edification while he was abroad. Prior to winning the fellowship to Rome, Cox had studied in New York City at both the National Academy of Design and the Art Students League from 1911 to 1916. Except for a stint as a first lieutenant with the American Red Cross in Italy in 1917 and 1918, Cox worked hard in Rome.

After his return to New York, he began to receive commissions for murals and decorative paintings for private homes, churches, and other buildings—both public and private. Among his earlier works were murals for Dumbarton Oaks in Washington, DC, and decorative paintings for both the National City Bank and the Continental Bank and for Grant's Tomb and Memorial—all in New York City. In 1952 he was commissioned to complete the last thirty-two feet of the frieze in the great rotunda of the United States Capitol building. He was delighted to receive this commission because of an early childhood experience. His parents had taken him to the Capitol building and he had noted the blank area under the dome. For over fifty years he had dreamed of being the person to complete that project.[4] The 300-foot mural had been begun in 1855 by the Italian artist Constantino Brumidi, who had died in 1880 after falling from a scaffold. His successor, Filippo Costaggini, died before the frieze was completed. Allyn Cox, therefore, did finish it, using scenes from the Civil War, the Spanish-American War, and the birth of the age of aviation—the first flight of the Wright brothers. President Dwight D. Eisenhower dedicated the completed rotunda frieze on May 11, 1954. At the apex of the rotunda was a 4,664 square foot mural Brumidi had finished in 1865, *The Apotheosis of George Washington*. In 1957 Cox received a commission to clean it, which he did by repainting the fresco to match the colors that had become soiled through the years. By 1988, however, at the cost of $500,000, a five-person restoration team "retouched about 5 per cent of the fresco in spots where the original paint had flaked off. The rest of their work involved removing dirt and Cox's paint," resulting in the wall painting becoming several shades brighter than it had been.[5]

Cox's career provided him with quite a few opportunities to work in Washington, D.C. High on the ceiling of the House of Representatives, he painted illustrative decorations of the Four Freedoms: Freedom from Want, Freedom from Fear, Freedom of Speech, and Freedom of Religion. In 1973 he began murals for the Great Experiment Hall on the House side of the Capitol building. He was undertaking a series of sixteen panels that began as a legislative history of the young America's bold experiment.[6] Down the hall he had painted scenes of his ancestor William Brewster from the Massachusetts Bay Colony, of Benjamin Franklin using his backyard to entertain important members of the Constitutional Convention in Philadelphia, of the origin of the Declaration of Independence, and of many other pivotal incidents in American history.

The major obstacle Cox faced in executing these projects was that of achieving the proper perspective—especially on the curving surfaces both of the Capitol ceiling and of the Great Experiment Hall. He met the challenge, however, with grit and determination. In order to pin down historical details accurately, he worked closely with the United States Capitol Historical Society; he also consulted with a committee from the Daughters of the American Revolution. Finally, he scrutinized his own vast collection of early American prints. But it was Cox who made the final decision about fidelity to historical detail.

Following a major heart attack early in 1980, Cox cut his schedule back to a three-day work week. The Capitol Historical Society did their bit by installing a motorized chair to haul him to and from his scaffolding. Nevertheless, he retired in December of 1981 and the age of eighty-five after having devoted thirty years to painting the Capitol. His assistant, Cliff Young, was assigned to complete the work. Young, too, had spent time in the Cornish area; he boarded with Mrs. George Ruggles in Plainfield and served as an assistant to Barry Faulkner, especially on the mural for the Cheshire County Savings Bank depicting the coming of the railroad (see below p. 194).

Less than a week before Allyn Cox died on September 26, 1982, he was honored at the Capitol building by a bipartisan group of political and artistic leaders for his distinguished career, particularly for those three decades devoted to that building. He was hailed as "a great artist" by House Speaker Thomas P. O'Neill, Jr., a Democrat from Massachusetts. The Senate majority leader, Howard H. Baker, Jr., a Republican from Tennessee, told Mr. Cox, "Your splendid work enjoys a special place in the art history of the world."[7]

ENDNOTES

1. *The Valley News*, West Lebanon, NH, July 27, 1981, p. 11.
2. Letter to Virginia Colby from Allyn Cox, dated July 31, 1982; Virginia Colby, Cornish Colony files.
3. Letter from Allyn Cox to Gail Furnas, Windsor librarian, September 1978, as quoted in *The Valley News*, August 1, 1981, p. 2.
4. *The Windsor Chronicle*, Windsor, VT, October 28, 1982, p. 1.
5. *The Valley News*, July 6, 1988.
6. *The Valley News*, July 27, 1981, p. 11.
7. Obituary, *The New York Times*, September 28, 1982, p. B12.

Figure 57, *Kenyon Cox as Pluto in* A Masque of "Ours," *1905.*

KENYON COX
1856 – 1919

and

LOUISE HOWLAND KING COX
1865 – 1945

KENYON COX

KENYON COX was born in Warren, Ohio, on October 27, 1856. His mother, Helen Finney Cox, was the daughter of Charles Grandison Finney, a famous evangelist and revivalist, an inspirer of several prominent abolitionists, and the president of Oberlin College (1851-1865). His father, Jacob Dolson Cox, had a distinguished career as a major general in the Union Army, governor of Ohio (1866-1868), secretary of the interior in President Ulysses S. Grant's administration (1869-1870), a congressman in the House of Representatives (1877-1879), dean of the Cincinnati Law School (1880-1897), and, during part of that period, president of the University of Cincinnati (1885-1889).

Kenyon persuaded his parents to permit him to study art. He enrolled at the McMicken School of Design, part of the University of Cincinnati. He found his studies uninspiring and moved on to the Pennsylvania Academy of the Fine Arts in Philadelphia. That institution also proved dull and he coaxed his parents into allowing him to go to Paris where he enrolled in the classes of Emile Carolus-Duran in 1877. He went to Italy with his close friend Theodore Robinson and returned in 1878 to the Académie Julian and enrolled with Jean-Léon Gérôme at the Ecole des Beaux Arts early in 1879. He returned to New York late in 1882 and soon established a formidable reputation as a draughtsman, a mural painter, and, eventually, as an art critic. He was aided in these pursuits by being an influential teacher both at the Art Students League, where he met his wife-to-be, Louise Howland King, and at the National Academy of Design.

His career as an art critic was a long one. He wrote for the *Nation* and *Scribner's* and did much of his reflective writing in Cornish.[1] He collected many of these essays, reviews, and articles into six books of criticism. Even before the debate about whether American art should follow the realists or the modernists, Cox confronted the issue Whistler and the aesthetic movement raised about "art for art's sake." For example, were Whistler's portraits "arrangements" and his landscapes "harmonies" or "nocturnes"? Cox offered the traditional academic definition that "in its essential nature, painting is the art of representing on a plane surface . . . the forms and colors of objects. Its origin is in the instinct of imitation. Its most fundamental appeal— not necessarily its highest appeal but its most universal and necessary one—is to the sense of recognition."[2] Despite the emphasis on imitation, the door is still left open for the viewer to rely on powers of recognition. Hence the response could be a recognition of "arrangement" alone. Three years before his death, however, he more clearly stated his definition of art, one that guided not only his own art but also his art criticism:

Figure 58. *Kenyon Cox,* Tolstoy, *from the original painting* en grisaille *done for* Century Magazine *in 1893 (vol. 46, p. 257).*

> The business of the painter as imitator is to give us, temporarily, the benefit of his power of vision, of his training and knowledge, of his perception of the significance of things, and by so doing to give us an unwonted sense of physical and mental efficiency which is in the highest degree pleasurable. We feel ourselves, for the moment, possessed of clearer senses, of more lively emotions, of greater intellectual powers, than we had imagined; we live more intensely and rejoice in our perceptions of this intensity of life.[3]

With this as a standard, it is not surprising, then, that Cox has gone down in art history for his attack on the International Exhibition of Modern Art of 1913: the famous—or infamous—Armory Show. His vitriol was poured into "The Modern Spirit in Art, 1913." Although he confessed that he "took to heart the admonition of the preface to the catalogue, that 'to be afraid of what is different or unfamiliar is to be afraid of life,'" he found himself unable "to sort out these people . . . to treat them seriously . . . Nor can I laugh. This thing is not amusing; it is heartrending and sickening." From Cox's standpoint, "the real meaning of this Cubist movement is nothing else than the total destruction of the art of painting . . . They have abolished the representation of nature and all forms of recognized and traditional decoration." The result was chaos: "The lack of discipline and the exaltation of the individual have been the destructive forces of modern art . . . Now all discipline has disappeared, all training is proclaimed useless, and individualism has reached the pitch of sheer insanity or triumphant charlatanism." Cox closed his jeremiad with advice to student and to the general public alike:

> To the student I would say: Distrust all short cuts to art or to glory. No work worth doing was ever done without long preparation and continuous endeavor. The success

Figure 59. *Kenyon Cox's studio, which no longer stands. Note the tall door which enabled Cox to move large murals.*

that is attained in a month will be forgotten in a year. To the public I would say: Do not allow yourselves to be blinded by the sophistries of the foolish dupes or the self-interested exploiters of all this charlatanry. Remember that it is for you that art is created, and judge honestly for yourselves whether this which calls itself art is useful to you or to the world. You are not infallible, but your instincts are right in the main, and you are, after all, the final judges. If your stomach revolts against this rubbish, it is because it is not fit for human food. Let no man persuade you to stuff yourselves with it.[4]

As a muralist he fulfilled commissions—many in his Cornish studio. There he worked on *The Sciences and the Arts* for the Library of Congress, *Plenty* for the Appellate Court House in New York City, allegorical images for the state capitol buildings of Minnesota, and a mural for the Essex County Court House in Newark, New Jersey, for which he used Ethel Barrymore as a model during her Cornish stay in 1906.[5] Cornish also inspired some of his paintings. He painted several portraits of Augustus Saint-Gaudens: one, done in 1888, is in the National Academy of Design; the other, a famous portrait, *Augustus Saint-Gaudens in his Studio in 1887*, was burned and redone in 1908—it is now in New York City's Metropolitan Museum. He also painted Lucia Fuller and Maxfield Parrish. His painting *The Education of Cupid* has as its background "a pure Cornish landscape . . . the extreme distance being Platt's river view."[6]

Kenyon and his wife Louise first came to Cornish as boarders at the Stephen Tracy farm. In her letter inquiring whether accommodations would be available, she notes that "Mrs. Prellwitz [Edith, Mrs. Henry] tells me you may be able to accommodate us this summer." Louise Cox would like "two rooms—in one of which we should like to be able to have a fire—and board for Mr. Cox, myself, and nurse, and child of two years.

Figure 60. *Residence of Kenyon and Louise Cox, Cornish, New Hampshire.*

We should want the rooms from about the middle of July until October." As an after-thought, she wanted to know what would be the "charge for a third room for a sitting room?"[7] That summer, with the help of Charles Platt, they bought land at John Free-man's mills and appeared on the Cornish tax rolls for the first time in 1897 as the own-ers of three acres. The land was situated on the Cornish-Plainfield line and was purchased with money that Louise had earned. Her son Allyn used to say that he could stand with one foot in Cornish and the other in Plainfield.[8] Kenyon's studio, which was built near the Blow-Me-Down Covered Bridge, was constructed with a huge door so that his murals could be removed easily.

When he and his wife called on other members of the Cornish Colony, their three children—Leonard, Caroline, and Allyn—often accompanied them. And for them he wrote and illustrated *Mixed Beasts,* a delightful collection of rhymes and pictures pub-lished in 1904 and recently reissued. Cox also was active in local plays: he was Pluto in *A Masque of "Ours": The Gods and the Golden Bowl* (1905) and the Crow in *Sanctuary: A Bird Masque* (1913). We have a brief vignette: he was "so temperamental that he had days when he did not speak. He never played a stroke of tennis, but he was fascinated by watching the game. He was very tall and thin and his face in repose had a fierce expres-sion exaggerated by his long, shaggy, black mustache."[9] But he was also someone with a "dry sense of humor [that] occasionally showed through, as when he asked his neigh-bor, the novelist Winston Churchill, to remove the bell from the lead cow in his herd. 'Its tintinnabulation in the early morning is somewhat insistent and very close at hand as, at that hour, the gentle ruminants like the shade of the trees along the line fence. I don't object to it, but the ladies seem to feel it is an interruption of their beauty sleep.' Churchill obliged."[10] Kenyon Cox died of tuberculosis March 17, 1919.

Figure 61. *Louise Cox as Thetis in* A Masque of "Ours," *1905.*

LOUISE HOWLAND KING COX

LOUISE COX was born in San Francisco in 1865 and not very much is known about her early life. She married Kenyon on June 30, 1892, at the home of her aunt, Mrs. M. B. Jones, in Belmont, Massachusetts.[11] After the couple had established a summer home in Cornish, Louise was able to enjoy her summers away from the pressures of the city. Financial worries plagued them, partly due to Kenyon's delicate health, but Kenyon's older brother, Jacob Dolson, Jr., often helped them out. He was the founder of a successful business, The Cleveland Twist and Drill Company.[12]

Nevertheless, Louise felt immediately at home in Cornish because she had known Lucia Fairchild Fuller previously, because she had known Emily Slade and Edith Mitchell Prellwitz at the Art Students League, and because she had studied with Thomas Dewing.[13] Homer Saint-Gaudens reported a story of her student days, noting that "I do hope the story of their courtship is correct. According to the annals of the Art Students League, Mrs. Cox was a student when Kenyon was a teacher. Said he one day, leaning over her work, 'What the devil is this?' To which she replied, 'Go to Hell and find out.' Whereat they were married and lived happily ever after."[14] Once they had settled in Cornish, they called their house "Monorada," a name derived from the botanical designation for the bee balm plant, *Monarda,* that grew profusely in the fields behind their house.[15]

Her contentment helped her in her art; she was happiest painting flowers and especially children. Stephen Parrish noted in his diary that "Cox came to get some roses for Mrs. C. to paint."[16] Portraits of children, however, were her true métier. In 1900 she did a *Madonna* for *The Woman's Home Companion* using Margaret Colby, the baby daughter of Morris and Mamie Colby, as her model.[17] Later she did a series of children's paintings for *The Woman's Home Companion* beginning with *Winter* in November of 1916 for which Elizabeth Ross posed. This portrait was followed by *Spring, Summer,* and *Autumn,* for which Floyd Tracy posed. Other portraits of Colony members' children included one of Arvia MacKaye, Percy MacKaye's youngest daughter; her own daughter Caroline; as well as *Master John Churchill* and *Little Miss Churchill;* the children of Winston Churchill; and *Mrs. Homer Saint-Gaudens and Son.* Both of these favorite subjects were included in what she exhibited at the Panama-Pacific Exposition in San Francisco in 1915: *Mayflowers* and *Daughter of Eve.* We are fortunate to have a review of her art by someone who strongly appreciated Louise Cox's work, but who is more famous as a novelist than as an art critic: Theodore Dreiser. "The work of Mrs. Kenyon Cox, who though partially obscured for a time by the prestige of her husband . . . is now receiving proper recognition. . . . The drawing, grouping, coloring, and interpretation [of *The Three Fates*] are in a way new to the subject, and easily place Mrs. Cox in the foremost ranks of American woman artists." Drieser also included an interesting comment from Louise about her conception of this work: "the faces of the Fates are young and beautiful, but almost expressionless. The heads are drooping, the eyes heavy as though half asleep. My idea is that they are merely instruments under the control of a higher power. They perform their work, they must do it, without will or wish of their own. It would be beyond human *or* superhuman endurance for any conscious instrument to bear for ages and ages the horrible responsibility placed upon such Fates."[18] Another one of her artistic activities was wood carving; in this craft she was joined by two others from the Colony: Rose Nichols and Emily Slade.

Her involvement in community endeavors included performing in *A Masque of "Ours": the Gods and the Golden Bowl,* in which her husband and three children also performed, and in doing the costumes

Figure 62. *Arvia MacKaye painted by Louise Cox, 1906.*

for the production of *The Rose and the Ring* done in H. O. Walker's studio during September of 1906. Again, all three children took part.

Following her husband's death in 1919, Louise sold the Cornish house and traveled in Europe; she bought and decorated a villa in Italy. After some deliberation, she moved to Hawaii and built a house there in 1929. The last house she would build was in Chappaqua, New York, near her daughter Caroline Lansing. She followed through on a long-cherished wish: to spend one of her last summers in a boarding house in Tyringham, Massachusetts, where she and Kenyon had stayed during their first summer together. Louise died in a nursing home in Windham, Connecticut, on December 11, 1945, at the age of eighty.[19] "Her body was cremated; her ashes were mixed with Kenyon's and scattered in Cornish."[20]

SUGGESTION FOR FURTHER READING

H. Wayne Morgan, ed., *An American Art Student in Paris: The Letters of Kenyon Cox, 1877-1882* (Kent, OH: Kent State University Press, 1986).

ENDNOTES

1. *A Circle of Friends: Art Colonies of Cornish and Dublin,* exhibition catalogue (Durham, NH: University Art Galleries, University of New Hampshire, 1985), p. 80.

2. Kenyon Cox, *What Is Painting? "Winslow Homer" and Other Essays* (New York: Norton, 1988), p. 94.

3. Kenyon Cox, "What is Painting?" *Art World* 1, October 1916, as quoted in H. Wayne Morgan, *Keepers of Culture* (Kent, OH: Kent State University Press, 1989), p. 23.

4. *Harper's Weekly,* March 15, 1913, p. 10; as quoted in John W. McCoubrey, *American Art 1700-1760: Sources and Documents* (Englewood Cliffs, NJ: Prentice Hall, 1965), pp. 193-196.

5. *A Circle of Friends,* p. 79.

6. A letter from Kenyon Cox to his son Allyn, June 15, 1917, Cox Papers, Avery Library, Columbia University, as quoted in *A Circle of Friends,* p. 80.

7. Letter sent from 75 West 55th Street, New York City, and dated January 29, 1896; copy in Virginia Colby, Cornish Colony files.

8. Letter to Virginia Colby dated September 4, 1982.

9. Margaret Homer Shurcliff, *Lively Days* (Taipei: Literature House, Ltd., 1965), p. 35.

10. Letter: Kenyon Cox to Winston Churchill, dated August 26, 1900; Churchill papers, Baker Library, Dartmouth College, Hanover, NH, as quoted in H. Wayne Morgan, *Kenyon Cox (1856-1919): A Life in American Art* (Kent, OH: Kent State University Press, 1994), p. 186.

11. Patricia C. Ronon, "Louise King Cox: Her Life and Work" (MA thesis, City University of New York, 1988), p. 18.

12. Ibid., p. 30

13. Ibid., p. 8.

14. Homer Saint-Gaudens, *The American Artist and His Times* (New York: Dodd, Mead, 1941), p. 156.

15. Ronon, p. 29.

16. Entry for July 19, 1903; Baker Library, Dartmouth College, Hanover, NH, gift of Marian and Roy Garrand.

17. Virginia Colby, Cornish Colony files.

18. Review of the "Work of Mrs. Kenyon Cox," *Cosmopolitan* (March 1898), p. 479.

19. Ronan, p. 44.

20. Morgan, pp. 244, 246.

Figure 63. *The garden and residence of Herbert Croly,*
designed by Charles A. Platt.

HERBERT D. CROLY

1869 – 1930

HERBERT DAVID CROLY was an author, editor, and political philosopher. The author of *The Promise of American Life*, "the progressive movement's bible, and the founding editor of *The New Republic*, the influential weekly journal of opinion, Croly virtually redefined the American national interest, and thereby laid the theoretical cornerstone for modern liberalism and the welfare state."[1]

He and his wife Louise (Emory) first came to Cornish in 1893 at the urging of Louise's best friend Ellen Biddle Shipman and her playwright husband Louis. For two summers the two couples shared a house, the farmhouse of Frank L. Johnson; it was eventually to become the home of Homer and Carlota Saint-Gaudens and is better known as "Barberry House." The Crolys were so enthralled with the area that they commissioned Charles A. Platt to design a house for them. *The Vermont Journal* noted in October of 1897 that Charles Platt had recently finished the house plans for the Crolys. It is not surprising, then, that the Crolys appear on the Cornish tax records in 1898, having bought part of the Bryant farm—they owned the property until the Burnham Carters purchased it in 1946. The tax records also show that until 1916 the Crolys were taxed each year for one or two horses and a cow. During part of this period, from 1900 until 1906, Croly served as editor of *The Architectural Record* and, while he was with the organization, wrote numerous articles about Charles Platt, his architect neighbor.[2]

The Crolys' contribution to the local community came in many forms. They spent most of their summers in Cornish from the 1890s until Herbert's death in 1930. Stephen Parrish noted in his diaries numerous visits with the Crolys. Herbert was later to meet his Harvard classmates Philip Littell and Justice Learned Hand in Cornish. Among his other close Cornish friends were Charles Platt, the Shipmans, George Rublee, and Norman Hapgood. Croly enjoyed playing tennis; apparently, though, he took his game very seriously. He also played poker and bridge. Mrs. Croly participated in community affairs, too. She signed "An Endorsement of Birth Control," and in 1911 was treasurer of the Cornfield Bird Club.[3]

Summers in Cornish gave Herbert Croly a respite from his deep commitment to American intellectual life. He first made his mark on that scene in 1909 with the publication of *The Promise of American Life.* Croly's vision of America's future included large, efficient corporations, whose power to exploit workers would be held in check by labor unions and whose effects on the general public would be regulated by a strong federal government.[4] In 1913 Willard and Dorothy Straight offered their moral and financial support to carry these ideas further and to establish a weekly opinion journal.[5] Croly gathered an impressive group of talented journalists that included a brilliant young political writer, Walter Lippmann, who was also a visitor in Cornish,[6] and his good friend and neighbor Philip Littell, who wrote a full page weekly column entitled "Books and Things." Thus, Croly's other major contribution to American thought, *The New Republic,* was born in 1914. Croly seemed an unlikely person to sway public opinion: he was painfully shy among strangers and sometimes barely spoke above a whisper. The journal, however, was neither reticent nor retiring. It attracted prominent contributors and championed such causes as academic freedom, the rights of blacks, women's suffrage, and birth control.[7] Croly was impressed by many of President Woodrow Wilson's reforms—from the creation of the Federal Reserve System to the establishment of an income tax. Consequently, *The New Republic* was often seen as a mouthpiece of the Wilson White House. The editors were extremely pleased when, in 1917, the President outlined a plan for "peace without victory." That phrase was one that *The New Republic* had coined and the plan itself incorporated many of the ideas that the journal had been advocating.

One of Croly's earlier journalistic endeavors was pretty much a "Grub Street" project, but it did have its link to Cornish. In 1912, at the behest of the Mark Hanna family (who even demanded the right to delete anything they might find objectionable about it), Croly agreed to turn out *Marcus Alonzo Hanna: His Life and Work.* He wrote his friend Learned Hand, "I must remain in Cornish until I get Uncle Mark well-planted in his printed grave."[8] It is generally believed that writing so favorably about so obviously an unprogressive person was a serious compromise of Croly's principles. But they were boldly reasserted as a result of an invitation from Harvard University to deliver the prestigious Godkin Lectures during the academic year of 1913-14. The ideas and principles of both *The Promise of American Life* and the Godkin Lectures found their way into Croly's second most important book, *Progressive Democracy.* It was published in 1914, just as the first issues of *The New Republic* became available to the public.[9]

The years after World War I left Croly, who had become enamored of the ideas of a mystic religious cult led by Georges I. Gurdjieff, a lonely fighter for unpopular liberal causes. A frustrated man, he died after a massive stroke in 1930. Mrs. Croly died in 1945 at her summer home in Berkeley, California, leaving no children. Both Mr. and Mrs. Croly are buried in Gilkey Cemetery on Stage Road in Plainfield, New Hampshire.

ENDNOTES

1. David Seideman, review of David W. Levy, *Herbert Croly of "The New Republic"* (Princeton, NJ: Princeton University Press, 1985) in *The New York Times Book Review,* July 14, 1985, p. 13.

2. For more on the interaction of Croly with Platt, especially the argument that artists of Platt's caliber were fundamental to Croly's firmly held conviction about "the promise of American life," see below p. 333 n. 22.

3. Virginia Colby, Cornish Colony files; her telephone number in 1911 was 106.

4. Levy, p. 221.

5. Dorothy Straight was the youngest daughter of William C. Whitney, a Wall Street financier and an active participant in Washington social life. Dorothy is said to have "considered it her special duty to 'keep alive in the privileged members of society the sense of responsibility for those less fortunate than themselves'"; see Levy, p. 186.

6. For more on Lippmann and Croly, see below pp. 486-487.

7. Perhaps Croly's interest in birth control resulted from his wife's concern for the cause. At any rate, he attended a support dinner in honor of Margaret Sanger, the birth control advocate and brief Cornish Colony resident, on the eve of her trial, January 17, 1916. She had been arrested for allegedly violating the Comstock laws, which prohibited dissemination of material considered obscene. There was information about contraception methods in the periodical she published, *The Woman Rebel.* Many celebrated intellectuals attended it, so no serious journalist could ignore such an occasion; see Madeline Gray, *Margaret Sanger* (New York: Richard Marek Publishers, 1979), p. 116; see also Ellen Chesler, *Women of Valor: Margaret Sanger and the Birth Control Movement in America* (New York: Simon and Schuster, 1992), pp. 139-40.

8. As quoted in Levy, p. 146.

9. Levy also quotes a note from Croly to Learned Hand, dated October 1913, from Cornish to the effect that he was "plugging away" at *Progressive Democracy,* "having a thoroughly good time—as I always do, when I lock myself up with my work" (p. 215).

CLARA POTTER DAVIDGE (TAYLOR)

1858 – 1921

CLARA, SOMETIMES CALLED CLARISSA, POTTER married Mason Chichester Davidge; she acquired the old Kingsbury Tavern in Plainfield, New Hampshire, built by the carpenter Asa Kingsbury in 1802.[1] Thus began her long association with the area, mainly as a patron of the arts. She came as a summer resident but in 1909 she "relinquished the lease of her house in Washington Square, New York City, and henceforth [made Plainfield] her permanent residence, and incidentally bec[a]me the largest taxpayer in town."[2]

Mrs. Davidge was the daughter of the Right Reverend Henry C. Potter, Episcopal bishop of New York. Her sister Mary married William Henry Hyde, an artist who lived in Cornish. Clara Davidge was also a friend of Everett Shinn, who first came to the Cornish Colony in 1902. After her husband died in 1901, she "drifted into antiques and decoration. Her early interest in this field led to her fame as 'the first interior decorator.'"[3] Mabel Dodge Luhan, in her inimitable manner, wrote:

> Clarissa Davidge was the unconventional one in her family: she was middle-aged and partially crippled so she walked with a limp. Animated, eccentric, rattle-brained Clara! Always dressed like the doll of any little girl of ten who has had recourse to the family ragbag and secured bits of gay silk, fur and lace, she was warmhearted, rather bad-tempered, and fond of expressing herself in a loud high-pitched voice in language rich with her own variations. . . . She collected old furniture and promising artists.[4]

She fulfilled her responsibility to "promising artists" in New York by taking over the management of the Madison Gallery in 1908—along with Henry Fitch Taylor. She did so primarily because she thought New York needed a new place for artists to exhibit their work, one that was not linked to the accepted canons of art then decreed mainly by the National Academy of Design. It was in a 1911 meeting at the Madison Gallery that the Association of American Painters and Sculptors was formed. And it was this group, the AAPS, that in 1913 organized an exhibition at the Sixty-Ninth Regiment Armory in New York known officially as the "International Exhibition of Modern Art," or more familiarly as "The Armory Show," with its far-reaching effects on the history of modern art in America. It was also in 1913 that Mrs. Davidge became Mrs. Henry Fitch Taylor; she married an artist who was a late convert to modern painting and someone with his own links to the Cornish Colony (see below pp. 402-404).

Clara fulfilled her role as a supporter of "promising artists" locally by purchasing several properties in Plainfield that she then made available to artists. For example, she bought the "Echo Farm" located on Old County Road and offered this farm to William and Marguerite Zorach for their use during the summer of 1917.[5] She actually proposed to give them the farm outright, but the Zorachs did not know how to accept such a generous offer. At one point, the potter Frank C. Applegate of Morrisville, Pennsylvania, came to Plainfield and stayed with the Zorachs. Clara decided to offer him the farm. Unlike the Zorachs, Applegate had no qualms about accepting her gift; he told her to make out a deed in his name, which she did. Applegate spent two summers there before moving on to Santa Fe, New Mexico. Clara also purchased an old mill on Daniels Road, originally built by David and Septimus Read, and converted it into living quarters. Although the mill had ceased operation about 1880, it quite handily served Langdon Mitchell, William Vaughn Moody, Willard Leroy Metcalf, Mattie Brown, and Frances Grimes as a good place in which to live and work. The mill's foundations still exist.

Clara was also an active and popular member of the Colony's busy social life. She was a frequent visitor at "Northcote," the home of Stephen Parrish. On August 8, 1905, he noted in his diary, "Evening dinner at Mrs. Davidge's. (The Whitings, Fullers, Mrs. Adams, Hart, John Blair, Miss Read, Miss Weir [daughter of Alden Weir], and Miss Blanchard were there.)"[6]

An interview with Marguerite Quimby provided several fascinating sidelights to Clara's life. She belonged to a group called "Unity," which had its headquarters in Lee's Summit, Missouri, and was an organization that emphasized constructive thinking, affirmative prayer, and spiritual healing. She believed that human beings are surrounded by a subjective mind and that this new thought pattern could produce positive results. Armed with these convictions, she started to work on her husband Henry Taylor in order to convince him to stop drinking. She never mentioned liquor, but every night she sat and willed him to stop his over-indulgence. She also applied the same technique to the famous poet Edwin Arlington Robinson. In both instances, it worked. Another one of her ideas resulted from her interest in comparing music and color; she theorized about how certain colors would register as specific musical notes. And finally, Mrs. Quimby revealed the fact that Clara used to rub her face with carrots every morning. Perhaps it is better that the reason for this cleansing remains a mystery.[7]

Clara's death was not one befitting such a devotee of art. Instead of visiting Cornish, she and her husband spent the summer of 1921 in a cottage on the estate of her brother Alonzo Potter at Smithtown, Long Island. She suffered from spinal trouble, which partially paralyzed her and caused her to use crutches and walk unsteadily. It is thought that, while walking from the cottage to the main house along a private road, she fell into a marsh, became "evidently stuck in the mud, and fainted in the struggle to free herself"; she drowned in water not more than two or three inches deep.[8]

A moving tribute to her noted that she:

> was devoted to art with a singleness of heart that is unusual. She loved the essential breath of life—that breath without which art does not exist, without which things are only paint or stone. And this love of art she made a force, turning her energy, her flaming enthusiasm, into helping painters . . . Clara Potter Taylor's vitality, her splen-

did optimism are gone, but the work she did is bearing fruit today, and we who among others benefited by her generosity and her affection cannot let her pass without a public recognition of our deep regret.

The letter is dated New York, November 10, 1921, and is signed by charter members of the Association of American Painters and Sculptors and such Armory Show luminaries as: George Bellows, D. Putnam Brinley, Walt Kuhn, Ernest Lawson (also a brief Cornish Colony resident), Elmer Livingston MacRae, Jerome Myers, and Allen Tucker.[9]

ENDNOTES

1. Deeds, Vol. 158, p. 443; Vol. 160, p. 74; Vol. 164, p. 227—Sullivan County Records, Newport, NH.

2. *The Weekly Enterprise*, Meriden, NH, May 26, 1909. The Plainfield correspondent continues with some commentary, lightly edited, relevant for anyone interested in the Cornish Colony:

   > a position held for the past few years by Albion E. Lang, who has paid a tax of $450 in Plainfield, besides a large tax in Cornish, ditto Winston Churchill, a heavy taxpayer in both towns, as is Admiral Folger, the Beaman Estate and Mr. Rubley [George Rublee]. Other big taxpayers are Herbert Adams, Louis Shipman, Dr. Heyward, Harry [Henry] Fuller, Mr. Hart, Maxfield Parrish, Mary Trueblood, Edith Lawrence, Mrs. Gohegan, Miss Watson, etc. Many others have bought building lots to become later on large taxpayers, if only proper encouragement be given them. (Mr. Rubley bought a building lot of forty-six acres paying for it $6000, but because he considered himself discriminated against, left Plainfield in disgust, leaving us in the lurch with an unsavory reputation, and then bought a $35,000 residence in Cornish where he is chucking out mints of money.) And these large taxes are but a small part of the benefit derived by the town from these city people.
   >
   > Before their advent a dozen or fifteen years ago, this part of the town was dead as a door-nail, so to speak. Houses in the village were unoccupied and going to decay, real estate so low in price that it was almost impossible to give it away, and now look at us, with our new three-story store building and unbeatable ball team. We are the envy of Meriden of whom we were formerly the despised. But who shouldn't feel thus, as they have the great KUA to keep them prosperous and stirred up.

   The "new three-story store building" is probably the Plainfield General Store, which was built three or four years prior to the "Plainfield Correspondent's" remarks.

3. Milton W. Brown, *The Story of the Armory Show* (New York: Abbeville Press, 1988), p. 94.

4. Ibid.; see also Mabel Dodge Luhan, *Movers and Shakers* (Albuquerque, NM: University of New Mexico Press, 1985, reprint of 1936 ed.), p. 123.

5. Roberta K. Tarbell, *Marguerite Zorach: The Early Years, 1908-1920* (published for the National Collection of Fine Arts by the Smithsonian Institution Press, Washington, DC, 1973), p. 48. See below p. 449 for another version of the episodes with the Zorachs and Applegates.

6. Baker Library, Dartmouth College, Hanover, NH.

7. Interview with Virginia Colby, November 12, 1979.

8. Clipping from *The New York Times*, November 11(?), 1921; Daniels scrapbook, Plainfield, NH.

9. Ibid.

THOMAS WILMER DEWING
1851 – 1927

and

MARIA OAKEY DEWING
1845 – 1927

THOMAS WILMER DEWING

THOMAS DEWING WAS ONE OF THE most significant painters among "The Ten"; in fact, he has been called "the Degas of the Ten American Painters."[1] Just as George de Forest Brush, another Cornish Colony member, idealized women, so did Dewing. The latter, however, was famous for "his artfully posed figures" arranged in a background of "subtly related color harmonies evoking a dream world of beauty in which time and logic play[ed] no role."[2] Some observers, even while he was alive, found his beautiful, dignified, and refined women rather saccharine. Dewing, though, described himself as halting a painting when it was "just sour enough to save it."[3]

Dewing was especially influenced by the Aesthetic Movement and its ideals as well as the vogue for Japanese prints. He "was an artist of profound aesthetic sensibility, as well as one of the most exquisite technicians and pictorial poets of the late nineteenth century."[4] James McNeill Whistler, who thought that there were only two artists of any

Figure 64. Summer *by Thomas Wilmer Dewing.*

175

importance in the late nineteenth century—Degas and himself—was an important influence on Dewing; they even shared the same patron: Charles Lang Freer.[5] Dewing's aestheticism, whether it came from Oscar Wilde, Swinburne, Rossetti, or Whistler, opened him up to criticism of inscrutability: "thin and mysterious exhalations floating amid flying blossomseeds through the ether on the wind of their own draperies, straining, bending, and yearning in all imaginable sentimental agonies, if sitting or walking."[6] If many of Dewing's contemporaries were striving for "the beauty of the actual," Dewing wished to replace such a goal with "the beauty of artifice." [7] His Cornish friend, neighbor, and devoted admirer Kenyon Cox said of Dewing's work that it depicted a "faint twilight country, this No-Man's Land full of pale faces and limbs swathed in binding draperies of uncertain color. . . . The subject is nothing."[8]

Thus when Dewing followed his friend Augustus Saint-Gaudens to Cornish in 1886, he was already an established artist. (Dewing grew up in Boston where he received his early training, crafted his draftsmanship in Paris, returned to Boston in 1878, and eventually settled in New York City in 1880 where he met Maria Oakey, already a well-known still-life and portrait painter; they married in 1881.) Upon his arrival in Cornish, Saint-Gaudens was gratified that Dewing considered himself "blood of the blood and bone of the bone of the country. He falls right into everything like a duck to water."[9] The rare interplay of sophisticated artists in a relaxing rural atmosphere led Dewing to remark that what he characterized as his "decorations" belonged "to the poetic and imaginative world where only a few choice spirits live."[10] Although he was somewhat of an artistic outsider, for almost twenty years Cornish provided him with a "few choice spirits."

In 1886 the Dewings rented an old farmhouse with adjacent buildings on what is now Platt Road from Charles Beaman; he painted first in "The Woodchuck Hole," a studio built by the carpenter George Ruggles. Dewing finally purchased the rented property in 1887 with a portrait of Beaman's wife, *Hettie Beaman*." Proud of their new house, Maria insisted that it be named "Doveridge" for the ancestral home of the Oakey family in Derbyshire, England. It must have been an environment conducive to work because Thomas Dewing is credited with painting over a dozen major canvases during his stay in Cornish and Maria Dewing finished quite a number of paintings here, too.

Although not a landscape painter, local birch saplings and trees figure in *Spring Moonlight* (originally called *In the Garden*) done between 1892 and 1894, in *Summer* done in 1890, and in *The White Birch* (1896-1899).[12] Mount Ascutney rises in the background of *Landscape with Figures* (originally entitled *Spring*) done in 1890. The model for the woman fishing in *Summer*, also done in 1890, is a Cornish Colony resident, Eleanor Hardy Bunker—who eventually married Charles Platt in 1893 and had her portrait painted by Dewing then. Other Cornish residents whose portraits he painted were Frances Houston (1880) and Charles Platt (1893). The inspiration for *The Hermit Thrush* (1890) was one of Dewing's favorite song birds and one quite common in the Cornish woods then. The gardens in Cornish, which were nationally famous, are significant in the composition of both *The Days* (1886) and *The Song* (1891).[13] Other of his works that are associated with Cornish include *The Recitation* (1891), *After Sunset* (1892), *Before Sunrise* (1895), *The Garland* (1899), *The Lute* (1901-1904), and *La Pêche* (1901-1904). Several of Dewing's works, also originating in Cornish and also rooted in his appreciation of the natural scene surrounding him, resulted from his interest in interior decoration: a pair of two-panel folding screens entitled *The Four Sylvan Sounds* (*The Sound of Falling Water and The Hermit Thrush* and *The Woodpecker and The Wind Through The Pine Trees*) done in 1897, a three-panel folding screen called *Morning Glories* for which his friend Stanford White, the famous architect, designed the frame, [14] and the painting on the lid of a Steinway piano that is now a permanent part of the White House's collection.[15] For all the natural elements in these works—and Dewing has been called "probably the finest American painter of screens at the time"[16]—Dewing's preference was for the female figure and portraits.

Dewing seemed to approach the social scene in Cornish with some ambivalence. In the main, despite "the feuds and intrigues that ran rampant in the art colony, with Thomas Dewing at the center of them all," he reveled in the social life, especially during his early years in Cornish. His social life did not diminish the fact that he "was a talented botanist who lavished almost as much passion on his vegetable and flower garden as he did on his painting." His "enthusiasms also extended to tableaux vivants, charades, and elaborate dinner parties that he planned to the last detail. Above all, Dewing loved elegance. He and his fellow artists identified with the established values of a venerated European past, erecting villas, planting Italianate gardens, and inveighing against the monied interlopers ('philistines,' they called them) who would undermine the social order to which their art appealed." Furthermore, within his social set, "recent arrivals to the art colony, such as the painters Kenyon Cox and his wife, Louise, and Henry B. Fuller and his wife, Lucia Fairchild, enthusiastically adopted Dewing's taste for carefully appointed Whistlerian interiors and well-planned dinner parties, which were as pleasing to the eye as they were to the palate."[17] To flatter his patron Charles Lang Freer during the latter's second visit to Cornish in 1894, Dewing organized an elaborate oriental masque. It was based on Javanese themes and costumes and was held at "High Court," the home for Annie Lazarus that Charles Platt had designed. On the other hand, both Hugh Wade and Homer Saint-Gaudens relate quips and occasions when Dewing found life at Cornish too social—and too expensive—for his tastes.[18] He left Cornish in 1905 and spent the summers in Green Hill, New Hampshire, and finally bought property in Fryeburg, Maine. He died in 1938, a "nearly forgotten" artist "living in a tenement building" in New York City.[19]

MARIA OAKEY DEWING

MANY OF THE DEWINGS' CONTEMPORARIES in Cornish acknowledge the importance of these two painters to the tone of their social lives while they were all together. So, it is not surprising that the couple is credited with beginning the garden craze—primarily because Maria (pronounced to rhyme with "papaya") needed flower models to paint.

Maria was born in New York City in 1845 and developed a serious interest in writing. Even in *From Attic to Cellar* (1879), *Beauty in Dress* (1881), and *Beauty in the Household* (1882), her artistic judgment was apparent. Gradually her interests shifted to art; she went to Paris to study with Thomas Couture then returned to America to study both with John La Farge, who, along with Winslow Homer, was a crucial figure in the development of American Impressionism, and later with William Morris Hunt in Boston. She married Dewing in 1881. "Six years his senior, the talented woman was Dewing's superior on several fronts. Not only had her training . . . equipped her with artistic credentials

Figure 65. Bed of Poppies *by Maria Oakey Dewing, 1909.*

that far outstripped his, her immediate circle of friends . . . also represented the group with which Dewing had sought to affiliate himself more closely. Added to these points of undeniable attraction were Maria's impressive connections with the intelligentsia of New England."[20] She was considered a founding member of the Society of American Artists, the group that broke away from the National Academy of Design in 1877. "A writer on household decoration and a devotee of Emerson, the attractive and strong-willed Maria and her friend, the artist Helena de Kay, maintained their own studio-apartment on Broadway at a time when such a thing was considered quite unconventional."[21]

Cornish offered her an excellent opportunity to perfect what she most preferred to do. "In her Cornish garden, she spent long hours studying the growth patterns, textures, and dispositions of individual plants in order to nurture her 'garden thirsty soul.'"[22] Although she insisted on what she called a "long apprenticeship in the garden," she firmly believed that a painter of nature was obliged to paint pictures not merely to reproduce reality. One of her most original contributions to depicting flowers was her procedure of beginning with the flower in its natural habitat but following through by arranging it on the canvas so that the viewer sensed the liveliness and animation of the flower itself. Often she would use a close-up, worm's eye view perspective on the flowers, highlighting objects in the foreground, providing an illusion of depth, and suggesting a natural setting through an asymmetrical arrangement within the picture frame so that a flower would continue to exist, so to say, beyond what was shown within the actual picture frame. As her friend Royal Cortissoz put it, "Mrs. Dewing's flowers have made for themselves a place apart in American painting. She gives us their character, their special texture, their special droop. She paints, literally, their portraits"; on a later occasion he noted that "she knew how to interpret the soul of a flower—but her principal aim was to make it a work of art."[23]

It is assumed that, while in Cornish, she painted many of her out-of-door paintings. But because her popularity declined rapidly, even during her lifetime, it is difficult to locate many of them. Jennifer Martin has established a checklist of some ten paintings; at least half of them seem to have been completed during the years she was in Cornish. Referring to one of them, *Poppies and Italian Mignonette*, which she had presented to Charles Lang Freer, she wrote: "I painted it at Cornish . . . [the] poppies grew in a large bed mixed with a tall white mignonette that grows wild in Italy and was tamed to the garden here by a nurseryman named Childs. I never saw it anywhere else than in our Cornish garden."[24] We also know that she did the floral background of *Hymen* (also known as *Wood Nymph*) done in 1886 and presented as a wedding present to Stanford and Bessie Smith White. Finally, she is likely to have done the floral background both for the screen *Morning Glories* that her husband completed in 1900, and for which Stanford White designed the frame, and for a large pre-Raphaelite painting in the Wadsworth Atheneum in Hartford, Connecticut, *The Days* finished in 1886. It may well be that, although she was an extremely talented painter, she restricted her art to floral painting so as not to compete with her husband. Maria Dewing died in 1927.

ENDNOTES

1. Richard J. Boyle, *American Impressionism* (Boston: Little, Brown, and Co., 1974), p. 173.

2. Susan Hobbs, "Thomas Wilmer Dewing: The Early Years, 1851-1885," *The American Art Journal* 13, 2 (1981), p. 5. Both this article and the one cited in note 5 need to be supplemented with Susan A. Hobbs, with an essay by Barbara Dayer Gallati, *The Art of Thomas Wilmer Dewing: Beauty Reconfigured*, exhibition catalogue (The Brooklyn Museum in association with the Smithsonian Institution Press, 1996).

3. Ibid., p. 6.

4. William H. Gerdts, *American Impressionism* (New York: Artabras, 1984), p. 178.

5. Freer even "underwrote Dewing's second studio in Cornish," something Dewing felt would "double" his output; see Susan Hobbs, "Thomas Dewing in Cornish, 1885-1905," *The American Art Journal* 17, 2 (Spring 1985), p. 18. It was in Cornish that Dewing introduced Freer to Charles A. Platt thus marking the beginning of quite a few commissions for Platt.

6. The critic "Greta" for the *Art Amateur* 2, March 1880, p. 75, as quoted in Hobbs, "Thomas Wilmer Dewing: The Early Years, 1851-1885," pp. 23-24.

7. Hobbs, "Thomas Wilmer Dewing: The Early Years, 1851-1885," p. 33.

8. Ibid, p. 34.

9. *The Reminiscences of Augustus Saint-Gaudens*, edited and amplified by Homer Saint-

Gaudens (New York: Century Co., 1913), Vol. 1, p. 323. The sculptor also modestly believed that the Cornish Colony thrived more because of what Dewing said about the surrounding beauty than from whatever praise he might have given it., Vol. 1, p. 317.

10. In a letter to Freer, February 16, 1901; see Hobbs, "Thomas Dewing in Cornish, 1885-1905." Even after a visit to Monet's Giverny, Dewing "wrote wistfully to Stanford White" that the village was "pretty . . . . but it is not New Hampshire"; Hobbs, *Beauty Reconfigured*, p. 26. That Cornish did not always suffice can be seen from his remark to Saint-Gaudens, "Why, Gussie, if you're not in New York, you're camping out," Homer Saint-Gaudens, *The American Artist and His Times* (New York: Dodd, Mead and Co., 1941), p. 139.

11. The tax records for Cornish indicate that the property transfer occurred in 1887; Because Beaman purchased the land originally from Chester Pike, the records refer to the ten acres as "part of Chester Pike Farm." Although Hobbs dates Dewing's arrival in Cornish as occurring in 1885, Saint-Gaudens in his *Reminiscences* clearly has him coming first in 1886 (Vol. 1, p. 322).

12. Most of the information in this paragraph comes from Hobbs, "Thomas Dewing in Cornish, 1885-1905." It should be supplemented by the relevant passages from Hobbs, *Beauty Reconfigured.*

13. Both Maria Oakey Dewing and Annie Lazarus are the subjects for this painting; Hobbs, *Beauty Reconfigured*, p. 132. For Dewing's "amorous relationship" with Annie Lazarus, see pp. 132-133 and for his "affair" with Lucia Fairchild Fuller, the model for Dewing's 1902 painting "A Portrait," see pp. 31, 70, 143.

14. Kathleen Pyne, "Classical Figures, A Folding Screen by Thomas Dewing," *Bulletin of the Detroit Institute of Art* 59, 1, 1981, pp. 5-15; see also Hobbs, *Beauty Reconfigured*, pp. 138-140.

15. Newspaper clipping (undated) from a scrapbook in the Windsor, VT, Library.

16. Gerdts, p. 178.

17. The quotations about Dewing's social life in Cornish come from Hobbs, *Beauty Reconfigured*, pp. 20-21; 27. For the first set of quotations, Hobbs cites the "Reminiscences of Frances Grimes."

18. Hugh Mason Wade, *A Brief History of Cornish* (Hanover, NH: University Press of New England, 1976; reprinted 1991), pp. 52, 54; Homer Saint-Gaudens, "The American Artist and His Times," p. 171.

19. Hobbs, *Beauty Reconfigured*, p. 43.

20. Ibid, p. 53. Hobbs believes that Maria is "the principal catalyst that brought about Dewing's shift from the French academic style he had acquired in Paris into the mode that marked him as an adherent to Pre-Raphaelitism in the context of the American Aesthetic movement" (pp. 53-54).

21. Hobbs, "Thomas Wilmer Dewing: The Early Years, 1851-1885," p. 27.

22. Jennifer Martin (Bienenstock), "Portraits of Flowers: The Out-of-Door Still-Life Paintings of Maria Oakey Dewing," *American Art Review* 4, (December 1977), p. 114.

23. Ibid., pp. 115-116.

24. Ibid., p. 118. Martin's article contains illustrations of both out-of-door and indoor still-life flower paintings Maria Dewing did; for an illustration of *Irises*, done in 1899 during her time in Cornish, see Virginia Tuttle Clayton, "Reminiscence and Revival: The Old-Fashioned Garden, 1890-1910," *The Magazine Antiques* 140, 4, April 1990, pp. 892-905.

FRANCES DUNCAN
1877 – 1972

EDUCATED AT DWIGHT MOODY'S NORTHFIELD SEMINARY in Northfield, Massachusetts, Frances Duncan had to work her way up from the bottom to establish her career. After many years of work in a nursery learning about plants and shrubs, she landed a job as an assistant editor for the popular magazine *Country Calendar,* an important publication in the country-life movement during the early decades of this century. When she became the *The Ladies' Home Journal*'s first garden editor in 1907, an influential position, she had already launched her career as a horticulture writer by visiting Cornish in 1905 to prepare an article on Maxfield Parrish's house and its gardens. The subtitle of her article in the *Country Calendar* for September 1905 clearly displays the perspective she brought to bear on all that she wrote, whether about Parrish or someone else: "art in craftsmanship." A dominant theme throughout all of her writing was that a garden was simply an outgrowth of the house, that a garden was an extension of the living room.

Her description of Parrish's garden at "The Oaks" recreated her visit early in 1905; it begins with passing "the Churchill Inn" and climbing "an unconscionably steep hill": "the site is, for Cornish, a thoroughly characteristic one—a rough sheep pasture which, seen from the distance, seems to rise up clear against the sky." From the loggia that Parrish has built, "one looks down a valley wonderfully rich in that picturesqueness of landscape which is so integral a part of Mr. Parrish's work." The article savors the craftsmanship Parrish displayed in designing and building the house; it "reflects his own skill at architecture, gardening, carpentry, and applied art." For example, the "kitchen over which William Morris, were he permitted to see it, would shed tears of joy . . . is perfectly finished, every detail of fine workmanship." An interesting sidelight to her visit was observing, in Parrish's as yet unfinished studio, "a marvel of a centaur, with barrel-hoop ribs and a [delightful] hock-action" that was to have a role "in the masque given by the Cornish Colony on the twentieth anniversary of its founding by Augustus Saint-Gaudens," that is *A Masque of "Ours": The Gods, and the Golden Bowl* presented on the grounds of "Aspet," June 22, 1905.[1]

The next year she returned to Cornish in order to write a comprehensive article with many photographs on "The Gardens of Cornish" for *The Century Magazine.* Cornish is "one of the most hopeful spots which any believer in the future of the American garden art can visit" because it is a place "where the art instinct is the strongest, and where desecrating and devitalizing standards do not obtain." A problem the terrain offers her contemporaries is not one necessarily faced today: the countryside "is not precisely what one might call 'gardenable'" because the "Cornish hills are bare." For this reason she finds much to admire in the work, which she calls "art," of Charles Platt because he "composed" both the house and the garden as well as adapting them to the contours of the site. In addition to mentioning Platt's own house, Duncan discusses "Highcourt," which Platt built for Annie Lazarus and was then owned by Norman Hapgood; she particularly commends the "composition" of Stephen Parrish's house "Northcote." The second feature of the Cornish gardens she admired was "the almost invariable subordination of the garden to the view." Again, "Highcourt" is praised because: "as

Figure 66. *The poplars at Augustus Saint-Gaudens's house, from Frances Duncan's "The Gardens of Cornish," published in* Century Magazine, *May 1906.*

one enters from the north, and looks directly through the wide doors to mountains far enough away in the blue distance to be seen in their dreamy, poetic beauty of outline, the wisdom of placing the gardens at the east of the house is at once felt; for, after lifting up one's eyes unto such hills, the gay color of the flower-beds would have seemed almost garish." Stephen Parrish's house and garden are almost inseparable; his garden is "one of the most satisfying and one of the most individual." Duncan pays a great deal of attention to the kinds of trees and plants that are appropriate for both the climate and the "composition" of the site. In doing so, she also discusses other members of the Colony: Henry O. Walker, Maxfield Parrish, Thomas Dewing, William Henry Hyde, Louis Evan Shipman, Kenyon Cox, Augustus Saint-Gaudens (to whom she was not shy about giving horticultural advice), Rose Standish Nichols, Herbert Croly, and Mrs. Frances C. Houston. In summarizing her fondness for Cornish gardens, she notes that they "are livable, lovable spots, on very intimate terms with their owners . . . Perhaps the intimacy of gardens and owners is due to the fact that no Cornish garden is given over to the care of a hireling—each is in the keeping of its owner." This bond inspired her to define her conception of an ideal garden: "it is not sacred and a thing apart . . . it is simply an outgrowth of the house, an out-of-door living room, to be used and changed if one pleases, until one finds the best possible arrangement."[2]

The following year *Country Life in America* published a major article that Duncan wrote about Stephen Parrish, "An Artist's New Hampshire Garden." She goes into great detail about what Parrish planted and why he did so as well as describing the effects of Cornish's cold winters on the plants.[3] More of her philosophy of gardening can be seen as she notes "the sincerity and delicate perception which are so integral a part of Mr. Parrish's work in his painting of landscapes are surely present in his garden craft, for gardening after all, is merely another expression of a man's art."[4] Two other Colony members about whose houses and gardens she wrote were Rose Nichols and Henry Fuller.

Cornish greatly influenced one of her contributions to a genre of writing popular in the early twentieth century known as the "garden novel." In 1914 Doubleday, Page brought out *My Garden Doctor* in which Cornish becomes the town of Enderby and in which Duncan "describes the healing effects of making a garden in the shadow of Mount Ascutney, among the low hills along the Connecticut." When *The New York Times* reviewed it, they instantly saw its relation to the country-life movement. They noted that her book "proclaims the gospel that Mother Earth is the best doctor for maladies of the nerves . . . better an abandoned farm than a sanatarium."[5]

Frances Duncan never owned property in Cornish, despite her love for the town, but she did rent several places. One was the Cherry Hill Farm on Dingleton Hill; the house and road it faced are now gone.[6] While she was here, she became quite caught up in the Women's Suffrage Movement and was a member of the Cornish Equal Suffrage League.[7] In 1908 she took in an eleven-year-old girl, Lavinia (Evelyn) Granger, to live with her because the girl's mother had recently died. When Lavinia was grown and married, her children affectionately referred to Frances Duncan as "Grammy Ducky."[8]

Eventually Duncan left Cornish and married John Manning on May 18, 1944. They moved to Burbank, California, where she became involved in advocating an increase in the number and quality of children's playgrounds. In addition to writing many articles and several books, she was the founder of the Woman's National Garden Association and the Cactus and Succulent Society of America. She died September 5, 1972, in Monrovia, California.[9]

ENDNOTES

1. The quotations in this paragraph come from Frances Duncan, "Maxfield Parrish's Home and How He Built It—Art in Craftsmanship," *The Country Calendar* 1, 5, September 1905, pp. 435-437.

2. See Frances Duncan, "The Gardens of Cornish," *The Century Magazine* 72, 1, May 1906, pp. 3-19. Of further interest is an article, "The Architectural Treatment of a Small Garden," that she "reshaped" based on a conversation with Charles Platt and Roger Riodan, pp. 35-36, in the same magazine. For her remarks about the garden Rose Nichols planned, see below p. 292.

3. *Country Life in America* 11, March 1907, pp. 516-520, 554, 556, 558.

4. Ibid., p. 556.

5. Both quotations in this paragraph are taken from Virginia Lopez Begg, "Frances Duncan: The 'New Woman' in the Garden," *Journal of the New England Garden History Society* 2, Fall 1992, pp. 32-33. Begg, p. 35, n. 1, also provides a list of Duncan's five other books: *Mary's Garden and How It Grew* (New York: The Century Company,

1904), *When Mother Let Us Garden* (New York: Moffat, Yard, 1909), *Roberta of Rose-berry Gardens* (Garden City, NY: Doubleday, Page, 1916), *The Joyous Art of Gardening* (New York: Charles Scribner's Sons, 1917), and *Home Vegetables and Small Fruits* (New York: Charles Scribner's Sons, 1918).

6. Interview: Virginia Colby with Frances Eastman, January 28, 1992.

7. Brochure, Cornish Equal Suffrage League, Cornish, NH, 1911; see also *The Los Angeles Times*, August 26, 1956, part 9, p. 9. The paper interviewed their former garden writer on the thirtieth anniversary of the passing of the Nineteenth Amendment to the Constitution. In her seventy-ninth year, she found "today's women, for all their boldness in displaying their persons and entering bars, are sissies and timid when it comes to political opinions and working for causes." See also below p. 470 for her marching activity and connection with Marie Dressler.

8. Interview: Virginia Colby with Frances Eastman, February 17, 1992.

9. See *The Los Angeles Times*, April 21, 1947, and Deborah E. Van Buren, "Landscape Architecture and Gardens in the Cornish Colony: the Careers of Rose Nichols, Ellen Shipman, and Frances Duncan," *Women's Studies* 14, 1988, pp. 367-388.

ISADORA DUNCAN
1878 – 1927

Figure 67. *Isadora Duncan, The Dover Street Studios, London. Hand inscribed by Isadora Duncan, "For my Friend Robert Barrett."*

ISADORA DUNCAN was one of the most significant figures in the history of the dance. Modern notions of the ballet originated in the extravagant displays in the courts of the Italian Renaissance. But in the early twentieth century, innovators in America were trying to free the dance from the formality traditional ballet required. "It was the combination of a ballet girl's body with the American untamed spirit that produced our first solo dancers and our first native art form. The difference between Isadora and the rest is that, as a creator of forms rather than of styles, she refused to settle for the commercial theater on any terms."[1]

Duncan, who grew up in poverty and insecurity in San Francisco and moved to New York City in 1918, was in the forefront of these efforts to effect a creative, living art based on free natural movement. She insisted that a dancer should seek to improvise movements rooted in the human body—she practically defined the solar plexus—and in the spontaneous rhythms of nature. To do so, even as a child, she would run barefoot along the Pacific shore imitating the ocean's rippling rhythms and the clouds' floating motions. Later, she would constantly refer to the solar plexus as the "central spring of all movement," even though most people had not given that area of the body a second thought prior to her announcement.

When she finally arrived in New York, she became the darling of high society by dancing in private performances both in the city and in the fashionable homes of Newport, Rhode Island. There she began to haunt museums to learn about Greek sculpture and to study the figures on Greek vases. She transformed these ideas into her interpretive dances that shocked audiences because she appeared in bare feet and wore only a loose fitting, clinging, and revealing tunic. Her tours took her from Carnegie Hall and the Metropolitan Opera House to London, where she danced before Queen Victoria, Paris, Vienna, Budapest, Berlin, and Moscow. Many people soon began to realize that her truly innovative contribution to the dance was her ability to dance and interpret the music, not merely to dance with or to the music.

Her innovations, however, did not meet with universal approval. A review, appearing in *The Nation* for November 14, 1912, of the book *Modern Dancing and Dancers* was not quite so enthralled with Duncan's achievements: "One regrets, after the author's sane

Figure 68. *Pen and ink drawing of Isadora Duncan dancing by Abraham Walkowitz.*

remarks . . . to find him gushing like a school girl over the artificial and ludicrous antics of Isadora Duncan in her efforts to revive classical dancing by assuming the attitudes of figures on Greek vases while 'interpreting' modern symphonies and piano pieces."[2] Nevertheless, that did not prevent someone like Walter Damrosch, who had his own connections with the Cornish Colony (see below p. 467), from being proud to play for her with his symphony orchestra.[3]

Her own connection with Cornish actually began in New York City where, in November of 1908, William Vaughn Moody and Percy MacKaye attended one of her performances and visited her in her studio later on: we "sat together there, spellbound as by some vision out of Beethoven's mind become then unbelievably corporeal; and afterward in Isadora's blue-curtained studio at the Windsor Arcade . . . I introduced to her our group of poets whom her autobiography refers to as 'young revolutionists.'"[4] The "big play" may well have been MacKaye's *Caliban, by the Yellow Sands,* a masque he wrote for the three hundredth anniversary of Shakespeare's death. Duncan danced at the opening performance in May of 1916. Arvia MacKaye's portrait of Isadora captures some of her beauty: "My memory of her as she came and sat beside us is of an unusually beautiful woman, in soft flowing garments, with large eyes of an almost tragic depth and beauty. It is the mystery and beauty of these large wonderful eyes which stays with me especially. There was an extraordinary harmony in her every motion, and it seemed as though she had just stepped out of an heroic, beauty-imbued age of former times."[5]

Percy MacKaye even considered sending Arvia to learn dance at Duncan's school for dance, one with extremely offbeat rules. Children had to be given over to her until they were twenty-one, they were to be between six and nine years of age, and possess "a certain amount of artistic feeling," but they were not charged any tuition.[6] None of her schools survived her death, but that did not prevent MacKaye from traveling to Palm Beach in 1917 where he helped sketch out a plan for a dancing school there. He had written a beautiful poem after seeing the children dance. Isadora, in gratitude presented him with an autographed picture of herself.[7]

In addition to MacKaye, the famous dancer had other admirers among the Cornish Colony. Marguerite Quimby remembered that Isadora stayed with the Rublees when she visited Cornish.[8] The two women had much in common since Juliet Rublee was also a dancer and danced at public functions—especially for *Sanctuary: A Bird Masque* that Percy MacKaye wrote for Ernest Harold Baynes in 1913. In either 1925 or 1926, shortly before her tragic death, Maxfield Parrish, Jr., recalled an evening when Isadora danced at a party in the music room in his father's house, "The Oaks." Apparently she was a bit past her prime by then: "her knees were cracking something awful. Everyone wanted to laugh but dared not. All of Cornish was there, and as the music room emptied and everybody walked out the front (red) door, M[axfield] P[arrish] and S[tephen] P[arrish] were at the front of the procession. M.P. said in a low voice to S.P., 'Her knees rang out like pistol shots,' and S.P., a convulsive laugher, broke up with uncontrolled hysterical laughter. Nobody in the procession heard what M.P. said, but they all exploded with laughter, knowing exactly what started the laughter, and each holding on to himself as long as he could. But once out on the greensward, everyone let go."[9]

Her life and loves have been frequently dramatized, but her death was surely a singular one. "Penniless and at the end of her career, she pretended that she wanted to buy a flashy Bugatti sport car, which she had delivered to her for a test ride with the handsome driver. Wearing a long, red scarf wrapped around her neck, she climbed in, announcing 'Adieu, mes amis, je vais à la gloire' ('Farewell, my friends, I go to glory'). As the car lurched forward, the scarf caught in the spokes of a wheel and she was strangled."[10]

ENDNOTES

1. Dale Harris, "Creators of a Native Art Form," a review of Elizabeth Kendall, *Where She Danced* and Marcia Siegel, *The Shapes of Change* in *The New York Times Book Review,* July 1, 1979, p. 9.

2. *The Nation* (95, #2472) November 14, 1912, p. 466.

3. *Bulletin for the New York Public Library,* Isadora Duncan Index, 76, 1972, pp. 181-198.

4. William Vaughn Moody, *Letters to Harriet,* edited with an introduction and conclusion by Percy MacKaye (Boston: Houghton Mifflin, 1935), p. 63; see also Arvia MacKaye Ege, *The Power of The Impossible: The Life Story of Percy and Marion MacKaye* (Falmouth, ME: The Kennebec River Press, 1992), p. 192, where it is noted that MacKaye is much interested in Duncan, "who is making quite an impression now. Rob Barrett is also much interested in her. Percy has an idea for a big play with Fred Converse, Margaret Anglin, Isadora Duncan, and himself."

5. Ege, p. 258.

6. *The New York Evening Sun,* November 20, 1914.

7. Interview: Virginia Colby with Christy MacKaye Barnes, August 4, 1980.

8. Interview: Virginia Colby with Marguerite Quimby, October 12, 1980.

9. Interview: Virginia Colby with Maxfield Parrish, Jr., March 26, 1979.

10. "The Creators," *U.S. News & World Report,* August 31/September 7, 1992, p. 103.

FINLEY PETER DUNNE
1867 – 1936

FINLEY PETER DUNNE, an American journalist and humorist, created the philosopher-saloonkeeper of Archey Road known throughout the country as "Mr. Dooley." The latter's criticisms from the political and social angle of the Spanish-American War and its results made Dunne famous both in England and the United States. He began his series with *Mr. Dooley in Peace and War.*

Franklin P. Adams, the well-known humorist, praised Dunne because "he revered the art of saying things perfectly; he hated slovenliness of thought and expression." Noting that the "Dooley" pieces were in reality "caustic and witty editorials written in the Irish dialect," Adams argued that "the expression of that social consciousness as articulated in the 'Dooley' sketches would never have been printed unless they had been written in dialect." Furthermore, Dunne wrote "maliciously" and "bitterly" because he "resented injustice . . . loathed sham, and . . . hated the selfish stupidity that went with them. Anger, and a warm sympathy for the underprivileged underlay about all the 'Dooley' sketches."[1]

Dunne spent the summer of 1903 in Cornish occupying the house of the artist Henry Oliver Walker. Stephen Parrish notes in his diary for May 22, 1903, that he "called at Dunne's (Mr. Dooley), who has Walker's house."[2]

In his own inimitable way, Mr. Dooley characterized the Cornish Colony in an article entitled "Mr. Dooley—On Vacation." Mr. Hennessy remarks, "as he dropped in for his usual morning call,"

> "Ye don't look much chang'd" . . .
> "Chang'd! No wan changes very much, Hinnissy, afther reachin' the age of dischreschun—which is about forty-five years" . . .
> "But where in th' wurruld have ye bein' all summer," asked Mr. Hennessy.
> "I've been baskin', Hinnissy, in th' blissful rays iv th' most illusthryus min iv th' counthry—th' poets an' thrue histhry writhers, an' sculpchoors, an' th' gr-reatest lights iv th' sinchoory—thims that inhabit stately manshuns in Cornish, an' stay most iv th' time in Noo-Yor-rk or Bosthon or Philidelphy or Windsor, or wan iv' th' big cities.
> "An' it's th' idale spot f'r wan to rest an' ray-coopirate; f'r ye can see the gould'n chain iv th' green mountains loomin' up in th' disthance, that'd make ye think iv th' ol'

Figure 69. Mr. *Dooley and Mr. Hennessy, by E. W. Kemble, frontispiece from* Mr. Dooley's Philosophy.

sod an' that ye was young again. An' to complate the pitchoor ye'er imaginayshun is dhrawin' f'r ye, ye've th' extinsive do-mains iv th' Kinnidays, thim as own'd half Tipp'rary in th' days iv Brian-bo-roo, stretchin' out in a glory'us pan-o-rammy befure ye. An' over for'ninst ye, raises th' proud walls iv th' house where th' constitooshun was born an' nurs'd, as Hogan wud say; an th' silf-same craydle in which th' mother iv raypublics rock'd th' green mountain state gintly to sleep.

"An' thin ye turn ye'er fataygu'd gaze on th' raysplindint Corbin Par-rk, where that gintl'man keeps his buffalos prancin' up an' down, thinkin' they ar-re not far from Saint Anthony's in Texas, while they're not a stone's throw fr'm Saint Gordon's in Noo-Hamsheer. But to lay eyes on th' deers, Hinnissy, 't w'ud do ye'er ol' heart gude—with their tall, noble antilleers lift'd proudly towards th' hivens—jist like the masts of me cousin George's flag ship, afther brav'ly sinkin' th' rottin' tubs iv th' hated Spanyards in Manila Bay. An' thin there's th' gran' scenes ye can't see until ye git down to 'em—th' toll-bridge an' th' cream'ry an' Hammon's folly an' th' majestic Connecticut with its placid wathers rollin' rapidly by, thryin' to bate me frind Winston with his noo automobele. There's nawthing like a vacayshun, Hinnissy—excipt wan spint in Cornish."[3]

ENDNOTES

1. The quotation in this paragraph came from Finley Peter Dunne, *Mr. Dooley at his Best*, ed. Elmer Ellis, foreword by Franklin P. Adams (New York: Scribner's Sons, 1938), pp. xiii, xvii, xviii.

2. Stephen Parrish, diary. Baker Library, Dartmouth College, Hanover, NH, gift of Marian and Roy Garrand.

3. Unidentified clipping, probably from 1904, from an unidentified scrapbook, Virginia Colby, Cornish Colony files.

JOHN ELLIOTT
1859 – 1925

Figure 70.

JOHN ELLIOTT, the artist and muralist, was born in Lincolnshire, England, on April 22, 1859. He studied in Paris at the Académie Julian under Carolus-Duran at the same time that Kenyon Cox and John Singer Sargent were students there. In 1878 he went to Rome, where he studied with Jose di Villegas, later the director of the Prado Museum and official painter to the Spanish Court. In Rome he also met his future wife, Maud Howe, the daughter of the author of "The Battle Hymn of the Republic," Julia Ward Howe. Both mother and daughter were on the Grand Tour. After years of casual meetings on the continent, John and Maud were married at Julia Howe's Boston home in 1887.

In characterizing his art, a contemporary critic noted that a "decorative quality of [an] intensely individual sort marks all of [his] landscapes and figure sketches . . . [he] sees nature from the decorator's standpoint, selecting mainly the facts of form and color that conform to a preconceived scheme of a harmony of line and tone."[1]

It is interesting to note that these general remarks were made at the end of the same year that John Elliott and his wife spent their first summer in Cornish where they had rented the home of Henry and Edith Prellwitz. Mrs. Frances Houston, as well as both Lucia and Henry Fuller, acted as the couple's sponsors in Cornish society. It did not take them long to become attached to the area. In 1904 they bought twenty acres of pasture land from Elmer DeGoosh along with some woodland from N. E. Williams and Walter Williams—all in Plainfield.[2] "Jack" Elliott named the little farm he bought "Farthest North" (now occupied by George Grabe). A friend, "Long Mike" Stillman, helped them design their new kitchen ell that, according to Maud was "the best of all the many kitchens I have presided over."[3] "Long Mike" was destined to play a heroic part in the history of American art. He was visiting the Elliotts in October of 1904, the night of the disastrous fire at the studio of Augustus Saint-Gaudens. Arriving early on the scene, Stillman noticed the unfinished statue of Phillips Brooks: "with one wrench he pulled the head of clay from its shoulders, and carried it to safety."[4] Shortly before his death, Saint-Gaudens, thanks to this valiant effort, was able to complete the monument, which was to be erected outside Trinity Church in Boston's Copley Square.

Although friends from far and near visited them while they summered here, Maud Elliott mentions that their particular friends in the area were the Herbert Adamses and

Figure 71. *"The Ocean Giant" from* The Great Sea Horse *by Isabel Anderson, illustrated by John Elliott, 1909.*

Finley Peter Dunne, the creator of Mr. Dooley. Both of them were active enough in Colony activities to have roles in the 1905 production of *Masque of "Ours": The Gods and the Golden Bowl* presented to Saint-Gaudens: John Elliott was Momus and Maud was Pomona. (In 1892 John Elliott had been commissioned to paint a fifty square-foot ceiling of the Boston Public Library, which he finished in 1901 as the huge *Triumph of Time* mural; since Saint-Gaudens was an advisor to the library project, Elliott probably knew Saint-Gaudens then.) But despite these influential connections, Maud was quick to point out that "our neighbor Farmer Read and his wife were our warm friends. Jack enjoyed forgathering with them far more than any social festivities. The farmers could teach him many things, and he never tired of their talk of 'crops an critters.' "[5]

Be that as it may, it was still Mount Ascutney that attracted him most. In a letter to Maud dated November 1, 1903, he writes "I am sitting out on the Houstons' piazza writing this, with the sun shining and a gentle warm breeze blowing and the wonderful 'mounting' in front of me—a deep plum colored bloom over it, so

Figure 72. *Studio of John Elliott at "Farthest North."*

beautiful that it is beyond description." In that same letter he announces the closing on the property that, according to Maud, "looked out upon a scene he called the Val d'Arno—it was so like the valley of the Arno near Florence."[6] As a matter of fact, there is quite a correlation between his feeling for the Cornish-Plainfield area and how he captures it on canvas, at least if we can credit the words of the same Boston art critic quoted above. In one view of Ascutney, "the birch trees, thrown up against the mountain almost in silhouette, yet with just a trace of modelling, a touch of local color, make extremely poetic passages, lovely in refinement of line." In another view "the pattern is as thoughtful as in the work of the great Japanese artists, and conjoined with it goes a certain sensibility to external reality that is occidental and practical. Still another noble view of the mountain is . . . a harmony of pale purples and yellows, all bound together with subtle little balances, thrusts and counterthrusts." And finally, "'Moonlight, Lawton's Valley' is a thoroughly masterful study of light falling over a meadow stream. The feeling of evening peace that suffuses it is doubtless due to the soothing color and values, which are particularly unobtrusive."[7]

The best record of Elliott's achievements as an artist, however, is Maud Elliott's book about her husband. In it she emerges as someone with whom to reckon, despite her tone of deference to him. She and her two sisters wrote a two-volume biography of their famous mother for which they won a Pulitzer Prize for biography.[8] Maud also took on some local obligations. She spoke at a meeting of the Mothers' and Daughters' Club in Plainfield. She describes the organization as one "for the farmers' wives, to help the women out of their very narrow lives by giving them a simple and exact account of the daily habits of life."[9] Nevertheless, she felt most at home with the "city folks," as Winston Churchill called them, because "the atmosphere of work counts for something too . . . it is stimulating to be among people of our own sort who observe as a sacred commandment the rule that nobody goes to anybody else's house till four or five in the afternoon."[10]

Although John Elliott worked in oil, pastels, silverpoints, and miniatures on ivory, his greatest achievements were works executed on a large scale. In addition to *The Triumph of Time* for the Boston Public Library, there was the huge twenty-five feet long and eleven feet high *Diana of the Tides* (now in the Paleontology Hall of The Smithsonian Institute in Washington, DC). It is "akin to the Boston Library ceiling in its employment of horses symbolically, its light, luminous color, and its subtle play of illumination."[11] Furthermore, it "is a striking example of modernity in art; an expression of the scientific spirit of this age in the traditional terms of gracious imagery inherited from classic times with the impersonations of natural forces as well as of emotional and primal passions that characterized the aesthetic conceptions of the ancients."[12] A similar allegorical painting, *The Story of the Vintage*, was done for Potter Palmer's private home in Chicago, Illinois, the entrepreneur who built Chicago's Palmer House Hotel. Elliott was also an excellent portraitist; he painted foreign royalty and did several famous portraits of his mother-in-law, of whom he was very fond.

Because Julia Ward Howe was a *grande dame* of Newport, Rhode Island society, the Elliotts spent a great deal of time there later in their lives. They were founders of the Newport, Rhode Island Art Association. In a "Tribute" that was connected with an exhibition of his works in 1925, we are reminded that "around the substantial and beautiful character of John Elliott, there was an aura of the charming culture, and the elevated taste that dwell only with those who seek and know the best. These attributes were drawn from . . . his long and intimate touch with whatever America has to give of truth and beauty."

ENDNOTES

1. Unidentified review from a December 1903 Boston newspaper, Windsor Library scrapbook, Windsor, VT.

2. Tax records, Plainfield, NH.

3. Maud Howe Elliott, *John Elliott: The Story of an Artist* (Boston and New York: Houghton Mifflin, 1930), p. 141.

4. Ibid., pp. 141-142.

5. Ibid., p. 143.

6. Ibid., p. 139-140. In an entry dated August 15, 1903, written in Cornish, she adds, "I never could describe the world I see from this hilltop—the mountain opposite is a sort of Fujiyama; people become magnetized by its beauty. Every morning we watch for the moment when the veil of mist is dropped and the dark blue beauty of Mount Ascutney shines out on us," Maud Howe Elliott, *Three Generations* (Boston: Little, Brown, and Company, 1923) p. 312; see also p. 313.

7. Unidentified review, Windsor Library scrapbook, Windsor, VT. Concerning the first quotation, Maud Elliott notes that "in Cornish, Jack made many paintings of the silver birch, his favorite tree," p. 142.

8. Laura E. Richards and Maud Howe Elliott, *Julia Ward Howe, 1819-1910* (New York and Boston: Houghton Mifflin, 1916).

9. Maud Howe Elliott, "Self-Help for Country Women," *Harper's Bazaar* 43, March 1909, pp. 269-273.

10. Maud Howe Elliott, *Three Generations*, p. 313.

11. Walter Prichard Eaton, "The Painter of 'Diana of the Tides,'" *Everybody's Magazine*, July 1910, p. 98.

12. Sylvester Baxter, "'Diana of the Tides': A Notable Gift to the Nation," *Art and Progress* 1, 7, May 1910, p. 195.

BARRY FAULKNER

1881 – 1966

ALTHOUGH THE PAINTER-MURALIST BARRY FAULKNER, who was born in Keene, New Hampshire, July 12, 1881, is most generally thought of in connection with the art colony in Dublin, New Hampshire, he also had strong ties with the Cornish Colony. When he was twenty years old, and through his friendship with Homer Saint-Gaudens during his freshman year at Harvard, Barry came to Cornish to visit both son and father—as well as the latter's studio: "The studio life at Cornish surprised and excited me. . . . Here was a world of collaboration in the arts, exhilarating and undreamed of."[1] In the years immediately after 1901—even until 1917, Faulkner was fortunate to visit "Aspet" on various occasions and to work in that famous studio under the guidance of "The Saint," as Saint-Gaudens was affectionately known to his assistants.

While he was in Cornish during his twenties, he became a founding member of the Cornish Equal Suffrage League in 1911.[2] He often boarded then with Mrs. George Ruggles and used Ruggles's studio. There he met Cliff Young, who later would assist Faulkner with two sets of murals: one, *The Constitution of the United States* and the *Declaration of Independence* done from 1934 to 1936 for the National Archives building in Washington, DC; the second, *The Opening of the Chesire Railroad, Keene, New Hampshire, May 16, 1848,* done in 1955 for the Chesire County Savings Bank in Keene, New Hampshire—what "was perhaps the most important commercial event in Keene's history—the first railway to cross Main Street."[3] Young continued his connection with Cornish by completing the murals in the United States Capitol Building that were left unfinished when Allyn Cox, Kenyon Cox's son, retired in 1981 at the age of eighty-five.

Cornish left a vivid impression on Faulkner. His description of it reminds us of its persistent beauty:

> The landscape of Cornish was a revelation of delight: the downpouring of the hills into rich meadows by the Connecticut River, the domination of Mount Ascutney, towering over land and river; the size and density of oak, maple, and birch, nourished by heavy river fogs and the grand bulk of the giant white pine, all these filled me with wonder. Aspet itself was rich in white pine, which often grew in protected gullies, and in one of these ravines, near the house, were a brook and icy swimming pool. There, as I splashed in it, the pines seemed to touch the sky.[4]

During World War I, Faulkner continued his connection with Cornish in a somewhat roundabout fashion. Faulkner was a cousin of Abbott Thayer, a bulwark of the Dublin Art Colony (see below pp. 504-505). He knew, worked, and studied with Thayer so that he was in a good position to paint the mural *Abbott Thayer: Painter and Scientist: In His New Hampshire Studio, Thayer Explains the Theory of Protective Coloration*, 1909 depicting Daniel Chester French, Mrs. Thayer, George de Forest Brush, Faulkner himself, Alexander James, Abbott Thayer, and Mary Thayer; the mural was done much later—in 1942—for the state house in Concord, New Hampshire. But back in 1909, because of his interest in the adaptive coloration of birds and animals to their environment, Thayer had published *Concealing Coloration in the Animal Kingdom*. Although he had a difficult time convincing military leaders of its potential, there eventually was a Camouflage Corps, the Fortieth Engineers, that became part of the United States Army. Its commanding officer was none other than Homer Saint-Gaudens; Faulkner enlisted in the unit, too, and was eventually commissioned as an officer. Another officer in the Camouflage Corps was Harry Thrasher, "a talented and good-natured Cornish lad,"[5] whom Faulkner had met in 1904 when he was living at the Westgate farm and they had both been assistants for Saint-Gaudens in his studio. Unfortunately, Faulkner had the unenviable duty of identifying Thrasher's body after a disastrous attack in "Death Valley" near Dravegny, France, in August of 1918. Following the war, Faulkner collaborated on a memorial to this slain

Fellow of the American Academy in Rome by designing a fresco for it; the memorial was sponsored by this organization (see below pp. 413-417) and also worked on by another Cornish Colony member, Paul Manship.

Figure 73. *Charles Platt, grandson of architect Charles A. Platt, posed for* The Childhood of Daniel Webster *mural in the New Hampshire state house, painted by Barry Faulkner.*

Figure 74. *A mural painted by Barry Faulkner in Elliot Community Hospital, now part of Keene State College.*

Charles and Eleanor Platt offered Barry Faulkner the use of a vacant room in their house in Cornish for a studio during the summer of 1933 and had little awareness of how that would lead to another Cornish connection for Faulkner. In 1933 the Platts found living accommodations for him with Ralph and Susie Jordan in Plainfield, and this was also a time when Frances Grimes urged him to buy a one-seated Ford Roadster.[6] Later during the early years of World War II, Faulkner persuaded Charles A. Platt, the son of William Platt and grandson of the Cornish Colony architect Charles A. Platt, to pose for a mural *The Childhood of Daniel Webster*, now part of the series done in 1942 for the state house in Concord, New Hampshire. It took a bit of coaxing, however: the mural shows a young Daniel Webster kneeling in front of a copy of the recently ratified Constitution, but the young Charles Platt agreed to pose only if he could do so in a new baseball uniform he had just received as a birthday present. Mr. Platt now maintains a house in Cornish and also serves as a trustee of the Saint-Gaudens Memorial. Incidentally, the mural scene is a general store in Salisbury, New Hampshire; the face of the proprietor's wife is that of Mrs. Archibald Cox (granddaughter of Maxwell Evarts, mother of the well-known Washington lawyer, and former late resident of Windsor, Vermont).

A final connection with the area was a series of mural panels Faulkner did for the Oregon State Capitol Building in 1937 and 1938. He drew the head of Hazel Gibson Amidon of Plainfield, who served as the model for the *Apple Girl* in one of the murals.

In the 1980s there were three local exhibitions that honored Barry Faulkner; the catalogues for these shows offer some interesting information. The Keene Public Library held a show when they dedicated the library's restored Faulkner drawings in April of 1984, the Indian Head National Bank issued a commemorative booklet in October of 1987 at their reopening and featured his *Men of Monadnock*, and the Historical Society of Cheshire County held a combined Harry Thrasher-Barry Faulkner show in November of 1987.

The moving tribute, recorded in the minutes of the American Academy in Rome at his death on October 2, 1966, can make Cornish proud of its association with him: "Barry Faulkner shared his wide interests with friends of all ages. He woke them to new aspects of the visual world. He saw the good and pointed out the fine and creative. He saw without prejudice the difference between one artist and another and one time and another. He was a delightful companion, a cultivated and civilized man, a wise critic, a distinguished artist. All his life he worked at his painting and worked for the arts."[7]

ENDNOTES

1. Barry Faulkner, *Barry Faulkner: Sketches from an Artist's Life* (Dublin, NH: William L. Bauhan, 1973), pp. 34-35.
2. Virginia Colby, Cornish Colony files.
3. Faulkner, p. 4.
4. Ibid., p. 32.
5. Ibid., p. 57.
6. Ibid., p. 139.
7. Ibid., pp. xi-xii.

ADMIRAL WILLIAM MAYHEW FOLGER
1844 – 1928

ADMIRAL FOLGER was a distinguished summer resident of Cornish for some thirty years. He bought property from Charles Gilkie on Platt Road in 1898. Descended from a long line of Nantucket seafarers, one of whom charted the waters of the Gulf Stream with the financial backing of Benjamin Franklin, Folger himself made no small contribution to naval history. He was graduated from the United States Naval Academy in 1864, briefly saw service in the Civil War, and was subsequently assigned to the Asiatic Squadron. He advanced steadily through the ranks and was appointed rear admiral in 1904. He saw service with the Washington Navy Yard and with the Bureau of Ordinance in Washington, which he headed from 1890 to 1903. During the Spanish American War he commanded the USS New Orleans which saw considerable action in Cuban waters. Earlier in 1898 he commanded the Philippine Squadron of the Asiatic Fleet, then headed the cruiser squadron of the Asiatic Fleet, and, shortly before his retirement in 1905 he was put in charge of the entire Asiatic Fleet.[1]

On the Cornish tax list, Admiral Folger is credited with owning fifty-two acres, two to three horses, two cows, and two carriages that, after 1914, became two vehicles. On the Plainfield tax records, he is listed as owning a sawmill yard; the rough lumber and framework for his house was cut from this mill.[2] But the nature of his commitment to agriculture is gently undercut by the testimony of Hubert Deming, his caretaker from 1918 to 1928:[3] "He was a hard one to work for. Everything had to be done by the clock, and the way he'd say. He didn't know anything about farming. He had a patch of potatoes and corn and he called it farming, but it was just amusement for him. It was like being in the navy to work for him. I always wondered why he didn't fire me or why I didn't quit. Each one kept one foot on the ground, I guess."[4]

While working for Admiral Folger, Mr. Deming lived in "The Snuff Box." This was a shingle cottage on the estate that was Mrs. Folger's project. She named it because she thought it looked like a little snuff box. So much so was it her project that she even had to pay the taxes on it.[5] But an earlier inhabitant, from 1904 to 1906, was the poet Percy MacKaye, who found great respite among those with interests similar to his in the Cornish Colony: "in the tiny Snuff Box [the MacKayes] took a deep breath and with the 'snuff of New England air' in their nostrils entered with joyful zest into the life of the far-flung neighborhood."[6]

Figure 75. *Admiral Folger's residence.*

The Folgers entered into the life of the community, too, and not merely in the summer. Stephen Parrish notes a good time spent at the Folgers' pond during an ice-skating party for the neighbors.[7] That the Folgers must have added to the wit of the Cornish Colony can be seen from an amusing interchange that is reported about them. The Admiral once said, "When I snap my finger, many men jump" and Mrs. Folger replied, "When I snap my finger, one man jumps."

Admiral Folger died in Cornish on July 22, 1928.

ENDNOTES

1. This paragraph is based on Hugh Mason Wade, *A Brief History of Cornish, New Hampshire: 1763-1974* (Hanover, NH: University Press of New England, 1976), p. 72 and the article on Admiral Folger in *The Encyclopedia Americana*, 1960 edition.

2. Cornish and Plainfield tax records. Mr. Edward Dannatt (1869-1947), a Windsor cabinetmaker, worked on Admiral Folger's house; interview: Virginia Colby with Marion Dannatt Trepanier, his daughter, July 14, 1982.

3. Interview: Virginia Colby with Hubert Deming, February 18, 1982, when Mr. Deming was ninety-four years old.

4. Bertha Emond, "Taming A Not So Wild West," *Impact* (Claremont, NH—Springfield, VT), October 30, 1977, C, 3. In this connection there is an interesting contemporary postal card showing some tiny mounds of grass in front of his house entitled "Second Crop at Admiral Folgar's [sic]."

5. She is listed on the Cornish tax records as owning one acre of land.

6. Arvia MacKaye Ege, *The Power of the Impossible: The Life Story of Percy and Marion MacKaye* (Falmouth, ME: The Kennebec River Press, 1992), p. 123.

7. Stephen Parrish, diary, November 20, 1905, Baker Library Collection, Dartmouth College, gift of Marian and Roy Garrand.

JAMES EARLE FRASER

1876 – 1953

THOUGH NOT EVERYONE may recognize his name, we all know at least one of James Earle Fraser's creations. In 1913 he designed the Indian or Buffalo Nickel with the head of an American Indian on one side and a buffalo on the other. Disappointed "that American coinage . . . might as well have belonged to any other country in the world," he sought to design a coin that "could be mistaken for no other coin in the world outside of the United States."[1] Then in 1915 he created a statue for the Panama-Pacific International Exposition in San Francisco World, *The End of the Trail*. This well-known image—often mistakenly thought to have been done by another person

who was briefly in the Cornish Colony, Frederick Remington—is a poignant one in which Fraser "sought to express the utter despair of this conquered people by showing the warrior and his mount at the end of their journey—'a weaker race . . . steadily pushed to the wall by a stronger [one],' as Fraser himself put it."[2] Although a replica of the statue now stands in San Francisco's Lincoln Park, at the Pacific end of the Transcontinental Lincoln Highway, Fraser had longed for it to have been cast in bronze and placed so that it would dominate a cliff overlooking the Pacific near San Francisco. As he phrased it, the statue would then be "driven at last to the edge of the continent. That would be, in very truth, 'The End of the Trail.'"[3]

Fraser was born in Winona, Minnesota, on November 4, 1876, and in the next year followed his father, a railroad contractor west, into the Dakota Territory; thus, as Fraser puts it, he was able to observe Indian life at first hand:

Figure 76. *The Buffalo Nickel designed by James Earle Fraser.*

[there] in the land that belonged to the Indians, and I saw them in their villages, crossing the prairies on their hunting expeditions. Often they stopped beside our ranch house; and camped and traded rabbits and other game for chickens. They seemed very happy until the order came to place them on reservations. One group after another was surrounded by soldiers and herded beyond the Missouri River. I realized that they were always being sent farther West, and I often heard my father say that the Indians would some day be pushed into the Pacific Ocean, and I think that accounted for my sympathetic feeling for them.[4]

Figure 77. *Fraser's* The End of the Trail, *1918.*

Eventually the family moved to Chicago where he entered the Art Institute and was inspired by the artistic excitement of the World's Colombian Exposition in 1893. He was determined to pursue his training in Paris, where he enrolled in the Ecole des Beaux-Arts. There his *Head of an Old Man* not only won the Wanamaker Prize at the American Art Exhibition in 1898 but also attracted the attention of one of the jurors, Augustus Saint-Gaudens. He promptly invited Fraser to work with him in his Paris studio and to return to the United States with him in 1900 so that he could continue working on the huge equestrian monument of General William Tecumseh Sherman (now in the Grand Army Plaza at New York's Fifth Avenue and Fifty-Ninth Street). For the next two years Fraser was Saint-Gaudens's leading assistant in Cornish where they worked on both the *Sherman Monument* and the *Memorial for Robert Louis Stevenson* for the Church of St. Giles in Edinburgh, Scotland.

Fraser shared in Saint-Gaudens's recreations as well as in his creations. "In the long list of Saint-Gaudens's pupils and assistants, Fraser was perhaps his favorite. Fraser was a vigorous athlete, a good-looking man of twenty-two or so, who could usually do with a hair-cut. He was good at any game, and he initiated Saint-Gaudens into the excitements of skating and hockey and the pleasures and exasperations of golf."[5] Beaman's Pond was the site for the skating and ice hockey; tobogganing was another favorite winter diversion. Along with many musical evenings, they enjoyed practical jokes together, too. Although Fraser lived and ate with what Faulkner calls his "patron," most assistants boarded outside "Aspet," thereby adding materially to the neighboring farmers' incomes. In 1902 Fraser set up his own studio on MacDougall Alley in Greenwich Village where his nearby neighbors, with New Hampshire connections, were George de Forest Brush, Witter Bynner, Barry Faulkner, Rockwell Kent, and Daniel Chester French. (Faulkner regarded "Jimmy Fraser" as "my standby, my elder brother, my advisor."[6]) Harry Thrasher of Plainfield, New Hampshire, was also a neighbor; Fraser had met him when they both were assistants for Saint-Gaudens and later had Thrasher work for him, too.

Fraser had fond memories of his association with Saint-Gaudens: "Those were pleasant years in Cornish and Paris, and busy ones, too, with energetic, kindly, and exacting Saint-Gaudens as the heart of what was going on. I suppose we should call ourselves extremely fortunate to have been associated with him, and with the detail of the things going on in that remarkable studio."[7] And of the studio itself, he wrote, "as I recall it, there were fifteen of us working at one time. . . . It was like Donatello at Padua except he had twenty-one sculptors to help him."[8]

Meanwhile, in 1901, the commissioners of Buffalo, New York's Pan-American Exposition wanted a special medal struck to honor the fine display of work that Saint-Gaudens had exhibited there. They asked Fraser to design it and thus started him on a long series of medal commissions. The most famous was the *Victory Medal* awarded to nearly five million people after World War I.[9] His wife, Laura Gardin, whom he married in 1913, was also a sculptor and medalist; her most famous work was one of the Congressional Medals of Honor.

A few of Fraser's other famous creations are the statue of Alexander Hamilton for the Treasury Building in Washington, DC, Fraser's first important public commission; a bust and also an equestrian group of Theodore Roosevelt, the former for the Senate wing of the United States Capitol Building and the latter, cast in bronze, is now in front of the American Museum of Natural History in New York City; a marble statue of Benjamin Franklin for the Franklin Institute in Philadelphia, Pennsylvania; a seated Lincoln that was placed at the head of the Transcontinental Lincoln Highway in Jersey City, New Jersey, so that Fraser graces both the beginning and the end of United States Highway, Route 30; *The Pioneer Woman*, 1927; and *The Buffalo Prayer*, 1931.

There were, finally, two more commissions involving his mentor. In 1926 he did a bust of Saint-Gaudens for the Hall of Fame of Great Americans at New York University that was unveiled by Augustus and Carlota Saint-Gaudens, his teacher's grandchildren. Then again in 1948, the Century Association organized a memorial exhibition to celebrate the birth of Saint-Gaudens and put Fraser in charge of the activities. He died five years later in Westport, Connecticut, where he had his final studio.

ENDNOTES

1. As quoted in the Catalogue, *James Earle Fraser: American Sculptor,* a Retrospective Exhibition of Bronzes from Works of 1913 to 1953, June 2-July 3, 1969 (New York: Kennedy Galleries, 1969), p. 12.

2. Wayne Craven, *Sculpture in America* (New York: Thomas Y. Crowell, 1968), p. 493.

3. Ibid.

4. Catalogue, p. 7.

5. Barry Faulkner, *Barry Faulkner: Sketches from an Artist's Life* (Dublin, NH: William L. Bauhan, 1973), p. 36.

6. Ibid., p. 55.

7. Catalogue, p. 26.

8. As quoted in John H. Dryfhout, *The Work of Augustus Saint-Gaudens* (Hanover, NH: University Press of New England, 1982), p. 316.

9. Craven, p. 492.

LUCIA FAIRCHILD FULLER
1870 – 1924

and

HENRY BROWN FULLER
1867 – 1934

Figure 78. *Lucia Fairchild Fuller as Proserpina in* A Masque of "Ours."

LUCIA FAIRCHILD FULLER

LUCIA FULLER was an extremely successful artist who frequently chose to create on a small scale. Frances Duncan admired her as an artist "of the subtle and exquisite miniatures."[1] Her artistic activity was somewhat compromised because her husband was subject to severe spells of depression. Furthermore, once they were separated, she was obliged to provide most of the income for meeting the family's expenses. She created several works with Cornish Colony associations. Augustus Saint-Gaudens asked her to do a portrait of his son Homer—for which she chose, in return, a copy of Saint-Gaudens' *Victory* and *The Puritan*. She also painted portraits of Sylvia Platt and Norman Hapgood as well as giving miniature lessons to Carlota Dolley Saint-Gaudens.[2]

One of her most visible works, which local legend asserted had Cornish Colony connections, now appears to have some remote connections, but not the one generally associated with it. It was believed that the brightly colored mural painting now affixed to the rear wall of the stage in the Blow-Me-Down Grange in Plainfield, New Hampshire, depicted some of Lucia Fairchild Fuller's neighbors—Tracy Spalding, Kate Davis, and Mrs. Eleanor Platt—in colonial guise as part of *The Women of Plymouth*.[3] Henry Fuller is said to have lent this painting to the Grange in 1900, but it originally was a commission Lucia Fairchild received in 1893—the year she married Henry Fuller—for the Woman's Building at the World's Columbian Exposition in Chicago. Although Lucia was assigned to create something for "one of the side murals intended for the Hall of Honor,"[4] Mary Cassat and Mary Louise Fairchild MacMonnies worked on tympana murals at either end of the Hall. Thus, the first, albeit tenuous, connection with Cornish—a coming together of names that we recognize today, but not necessarily one the women could have know about them. Five years earlier, in 1888, the

203

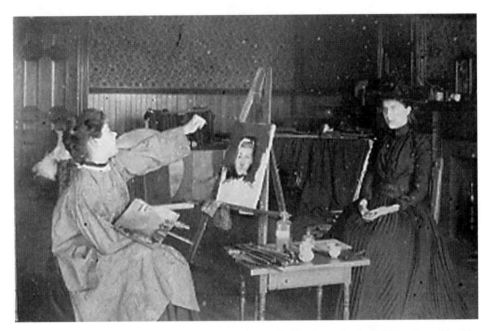

Figure 79. *Lucia Fuller at the easel, painting Mildred Howells, daughter of writer William Dean Howells.*

year after he finished assisting Augustus Saint-Gaudens in the latter's Cornish studio, Mary MacMonnies had married the famous sculptor; they would, however, eventually choose to spend their summers near Monet's Giverny rather than in Cornish (see below pp. 267-270).

A second connection to Plainfield comes in the form of Maud Howe Elliott, who would first come to the Cornish Colony ten years later and six years after the Fullers arrived. In 1893 she wrote quite positively of Fuller's huge work—the unframed canvas measures eleven by twelve feet: "the thought behind the picture needs no criticism, it is an assertion of the prime duties of woman, the home-maker and care-taker; it is a hint full of significance to our day and generation, reminding us that unless the higher education now open to our sex makes women better and wiser wives and mothers, it is a failure."[5]

This comment, while it is interesting from the point of view of two people who would eventually live in Plainfield, is also interesting for what it may suggest about the importance of this work in Lucia Fuller's life. In this connection Rawson makes a significant point. She notes that "the choice of subject matter was left to the artist, and Fuller's mural depicts Puritan women and children performing daily chores. The women spin, wash dishes, teach the children, and interact with one another." But she goes on to point out that Maud Elliott's remarks do not adequately define why Fuller chose this subject. "Not only is the education of children, female children, specifically, one of the major scenes in the mural, but it is the women who are responsible for that education. The main woman talking to the children has a book open on her lap. She is not merely a teacher of the responsibilities of the home-maker, although the women clearly are proficient in those areas as well, but it is book-learning that is specifically depicted. The subject of the mural is the coexistence of education, home-making, and child-rearing, in addition to the community and closeness of the women."[6] Lucia Fuller had too much at stake both as an educated woman and as a talented artist. She would never have substituted Maud Howe Elliott's definition of "the thought behind" *The Women of Plymouth* for her own statement of its intent.

Lucia Fairchild Fuller's diary is a mine of interesting information. Not only is it useful for her glimpses into the life and opinions of John Singer Sargent, whom she knew very well as both a friend and teacher,[7] but it is also revealing about her private life and her life among the Cornish Colony inhabitants. It also describes several occasions when she took her dearly loved children to Windsor, Vermont, by using the ferry that was then in use near the Plainfield-Cornish boundary line.[8]

Figure 80. *A profile of Mildred Howells by Lucia Fairchild Fuller.*

Although her earliest efforts were murals, she soon shifted her primary emphasis to miniatures.[9] Indeed, she was a founding member of the American Society of Miniature Painters in 1899 and its president in 1913; she was also a member of the Pennsylvania Society of Miniature Painters. She won a bronze medal at the International Exposition in Paris in 1900, a silver medal at the Pan-American Exposition in Buffalo in 1901, and a gold medal at the Louisiana Purchase Exposition in Saint Louis in 1904. She entered five of her works in the Panama-Pacific International Exposition at San Francisco in 1915 and three of them at the Dartmouth College Exhibition of Cornish Colony Artists in 1916.

After 1911 multiple sclerosis severely hampered her artistic activity. She died in 1924.

Figure 81. The Women of Plymouth *by Lucia Fairchild Fuller, a mural at the Blow-Me-Down Grange in Plainfield, New Hampshire.*

HENRY BROWN FULLER

Figure 82. Triumph of Truth Over Error *by Henry Brown Fuller, 1907.*

HENRY BROWN FULLER was the son of George Fuller (1822-1884), a Tonalist painter with an international reputation. His son, inheriting his father's talent and interest in art, developed into a painter of classical and allegorical works that typified the American Renaissance. Henry's painting, *Illusions,* finished in Cornish in 1901 (collection of the Smithsonian National Museum of American Art), is a well-known, representative example. Frances Duncan described him as "an artist of note, although his painting is perhaps of too delicately lovely and elusive a quality ever to become wildly popular."[10]

Both of them had similar training. At various periods they both studied under Dennis Bunker at the Cowles Art School in Boston and under William Merritt Chase and Henry Siddons Mowbray at the Art Students League in New York City. They married in 1893 and came to the Cornish-Plainfield area in 1897 with their two children, Clara and Charles. They purchased the Solomon Stone house on Route 12A in Plainfield. They soon renovated the house, which was built around three sides of a courtyard with a pillared portico facing the court. The house was almost completely destroyed by fire in 1899 so the Fullers decided to rebuild only the main part of the house and to leave the pillars from the former portico standing. Eventually they had a twelve by twenty-eight foot swimming pool dug and added it on to the courtyard at a cost of $200; then they had a wall that incorporated the pillars constructed on all four sides of the courtyard.[11]

The pool was the delight of the neighborhood children; indeed, the Fullers participated rather fully in the social life of the Cornish Colony. For *A Masque of "Ours": The Gods, and the Golden Bowl,* Lucia played the part of Proserpina and Henry was Apollo. Furthermore, the two of them built and decorated a Greek chariot that bore Augusta and Augustus Saint-Gaudens off from the play and returned them triumphantly to the studio.[12] The following year many of the children of the Cornish Colony performed a play, Thackeray's *The Rose and the Ring;* they were "coached" by Ethel Barrymore. Lucia Fuller's contribution was painting the scenery and acting as stage manager. Her daughter Clara took the part of the queen and her son Charles played Prince Bulbo.[13] Lucia also adapted Scott's *Ivanhoe* for the local children to show off their theatrical skills. The children had carpentry lessons at the house of the Nicholses, and Clara was enrolled in school locally. Among the adults of the Colony, the Fullers' tennis courts were often the center of interest. In addition to Henry, the artist Everett Shinn, the actor John Blair, the social philosopher Herbert Croly, and *Collier's* editor Norman Hapgood all took good advantage of their courts. A final clue to their social life comes from Stephen Parrish. His diaries frequently indicate that he attended dinner parties and other social affairs at the Fullers', as well as showing that he often entertained them at "Northcote."

Although they both accomplished a great deal of work while they were in Cornish, it would seem that their social life fared better than their marriage. The couple separated amicably in 1905. Henry went to Deerfield, Massachusetts, to live with his mother, though he paid occasional visits to the area in subsequent summers. In 1906 they rented their house to Ethel Barrymore; later they rented it to Ernest Lawson, who was represented in the Armory Show, and his family, as well as to William and Marguerite Zorach and their family.

Two of Henry Fuller's most famous paintings were done while he was part of the Cornish Colony. *Illusions* was done in 1900 and 1901; the Connecticut River and Mount Ascutney are visible in its background. It received a medal at the Pan-American Exposition in 1901 and was immediately responsible for Fuller's becoming an Associate of the National Academy. Another painting conceived and worked on in the area caused a great deal of furor, *The Triumph of Truth Over Error*. This ten foot by eight foot canvas was inspired by Mary Baker Eddy and the Christian Science movement. It was the first painting by an artist of Fuller's rank to illustrate a text from her book, *Science and Health*. Fuller, then a Christian Scientist, said that his painting was designed to illustrate Mrs. Eddy's principles that "Truth guards the gateway to harmony" (*Science and Health*, p. 537, 15) and "Truth destroys falsity and error, for light and darkness cannot dwell together" (p. 474, 34). Fuller's own notes describe the allegory:

> Truth is represented in the form of full womanhood, energized and glorified by faith. Her wings typify Omni-Presence. She holds a scythe, the familiar symbol of destruction—which she has taken from the impotent fingers of Error. With her right hand extended, she bars the further progress of Illusion—Error. Truth's presence brings victory. There is no struggle. Truth triumphs by force of being. The shrinking form of Error acknowledges the divine authority with which God has endowed Truth. Error has one hand raised to screen his countenance from the calm eyes of Truth. This figure of Error typifies non-existence.[14]

The comments of Frances Duncan on this painting are an interesting example of a Cornish Colonist's first-hand opinion: *The Triumph of Truth Over Error* "follow[s] in the train of that series of ideal figure pictures through which Mr. Fuller has gradually become known. . . in [it] . . . one sees the full stature of the artist: there is in it a stronger note and a more vivid color. In color the picture is striking. The outer draperies of the figure of Truth are an intense red, and the white radiance of the figure itself triumphs over the sinister blackness of Error and the somber clouds below, as if Truth had vanquished not only the embodiment of darkness, but Night itself."[14]

When *The Triumph of Truth Over Error* won the Carnegie Prize of $500 at the winter exhibition of the National Academy of Design in 1908, many critics believed that the prize should be withdrawn because Fuller indicated that he had had assistance in completing it. He credited two artists associated with the Cornish Colony: Everett Shinn for help in its execution and Augustus Saint-Gaudens for "advice and encouragement concerning the whole question of a new religious art." Others who received his acknowledged gratitude were William Chadwick and two men not generally associated with the allegorical style—William Glackens and George Luks.[15] Even considering the quality of those who helped him, it did little good to argue, as Fuller was quick to do, that most of the old masters had always had assistants to help them with the preliminary work on an undertaking—especially something on that scale. As one paper commented at the time, Fuller "must know whether he has carried out his plan with somebody's aid or whether somebody else has aided him in finding a plan to be carried out. In one case, he is master; in the other a manufacturer employing specialists."[16] Be that as it may, Fuller won a silver medal for the painting at the Panama-Pacific International Exposition in San Francisco in 1915. It was finally sold in 1930 to a California couple who then donated it to Principia College in Elsah, Illinois, where it still remains.

Although Fuller was noted for inventing in 1919 a new etching technique, mellowtint, he is best remembered for his paintings. In addition to *The Fates*, owned by the Corcoran Gallery in Washington, DC, and *The Mother and Child*, he also did some canvases related to the Cornish Colony: portraits of George Rublee and Margaret Littell; a portrait of Ebba Bohm, an auburn-haired Swedish model who lived with the Fullers; and a painting of Mount Ascutney. His connections with the Colony also led to an involvement with Ireland. After Augustus Saint-Gaudens completed a statue of Charles Stewart Parnell, the late nineteenth-century Irish nationalist leader, a branch of the United Irish League of America was formed in the area and Henry Fuller became its president.[17] And finally, Fuller showed two paintings in the Exhibition of Cornish Colony Artists at Dartmouth College in 1916.[18] Fuller died in 1934.

ENDNOTES

1. Frances Duncan, "A Swimming Pool at Cornish," *Country Life in America,* July 1906, pp. 302-303.

2. Furthermore she was the model for Thomas Dewing's painting *A Portrait* (1902); for discussion of their "affair," see Susan A. Hobbs, with an essay by Barbara Dayer Gallati, *The Art of Thomas Wilmer Dewing: Beauty Reconfigured,* exhibition catalogue (The Brooklyn Museum in association with the Smithsonian Institution Press, 1996), pp. 31, 70, 143.

3. This is what Priscilla Tracy Hodgeman told Virginia Colby in an interview, September 10, 1983. Since the Fullers came to Plainfield in 1897, four years after the mural painting was completed, Lucia Fuller must have used other models. Some people at the time believed that the mural painting may have been rejected because the tree stumps in it look sawed rather than axed—as would have been appropriate to the seventeenth century.

4. Charlene G. Garfinkle, "Lucia Fairchild Fuller's 'Lost' Woman's Building Mural." *American Art* 7:1 (Winter 1993), p. 2. Basing her assertion on period photographs, Garfinkle adds that "Fuller's mural was on the northwest wall of the Hall of Honor," p. 3.

5. Maud Howe Elliott, ed., *Art and Handicraft in the Women's Building of the World's Columbian Exposition* (New York: Goupil & Co., 1893), p. 33, as quoted in a copyrighted paper submitted by Kathryn E. Rawson as a Senior Thesis to the Art History Department at Smith College, 1995, p. 9; courtesy of Judith Nyhus, Curator/Registrar, Saint-Gaudens National Historic Site.

6. Rawson, pp. 9-10.

7. Lucia Miller, "John Singer Sargent in the Diaries of Lucia Fairchild, 1890-1891," *Archives of American Art Journal* 26, 4 (1986), pp. 2-16.

8. One such occasion is noted in her diary for September 10, 1903, Baker Library, Dartmouth College, Hanover, NH.

9. Lucia Fairchild Fuller wrote two articles about miniature: "Modern American Miniature Painters," *Scribner's Magazine* (March 1920) and "The Miniature as an Heirloom," *Arts and Decoration* (May 1922). For its Cornish Colony connection, see also a discussion of her work in Homer Saint-Gaudens, "Modern American Miniature Painters," *The Critic* 47, 6 (December 1905), pp. 517-529.

10. Duncan, "Swimming Pool," pp. 302-303.

11. Ibid., pp. 303-04.

12. Frances Grimes, "Reminiscences," typescript, Dartmouth College Library, quoted in *A Circle of Friends: Art Colonies of Cornish and Dublin,* exhibition catalogue (Durham, NH: University Art Galleries, University of New Hampshire, 1985), p. 111, n. 3.

13. Edith Leckie, "Children Mummers of the Cornish Colony," unidentified magazine article in the Cornish Colony file, September 1906, Baker Library, Dartmouth College, Hanover, NH.

14. Proceedings at the unveiling of the painting during its presentation to Principia College, June 5, 1931, and printed in the college's alumni magazine.

15. *The Century Magazine* 75:6, April 1908, p. 957.

16. Unidentified newspaper clipping, Saint-Gaudens Papers, Box 40, Baker Library, Dartmouth College, Hanover, NH.

17. An unidentified issue of the *New York Evening Post,* Virginia Colby, Cornish Colony files.

18. "Noted Irish Leader in Windsor," unidentified newspaper clipping, Windsor, VT, Public Library scrapbook.

19. George Breed Zug, "Exhibition of Cornish Artists," *Art and Archaeology,* April 1916, pp. 203-205; *Dartmouth Alumni Magazine,* March 1916, pp. 207-211.

Figure 83. *The Fuller Sisters of Dorset, England: Cynthia, with Irish harp, Dorothy, and Rosalind.*

THE
FULLER SISTERS

A DIMINUTIVE PLASTER-OF-PARIS SCULPTURE of three dancers, which graces the shelves of the Cornish library, and a pamphlet, "Echoes of the Fuller Sisters,"[1] written by a former teacher in Cornish who was brought here by the Barretts both establish a connection that is an interesting one for the cultural life of Cornish. The Fuller sisters first came to Cornish in July of 1915 at the invitation of Percy MacKaye and his wife. The girls stayed a month at "Hilltop," the newly-finished "little white house belonging to the MacKayes, which was perched up high on a hill overlooking a most beautiful valley with the mountains beyond."[2] Toward the end of their first visit, they gave a recital at "The Oaks," Maxfield Parrish's house in Plainfield, on August 7, 1915, attended by a number of guests including Margaret, the daughter of President Woodrow Wilson.[3] They returned to Cornish as guests of the Barretts at the end of September and the beginning of October. During their visit they varied their locale by alternating between the Japanese-style "Glass House" on Dingleton Hill and a "nice white farmhouse which also belongs to the Barretts."[4] The couple had "engaged [the Fuller sisters] to teach the villagers of Cornish some English country dances and the village children the Singing Games."[5] The sisters were so entranced with the Barretts: "Mr. and Mrs. Barrett, whom we called 'Gypsy Davie' and 'Lady Ba' are charming people who live and look like gypsies."[6]

Dorothy, Rosalind, and Cynthia Fuller were three sisters from Sturminster New-ton, Dorset, England. They grew up learning to sing from their mother. As time went on, they became more and more interested in the then relatively unworked field of

British balladry and folk songs. They gathered their songs from all parts of England, Scotland, Ireland, and Wales.

The sisters first came to America in 1912 to give three recitals of their folk songs in Chicago. They eventually gave more than eighty recitals in many cities, especially in the eastern half of the United States. Their performances revived interest in the old folk and country songs. The Fuller sisters were applauded for their skillful interpretation and perfection of enunciation.[7] The following comment is from *The Boston-Transcript:*

> The singing of the Misses Fuller was exquisite. There was nothing of the drawingroom or studio about their voices. They maintained completely the straightforward objectiveness necessary to folk music, never for a moment seeming to be superior to the songs or to be personalities in their own right. The important thing was to get the song sung, distinctly, simply, and joyously. Their dramatic gestures and dance steps seemed to be perfectly spontaneous and never studied. The evening was one of pure delight.

During their recitals, "sometimes Dorothy sings; sometimes Rosalind; again each answers each in dialogued duet . . . or all three in a refrain. Cynthia, whether she sings or not, accompanies the others with the soft tones, gentle coloring, and pleasant pulsating rhythm of the Irish harp." Another contemporary critic added that: "Their music appeals to all. Children are delighted with them, as are the parents; musicians and non-musicians alike rejoice in their performances. They have performed at Bryn Mawr, Wellesley, Smith College, Radcliffe, Mount Holyoke, Harvard, Princeton, Columbia University, Leland Stanford University, and the New England Conservatory of Music. They are a very picturesque group in early Victorian costume."

The Fuller sisters' invitations to Cornish resulted in the following story, entitled "A Cornish Festival." It proves that the sisters delighted in their ability to bring people together from every corner of the town.

A CORNISH FESTIVAL

It is amazing how things happen. The Fuller sisters grew up singing ballads in an England that had almost forgotten her folk songs. Cecil Sharp[8] had come to the rescue and begun collecting them from the lips of the few who still remembered them. The Fullers helped him. They went straight to a ballad's heart. They knew the truest of its many versions.

At one of Cecil Sharp's gatherings when they were displaying their finds, an American woman said to Rosalind: "You should go to America." Rosalind went home filled with the spirit of adventure, filled her sisters with it, persuaded her father, in whose breast that little affair of '76 still rankled, promised her mother that they would mind their brother, Walter, to whose care she committed them, and away they sailed with a tiny purse and one letter to a professor at Columbia University.

They sang in most of the colleges of the East that first autumn, and returning the next year and the next they sang from coast to coast, from Florida to Wyoming. When they did the "Roman Soldiers" for President Wilson at the White House, "That's war in a nutshell," he said. The Fuller sisters have become a tradition here in America. But there is one place—in our own New England—where they are more than a tradition. There they came across old English songs; even discovered some they hadn't known before.

It happened that one night the girls found themselves on the platform of a lonely old Townhouse in the New Hampshire hills. Stable lanterns lighted the place—lanterns came swinging on rear axles of buggies up and down slow miles of country road. A farmer audience crowded rude benches, men and women of old English stock, familiar with the things the ballads dealt with, "a darling audience," Rosalind called them. The tale of a cheese set them rocking with laughter. The tragedy of "Lord Rendal" went home.

When it was time for everyone to go home to bed Rosalind said, "The concert is over but wouldn't some of you like to stay and play games with us?" They would, and they did. It was after midnight when the last lantern was carried out and swung from the pole of a long, low-hung farm wagon. The three girls climbed in and lay down on new mown hay, still singing, while the farm team plodded up a long, steep hill. They had to walk a little way in the dark of the forest road. Gypsy Davy went ahead and the three groped timidly behind them, reaching for each other with little cries. "Where's Cynthia?" "Dorothy, are you there?" "Oh! I'm in the hedge!"—there wasn't any hedge—"Someone is treading on my slipper ribbon!" Swaying crinolines and little slippers were never meant for such rude roads. Back in the wagon again, the stern Gypsy forbade talk, but that didn't silence them. They couldn't be quiet. They made the farmer stop at darkened houses and sang to the sleepers there. It was very late indeed when the wagon drew up before a little white farmhouse, and the horses were unhitched, and the girls went in to go to bed—but they wouldn't go to bed until they had been promised that they might come again to this dear place and leave something lasting behind them. Thrilling plans were drawn up that very night for a whole week of songs and games—a "Singing Festival."

The news spread rapidly through the Cornish hills and there was eager preparation. The Fuller sisters, going about singing in cities, kept thinking of that festival week to come in Country Cornish.

So one morning in early autumn there they were again, not in crinolines this time but in little frocks that made them look very slight, walking through the cornfields to Deacon Wark's back yard,[9] singing as they came: "The Road is Very Dusty"—And the dear old Deacon, in his eighties, all in a flutter, was saying, "It is the wits. They want a penny. I must get them a penny," and then they were in the big clean kitchen and the Deacon was saying, "They're the real old country girls. 'Tis the great day of my life." And in no time at all he was coming down from the attic with an old fiddle he had made himself forty years before, fiddling as he came. And presently, big farm boots and all, he was doing a Highland Fling. They learned a reel as he and his wife used to dance it in Scotland, "with never a rude thought," and Rosalind, whose swaying grace was of a sort to make dance lovers catch their breath, heard herself being rebuked: "Ye'll dance it as neatly as ye can, like my wife." So his wife, in her long blue calico gown did the intricate step with almost imperceptible motion, and Rosalind meekly watched and did her best. She said afterwards it was one of the hardest things she had ever done.

That was the beginning of a week that was to have a touch of immortality about it. 'Twas on a Monday morning when the singing three and the little harp and a pair of gypsies piled into the long blue wagon and the farm team plodded up hill once more and jogged down. The wagon body hung so low it bumped on rocks sometimes. There was singing in the wagon, and there was Morris dancing down the road. When a lonely little schoolhouse came in sight, high on a hillside, the voices and the harp drew its children shyly to the door. And in a minute there they all were, Rosalind and Dorothy and the children dancing on the green, but Cynthia sat on the hay and twanged the harp strings, her lovely head barely reaching to the top of one big blue wheel.

'Twas on a Monday evening the people in one of the little groups of houses that hide among those sparsely settled hills met in the Grange for a singing lesson—forty men on one side of the hall, more women on the other, Dorothy in a corner at the front sketching, Cynthia harping near her, and Rosalind skipping between them and the company, up and down the aisle, hoping, believing, desiring the song straight out of those self-conscious folk. They worked an hour and a half on "My Man John" that night, and met every night for the rest of the week to practice for the concert come Saturday night in the Townhouse. So all through the week each school had its game, each neighborhood its song.

Tuesday night South Cornish filled a farmhouse to overflowing—parlor, kitchen, bed-room, stairs. There the song was "When Shall We Be Married, John." Wednesday night the Center assembled in the supper room of the old brick church for "Mowing the Barley."

Thursday night the familiar "O No John" rang through the old house where Chief Justice Chase was born. Some of his descendants were in the company. That was on the River Road. Friday night at Cornish Mills it was "Robin-a-Thrush."

So all the hills and dales came under the singing spell. Someone heard Farmer Brown on his way to the creamery singing "O madam, I will give to you the keys of my heart." The cows went to pasture to: "Ransy, tansy, tiddlemans all." The hay went down before "Mow-ow." Indeed rumor had it that Farmer Barton, known as a sober, steady man, forgot his work and fiddled all day long, after the blue wagon had stopped before his hayfield and the sweet three had danced with the "Gypsy Davy" to his fiddling. Rumor still persists that it was two whole weeks before he did get back to his work again. Luckily the sunshine lasted.

Each night a different house proudly sheltered the singing girls and each morning before leave taking they sang before the door: "God Bless th' Master of This House."

Saturday night, when the chores were done, the swinging buggy lanterns, making great wheel shadows on the bushes by the roadside, began to draw up about the Townhouse.

The news of the Festival had reached the City Colony in a far corner of the hills, and gone much further afield than that. All outsiders had to be warned off. Rosalind herself, telephoning from a farmhouse kitchen, begged the President's daughter to stay away: "If you come, nothing at all will happen." Guards were stationed along the road to turn city folk away and none got by. But everybody in the big country family came, except the bedridden, and they came in spirit, for none of them had been forgotten on the rounds of the blue wagon.

The Townhouse was all scrubbed and shining, and the windows all open—nailed open. Thick-set wild flowers hid the fact that dangerous night air was entering. The door-keeper urged the aged to keep their overcoats. The erring farmer Barton was there with his precious fiddle, and Deacon Wark with his, and octogenarian Amos Spaulding, when his turn came, took off his black coat and sitting, shirt-sleeved, beat an intricate kind of "Peas Porridge Hot" on his knees to the time of the fiddling.

Cornish Flat set the ball rolling with "My Man John," which they did with inspiring fervor—twenty men for the Lord, a dozen for John, and all the women and girls for the lady.

We must admit it had not been a united family, this that gathered in the Townhouse. Indeed that place had been chosen because only there could all the warring factions meet on neutral ground. There were family feuds which had kept whole groups on not-speaking terms for generations, and one small settlement despised another. But that night each school did its game, each group its song, and every one cheered, without reserve and without discrimination. They stamped!

Those songs are easy to find in Cornish now, and the Cornish boys and girls, going out to seek their fortunes, carry them far and wide.[10]

ENDNOTES

1. Alice Mansur published "Echoes of the Fuller Sisters" in 1929; Virginia Colby, Cornish Colony files. For more on Robert L. Barrett, see above pp. 130-134.

2. Carol Odell, "The Fuller Sisters: Fourth Tour of America, Part 2, October 1914-May 20, 1916," p. 31, unpublished manuscript, Virginia Colby, Cornish Colony files; courtesy of Carol Odell, Dorothy Fuller's daughter. See also Arvia MacKaye Ege, *The Power of the Impossible: The Life Story of Percy and Marion MacKaye* (Falmouth, ME: The Kennebec River Press, 1992, pp. 255-56. For more on this friendship with Maxfield Parrish, see below p. 309.

3. Arthur S. Link, ed., *The Papers of Woodrow Wilson* (Princeton, NJ: Princeton University Press, 1978), 34, [1915], p. 128.

4. Cynthia Fuller to her mother, September 19, 1915, Virginia Colby, Cornish Colony files; courtesy of Carol Odell. The farmhouse was at the foot of the hill; it was here that the meals for the "Glass House" were prepared and then sent up the hill by two mules.

5. Dorothy Fuller to her parents, September 18, 1915, Virginia Colby, Cornish Colony files; courtesy of Carol Odell.

6. Rosalind Fuller to her parents, September 28, 1915, Virginia Colby, Cornish Colony files; courtesy of Carol Odell. It is unclear whether the Fuller sisters gave them this nickname or whether it was already a generally accepted one. At any rate, when the Barretts wrote their *Himalayan Letter* in 1927, they decided to incorporate "Gypsy Davy," which the Fuller sisters sometimes spelled "Davy" and sometimes "Davies," and "Lady Ba" into its title.

7. George H. Stowell Library, Cornish Flat, files for this and the following contemporary quotations.

8. Cecil Sharp (1859-1924) was an English musician known primarily for his interest in English folk music. He founded the English Folk Dance Society in 1911. He came to America to track down American folk songs of English origin, which he did from 1911 to 1918, in the Appalachia Mountains. His results were published in 1917: *English Folk Songs for the Southern Appalachia Mountains* (with O. D. Campbell).

9. The "backyard" referred to belonged to the house currently owned by Wendell Garrett (1996) near the corner of Saint-Gaudens Road and Hell Hollow Road in Cornish. It once belonged to Josiah Stone; his portrait and one of his wife are on display at the Cornish Historical Society. Rosalind Fuller commented on a later occasion:

> There was tremendous applause for every item—but I think the most went when an old man called Mr. Wark—the same that had played the fiddle for me to "leg it" a month before— came up on the platform to dance the Highland Fling with me. Of course, I didn't know a step really, but I watched his legs and did as he did. We jigged and jigged, and when we ended "the house rose," as the saying goes. He was as proud as a peacock and as excited as a school boy. He is like Smee in *Peter Pan* to look at and is over seventy-eight years old.

(Letter to her mother, September 28, 1915, Virginia Colby, Cornish Colony files; courtesy of Carol Odell.)

10. "Echoes of the Fuller Sisters," George H. Stowell Library booklet, No. 12, with a preface by Katherine Ellis Barrett, printed by the Torrence Printing Company, Charles City, IA, 1929. A heart-warming moment occurred at the September 5, 1994, meeting of the Cornish Historical Society. After Carol Odell had held the audience spellbound with her account of the Fuller sisters, one member, Lawrence Hilliard, thrilled her with his boyhood memories of actually being at one of the Fuller sisters' performances in Cornish.

Figure 84.

GARDENS IN THE CORNISH COLONY

WITH EACH NEW SPRING, thoughts of garden projects formed in the dead of winter begin to percolate anew. Some may recall the time when the town was noted in nation-wide publications because of the elaborate gardens its famous residents maintained.

In 1906 Frances Duncan featured "The Gardens of Cornish" in *The Century Maga-zine*. She believed that what typified the local gardens was the fact that they were "an outgrowth of the house, an out-of-door living-room" to be used and enjoyed as much as possible by the owners and their guests. Most houses had verandas, or loggias, or a suitable area where, weather permitting, meals were enjoyed outdoors. She noted that many of the local gardens contained lily pools, which were usually round beds of perennials, and cutting gardens. Fruit trees would generally be arranged on the outer perimeter. The central feature for the majority of these gardens, however, was a promi-nent view of Mount Ascutney in nearby Vermont.[1]

Many of the early artists who chose Cornish for their vacation homes were inter-ested in gardens. Augustus Saint-Gaudens, the first to arrive, preferred flowers of the old-fashioned sort: dahlias, phlox, and sweet William. Nevertheless, with the many assistants he employed to work in the studios and with his numerous guests, vegeta-bles held an important place in his garden. His garden plan even provided for open spaces so that he and his guests could enjoy lawn bowling in the summer and tobog-ganing in the winter. The Thomas Dewings arrived in 1886 and purchased ten acres of the Chester Pike farm. Maria Oakey Dewing was a distinguished painter of flowers so she and her husband are credited with introducing the passion for flower gardening to the Colony.

A third early resident, Charles A. Platt, a painter, etcher, and architect, designed many of the houses the Colonists built. Consequently, he exerted a distinct influence on the architecture and the garden layout of numerous residents. Because of his strong connections with the American Renaissance movement, Platt was partial to the more

Figure 85. *Anne Parrish in Stephen Parrish's garden at "Northcote."*

formal gardens such as those found in Italy. He even published a book in 1894 entitled *Italian Gardens.* Numerous articles featuring Platt's houses and their gardens appeared while these characteristics were in vogue. "High Court," which he designed in the Italian villa manner for Annie Lazarus and which was later owned by Norman Hapgood, the editor of *Collier's Magazine,* was featured in a photo essay in the June 1902 issue of *House and Garden.*[2] In presenting "an impression of Cornish" that emphasizes the Italian feel of the gardens at "High Court," Helen W. Henderson notes that "Lombardy poplars figure conspicuously from every viewpoint, while a nearer inspection reveals a wealth of sunken gardens and terraced lawns."[3]

Although not a Platt-designed house, Henderson has words of praise for another Cornish Colonist, Everett Shinn, and his first wife Florence Scovel Shinn, for their use of the natural setting to provide beauty: "The natural beauties of the grounds are great. Six huge maple sugar trees screen the house on the east side, and the ledges of granite exposed about the summit of the hill, upon which the house stands, are in themselves immensely decorative."[4]

It seems Cornish gardeners were exceedingly skillful in utilizing the natural setting and the materials at hand. Maxfield Parrish took advantage of several fine old oaks that were used to determine the "proper" location of his house—even appropriately naming his house "The Oaks." On the other hand, he wisely decided against planting the ever-popular Lombardy poplar because they would have diminished the effect of the splendid oaks and also been out of keeping with the style of the house.[5]

In 1908 Frances Duncan returned to Cornish and was highly complimentary of Rose Nichols, who not only wrote books on gardens but followed her own advice when creating the garden at her father's house, "Mastlands." The focal point was the center of the garden where two main paths intersected. Gravel widened into a circle, surrounding a pool about nine feet in diameter. The pool was framed with three wooden seats that blended unobtrusively with the setting.[6]

"The Gardens of Cornish" were again featured in 1914 in a national publication when May Wilkinson Mount went into ecstasies about the beauty of the gardens of Winston Churchill's "Harlakenden," one of the more elegant of the Colony's houses:

> Close about the house crowds the gardens, borders, and beds of perennials, sheltered in the wings of the house, which form a court in the front. The park, which consists of 700 acres, comes directly up to the dwelling, which is set on top of a hill that commands views of the Green Mountains, the valley of the Connecticut River, and the nearer New Hampshire hills. A garden entrance in the rear leads to a semicircular lawn, enclosed by a low stone wall, at the back of the house, and here, from the tiled outdoor living room, one may gaze upon the most beautiful landscape to be seen from Cornish. Winston Churchill himself laid out the gardens and park in the Old English style, planned roadways and drives, and thinned the woods, mostly native white pine mingled with oak and maple.[7]

In her comment on the gardening craze in Cornish in general, and on the garden Charles A. Platt planned for Emily and Augusta Slade in particular, Rose Standish Nichols echoed a common comparison of the local landscape with that of Italy:

> Few parts of New England bear so strong a resemblance to an Italian landscape as the hills rising above the banks of the Connecticut River opposite the peaks of Mount Ascutney. Here in the township of Cornish . . . came to settle a little colony of sculptors, painters, and writers . . . . Apart from the practice of his own particular art, each was intent upon making his place a little paradise. Charming gardens were created by struggling artists who hardly knew the commonest flowers by name, but who were thoroughly conversant with the principles of design. Every householder was his own head gardener and landscape architect, though subject to much constructive criticism from his neighbors. An intense love of beauty, as expressed both in art and nature, and a genuine community spirit were the mainsprings of action.[8]

With all this passion for gardening permeating the Colony, Stephen Parrish, Maxfield's father, was probably the most intense, fervent gardener of them all. He even succeeded in developing elaborate gardens on a very challenging hillside. To take advantage of the views, Parrish located the main garden in line with the often spectacular sunsets. Journals that he kept from 1893 to 1911 provide extremely detailed descriptions of his horticultural activities. He maintained a thorough account of weather conditions and consistently referred to plants, shrubs, and trees by their correct botanical names. Seedlings were started early in the greenhouse. Much rearranging took place when a new flowerbed was established or a new shipment of stock was received from one of his Massachusetts suppliers. Parrish employed one garden helper unless special work had to be done. He could usually be found working beside the hired hand cultivating, transplanting, and performing even the most menial of garden chores. And his work did not go unnoticed. *House and Garden* published a feature article in 1902 entitled "A Day at Northcote," which gave the highly detailed planning diagrams for Parrish's various gardens; *Country Life in America* featured his gardens in 1907, and they used a photograph of the garden walk and lily pool on its cover in 1908.[9]

SUGGESTIONS FOR FURTHER READING

(The Endnotes for the chapters on the following people will also supply relevant information: Frances Duncan, Rose Nichols, Stephen Parrish, Ellen Shipman, and Augusta and Emily Slade.)

Virginia Lopez Begg, "The 'New Woman' in the Garden," *Journal of the New England Garden History Society* 2, Fall 1992, pp. 29-35.

Charles A. Birnhaum and Lisa E. Crowder, ed., *Pioneers of American Landscape Design* (Washington, DC: US Department of the Interior, 1993).

Virginia Tuttle Clayton, "Reminiscence and Revival: The Old-Fashioned Garden, 1890-1910," *The Magazine Antiques*, April 1990.

Madison Cox and Erica Lennard, *Artists' Gardens: from Claude Monet to Jennifer Bartlett* (New York: Harry N. Abrams, Inc., 1993), pp. 32-39.

May Brawley Hill, "Grandmother's Garden," *The Magazine Antiques*, November 1992 and *Grandmother's Garden: The Old-Fashioned American Garden*, 1865-1915 (New York: Harry N. Abrams, Inc., 1995), pp. 101-109.

Guy Lowell, ed., *American Gardens* (Boston: Houghton Mifflin, 1902), features the gardens of Herbert Croly, Rose Nichols, Charles A. Platt, Stephen Parrish, and Augustus Saint-Gaudens.

William Noble, "Northcote: An Artist's New Hampshire Garden," *Journal of the New England Garden History Society* 2, Fall 1992, pp. 1-9.

Louise Shelton, *Beautiful Gardens in America* (New York: Charles Scribner's Sons, 1915), revised 1924, features the gardens of Mrs. William H. Hyde, Stephen Parrish, Esq., Mr. and Mrs. Charles A. Platt, Miss Augusta P. Slade, and Mrs. Augusta Saint-Gaudens.

ENDNOTES

1. Frances Duncan, "The Gardens of Cornish," *The Century Magazine* 72, 1, May 1906, pp. 3-19; see above pp. 181-184.

2. Platt's work received a great deal of attention during the first two decades of this century: Herbert Croly, "The House and Garden of Mr. Charles A. Platt," *House and Garden* 1, December 1901; "Entrance Gate of Mr. Platt's Garden," *House and Garden*, June 1902; Herbert Croly, "An American Landscape Architect," *The House Beautiful*, October 1906, pp. 11-12, 14; and "The New Hampshire Garden of Charles A. Platt," *House and Garden*, April 1924, pp. 66-67.

3. Helen W. Henderson, "An Impression of Cornish," *The Lamp*, October 1903.

4. Ibid.

5. Frances Duncan, "Maxfield Parrish's Home and How He Built It—Art in Craftsmanship," *The Country Calendar*, September 1905, pp. 435-37.

6. Frances Duncan, "A Cornish Garden," *Country Life in America*, March 1908; see below pp. 290-295.

7. May Wilkinson Mount, "The Gardens of Cornish," *Suburban Life*, March 1914.

8. Rose Standish Nichols, "A Hilltop Garden in New Hampshire," *The House Beautiful*, Vol. 55 (March, 1924), p. 237; see below p. 401, ns. 9 & 10.

9. Stephen Parrish, diary, Baker Library, Dartmouth College, Hanover, NH, gift of Marian and Roy Garrand; "A Day at Northcote, New Hampshire," photographs by Herbert C. Wise, *House and Garden*, June 1902, pp. 240-251; Frances Duncan, "An Artist's New Hampshire Garden," *Country Life in America*, March 1907, pp. 516-520, 556-568; and "Stephen Parrish's Garden at Cornish," *Country Life in America*, March 1908, features a cover design as well.

FRANCES GRIMES
1869 – 1963

FRANCES GRIMES is best remembered today for both her bas-reliefs, particularly those of children, and her discriminating portrait busts. She worked in plaster and bronze, but it is her efforts in marble that reveal her talent most effectively. In her day she was noted for her insistence on exercising full control over her marble creations and not relegating their completion to skilled assistants. Her interest and her ability in drawing, modeling, and carving, exhibited first in her hometown of Braceville, Ohio, where she was born in January of 1869, led to Brooklyn, New York, and the Pratt Institute upon her graduation from high school so that she might pursue her education in art. Because of her proficiency in cutting and carving marble, she was hired by her teacher, Herbert Adams, in 1894 and soon began teaching "the less forward pupils," especially in clay modeling and was listed as an assistant in clay modeling by 1900.[1] Grimes followed Adams to Cornish for the first time in 1894 and returned regularly from 1895-1900. As an apprentice sculptor, she lived with Herbert and Adeline Pond Adams in a little cottage on Freeman Hill owned by Charles C. Beaman. The house had been originally assembled from some out-buildings for George de Forest Brush; it no longer stands.

After six years as a studio assistant to Adams, he introduced her to Augustus Saint-Gaudens, and she began working for him. Affectionately known as "Grimsey," although she would have preferred the more alluring "Francesca," one of her studio mates described the new arrival as "a beautiful woman of thirty with a lovely speaking voice. She moved with languid grace. The languor was deceptive for her character was alert and vigorous, her mind clear and searching. She was wise and discreet and she became Saint-Gaudens's confidante, and stayed with him until his death."[2] Her affinity for him was remarkable: "she appeared to have almost the power of second sight in the sympathy with which she could divine his intentions and perform whatever he wished done"; his affinity for her was no less real: "during his lifetime, Saint-Gaudens had said of her that there was no one on whose fidelity to his own mind's wish he could so wholly reply."[3] Proof of this bond can be seen in the significant projects of his with which Grimes was involved: a version of the *Robert Louis Stevenson* relief (1899-1903), *The Pilgrim* (1903-1904), *The Phillips Brooks Monument* (1896-1907), the bronze bust of *William C. Whitney* (1905-1907), and, after the death of Saint-Gaudens, the com-

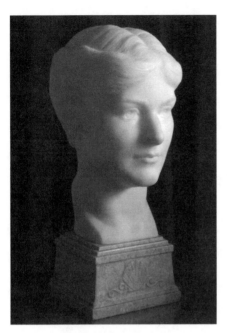

Figure 86. *Portrait bust of Mrs. Learned Hand by Frances Grimes.*

pletion of the *Albright Caryatids* (1906-1908).[4] Her "Reminiscences" are a precious document for what they reveal not only about the life of Cornish Colony members but also about her mentor: "He was a great instructor and took the trouble to have us get experience for ourselves from the work we were doing for him. He would stop to make drawings of the muscles of the arm in different positions when he was explaining a gesture he wanted carried out or talk at some length on an element of beauty involved in what he wanted modeled."[5]

While she was at the studio, he encouraged her to pursue independent work. She modeled a bust of Bishop Henry C. Potter, the father of Mrs. Henry Fitch Taylor, and of Mrs. William Henry Hyde—both members of the Colony; the bust is in the Grace Church of New York City. Other portraits of her Cornish Colony neighbors include a bas-relief of Clarissa and Eleanor Platt and of Frances Hand; her bas-relief of Arthur Whiting is in the New York Public Library's music library at Lincoln Center. John Edgar Chamberlin spoke rather highly of her portrait bust of Winston Churchill: "Frances Grimes . . . was a pupil of Augustus Saint-Gaudens, and his influence shows in the rather cold and cameo-like formality of her bas-reliefs. All of her work has even more than an Hellenic repose. But it is beautiful in its perfect grace; and the portrait bust of Winston Churchill, and a study head once made in Saint-Gaudens's studio, reveal enthusiasm and inspiration as well as a most careful elaboration."[6] Another bas-relief that was especially admired was of Anne Parrish, the cousin of Stephen Parrish, who wrote: "With Anne, drove over to Saint-Gaudens's and brought home plaster cast of Anne made by Frances Grimes. It was commenced nearly two years ago and is a beautiful work of art and a perfect likeness."[7] Later, in exchange for this bas-relief, Parrish painted a picture for Frances Grimes.

During her early years in Cornish, she stayed with a variety of local people. During the winter of 1900-1901, she and Frances Houston decided to spend the winter in Cornish. It was the first time either one of them "spent a winter in a cold climate in the country and much of our time was spent in finding combinations of clothes to keep us warm. A comfortable life was occupation enough, but Frances found time to paint almost every morning, and I posed for her."[8] Frances, along with Elsie Ward and Henry Hering, two other assistants Saint-Gaudens employed, stayed at the Westgate farm just up the road from the studio. In 1906 Stephen Parrish noted in his diary that she was staying at the Bryants'. Later, in 1910, she lived in Clara Davidge's renovated old mill in Plainfield.

She was an active participant in the Colony's social activities. From a design of Maxfield Parrish's, she and Henry Hering fashioned the two large, gilded masks in 1905 for *A Masque of 'Ours:' The Gods and the Golden Bowl*. She played the part of Iris, the goddess of the rainbow and a messenger of the gods: "The music began—with exquisite wood sounds. Then from between the curtain folds stepped the diaphanous form of Iris, acted by Miss Frances Grimes, the sculptress, in a gown of many-colored chiffons with a staff of purple iris, and the same in her hair, who gave Percy's *Prologue* very appealingly."[9] The story goes that quite early in her association with the Colony, Herbert Adams said that women ought to take care about what they wore to picnics; they should wear white or bright colors. From then on, Frances always wore white to picnics.[10]

There are a few other records of her activities in Cornish. In the "Cornish Library Notes," unfortunately undated, there is an item that "Cornish School #2 (located on Saint-Gaudens Road) was very thoroughly cleaned by five volunteers, five women living in the neighborhood, Mrs. Philip Littell, Mrs. Leaned Hand, Mrs. George Rublee, Miss Frances Arnold, and Miss Grimes." For many years, she lived in a little house on Stage Road near Route 12A in Plainfield. There is also a later indication of her local involvement: on August 27, 1941, she assisted with the "British War Relief Society Auction" in Plainfield.[11]

Once she left Cornish, she moved to New York and established a studio at 17A Macdougal Alley. At one point, *The New York Times* carried a story headed "Sculptor's Wooing of His Adored Sculptress Lands Him in Bellevue." It seems that "Augustus J. Jaegers, the sculptor in this melancholy romance" foisted his unwanted attentions on Frances Grimes "for years and years and years" until she—"wearied of his wistful eyes," and irked at having "to fish his love notes out of her wet clay"—"answered them all in one document, and that—the pity of it—a summons." The hapless suitor persisted in a less obtrusive vein: "he wandered about Macdougal Alley several times a day, and now and then he thrust a note to its fate through the slit in the door of 17A." Finally, Frances hauled him into a court "flanked by unsentimental court officers, mingled with many common persons and breathing an atmosphere which he felt quite properly was alien and inhospitable to an intimate tale of love and art . . . when the proceedings were over, the sculptor went to Bellevue Hospital for a five-days' examination and the sculptress retreated to perfect peace at 17A Macdougal Alley."[12]

For her final "perfect peace," Frances Grimes returned to the Chase Cemetery in Cornish. She died in New York City on November 9, 1963.

ENDNOTES

1. Lucia Fairchild Fuller, "Frances Grimes: A Sculptor in Whose Works One Reads Delicacy and Intelligence," *Arts and Decoration* 14, November 1920, p. 34; see the Pratt Institute Catalogue for 1900-1901.

2. Barry Faulkner, *Sketches from an Artist's Life* (Dublin, NH: William L. Bauhan, 1973), pp. 35-36.

3. Fuller, loc. cit.

4. She completed the remaining six of the eight caryatids on the Albright (Knox) Gallery. For further information about other projects of his on which Grimes was involved, see the Index of John H. Dryfhout, *The Work of Augustus Saint-Gaudens* (Hanover, NH: University Press of New England, 1982), p. 349.

5. Quoted in Dryfhout, p. 31.

6. Undated, unidentified clipping in the Archives of American Art, The Smithsonian Institution, Microfilm Reel #N 738.

7. Stephen Parrish, diary, September 8, 1905, Baker Library, Dartmouth College, Hanover, NH, gift of Marian and Roy Garrand.

8. Frances Grimes, "Reminiscences," typescript, Baker Library, Dartmouth College, Hanover, NH. This typescript is a treasure trove of tales about the personalities, dinner parties, plays, musicals, and social activity of the Cornish Colony. She pulls no punches about the people whom she discusses.

9. Arvia MacKaye Ege, *The Power of the Impossible: The Life Story of Percy and Marion MacKaye* (Falmouth, ME: The Kennebec River Press, 1992), p. 129, quoting from the diary of Marion MacKaye. The *Prologue* was a brief tribute in verse to Saint-Gaudens as artist and neighbor.

10. Grimes.

11. Both these items are from newspaper clippings in the files of Virginia Colby.

12. Undated newspaper clipping from the files of Virginia Colby. An Albert Jaegers (1868-1925) is mentioned in Dryfhout, pp. 260, 315-316, as being first a student of Augustus Saint-Gaudens at the Art Students League in New York and later one of his assistants; while he was in Cornish, Jaegers worked on the bronze relief of Henry W. Maxwell (1903). An entry in Stephen Parrish's diary for April 28, 1903, indicates that he had "Frances Grimes and Mr. Jaegers to dinner"; diary, Baker Library, Dartmouth College, Hanover, NH, gift of Marian and Roy Garrand.

Figure 87. *Portrait of Learned Hand
by Will Hollingsworth.*

LEARNED HAND
1872 – 1961

JUDGE LEARNED HAND was chief judge of the busiest federal appeals court in the United States, the Second Circuit Court of Appeals in New York City. His trenchant opinions caused him to be the most frequently quoted American jurist since Oliver Wendell Holmes. At the time of his death, he had served as a federal judge for fifty-two years—more than any other judge. He was admired as much for the precision that governed his legal mind as the spirit that infused his legal philosophy. In 1950 he wrote a famous opinion that upheld the conviction of eleven major Communist leaders in the United States on charges of conspiracy to teach and to advocate the overthrow of the government by force and violence: "The advocacy of violence may or may not fail; but in neither case can there be any 'right' to use it. Revolutions are often 'right,' but a 'right of revolution' is a contradiction in terms, for a society which acknowledged it could not stop at tolerating conspiracies to overthrow it but must include their execution."[1]

The meticulous attention that he required in his court was also applied in writing his decisions. Judge Hand "invariably wrote three or four drafts of every opinion in longhand on yellow foolscap before the language and reasoning finally satisfied him." His celebrated opinion in the case of the *United States v. Aluminum Co. of America*, "in which he ruled that 'good' monopolies had no more legality than 'bad' monopolies, was distilled from forty thousand pages and four years of testimony, has been a model for every subsequent antitrust suit."[2]

After he was graduated summa cum laude from Harvard College, where he studied with George Santayana, Josiah Royce, and William James, he went on to Harvard Law School, graduating in 1896. In 1939, his alma mater awarded him with an honorary degree of Doctor of Laws. Ten years later, in April of 1949, a bust of Judge Hand, a gift of the law clerks who had served under him, was presented to the Harvard Law School.[3]

In 1902 Judge Hand married Frances Fincke, one of whose Bryn Mawr classmates was Frances Arnold. Whether as a result of that friendship or for some other reason, the couple decided in 1908 to spend their summers in Cornish. Stephen Parrish noted in his diary the beginning of calls to and from the Hands in September. For example, "the Hands called here in our absence"; "evening, a supper party (the Hands and

Frances Arnold). Had an exhibition of my pictures afterwards, the Hands selecting one"; and "Fanny Hand in A.M. and selected a picture."[4] In 1910 the couple began to rent "summer homes" in Cornish for their summers "virtually every year; . . . in 1919, they bought a house in Cornish and used it as their country house for the rest of their lives."; Mrs. Hand "had been enchanted by Cornish" and "had been introduced to the community's intellectual ferment. . . . She loved the more spacious countryside of New Hampshire, knowing that it would inspire richer engagement with nature and wider opportunities for long walks and gardening."[5] Frances Hand officially appeared on the Cornish tax list only in 1922; she was credited with owning thirteen acres that were formerly the William Hyde property—and previously had belonged to Thomas Dewing. They had three daughters: Mary, who became Mrs. Morris Darrell; Frances, who became Mrs. Robert M. Ferguson; and Constance, who became Mrs. Newbold Morris. Maxfield Parrish used two of the daughters, before they were married, as models in his painting "Hilltop," done in the early 1920s.[6] Frances Fincke Hand was quite active in the women's suffrage movement both in Cornish and in New York, where she frequently marched in parades. She remarked that "the first time I marched in a parade, my husband told me he was going to pull down the shade, but after that he marched with me."[7]

Judge Hand died in 1961 and Mrs. Hand died two years later. A fitting epitaph can be found in a speech he delivered in Central Park to 150,000 recently naturalized Americans in 1944: "The spirit of liberty is the spirit which is not too sure that it is right; the spirit of liberty is the spirit which seeks to understand the minds of other men and women; the spirit of liberty remembers that not even a sparrow falls to earth unheeded; the spirit of liberty is the spirit of Him who, nearly two thousand years ago, taught mankind that lesson it has never learned, but has never quite forgotten: that there may be a kingdom where the least shall be heard and considered side by side with the greatest."[8]

ENDNOTES

1. Irving Dilliard, *The Spirit of Liberty: Papers and Addresses of Learned Hand* (New York: Alfred A. Knopf, 1960), pp. xv-xvi; see *Time*, the issue following his death in August of 1961, p. 16.

2. Dilliard, p. xiv.

3. Newspaper clipping, *New York Times*, March 30, 1947, Virginia Colby, Cornish Colony files.

4. Entries for September 11, 17, and 26. Stephen Parrish, diary, Baker Library, Dartmouth Colllege, Hanover, NH, gift of Marian and Roy Garrand. The Hands may have been included in his entry for October 1: "sudden exodus beginning of our summer neighbors."

5. Gerald Gunther, *Learned Hand: The Man and the Judge* (New York: Knopf, 1994), p. 172. Gunther is the source of the friendship between Judge Hand, Frances Hand, and Louis Dow, a professor of French at Dartmouth College.

6. Interview: Virginia Colby with Sue Lewin Colby, 1975.

7. As quoted in an obituary, *The Washington Post*, December 14, 1963.

8. Dilliard, p. 190.

Figure 88. *Norman Hapgood's masthead "Seen from the Study Window,"* Collier's Weekly, *Feb. 28, 1903.*

NORMAN HAPGOOD
1868 – 1937

NORMAN HAPGOOD, a prominent American journalist and author, edited *Collier's Weekly* from 1903 to 1912, *Harper's Weekly* from 1913 to 1916, and later, from 1922 to 1925, *Hearst's International Magazine*. At *Collier's* he wrote a column that ranged widely and yet incisively over the current literary scene; its title provides a clue as to the type of man he was: "Seen from the Study Window: Thoughts Which Sometimes Get Lost in the Bustle of Busy Life." Later in his editorial career, he briefly summarized his aim as an editor:

> Somewhere around 1908 a famous American declared that intellectual leadership had passed from the universities to the popular magazines. If he lived today, where would he place such leadership? Many believe that this leading quality has gone forever from the magazines. It was inseparable from individuality. When a product is standardized, it ceases to be individual. . . . The mind is different. . . . Editors have much responsibility. Charles Darwin said, "We are apt to look at progress as normal in human society, but history refutes this." The editor who does not think of making our grandchildren wiser, more enlightened than we are, is unworthy of his post.[1]

He was generally considered to hold liberal opinions. Characterizing a book he had written in the aftermath of World War I, a period of shifting alliances—both political and intellectual ones—a reviewer commented:

> Writing out of a long and varied experience as student, author, editor, and public man, and with an enviable record of courage in championing good causes and opposing wrong, he is trying only to analyze a period of transition. There are unhappily many who will find even his moderate progressivism too vigorous for their blood, but we suspect that historians will characterize as an advance the hour which he has described.[2]

Although written at an earlier period, and with some fatuous flippancy, Mabel Dodge Luhan was someone who found Hapgood too radical: "I . . . used . . . to stay overnight with the Hapgoods . . . Norman had been with [Lincoln] Steffens as dramatic critic. He was also a radical. . . . He was the editor, now, of *Collier's Weekly*, a magazine that was considered very broadminded . . . Norman [was] in New York, living [an] intellectual li[f]e, being broadminded, advocating 'public ownership,' and other communistic principles."[3]

He brought some of his New York connections, as well as his ideas, to Cornish in 1903 when he first appeared on the Cornish tax list after he bought "High Court" from Annie Lazarus, who was married to the artist John Humphreys Johnston. Two years later, the gate to his house was the subject of an illustration in *The Country Calendar*, though identified as being in "Windsor, Vermont."[4] A strong advocate of the benefits of the local area, he was responsible for persuading two subsequent Colony residents to consider the idea of summering in New Hampshire. He was an early advocate of the poetry and drama of Percy MacKaye and the person who introduced the Cornish Colony to MacKaye.[5] More significantly, his "glowing account" of Winston Churchill's palatial "Harlakenden" induced President Woodrow Wilson and his first wife Ellen Axson Wilson to spend the summer of 1913 renting the house.[6] One further connection, through *Collier's*, was with Maxfield Parrish, provided sixty-six covers for the magazine, all but a few executed while Hapgood was associated with the magazine and living in Cornish.[7]

There is much evidence of his participation in community events and hence his commitment to Cornish. "The Cornish Library Notes" frequently lists his contribution of books, both those he had written and autographed as well as those from his library, and he gave an address at the Plainfield Old Home Day.[8] The frequent references to him at social events in the diaries of Stephen Parrish indicate that he was popular on the social circuit as well.

On two occasions he combined his interest in drama with his regard for Cornish. In the famous *A Masque of "Ours": The Gods and the Golden Bowl*, he played the part of Charon when it was presented to Augustus Saint-Gaudens in the summer of 1905. Then, when *Sanctuary: A Bird Masque* was performed for a second time at the Hotel Astor in New York City on February 24, 1914—with the same cast as had been in the Meriden, New Hampshire, performance the previous year—he was one of the participants in a discussion following Percy MacKaye's lecture "The Relation of the Art of the Theatre to Wild Nature Conversation."[9]

Norman Hapgood died in New York on April 29, 1937.

SUGGESTION FOR FURTHER READING

Michael Marcaccio, *The Hapgoods: Three Earnest Brothers* (Charlottesville, VA: University Press of Virginia, 1977).

ENDNOTES

1. "Norman Hapgood Writes About Harding, Taft and Queen Elizabeth," *Hearst's International*, March 1922, p. 7.

2. William MacDonald, reviewing *The Advancing Hour* in *The Nation* 111, #2884, October 13, 1920, p. 427.

3. Mabel Dodge Luhan, *Movers and Shakers* (Albuquerque, NM: University of New Mexico Press, 1936, reprinted 1985), p. 56.

4. *The Country Calendar* 1, 5, September 1905, p. 450.

5. Arvia MacKaye Ege, *The Power of the Impossible: The Life Story of Percy and Marion MacKaye* (Falmouth, ME: The Kennebec River Press, 1992), p. 121.

6. Hugh Mason Wade, *A Brief History of Cornish, 1763-1974* (Hanover, NH: University Press of New England, 1976), p. 76.

7. Coy Ludwig, *Maxfield Parrish* (New York: Watson-Guptill, 1973), p. 208.

8. Virginia Colby, Cornish Colony files.

9. Invitation to the play, February 24, 1914, Virginia Colby, Cornish Colony files.

Figure 89. *Self-portrait.*

WILLIAM HOWARD HART
1863 – 1937

WILLIAM HOWARD HART, a landscape and portrait painter, received his artistic training in New York under J. Alden Weir and at the Art Students League as well as in Paris at the Académie Julian under Gustave Boulanger and Jules-Joseph Lefebvre in the 1890s. Several of his works center on the Cornish scene. In 1896, he painted *Country Lane Landscape;* two others of his works, *Hayfield, Summer* and *Landscape with Mt. Ascutney,* are landscapes with a local focus. His *Portrait of Mrs. Herbert Adams, Woman in a Garden,* and *Mrs. Herbert Adams at Home* are owned locally by Cornish residents. He exhibited two of his figure paintings in an exhibition of Cornish artists at Dartmouth College in 1916.[1] Elsewhere he exhibited *Lady in Shawl* and *Girl in Cloak* at the 27th Annual Exhibition of the Society of American Artists in 1905. Among his friends and neighbors in the Cornish Colony, however, Hart was respected for his passion for drama as much as for his devotion to art.

Shortly after his return from Paris, Herbert and Adeline Adams invited him to come to Cornish; he boarded with them at Stephen A. Tracy's farmhouse.[2] He turned up on the Plainfield tax list in 1909 when he purchased part of the Lewin property adjacent to the house of his close friends, the Adamses, off Stage Road in Plainfield.[3] The house on the property was "an old New England farmhouse of the usual kind," but Hart did "just enough to it and to its surroundings to bring out its modest but manifest possibilities." In fact, "people who propose to 'do over' New England farmhouses would do well to examine this example. They could scarcely better the instruction; but they could learn there from the cost of architectural interest, of which such farmhouses are capable and the way in which this interest can be brought out." Hart added two dormer windows and a porch at one end of the house, built a terrace to provide a flat area in front of it, planted vines and shrubbery "in the right places," enclosed the entrance door with a lattice, and encircled the house and lawn with flower beds. Consequently, "it would be difficult to find elsewhere in this country an effect equally as charming obtained by the use of such extremely simple and inexpensive means."[4] (The original house has been torn down and rebuilt as part of the Powerhouse Complex in West Lebanon, New Hampshire, where it is labeled as "The Charles Gilkey House, Plainfield, New Hampshire, ca. 1799.")

Figure 90. *A painting of Howard Hart's cottage by Henry Prellwitz.*

Once his house was in order, Hart could devote himself to art and to a favorite pastime for members of the Cornish Colony: organizing, rehearsing, and presenting plays. To encourage this interest, Herbert Adams constructed an amphitheater in the woods behind his house and Hart's where many theatrical productions were mounted. Hart's own interest in dramatics led him in several different directions. First, he offered a stage to the town of Plainfield. Article X of the 1916 Plainfield Annual Town Report reads: "To see if the town will vote to raise the sum of three hundred dollars to build a foundation at the east end of the town hall at Plainfield in accordance with a proposition submitted by William H. Hart."[5] Once the town agreed to provide the foundation, Hart and his associates pledged themselves to finance the rest, including the stage and lights. Hart donated the latest in stage lighting and Maxfield Parrish in 1916 painted a scene of Mount Ascutney; his design was reproduced for a backdrop augmented by six panels for the wings. It is unknown whether Parrish actually painted any of it himself. One theory is that professional scene painters reproduced the study on the town hall stage backdrop and wings.[6] They are still used today. The stage had the reputation for being the most beautiful one north of Boston.[7] Hart, for his part, donated the latest in stage lighting; the lights can be made to create the impression of daybreak, dusk, twilight, and all graduations of daylight in between. Its inaugural production was an operetta, *The Woodland Princess*, on Old Home Day, August 11, 1916. A reviewer noted that it "was given by the children of Cornish and it would be difficult to find a more enthusiastic audience than that which broke into applause at the sight of the charming little stage in its green lattice frame, and never stopped from the time that the red velvet curtains parted on Mr. Parrish's lovely woodland scene until the audience rose to its feet and joined enthusiastically in informing Mr. Hart that he was a jolly good fellow, sung with considerable emphasis . . . all the audience . . . rose to their feet to . . . name . . . the one who had made that and many other such evenings possible—Howard Hart."[8]

Hart's second significant contribution to local dramatics was his organization in the 1930s of the "Howard Hart Players," a drama group of local players. They produced plays such as *Hansel and Gretel* in 1937 and 1938, *The Late Christopher Bean* in 1938, and *Folk Dance Festival* also in 1938. On a more personal basis, Hart did some acting of his own. In the 1905 production of *A Masque of "Ours": The Gods and the Golden Bowl*, he was Silenus, the satyr leader, and in the 1913 production of *Sanctuary: A Bird Masque*, he was in charge of the properties and played the Evening Grosbeak.[9]

Hart died, unmarried, on February 20, 1937, and bequeathed most of his estate to Herbert Adams.[10]

ENDNOTES

1. George Breed Zug, "Exhibition of Cornish Artists," *Art and Archaeology*, April 1916, pp. 203-205; see also *Dartmouth Alumni Magazine*, March 1916, pp. 207-211.

2. Letter from Mrs. Herbert Adams to Stephen A. Tracy, dated May 19, but no year given; the letter is in the collection of Dorothy Tracy, Cornish, NH. Because the earliest dated painting Hart did in Cornish is 1896, that may be the date of this letter. Frances Grimes recalls that the Adamses came to Cornish in 1894 for the first time and returned next in 1896 when they boarded with Stephen A. Tracy; see the "Reminiscences of Frances Grimes," Saint-Gaudens Papers, Baker Library, Dartmouth College, Hanover, NH.

3. The Plainfield town tax records list Hart as a non-resident taxpayer from 1909 to 1935.

4. Unsigned, illustrated article in *The Architectural Record*, October 1907, pp. 280-282. The article contains an interesting glimpse into contemporary architectural values. "These [New England] farmhouses, as we all know, were frequently in themselves well-proportioned little buildings, with a certain definite architectural character, which counted in spite of the neglect with which they have been usually treated by their inhabitants; but whether from poverty, from the lack of the proper educational influences, or from sheer insensibility, the farmer rarely made any attempt to give his neat little house the advantage of a proper setting. At its best, the New England farmhouse was nothing more than tidy; and the planting in its vicinity never consisted of more than a few trees, a lilac or two, and occasionally a border of annual flowers. The effect is usually so bare and arid that one feels like weeping at the sight of such widespread neglect of the decent comeliness of domestic life."

5. The Annual Report for 1917 notes that the foundation for the town hall addition had cost the town $270; see below p. 311.

6. Letter from Maxfield Parrish, Jr., to Plainfield Selectman Stephen H. Taylor, June 18, 1977; Plainfield Historical Society.

7. Virginia Reed Colby, "Stephen and Maxfield Parrish in New Hampshire," *The Magazine Antiques* 115, June 1979, p. 1297. The sketch for the backdrop is in a private collection, Los Angeles, CA.

8. Clara Westgate's scrapbook, Virginia Colby, Cornish Colony files.

9. Records, Cornish Historical Society, Cornish, NH.

10. Probate Court Records, Newport, NH, File #9366.

Figure 91. *Portrait of Ethel Barrymore by Frances Houston.*

FRANCES C. LYONS HOUSTON
1851 – 1906

LITTLE HAS BEEN WRITTEN on a well-known, turn-of-the-century artist who was a beloved member of the Cornish Colony: Mrs. Frances C. Houston. Primarily a portrait painter, she was born in Hudson, Michigan, in 1851, the daughter of Lafayette A. Lyons and Charlotte M. Hand. At a time when a woman rarely entered upon a professional career, she studied in Paris both with Jean-Léon Gérôme and with Gustave Boulanger and Jules-Joseph Lefebvre at the Académie Julian. Returning to America, she married William C. Houston in 1874; the couple then established their residence in Boston. But Mrs. Houston continued to exhibit widely both here and abroad. She was awarded a bronze medal at both the Georgia International Exhibition of 1895 and the 1901 Pan-American Exhibition in Buffalo. She also won a medal for *Larghetto*, a study of three young female musicians with subtle gradations of color, at the Louisiana Purchase Exposition at St. Louis in 1904. She was a member of both the Boston and New York watercolor societies. Abroad, she exhibited in London, Paris, and Naples. Her work was chosen for the Paris Salon of 1890, and she won an Honorable Mention at the 1900 Exposition Universelle in Paris. For her portrait of Cavaliere Francesco Mancini, the Società Artistica Napolitana elected her its only woman member. Contemporary opinion of her was high: "her extraordinary talent, her unusual technical ability, and her exquisite sense of beauty all met with an immediate recognition. . . . She was an artist of immense range; her portraits show a rare strength and feeling for character, with a delicacy and charm of handling and of color which are missed in most of the art of our day."[1]

One artist of that day in whose work these qualities certainly were not missing and someone whom Frances Houston greatly admired actually urged the couple to come to Cornish: Thomas Dewing. He had painted Frances's portrait probably in 1880 and, as he did with many of his friends, invited the Houstons to try New Hampshire during the summer. Her arrival in Cornish did not go unnoticed.[2] A report in an 1891 number of *The Vermont Journal* noted that the William Houstons were boarding with the George S. Ruggles family while they were looking for property in the area. They eventually purchased twenty acres from Charles Beaman, land that had been part of the Pike farm and that was adjacent to the house of Annie Lazarus.[3] There they built "Crossways," an English-style house designed by the well-known Boston architect J. W. Beale. Frances Grimes thought that "it was more luxurious than any of the houses at that time except High Court [owned by Annie Lazarus]. The life in it freer from restraint, the food richer, Italian rather than French. It set new standards of hospitality. Mr. Houston—Uncle Billy as he was called—was an invalid, limited to a wheeled chair."[4]

After moving to the area, Frances Houston took a strong interest in local affairs. In 1897, with Mrs. Henry Oliver Walker, she helped organize the Mothers' and Daughters' Club in Plainfield. When the clubhouse was built in 1901, Mrs. Houston was instrumental in starting the Mothers' and Daughters' Rug Industry. She suggested that instead of a "rag carpet of historic fame, made on the old-fashioned loom, a rug might be made of prettier and more harmonious color with some attempt at design."[5] The rug industry flourished—thanks to the ability of some Cornish Colony members to sell their rugs to their friends in Boston and New York. She and her husband were also instrumental in refurbishing the Methodist-Unitarian Church.[6]

Other of her activities locally included playing the role of Ceres in *A Masque of "Ours": The Gods and the Golden Bowl* (1905) and entertaining guests on the family's popular tennis court that was built on a plateau surrounded by pines. Margaret Homer Shurcliff noted that "the popularity and wit of the players always drew a large gallery. Charlotte Houston herself, a famous beauty often painted by artists, was generally at the court. With her was her dear father, in a wheelchair. He had been beaten up in the street by thugs—a case of mistaken identity."[7] One of the 1898 social season's highlights was the wedding of Charlotte to John Fairchild, Lucia Fairchild Fuller's brother. The eleven o'clock ceremony took place in the music room of "Crossways" and was conducted by Rev. Charles Ames of Boston with "the official part, which made them man and wife, conducted by Mr. W. P. Thrasher of Plainfield."[8] The invited guest list reads as if it were a Who's Who of the Cornish Colony with many local people attending, too: Mr. and Mrs. S. A. Tracy, Mr. and Mrs. George Ruggles, Mr. and Mrs. Curt Lewin, Mr. and Mrs. Jerome Wilder, and Mr. George Austin. The following week Charles C. Beaman gave a ball in his pavilion in honor of the bride and groom.

The year before she died, Frances exhibited twenty-three paintings at the St. Botolph Club in Boston, a private dining and residential club devoted to promoting the arts. Included in this 1905 show were a number of paintings involving local subjects. There was a portrait of Mrs. Winston Churchill which was described as "an individual one, holding the attention by its reserved qualities. The attitude of the figure is dignified, but most natural, and the whole tone of the picture is quiet. The only bright color is in the flesh tones of the face, and the dash of brilliant green in the hat. The hair, too, is bright, but kept subordinate to the whole." Secondly, there was a portrait of Richard Mann, "the little modern, most American boy, holding a puppy in his arms . . . Mrs. Houston has caught the real spirit of small boyhood, and also expressed the child's striking individuality." A third painting was of her daughter Charlotte; it is variously known as *Summer* and *Mrs. J. C. Fairchild and Children*. It depicts Charlotte Houston Fairchild "standing under the shadow of a tree with her little girl Frances [named for her grandmother?], dressed in a short white gown, at her right, and her little boy in a white flannel suit at her left, both nestling close to their mother." The account continued, noting that there was another portrait of Charlotte, painted before 1898, hanging on an adjacent wall. "Mrs. Fairchild, who is quite as beautiful as a matron as when in her teens . . . is wearing a gown of white filmy material with pale pink roses and rosebuds, with delicate green leaves and vines—thoroughly harmonious with its setting—and a fall of lace around the decollete bodice. The distant dark blue hills of Windsor, Vermont, and a bit of bright blue sky and the nearer green hills and trees add to the whole charming effect and make an admirable background for this truly decorative group."[9] Finally, there was a portrait, *Ellen*, loaned by Louis Evan Shipman.

Thomas W. Dewing wrote an important statement about the last picture she painted, a portrait of Ethel Barrymore done while both women were in Cornish during the summer of 1906; it accompanied a photograph of the painting in *The Century Magazine*. "Mrs. Houston's canvases have great technical value, as this charming portrait shows, and its publication may call attention to the importance of contemporary art in America. . . . The two qualities that gave distinction to Mrs. Houston's work were undoubtedly her sense of style and her sense of beauty. . . . She worked quietly, satisfied with the job of creating many forms of beauty in pottery, goldsmith's work, and gardening, in which branches of art she was an adept."[10] After her death in October of 1906, this portrait, which remained unfinished, was also exhibited at a memorial exhibition of fifty of her works held in the Doll and Richards Gallery on Boston's Newbury Street. It was described as "not only a portrait, but . . . an impression of Miss Barrymore's versatility and ever-changing and elusive beauty. The graceful pose, with slender arms extended upon the knees, the individual poise of the head and the wonderful dark eyes, the semi-classic dress of grey blue, the unobtrusive background, and the general color arrangement, make a most agreeable impression."[11]

ENDNOTES

1. Obituary, unidentified Boston newspaper, Virginia Colby, Cornish Colony files.
2. For a discussion of this portrait and the autoradiographs done on it, see Susan A. Hobbs, with an essay by Barbara Dayer Gallati, *The Art of Thomas Wilmer Dewing: Beauty Reconfigured*, exhibition catalogue (The Brooklyn Museum in association with the Smithsonian Institution Press, 1996), pp. 91-92.
3. Tax records, Cornish, NH.
4. As quoted in *A Circle of Friends: Art Colonies of Cornish and Dublin*, exhibition catalogue, (Durham, NH: University Art Galleries, University of New Hampshire, 1985) p. 134. Frances Grimes was recalling the winter of 1900-01 that she spent there; her "Reminiscences" are in Baker Library, Dartmouth College, Hanover, NH.
5. Virginia Colby, Cornish Colony files.
6. See above pp. 76-77 for the story of this building that has had its secular uses too—as the Cornish Grange Hall and, more recently, the Selectmen's Office.
7. Margaret Homer Shurcliff, *Lively Days* (Taipei: Literature House, Ltd., 1965), p. 35.
8. Virginia Colby, Cornish Colony files.
9. Ibid.
10. *The Century Magazine* 75, April 1908, p. 957.
11. Virginia Colby, Cornish Colony files.

Figure 92. *Self portrait.*

WILLIAM HENRY HYDE
1856 – 1943

WILLIAM HENRY HYDE was a painter of portraits and landscapes as well as being a popular illustrator for such magazines as *Century, Harper's,* and *Scribner's.* He studied painting in Paris with Gustave Boulanger and Jules-Joseph Lefebvre at the Académie Julian. He was a member of the Society of American Artists, a group founded in opposition to the more conservative National Academy of Design, although he became an associate member of the Academy in 1900. At the Lousiana Purchase Exposition at St. Louis in 1904, he exhibited a portrait of his wife and at the Panama-Pacific International Exposition at San Francisco in 1915, he showed a portrait entitled *Vera,* which may have been a picture of Mrs. William Beaman.[1] At the Century Club in New York in 1909, he exhibited eighteen portraits, several of which had a connection with Cornish: a portrait of Mrs. John Blair, whose husband directed *A Masque of "Ours": The Gods and the Golden Bowl*; one of Mrs. Winston Churchill, the wife of the novelist; one of Miss Sylvia Hyde, his daughter; one of Miss S. L. Potter, his sister-in-law; and one of Frank H. Potter, Esq., his brother-in-law.[2] Other of his Cornish-related paintings include landscapes of local scenes and of *Ascutney Mountain.*[3]

He first appeared on the Cornish tax rolls in 1906 as the new owner of the former house belonging to Thomas W. Dewing. Yet, Hyde was in Cornish the previous summer because he played the part of Leander in *A Masque of "Ours:" The Gods and the Golden Bowl.*[4] During that summer, he rented the Dewing house with his wife, Mary Potter Hyde, who was the sister of Clara Davidge and the daughter of the Right Reverend Henry C. Potter, Episcopal Bishop of New York. (Clara Davidge had actually first come to Cornish in 1904.) The Colony's social life claimed much of their attention during their summers. Their daughter Sylvia played the part of Giglio in the play *The Rose and the Ring,* a play for children that Ethel Barrymore coached during her summer here in 1906. The play's scenery was painted by Lucia Fuller and Louise Cox arranged the costumes. Following the program, tea was served at the home of H. O. Walker. The performance was a benefit for the St. John's Guild; it netted the group $260.[5] Later in their lives, both Hydes were active in the Cornish Equal Suffrage League.[6] A final tidbit of

Figure 93. *Residence of William Henry Hyde.*

information about the Hydes: when they left Cornish after the summer of 1905, they deposited their pet cat with Stephen Parrish.[7]

ENDNOTES

1. *A Circle of Friends: Art Colonies of Cornish and Dublin*, exhibition catalogue, (Durham, NH: University Art Galleries, University of New Hampshire, 1985) p. 134.

2. Catalogue, "Exhibition of Paintings, Sketches, and Drawings by Kenneth Frazier, Birge Harrison, William H. Hyde, and Allen Tucker at the Century Club" (1909), Virginia Colby, Cornish Colony files.

3. *A Circle of Friends*, pp. 91, 134.

4. Hyde's name is included among those listed on the medallions that Saint-Gaudens made for each participant.

5. September 1906 clipping from an unnamed magazine, Cornish Colony file, Baker Library, Dartmouth College, Hanover, NH.

6. Cornish Equal Suffrage League brochure, 1911, Cornish Historical Society files, Cornish, NH.

7. Stephen Parrish diary, entry for October 28, 1905, Baker Library, Dartmouth College, Hanover, NH, gift of Marian and Roy Garrand.

ALBION E. LANG
1849 – 1938

ALBION LANG was among the third wave of residents of the Cornish Colony—affluent people who arrived after the sculptors and artists, who preceded the writers. The third group sought the lively conversation and excitement of their creative neighbors. Lang, born in Huntington, Ohio, on September 13, 1849, arrived in 1905 from Toledo, Ohio, where he had made his fortune in streetcar service in northwestern Ohio. His wife Mary's brother was Admiral William Mayhew Folger, who had come to Cornish in 1901. In the context of this influx, Child remarks that:

> Of course Cornish could never have attained the elaborate limits of the country around Lenox, Massachusetts, or Dublin, New Hampshire. Those regions are controlled by bankers or businessmen, who back their original purchases by large fortunes. While here, with scarcely an exception, most of the residents, after the fashion of artists, live to the extent of their incomes. It is strange, indeed, that this genuinely rich, element has never crept in, yet such is the fact, with the exception of . . . Dr. George Hayward of Boston . . . and of Mr. Albion E. Lang of Toledo, Ohio, who in 1905 bought land of Mr. Frank J. Chadbourne, just north of Doctor Hayward's.[1]

The land they bought, which also included part of the Chapman farm, was on the Cornish-Plainfield line. Consequently, the Langs paid taxes in both communities. They were consistently taxed for horses and cows and, during some years, for fowl, hogs, and sheep. In 1907, for example, the Cornish tax records reveal that Lang was taxed for five horses, four cows, five neat stock, sixteen sheep, one automobile, and four carriages.[2] At a later date, *The Weekly Enterprise* remarked that "Albion Lang has been the largest taxpayer in Plainfield for the last few years, paying $450 plus a tax in Cornish."[3] The farm itself consisted of a slaughterhouse, a hen house, a large grain bin, and an ice house. On the side of the barn was a wash rack to which the vehicles were driven so that they could be washed. For a number of years, Burtel Philbrick operated the farm for the Langs.

The house, known as "Highlands," was a twenty-seven room mansion with three furnaces designed by the New York City architectural firm of Gay and Nash. Stephen Parrish noted in his diary on September 28, 1905: "I am in despair at the inability to get any 'help,' including a stonemason to lay the new wall south of the present garden.

Figure 94. *Architect's drawing of Albion Lang's house.*

Lang's new house takes all the men available."[4] In fact, many local people were involved with the Lang estate. Edward M. Dannatt, a Windsor cabinetmaker, did fine woodwork for it, and among those who served as caretakers were William Jenney and Francis Perry.

The Langs devoted much of their time, energy, and money to local philanthropic concerns as well as local issues. They substantially aided in the renovations of the former Methodist church when it was taken over by the Unitarians in 1905.[5] Mr. Lang was a member of the Plainfield Progressive League, which was organized in the winter of 1908-09.[6] Both of them were members of the Cornish Equal Suffrage League. Mrs. Lang was a member of the Mothers' and Daughters' Club of Plainfield. The two of them were generous contributors to the Meriden Bird Sanctuary.[7] And they contributed books and magazine subscriptions to the Plainfield and Cornish libraries.[8] Mr. Lang frequently participated in the Old Home Day celebrations of both towns— often serving as a speaker.

As for local issues, in 1906, the issue of "freeing" the toll bridge across the Connecticut River, so that no fees would be charged for using it, was one to which Albion Lang spoke, as well as William Balloch—both listed as being from Cornish.[9] Water was an issue in which Lang was keenly interested. At one point, he wanted to give Plainfield running water. To do so, the pipes had to run through the Shipman property, but they refused to grant permission for the pipes to be laid through their land. Thus, Plainfield never got access to Lang's promise of water. Meriden, however, was somewhat luckier. In November of 1927, there was a fire on the high ground in Meriden near Kimball Union Academy. A solution for an area difficult to protect came in the form of "a large storage of water" and the installation of "a pump for use in case of fire." But, "if water is to be stored, why not make some other use of it? Gradually, there evolved the plan of a swimming pool which might serve the double purpose of protection for fire and recreation for students in fall and spring, and for guests in summer. A new friend of the Academy was found in the person of Albion E. Lang, a summer resident of Plainfield who has become a citizen of the town, highly respected for his public spirit and personal qualities, and who provided generously for the construction of the pool and placing of the pump."[10]

The subsequent history of the Langs' connection with the area is an ironic comment on this concern with fire and water. Following the death of Mary in 1931, Albion Lang's sister Lily came to stay with him; he died at the age of eighty-nine in 1938 and Lily G. Lang died in 1939 at the age of eighty-two. But "Highlands" had an even sadder end. The huge estate burned to the ground on the night of April 11, 1945, under suspicious circumstances. In October and November of that year, there was a lengthy, sensational trial in Newport, New Hampshire. For three weeks, spectacular banner headlines, mostly concerning the alleged suspicious actions on the part of Arthur W. Fedor, a wealthy realtor from Linden, New Jersey, screamed from the Claremont, New Hampshire, *Daily Eagle.* The facts the prosecution established "beyond a reasonable doubt" were that Fedor had bought the Lang house for $6,000, that he had insured it for $80,000, that the house was a total loss, and that Fedor was in Plainfield at six o'clock the morning after the fire. The house's value in 1945 was determined to be $180,000. But the defense lawyers, with witnesses and laboratory tests, were able successfully to challenge the circumstantial evidence, some of which involved the testimony of such local people as Otis William Jordan, fire warden of Plainfield; Plainfield Selectman Francis E. Atwood and his wife; Sheriff James F. McCusker; Mr. Herbert Hodgeman, a deputy sheriff; and Palmer C. Read, Jr., a Plainfield farmer and deputy forest fire warden. Fedor was finally acquitted on November 21, 1945.[11]

ENDNOTES

1. William H. Child, *History of the Town of Cornish with Genealogical Record: 1763-1910.* (Concord, NH: The Rumford Press, 1911?), Vol. 1, p. 224.

2. Cornish town tax records, Cornish, NH.

3. May 26, 1909.

4. Stephen Parrish, diary, Baker Library, Dartmouth College, Hanover, NH, gift of Marian and Roy Garrand.

5. Hugh Mason Wade, *A Brief History of Cornish, 1763-1974* (Hanover, NH: University Press of New England, 1976), p. 30; this church, used originally by the Methodists, became the Cornish Grange Hall, and now houses the office of the Board of Selectmen—see above pp. 76-77.

6. Virginia Colby, Cornish Colony files.

7. Newspaper clippings, not dated, Daniels scrapbook, Plainfield, NH.

8. Cornish Library scrapbook, George Stowell Library, Cornish Flat, NH.

9. Windsor Library scrapbook, July 10, 1906, Windsor, VT.

10. *Kimball Union Academy Bulletin,* August and December 1929, pp. 2-4.

11. For a complete set of newspaper clippings about the trial from the Claremont *Daily Eagle,* see Virginia Colby, Cornish Colony files.

Figure 95. *Grace Lawrence at about age 13.*

GRACE LAWRENCE
(TAYLOR)
1871 – 1940

GRACE LAWRENCE AND HER SISTER EDITH were the daughters of De Witt Clinton Lawrence (1830-1897) and Adeline Elizabeth (Hoe) Lawrence (1836-1882). Grace attended the Capen School, later Miss Burnham's School, in Northampton, Massachusetts. The two sisters came to Cornish in 1891 when Grace was twenty;[1] they were alerted to the area because their aunt, Annie Corbin Hoe, was Charles A. Platt's first wife. (In 1887, she died in childbirth eleven months after their marriage in 1886.[2])

At first the two sisters lived at "Chaseholme," the Beaman house now belonging to Anthony Neidecker (1996), and then at the "Turnpike House," another Beaman house on the other side of 12A near the intersection of Saint-Gaudens Road—a house that no longer exists. The sisters soon bought a two-acre lot from George Freeman at the top of Freeman Hill in Plainfield, up from where Maxfield Parrish was later to select a lot and on the other side of the road. Having paid $400 for the property, the sisters caused quite a local stir because everyone thought the price was exorbitant.[3]

But this was just the beginning of their expenses. Because of their family connection with Charles A. Platt, they were easily able to persuade him to design their new house in 1890. Platt was intent on remedying some design problems with "High Court" and carefully crafted what locally was his smallest "and most charming [house]. The traditional character of its center-hall plan was modified by the large windows with narrow muntins, the wide-board siding, deep overhanging eaves, and loggia" on the west side so that its inhabitants could readily enjoy a view of Mount Ascutney. He had found, however, that "High Court's" "low-hipped, shingled roof . . . trembled under the heavy New Hampshire snowfalls so . . . Platt increased the pitch of the hipped roof while retaining the deep overhang, thus creating a charming compromise between the New England farmhouse and the Italian villa. Instead of stucco, he used grooved, horizontal boards which were unplaned to enliven the texture of the surface. Finally, he abandoned the U-shape plan for a center-hall building with a loggia at one end."[4] Since Grace was a concert pianist and a frequent soloist with the Kneisel Quartet, the west parlor was designed as a drawing room for her small, local recitals and the loggia could be used for any overflow. Edith's interests, however, required no such adjustments because they were in horses and gardening. They agreed to call the house "Hilltop."

Music became a central element in establishing Grace Lawrence's relationship with other members of the Cornish Colony. She played the part of Calypso in *A Masque of "Ours": The Gods and the Golden Bowl* in 1905. More impor-

Figure 96. *Grace Lawrence Taylor at the piano.*

tantly, she gave concerts with Arthur Whiting, a conductor and composer, whose pieces were performed by the symphony orchestras of Boston, Pittsburgh, and Cincinnati. Stephen Parrish was one member of the Cornish Colony who genuinely appreciated Grace's talent. There are many references in his diaries to social contacts between the Lawrence sisters and his cousin Anne, who lived with him after his wife's death. For example, on July 2, 1899, he notes, "Grace Arnold and Grace Lawrence to lunch, music all day. A very delightful Sunday." Because of the distance between their two houses, the Lawrence sisters would often spend the night at the Parrishes and then return home the following day. Parrish was consistently impressed with Grace Arnold's beautiful contralto voice as well as Grace Lawrence's sensitive accompaniment.[5] In addition to the Sunday-afternoon chamber music concerts at "Hilltop," Grace Lawrence also played at the homes of Maxfield Parrish, Charles A. Platt, and Winston Churchill.[6] She presented a musical program at the wedding of Mabel Harlakenden Churchill to Allan M. Butler for which "most of Cornish" was invited.[7] Only a few months before her death, she played Robert Schumann's "Carnival" for a group of friends at Mrs. Bullard's house in Windsor, Vermont.

On a more intimate scale, music created numerous personal contacts. She was a great influence on and inspiration to her family; she instilled in them a love and appreciation for good music. She helped several local people, Marguerite Quimby, for example, with their music. And Frances Arnold, who loved to bind books using beautifully marbled endpapers made in Italy, bound some of Grace Lawrence's music for her. Proof that music resulted in extensive entertaining within the Colony can be found in the large number of table linens, china, glassware, and flatware included in her inventory.[8]

In 1906, Grace Lawrence married Robert Longley Taylor (1861-1923). Because Professor Taylor taught Romance Languages at Dartmouth College, the couple moved to Norwich, Vermont, where they lived from 1906 to 1913 in the house now owned by the Norwich Historical Society. Not all contact with the Cornish Colony was broken, however: Anne Parrish often took the train from Windsor and stayed with them on overnight visits.[9] The Taylors had three children: Lawrence Hoe Taylor (1910-1981), Philip Longley Taylor (b. 1912), and Rosamond (Taylor) Burling Edmondson (b. 1915). The Taylors moved to Williamstown, Massachusetts, where Dr. Taylor taught Romance Languages at Williams College until his death in 1923. Grace Lawrence Taylor died in April 1940 and is buried in Williamstown.

ENDNOTES

1. Interview: Virginia Colby with Rosamond (Taylor) Burling Edmondson, July 1, 1987.

2. Keith N. Morgan, *Charles A. Platt: The Artist as Architect* (Cambridge, MA: The MIT Press, 1985), pp. 22, 241.

3. Frances Grimes, "Reminiscences," Reel #36, frame #408, Baker Library, Dartmouth College, Hanover, NH.

4. Keith N. Morgan, "Charles A. Platt's Houses and Gardens in Cornish, New Hampshire," *The Magazine Antiques* 122:1, July 1982, pp. 122, 124-25.

5. See especially his diary entry for October 11, 1903, when he attended church services in Plainfield and heard the two. For more on the Grace Arnold mentioned in the diary and the Frances Arnold mentioned in the next paragraph, see below pp. 459-460, especially n. 3.

6. Interview: Colby/Edmondson.

7. Daniels scrapbook, Plainfield, NH.

8. Probate File, Hall of Records, Newport, NH.

9. Stephen Parrish, diary, entry for December 2, 1907, Baker Library, Dartmouth College, Hanover, NH, gift of Marian and Roy Garrand.

Figure 97. The Boat House *by Ernest Lawson* .

ERNEST LAWSON
1873 – 1939

ERNEST LAWSON was born in Halifax, Nova Scotia, on March 22, 1873. At fifteen, he moved to Kansas City with his parents and entered the Kansas City Art League School. In 1890, he came to New York City to study at the Art Students League with John Twachtman, who became a strong influence on Lawson's subsequent work. During the next two years, Lawson joined the art school Twachtman and J. Alden Weir established at Cos Cob, Connecticut. In 1893 he went to France and enrolled in the Académie Julian under Jean-Paul Laurens and Benjamin Constant. He visited Moret-sur-Loing where he came in contact with the French Impressionist Alfred Sisley's work and it too became an important early influence on his painting. While he was in Paris, he shared a studio with Somerset Maugham, who based the character of Frederick Lawson, the emotional artist in *Of Human Bondage*, on Ernest Lawson. Some of this same intense feeling can be seen from Ernest Lawson's remarks about how he painted:

> Color affects me like music affects some persons . . . emotionally . . . I like to play with colors . . . like a composer playing with counterpoint in music. It's sort of a rhythmic proposition. You try one color scheme in a sort of contrapuntal fashion, and you get one effect. And you try something else, and you get another effect. We don't actually copy nature in art. Nature merely suggests something to us which we add to our own ideas. Impressions in nature are merely jumping off points for artistic creations.[1]

In 1894, he returned to America and married Ella Holman, an art teacher with whom he had studied in Kansas City. Thus, this American Impressionist, though not linked to the earlier impressionism of "The Ten," soon became associated with "The Eight"; many of his early paintings are indicative of the urban emphasis associated with "The Ashcan School," some of whom were also numbered among "The Eight."[2] He earned a silver medal at the Universal Exposition in St. Louis in 1904 and the Jennie Sesnan Gold Medal from the Pennsylvania Academy of the Fine Arts in 1907; in 1915, he received gold medals from the National Academy of Design and from the Panama-Pacific International Exposition in San Francisco. He had three paintings in the International Exhibition of Modern Art—the Armory Show—in 1913. He was made an associate member of the National Academy of Design in 1908 and a full academician in 1917.

Lawson came to the Cornish Colony during the summers of 1919 and 1920 when he rented the house of Lucia and Henry Fuller in Plainfield.[3] In the landscapes of this period, "the gritty speed of New York was replaced by rural serenity."[4] As was true of many of the artists who came to the area, the grandeur of Mount Ascutney and the Connecticut River Valley captivated Lawson.[5] His *New England Birches* (also called *Mt. Ascutney, N.H.*, c. 1920, Phillips Collection, Washington, DC) shows the mountain through a screen of delicate birches. (Note that it is he who geographically misplaced his subject when putting a title on the painting.) Another painting, entitled *Ploughing*, formerly in the Los Angeles County Museum of Art, may be one of a ploughing farmer and his horse working against a background of Mount Ascutney. Other of his Cornish landscapes include *Vanishing Mist* (also called *Rising Mist*, Carnegie Institute), *After Rain* (also called *Vanishing Mists*, c. 1920, Phillips Collection), and possibly *Winter Hills* in the Ira Glackens Collection—Ira's father William was one of Lawson's best friends.

Not only was 1920 the last summer he spent in New Hampshire, it was also the last year he and his family lived together. Lawson went out West and taught art in Kansas City and at the Broadmoor Art Academy in Colorado Springs. He won several prizes and medals during this period and, suffering from rheumatoid arthritis which allowed him rare periods of being able to paint, he moved to Coral Gables, Florida. Toward the end of the Depression, he recuperated enough to receive a Federal Arts Program mural commission for the post office in Short Hills, New Jersey, that he completed in the summer of 1939. In December of that year, morose at the death of William Glackens and suffering from both a serious depression and a severe drinking problem, his body was found on the beach at Miami, a probable victim of a heart attack brought on by a gang of marauding young robbers and assaulters.[6]

ENDNOTES

1. William H. Gerdts, *American Impressionism* (New York: Artabras, 1984), p. 278.

2. For more information on this group, one of who was Everett Shinn—a Cornish colony member—see above p. 119, n. 4.

3. See the Fuller Papers, Baker Library, Dartmouth College, Hanover, NH.

4. Gerdts, p. 278.

5. Lawson "has a secure place in the affections of art lovers. A many-sided, delightful and companionable personality, he has instinctively shrunk from the usual methods of the business artist in placing his work. If there is one outstanding virtue of Ernest Lawson's work, it is that of distinctive Americanism; he does not find it necessary to change our fine Westchester hills into the Vosges or the Ardennes, and he has been content to paint the Hudson River and Connecticut Valley so that they look like part of Uncle Sam's country"; quoted in Henry and Sidney Berry-Hill, *Ernest Lawson: American Impressionist, 1873-1939* (Leigh-on-Sea, England: F. Lewis, Publishers, Ltd., 1968), p. 39.

6. Dennis R. Anderson, *Ernest Lawson Exhibition*, exhibition catalogue (New York: ACA Galleries, 1976), p. 9.

ANNIE LAZARUS
1859 – 1945

ANNIE LAZARUS was a younger sister of Emma Lazarus, the poet who wrote the sonnet "The New Colossus." We all know this poem's closing lines because they appear on the Statue of Library: "Give me your tired, your poor,/Your huddled masses yearning to breathe free,/The wretched refuse of your teeming shore./Send these, the homeless, tempest-lost to me./I lift my lamp beside the golden door!" Both women were from a New York City banking family that regarded itself as members of the "Jewish Nobility."[1] Annie was also a friend of William M. Evarts, whose son-in-law was Charles Cotesworth Beaman, the man chiefly responsible for the settlement of the Cornish Art Colony. Annie Lazarus, no doubt, wanted to be in Cornish because she was a patron of the arts. Though he was a good friend of her sister, Emma, Thomas W. Dewing once remarked, "[Annie] must take great pleasure in looking down from her palace on the artists working in the ghetto below."[2]

She first appeared on the Cornish tax list as the owner of thirty acres of land that had been "on the western edge of the Austin farm."[3] *The Vermont Journal* notes the next step: "the road is now completed to the site of Miss Lazarus's summer residence, and workmen are excavating for the foundation of the house, the cornerstone of which will be laid Saturday, with appropriate exercises in which all the 'New Yorkers' will participate."[4] Several local people were involved in building the house. Charles Read contracted to furnish 15,000 feet of lumber for it, the Flowers brothers of Hartland, Vermont, laid its chimneys, and Edward Dannatt, a cabinetmaker from Windsor, was one of its carpenters. During the actual period of construction, Stephen A. Tracy provided a place for Miss Lazarus to stay.

"High Court," a name chosen by Annie herself, was an early triumph of Charles A. Platt, one of the best residential architects in America and a member of the Cornish Colony. The house was begun in 1890 and completed in 1891; it "immediately became a landmark of the area and a harbinger of Platt's later work . . . [it was an] early non-urban example of the classical-Renaissance formula that came to dominate American architecture in the 1890s."[5] Platt wrote his friend Stanford White, "What I want to build is an Italian villa three sides of a court with a collonade[sic] in the middle. The wings to be one story and the main part two."[6] Platt, intent on integrating the house

Figure 98.
*Charles A. Platt's
"High Court"
(1890-1891).*

with its surroundings, positioned the house to take full advantage of the view of Mount Ascutney. In fact, he approached the siting and landscaping problems the house presented "from the perspective of a landscape painter"—even painting a picture of Lazarus's house as seen from his own garden across the road and "farther down the hill. . . . He designed the entrance drive to circle around the hill and approach the house on the side away from the main vista. Rows of hemlocks, backed by poplars, channeled the visitor to the door and prevented an early view" of the panoramic prospect out to Mount Ascutney.[7] The house was focused on a central axis that brought the visitor "into the rear courtyard which framed a panorama of the valley. Mount Ascutney only became visible as one walked to the edge of the terrace. To conceal these views until the precise moment was one of Platt's major objectives in the design of High Court."[8] Morgan goes on to argue that Platt also employed a technique of landscape painting to incorporate the building into its surroundings: attention to depth recession. He quotes one of Platt's rare comments in 1912 on his activity: "To a house set high upon a hill, the ground falling away from it with some abruptness, the whole site chosen for the view, the landscape gardener will give surroundings of the utmost simplicity that they may not compete with or disturb the larger without. This was recognized in the Frascati villas of Italy, which were terraced to give a view of the distant Campagna, and in America there was an example in High Court."[9]

Unfortunately, the original "High Court" burned in 1896. *The Vermont Journal* of July 18, 1896, reported that "the summer residence of Miss Annie Lazarus of New York in Cornish, N. H., was destroyed by fire, early Thursday morning. The alarm was sounded by a locomotive whistle, and a number of Windsorites responded to the call for assistance. The house was burned to the ground, but nearly all of its contents were saved. The fire is supposed to have been caused by ashes in a barrel in the cellar. The house will be rebuilt at once."[10] The stucco over wood structure was rebuilt in 1896, this time from red brick that was whitewashed.[11]

By 1901 Annie Lazarus had married the artist John Humphreys Johnston. In 1902 she sold "High Court" to Norman Hapgood; she and her husband moved to Italy and lived there among the international set. Subsequently, "High Court" was owned by: A. Conger Goodyear; at his death his wife married an architect from Boston, John Ames; and later by James L. Farley, whose wife had been "previously married to Creighton Churchill, the younger son of the novelist."[12]

ENDNOTES

1. Heinrich E. Jacob, *The World of Emma Lazarus* (New York: Shocken Books, 1949), p. 15. Although the Statue of Liberty was dedicated in 1886, the lines from Emma's poem were put on a plaque and attached to the statue's pedestal in 1903 at the instigation of her friend Georgiana Schuyler. Emma died before this commemoration—in 1887.

2. Hugh Mason Wade, *A Brief History of Cornish: 1763-1974* (Hanover, NH: University Press of New England, 1976), p. 54. Both Maria Oakey Dewing and Annie Lazarus are the subjects for Dewing's 1891 painting *The Song*, done in Cornish; for Dewing's "amorous relationship" with Annie Lazarus, see Susan A. Hobbs, with an essay by Barbara Dayer Gallati, *The Art of Thomas Wilmer Dewing: Beauty Reconfigured*, exhibition catalogue (The Brooklyn Museum in association with the Smithsonian Institution Press, 1996), pp. 132-133.

3. William H. Child, *History of the Town of Cornish with Genealogical Record: 1763-1910*, (Concord, NH: The Rumford Press, 1911?), Vol. 1, p. 224. The full quotation reads: "At about this time, too, in 1890, Mr. Dewing's friend, Miss Emma Lazarus of New York, set up her home, 'High Court,' on the western edge of the Austin Farm." As is true of many people familiar with Emma's famous lines of poetry, Child confuses Emma with Annie. Emma had been dead three years.

4. September 13, 1890, Virginia Colby, Cornish Colony files.

5. Keith N. Morgan, *Charles A. Platt: The Artist as Architect* (Cambridge, MA: The MIT Press, 1985), pp. 29, 32.

6. As quoted in Morgan, p. 29.

7. Ibid., pp. 33-35.

8. Ibid., p. 35.

9. As quoted in Morgan, p. 35; from *Architecture* 26, August 1912, p. 142. Note that Platt refers to his activity not as that of an architect but as "landscape gardener." It is also interesting to note the Cornish connection with "the Frascati villas of Italy." Maxfield Parrish illustrated both the Reservoir at the Villa Falconeri in Frascati and the Cascade at the Villa Torlonia in Frascati for *Italian Villas and Their Gardens* by Edith Wharton and pictures by Maxfield Parrish (New York: The Century Company, 1904), opposite pp. 5 and 8.

10. Windsor Library scrapbook. Another account reads: "Claremont people who chanced to observe the northern horizon in the early morning hours of Thursday, noticed the sky lurid with fire. . . . The fire was discovered by a domestic, who aroused the inmates of the house. Efforts to extinguish the flames were fruitless, as they started in a lot of dry birch wood, and burned furiously. Considerable household furniture, paintings, etc., were saved, but the house was totally destroyed. The property was insured, $6000 on the house. . . . The fire is thought to have been caused by rats and matches."; Albert Read scrapbook. Both sources are in Virginia Colby, Cornish Colony files.

11. See the illustrations that accompany an article in *House and Garden*, June 1901 [1902], pp. 413-415.

12. Wade, p. 55.

CURTIS LEWIN AND HIS ACOCUNT BOOKS
1850 – 1906

THE CORNISH HISTORICAL SOCIETY is fortunate to own the account books beginning with the year 1893 from the butcher shop run by Curtis Lewin on the south end of Prospect Hill in Plainfield, New Hampshire. The adept social historian can derive interesting information and devise significant hypotheses from this kind of primary evidence. These account books offer a rare glimpse into the lives of many Cornish Colonists. For example, these books show that one secret of Curtis Lewin's success was his ability to befriend many of the cooks who worked in the houses of Colony members.

At the turn of the century, there were several Lewins in the Upper Valley engaged in the meat business: B. E. Lewin of Hanover was a dealer in fresh and salted meats, Benny Lewin of Plainfield was a butcher, and so was Curtis Lewin. His accounts indicate that he did a great deal of business in Plainfield, Cornish, and Windsor. He had seven or eight meat wagons that would travel eight or ten miles in all directions delivering the meat orders to his customers. In Windsor they would call on the Cabot, Cone, and Jarvis families as well as those of Max Evarts, William Evarts, and Dr. Brewster.

Regular, faithful customers from among the Cornish Colony members listed in the early account books included Annie Lazarus, who purchased 5¾ pounds of beef for 96 cents and 9 pounds of veal for $1.50; Charles A. Platt, who had one tremendous order of 13½ pounds of mutton for $2.70; Henry Oliver Walker; Thomas W. Dewing; and Dr. Nichols. By 1898 the account books register many more people associated with the Colony: Herbert Adams, Kenyon Cox, Herbert Croly, Henry Fuller, Samuel Isham, Maxfield Parrish, Arthur Whiting (the composer, conductor, pianist, and member of the Kneisel Quartet), and Mr. Kneisel himself—the founder of the quartet. Even James Tasker, the well-known builder of local covered bridges, was a frequent customer.

What kind of hypotheses, therefore, can be drawn from these entries? That the prices, judged even by contemporary standards, seem low suggests that transportation costs were not added onto prices; hence, it was cheaper to buy in rural markets rather than in urban ones. That a large number of people must have been dining at the Platts'. That the increase in the number of Colony members from 1893 to 1898 is indicative of the growing popularity and reputation of the Colony as "the place to be."

Here are some more facts. What hypotheses do they suggest to you? l) George Ruggles, Stephen A. Tracy, Frank Johnson, and the Egglestons all ordered quantities of beef, veal, and mutton. (These were families that took in boarders from the Colony, so their orders were proportionately higher than the norm.) 2) Frances Houston ordered quantities of liver. (Either she was excessively fond of liver—or her cat was.) 3) George de Forest Brush, according to the number of entries, was an extremely faithful customer. (That he probably did not spend all his dinner hours in the tepee that he pitched on Saint-Gaudens's field near Blow-Me-Down Brook.) 4) The number of entries for Stephen Parrish are greater in 1895 than in 1893. (That, in fact, once his house was finished and he was settled in it, he became a more frequent customer.)

The number of entries, in general, offer useful, concrete proof that entertaining at dinner parties was a principal diversion among Cornish Colony members. For this fact, there exists much corroborating evidence in addition to these account books; letters often refer to these gala affairs. Finally, the entries in these books are useful in helping us to determine exactly what years certain people summered locally and how late into the autumn they remained.

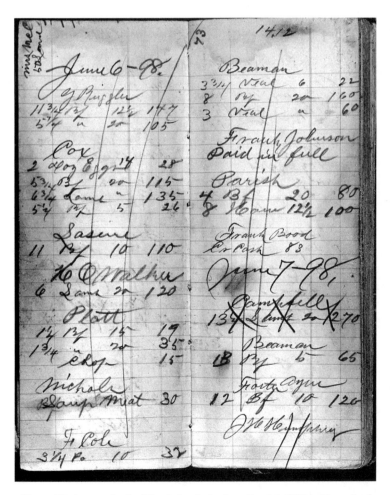

Figure 99. *Account book of Curtis Lewin for June 6 and 7, 1898, with entries for the Ruggles, Cox, Platt, Nichols, Beaman, and Parrish families.*

SUSAN L. LEWIN (COLBY)
1889 – 1978

Figure 100. *Sue Lewin posing for Maxfield Parrish's* The Tea Tray.

FOR MAXFIELD PARRISH, SUE LEWIN was the perfect model. "Professional models, he once remarked, seemed to lack the quality of innocence that was necessary for the kind of paintings he made."[1] She was able to capture exactly the mood and the pose that he required. Hence, it is not surprising that she modeled for more paintings than any of his other models.

Sue, the daughter of Elmer and Nellie (Westgate) Lewin, was born in Hartland, Vermont, on November 22, 1889. In 1905, at the age of sixteen, she went to "The Oaks" and began what was to be a fifty-five-year association with the Parrish family. That was also the year she first posed for Parrish and his *Land of Make Believe*, a painting not used as an illustration until the frontispiece cover of the August 1912 number of *Scribner's Magazine*.

In addition to working for the family and posing for Maxfield Parrish, Sue also made most of the costumes she wore out of drapery fabric or cheesecloth. She "turned [them] out on a small hand crank 'Wilcox & Gibbs' sewing machine, once owned by Parrish's grandmother, Susan Maxfield Parrish."[2] When Sue was not working on these tasks, she enjoyed her bridge club that met regularly. At the point when refreshments were to be served, Maxfield Parrish could generally be counted on to turn up.[3]

Modeling for him, however, was a significant assignment in itself. In 1910, Edward Bok, the editor of the *Ladies' Home Journal*, with its headquarters in the Curtis Publishing Company building in Philadelphia, Pennsylvania, commissioned Parrish to paint eighteen murals for the female employees' dining room on the top floor. The murals were to be on a large scale—10 feet 8½ inches by 3 feet 5 inches, those in the corner were even larger—and the theme was a *Florentine Fête* in which groups of young and happy people would be seen going to a carnival. In a letter to Bok dated July 27, 1911, Parrish noted dryly:

All the people are youths and girls; nobody seems old. It may be a gathering of only young people, or it may be a land where there is youth, and nobody grows old at all. . . . What is the meaning of it all? It doesn't mean an earthly thing, not even a ghost of an allegory: no science enlightening agriculture: nobody enlightening anything. The endeavor is to present a painting which will give pleasure without tiring the intellect: something beautiful to look upon: a good place to be in. Nothing more.[4]

This commission, on which Parrish worked assiduously until 1913 (the final panel was not completed until 1916), was among Parrish's most significant artistic triumphs. For most of the many figures, in all their variety of poses, Sue Lewin was the model.

There is an interesting aspect to Parrish's working methods illustrated by Sue's modeling in the studies for these murals. Parrish was such a meticulous artist that for a model to hold a pose for the length of time it took him to prepare a canvas would be the equivalent of "cruel and unusual punishment." Consequently, he constantly used a camera to fix an image of the human form and then painted it from the photographic print.[5] We are fortunate to have many of the glass plates Parrish made. Several of those used for the *Florentine Fête* mural show Sue in photographic studies for three of the panels. *Stairway to Summer* shows her in a walking pose, though she is actually leaning on a chair for support, dressed in an outfit appropriate for a carnival, with her eyes cast down and holding a lute. In *A Rose for Reward*, she wears a long, flowing gown with its folds carefully arranged for the effect of drapery with a wide, fringed scarf extending to the floor and belted at her waist; there is a ribbon in her hair, and she appears to be bowing, head and eyes cast down. In *Sweet Nothings*, she leans on a support in a pose enabling her to hear the "sweet nothings" from below; she is wearing a satin gown with puffed sleeves gathered by wide, jeweled armbands and a necklace; her hair falls loosely as it frames her pensively smiling face.[6] Each of these photographs has in its background several almost indistinguishable elements frozen in it for posterity from Parrish's studio—an easel, a chair, an open door with a stairway.

Because of her photogenic beauty, Sue Lewin posed for many paintings used on the magazine covers of both *Collier's, The National Weekly*—notably *The Lantern Bearers* and *The Idiot* (also known as *The Book Lover*), and *Hearst's Magazine*—notably *Reveries* (though the magazine was never released with the painting on the cover), and *Scribner's Magazine*. She posed for the male and female figures in *The Rubaiyat*, a decorative gift box for Crane's chocolates, and those of the four figures on the double-sided *Tea Tray*, a signboard for a friend's tea house. In the bookplate for the *Knave of Hearts*, she had to rest her elbow on a bottle to hold the pose long enough to get it right. She modeled for two of the faces in *The Pied Piper*, a mural for the Palace Hotel in San Francisco done in 1909 and two of the adult girls in *The Venetian Lamp Lighter*. Some of Parrish's other works for which Sue Lewin posed include advertisements for Jello (*Polly Put the Kettle on We'll all Make Jello* and *Jello: The King and Queen Might Eat Thereof and Noblemen Besides*), Djer-Kiss Cosmetics, General Electric Mazda Lamps (*Primitive Man*), Oneida Community Silver Plate, Swift's Premium Ham, and a poster for the Red Cross during World War I as well as such individual paintings as *The Enchanted Prince, The Little Chef, Griselda,* and *The Garden of Allah.* Although this is not a definitive list of her contributions as a model, these examples do suggest how popular a model she was for him (see below pp. 307-308).[7]

In 1960, Sue Lewin, at the age of seventy-one, married a childhood sweetheart, Earle W. Colby, and left "The Oaks" forever. She died January 27, 1978, and is buried in the Plain Cemetery in Plainfield.

ENDNOTES

1. Coy Ludwig, *Maxfield Parrish* (New York: Watson-Guptil Publications, 1973), p. 200.

2. Les Allen Ferry, *The Make Believe World of Sue Lewin* (Los Angeles: Republic Corporation, Continental Graphics Division, 1978), p. 8.

3. Interview: Virginia Colby with Marian Garrand, June 17, 1979. In addition to Mrs. Garrand, other members of the bridge club were Hazel Amidon, Edith Jordan, Ellen Maylin, Lucy Northrop, Ruth Northrop, and Lucille Read.

4. As quoted in Ludwig, p. 162.

5. See the fascinating remarks his son, Maxfield Parrish, Jr., made about "Maxfield Parrish and Photography" reprinted in Ludwig, pp. 198-200.

6. These studies are reproduced in Ferry, pp. 32-33, 45. Interestingly enough, in the 1905 photographic study for the *Land of Make Believe*, Sue appears to be carrying the same fringed scarf-belt she had on in the study for *A Rose for Reward*; see Ferry, p. 39.

7. For another view of Sue Lewin as Parrish's model, see Alma Gilbert, *The Make Believe World of Maxfield Parrish and Sue Lewin* (San Francisco: Pomegranate Artbooks, 1990) and the relevant passages in Alma Gilbert, *Maxfield Parrish: The Masterworks* (Berkeley, CA: Ten Speed Press, 1992), esp. pp. 17; 19-20.

PHILIP LITTELL
1868 – 1943

PHILIP LITTELL'S connection with Cornish was established in his youth through his Harvard University roommate, George Rublee. The latter persuaded him to come to Cornish in 1906 when Littell and his wife, Fanny Whittemore from Milwaukee, Wisconsin, stayed at "Chaseholme." In subsequent years they stayed at "The Turnpike" house, the Westgates' and Winston Churchill's "Farm House."[1] In 1912, they rented Arthur Whiting's house, which he had built in 1893 on land that was part of Edward Bryant's farm. Eventually the Littells settled in their house on Littell Road.

As it turned out, summering in Cornish cemented his friendship with Herbert Croly, who also bought some pasture land from Bryant above Littell's. Having begun his career by working on the *Milwaukee Sentinel,* a newspaper owned by George Rublee's family, Littell became the literary editor of Croly's magazine, *The New Republic.* He wrote a column for it called "Books and Things"; in 1919, Littell published a collection of his pieces, entitled appropriately, *Books and Things.* While living in "The Turnpike," Littell adapted a novel, William J. Locke's *Simple Septimus,* for the New York stage; it was a vehicle for the famous actor George Arliss.[2] Later in his life, he served on the editorial board of the *New York Evening Post* and published *This Way Out* in 1923.

As for their activities in Cornish, the Littells were listed as members of the Cornish Equal Suffrage League in 1911 and Mrs. Littell signed an "Endorsement of Birth Control." Philip Littell and George Rublee were enthusiastic tennis players. And, thanks to the "Cornish Library Notes," we know that "School No. 2 was very thoroughly cleaned by five volunteers, five women living in the neighborhood: Mrs. Philip Littell, Mrs. Learned Hand, Mrs. George Rublee, Mrs. Frances Arnold, and Miss Grimes."[3] (Although it is no longer standing, School No. 2 was located on the north side of Saint-Gaudens Road, a bit west of the Saint-Gaudens National Historic Site.)

Both Fanny and Philip Littell are buried in the Chase Cemetery in Cornish.

Their children, interestingly enough, each had a firm connection with Cornish. In 1924, their eldest son Robert married Anita Damrosch, the daughter of the famous conductor Walter Damrosch, who rented "High Court" in the early 1920s (see below p. 467). In 1934, he brought out "a Cornish novel, *Candles in the Storm,*" a satire based on "Percy MacKaye's philosophy that society, and particularly immediate neighbors, should support poets."[4] As did his father, Robert Littell wrote for *The New Republic*, as both a staff member and later as an associate editor; he also served as a columnist and drama critic for *The New York World*. In collaboration with his brother-in-law Sidney Howard, Robert wrote a comedy *Gather Ye Rosebuds*. He also had a distinguished career as a public servant. After World War I, he worked in London for the Allied Maritime Transport Council and served in Paris as a secretary for President Herbert Hoover's American relief administration. Shortly before World War II, he joined the staff of the *Reader's Digest* and served the magazine as a war correspondent both in England and in Normandy and as an editor. He died in 1963. The Littell's younger son, Whittemore, worked in the 1930s for an organization, the Commonwealth Fund, that sponsored graduate students from England when they came to study at universities in this country; notable among this group was Alistair Cooke, a venerable arbiter of "masterpiece" culture. During World War II, Whittemore worked in Concord, New Hampshire, in civil defense work and also taught at Dartmouth College—first V-12 midshipmen and later physics. After teaching at the Fountain Valley School in Colorado Springs, Colorado, for twenty-six years, he returned to Cornish in 1986 and died here in 1992. Finally, the Littell's only daughter Margaret married William Platt, the architect son of Charles A. Platt, and lived in Cornish for many years.[5]

ENDNOTES

1. Hugh Mason Wade, *A Brief History of Cornish: 1763-1974* (Hanover, NH: University Press of New England, 1976), p. 70, notes that "The Turnpike" was "an old house that formerly stood at the northern end of the long river meadow above the Windsor Bridge and was one of Charles Beaman's numerous acquisitions from Chester Pike." "Chaseholme" was "another old Beaman house to the northward."

2. Ibid.; William H. Child, *History of the Town of Cornish with Genealogical Record: 1763-1910* (Concord, NH: The Rumford Press, 1911?), Vol. 1, pp. 229-230, refers to Littell as a "dramatist" and his "Simple Septimus" as "a charming adaptation."

3. An undated newspaper clipping; Virginia Colby, Cornish Colony files.

4. Wade, p. 73.

5. Much of the information on Robert Littell comes from a 1963 obituary, Virginia Colby, Cornish Colony files. For the information on Whittemore and Margaret Littell, see Wade, pp. 70-71, and the article in the *Windsor Chronicle*, Windsor, VT, for Friday, June 20, 1986.

BENTON MACKAYE
1879 – 1975

IN "A CAPSULE HISTORY OF CONSERVATION," our sometime Vermont neighbor Wallace Stegner has recently reminded us, in case our memories need jogging, that Benton MacKaye was one of the founders of The Wilderness Society.[1] And in 1987, when people celebrated the fiftieth anniversary of the establishment of the Appalachian Trail, we were also reminded that the "Father of the Appalachian Trail" was none other than Benton MacKaye. Perhaps, then, his connections with Cornish need further elaboration. Although it is stretching matters to categorize him among the members of the Cornish Colony, he loved the New Hampshire hills—both those in the White Mountains and those of the local variety. He knew the latter because of his frequent visits to his brother Percy's house "Hilltop"—both in the heyday of the Colony and in 1956, the year of Percy's death.[2] From all reports Benton was quite a companionable man; Stephen Parrish frequently noted in his diary the fact that he had enjoyed a visit with Benton MacKaye.

The fifth son of the famous American actor Steele MacKaye, Benton was born March 6, 1879. His father "had known Emerson and Thoreau and other New England Transcendentalists, and had given his family's life an air both of his seriousness and of erratic instability. Young Benton early reacted against the mercurial impracticality of his idealistic father, but he absorbed his idealism grounded in a Thoreauvian appreciation of practical ways and means."[3] The connection with Thoreau appears frequently in discussions of MacKaye: "With his black hair, his lean face, his gift for picturesque epithets and oaths, his campfire stories, he might seem from the outside the archetypal Yankee, almost the stage Yankee. Though he was so different in character from Thoreau, he figures for me as Thoreau's latest continuator: a Yankee of the Yankees, tart as a wild apple, sweet as a hickory nut—though to more philistine minds he must often have seemed, to use Mackaye's own words, 'wild as a wolf, and crazy as a loon.'"[4]

Benton's exploration of the then rural area around his home in Shirley Center, in central Massachusetts near the New Hampshire border, led to his interest in becoming what he termed a "geotechnist." He defined such a profession as being applicable to someone interested in "the applied science of making the earth more habitable."[5] In fact, it lay at the heart of a massive work that was to have been the capstone of his career, "The

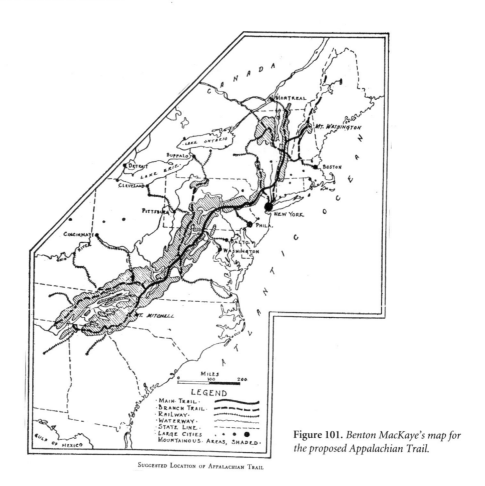

SUGGESTED LOCATION OF APPALACHIAN TRAIL

Figure 101. *Benton MacKaye's map for the proposed Appalachian Trail.*

Geotechnics of North America." It has unfortunately never been published, although some of its substance appears in *From Geography to Geotechnics*.[6] In pursuit of his "geo-technic" career, he went to Harvard, where he earned a BA and then an AM in forestry, and later went to work for Gifford Pinchot in the US Forest Service. There he wrote "numerous technical reports on forestry which began to have a more social orientation after his marriage in 1915 to the noted suffragist Jessie Stubbs."[7]

In October of 1921, he published "An Appalachian Trail, A Project in Regional Planning" in the *Journal of the American Institute of Architects*, the first of MacKaye's many legacies to his country. "It may have been in 1891, while I was listening to bearded, one-armed Major John Wesley Powell recount to an enthralled audience in Washington City his historic trip through the Grand Canyon.... It may have been in 1897, in the White Mountains of New Hampshire, as Sturgis Pray and I struggled through a tangled blowdown.... Or it may have been in 1900 when I stood with another friend, Horace Hildreth, viewing the heights of the Green Mountains... [that] the notion of an Appalachian Trail occurred to me."[8]

MacKaye wanted to insure that office workers and factory employees would be able to spend part of their vacations in an outdoor environment. Furthermore, he believed that there should be camping areas, especially in the heavily populated eastern part of the United States, so that people could drive to them easily and enjoy them readily. He really aimed at a cooperative camping life that would draw people out of the cities, expose them to life in the country, and inspire them eventually to settle in less populated areas. Thus he would create a series of recreational communities throughout the Appalachian chain of mountains from Maine to Georgia connected by a walking trail. Its purpose was to establish a more extensive as well as systematic development of outdoor community life. (The housing and community component in his vision perhaps explains why the project was initially published in a journal for architects.) As he said of the trail in one of the last articles he published before he died:

> I find in this a note of optimism for our sometimes gloomy world. With pollution and over-population spawning a sprawling urban desert, I am encouraged by the knowledge that there are millions of Americans who care about wilderness and mountains; who go forth for strength to Mother Earth; who defend her domain and seek her secrets. I am proud to have played a role in the birth of the Appalachian Trail. And I am proud of the generations of hikers who have made my dream a reality.[9]

His concern for wilderness led to his second major legacy: The Wilderness Society. Planning and advocacy for it began at a famous meeting in the Great Smoky Mountains in 1934 that included MacKaye, Harvey Broome, Bernard Frank, and Robert Marshall. The latter was one of the first to write about organizing such a society, but Aldo Leopold was its prophet—his principles can be read in his posthumously published *Sand County Almanac.* Leopold, along with Harold C. Anderson, Ernest C. Oberholtzer, and Robert Sterling Yard, officially organized The Wilderness Society in 1935 and Benton MacKaye was elected as the group's first vice-president in 1937; from 1945 to 1950, MacKaye was its president and from 1950 until his death, he was its honorary president. The principles he was acting upon as he saw the society take hold in America were clear:

> The whole object of conservation is, of course, to emulate nature's successes; this is not to make tamed land wild, but to make subnormal land normal. . . . Wilderness is the "perfect norm"; it is wild or untouched land as distinguished from domesticated cornfield, pasture, or farm woodlot; it is the product of paleontology. Wilderness is a reservoir of stored experiences in the ways of life before man. . . . Wilderness is two things—fact and feeling. It is a fund of knowledge and a spring of influence. It is the ultimate source of health—terrestrial and human.[10]

For MacKaye, the wilderness was never "the last refuge of despairing hermits, who might escape from the complexities and mischiefs of civilized life. . . . Like Thoreau, MacKaye appreciated the communal values of the New England village."[11] For him, each environment human beings inhabited was "complementary and . . . necessary for man's full development. If the preservation and restoration of natural resources was central to his whole life work, this was not to retreat from civilization but to make both the natural and the cultural environment serve man."[12]

Before leaving the career of this committed environmentalist, it should be noted that a quick glance at his bibliography is immediate proof of the enormous impact Benton MacKaye had on the world around him. There are reports for regional planning associations during the 1920s, a watershed article in 1930 called "The Townless Highway" that argues for a system of limited-access highways of the interstate variety, recommendations for both the Tennessee Valley Association and the Rural Electrification Administration (for which he worked in St. Louis), and discussions of conservation, wilderness, atomic energy, and region-wide planning issues that continue on into the 1960s and early 1970s.[13]

ENDNOTES

1. This essay first appeared in the *Smithsonian*, April 1990, and was reprinted in *Where the Bluebird Sings to the Lemonade Springs* (New York: Random House, 1992; Penguin Books, 1993).

2. Arvia MacKaye Ege, *The Power of the Impossible: The Life Story of Percy and Marion MacKaye* (Falmouth, ME: The Kennebec River Press, 1992), pp. 672-673.

3. Paul T. Bryant, "MacKaye as Writer," in an issue of The Wilderness Society's magazine designed as a tribute to Benton MacKaye: *The Living Wilderness*, Vol. 39, #132, January-March 1976, p. 31.

4. Lewis Mumford, "Benton MacKaye as Regional Planner," *The Living Wilderness*, p. 14. Mumford, MacKaye's good friend and collaborator, goes on to mention that MacKaye did not begin reading Thoreau until the late 1920s.

5. Crista Rahmann Renza, "The MacKaye Family papers," *Dartmouth College Library Bulletin*, Vol. 22 (ns), #1, November 1981, p. 18.

6. Paul T. Bryant, ed., *From Geography to Geotechnics* (Urbana, IL: University of Illinois Press, 1968), based on a series of publications in *The Survey* from October 1950 to June 1951; *A Two-Year Course in Geotechnics* was privately printed in Shirley Center, MA, in 1972.

7. Renza, p. 18.

8. Forward to Ronald M. Fisher, *The Appalachian Trail* (Washington, DC: The National Geographic Society, 1972); quoted in Paul H. Oehser, "Yankee Trailblazer," *The Living Wilderness* (1976), pp. 8-9.

9. As quoted in Oehser, p. 9. And savoring that reality was extremely important to him. So much so that "Benton would become acerbic if any hiker mentioned that he had hiked the trail in record time. He believed that a prize should be given to the person who hiked the trail in the longest time." Harley P. Holden, MacKaye's literary executor, letter to *Appalachian Trailway News* 55.5, November-December 1994, p. 3.

10. As quoted in George Marshall, "Benton as Wilderness Philosopher," *The Living Wilderness* (1976), p. 11

11. Mumford, p. 17.

12. Mumford, loc. cit.

13. Marshall, pp. 33-34.

PERCY MACKAYE
1875 – 1956

PERCY MACKAYE was a significant poet and dramatist who played a major role in the revival of interest in poetic drama in the early part of this century. But popular taste in the theater was then governed mostly by realism and naturalism; even the elements of folklore and social conscience that MacKaye championed had difficulty finding widespread appeal. Furthermore, melodramas in the nineteenth-century style as well as the star system worked against the kinds of plays he wrote. Nevertheless, MacKaye's delight in spectacle, which found expression in masques done locally and throughout America, helped to attract audiences.

This ability he may well have learned from his father, (James) Steele MacKaye (1842-1894), who was a famous nineteenth-century producer and actor, known especially for his performances as Hamlet. Steele MacKaye sought to adapt the European idea of a repertory theater in New York, produced his own play *Hazel Kirke* that had a two-year run, and built the Lyceum Theater where he set up New York's first acting school. Just before he died, he was planning a vast "Spectatorium" at the World's Columbian Exposition at Chicago in 1893. Although it was never constructed, it was designed to introduce the latest developments in stage equipment. Childe Hassam did a large watercolor of it, so we have some idea of what its impressive scale could have been. It certainly would have given his son a standard by which to measure his yearning for spectacle.

Percy MacKaye arrived in Cornish in the summer of 1904 after writing *The Canterbury Pilgrims* and *The Scarecrow* in 1903, though neither play was staged until later in that decade.[1] Before he finally had his own home, "Hilltop," built on Dodge Road in Plainfield with the help of Ned Waite and Gene Rice, MacKaye rented three different places. During the summers of 1904 and 1905, at the urging of Norman Hapgood, he rented the "Snuff Box House," which belonged to Admiral Folger, where he wrote *Fenris the Wolf.* He also stayed in the Fullers's house and boarded at the Tracys's house in 1906. From 1906 until 1912, he stayed at "The Wayside," a house that once stood on the corner of Lang and Hayward Roads.[2] A large part of *Jeanne d'Arc,* a play written in 1905 and published in 1906 that brought him much fame, was written while MacKaye occupied "The Woodchuck Hole," the studio built about 1890 by a local carpenter, George Ruggles.[3] Once he was settled at "Hilltop," he had the studio from "The Wayside" moved up

Figure 103. *Percy MacKaye's studio at his home "Hilltop" in Plainfield.*

to his new home. There he wrote several works based on New England life among which were *Yankee Fantasies,* 1912, a series of one-act folk plays, and *Gettysburg: A Woodshed Commentary,* based on the life of a neighboring farmer, Link Chapman.

His wife Marion lovingly described their life in Cornish during February of 1905: "Percy and I walk miles on our snowshoes, going through the woods, over the pastures with their big drifts and sliding, seated on the snowshoes, down the icy places. . . . The other day we went to the Smoot place and came upon countless rabbit tracks. . . . Suddenly we saw some *very* large tracks which looked as if a man had been there. We wondered who it could be and sat down on the piazza of the empty house . . . they were the tracks of a small bear and not only one but two." Cornish life during the winter was not without its tribulations: "We have been having a dreadful time with our water pipes freezing, much to Percy's disgust, as he has been wielding a pick-axe. However, he has had the whole neighborhood to help him—Louis Shipman, Harry Fuller, Max-field Parrish, and others, not to mention good old Columbus Jordan, who has been working the pump for an hour to fill the tank from the well sweep." On the other hand, there were some pleasant diversions to compensate for these inconveniences: "We went up to Maxfield Parrish's to a chick-a-dee dinner—that means the 'winter folk' here—Mr. Harry Fuller, Mr. and Mrs. Louis Shipman, the playwright, and Mr. Biddle were also there. We had a wonderful dinner (of squabs, wines, etc.) as we always do there. The witticisms just flowed from Mr. Parrish's lips! He is a very brilliant fellow, hardly a moment when these sallies are not amusing and delighting." And there follows Marion MacKaye's interesting description of the artist at work: "He showed us some of his new pictures. They are very decorative and extremely colorful—the famous Parrish blue appearing again and again, so vivid and luminous. He told us how he uses special methods in order to get them so brilliant, applying many glazes, etc. Later he took us out into his wonderful shop, where he makes everything from brass latches, hinges, tables, to plumbing feats—I can't begin to say what—it is like an alchemist's shop."[4]

The experience of winter finds its way into many of MacKaye's poems. Although there is no way of knowing whether the following poem was also written during the same winter, it does refer to the moon of St. Agnes, and it certainly sounds as if its images depict a wintry Cornish scene recollected in tranquillity:

Steep ran the hill-road out of the wood:
>Lambent, below us
>Flushed in the valley
>Snow-colored twilight—
>>Black isles of pines.

Hushed the cold tinklings, shuddered the sleigh:
>Round the horizon,
>Keen and auroral,
>Burned on the hill-lines.
>>Inexpressible rose.

Snorted the silvery breath of the horse:
>Into the silken
>Quivering silence,
>Slid like a snowflake
>>Saint Agnes' moon.[5]

But the "quivering silence" of a winter's night must eventually give way to a time "when first the pussy-willow shows/Her fairy muffs of gray." And MacKaye can transport us into a mood whose magic spell is clearly cast by Cornish:

For now through all of nature that we love
A vernal change, like love's, has late begun;
>The northing sun
That nightly from Ascutney shall remove
>Farther its setting, fills
The valley-chalice of the Cornish hills
With wine of warmer splendors . . .
>More seldom sounds the frosty axe,
>And by the rabbit-run
Our quaint embroideries of snowshoe tracks
>Grow softly blurred and charr'd . . .[6]

But the time spent in "the valley-chalice of the Cornish hills," though a great source of inspiration and a respite, was balanced by MacKaye's literary concerns that required extensive periods away from New Hampshire. Driven by a conviction that poetic drama was the best "means for most truly revealing the life and destiny of man in every historic age, including [his] own, [MacKaye was] impelled by a powerful impulse to develop in America drama of spiritual depth commensurate with the great dramas of past epochs, yet nonetheless modern and indicative of the future. From boyhood, this had been Percy MacKaye's unerring goal, and to find others who shared a like striving added fresh impetus to his efforts and aspirations."[7] Two of those "others" he found in New York and proudly brought to Cornish were William Vaughn Moody and Edwin

Figure 104. *Percy MacKaye, photographed by Arnold Genthe, 1912.*

Arlington Robinson. They must have recognized in him the same "divine fire" that Rosalind Fuller saw when she wrote her parents:

> I wish I could describe the MacKayes, but I fail miserably before such a task. I can only say that a divine fire burns in Percy MacKaye's soul and shines through his eyes—and I wish I could tell of the interesting, burning arguments we have had about War and Socialism. He is a peace man, but not such a pacifist as I am. He does not go so far—he is a little nervous of expecting too much—to hear him say, "But, Rosalind," is like music—indeed, he makes all our three names sound like poems.[8]

In Cornish, however, there were those who responded to his "divine fire" and enabled him to realize his artistic longings, particularly in connection with his lofty ideas about public pageantry. He began with the high-minded notion, expressed in *The Playhouse and the Play* and *The Civic Theatre in Relation to the Redemption of Leisure*, that the theater as an institution had a redemptive potential and that individual plays should educate their audiences by promoting civic responsibility. Toward this end, MacKaye revived public pageantry that might start out as a spectacular procession and result in dramatic productions that were performed outdoors not by professional actors but by local amateurs. Cornish in June of 1905 was the setting for the first publicized pageant, the locally famous *A Masque of "Ours": The Gods and the Golden Bowl*, written by Louis Evan Shipman. As Marion MacKaye noted, "it is to be a meeting of the Greek Deities, enacted by all the Cornishites coming in Greek costume, and Saint-Gaudens himself, as a saint, is to be taken into the society of the gods. The original idea was Harry Fuller's. Percy is to make the scenario and Parrish to help. The three are to do it."[9] (In addition to providing the scenario, MacKaye also wrote the Prologue.) Some of the elements of the masque carried out the idea that pageantry and spectacle were the order of the day:

> the music was played by a group from the Boston Symphony Orchestra—a small orchestra with harp, woodwinds, etc., and was led by Arthur Whiting. The whole colony took part, all in magnificent costumes. . . . At the center of the stage was a beautifully sculptured altar, while on either side hung great garlands of laurel and flowers. In front of the altar were two thrones, and on the sides benches for the gods. . . . After Jupiter and Juno were seated on the thrones, great clouds of smoke came up from the ravine behind the scenes and out of these clouds the gods gradually appeared. . . . There were also groups of nymphs and satyrs, the three graces, the god Pan with a rollicking assemblage about him, the Muses in gold and white, etc. Percy, as Mercury, was constantly running in and out during the entire Masque, as he introduced and announced the different groups. He wore lovely white wings on his feet and a little hat, and had a Mercury staff made by

Ernest Hill, the local carpenter. . . . Finally accompanied by the whole dramatis personae, [Minerva] came forward and with impressive effect presented a golden bowl to Saint-Gaudens—as the sign of his supremacy. And now, taking him with them—the gods, headed by Jupiter and June, led the players around through the audience and back to the stage, till finally the whole procession, still singing, mounted the hill to the studio. Around about the great chariot, carrying Mr. and Mrs. Saint-Gaudens, gamboled Fred Parrish, in his amazing get-up as a centaur, together with the little children of the Colony, among them Robin, in a little white tunic and green chaplet with sandals.[10]

MacKaye's interest in community drama was carried a step further when later Ernest Harold Baynes, representing the Meriden Bird Club, asked him to help dedicate the opening of their new sanctuary in 1913. He obliged with *Sanctuary: A Bird Masque*, the work for which, in Cornish, he is probably best remembered. But this poetic drama also alerted the entire country to the issues of ceasing to slaughter birds so that their feathers might be used on hats and clothing, of safeguarding them with year-round sanctuaries, and of feeding them during the winter. MacKaye's play received national attention—as well as notices in French and German newspapers—and performances throughout America stimulated the organization of over one hundred bird clubs. Other family members were involved in it: the Prologue, "The Hermit Thrush," was written by Arvia MacKaye, the MacKaye's eleven-year-old daughter, and MacKaye himself played the role of Alwyn, the poet. Mrs. Ellen Axson Wilson wrote MacKaye shortly after the Meriden performance that "Mr. Wilson, who, of course, has the experience which I lack in such matters, says he never knew anything of the sort so well and gracefully done—so charmingly conceived and carried out!"[11]

MacKaye's ideas about poetic pageantry also appealed to people beyond the confines of Cornish. In 1910, with the help of another member of the Colony, John Alexander, he created the *Masque of Labor*, a five-year Fourth of July project that was established in Pittsburgh, Pennsylvania. Then in 1914, he created the most spectacular of his masques, a civic masque done in St. Louis, Missouri, to commemorate the sesquicentennial of the city's founding and performed along the banks of the Mississippi before 500,000 people with a cast of 7,500 actors, actresses, and musicians. Of the crowd, Ernest Harold Baynes said, "Here was an ocean of faces . . . I can compare [it] with nothing I have ever seen, save perchance the growing corn on a rolling western plain."[12] And finally, there was *Caliban, by the Yellow Sands*, to commemorate the tercentenary of the death of William Shakespeare. The only time Isadora Duncan ever danced in public outside her own productions was at the masque's opening night in New York, May 24, 1916. Again Baynes wrote in the *Boston Evening Transcript* of the enormous preparations required for the 5,000 participants in this community pageant and masque: "I began to realize something of the magnitude of 'Caliban'—something of the enormous amount of organization which must have been necessary to recruit, teach, rehearse, amuse and protect so large a body, drawn from so many nationalities, so many classes, before they could be welded into one effective cast, capable of presenting a great and beautiful drama."[13]

Closer to home, however, the MacKayes were very active members of the Cornish Colony and participated in the local community until their deaths. There is a delightful portrait of one social occasion:

On Saturday night, we had a Café Chantant at the Town hall in the little town of Plain-field. We tied our horse in Louis Shipman's barn. Then we walked to the Town Hall, which was surrounded with carriages. It was trimmed on the inside with pine trees, and the stage was gotten up most artistically by Mr. Hart. . . . The old English songs linger in my memory with great sweetness, being done simply and with tender, deep feeling by Margaret Beaman. A Scottish ballad was done by Percy. He had on a great MacKaye plaid shawl, draped in the Scotch way, as shown by Mr. Barrett, bare neck and arms, trousers laced crosswise to the knee, a black brigand-like hat and feather, as he came striding onto the stage. He was a most tragic wonder, his amazing face taking on all the shades of meaning as he did the weird and dreadful ballad, "Edward, Edward!" It was consummately done, but [terrifying]. Miss Grimes, the little sculp-tress, said to me, "Heavens, aren't you afraid of him!" Then came the well-known cha-rades between Harry Fuller and Fred Parrish. Then Mr. Rublee dressed as a small girl in short frock, sash, and socks. As he is six feet five and one-half inch tall, he was too funny for words. The naturalist over at Corbin's Park, Harold Baynes, brought a small wild boar into the stage to have his bottle of milk. We had a wonderfully good time and talked with everybody.[14]

As a furthermore contribution to Cornish life, Percy used to entertain his friends by reading his poems or plays aloud. In a diary entry, Stephen Parrish wrote: "Evening Percy MacKaye read his play *Jeanne d'Arc* in his studio at Ruggles' to a company of 21 persons—all the Colony here at present." There are two more brief notices of the play. On October 11, 1906, Parrish noted, "Left for Phila. to see first performance of *Jeanne d'Arc* by Percy at the new Lyric Theatre—Sothern and Julia Marlow" and on October 15: "Play a success. Met the actors."[15] Cornish Colony artists took note of the family. Carlota Saint-Gaudens painted a portrait of Percy, and Arvia MacKaye, the oldest of the MacKaye's two daughters was a subject for a sculpture by Frances Grimes and a portrait by Louise Cox. Local recog-nition for Percy's contributions came in the form of an honorary degree from Dartmouth College in 1914: "Master of Arts to Percy MacKaye, poet, dramatist, critic, whose large vision of the theatre includes the pageantry and idealism of all men."

But recognition for his talents was not limited to this region. He was the first Ameri-can fellow in poetry and drama at Miami University, Ohio, in 1920. This honor came as no surprise to Maxfield Parrish, who let it be known that "Percy is the best possible per-son to be a poet in residence, because he's a poet twenty-four hours a day."[16] For his fifti-eth birthday in 1925, a huge tribute was organized for him to which Witter Bynner, Walter Damrosch, Hamlin Garland, Walter Lippmann, Langdon Mitchell, and Ridgely Torrence—all of whom had spent time in Cornish—as well as Henry Seidel Canby, Padraic Calum, Frank S. Converse, John Erskine, Robert Frost, Herbert Hoover, Charles Evans Hughes, Robert Underwood Johnson, Vachel Lindsay, Amy Lowell, Edward Markham, Don Marquis, Edgar Lee Masters, Albert Bigelow Paine, Bliss Perry, Edward Arlington Robinson, Sara Teasdale, and Hendrik Van Loon contributed.[17] He spent the summer of 1930 as a resident of the prestigious MacDowell Colony in Peterborough, New Hampshire. He was a member of both the National Institute of Arts and Letters and the Poetry Society of America. A national testimonial was organized for his seventieth birthday on March 16, 1945. Lewis Mumford's praise was typical: "Percy MacKaye's imagination has enriched and blessed America; his works are a direct manifestation of that better world for which we all must live and fight and die."[18] On this occasion, his publisher announced *The Mystery of Hamlet, King of Denmark, or What You Will,* a tetralogy based on the Hamlet legend. When these four verse plays were finally produced, no small task for a theatrical company, the *New York Times* sent its best drama critic, Brooks Atkinson, to California so that he could cover the performances in repertory. He commented that MacKaye's "characters are especially well-imagined and defined. And his verse is neither an insipid or pompous imitation of Shakespeare, but genuine poetry . . . MacKaye accepts a considerable challenge . . . because he is a genuine poet in a venerable tradition."[19]

Marion MacKaye died on June 1, 1939, during a visit to France, and Percy MacKaye died in Cornish, August 30, 1956.

ENDNOTES

1. *The Scarecrow* was reviewed by Clive Barnes, the drama critic of *The New York Times,* during a revival at Washington's Kennedy Center in 1975: "*The Scarecrow* is frankly a dramatic eccentricity, a play of no particular consequence perhaps, but on its own crazy terms it works most triumphantly." After noting that "the writing is terrible and [the] symbolism is corny," Barnes is nevertheless forced to admit that "what MacKaye has done here is to somehow create the magic—and it is magic, pure illusion—of theatrical characters." And with excellent acting, which the revival apparently supplied in abundance, this "poor but engaging play" became "fascinating": "MacKaye . . . this enormously experienced man of the theater must have realized what would have happened to his play when it fell into such sure hands." From a review, Virginia Colby, Cornish Colony files. (There was a New York revival in 1953, three years before Percy MacKaye died.) Incidentally, *The Canterbury Pilgrims* was presented by the "Coburn Players . . . on Tuesday, August 10th, at 8:15 P. M. in the Saint Gaudens' Woods. Mrs. George Rublee will dance between Acts II and III. Price of seats, $2. and $1. on sale at Mr. Homer Saint Gaudens' . . ."; a copy exists in the Cornish Historical Society files, Lagercrantz Collection.

2. Edwin Osgood Grover, ed., *Annals of an Era: Percy MacKaye and the MacKaye Family, 1826-1932* (Washington, DC: Published under the auspices of Dartmouth College, 1932), pp. xxxiii-xxxiv.

3. An inscription in a copy of *Jeanne d'Arc* owned by Anne Ruggles Curfman reads, "To Mr. and Mrs. George Ruggles, in whose studio much of this play was written, from their neighbor," signed Percy MacKaye. MacKaye's annotation of William Vaughn Moody, *Letters to Harriet* (Boston and New York: Houghton Mifflin, 1935), p. 277, indicates that "the elaborate stage arrangements" for this play "included new experiments in stage lighting and mechanics conducted by Abbott H. Thayer, assisted by Rockwell Kent and Barry Faulkner, based on Thayer's discoveries in protective coloration."

4. Arvia MacKaye Ege, *The Power of the Impossible: The Life Story of Percy and Marion MacKaye* (Falmouth, ME: The Kennebec River Press, 1992), pp. 123-124, describing February 5 and February 11, 1905. The Smoot house is a Charles Platt house near the corner of Thrasher Road and Lang Road, occupied by Rosamond Edmondson in 1996.

5. Percy MacKaye, *Poems* (New York: Macmillan, 1909), p. 168. St. Agnes is the patron saint of virtuous virgins. The story has it that if a young girl follows the prescribed ritual, a vision of her future husband will come to her on the evening prior to St. Agnes'

Day, January 20. Because of its associations with Keats's poem and because Percy MacKaye proposed to Marion Morse in a letter that was to be opened on the eve of St. Agnes in 1897, it was an evening special to the devoted couple.

6. MacKaye, p. 167.

7. Ege, pp. 136-137.

8. Rosalind Fuller to her parents, written "next door to the President of the US.," August 4, 1915, Virginia Colby, Cornish Colony files, courtesy of Carol Odell. The Fuller sisters were staying with Rose Standish Nichols, a niece of Augusta Saint-Gaudens. The house was the former Chester Pike farm that the Nicholses christened "Mastlands." It is adjacent to Winston Churchill's "Harlakenden," the house President Wilson was renting that summer. The Fuller sisters were so impressed with Percy MacKaye's pacifism that they included several peace songs in their Cornish programs. "Later, Miss Nichols drives [the Fuller sisters] to a large Peace Meeting in Windsor, where they changed into their Victorian dresses and sang to many young men from the ammunition factories nearby. 'The audience we sang to was very interesting,' wrote Cynthia [Fuller] . . .'there were many of these factory men—rough, dirty men—listening to the words *against* what they were helping to make—then there were middle-class men and their wives. They all seemed very intent and listened to every word.'"; Carol Odell, "The Fuller Sisters: Fourth Tour of America, Part 2, October 1914-May 20, 1916," unpublished manuscript, p. 39, Virginia Colby, Cornish Colony files.

9. Ege, p. 128. In his annotation of Moody, *Letters to Harriet*, MacKaye specifies that the Masque was "written by Louis Evan Shipman with Prologue by P.M-K.," (p. 425).

10. Ibid., pp. 128-130. Robin was Robert (Robin) Keith MacKaye, the MacKaye's eldest child, born in 1899. For a newspaper account of this event, see pp. 366-367.

11. Ibid., p. 241; see above pp. 141-143. For more on Wilson's attendance, see below pp. 502-503, n. 3.

12. "The Biggest Show Ever Staged," *Boston Evening Transcript*, June 20, 1914; Virginia Colby, Cornish Colony files. See also Ege, p. 249.

13. Ege, p. 285.

14. In August of 1905; Ege, pp. 131-32. For "terrifying" in the quotation, Marion MacKaye used "terrible," in trying to convey the sense of Percy "inspiring alarm or intense fear" during his rendition of the grisly Scottish ballad.

15. Stephen Parrish, diary, Baker Library, Dartmouth College, Hanover, NH, gift of Marian and Roy Garrand. This may be the reading Marion MacKaye describes in Ege, pp. 134-135. "Sothern" is Edward Hugh Sothern (1859-1933), a leading actor, especially at Steele MacKaye's Lyceum Theatre, and a good friend of Percy's; Julia Marlow [Sarah Frances Frost] (1866-1950) was a leading actress and Sothern's second wife—the two together were known for their roles in Shakespeare's plays. Julia Marlow and MacKaye had a terrible row over *Jeanne d'Arc*, but the two men remained steadfast friends (Ege, pp. 145-147).

16. Hugh Mason Wade, *A Brief History of Cornish: 1763-1974* (Hanover, NH: University Press of New England, 1976), p. 72.

17. *Percy MacKaye on His Fiftieth Birthday*, a copy of which is in the collection of the Cornish Historical Society.

18. *Memoir of the Occasion Celebrating Percy MacKaye's Seventieth Birthday*, a copy of which is in the collection of the Cornish Historical Society.

19. April 24, 1949, from the Daniels scrapbook, Virginia Colby, Cornish Colony files.

FREDERICK WILLIAM MACMONNIES
1863 – 1937

AUGUSTUS SAINT-GAUDENS BELIEVED that "MacMonnies is a man who has the touch of genius and everything he does is valuable, no matter whether one quite likes the subjects or manner of treatment. I think that the city of Brooklyn should possess replicas of everything he has done."[1] This was not altogether a playful remark. It was inspired in part by a statue of James Stranahan that MacMonnies did for Prospect Park in Brooklyn. The statue elicited great admiration from his contemporaries because his "inventiveness . . . introduced a new realism for the portrait statue, setting the figure in an ordinary 'slice-of-life' action with neither costume nor pose to personify his fame. Stranahan is represented in contemporary attire, so naturally that he appears to be walking out the door, with coat over his arm, gloves in one hand, and silk hat in the other. This fashionable and modern top hat had never before appeared in portrait sculpture."[2] But Saint-Gaudens's remark may also have been inspired by the fact that MacMonnies was Brooklyn born and bred: September 28, 1863. His father was an importer and his mother was a first cousin four generations removed of Benjamin West.[3]

Saint-Gaudens was the first to recognize the innate talent of the young man. He taught the seventeen-year-old MacMonnies at the Art Students League in New York and then hired him as an assistant in his New York studio for about four years, bringing him to Cornish during the summer of 1885. While in New Hampshire, MacMonnies did extensive work on the *Eli Bates Fountain*, also known as *Storks at Play*, that is currently in Chicago's Lincoln Park; he may also have worked on the fountain "again briefly from 1886 to 1887."[4] Prior to his Cornish stay, MacMonnies had worked with Saint-Gaudens on the decorations for the Henry Villard House (1881-1883) and the house of Cornelius Vanderbilt II (1881-1883).[5] His connection with Cornish was strong enough for three of his sculptures to be included in the exhibition of Cornish artists held in 1916. "One undergraduate remarked that he knew nothing about art but that he could see that MacMonnies's 'Nathan Hale' looked like a hero."[6]

This was a copy of the same statue that had been erected in New York's City Hall Park. Saint-Gaudens had prompted MacMonnies to enter a competition for its commission in 1889. MacMonnies's *Nathan Hale* became his "most expressive public monument . . . a convincing reality infuses the tense figure, from the finely rendered textures of wrinkles and creases in the clothing, to the expressive gesture of bound hands and disdainful head. The impressionistic, animated and slightly unfinished surface has more immediacy than the studied, overworked portrait statues created by many of MacMonnies's well-known contemporaries."[7]

The greatest influence on MacMonnies's life that Saint-Gaudens probably had was his advice for the young sculptor to go to Paris to continue his studies. MacMonnies happily followed the advice; it paid off handsomely. He won in two successive years the highest prize available to foreigners at the Ecole des Beaux-Arts. But it was his *Diana* that brought him instant international acclaim when it was awarded an honorable mention at the Paris Salon of 1889.[8] Nevertheless, Saint-Gaudens's advisory capacity for the World's Columbian Exposition of 1893 in Chicago was also important to MacMonnies's career. By this time, however, MacMonnies had achieved great success in France, too; he wanted his reputation not to be dependent on the recommendation of others. So anxious was he, that "MacMonnies refused to work under Saint-Gaudens's direction or in collaboration with him."[9] As proof of his conviction and self-confidence, he executed a colossal sculpture *The Triumph of Columbia* or *The Barge of State* that commanded the lagoon at the Chicago Fair's Court of Honor:

Figure 105. Bacchante and Infant Faun *by Frederick MacMonnies, 1893.*

In a ship vaguely reminiscent of the one that carried Christopher Columbus... were numerous allegorical figures, led by a winged Fame at the prow... it... was propelled by eight mighty maidens who represented the Arts (Music, Architecture, Sculpture, Painting) and the Industries (Agriculture, Science, Industry, Commerce), and it was guided by an aged and bearded Father Time at the helm. Perched high on a throne, which rests on a pedestal decorated with *putti* and festoons, sits triumphant Columbia holding a torch in her right hand. What probably was intended to be an imitation of the Renaissance style actually became Baroque in its exuberance and in the lavishness of its classical decorative motifs.[10]

It is true that MacMonnies "felt a kinship with the Italian Renaissance, but [what] took his fancy was the representation of the mischievous joy of childhood. 'Pan of Rohallion,' the 'Boy and Duck' fountain, and the 'Running Cupid' all show this affinity."[11] Both of these affinities eventually got him in trouble—so much so that he was "banned in Boston." The statue that did it was called *Bacchante and Infant Faun* and it came as a gift to the Boston Public Library from Charles McKim, whose prestigious architectural firm McKim, Mead, and White had designed the library. Some Bostonians admired it for its "vitality and gaiety, and its suggestion of the joy of life" and McKim for giving Boston "one of the few admirable examples of imaginative sculpture in public places in America."[12] The majority, however, held a radically different view:

A firestorm of protest, fanned by an avid press, questioned the appropriateness of the statue for the library because of its explicit nakedness, depiction of debauched motherhood, and certainty to encourage drunkenness and other libertine behavior. The naturalism and liveliness of MacMonnies's work were also a problem for viewers accustomed to the smooth, neutral idealization of the prevailing neoclassical figure style. Moreover, the model had not been a classical statue but a young Parisian, Eugénie Pasque, who also appeared in Charles Dana Gibson's "Gibson Girl" magazine illustrations . . ."Bacchante" was deemed a "menace to the Commonwealth." Reflecting the convictions of many religious groups, the Baptist ministers of Boston adopted a resolution declaring that "the statue of Bacchante represents reckless abandon to sensual pleasure, thoughtlessness, intoxication, and the supreme reign of the grosser nature." "Bacchante" soon became a *cause célèbre*. Songs and poems were written about her, cartoons drawn, and the "Bacchante Skip" invented for ballroom dancing.

Finally McKim removed the statue and offered it to the Metropolitan Museum of Art in New York whose trustees rose above the hullabaloo that even pursued her there and placed her in the entrance hall of the museum. MacMonnies, meanwhile, was in Paris far away from—and above—the controversy, which focused all the more attention on him and brought him all the more commissions. He made marble and bronze castings of her so that in museums throughout the United States, there are Bacchantes in a variety of sizes. In 1993, a cast was made of the one in the Boston Museum of Fine Arts. The *Bacchante*, although not in her original form, finally made her way back to the Boston Public Library.

In 1905, MacMonnies opened a studio and school in Claude Monet's village of Giverny. In 1888 he had married the American painter Mary Louise Fairchild, whose paintings he admired, and the couple began annually to rent a house in the art colony and finally bought one there.[13] Painting occupied more of his time as he grew older, though he continued to sculpt. One of his final commissions was a huge "130-foot-high monument commemorating the Battle of the Marne, which was paid for by the contributions of four million Americans . . . A titanic nude female, representing a defiant France, turns eastward toward Germany and holds in her arms a mortally wounded nude male figure."[14] It was not erected until 1936, and MacMonnies died of pneumonia the following year.

ENDNOTES

1. *The Reminiscences of Augustus Saint-Gaudens,* edited and amplified by Homer Saint-Gaudens (New York: Century Co., 1913), Vol. 2, p. 52.

2. Ethelyn Adina Gordon (chapter on MacMonnies), *Frederick William MacMonnies (1863-1937), Mary Fairchild MacMonnies (1856-1946): deux artistes américains à Giverny* (Vernon, France: Musée Municipal A.-G. Poulain, 1988), p. 41.

3. Gordon, p. 31.

4. John H. Dryfhout, *The Work of Augustus Saint-Gaudens* (Hanover, NH: University Press of New England, 1982), p. 156.

5. Ibid., pp. 8, 131, 134.

6. George Breed Zug, "Exhibition of Cornish Artists," *Dartmouth Alumni Magazine* (March 1916), p. 203.

7. Gordon, p. 41.

8. H. H. Greer, "Frederick MacMonnies, Sculptor," *Brush and Pencil* X, 1, April 1902, p. 5.

9. Gordon, p. 41. She quotes MacMonnies as saying, "I will not work for anybody any longer. I am going to work for myself the rest of my life." She also refers to the "intense love-hate relationship" between the two men. "Saint-Gaudens's jealousy, competitiveness, desire to be the respected and adored patriarch, and fear that he was not appreciated or honored in France as highly as his protégé, often made him abrasive and sarcastic toward the younger sculptor. Fierce pride, over-sensitivity, driving ambition, and over-confidence at early successes made MacMonnies at times aloof from his master, or unwilling to collaborate with him. Yet each respected the other's ability. They loved each other deeply and frequently assisted each other in personal and professional matters" (p. 31).

10. Wayne Craven, *Sculpture in America* (New York: Thomas Y. Crowell, 1968), p. 424.

11. Beatrice Gilman Proske, *Brookgreen Gardens Sculpture* (Brookgreen Gardens, SC: Brookgreen Gardens Trustees, 1968), p. 34.

12. This quotation and the information in this paragraph come from Gilian Wohlauer, "The Bacchante is Back: BPL Welcomes its Prodigal Daughter," *Preview* (Boston Museum of Fine Arts, July-August 1993), pp. 3-4. A copy in marble of "Bacchante and Infant Faun" is in San Simeon, the former home of William Randolph Hearst in California; it is now a museum.

13. William H. Gerdts, *American Impressionism* (New York: Artabras, 1984), p. 261.

14. Craven, p. 428.

Figure 106. *Paul Manship in 1915,*
photographed by De Witt Clinton Ward.

PAUL MANSHIP
1885 – 1966

PAUL MANSHIP was a gifted, prolific sculptor; during the 1920s and 1930s he was considered America's most popular sculptor. "He pursued a path that led directly between the ultraconservative, old-guard realist-academicians and the wildly experimental and adventurous avant-garde of modern art . . . his subjects and even his style sprang from antiquity and were therefore acceptable to the men of the academies, yet his work incorporated something of the simplification and abstraction of the new art. In the end, however, the latter would allow no compromise, and Manship was branded, in the most derogatory sense, an 'academician.'"[1] Be that as it may, Manship's most characteristic sculpture epitomizes what we call the Art Deco style:

> Without his knowing it, and before the term was coined, Manship participated in the formation of our era's most popular and long-lived style of art and decoration. . . . Art Deco reconciled art and industry; it incorporated modernist-inspired form, academic formalisms and literary references, citations from antiquity, and a rakish love of speed that typified the modern era and recalled the energetic expressions of Futurism—itself the spawn of Cubism. These sources merged into a consistent fashion with the potential for universal application in textiles, buildings, graphic design, household utensils and garments . . . Manship never advocated this style; the formulation of his artistic goals and style predated . . . any stylistic association with Art Deco. Nevertheless, he advocated the creation of a new sculpture that would harmonize with the flow of the modern world as a fitting component of the new architecture, its buildings, parks, plazas, and rising cityscapes.[2]

As is true with many pieces of sculpture, we all know what is perhaps his most famous creation—even though few people could probably come up with the name of its creator: the gilded bronze statue of the *Prometheus Fountain* at the Rockefeller Center in New York City that clearly represents the most salient features of American Art Deco. In July of 1932, the Center's Board of Directors commissioned Manship to sculpt a piece destined to be placed against the west wall of the sunken plaza and skating rink and with the RCA Building as its towering backdrop. Since it was dedicated in January of 1934, it is obvious that he worked fast. Faster, no doubt, then he would have

Figure 107. *Paul Manship around 1920, photographed by De Witt Clinton Ward.*

preferred: "'No artist is ever entirely satisfied with the work he creates. I'd naturally welcome the opportunity of doing the whole fountain group over again.' Thus, Manship's best-known work is a sculpture he more or less dismissed. The situation recalled Herbert Adams's warning to Oliver La Farge in 1913 that Manship might "'do American art an incalculable good, if, as Adams had cautioned, fate 'didn't let the architects ruin him by giving him a lot of big work which must be hastily executed.'"[3]

Manship was born in St. Paul, Minnesota, and received his early training at the city's Institute of Art. He began his career as a painter but wisely switched to sculpture once he realized, after making the grass in a landscape bright red, that he was color blind.[4]

At nineteen, he came east to study and in 1909 won a coveted three-year fellowship to the American Academy in Rome. That was the year he met two men who may have had a hand in getting him to come to Cornish for several summers: Barry Faulkner and Charles A. Platt.

Faulkner speaks very warmly of his friendship with Manship: "Paul struck a fresh note in American sculpture, a note of lyric grace and robust humor expressed with exquisite technical skill. I know of no man with a keener intelligence and more avid curiosity as to all forms of art and their techniques. At work his concentration was formidable but when he relaxed he was a kind, genial and humorous companion.[5] In 1916, Manship began a series of bronze portrait medals of his friends; one side was an image of the artist's head and on the other was an allegorical representation of some aspect of the friend's art.[6] The first one of the series, with the motto "to the ultimate do we pursue the ideal," was a medal of Faulkner who, in 1909, had painted a portrait of Manship. Several years later, in 1922 and 1923, Barry Faulkner and Paul Manship, as well as the architect Eric Gugler, cooperated on a commission for the American Academy of Rome: a memorial to Harry Thrasher, a resident of Plainfield who had been an assistant to Augustus Saint-Gaudens and a winner of a scholarship to the Academy.[7]

As if to cement the Cornish connection, both Manship and Faulkner were frequent guests at the Cornish house of Charles A. Platt.[8] Manship met Platt, a trustee of the American Academy in Rome, and also did a portrait medal of him in Rome in the winter of 1918-1919. Platt, in turn, often turned to Manship for garden sculpture to complement his houses and landscapes.[9]

Figure 108. Diana, *1921*.

During these early years of Manship's career, there was another connection with Cornish, although neither man would have known it at that time. Immediately upon his return from Rome, Manship, as a former student of the American Academy, entered ten pieces of sculpture at an exhibition of the Architectural League in the Fine Arts Building of New York. Unaware of what was soon to become a more neighborly connection, Kenyon Cox opened his review in February of 1913 of Manship's work by noting that, "There is no rarer or more delightful sensation than the recognition of a new and genuine talent." Cox went on to admire Manship's determination to be his own man. Contrary to some reports that his work was "extremely mannered," Cox thought Manship's pieces "seem the experiments of a young man in search of his manner—a young man who has, fortunately, an eye for the art of the past as well as for the nature of all times, and who is not willing to submit himself to the dominating influence of his own time. And if the mixed style he has employed in them should harden into a premature mannerism, as I do not believe it will, it would, at least, have the merit of being his own mannerism, not that weak reflection of the mannerism of Rodin which seems to be the stock in trade of most of our younger sculptors." Little did Cox realize that he would soon be close enough to Manship, in both New York and Cornish, to "watch his future with the deepest interest, and [I] shall hope that he will prove to have the enduring patience, the indefatigable industry, the high seriousness of purpose, which are, to less than the talent which he assuredly possesses, necessary to the making of a great artist."[10]

Manship married Isabel McIlwaine on New Year's Day of 1913. The couple had their first daughter Pauline in December, then spent the summers of 1915, 1916, 1917, and 1927—the year his son John was born—in Cornish.[11] During their first summer here, they rented the house of Henry and Lucia Fuller in Plainfield. Within the family, it was known as "Mellakunk Lodge" since Pauline had referred to it that way because of a nearby family of skunks.[12] Later, the Manships stayed in the Wood cottage on Freeman Road, which George de Forest Brush had used earlier, and at the Churchill Inn.[13] They also boarded with Mrs. George S. Ruggles and rented the Ruggles' studio, "the Woodchuck Hole," which Mr. Ruggles had built to accommodate the New York artists. It may also have sheltered Gaston Lachaise, who served as Manship's first assistant from 1914 to 1921 and accompanied Manship to Cornish for two summers.[14]

Figure 109. *Adam.*

Paul Manship must have enjoyed his time in Cornish because he is referred to as a wicked croquet player[15] and because of the firm friendships he made. In addition to those already mentioned, he also formed a close relationship with Maxfield Parrish. During Manship's first summer in Cornish, Parrish, who was one of the first members of the Colony to own a car, invited both Barry Faulkner and him on an extended motor trip through New Hampshire and on to Manship's first visit to Cape Ann, Massachusetts, an "area that was later to be so important to him."[16] Maxfield Parrish was also the subject of one of Manship's bronze portrait medals. The allegorical emblem he chose for Parrish was the winged horse Pegasus, "which was a symbol in Manship's oeuvre for artistic inspiration."[17]

The years during which Manship summered in Cornish were also the years of some of his best-known early works: *Salome,* 1915 (the Smithsonian Institution's National Museum of American Art); *Dancers and Gazelles,* 1916, for which he received the National Academy of Design's Helen Foster Barnett Prize in 1917 (New York's Metropolitan Museum of Art); *Flight of Night,* 1916 (the Wadsworth Athenaeum, Hartford, Connecticut); *Indian* and *Pronghorn Antelope,* both done in 1917 (Mead Art Museum, Amherst, Massachusetts); and the *Venus Anadyomene Fountain,* 1927 (Addison Gallery of American Art, Phillips Academy, Andover, Massachusetts). During his first summer in Cornish, Manship sketched out both *Diana* and *Actaeon,* gilded bronze statues completed in 1924 and currently in Murrells Inlet, South Carolina, at the Brookgreen Gardens.[18]

The list of Manship's awards and honors is long and distinguished: he was elected an associate of the National Academy of Design in 1914 and an academician in 1916; he was elected to the National Institute of Arts and Letters in 1920, he became a fellow of the American Academy of Art and Sciences in 1931; he was elected president of various groups—the National Sculpture Society in 1939, the American Academy of Arts and Letters in 1948, and the Century Club in 1950. Locally, he exhibited four pieces in an exhibition of Cornish artists at Dartmouth College in 1916,[19] and he served as a trustee of the Saint-Gaudens Memorial.

A radical change in taste for abstract sculpture resulted in Manship's reputation being at its nadir when he died on January 28, 1966. A quarter of a century later, however, his works are highly respected and valued not only for their representation of a significant period in art history but also for their possession of an intrinsic beauty.

ENDNOTES

1. Wayne Craven, *Sculpture in America* (New York: Thomas Y. Crowell, 1968), p. 565.

2. Harry Rand, "The Stature of Paul Manship" in *Paul Manship: Changing Taste in America*, exhibition catalog (St. Paul, Minnesota Museum of Art, 1985), pp. 20-22. To put this style into a perspective proper to sculpture, Craven notes that Karl Bitter (1867-1915), an accomplished sculptor who began working in the tradition of the Ecole des Beaux-Arts, started to experiment in strongly stylized abstraction of form with the two figures that embellished the doorway of the First National Bank of Cleveland in 1908. Thus, five years before the Armory Show, he was creating sculpture that fit "harmoniously with the new architectural theory, which was based on the beauty of the simplicity of geometric designs. . . . It was a very important step and in following years, this sculptural stylization gained momentum, reaching its fullest realization in the work of Paul Manship" (Craven, p. 472).

3. As quoted in Harry Rand, *Paul Manship* (Washington, DC: The Smithsonian Institution Press, 1989), p. 141; Exhibition Catalogue for the National Museum of American Art; see also Rand, p. 28.

4. John Manship, *Paul Manship* (New York: Abbeville Press, 1989), p. 15.

5. Barry Faulkner, *Barry Faulkner: Sketches from an Artist's Life* (Dublin, NH: William L. Bauhan, 1973), p. 82.

6. John Manship, p. 75; the series may have begun in 1915, see *A Circle of Friends: Art Colonies of Cornish and Dublin*, exhibition catalogue, (Durham, NH: University Art Galleries, University of New Hampshire, 1985) p. 94.

7. Faulkner, p. 112; see above p. 195 and below pp. 413-417.

8. Geoffrey Platt, "A Memoir," in Keith N. Morgan, *Charles A. Platt: The Artist as Architect* (Cambridge, MA: MIT Press, 1985), p. 202.

9. *A Circle of Friends*, p. 94; see also "Garden Statuary by Paul Manship," *House and Garden*, June 1921, p. 62.

10. Kenyon Cox, "A New Sculptor," *The Nation* 96, February 13, 1913, pp. 162-63; see also Rand, p. 28.

11. Letter from Paul Manship's son John to Virginia Colby, August 22, 1985.

12. John Manship, p. 75.

13. Hugh Mason Wade, *A Brief History of Cornish: 1763-1974* (Hanover, NH: University Press of New England, 1976), p. 73.

14. Craven, pp. 599-600; *A Circle of Friends*, p. 94.

15. Platt, p. 201.

16. John Manship, p. 75.

17. Ibid.

18. Beatrice Gilman Proske, *Brookgreen Gardens Sculpture* (Brookgreen Gardens, SC: Brookgreen Gardens Trustees, 1968), p. 290. These sculptures can also be seen elsewhere: the *Diana* at the Gardner Museum, the Carnegie Institute, and Ball State College, and the *Actaeon* at the Detroit Museum of Art, the Carnegie Institute, and the National Museum of American Art; *A Circle of Friends*, p. 94.

19. George Breed Zug, "Exhibition of Cornish Artists," *Art and Archaeology*, April 1916, pp. 203-205; *Dartmouth Alumni Magazine*, March 1916, pp. 207-211. The title of three of the works exhibited are: *Centaur and Dryad*, *Satyr and Sleeping Nymph*, and *Wrestler*; *A Circle of Friends*, p. 134.

WILLARD LEROY METCALF
1858 – 1925

WILLARD METCALF belonged to the group of artists that came to be known as "The Ten American Painters." Contemporaries and subsequent generations considered these ten men to be an "academy of American Impressionism."[1] Metcalf, however, had a rather inauspicious beginning for an "academician." It was not until he was forty that he decided to renounce his career as a successful book illustrator. He worked for *Harper's Magazine* and the *Century Magazine*, for whom he illustrated a series of very popular pictures of Zuni life, as well as for *Scribner's Magazine*. Plagued by a drinking problem and distraught at his failing marriage, he "went off to the Maine woods to think and to paint. He stayed in Maine for a year and when he came back to New York, he had decided to devote all of his time to painting."[2] Thus, he drew on his study with George Loring Brown, sometimes called "the American Claude," on his training at both the Boston Museum School and the Académie Julian in Paris under Boulanger and Lefebvre, and on time spent at Giverny.

Metcalf was an accomplished, acclaimed artist by the time he first came to Cornish in 1909 at the invitation of the playwright and poet Louis Evan Shipman, both members of the Players Club in New York City. Homer Saint-Gaudens commented that:

> Metcalf was another of those old cronies who met for lunch each day at the Round Table of the Players Club. As the son of my father, I was admitted to the group, where I sat in proper silent admiration. That circle was possessed of a humorous, mildly salacious, verbosely balanced, and altogether pleasant view of life, which concerned itself with loaves of specially made rye bread provided by my father and a special type of Italian cheese sponsored by Richard H. Hunt. Metcalf did his share. He knew how to talk. He knew how to observe the world. He knew how to paint.[3]

It is clear from a painting done later, *Winter Afternoon, 1917*, that Metcalf stayed in the Shipman's house, "Brook Place" located on the Meriden Stage Road, because he incorporated it into the painting. It is possible that is where he stayed during each visit to the area. During his first year, Stephen Parrish noted "Evening to Fred's [Maxfield Parrish] to dinner. The Shipmans and Metcalf, the painter."[4] It is also clear that Metcalf enjoyed the quiet tranquility of a New Hampshire winter. The many beautiful snow scenes he painted brought him high critical acclaim and solid financial rewards. A painting done in 1909 during his first winter in Cornish, *Icebound* (now in the Art Institute of

Figure 110. Winter Afternoon (The Louis Shipman House, Cornish, New Hampshire) *by Willard Metcalf, 1917.*

Chicago), drew high praise in the *New York Herald* when it was part of his one-man show at New York's Montross Gallery in 1910: it "reveals the poetry of winter. There is an eerie beauty in the play of light and shadow upon snow and ice surrounding the open channel of the brook."[5] Both this painting and another winter scene done that first year in Cornish, *The White Veil #1* (now in the Museum of Art at the Rhode Island School of Design), are dominated by strong diagonals, a means by which he characteristically organized his compositions. Contemporaries were aware that he was strengthening his pictures as well as capturing the beauty of snow, but de Veer correctly calls attention to the "oddly distinctive feeling of *warmth* that Metcalf conveys in this scene of gently falling snow. The unusual tone of the sky perhaps accounts for the impression of winter made as welcome and easy as a summer's day."[6] Even his contemporaries responded strongly to his ability, perhaps even better than John Twachtman's skill, to render winter tangibly: "Metcalf shows us the winsome side of winter, not the frosty air, the biting cold, but the caressing touch of the golden sunlight, the soft mantle of snow resting ever so lightly on the shoulders of the world."[7]

Two years later Metcalf returned to Cornish as part of his honeymoon with his new bride, Henriette Alice McCrea, thirty-three years his junior. Charles Adams Platt lent his house to the pair. "Calling herself his 'willing slave,' Henriette eagerly toted Willard's canvases while learning at firsthand the meaning of plein-air painting in bitterly cold New England weather. She found her husband firm in his commitment to paint from nature, retiring to the studio only for the finishing touches."[8] As de Veer also points out, her "energy and health warmed to the wintry setting; in woolen cap and ulster she hiked through the snow with him to painting sites. For a time, she set aside her own aspiration in the dramatic and literary world for Metcalf's career."[9] And his career, thanks to the work produced that winter and later in the summer of 1911, was burgeoning. *Thawing Brook, #1, The Hush of Winter,* and *Cornish Hills* are striking renditions of winter; they are vivid witnesses to the special affinity between artist and subject. *Cornish Hills* now has the dubious distinction of being enshrined as a Christmas card, but when it was first exhibited, it elicited delighted esteem. In it "Metcalf stands at the zenith of his reputation as the foremost landscape painter."[10]

That summer Metcalf once more came back to the area and stayed through the fall. This time he stayed in less well-appointed lodgings: the old mill on Daniels Road, originally built by David and Septimus Read, that Clarissa (Potter) Davidge—later Mrs. Henry Fitch Taylor—had converted into living quarters. The social life of the Colony, however, more than compensated for any discomfort. Metcalf and his wife were entertained by Maxfield Parrish, Homer Saint-Gaudens, Witter Bynner, and Louis Shipman.[11] Moreover, the canvases he completed are among his best work. *The Village—September Morning* clearly depicts Plainfield, New Hampshire, on a crisp, early fall morning.[12] *Blow-Me-Down*, as its alternate title *Flickering Shadows* indicates, is as much about *Flickering Shadows* as it is about the local brook. It caught the attention of a painter and writer on Impressionism, Arthur Hoeber, who considered it "a veritable tour de force . . . an achievement where each touch seems just right, when the observer [Metcalf] is intelligent and the technique is about the last word."[13] This was also the summer for *Le Sillon*, a French title suggested by his wife, to call attention to the "furrow" that "creased an expanse of rough meadow inviting the eye to follow a double path of light and texture"[14] and *Green Idleness*; it is not clear whether or not *The Red Bridge* was painted locally, but it does not appear to be. That fall he did *Symphony in Yellow*, also known as *October Afternoon*, with Plainfield in the background.

Metcalf's subsequent visits to the area were of a briefer duration. Early in 1913, Metcalf took a quick, solitary trip to New Hampshire that produced four wintry landscapes, among them "'The Winter's Festival,' which depicts a site close to the Shipmans' house in Plainfield and the Japanesque quality of 'Winter in New Hampshire,' which possibly also dates from 1913."[15] While staying at the Shipmans' house in 1917, he finished about six winter scenes, among them the *Winter Afternoon, 1917* already referred to and *The White Pasture* (now in the Freer Gallery of Art in Washington, DC). Finally, in 1920, it is believed that he painted one of the last paintings based on a local scene, *Hauling Wood* (now in the Addison Gallery of American Art at Phillips Academy). In it Metcalf "departed from his usual practice and included the figure of a man and a team of horses alongside a sizable woodpile. His choice of a higher elevation from which to paint the scene adds appreciably to the interest of the picture."[16]

Metcalf's contribution to American art is considerable. He came to be called "the poet laureate of the New England hills,"[17] though those hills were not exclusively in the Cornish and Plainfield area. He also painted in Maine, Vermont, Massachusetts, and Connecticut. More importantly, he took a technique and an aesthetic from abroad and made it distinctly American. "Almost all American Impressionists were interpreted by their champions as striving to adapt the style, but Metcalf was seen as the truly American Impressionist."[18] Royal Cortissoz, an admirer of Metcalf and a friend of many members of the Cornish Colony, was especially impressed with his ability to paint the "truth to the very soul of the American landscape. . . . The indefinable elements which make our brooks and pastures intensely and unforgettably American are curiously eloquent in [Metcalf's] pictures. I return with a special appreciation to the Americanism of his art, to the sincerity and force with which he puts familiar motives before us. He got into his canvases the simple, lovable truths which, perhaps, only an American can feel to the uppermost in our apple trees and our winding streams . . . an inheritor of the very essence of American art."[19]

ENDNOTES

1. William H. Gerdts, *American Impressionism* (New York: Artabras, 1984), p. 171

2. Richard J. Boyle, *American Impressionism* (Boston: Little, Brown, and Co., 1974), p. 170.

3. Homer Saint-Gaudens, *The American Artist and His Times* (New York: Dodd, Mead, 1941), p. 197.

4. Stephen Parrish, diary, Baker Library, Dartmouth College, Hanover, NH, gift of Marian and Roy Garrand.

5. Elizabeth de Veer, "Willard Metcalf in Cornish, New Hampshire," *The Magazine Antiques* 126, 5, November 1984, p. 1208. The anonymous critic may be echoing the title of an 1888 painting that is the basis for the title of the *catalogue raisonné* published by Elizabeth de Veer and Richard J. Boyle, *Sunlight and Shadow: The Life and Art of Willard L. Metcalf* (New York: Abbeville Press, 1987). "The strong contrasts of light and shade in 'Sunlight and Shadow,' with their implications of swift changes of mood and a recognition, perhaps, of the 'dark' side of life, could be taken as a symbol of the artist's work and possibly his personality." (de Veer, *Sunlight and Shadow*, p. 170).

6. De Veer, *The Magazine Antiques*, p. 1210.

7. An anonymous critic in the *Washington Post*, January 11, 1925, two months before Metcalf's death, as quoted in de Veer, *The Magazine Antiques*, p. 1214. The same critic hailed Metcalf as "one of those who has placed an indelible stamp upon American art and who will leave behind him in the record of his life's achievements for the uplift and joy of future generations a priceless heritage," quoted in de Veer, *Sunlight and Shadow*, p. 243.

8. de Veer, *The Magazine Antiques*, p. 1211.

9. de Veer, *Sunlight and Shadow*, p. 103.

10. An anonymous critic in the *New York Evening World*, March 22, 1911, as quoted in de Veer, *The Magazine Antiques*, p. 1211, and de Veer, *Sunlight and Shadow*, p. 104. *Thawing Brook, #1* has as a variant title *Winter Shadows*, ibid., p. 263.

11. de Veer, *The Magazine Antiques*, p. 1212.

12. Variant titles for this painting are: *September Morning, New England Village at Cornish, NH*, and *September Morning, Cornish* (de Veer, *Sunlight and Shadow*, p. 263).

13. In the *New York Evening Globe*, January 3, 1912, as quoted in de Veer, *The Magazine Antiques*, p. 1213.

14. de Veer, *The Magazine Antiques*, p. 1213.

15. Ibid.

16. Ibid., p. 1214.

17. Walter Jack Duncan, Foreword to the Catalogue accompanying an exhibition of Metcalf's paintings at the Corcoran Gallery of Art, Washington, DC, January 3 to February 1, 1925.

18. Gerdts, p. 199.

19. "Willard Leroy Metcalf," in *Commemorative Tributes of the American Academy of Arts and Letters, 1905-1941* (New York, 1942), pp. 511, 181, as quoted in Gerdts, p. 199.

Figure 111.

MOST SURVEYS OF AMERICAN LITERARY HISTORY treat William Vaughn Moody with a great deal of respect. He is thought to stand out from the turn-of-the-century poets and to have had the "most substantial mind" of his generation, although he died "while he was still growing as a poet and thinker."[1] As with his good friend Percy MacKaye, Moody combined a love of poetry with an interest in the theater. A melancholy permeates his trilogy *The Masque of Judgment* (1900), *The Fire-Bringer* (1904), and the unfinished *The Death of Eve* (1912). This tone "was rooted in doubt and disillusionment" primarily because Moody "undertook to set forth in verse-drama the central problem of humanity: the rebellion of man against God and the final resolution of mortal conflict in moral idealism. . . . Moody's idealism looked backward rather than forward, and his call was for a return to the old values and solutions rather than for an honest confronting of the problems of the world of science and the machine."[2] He also wrote two prose plays concerned with social problems of his day: *The Great Divide* (1906) and *The Faith Healer* (1909).

Moody was born in Spencer, Indiana, on July 8, 1869, studied at Harvard University as both an undergraduate and graduate student, traveled in Europe and the United States, and began teaching in 1895 at the University of Chicago as an instructor and then as an assistant professor in the English Department. Once he finished *A History of English Literature*, which he wrote in collaboration with Robert Morss Lovett in 1902, he gave up his teaching position in 1903 and devoted his life to writing.

Moody first came to Cornish in February of 1906 in order to visit Percy MacKaye, who was then living in Admiral Folger's "Snuff Box House." Moody describes his first winter in Cornish to Harriet Converse Tilden Brainerd, whom he was to marry on May 7, 1909:

I am just back from Cornish, which turned out to be a most enchanting spot, at least in its winter dress. From the wooded river wind deeply wooded roads slowly upward through high-hung pastures to broad acclivities of woodland and rocky open, with wide prospects unfolding on every side, and across the river the delicately majestic blue figure of Mount Ascutney—one of the most lovable mountain-forms it has ever been my lot to behold. The place combines intimate loveliness with a sense of large freedom in a remarkable way, and the distinction of the land-scape is carried out with rare harmony in the human beings which inhabit it. I saw, of course, only the winter colony— Maxfield Parrish and Saint-Gaudens being the chief figures—but I saw also a dozen houses and gardens belonging to absentees, of such faultless taste and pure charm that they proclaimed aloud

Figure 112. *Frontispiece from Moody's* Selected Poems, *1931.*

their possessors as people worth knowing. Torrence and I were given a royal welcome. The first night there was a snowshoe and sleighing party in our honor, the supper cooked over bonfires in the woods. The next night there was a small party and supper at Saint-Gaudens's, and the third night brought forth a larger festivity at the Parrishes'. Saint-Gaudens was a pure delight. MacKaye's little home is a very sweet place. He has two adorable children, a boy of six and a girl of four, and a very pretty wife. The weather was prime, crisp, and clear, with an unspeakable moon.[3]

Augustus Saint-Gaudens, in addition to being a focal point of the Cornish Colony, acted as a great inspiration to its members. The circumstances and passions surrounding the Spanish American War may be alien to us today, but they form the context of one of Moody's finest poems, "An Ode in Time of Hesitation," written in 1900. It begins:

> Before the solemn bronze Saint-Gaudens made
> To thrill the heedless passer's heart with awe,
> And set here in the city's talk and trade
> To the good memory of Robert Shaw,
> This bright March morn I stand,
> And hear the distant spring come up the land.

The poem continues in the "lest we forget" vein:

> This delicate and proud New England soul
> Who leads despisèd men, with just-unshackled feet,

Up the large ways where death and glory meet,
To show all peoples that our shame is done,
That once more we are clean and spirit-whole.
Crouched in the sea fog on the moaning sand
All night he lay, speaking some simple word
From hour to hour to the slow minds that heard,
Holding each poor life gently in his hand
And breathing on the base rejected clay
Till each dark face shone mystical and grand
Against the breaking day . . .
Then upward, where the shadowy bastion loomed
Huge on the mountain in the wet sea light,
Whence now, and now, infernal flowerage bloomed,
Bloomed, burst, and scattered down its deadly seed,—
They swept, and died like freemen on the height,
Like freeman, and like men of noble breed;
And when the battle fell away at night
By hasty and contemptuous hands were thrust
Obscurely in a common grave with him
The fair-haired keeper of their love and trust.
Now limb doth mingle with dissolved limb
In nature's busy old democracy
To flush the mountain laurel when she blows
Sweet by the southern sea . . .[4]

Of course, while Moody was in Cornish, he had the ordinary problems of any visitor in those days. Returning in May of 1906 for a second visit, he wrote Harriet that "the place is as lovely as I had remembered it, and everybody vastly hospitable and kind. I am not at all confident, however, of being able to locate myself in a way advantageous for the job I have on hand. The boarding facilities of the place seem very meagre." Several days later, though, "solemn deputations are to be made to various goodwives and spinsters who have been wavering in their minds, and a concerted attempt will be made to break down their hostility to me as a stranger and a city-chap. The country people are as con-servative here as if no 'Colony' had ever troubled their world-old scheme of life." By the end of that same day he was "established in a big cool room, under the care of a motherly New England woman, whose dialect and view of life are alone worth twice per week what in her utmost stretch of thrift she has had the courage to charge me. I have four windows, two opening on a leafy road and the sunset, two northward on growing fields, a sheep-pasture, and distant hills, at this hour of five in the afternoon as blue as the hills of Beulah." At this point, he has yet to encounter Ethel Barrymore: "on the other side of the road is a house belonging to one Harry Fuller, a landscape painter, rented for the summer to Ethel Barrymore. I expect to enjoy her, but I rather dread the crowd she will have about her."[5] Noting with mixed pleasure that she has a tennis court by her house is the first step in his being won over to her side (see his remarks about her progress through Cornish, above pp. 135-137).

The landscape, of course, was a decisive factor in his admiration of the place and his desire to be in the area. As with the painter John Elliott, Moody saw the countryside filtered through Tuscan lenses. Because he had hiked and tramped through Tuscany and northern Italy with his friend, Ferdinand Schevill, a scholar who was to write about Florence and Siena, this description shows that what he saw was important to him:

> The country here is at this moment wholly divine, warm sun and crisp breezes, shad-bushes and apple trees in their glory, more birds with more song in their gullets than I ever saw in all my life together. Blow-Me-Down Brook (that's its real name!) singing through miles of yellow willow between fresh ploughed fields, pine woods, and rocky sheep pastures, the whole country rolling into hill-forms of almost Tuscan grace, from any of which the climber can command leagues of delicious misty blue distance! You can see I have fallen in love with it.[6]

Moody's delight in his physical surroundings is matched by his enjoyment of the social scene—even when it involved Ethel Barrymore:

> The social life here is charmingly simple and free from stiffness, the people both open hearted and clever, (not a frequent coincidence of qualities) and I am enjoying the kind of summer colony existence for the first time in my life.
>
> I see Miss Barrymore every day and like her immensely. She is simple, hearty and boyish as can be imagined. She has a tennis court and a great cement-lined bathing pool, both of which we indulge in early every day, and the combination, with a high-ball and a cigarette afterwards on the big stone-flagged porch, is difficult to beat.
>
> She is preparing to stage—in the studio of their house here—a one-act play of my friend and chum, Percy MacKaye, and I have been asked to undertake one of the parts—that of a Maine sea-captain. I don't quite see myself as a Maine sea-captain, and besides I am far too busy to spend the time required for rehearsals, but I am tempted nevertheless to go in for it, for the *fun* of the thing.[7]

Even though he had been frantically rewriting a play he called *A Sabine Woman*, known today as the prose drama *The Great Divide*, he still had time for doing things for the "fun of it." As he could write Harriet on July 2, 1906, "Cornish is very gay—for Cornish. I am refusing everything but dinner invitations, of which I have seven at least to the week. After the day's work in seclusion, it is refreshing to meet people in the informal way practiced here, and to eat a good dinner in witty company. I fear I could easily contract the dining-out habit, which has killed so many good poets."[8] But the social scene was not always dinners and conversations. Several weeks later, he is planning a hiking expedition and entranced by his surroundings:

> It is blazing, or rather smotheringly hot here. Hotter than it was in [New York]. Of course, it is unprecedented in the experience of the oldest inhabitant. MacKaye and I, with perhaps two other men, are waiting for a cool spell in order to climb Mount Ascutney. We expect to spend the night up there in an abandoned stone house, and come back the next morning. Aside from the prostrating heat, the country is lovely. I have never seen such color—in New England—as these glowing days bring out in hills and woods and river, and the nights are beyond words wonderful—stars twice as big as they ought to be. Yesterday, I saw a deer in the road near Parrish's. It was a full-grown doe, nearly as tall as a man. It watched me approach until I was scarcely fifty feet away, and then, appar-

ently without fear, merely from a sense of bashfulness, dropped into the bushes and *floated off* (literally) across a field of high grass, moving like a swallow. There has been no "open season" now for three years, and the gentle creatures have two more years of respite. Then the ghastly business of extermination will begin again.[9]

Finally, there is a frosty description of a winter visit in 1908 immediately upon completing his prose play *The Faith Healer*. Despite her dislike of the play, Mrs. Davidge invited him to stay with her at "Kingsbury Tavern"; he left New York with his friend Ridgely Torrence, a poet and managing editor of *The Critic*. "The second day after arriving at Cornish (with Torrence) the thermometer dropped out of sight, and the resources of the Davidge 'tavern' were taxed to the breaking point to keep the breath of life in our bodies. As soon as the intense cold moderated, the heavens opened and incredible quantities of snow buried us out of sight for several days. It was a great experience, though strenuous; both of us had gone up to Cornish quite inadequately furnished with winter clothes and wrappings."[10]

Shortly thereafter, the "letters to Harriet" ceased. They were married in Canada the following year, after she had divorced her former husband and "devoted herself to providing her mother with a comfortable living."[11] Their life together, however, was brief. William Vaughn Moody died on October 17, 1910; he had caught typhoid fever, which was followed by a brain tumor. His ashes were scattered over the waves at Far Rockaway Beach by his wife, his sister Charlotte, Ridgely Torrence, and Ferdinand Schevill.[12]

ENDNOTES

1. Kenneth Rexroth, *American Poetry in the Twentieth Century* (New York: Herder and Herder, 1971), p. 24. John M. Manly in the introduction to *The Poem and Plays of William Vaughn Moody* (Boston and New York: Houghton Mifflin, 1912), Vol. 1, p. xxx, notes that to the issues brought up in his plays "he brought the richest intellectual and emotional development possessed by any American poet."

2. Robert E. Spiller, *The Cycle of American Literature* (New York: New American Library—Mentor, 1957), pp. 159-160.

3. William Vaughn Moody, *Letters to Harriet*, edited, with introduction and conclusion by Percy MacKaye (Boston and New York: Houghton Mifflin, 1935), p. 251; the letter was dated New York, February 13, 1906. The poet Ridgely Torrence was a good friend of both Moody and MacKaye; see below pp. 505-506. This same letter is also in Arvia MacKaye Ege, *The Power of the Impossible: The Life Story of Percy and Marion MacKaye* (Falmouth, ME: The Kennebec River Press, 1992), pp. 139-140. The children Moody refers to are Robin, born in 1899, and Arvia, born in 1902.

4. Manly, Vol. l, p. 15, 19-20. Moody notes that his poem was occasioned by "seeing at Boston the statue of Robert Gould Shaw, killed while storming Fort Wagner, July 18, 1863, at the head of the first enlisted negro regiment, the Fifty-fourth Massachusetts." For a remark of Saint-Gaudens about the Shaw Memorial, see below p. 361.

5. Moody, pp. 268-269. Some of this material is also in Ege, p. 140. The house he rented was a brick house belonging to Mrs. Eggleston on the current Route 12A in Plainfield.

6. Moody, p 273; see also Ege, p. 140. Within the week he was "asked to supper at the Hapgoods', so must stop. They have a wonderful place, hung high in the face of mountain and river, the landscape, the garden in the foreground, and the house itself,

subtly suggestive of Tuscany, but still with the good Yankee flavor" (Moody, p. 276). Norman Hapgood had bought "High Court," designed by Charles A. Platt, from Annie Lazarus.

7. Moody, p. 68, in a letter dated Cornish, July 2, 1906, to his devoted sister Charlotte, who often nursed him. The play was *Nereida* later published in MacKaye's *Yankee Fantasies* (1912) as *The Cat-Boat*; see MacKaye's annotation to Moody, p. 425.

8. Ibid., p. 287.

9. Ibid., p. 292.

10. Ibid., p. 353; letter dated February 6, 1908, from Boston.

11. MacKaye's annotation, Moody, p. 436.

12. Several of Moody's friends wrote poems in tribute to him. See below pp. 499-500, n. 2 for one by Edwin Arlington Robinson and p. 506, n. 2 for one in memory of Moody by Ridgely Torrence.

THE MOTHERS' AND DAUGHTERS' CLUB
IN PLAINFIELD

THE MOTHERS' AND DAUGHTERS' CLUB was organized at a meeting in the town hall under the direction of Cornish Colony members Frances (Mrs. William C.) Houston, Laura (Mrs. Henry Oliver) Walker, Eleanor (Mrs. Charles A.) Platt, and Miss Grace Arnold in August of 1897. They wanted to form a group "that should embrace the sojourners from the city and the country women, so that interest might be shared and helpful work done together." In 1911, the club noted in the *Weekly Enterprise* that "The club was formed solely for the women of the community—to draw them out of their circumscribed home life, to make them better acquainted with the women of the 'city colony,' and to help them in every way possible—the constitution of the club reads thus: Object—Its object shall be the mutual improvement of its members, also to promote social and philanthropic work in our midst."[1]

Initially, the meetings were held twice a month for eight months of the year in a room hired for that purpose. It soon became apparent that the organization needed its own building. In 1901, Curtis Lewin, the owner of a local butcher shop, donated land on Route 12A expressly for a clubhouse to be finished within two year's time. The eminent local architect Charles A. Platt designed the building and the novelist Winston Churchill donated the oak floor. Many local citizens donated their time and ingenuity; for example, George Ruggles, Harvey Plummer, W. B. Eggleston, and E. G. Kenyon. Its total cost "including donations was $1,093.17." Thus, the clubhouse was built within the time frame Lewin specified and, as of March 1982, it "is now listed on the National Register of Historic Places as the first women's clubhouse in the state of New Hampshire" and the site of the "first home-based crafts industry in New Hampshire."[2] Many Colony members were also involved in outfitting the clubhouse. Mrs. Maxfield Parrish, Mrs. H. O. Walker, Mr. Charles C. Burlingame, the New York lawyer, and Frances Houston all donated books for the library. Mrs. C. C. Beaman loaned a piano, Stephen Parrish donated a large volume of animal photographs, and Mrs. Albion Lang presented the club with seven dozen teaspoons.

The topics for the earliest meetings were talks the "city ladies" gave about their various trips. "The tired farmers' wives found at once that here was a new stimulus in life, and they appreciated the efforts made in their behalf and have always been most enthusiastic and grateful." Programs were expanded to include book reviews and more instructive subjects such as studies in household bacteriology and child rearing. "The ladies of

Figure 113. *Women working on rugs at the Mothers' and Daughters' Club, Plainfield.*

the summer colony soon decided that something more stimulating than that sort of thing was needed, and they decided to start some industry that would be both entertaining and lucrative. They decided upon rug and carpet making and general weaving." This project for a "Mothers' and Daughters' Industry" was a particularly good choice because a few homemade rugs had already been made and sold to raise money to build the clubhouse. Frances Houston and Laura Walker headed the project because they were artists; they assumed the job of designing the rugs and choosing the colors. Their contacts in the cities opened many markets for the rugs. Thus, "the farmers' wives from far and near belong, and women who were old before their time and for whom life stretched before as a dreary round of uninteresting toil have discovered new joys in existence, in making money for themselves and families, and having the most delightful intercourse with intellectual and charming women from the city."[3]

Soon this rugmaking venture became a highly organized business. The first winter, enough material was prepared so that the group finished twenty rugs. They were quickly sold and orders for forty more happily taken. This time new material had to be used. Marion L. (Mrs. George S.) Ruggles was appointed manager; she was responsible for buying all the material, doling out the work to the women, taking orders, packing and shipping all the goods, and maintaining the accounts. She bought all white outing-flannel cloth in lots from 500 to 1000 yards. "Instead of hard material, like new denim, [she] hit upon the use of torn strips of dyed Canton flannel, which gives a fluffy softness which is a very desirable quality."[4] It was then torn into strips for dying, the most strenuous step in the process. They used primarily natural dyes taken from barks of trees, onion skins, golden rod, and indigo. Once Laura Walker was "walking on the seashore in Mantoloking, New Jersey, where parts of a wrecked ship had washed up after a disastrous storm. Among the wreckage was a quantity of purple wood; it turned out to be logwood from Jamaica. . . . She picked up some little pieces and sent them to Plainfield, where they made dyes for many a piece of cotton."[5] Following the dye bath, the strips were hung outdoors in the sun and rain to set the fastness of the color. Next, they were washed in soap and water and dried again. Once the strips were dyed, they were tied up in bundles, each of which would make enough prepared material for one rug. These were taken to a sewer who would return them sewn and ready for weaving to the manager. After a rug had been ordered, the manager selected the colors required and carried the material and the design of the rug ordered to the weaver. Because the looms were old and heavy, this step also required strength to complete. The weaving was done at the clubhouse where a loom had been set up. At first they had only one loom, then a new, lighter-weight Swedish loom was bought and people were given lessons in twine weaving so that they could make curtains, bed coverlets, and tablecloths. Eventually, there were five looms and plenty of work. The final step in the process was done by the finisher, who looked the rug over on both sides, fastened any loose threads, sewed down the ends of the strips which were woven in so that the design was clear, knotted the fringe, and sewed on the club's trademark, designed by Frances Houston.

As Mrs. Ruggles noted in 1904, "Of course, there is not work enough to keep all the helpers busy all the time, nor is such the intention. It simply provides a pleasant occupation for spare moments in the home, and while profitable so far as dollars and cents are concerned, has also been an artistic education in itself, all the workers having learned more in the past two years in regard to color schemes, harmonious designs, the use of soft shades and avoidance of crude colors, etc., than they otherwise would have learned in a lifetime."[6] Nevertheless, their "Industry" lasted a good fifteen years, from about 1900 to 1915. They were so successful that they were able to supply the clubhouse with electricity in 1914. The occasion was special enough to warrant a celebration: an oyster supper attended by a hundred people. The reason for this success, however, was the weaving and the rugs. Most of the rugs were 3 feet by 6 feet; their price was determined by the complexity of the design. "To illustrate: a rug with designs, 3 feet x 6 feet would be $6; one, 27 inches x 1½ yards, same design, $5, because in either case the difficulty in weaving lies in putting in the figures, and as there are the same number in the smaller as in the larger sizes, the cost of weaving is nearly the same, and the only reduction in the cost of making is in the amount of material used."[7]

The program for 1906-1907 was the first to include a quotation from John Ruskin as the club's motto: "Wife means weaver. You must be either housewives or house moths— remember that. In the deep sense you must either weave men's fortunes and embroider them or feed upon them and bring them to decay."[8] Later in the twentieth century, the sentiments of the English leader of the Arts and Crafts Movement became outdated as more and more women began working and holding full-time positions. Furthermore, it became increasingly difficult for the club to meet expenses, especially their tax bill. So, in 1979, the women deeded the clubhouse to the Plainfield Historical Society, reserving the use of the building for their meetings. Yet even today, the spirit and ideals of the founders persist: "the educational part of our original ways—the *studying* of things, should be kept up. And we should keep our eyes open to see where we can help each other where help is needed, either in material ways, or in 'holding up of the hands' of those less strong among us and always in *loving kindness*—for after all, we each one are in need of kindness and affection of being understood."[9]

ENDNOTES

1. *Weekly Enterprise*, Meriden, NH, Vol. 3, #20, March 30, 1911, p. 1.

2. See the chapter on the group by Beatrice Clark, Philip Zea and Nancy Norwalk, eds., *Choice White Pines and Good Land: A History of Plainfield and Meriden, New Hampshire* (Portsmouth, NH: Peter E. Randall, 1991), p. 204.

3. The quotations in this paragraph come from Elizabeth Van Horne, "Pleasure and Profit for Farmers' Wives," *Leslie's Illustrated Weekly Newspaper*, November 7, 1912, p. 470.

4. Candace Wheeler, "Home Weaving in Country Houses," *Country Life in America*, July 1903, p. 199.

5. Mary D. Marshall, "Money-Making for Women—A Rug Industry in the New Hampshire Hills," *The Twentieth Century Home*, September 1904. Mantoloking, NJ, is near Lakewood, where the Fullers lived when they were not in Plainfield.

6. Mrs. G. S. Ruggles, Manager, *Mothers' and Daughters' Industry* (Plainfield, NH, December 1, 1904), p. 10.

7. Ibid., p. 13.

8. Clark, p. 201.

9. As quoted in Clark, p. 209.

ROSE STANDISH NICHOLS
1872 – 1960

ROSE STANDISH NICHOLS was a pioneer in a discipline that in her day was itself a fledgling one: landscape architecture. In fact, she is frequently referred to as the first female landscape architect in America. She began by studying horticulture with Mrs. Benjamin Watson; it was then that she decided to emphasize a formal "style in gardens, revived in England" at the expense of the then more popular "sinuosities of the romantic school."[1] She also studied architectural drawing with the well-known New York architect Thomas Hastings, an acquaintance of her uncle, Augustus Saint-Gaudens. And, from her Cornish neighbor Charles A. Platt, she learned architectural layout. Further studies at the Massachusetts Institute of Technology, then London, and finally at the Ecole des Beaux Arts in Paris increased her knowledge of landscape architecture and enabled her to perfect her ability to adapt European styles to ornamental garden designs. In time this skill was to become her hallmark. She was, however, treading on controversial ground—a fact that rarely troubled her. In the early 1890s, there was a great debate in Europe and America about whether gardens should follow a "naturalized garden layout" or be "formally organized compositions."[2] During her lifetime, she made over thirty trips to Europe so that her visits could complement her academic studies. Her first attempt to put what she had learned into practice was her garden in Cornish. By 1904, the year when Edith Wharton brought out *Italian Villas and Their Gardens*, with Maxfield Parrish's illustrations, the taste for formal landscape was widespread.

It was quite natural for Rose Nichols to come to Cornish because it was the summer residence of her aunt and uncle: Augusta Homer Saint-Gaudens and Augustus Saint-Gaudens. While they were in Europe during the summer of 1889, Rose and her family stayed in "Aspet."[3] Rose had a particularly "stimulating" summer in the company of the Thomas Dewings, the Herbert Adamses, the Charles Platts, and the Henry Prellwitzes. Her sister Margaret was somewhat more ambivalent about Cornish: "At that time, Cornish was farming country and had only a few summer residents, but each was distinguished in one way or another, with artists and writers predominating . . . my artistic sister, Rose . . . set her heart on our buying a place in Cornish . . . while I had very little enthusiasm for faraway Cornish with no marsh, no ocean, and no friends, I did like the idea of having a place of our own. Rose had her way." She finally persuaded her father, Dr. Arthur Nichols, a prominent Boston homeopathic physician, to buy a summer place

Figure 114. *"Mastlands," home of Rose Standish Nichols.*

for his wife, Augusta Saint-Gaudens's sister, and their three daughters: Rose, Marian, and Margaret. The following winter they decided on the Chester Pike farm, which "consisted of a commonplace house of the period of 1860, with many sheds and two big barns, a small cottage with more barns, and about 150 acres of flat land extending from Blow-Me-Down Brook to the Connecticut River." The proud new owners called it "Mastlands" because of the tall pines on the land. This name was appropriate: Cornish had been settled by the king's men who so admired its tall pines that they established a Mast Camp in the vicinity, harvested the trees, and floated them down the Connecticut River to Long Island Sound to be used as masts for the Royal Navy. By 1892, Dr. Nichols and his family had moved to their summer home, having added dormers and a large square piazza to it; Rose enthusiastically designed a charming walled garden for it.[4]

As her horticultural interests became more professional, so did her contributions to the field. She wrote many articles on gardening and garden design for *The House Beautiful.* It is not surprising that she demonstrated many of her points by drawing upon her local experience. One, entitled "How Not to Make a Flower Garden," was illustrated by a picture of Mount Ascutney rising "in majesty in the distance" and a picture of "a wilder portion of the Connecticut Garden," which she describes as being "located on a flat stretch of the purest sand, interesting from a geological standpoint as a reminiscence of the glacial period, but almost as baffling as a bottomless pit to the would-be-gardener."[5] A year later in "The Use and Abuse of Evergreens," she noted that "as an avenue or roadside tree, the pine is of great value. It furnishes shade in summer and protection from the wind in winter, while unlike deciduous trees, it does not litter up the ground with leaves. At Cornish, New Hampshire, my father planted a double row of white pines spaced about twenty feet apart on each side of the highway for a stretch of perhaps half a mile. These trees, four or five feet high when planted fifteen years ago, are over thirty feet and none I think have died."[6] (If only Rose Nichols and her father could see Route 12A today, wouldn't they be proud?) And later that same year, in a discussion of "How to Make a Small Garden," she pointed out that "the style of the garden should obviously correspond to its environment, especially to any permanent architectural feature such as an adjoining house or to the marked characteristics of the landscape." The manner in which

Charles A. Platt had brought Mount Ascutney into the "Garden at High Court, Cornish, Vt," was praised because it showed "how the distant view can be made to count as part of the garden and how the architectural framework binds both harmoniously together. The parapet shuts out the middle distance and enhances the impressive contour of Mt. Ascutney, while the flowerpots planted with dwarf apple trees furnish just the right vertical accents in contrast to the horizontal lines dominating the landscape."[7]

What she accomplished in her own Cornish garden is best left to Frances Duncan to describe. Its tasteful serenity and comfort drew her praise because "the ideal garden" for a house in the country "is not an exhibition grounds, nor even a flower show, but a lovable place where one is inclined to lounge or read in undisturbed peace." As for the garden's design, it "is simple and straightforward. Two broad paths cross each other at right angles and divide the garden into four parts. . . . In the centre of the garden, where the two main paths intersect, the gravel widens into a circle within which is a pool some nine feet in diameter, over which spreads the branches of the apple tree, which seems to have grown there for that especial purpose." In fact, Rose Nichols actually designed the garden so that its focal point would be the crooked, gnarled old apple tree that had once been standing in the middle of a field. "A good garden, if it have any pretext of regularity, is made on the same axis as the house, else its symmetry profiteth nothing. The broad path which divided the garden in halves left this tree a little to the west of the centre; the width of the garden was so arranged that the longitudinal path left the tree just north of it . . . it now stands . . . reflected in the quiet water below, it gives a touch of serenity and repose to the whole garden." Fortunately, there are curved wooden seats, "green painted affairs," not ostentatious "marble *exedrae* or pseudo-marble benches to disturb with an alien note the quiet charm of the place." Frances Duncan was particularly strong on this point, because "in garden-making as in the higher form of art, what to omit, when to stop in decoration, is no small test of a man's taste, for over-adornment, until the garden is out of scale with the house, is one of the most easily committable sins in the gardener's Decalogue." After describing the use of dwarf fruit trees to suggest scale and the pruning methods used, she drew to a close by pointing out that "interesting as this garden is in design, one of its chief charms is its color scheme." Color was a subject to which Rose Nichols paid a great deal of attention—she even wrote an article, "Color in the Garden," for *The Country Calendar*, (October 1905, p. 541). It is clear, however, that Frances Duncan considers Rose Nichols to be one of the most professional garden architects she knows:

> Miss Nichols is doubtless best known as the author of a gardening book done with an unusual degree of care and intelligence. But to write of gardens is one thing, to make them another. There be many garden writers who say unto the reader "Lo here" and "Lo there" is the place to plant, but their actual knowledge of the subject is slenderness itself. Rare indeed is it when in garden matters precept and practice are met together in the same person. For which reason, it is refreshing to know that Miss Nichols can make a garden as well as books about them, and her garden at Cornish was well worth making.[8]

Her interests ranged widely; they were not limited to gardening. She made a special study of embroidery and completed a canopy done in crewel work for her lovely Sheraton poster bed at her home on Boston's Beacon Hill. No more able not to write about what she practiced with her needle than what she did in her garden, she wrote an article for *Ladies' Home Journal* on crewel work. Furthermore, since she so loved to use her hands, she became interested in wood carving and took lessons from Carl Larson, a teacher at Mrs. Pauline Shaw's co-ed school. While in Cornish, she carved a set of four chairs using a family antique Jacobean chair as a pattern. These chairs, too, are in her Beacon Hill house, now the Nichols' House Museum at 55 Mt. Vernon Street, the only Beacon Hill house open to the public.[9]

And her interests were of an intellectual sort as well. "It was the spirit of the Puritans to try to broaden their interests toward wide horizons, and that same spirit I've tried to keep alive in everything I've ever done."[10] She was quick to join the Cornish Equal Suffrage League in 1911. In Boston, her reputation was high because of her "Sunday afternoon teas." She combined her intellectual interests with social ones. She would invite people from all walks of life—scholars, artists, scientists, theologians—as well as from every race and culture to discuss current political and religious issues. These events dovetailed with the Beacon Hill Reading Club, which she founded even before she came to Cornish. The club met weekly during the winter at various members' houses; the hostess selected the topic and the reading and then led lively discussions. There were also occasions when the opera singer Louise Homer sang, accompanied by her husband Sidney Homer, a first cousin of both Augusta Homer Saint-Gaudens and Rose Nichols. Other guests included Jane Addams, the noted American social worker; Norman Angell, the English author and activist who won the Nobel Peace Prize in 1933; Mrs. Malburg, a member of the Finnish Parliament; the novelist John Phillips Marquand; Colonel Laurence Bunker, one of General MacArthur's chief advisers in Tokyo; and Godfrey Lowell Cabot. Her interest in the peace movement led her to invite members of the Fellowship of Reconciliation and her interest in international affairs led her to welcome representatives of the Women's International League for Peace and Freedom. During the first World War she took up the cause of small European nations and founded the League of Small Nations which became the parent of the Foreign Policy Association, a club that now exists throughout the country.[11]

With these commitments, it was natural for her to be one of the founding members, along with Mrs. Woodrow Wilson, Mrs. Winston Churchill, and Mrs. Maxfield Parrish, of the Cornish Discussion Club, an organization with goals similar to those she fostered in Boston. What people said was as interesting to her as the people themselves. As Lydia Parrish noted in her diary, "Rose Nichols is very interested in people and sidelights on their characters are almost a passion with her. She handles their actions and characters in such a light, interesting way that until afterwards you do not realize that it is gossip on a very high plane."[12] We can get some idea of what went on in the meetings of the Discussion Club and what their subjects were from the letters Mrs. Ellen Wilson wrote her husband in the White House: "the subject was one about which we would all naturally know something, viz. the education of girls" (July 22, 1913); "the duty on pictures" (August 5); "does human nature change" (August 11); "what constitutes a good citizen" (August 12); "how can we promote a fuller and more general appreciation of *American* art?" (August 19); "the simple life—what is it and is it worth while?" (September 9). In 1915, after the death of Ellen Wilson, the President was courting Mrs. Edith Bolling Galt, who visited Cornish with the President's daughters. She, too, wrote him her impressions of the Discussion Club's meetings, though they were somewhat less rosy than his first wife's: "We had to hurry back on account of the 'Discussion Club' . . . [it] was about the most amusing thing I have heard in a long time, and no one knew a bit more when we left than when we arrived. But lots of women had talked a great deal." (July 21, 1915)[13]

Two final notes about Rose Standish Nichols. An index of her importance to the Colony is the fact that she took the part of Polyhymnia in the 1905 performance of *A Masque of "Ours": The Gods and the Golden Bowl*. But after her death in 1960 many of her manuscripts, journals, and drawings were destroyed.

ENDNOTES

1. As quoted in George Taloumis, *Boston Sunday Globe*, September 16, 1956, section C, p. 22. For more on Nichols's career, see Deborah E. Van Buren, "Landscape Architecture and Gardens in the Cornish Colony: the Careers of Rose Nichols, Ellen Shipman, and Frances Duncan," *Women's Studies* 14, 1988, pp. 367-388.

2. Charles A. Platt, *Italian Gardens*, with an overview by Keith N. Morgan (Portland, OR: Sagapress/Timber Press, 1993), p. 119; for more on this issue, see the "Overview," pp. 97-142.

3. Rose Nichols was so close to her uncle that after his death she edited and published some of his letters to her in *McClare's Magazine* 31:6, October 1908, pp. 603-615 and 32:1, November 1908, pp. 1-16.

4. The information in this paragraph comes from Margaret Homer Shurcliff, *Lively Days: Some Memoirs of Margaret Homer Shurcliff* (Taipei: Literature House, Ltd., 1965), p. 34.

5. *The House Beautiful*, September 1911, p. 103.

6. *The House Beautiful*, June 1912, p. 1.

7. *The House Beautiful*, August 1912, p. 88. Later, she uses her own garden, with a "large Sicilian oil jar on a mill-stone in the center of a circle of grass" to illustrate "the intimate relationship between a house and garden, where grass has gradually taken the place of many of the flowerbeds, much to the improvement of the appearance of the garden and to the economy with which it can be kept in order. There are many points to be mastered"; (p. 88) for her thoughts on the Slade sisters' garden, see below p. 400.

8. The quotations in this paragraph come from Frances Duncan, "A Cornish Garden," *Country Life in America*, March 1908, pp. 507-508; see also Guy Lowell, ed., *American Gardens* (Boston: Houghton Mifflin, 1902) for another admiring account of her Cornish garden. The book Duncan refers to is *English Pleasure Gardens*, which Nichols published in 1902. Other important books that she wrote are *Spanish and Portuguese Gardens* (1924) and *Italian Pleasure Gardens* (1928).

9. The house has been open to the public since the early 1960s. Built in 1804, it is of a Federal design and was updated in the 1930s. Her father's office remains about the same, with his medical books and desk where he saw his patients. There are oriental rugs on the wood floors. In the parlor, a large French tapestry hangs on one wall and on another wall a painting of an ancestor, Thomas Johnson. Rose's carved chairs are in the dining room along with a pair of Paul Manship's *Adam* and *Eve*, which are on the mantle. In Rose's bedroom is her poster bed with the crewel work and a painting of her by Daisy Pumpelly of Dublin, NH. In the guest room hangs a portrait of Rose by Polly Thayer.

10. George Taloumis, *Boston Sunday Globe,* September 16, 1956.

11. Ibid.

12. Lydia Parrish, diary, entry for January 15, 1904; copy, Virginia Colby, Cornish Colony files.

13. The quotations in this paragraph come from Arthur S. Link, ed., *The Papers of Woodrow Wilson* (Princeton, NJ: Princeton University Press, 1976), Vol. 28, pp. 63, 120, 143, 146, 194-95, 269; Vol. 34, pp. 7-8. For the full context of all these quotations, see below pp. 430, 432, 433-434, 435-436.

Figure 115. *Lydia Parrish and her daughter, Jean, from an autochrome by B. Martin Justice, c. 1913.*

LYDIA AUSTIN PARRISH
1872 – 1953

HISTORY HAS BEEN UNFAIR to Lydia Austin Parrish. Although her fame now may rest on the fact that she was Maxfield Parrish's wife, she deserves to be recognized for her own accomplishments. Her book *Slave Songs of the Georgia Sea Islands*, published in 1935, was hailed as "a singularly sincere and valuable contribution to the subject of Afro-American song."[1] And, had she not been an instructor of painting at Philadelphia's Drexel Institute, she might not have had the opportunity to encounter her future husband.

The two first met in 1894. "Miss Austin, the daughter of a Quaker family from Woodstown, New Jersey, was an exceptionally attractive woman whose intelligence and enthusiasm impressed those who met her. She and Maxfield Parrish became close friends, and after a courtship of more than a year they were married on Saturday, June 1, 1895, in Philadelphia."[2] Three years later Parrish bought land on a Plainfield, New Hampshire hillside. During the construction of their house, which he would call "The Oaks" and help to design and build, the couple stayed with Stephen Parrish, Maxfield's father, whose hillside house was across the valley in Cornish. They also boarded at Stephen Alden Tracy's place down the road from Stephen Parrish's house. By the end of the year, *The Vermont Journal* would note that "Fred Parrish will move to his new house in a few days."[3]

Household duties and child rearing kept Lydia busy during her early years in the area. John Dillwyn was born in 1904,[4] Maxfield, Jr., in 1906, Stephen in 1909, and their only daughter, Jean, in 1911. Lydia had help from several local people in educating her brood. Lucy Ruggles Bishop tutored the Parrish children in all of their subjects and was especially appreciative of the pictures the young Maxfield drew on the margins of his papers.[5] Marguerite Lewin Quimby was the children's music teacher. As for help around the house, Lydia employed Miss Hattie Read, of Cornish, for seventeen years.

Lydia Parrish's interest in children took several forms. On the one hand, a diary entry is proof of her delight in a performance that the children of the Colonists put on:

Fred finished the poster for "Ivanhoe" just in time and we got it over to Houstons' 20 min. before performance began—It was really wonderful! Over a hundred people. The children and the scenery were so pretty—The children knew their parts so well-required so little prompting-and three were really excellent actors—Charles Fuller—first of all—Sylvia Hyde as Rebecca—Charlie Fuller as Isaac of York and Allyn Cox as Wamba—Leonard Cox as Brian Bois de Guilbert and Ellen Shipman as Cedric were wonders at remembering their many lines and they were very spirited. Edwin Prellwitz was the only drawback—a strange child—Lucia Fuller as playwright and stage manager was a marvel and the enthusiasm of the audience must have repaid her for the vast amount of care and thought she had put in the performance. She says being so near blind this summer that the work has been her salvation (entry for September 17, 1904).

On the other hand, ten years later Lydia was instrumental in a significant school project. In autumn of 1914, as the storm clouds of World War I were gathering, she organized the young people of Cornish and Plainfield into the planning and maintenance of school gardens. Local children who participated included Erwin Williams, Max Plummer, who was the youngest member, Stephen Plummer, Ruth Whitaker, Benjamin Lewis, Sylvia Waite, Adelbert Westgate, Grace Whitaker, and Rachel Daniels. Prizes were awarded for the best spring and the best autumn garden.[6] Her motive for organizing these gardens was an admirable one: "We do want to keep our boys and girls at home if they show any inclination for staying and to give them the training that will help them to get the best out of country life, instead of only the training that fits them for city conditions. Enable them to take pride in being producers instead of consumers only."[7]

Her involvement in community affairs had its social aspects as well. She was a member of the Cornish Equal Suffrage League, the Cornish Discussion Club, and active in the Mothers' and Daughters' Club of Plainfield. She and her husband especially enjoyed entertaining. Her diary and that of her father-in-law Stephen Parrish are replete with references to dinner parties, often with elaborate menu descriptions. The list of those invited reads as if it were a census of the Cornish Colony's "in" members. Stephen Parrish's accounts are brief and factual, but Lydia's make it clear who her favorite—and not so favorite—guests were.

It is obvious that members of the Cornish Colony played as hard as they worked. Maxfield Parrish, Jr., saved a newspaper clipping that is humorous proof of the fun they had. The day after the celebration of the fifteenth anniversary of Lydia and Maxfield Parrish's wedding, June 2, 1910, Winston Churchill commissioned a fake copy of the *Windsor Journal* to run the following tongue-in-cheek story, complete with false photographs of the "model couple." Churchill saw to it that a copy was given each participant; the by-line is "From Our Special Correspondent":

Figure 116. *Title page and frontispiece from* Slave Songs of the Georgia Sea Islands *by Lydia Parrish.*

Smiling faces greeted Mrs. Lydia Parrish and her husband at their residence on the Plainfield road, Wednesday night, on the happy occasion of their wedding anniversary. Mr. Parrish has been well known as a temperance man for years. The genial Prof. Dow came over from Hanover in his auto. Farmer and Mrs. Louise Croly arrived behind their horse, Belle, and Mrs. Mabel Churchill, to say nothing of the "Doc," who recently signed the pledge, made up the complement of old friends. Many reminiscences were indulged in, and one of the pleasantest features of the evening was a song, "O Promise Me!" charmingly rendered by H. B. Croly. The genial professor from Occom Ridge, Hanover, presented the happy couple with an easel destined to contain the crayon portrait of the family. Those who have had a glimpse of this assure us that it is one of the handsomest things ever brought to Plainfield. The professor then recited "Honi Soit qui Mal y Pense" with terrific effect, and ended with a graceful and original composition, an eulogium on the joys of marriage, a delicate compliment to the host and hostess. Mrs. Mabel Churchill declaimed, "O Woman, where is thy Sting, O Man, where is thy Victory." Mrs. Louise Croly, "Oats, peas, beans, and barley grows." Her present was a rococo ice pitcher, imported by Tuxbury's, Windsor, which swings on a stand. A collation was served of all kinds of pie, and the baked beans which have made Mrs. Lydia Parrish famous. Doc Churchill's present, we neglected to say, was a chased carburetor, which, when not in use may be employed as a centerpiece.[8]

Maxfield Parrish, Jr., wryly commented that "this was sort of a commemorative gift like Saint-Gaudens's 1905 Masque, though, of course, it cost one one-hundredth as much and wasn't exactly art: more an artful hoax."

Such frivolity, however, did not prevent Lydia from her work on *Slave Songs of the*

Georgia Sea Islands. Mrs. Parrish first went to the Sea Islands off the coast of Georgia in 1912. This was a particularly busy period for Maxfield Parrish; he found it difficult to complete his many commissions because of the interruptions and the fact that he had no studio there. Gradually, they agreed that she would head south in the winters and return to Cornish for the summers. Years later, after she published an article on "The Plantation Songs of Our Old Negro Slaves," Maxfield dryly noted, "It never occurred to me that she could write."9 But write she could. She eventually bought a place on St. Simons Island on the site where the English drove the Spanish out of the American settlements in 1742 at the Battle of Bloody Marsh. There, she devoted herself to learning more about the music she heard, especially that sung by the older African-Americans. Some of them were born slaves and many were children of former slaves. By virtue of returning year after year, she gained their confidence so that they would unselfconsciously sing, dance, and chant for her and tell her their lore of stories. The distinguished folklorist Carl Carmer summarizes the importance of the study that took her virtually a lifetime to complete: "Mrs. Parrish proves to be on the right side of most controversial issues that have risen since Americans have been seriously studying the ancestral music of our Negro citizens. She points out that our system of notation cannot even intimate what happens musically when a group of Negroes sings one of these songs, and she adds the inevitable corollary that choruses may not be formally drilled in singing them without the loss not only of spontaneity but of musical quality. She denies emphatically that the slave songs are Negro adaptations of white words and music and offers adequate proof of her contention, though it would seem now that the point needs no further proving."10 The book describes the early history of slave songs and how they were preserved, discusses the evidence and examples of the African survivals on the Georgia coast, and describes shout songs, ring-play, dance, and fiddle songs, religious songs, and work songs. She avoids the term "spiritual" because "today it is applied to almost any religious song in Negro dialect, regardless of its age or origin, and because of its indiscriminate use I have suppressed it whenever possible."11 There is an amusing anecdote of Mrs. Parrish "tell[ing] the Negroes interesting things about themselves, and the Negroes listen[ing] politely." She explains that the phrase "shout songs" really means dance songs "accompanied by a slow, circular, dancing movement." Something her audience readily acknowledges. "But it takes Mrs. Parrish, backed up by Dr. Lorenzo D. Turner, the Negro research scholar, to teach them that the word 'shout' is derived from an Arabic word 'saut,' which means 'to dance counterclockwise around a shrine in the inner temple."12 In addition to Maxfield Parrish, Jr., taking some of the photographs for the *Country Life* article, the transcriptions of the music in *Slave Songs* was done by Creighton Churchill, son of the novelist Winston Churchill, and by Robert MacGimsey.

Lydia Parrish also prepared another two-volume study of English Loyalists during the Revolutionary War, but it was never published. The manuscript is in the library of Harvard University.

While still at her home on St. Simons Island, Mrs. Parrish died in 1953.

ENDNOTES

1. Olin Downes, Preface in Lydia Austin Parrish, *Slave Songs of the Georgia Sea Islands* (New York: Creative Age Press, 1942), p. xxvii.

2. Coy Ludwig, *Maxfield Parrish* (New York: Watson-Guptill, 1973), p. 15.

3. Issue of December 24, 1898. To his friends, Maxfield Parrish was known by his given name Frederick, or, simply, Fred.

4. There are several interesting notes in her diary about her concern for her first-born child: "Stopped at Coxes—Louise gave me the first tiny garment which I prize immensely" (entry for August 4, 1904); "Went to the Churchills and was initiated into the mysteries of the baby bath—his clothing and feeding—I hope I shall be able to get as attractive and capable nurses as he has" (August 10); "Went over to Northcote and got Fred's baby clothes" (August 23).

5. Interview: Lucy Ruggles Bishop with Virginia Colby, July 27, 1979.

6. Lydia Parrish's article in the *Sullivan County Farmer's Advisor,* Newport, NH, 2:2, February 1916, p. 1. The article points out that "Benj. [Lewis] had two long rows of potatoes, the same of corn, fine corn, too, some of which was sent to President Wilson's family along with some of Sylvia's [Waite] beans, the President's garden being smaller than ours," p. 2.

7. Ibid., p. 3.

8. See Virginia Colby files for a copy of the clipping, dated June 2, 1910, and Maxfield Parrish, Jr.'s, comments, dated January 30, 1975. The spoof's reference to automobiles is an interesting one. They were not too prevalent at the time, though Maxfield Parrish had owned a number of them before the following advertisement appeared in 1913: "Wanted—A small, light, second-hand sleigh for my 650 ob. pony. I wish to sell my excellent driving horse, not afraid of automobiles, as I have no further use for him. Price reasonable for cash. Mrs. Maxfield Parrish"; Virginia Colby, Cornish Colony files, W. Williams's scrapbook.

9. As quoted by Margaret Case Harriman, "Nirvana is Near Savannah," *The New Yorker,* February 3, 1940, p. 53. Lydia's article can be found in *Country Life,* 69:2, December 1935, pp. 54 ff.

10. *New York Times Book Review,* July 5, 1942, p. 8.

11. Parrish, *Slave Songs,* pp. ix-x.

12. Harriman, p. 54.

Figure 117. *Column heading painted for* Collier's *by Maxfield Parrish.*

A REMARK HIS FATHER once made about his son, "Fred is more of an artisan than an artist," raises two puzzling questions: why is his son called "Fred" and how accurate an assessment is one that concentrates on the artisanship rather than the art of Maxfield Parrish? The answer to the first question is easy; it leads us down a fairly straight-forward biographical path. The answer to the second question, however, takes us through the maze of art criticism in its attempts to come to terms with Parrish's complicated "combination of mechanic and poet."[1] We can never lose sight of the fact that it is precisely this blend that creates "the unique world of fantasy and romance" that "strikes modern viewers with no less power than it did nearly a century ago when Parrish first became known to the public."[2]

Parrish, born July 25, 1870, in Philadelphia, Pennsylvania, was christened Frederick Parrish. He later decided that he liked the ring of the maiden name of his paternal grandmother, Susanna Maxfield, and took it as both his middle name and his signature name. His family and friends, though, continued to call him Fred throughout his life. And there is probably no point during his lifetime that these same people would not have agreed with the foresightful judgment his father passed on his three-day-old son: "Fred is certainly rebellious and shows even at this early age a decided temper and a determined will."[3] These characteristics were to stand him in good stead as he acquired the artistic techniques that would develop the talent his father saw early in his son's life. Determination and independence were also necessary so that Maxfield Parrish could develop his career along lines that he defined. After all, "Parrish worked entirely outside the several schools or movements that emerged in American art during the more than sixty-five years in which he was active. In every sense he was an independent artist. Reflected in both his life style and his painting style is his determination to be his own man. . . . He established rigid standards for himself, and when a commission called for him to make an advertising design, he approached it with the same concern for aesthetic beauty and technical perfection as he did his other art."[4]

The Quaker tradition he was born into led him to Haverford College from 1888 to 1891; his intention while a college student was to become an architect. He had already been introduced to art during an extended European tour with his parents from 1884

Figure 118. *House and garden at Parrish's estate, "The Oaks."*

to 1886. Once he graduated from college, he asserted his preference for art over architecture in 1892 by entering the Pennsylvania Academy of the Fine Arts in Philadelphia only six years after Thomas Eakins had shaken that venerable institution with the "loincloth incident." There, Parrish studied for two years under Robert W. Vonnoh and Thomas P. Anshutz. Although he was never officially registered at the Drexel Institute, he briefly audited classes there taught by Howard Pyle. At Drexel he met his future wife, Lydia Austin, where she was a painting instructor. They were married on the first day of June in 1895; shortly thereafter Parrish went to Europe without her for about two months to observe both the current salons and again to look more carefully at the great art of Europe's past.

What he saw, and how it impressed him, came at a turning point in his career. His descriptions in letters to his bride provide us with several clues to his further development. On the one hand, he was impressed with the old masters. Fifteenth- and sixteenth-century Flemish and Dutch painters "were a perfect revelation to me"; the Louvre showed him "one glorious mosaic of richness. What an awesome feeling it is to be in such a presence," and its *La Mise au Tombeau* (*The Entombment [of Christ]*) by Titian "simply haunts me. I dream about beautiful reds and blues and greens and glorious whites. The color in that picture is pure magic." From such inspiration as these traditional paintings may have come his heightened sense of color and his interest in achieving them through a complicated glazing process. On the other hand, he was in the immediate presence of 1890s Europe, and especially of Paris. Its salons left him cold: "Of the avenues and avenues of pictures there is not one good thing: not one. The most interesting thing is to see what frightful subjects some have taken, and see which Frenchman had the most original idea of blood. There are many examples worth dwelling upon . . . one . . . is the canvas of a man who has gone straight to the slaughter house for this subject. There before us is a colossal representation of a newly cut-open ox, dripping, swimming, wallowing in crimson, animal blood!" Although Parrish would always admire art firmly grounded in reality, apparently the realism that was then in vogue—both in America and Europe—could go too far for his tastes. Nevertheless, while he was in Paris, his aversion did not preclude his socializing with some of the men who would become the best known representatives of American realism. He wrote Lydia that he "took lunch with Henri, Schofield, and Glackens and had a fine time." The atmosphere of Paris also had its role to play, albeit on a more personal note. He could be nostalgic both for his bride and for Europe's great art: "I am sitting in the Tuileries watching the twilight: a glorious place to be alone in and wish one were not. This evening is simply heavenly—such gray twilights! One does not wonder that the old masters put such beautiful ones behind their madonnas."[5]

Meanwhile his father had come to Cornish; in 1893 Stephen Parrish started the long-term project of building "Northcote." Five years later, "Fred bought 19 acres of land today from Chas. A. Williams. 19 acres @ $50—$950. I advanced him the money."[6] Thus, on a sheep pasture strewn with rocks and trees in Plainfield, he began construction of "The Oaks." The vista from the site was probably given more consideration than the site itself: during construction when the men encountered a large section of ledge, instead of blasting it out, Parrish merely built over it creating a ground floor on two levels. George S. Ruggles, his chief carpenter and a man soon to become his boon companion, commented that "the house started as a rectangle and then [Parrish] built east, west, north, south, and up."[7] Although the house began on an unassuming scale—a place for raising four children[8] as well as for Parrish's work—it soon became one of the Colony's premier houses, featured in many architectural and home magazines.

Parrish and his wife sensibly added onto the house and land gradually. It was not until 1905 that he built a separate studio about forty paces from the house on its northern, rear side. Parrish's love for his studio is everywhere apparent and it offers a possible explanation for his father's remark about his "artisan" son. It was his special affinity for the studio that led even Maxfield Parrish to refer to himself as a "machinist who paints." Parrish once parried an interviewer's question, "Isn't it unusual to find an artist who likes to fool around with machinery," with the assertion, "In the first place, it's just the opposite. You mean a machinist who paints pictures . . . I just happened to slide into painting as a profession. . . . The tool makers of the Connecticut Valley used to be famous, you know."[9] So, it is no wonder that the studio's ground floor consisted of a fully equipped machine shop. In addition it contained lathes, drill presses, and presses to glue paper and canvas to panels. There were also a shaper, two South Bend lathes, a 9" swing and a 12" swing for metal work, and a Star lathe for small wood work. The German drill press had a variable speed transmission.[10] He would use this machinery to help him make many of the beautiful brass latches used in both "Northcote" and "The Oaks."[11] And it was on the wood lathe in this shop that Parrish turned the small wooden models as well as the wooden urns, vases, and furniture that he often used in his paintings.[12] In order to prepare a guide for a painting, especially in

Figure 119. *Maxfield Parrish at one of the lathes in his machine shop.*

the landscapes that he turned to toward the end of his career, he would sometimes set up a small scene with a model house—or whatever the painting-to-be called for—he had made in the shop. Then he would carefully arrange it under the light of a floor lamp, so that the proper shadows were cast, and, finally, photograph it. Conveniently enough, there was a large, well-equipped darkroom in the studio so that he could do his own developing. Parrish would wryly explain to any visitors exclaiming over how elaborate his shop was, that he had to paint in order to earn enough money to buy all the machinery in which he took so much delight. The studio had its comforts, too. A large room had a pot-bellied stove in it so that Parrish could be warm in winter; it was also useful throughout the year for drying the special glazes on his paintings. Because of the meticulous process necessary for his paintings to acquire their intense color, he generally had many paintings in progress simultaneously. He had to paint a segment of the canvas, apply a glaze to it, and then wait for that section to dry before painting the next coat over it or near it. Each layer had to dry thoroughly before the next color could be applied.[13] There were two painting rooms in the studio; both had large, high windows equipped with worm and gear segments to open and close them at the touch of a lever. The larger of the two rooms was built to accommodate his huge mural panels. Furthermore, there was a trap door in the floor; when it was opened, the mural panels could be lowered into the garage below. Thus, all the tricky maneuvers to get them down the stairway were eliminated.

Parrish's mural commissions rank among his more important creations. Their completion was often the occasion of local socializing. Before they or his significant paintings were crated and shipped off to their destination, Parrish would frequently hold an "open house" to which he would invite friends and neighbors so they could view them. On October 24, 1909, Stephen Parrish noted "P.M. drove over to Fred's to see his decoration "The Pied Piper of Hamelin" (for a San Francisco Hotel). Everybody there."[14] He is referring to the mural, which is still in place, for the Sheraton Palace; two of Parrish's children as well as Sue Lewin served as models for it.

Local affairs as well as social affairs were part of a strong commitment to the area on the part of the Parrishes. They were both members of the Cornish Equal Suffrage League and Parrish was listed as a substantial contributor to the Meriden Bird Sanctuary organized by his friend Ernest Harold Baynes in 1913, and he was on the committee that sponsored *Sanctuary: A Bird Masque.* Earlier he participated in the most outstanding event in the life of the Cornish Colony: the 1905 production of *A Masque of "Ours": The Gods*

Figure 120. *Parrish's Gnome costume design for a proposed theatrical production of* Snow White.

and the Golden Bowl. Curtains for the outdoor stage were suspended between two pine trees; they were held in place by two large gilded masks that Parrish designed and executed. Furthermore, he played the role of Chiron, a wise and beneficent centaur whose fanciful costume he designed. It consisted of a rib cage made of barrel staves and wooden hind legs on wheels. They, in turn, were connected to Parrish's own legs by steel rods so that they moved with him as he walked. As his son later recalled:

> The hollow body of the centaur was attached to the body of a man by two large leather thongs and brass buckles, I believe worn inside the jockey's shirt and going in through four holes in the back. The body was hollow and remarkably light, made, as I remember, out of papier-mâché reinforced with thin wooden stringers like an airplane fuselage. The rear hips were flattened but the hind legs were curved to simulate the rounded rump of a horse and the hip joints consisted of a single long steel bolt passing through the body on which the legs swivelled. The hoofs were slotted and in them were wooden rollers on a steel pivot so in walking around, the rear hoofs wouldn't get stuck in holes in the ground or in the turf. The connecting rods were low and inconspicuous, and painted dark so as not to be noticed by the audience. The body was painted a dirty creamy white with the most improbable patches, as I remember, greyish blue. . . . The

305

front end of the connecting rods ended in swivels and straps, black to match—or it might have been russet?—the riding boots of the wearer. Dad told me last summer the cap was scarlet and the scarf either blue or green. The tail was wavy and real-looking, but I don't remember if it was cords or real horse hair. It was made for a grown man and us kids found it when we were too small to make it work, but as near as I can remember, Dad attached no value to it once it had been used, and let us play with it until it went to pieces. A pity, for it was a beautifully made thing and would have been usable now if we hadn't found it.[15]

Regrettably the costume is now lost, but surely it is another example of Maxfield Parrish—the artisan as artist.

The ability of the Parrishes to entertain at "The Oaks" was considerably enhanced in 1906, one year after the studio was built, when the couple completed the west wing, known as the music room: "it was about twenty feet wide, forty feet long, and almost fourteen feet high. The parquet floors were oak, and the oak-paneled walls were stained a dull grey black, as was the beamed ceiling." A stage was built at one end where Parrish himself frequently starred in charades, one of his favorite—as well as the Colony's— forms of entertainment.[16] As his career and its attendant obligations expanded, the house and its environs became a haven to him. The following passage from a letter written in 1932 suggests not only what a refuge "The Oaks" was but also what may well have been an inspiration for "Parrish blue":

As you descend some steps from the upper level to the house terrace, through old oak trunks and branches, you have a confused sensation that there is something grand going to happen. There is blue distance, infinite distance, seen through this hole and that, a sense of great space and glorious things in store for you, if only you go a little further to grasp it all. It takes your breath away a little, as there seems to be just blue forms ahead and no floor. Then you come upon the lower terrace, and over a level stone wall you see it all: hills and woodlands, high pastures, and beyond them, more and bluer hills, from New Hampshire on one side and from Vermont on the other, come tumbling down into the broad valley of the Connecticut, with one grand mountain over it all.[17]

Although one can still retrace the steps and recapture the vista, the house itself burned to the ground in 1979, thirteen years after Parrish died.

The career this house and its environs nurtured was launched shortly before his arrival in New Hampshire, but its full flowering occurred here. The range of illustrations that Parrish did for books, magazines and their covers, advertisements and posters, calendars, greeting cards, art prints and mural designs is much too extensive to discuss in this context. But it might be interesting to try to identify some aspect in each of these categories that has a local association or connection.

An early magazine illustration elicited a warm response from Augustus Saint-Gaudens. Although he worked on the illustrations for John Milton's poem "L'Allegro" while at Saranac Lake in 1900 and 1901, the background of "Straight mine eyes hath caught new pleasures" reminds some viewers of a valley scene set against a background with Mount Ascutney's profile in it. Whether it actually is, when the illustrations came out in the *Century Magazine* for December 1901, Saint-Gaudens wrote him:

The[y] . . . are superb, and I want to tell you how they impressed me. They are *big* and on looking at them I feel that choking sensation that one has only in the presence of the really swell thing. The shepherd on the hill, the poet in the valley are great in composition and with the blithesome maid are among the most beautiful things I have ever seen. . . . It is always an astonishment to me how after all the fine things that have been done and which seem to have exhausted all the possibilities of beauty, some man like you will come along and strike another note just as distinctive and just as fine. It is encouraging and stimulating.[18]

Self-caricature was a common element in Parrish's earliest book illustrations. His portrait of *Saint Nicholas*, done for the reprinting of Washington Irving's *Knickerbocker's History of New York* in 1900, lacks any specific local connection, but it looks a lot like Parrish—as does the person in the title page illustration for Kenneth Grahame's *Dream Days* (dated June 1900; book published in 1902).[19] Finally, the illustrations for *The Knave of Hearts* (1925), written by Louise Saunders who summered in both Cornish and Windsor, Vermont, with her husband Maxwell Perkins, have numerous local associations—from the self-caricature in *The Manager Draws the Curtains* to the frequent use of Sue Lewin as model, especially for the bookplate.

There is a fine picture of Parrish at work in his studio setting up for an illustration of a poem entitled "Potpourri" published in the August 1905 number of *Scribner's*.[20] It is an excellent example of the extent to which Parrish would go so that he might achieve a realistic basis for what most readers would see as an ethereal fantasy depicting the quotation, "Ah never in this world were there such roses/As once from that enchanted trellis hung." The photograph shows the elaborate arrangement of string necessary so that he can trip the shutter of the camera. Thus he is able to freeze the model, himself, in just the proper position. In the photo we see a naked Parrish bending over and holding onto a

handle at a 45 degree angle in his left hand while his right hand is curled around the string to the camera. In the illustration, however, we see an idealized youth plucking the enchanted roses" in an idealized garden from a blossomy bower with both hands—in precisely the same position, of course, as the photograph.

Clearly other magazine art has Parrish in it, for example *The Sandman* in the *Century Magazine*, March 1905. The most important of

Figure 121. *Mask designed originally as part of the stage set decoration for* A Masque of "Ours." *This is one of a number of small reproductions.*

his local models, Sue Lewin, posed for all six figures of *The Lantern Bearers*, which was the cover design for the December 10, 1910, issue of *Collier's Magazine*. There also exists a photograph of the preparations for *The Idiot* (also known as *The Book Lover*) that formed the *Collier's* cover of September 24, 1910. In addition to showing Sue Lewin posing in Parrish's studio perched on one of his chairs in the costume of the illustration so that the general contours as well as the folds of the vivid cloth fall correctly, there is just a glimpse of Parrish's head as he is studying the scene.[21] There are even those who would say that the final version, instead of retaining Sue Lewin, replaces the subject with a self-caricature of Parrish. In addition to using himself and Sue Lewin as models, he also drew upon other people from the local scene: Kathleen Philbrick Read, Arlene Jenney Wilson, George Ruggles, Kitty Owen, Sam Clark with his team of horses, Judge Learned Hand's two daughters, and his own daughter Jean.

As for advertisement and poster art, Maxfield Parish's *Jack Sprat* appeared as an advertisement for Swift's Premium Ham in the *Ladies' Home Journal* for November 1921. It was also distributed to grocery stores as a poster. This is one of the many instances Parrish pictured his domestic surroundings: the window is one of those in his music room and the chairs are from his living room. The models for it may be George Ruggles and Sue Lewin. A clearer example of Sue Lewin working for an advertisement is documented in a photograph. She is caught in a precarious position with a sheet behind her firmly holding onto a rope and the drapery of her gown arranged flowingly over her left thigh and knee. In the final Djer-Kiss cosmetic advertisement, done in 1916, she becomes an innocent damsel holding on gracefully with one hand to a swing that wafts her through a flower arbor; the awkward sheet metamorphoses into a rugged landscape—its folds representing crags and the faces of rocky mountains.[22]

Of all the art prints Parrish produced, none is more famous than *Daybreak* (1922, New York Graphic Society). One quality that sets it apart from his other creations is his use of beautiful, vivid hues enhanced by his special glazing process; these features produced the "Parrish blue" for which he is so well known. When he saw proofs before the final lithograph edition was published in 1923, Parrish was concerned how the "relative values" of the colors he had chosen would reproduce. Clearly he did not want to be too niggling in his critique, but just as clearly he did want the blue to be accurate: "It might be better, too, if the water was not quite so intense a blue; it looks a little out of color scheme. These are minor suggestions as I think it a very faithful reproduction."[23] As for the local connection, Parrish's own fingerprints appear in the mountains where he patted a glaze to achieve precisely the right density and the models are those he would have known well: his daughter Jean, who was born in 1911, is the standing girl and a friend of the family Kitty Owen, the granddaughter of William Jennings Bryan, is the girl lying on her back.

Although the two girls in *Daybreak* are not on a rock, Parrish was tiring of this type of "rubber stamp" image. Toward the end of his career Parrish gladly turned to unpeopled landscapes. The shift began in 1931 when Parrish told an Associated Press interviewer: "I'm done with girls on rocks. I've painted them for thirteen years and I could paint them and sell them for thirteen more. That's the peril of the commercial art game. It tempts a man to repeat himself. It's an awful thing to get to be a rubber stamp. I'm quitting my rut now while I'm still able. . . . My present guess is that landscapes are coming in for magazine covers, advertisement and illustrations. . . . There are always pretty girls on every city street, but a man can't step out of the subway and watch the clouds playing with the top of Mount Ascutney. It's the unattainable that appeals. Next best thing to seeing the ocean or the hills or the woods is enjoying a painting of them."[24] The public was equally delighted with his decision. When Brown and Bigelow, the calendar and greeting card company, informed him that his *Elm, Late Afternoon*, which they published in 1936 as *Peaceful Valley*, was a huge popular success, Parrish wrote them of the pleasure he took in painting landscapes: "It means a lot to me, for I have felt for a number of years that I have a better grasp on landscape than on any other subject." (Ludwig's comment on this sentence is significant: "At sixty-four, an age at which many men are retiring, Parrish was entering full speed into a new phase of his career."[25]) From a local point of view, this new concentration on landscape resulted in many familiar views being incorporated into paintings that Brown and Bigelow subsequently published. Views of Plainfield, Mount Ascutney, Windsor, Vermont, and Norwich, Vermont, as well as local farms are plainly visible on both the cards and calendars Parrish did from the thirties through the fifties.

Finally, the sketches for both his private commissions and his large-scale murals include local elements. Rosalind, Cynthia, and Dorothy Fuller, sisters who took Cornish by storm twice in 1915 (see above pp. 211-215), posed frequently for him.[26] The earthenware jars used in both of these works and in many of Parrish's paintings are quite similar to one that used to be near the western facade of "The Oaks," a gift from his friend and neighbor, Charles A. Platt.[27] Sue Lewin is again photographed in exactly the same position as one of the women in the 1913 *Sweet Nothings* mural done for the female employees' dining room at the Curtis Publishing Company's building in Philadelphia, Pennsylvania.[28]

To return to Stephen Parrish's notion of his son as an "artisan," it should be clear from the foregoing discussion of his local connections that, however grounded locally they may be, much more is at work in Maxfield Parrish's art. What many admirers see as the spontaneous, idealized freedom, especially visible in *The Dinkey Bird*, is actually the result of meticulous craft, painstakingly thought through in advance of any commission. He does not simply recreate what is immediate, visible, or familiar to him. For all the reality of New Hampshire sunsets—winter or summer ones—found again and again in his landscapes, there is the inescapable fact that we are also aware of the artist shaping his own vision of that reality. As Ludwig points out, "especially in his later landscapes, he often treated real objects unrealistically, giving them the appearance of reality through accurate form, but imposing his own effects of light and color. . . . The lighting that he frequently chose to use, a kind of theatrical backlighting that is rare though not entirely absent in nature, further emphasized the artist's concepts rather than nature's creations." To emphasize that important distinction, Ludwig goes on to quote a significant explanation of his aesthetic from Parrish himself: "Just a faithful 'portrait' of a locality, factual, would never do. My theory is that you should use all the objects in nature . . . just as stage properties on which to hang your idea, the end in view, the elusive qualities of a day, in fact all the qualities that give a body the delights of the out of doors. . . .'Realism' of impression, the mood of the moment, yes, but not the realism of things."[29]

Figure 122. *Stage set designed in 1916 by Maxfield Parrish for*
The Woodland Princess, *Plainfield Town Hall.*

It may be that Parrish's continued appeal, especially in this age of uncertainty, is his insistence that we can soar with his gossamer fantasy at the same time as we are grounded in his vivid reality. We know where we are even as we are being taken away from it. Adeline Adams, his friend and neighbor and an acute observer of art, phrased this sense of his popular appeal this way: "His genius, fundamentally aristocratic, has been dedicated by choice to democratic ends. It has been joyously used for the greater glory of weekday things like chairs and tables, door-latches and water-works. It has brought the canyons of our country to the canyons of our cities. It has shed gaiety on our street corners, our news stands, and even our bargain counters. And perhaps in these days when democratic ideals are getting so badly battered, our brightest hope for democracy lies in the fact that aristocrats of the Maxfield Parrish type are still up and doing, moving Heaven and earth in their delight in a day's work that shall somehow bring 'the best' a little nearer to everybody, and everybody a little nearer to 'the best.' "[30]

Parrish died in 1966 at the age of 95; his ashes are buried in the Plainfield Plain Cemetery.

MAXFIELD PARRISH AND THE STAGE SET
AT PLAINFIELD'S TOWN HALL

In 1916 William Howard Hart (see above pp. 229-231) persuaded Maxfield Parrish to paint a landscape to serve as a stage set and backdrop for the town hall in Plainfield, New Hampshire. Parrish painted a forest scene with a lake—or perhaps the Connecticut River—in the center and Mount Ascutney as the central focus. No proof has been found as to exactly what the method of painting was or if Parrish himself did any of the actual painting on the stage set. It was Maxfield Parrish, Jr.'s, theory that by creating a grid for the original design and then projecting it onto a large canvas, Parrish showed professional scenery painters how to reproduce the entire set: a long, horizontal backdrop, six wings, and three overhead drapes.[31] The linen-like material for the set was manufactured by the Indian Head Mills in Nashua, New Hampshire. In addition to giving the set to Plainfield, Hart, an artist noted for his landscapes and portraits as well as for his theatrical designs, donated the latest in stage lighting to the town. Even today, the lights can be made to simulate daybreak, dusk, twilight plus graduations of daylight in between.

The entire idea can be traced to an item on a warrant offered Plainfield in 1916. Article X of the Annual Town Report reads: "To see if the town will vote to raise the sum of three hundred dollars to build a foundation at the east end of the town hall at Plainfield in accordance with a proposition submitted to William H. Hart." The 1917 Town Report notes that the foundation for the hall's addition had cost $270. Hart proposed that if the town would commit itself to the addition, he and his associates would finance the rest.

Over time this "most beautiful stage north of Boston," while still beautiful, showed signs of use: the paint had flaked, it was torn and spotted with water marks—not to mention dust and cigarette smoke. The town worked hard, however, to restore their treasure. They were spurred on by Richard Stoddard, an authority on American theater scenery, who wrote: "The Parrish set has considerable historical importance. Very little actual scenery . . . has survived from the American theater before 1920 . . . the Plainfield set is remarkable, then, not only because so little such scenery has survived, but it was designed by and painted under the supervision of a celebrated American artist. In this respect, the Parrish set appears to be unique. The Plainfield set is also notable because it is not a stock scene, but rather a view of a well-known Plainfield landmark."[32] Armed with an estimate of $23,600 from the Williamstown Regional Art Conservation Laboratory of Williamstown, Massachusetts, the Plainfield Historical Society set out to raise the money from concerned citizens, grants from charitable organizations and foundations, and the many Parrish enthusiasts throughout the country.

Victory was achieved in 1993. In October, five conservators from Williamstown "worked nine days to preserve the set. The scenery was vacuumed very gently, tears were repaired with muslin and heat set film. The main backdrop and overhead drapes were backed with muslin, and obvious losses and disturbing abrasions were inpainted with a reversible medium of the same flat matte and non-reflectance as the original paint. The conservators also backed and reinforced the side panels with corrugated plastic. Care was taken to document and preserve signatures on the backs of the wings. Old shipping labels were re-attached."[33] One of the remarkable discoveries during this process was that, even after seventy-seven years, "the glue fixative was still holding well . . . and only the edges of the backdrop and wings needed the treatment [of spraying ethulose as a fixative]."[34]

Everyone can rejoice in the unstinting energy of the community to save this precious monument. The Plainfield Town Hall was placed on the National Register of Historic Places in 1985; it is also included on the National List of Historic Theater Buildings.

ENDNOTES

1. This combination and his father's quotation come from Homer Saint-Gaudens, "Maxfield Parrish," *The Critic*, 46:6, June 1905, p. 512.

2. Laurence S. Cutler, Judy Goffman, and The American Illustrators Gallery, *Maxfield Parrish* (New York: Bison Group, 1993), p. 6. For more elaboration on this point, see also *Maxfield Parrish: A Retrospective*, an exhibition catalogue for an exhibition curated

and assembled by Judy Goffman Cutler and organized and produced by Laurence S. Cutler in 1995.

3. Letter from Stephen Parrish to Dillwyn and Susanna Maxfield Parrish, dated July 28, 1870, as quoted in Coy Ludwig, *Maxfield Parrish* (New York: Watson-Guptill, 1973), p. 11.

4. Ludwig, p. 201.

5. The quotations from his letters to his wife are found in Ludwig, pp. 16-17.

6. Stephen Parrish, diary, entry for June 8, 1898; Special Collections, Baker Library, Dartmouth College, Hanover, NH, gift of Marian and Roy Garrand.

7. Virginia Reed Colby, "Stephen and Maxfield Parrish in New Hampshire," *The Magazine Antiques*, 115:6, June 1979, p. 1293; for more on Ruggles, see below pp. 349-351.

8. John Dillwyn Parrish lived from 1904 until 1969; Maxfield Parrish, Jr., lived from 1906 until 1983; Stephen Parrish II was born in 1909, and Jean Parrish was born in 1911.

9. *The Literary Digest*, May 12, 1923, as quoted by Charles A. Merrill, *The Boston Globe*, April 15, 1923. As this quotation has been repeated by subsequent commentators, it has become distorted to "a mechanic who paints." The confusion may be partially attributed to the fact that the title of the *Globe* article reads "Did You Ever Hear of Maxfield Parrish? 'Who, the artist?'—'No, the mechanic!" It was this mechanical turn of mind that led to several labor-saving devices he rigged up for "The Oaks." One was a set of tracks and a car used to bring wood from the woodpile into the house; it was then loaded onto an elevator and brought upstairs to the fireplace. Another invention was a birdbath, located on the roof, that was filled through a copper tube leading up to it from the water supply. On the second floor above the rear door on the north side of he house, there was a large circle with the Roman numerals I through V painted on it and a single pointer, beautifully carved by Parrish. The position of the pointer indicated the water level in the attic storage tanks that Parrish installed.

10. Interview: Virginia Colby with William S. Clark, Plainfield, NH, August 24, 1984.

11. Dalton Wylie, "Artistic Builders' Hardware," *Country Life in America*, 12:6, October 1907, p. 670; there, too, he made the handsome brass handle for tightening the net at the Houstons' tennis court, a social center for many people from the Cornish Colony.

12. He used a handcrafted model of the Daniels' farmhouse in the 1942 painting *Little Brook Farm* that became the Brown and Bigelow calendar for 1945, *Sunup*. In his shop he also built the model of a wooden chair used in both the *Tea Tray* sign (1914, private collection) and the *Jell-O* advertisement, *Jello: The King and Queen Might Eat Thereof and Nobleman Besides* (1921).

13. Ludwig, pp. 195-198, based on an explanation by Maxfield Parrish, Jr., is particularly helpful on the glazing process. In fact, Ludwig's eighth chapter is very informative on Parrish's techniques in general. (For Marion MacKaye's description of his work habits and studio, see above p. 260.)

14. Stephen Parrish, diary, Special Collections, Baker Library, Dartmouth College, Hanover, NH, gift of Marian and Roy Garrand.

15. Letter from Maxfield Parrish, Jr., to Frank O. Spinney, probably written in 1964, Virginia Colby, Cornish Colony files. See also Colby, *Magazine Antiques*, pp. 1297-1298, n. 2. The costume is illustrated in Virginia Reed Colby, "A Museum for Maxfield Parrish," *The Art Gallery Magazine*, August/September 1978, p. 62, and on the cover of the Cornish, NH, 1993, Phone Directory and Handbook.

16. Colby, *Magazine Antiques*, p. 1293; see also Ruth Boyle, "A House that 'Just Grew,'" *Good Housekeeping*, 88:4, April 1919, p. 45, and "House of Maxfield Parrish," *Architectural Record*, 22:4, October 1907, pp. 272-279, article unsigned.

17. Letter to Irénée du Pont, one of Parrish's friends and patrons, April 13, 1932, as quoted in Ludwig, p. 17.

18. Letter dated December 5, 1901, as quoted in Ludwig, p. 62. Parrish was in the Adirondacks to recuperate from tuberculosis.

19. Parrish was at Saranac Lake, NY, where he "spent the winter of 1900-1901. Most of the remaining illustrations [for *Dream Days*] were made in Plainfield the following summer," Ludwig, p. 29; it is true, however, that this quotation does not prove he did the title page illustration in Plainfield.

20. See Ludwig, pp. 192-193, for reproductions both of the illustration and the photograph. For Parrish's connections with photographers connected with the Cornish Colony, see below pp. 476-478.

21. See Les Allen Ferry, *The Make Believe World of Sue Lewin* (Los Angeles: Republic Corporation, Continental Graphics Division, 1978), pp. 14-15. For another view of Sue Lewin as Parrish's model, see Alma Gilbert, *The Make Believe World of Maxfield Parrish and Sue Lewin* (San Francisco: Pomegranate Artbooks, 1990) and the relevant passages in Alma Gilbert, *Maxfield Parrish: The Masterworks* (Berkeley, CA: Ten Speed Press, 1992), esp. pp. 17, 19-20.

22. Ibid., pp. 16-17.

23. Ludwig, p. 143.

24. As quoted in Ludwig, p. 129; the interview was published April 27, 1931.

25. Letter dated January 1, 1935, as quoted in Ludwig, p. 173.

26. Dorothy Fuller writes her parents, "I took a hasty tip on how to use chalk for drawing from Maxfield Parrish. . . . I should like to get some more tips from Maxfield. . . . but . . . I don't think [his wife] thinks Maxfield ought to give his secrets away! (August 12, 1915), courtesy of her daughter, Carol Odell; Virginia Colby, Cornish Colony files. Carol Odell writes of the scene at Percy MacKaye's house "Hilltop" that, "Maxfield Parrish, and his wife and children, walked over from their house every morning and were particularly enthusiastic—the children and their mother joining in, while Maxfield Parrish often sketched," Carol Odell, "The Fuller Sisters: Fourth Tour of America, Part 2, October 1914-May 20, 1916," p. 36, unpublished manuscript, Virginia Colby, Cornish Colony files, courtesy of Carol Odell. In private correspondence to Virgina Colby, Carol Odell writes, "my mother writes in her diaries that [Maxfield Parrish] is sketching them all the time—and later recognizes some poses that they did for him in his illustrations. He was entranced that they were always together in threes" (April 26, 1994). Hence, Virginia Colby believed that the Fuller sisters are the basis both for a sketch that Parrish subsequently turned into an overmantle panel painted for Philip C. Collins of Wyncote, Pennsylvania, in 1920 and for the more familiar "Garden of Allah." There they are, from left to right, Cynthia, Rosalind, and Dorothy. The painting was used on a Crane Chocolate gift box and on a House of Art print published in 1918.

27. See Colby, *The Magazine Antiques*, p. 1292, for a picture of the red-earthenware jug.

28. Ferry, pp. 44-45.

29. Letter to Jerome Connolly dated May 5, 1952, as quoted in Ludwig, p. 202.

30. Adeline Adams, "The Art of Maxfield Parrish," *The American Magazine of Art*, 9:3, January 1918, p. 101.

31. Letter from Maxfield Parrish, Jr., to Selectman Stephen H. Taylor, dated June 18, 1977.

32. Brochure published by the Maxfield Parrish Stage Set Committee of the Plainfield Historical Society, 1991.

33. Program for "A Celebration of the Maxfield Parrish Stage Set Preservation," November 7, 1993.

34. "Maxfield Parrish Stage Set Preservation Update," published by the Maxfield Parrish Stage Set Committee of the Plainfield Historical Society, October 1993. For more on Parrish locally, see Jerold Wikoff, *The Upper Valley: An Illustrated Tour Along the Connecticut River Before the Twentieth Century* (Chelsea, VT: Chelsea Green Publishing Company, 1985), pp. 172-177.

Figure 123.

STEPHEN PARRISH
1846 – 1938

ALTHOUGH THE ACCOMPLISHMENTS of his famous son often overshadowed the career of Stephen Parrish, he merits consideration for his own distinguished achievements. Comments from his contemporaries and modern observers bear out this assertion. In 1883, a shrewd observer of the attempt by American etchers to carve a niche for themselves in a rapidly expanding market in Europe and America readily acknowledges his popularity: "Mr. Stephen Parrish, whom I should put . . . in the very first rank of our home-keeping etchers . . . is the most popular of them all, [he] has tried his hand at themes of many sorts, but his name is essentially associated with seaboard scenes. Our ragged fisher-villages, with their rocky foundations and primitive vessels, have found in him a first and most clear-voiced interpreter."[1] And still in the context of his contributions to etching, a modern art historian puts the point more succinctly: "In black and white, Parrish's work has an absolute unity of form, color, and mood, and his *oeuvre* represents a high point for the entire decade [of the 1880s]."[2] In addition to his significance as an etcher, which will be what is concentrated on here, Parrish was also an excellent painter. Finally, his passion for gardening caused him to be highly regarded by those frequent commentators on the special gardens of the Cornish Colony.

Parrish was born in Philadelphia, Pennsylvania, on July 9, 1846, the son of a prominent Quaker family. Although he was given art lessons as a boy, a brief trip to Europe in 1867 provided the impetus for his appreciation of art. He started his adult life, however, in a coal business (1867-1870); after he married Elizabeth Bancroft in 1869, he bought a stationery store and ran it until 1877. Neither commercial venture was much to his taste; in his early thirties he decided to devote himself to art. Yet, by 1879 he had sold only seven of the thirty-three canvases he had painted. Aware that etching was much in vogue, he began his studies with the famous painter and etcher Peter Moran in 1879. Reflecting on these early years in 1887, he wrote his friend, the etching enthusiast and critic Sylvester Rosa Koehler, that he lamented having wasted "thirteen years of his best life in business to wake up in middle life to the consciousness that there was something better in him."[3]

The same year that he decided to take up etching he happened to meet Charles A. Platt while vacationing near Lake George. They were to become fast friends and, eventually in Cornish, close neighbors. The two of them enjoyed painting and sketching together. In fact, Platt's earliest extant letter describes an excursion to Warrensburgh, New York, in 1879 accompanied by Stephen Parrish: "The trip was not quite as successful in a sketching point of view, as I expected it would be. The character of the scenes and landscape was so different from that which I had been accustomed to sketch from, that it was with no small difficulty that I chose my subjects and painted them. In fact I made so many deviations from the scenes as they were, that they could hardly be recognized by the natives, who crowded around me and Mr. Parrish whenever they had a chance."[4] Etching, however, was to be the medium that drew the two men together. Because Parrish taught Platt how to etch, Platt came to regard Parrish as his mentor.

And for good reason. The decade of the 1880s was to see Parrish join the ranks of America's most significant etchers in what has come to be called the American Painter-Etcher Movement. The financial prosperity America enjoyed after the Civil War made it increasingly possible for many people to own original art. Naturally, there were a few, more than before the 1860s, who could afford paintings. But the middle class also wanted original art of its own. "For people of the late 1870s and 1880s, etching was more of an artistic novelty than the steel engravings and chromolithographs with which they had grown up. The men and women who championed [etching] were mostly artists . . . using etching to create original works, not just copies."[5] Parrish's 1882 etching *Gloucester Harbor* (S.P. #74) is a rare exception to his copying another artist's work. It is a reproductive etching deftly capturing the atmospheric qualities of William Morris Hunt's 1877 painting with the same title. One of the reasons why the mania for etchings faded, however, was precisely one of the reasons why it at first was so popular: modern reproductive techniques made etchings readily available. "The goal of etching was to have an 'autographic' quality—the stamp of the individual artist's hand—and yet, because it could be made in multiples, an etching could be owned by more than one person."[6] Thus, with this accessibility, the stamp of an etching's originality was called into question. Once the quality of originality was debased it no longer was a mark of distinction that set etching apart from the other arts. Although these factors were eventually to become relevant to Parrish's career, at the outset his enthusiasm for and commitment to etching was high.

So high, indeed, that he affirmed his interest in etching by urging the founding of the Philadelphia Society of Etchers in 1880. He, along with Peter Moran, Stephen James Ferris, Joseph Pennell, and Henry Rankin Poore, were its founding members; Parrish was its secretary and was appointed to a committee to draft its constitution and by-laws. "Parrish's membership . . . was short-lived as he resigned in December 1881 to pursue his artistic interest in New England and New York where he joined the New York Etching Club."[7] In order to bring his work to the public view, he entered a number of shows in Philadelphia, New York, and Boston. In 1881, once the English

Figure 124. Low Time—Bay of Fundy *etching by Stephen Parrish (1881, S.P. #64).*

surgeon and etcher Seymour Haden established the Royal Society of Etchers and Painters and held its opening exhibition, he was one of the few Americans whose entries were accepted. Furthermore, he was elected to its membership on the basis of the quality of those entries.[8] He later joined the important New York Etching Club and became categorized, accurately or not, as a member—along with Charles A. Platt—of the "school of Seymour Haden." Although Hitchcock has his reservations about the validity of this designation, he clearly admires the vigor of Parrish's *Low Tide—Bay of Fundy* with its "strong lines of stranded vessels outstanding against a brilliant sky, balanced by quaint houses on the shore, and with another touch added in the expressive figures on the beach."[9] In addition to exhibitions in the major cities in America, Parrish had his etchings shown at the World's Columbian Exposition in Chicago in 1892; abroad his etchings were exhibited in London, Paris, Munich, and Vienna.

Attempts to specify what is excellent about Parrish's etchings generally refer to the quality of his line. In fact, this was a feature in which he was very much interested. In his own attempt to define the "character" of an "etched line," he wrote that it has nothing to do with the physical characteristics of a line, which depend "largely on irregular biting or greater or less pressure of the needle or inequalities in the copper, etc." Rather, it refers to "the way the lines are made. A few expressive lines properly treated standing for so much more than the same lines treated in a mechanical manner, as in Engraving for instance." He continues with a paragraph that provides a particularly good insight into his frame of mind as an artist: "I think . . . that it does not help the art, nor any other, to discuss this & that merit in a meaningless way. Indeed I think there is a danger in this age of investigation of too much theorizing and too little honest work. All kinds are admissible and enjoyable if they are good."[10] It is true that he applied himself to his work; he must

317

Figure 125. Bridge at Paluel Normandie *etching by Stephen Parrish, c. 1891.*

indeed have enjoyed his artistic career—in part because the public responded to his etchings so positively. With the nature of his line still an important factor, a modern art historian accounts for his popularity in this manner: "The nature of Parrish's popularity resulted not only from his choice of subjects but the techniques by which he etched them. He had a very good control over his etched line, and he was adept at using this line to create dense areas of shadow on the rocks, boats, buildings, and foliage that make his images. This shadow gives a substance and accent to forms, becoming a distinctive element of his etchings." His technical control laid the groundwork for another reason for his popularity. "Parrish . . . employed extensively . . . an acid tint or wash that would print very delicate, transparent tone across broad areas of plate. He often used this technique for creating luminous skies, by a gradation of tone from light on the horizon to darker above. The sky is an important part of Parrish's images . . . it offered the means to suggest specific times and moods. For Parrish it was a twilight sky, and the predominant mood suggested is one of reflectiveness and stillness . . . the very elements of quietude, of picturesqueness, or even of sentiment that appealed to Stephen Parrish's contemporaries . . . appeal to us today for very much the same reasons."[11] But even his popularity as an etcher of picturesque scenes did not deter him from exciting experimentation. And although these attempts are valued as such by those who appreciate the art of etching, they still sold well to his general public. "Parrish is unusual in that he would occasionally etch a subject devoid—or almost so—of any picturesque forms. He can offer the most barren of landscapes: massive rocks and little else sitting on or in the earth. Parrish will strive through line and plate tone to create tones and forms that have their own intrinsic interest apart from the subject matter of the print."[12]

At the same time as his fame as an etcher was spreading, he continued to paint. His own comments are interesting about the interrelationship of the two disciplines. Referring to an etching he did in February of 1880, *November* (S.P. #12), he tells his friend Sylvester Rosa Koehler that, "I have painted this same subject with more of the effect of evening, and the painting is far superior to the etchings." It seems, too, that work in one medium stimulated activity in the other. "I shall now turn my attention for a time more to painting, putting aside the needle for a time. I find the two play well into each other's hand and each acts as a relaxation to the other." A year later he remarks to Koehler that, "for the time painting lies dormant but I believe in doing that which is most enjoyable at the time and just now the needle seems handier to hold than the brush."[13]

Handling the brush, however, had been an interest ever since his first visit to Europe in 1867. While visiting the "Palace of the Grand Exposition" in Paris, he noted in his diary that, "I never knew before that men could do some things which this day I have seen and wondered at. I never knew that the art of painting was such a vast and splendid profession. There are some effects produced on canvas which I never conceived the possibility of before. . . . There is one thing *certain*, however, that is, they paint *differently* in this country than in our own. The European paintings have a certain massiveness and breadth and coloring and effect which I have never seen in any picture painted in the United States."[14] There are a number of correspondences between scenes that he both etched and painted; more often than not he would incorporate elements from etching, such as a dead tree leaning at a precarious angle, into paintings, though marine scenes were favorites in both media. Although he would often start a painting with a rough sketch, sometimes "he would do a meticulously drawn, almost etching-like fine point India ink drawing. . . . Probably the most frequent method of attacking a painted project was to sketch it up in pencil first, getting the important boundaries between dark and light very carefully positioned, and accurately drawn, and dub in the non-contrasty parts sort of crudely, then carefully work out the areas of value in the studio after much studying the subject with his eye only. Or so he told us grandchildren when we wanted him to tell us how to paint. . . . He said getting the dark and lights right was far more important than the color."[15]

What is interesting about his painting career from the point of view of Cornish is the number of scenes he painted with local elements in them; for example there is: *In White River Valley, Vermont* (c. 1895); *Blow-Me-Down Brook, Cornish, New Hampshire* (1915); *Rocky Pasture, Cornish, New Hampshire* (n.d.); *On the Connecticut, Plainfield, Vermont [sic]* (n.d.); *Rocky Field and Brook, Plainfield, New Hampshire* (n.d.); *Northcote (home of Stephen Parrish), Cornish, New Hampshire* (n.d.); *Red Barn, Winter, Plainfield, New Hampshire* (c. 1923); and *East of Plainfield, New Hampshire* (1923).[16] Not only did the local scenery inspire him, but the local population collected his work: "the best sales of all were from off his easel in Cornish, N.H. All the more wealthy Cornish Colony people bought many pictures by him, and by 1920 he had almost completely given up sending pictures to exhibitions or galleries."[17]

But perhaps the local scene that was most inspiring to him was his very own garden. It graced his painting, *Garden Stairway*, done around 1907, and the cover of both the March 1908 issue of *Country Life in America* and the March 1912 issue of *American Home and Gardens*. The garden, however, was dependent on the house he built; almost ten years elapsed between the time he began it and his return to active painting.[18] Coming at the invitation of Charles A. Platt, Parrish was one of the earliest arrivals to the Cornish Colony. In the early 1890s, he and his wife boarded with Stephen Alden Tracy and his wife Agnes; then, in 1893, he purchased eighteen acres of land across the road from the Tracys'.[19] The noted Philadelphia architect Wilson Eyre (1858-1944) was engaged to design the house, which would be called "Northcote"—Parrish and his contemporaries sometimes spelled it "Northcôte." The *Vermont Journal* noted on July 22, 1893, that "Superintendent Fred Waite with assistant carpenters began work on Stephen Parrish's house Tuesday." An early visitor to the house was impressed with its lack of pretension: "Just as all the parts of this charming place combine to make a delightful harmony, so are Northcôte and its owner a unity. . . . The owner's nature is reflected everywhere in all the details of the house and grounds. Thus the individuality of the place is indissolubly established. Modest retirement is the note which pervades it. Simplicity and absence of pretence are everywhere apparent. The house itself is neither large nor elaborate; but the house when finished was only a bare form, around which all the natural charms of the place have since been carefully trained by a patient growth."[20] Parrish had the distinction of being the only famous Colonist to construct his kitchen so that it, not the living room or drawing room, would have a direct view of Mount Ascutney.[21] It was not until 1902 that he noted in his diary that "I establish a studio"; previously he had been preoccupied with "Northcote," building a greenhouse, a shop, a stable for his horse Betty, and planning and laying out his extensive gardens.

Parrish's horticultural interests were as strong as his artistic interests; they both offered him equal pleasure. He had the reputation for conceiving the most elaborate gardens among those in the Cornish Colony. As was true of the other fine houses, his, too, was a good union of architecture, garden site, and garden plan. With slightly more than two acres of garden plot, he realized a garden that was held to be a paragon in its time and a source of inspiration to landscape architects today. Taking advantage of the views from "Northcote," Parrish located the main garden path in line with the sunset. At the end of this path stood a tall, white pine tree with spreading branches; underneath it was a curved seat thirty feet long—a favorite gathering place for his family and many visitors. In fact, "nothing in the garden-craft at Northcote is so thoroughly artistic as the treatment of a magnificent old pine which is at the end of the grass walk around the hill . . . the great tree [is] . . . a magnificent old giant—irregular, weather-battered, the great limbs stanch and sinewy, in spite of the century and more it has kept its outlook over the valley. . . . Here any touch of ostensible gardening would have been an intrusion, and Mr. Parrish has been content to let the great pine dominate the place unchallenged."[22] Another commentator on the effect of this spot thought that "the effect is indescribably Japanesque. The gnarled tree, with its contorted boughs low-sweeping, the distant mountain and the near-by valley, lined on its opposite slope with straight-trunked trees,

Figure 126. On the Schroon—Drought *etching by Stephen Parrish (1890, S.P. #6b).*

makes one almost expect Hokusai's signature to dangle on a pink panel against the sky."[23] As for the total effect of the garden, the often reproduced photograph taken in the summer of 1898 of Anne Parrish, his cousin, "standing in the garden captures something of the feeling of [the garden's] style, its individuality as well as its nod toward the cottage garden style that crowded together all sorts of hardy, garden-worthy plants. . . . In 1905, the paths were widened and two raised beds were removed so Parrish could build a nine-foot-wide, round, sunken lily pool. . . . Here too the painter was at work in the garden: seated on the bench under the pergola, the eye danced along the cascading annuals and the clusters of blue Otaksa hydrangea which reflected on the surface of the pool, then up through the colorfully planted raised beds bordering the steps and out across a small orchard of apple trees on the lawn. The water lilies were eventually removed from the pool because they interfered with the reflection of the garden on its still water."[24]

Although Stephen Parrish often appears to be a quiet, retiring person devoted to his twin passions of art and gardening, he took an active part in the Cornish Colony's social life. Entries in his diary are governed primarily by gardening activities and pre-occupations, meticulous attention to weather details, and records of specific birds' first and last appearance. Nevertheless, in tantalizingly brief but amazingly frequent jottings, he refers to numerous callers and dinner guests as well as to social occasions and their participants during the years from 1893 to 1910. He played the role of Nestor in the 1905 production of *A Masque of "Ours": The Gods and the Golden Bowl* and he was Cardinal Bird in Percy MacKaye's *Sanctuary: A Bird Masque* when it was performed in Meriden in 1913.

Stephen Parrish died at "Northcote" on May 15, 1938, at the age of 92. He left a legacy of beautiful etchings and paintings, which may be found in private collections and museums throughout America, and a garden the equal of many of the more professional landscape architects of the Cornish Colony.

ENDNOTES

1. M. [Marianna] G. van Rensselar, "American Etchers," *The Century Magazine,* 3:4 (n.s.), February 1883, p. 495, as quoted by Rona Schneider, *Stephen Parrish,* exhibition catalogue (Gloucester, MA: Cape Ann Historical Association, 1986), pp. 17-18. In contrast to "home-keeping etchers" in the quotation, Mrs. Schuyler van Rensselar had in mind such expatriate etchers as Whistler and Mary Cassatt as well as Otto Bacher and Frank Duveneck.

2. Thomas P. Bruhn, *American Etching: The 1880s* (Storrs, CT: The William Benton Museum of Art, The University of Connecticut, 1985), p. 113.

3. As quoted in Schneider, p. 8.

4. Letter to John H. Platt, September 14, 1879, as quoted in Keith N. Morgan, "The Architecture and Landscapes of Charles A. Platt" (PhD dissertation, Brown University, 1978), p. 20.

5. Bruhn, p. 7.

6. Schneider, p. 11.

7. William C. Patterson, "The Philadelphia Society of Etchers," *Imprint* 19:2, Autumn 1994, p. 20.

8. J. R. W. Hitchcock, *Etching in America* (New York: White, Stokes, and Allen, 1886), pp. 36-37.

9. Ibid., pp. 81, 83—he is referring to the etching Parrish numbered 64, done in 1881. Hitchcock adds that "this is perhaps the only American etching which has been purchased for one of the great continental collections, that at Vienna, of which Adam Bartsch was the curator seventy years ago"; Bartsch, famous for his twenty-one volume catalogue of engravers, was director of the Imperial Print Collection in Vienna. It is worth noting that for all Hitchcock's pride in American etching, he still takes comfort in Parrish's etchings being honored with a European accolade. Parrish kept a record of all his etchings and paintings; it is now in a private collection. Two other accounts are *A Catalogue of Etchings by Stephen Parrish (18790-1883) with Descriptions of the Plates and Ten Etchings Made for this Work—nine of which are reduced copies of plates mentioned in the text,* a listing of eighty-six plates that Parrish himself published in an edition of fifty copies in Philadelphia during the early 1880s and a *Catalogue of S. Parrish's Complete Work on Exhibition at the Gallery of H. Wunderlich and Co.* (New York, 1886).

10. From a letter to an unknown correspondent as quoted in Rona Schneider, *American Painter Etchings: 1853-1908* (New York: The Grolier Club, 1989), p. 12.

11. Bruhn, pp. 112-13.

12. Ibid., p. 118, discussing *Northern Moorland* (S. P. #42), *An Old Farm Near the Sea* (S. P. #44), and *Rocks of Cape Ann* (S. P. #45) done in March and April of 1881.

13. The quotations in this paragraph come from Maureen C. O'Brien and Patricia C. F. Mandel, *The American Painter-Etcher Movement* (Southampton, NY: The Parrish Art Museum, 1984), p. 41. They also quote the statement from his "Record of Painting & Etchings," that "From March until October [1881] principally Etching." For more on

the *November* etching, see Bruhn, p. 114. During this period, Parrish was also contributing etchings to illustrate books; for example, as did his friend Charles Platt, he made one for Dean Sage, *The Restigouche and Its Salmon Fishing* (Edinburgh: David Douglas, 1888), reprinted in 1923 by the Angler's and Shooter's Press, Goshen, CT; the Restigouche River is in northwest New Brunswick, west of Dalhousie. For Parrish's relation to the revival of etching in Canada, see Rosemarie L. Tovell, *A New Class of Art: The Artist's Print in Canadian Art, 1877-1920* (Ottawa: The National Gallery of Canada, 1966), pp. 31, 43, 48, 50, 63-64; the Charles H. Platt mentioned in this context is Charles Adams Platt.

14. As quoted in Maxfield Parrish, Jr., *Stephen Parrish: 1846-1938* (Boston: Vose Galleries, 1982), pp. 8-9.

15. Ibid., pp. 9-10.

16. As catalogued in Parrish, p. 13. In addition, *A Circle of Friends: Art Colonies of Cornish and Dublin*, exhibition catalogue (Durham, NH: University Art Galleries, University of New Hampshire, 1985) lists "Read's Farm" (n.d.), p. 100 and p. 135, n. 9 to "Stephen Parrish" entry.

17. Parrish, p. 8. On September 17, 1908, Stephen Parrish notes, "Framing and cleaning pictures in the studio and bringing them over to the house. Evening supper party. Had an exhibition of my pictures afterwards. Judge and Mrs. Learned Hand selecting one," diary, Special Collections, Baker Library, Dartmouth College, gift of Marian and Roy Garrand.

18. "In 1903, ten years after he had started the house, he wrote in his diary, 'Painting in Studio all day. Have taken it up again after years of neglect.' He kept painting from then on until about 1923 to 1926, stopping only when forced to by a stroke which partially paralyzed his left arm and left leg" (Parrish, p. 12).

19. Letters from Parrish to Tracy, collection of Dorothy Tracy, Cornish, NH; see also Cornish tax records.

20. Herbert C. Wise, "A Day at Northcôte, New Hampshire," *House and Garden*, June 1902, pp. 248-249; Wise was a partner in Eyre's firm and hence giving the house its first architectural review.

21. Virginia Reed Colby, "Stephen and Maxfield Parrish in New Hampshire," *The Magazine Antiques* 115:6, June 1979, p. 1290; see also *A Circle of Friends*, p. 135, "Stephen Parrish," n. 6.

22. Frances Duncan, "An Artist's New Hampshire Garden," *Country Life in America*, March 1907, p. 556.

23. Hazel W. Henderson, "An Impression of Cornish," *The Lamp* 27, October 1903, p. 191.

24. William Noble, "Northcote: An Artist's New Hampshire Garden," *Journal of the New England Garden History Society* 2, Fall 1992, pp. 5-6.

CHARLES ADAMS PLATT
1861 – 1933

CHARLES A. PLATT, renowned in his day as an etcher, painter, landscape designer, and architect certainly left a noteworthy legacy not only to Cornish but to the United States. As his good friend Royal Cortissoz, put it, "To spend a long life in the creation of works of beauty, to care unswervingly for the things of the spirit and the mind, to wake the love of innumerable friends through the promptings of a generous heart—to do all this is surely to fulfill a high destiny. Such was the achievement of Charles A. Platt. He was an artist in the core of his being."[1] In fact, it is indicative of the centrality of his place in the American Renaissance that his contributions to the history of American art successfully fit into so many categories.

Born in New York City in 1861 to a prominent family with important cultural and social connections, Platt's early training began in 1878 at the age of seventeen and included study at the Antique School of the National Academy of Design during the day and painting classes at the Art Students League at night. He spent most of the years from 1882 to 1887 in Paris studying at the Académie Julian with the painters Jules Lefebvre and Gustave Boulanger and traveling both in England and on the continent. But prior to leaving for Europe he met someone who not only was to have a significant impact on his artistic career but who was also to become his neighbor in Cornish: Stephen Parrish.

The two first met while they were both vacationing separately at Bolton's Landing on Lake George in 1879. He was so taken with Parrish's talent at etching, that he virtually apprenticed himself to Parrish and was invited the following summer to be with Parrish in Gloucester, Massachusetts. By 1881, a contemporary could write that "Charles A. Platt is, if not the youngest, one of the youngest, of the school of American etchers which has developed with such surprising rapidity within a few years ... His first plate was etched in December of last year and the art had such fascination for him that he devoted much more time to it than he had originally intended, to the neglect of his studies in drawing and painting."[2] Although most keen-eyed, contemporary observers were aware of his stylistic affinity for Parrish's etching manner, Platt was quite conscious of the dominant influences on etching coming, then, from England: Seymour Haden and the American James McNeill Whistler, who was living in England. "Platt adopted some of Whistler's effect of understatement in presentation, but he followed Haden more closely in his concern for careful craftsmanship to create

324

Figure 127. Little River, Hartford *etching by Charles A. Platt (1881, Rice #18).*

more exciting effects of light, water, and atmosphere."[3] Nevertheless, it seems quite clear that Platt's "ease in mastering the techniques of etching forecast his later shifts to landscape design and architecture, again without any academic training. But Platt was not a facile dilettante. Regardless of medium, he approached his work with total seriousness, taught himself the necessary skills, and evolved a personal style."[4] And certainly the judgment of one of his contemporaries goes a long way in defining Platt's significance in the history of American etching: "In the long history of art, not more than ten or twelve men became great etchers, and of these only a few had the true 'etcher's touch'—it cannot be taught, it cannot be acquired, it must be inborn. Among all our etchers of talent *one* only had this gift—Charles A. Platt."[5] Colman's judgment is a knowledgeable one: he painted frequently in the White Mountains and was one of the stalwarts of the American Painter-Etcher Movement in the 1880s.

Platt did not forgo his interest in etching while in Europe, but his primary interest while there was painting. These were very formative years for him as he perfected his technique in both landscapes and marine subjects. He also began several friendships to be developed later when they were all in Cornish—with George de Forest Brush, Kenyon Cox, and Willard Metcalf. Furthermore, his interest in architecture was piqued by his friends' excitement for their studies at the Ecole des Beaux-Arts and his own failure to be admitted to its architectural study group. Perhaps the most significant development for his career during these years in Europe was a shift in his aesthetic views that affected his entire artistic output. Prior to his European tour, his subjects had frequently been picturesque scenes of quaint fishing villages with dilapidated buildings and active harbors. In Europe, however, he was exposed to notions about the value of art for art's sake. Thus, he developed a more classic, formal sense of what he thought constituted the artist's duty, namely, to render the beautiful. Although he was never a follower of the stylized art of the art-for-art's sake movement, we can see him working out the idea of an artist's duty in the following extracts from two of his frequent and devoted letters home to his parents. In April of 1884, he wrote, "An artist should interest one's sense of the beautiful and make that his great object. He must have a subject, of course, but he should *use* the subject to make his picture and not use the picture to render his subject." While in February of 1885, he was a bit more expansive: "I think it is often difficult to separate the beautiful from what is curious and extraordinary . . . I find that I carry with me longer and with constantly recurring charm the impression of something beautiful, while the effect of the wonderful and curious and seemingly picturesque may be remembered just as long but never with the same pleasure."[6]

A contemporary and loyal admirer, Royal Cortissoz, clearly saw the direction Platt was going during these years. His remarks are interesting because they make a distinction between Platt the etcher and Platt the painter, the next phase of his career:

Platt's etchings interested me . . . for their easy composition, their unforced picturesqueness and their strong line. He early imbibed the principle on which Whistler laid such stress, using the art of omission with almost unfailing judgment. He knew his craft, and, besides, there cropped out abundantly in his etchings that sense of beauty. . . . Nevertheless, it was in his paintings . . . that he really stirred me. . . . The important thing was what I can only describe as a new and very fine personal quality that embraced, with notable simplicity of design and very clean, competent brush work, the sentiment of the American scene portrayed . . . he had something to say. The beauty that he loved he did not see in deftly manipulated paint alone but in the hills and skies and he gave these their chance. He did more than that. He painted them fervently and understandingly, and I can realize . . . the lift that one got on coming across a picture of his. . . . It revived Nature's spell, gave you a taste of her invigorating airs, and so often too, brought home to the spectator her breadth and dignity. That is the essential impression I have preserved from all my meetings with Platt's pictures, an impression of delicacy and strength, of a kind of masculine serenity. He has been one of the skillfulest of American painters and one of the sincerest.[7]

These characteristics can be seen in the two etchings done in 1920 based on local subjects, *Meadow Brook* and *The Mountain, Cornish in Winter* as well as paintings of *Clouds, Garden in Winter, Garden in Summer, High Court, Road to Highcourt* (all in local private collections), and *Cornish Landscape*, in the collection of the Corcoran Gallery of Art, Washington, DC.

This notion of the beautiful found its primary outlet not so much in his paintings as it did in his contributions to landscape design and architecture. But before dealing with these topics, his personal life is of interest, especially as it bears on his connection with the Cornish Colony. In contrast to the years of opportunity and experience in Europe, Platt was beset with a number of tragedies. Within several months of his marriage to Annie Corbin Hoe in April of 1886, both his father and father-in-law died. Then in March of 1887, he was dealt a crushing blow: his wife Annie died in giving birth to twin daughters. During the summer of 1889, Platt accepted the invitation of a friend from his Paris days, Henry O. Walker, to join him in Cornish. A few weeks sketching in the vicinity and meeting the group of artists that had gathered in the Cor-

Figure 128. Buttermilk Channel *etching by Charles A. Platt, showing but not featuring the three-year old Statue of Liberty (1889, Rice #107).*

nish hills provided the necessary stimulus for Platt's recovery from grief. Furthermore, Cornish offered a marked contrast to the horizontal landscapes of Holland and the New England coast; they provided Platt with a challenging opportunity to explore and expand his artistic interests. Rather than France or Italy or the Netherlands, it would appear that Cornish, New Hampshire, "played a pivotal role in [his] personal and artistic development. . . . The houses and gardens that he designed for himself and for his Cornish neighbors allowed him to experiment with the ideas he had formulated . . . and to gain practical experience in the design and construction of 'small estates.' This early work in the New Hampshire hills led directly to his national reputation as a domestic architect and garden designer."[8]

Platt's first project in Cornish was to construct his own house and garden. He purchased land from Chester Pike south and adjacent to Henry O. Walker's property. There he built a house with a studio and gardens that he worked on and added to from 1890 until 1912. Just as Rose Nichols sought to keep an old apple tree as a central focus to her garden, so Platt chose to retain one on his house site, "the remnant of a former orchard. . . . The piazza . . . has been designed not in relation to the house itself, but rather as the crowning feature of the lateral pathway leading down through the several levels of the garden. The garden is not, however, the only thing worth seeing from the piazza. The rich and tender beauty of the whole valley lies stretched out before the observer." Thus, contrary to what was then in vogue, Platt did not choose his site in order to highlight a view of Mount Ascutney. As for the house, its earliest section had five central bays with a loggia on the west side; a wing with a parlor was not added until

1904. "The design of the house has been subordinated obviously to its surroundings and it takes its place in them with unobtrusive propriety. It is a low two-story and attic structure, a little Italian in feeling, but with nothing exotic in the impression it makes."[9] That very first summer he also received a commission to design and build a house and garden for Annie Lazarus (see above pp. 245-247). Called "High Court," this commission launched him on his career in architecture and landscape design; it occupied him from 1890 to 1891. But it did so with some initial trepidation on his part. Aware that he was a novice without any formal training in architecture, he wrote his good friend Stanford White, one of the busiest architects of the "Gilded Age," that he needed some trained help in designing "High Court": "Haven't you got *some photo*, or something that *would help* me in regard to detail? Can you give the address of a man who will make a perspective of the plan when I get it drawn out?"[10]

But he was not in need of help for long because during the early years of the 1890s he resolutely set out to perfect his skills in both architecture and landscape architecture. In 1892, the year after "High Court" was finished, he and his younger brother William spent six months in Italy touring and studying the major villas of the Italian Renaissance. William had recently began studying landscape architecture with Frederick Law Olmsted, the designer of New York's Central Park and a firm believer in naturalistic, "picturesque" landscapes. Platt explains that "I got interested in landscape gardening . . . through the fact that my youngest brother had adopted landscape gardening as a profession. I was very much interested in his studies and felt that they [Olmsted and his associates] were not teaching him on the side of landscape architecture that interested me the most—that is, the purely architectural side of it. So I decided to take him abroad and go through the great gardens of Europe with a camera, etc., prepared to study them and make drawings."[11] The trip not only led to the articles in *Harper's Magazine* (1893) and the book *Italian Gardens* (1894),[12] but, while they were returning to America, it also led to the beginning of Platt's courting of Eleanor Hardy Bunker. She was the wife of Platt's good friend, the painter Dennis Bunker, who had died of pneumonia three months after his marriage to Eleanor in 1889. Platt married her in 1893. But while Charles Platt remained in Paris in 1892, his brother William, to whom Charles was deeply devoted, returned to America and drowned while vacationing in Maine.

Upon Charles Platt's return to America in 1892, his career soon developed into a formidable one. The list of buildings, gardens, and projects that Keith Morgan compiled for his study extends over twenty-two pages. In the immediate Cornish and Plainfield area, Platt received commissions from Henry O. Walker (1890); Grace and Edith Lawrence, the nieces of his first wife Annie C. Hoe (1896); Herbert Croly (1897, 1902, 1904); Mary B. Smoot (1899); Winston Churchill, "Harlakenden House" (1901-1904); a farmhouse on Freeman Road (1903, 1914); Herbert Adams (1903); and Augusta and Emily Slade "Dingleton House" (1904, 1905). From people associated with the Cornish Colony, he received a commission from Norman Hapgood to work on his New York City town house (1905); he made some alterations on the pedestal of *The Pilgrim* by Augustus Saint-Gaudens located in Philadelphia, Pennsylvania (1905); he designed alterations for Ellen Shipman's town house in New York City (1919); he worked on plans for the pedestal and landscape treatment of the Herbert Adams War

Figure 129. *Architect Charles A. Platt's house and garden.*

Memorial in Winchester, Massachusetts (1926); and he was involved with plans for Carpenter Hall, Sanborn House, and the Tuck School at Dartmouth College (1926-1931). In 1902 he designed the Mothers' and Daughters' Clubhouse, now the home of the Plainfield Historical Society, Plainfield, New Hampshire. Morgan notes further that Kenyon Cox incorporated the view from Platt's garden into a painting that has now been lost and that Platt influenced both Maxfield Parrish in his designs for "The Oaks" and Ellen Shipman in her study of landscape design.[13]

A final local connection is with Edward C. Waite, Jr., and his nephew Schel Lewis. "Ned" Waite was a well-known builder of dams and an excellent carpenter who served as Platt's contractor: he did the paneling at "Harlakenden House," a Platt commission; Percy MacKaye's "Hilltop"; the front portico of the Philip Read Memorial Library in Plainfield; and the floor of the Plainfield Town Hall.[14] His nephew Schel Lewis joined Platt in 1907 as an office boy and became one of Platt's most trusted model builders and renderers, preparing finished perspective drawings that gave prospective clients a better idea of how their final commission would look. "Platt taught him a rapid rendering technique using charcoal and the flat edge of a pencil on tracing paper placed over a measured drawing."[15] Lewis spent an entire year working on the drawings for the Freer Gallery in Washington, DC; eventually he became so good at his job that he went into private practice during the 1920s.

Herbert Croly is a good person to turn to for a summary judgment on the career of this twentieth-century Renaissance man because Croly was a friend, a neighbor, and, from 1900 until 1906, an editor of *The Architectural Record*. To begin with, Platt "enlarged the scope of architectural design in this country and opened up a whole new field for its practice." Platt was one of the first architects to realize "that the lay-out of the grounds, the plan and design and the location of the buildings, and the situation, the planting, and the character of the flower garden should all be part of a single architectural scheme." To minimize the "Italianate" flavor of Platt's garden design, Croly points out that "Mr. Platt's work . . . is derived from Italian models only in the sense that the technical traditions of any art must be derived from its most perfect examples. What he is really trying to do is, not to reproduce Italian gardens in this country, but to apply to the design of American houses and gardens the principles which were used by the architects of Italian villas in the seventeenth century." And to do so for no other reason than Platt's belief that these principles, when applied to the specific problems confronting an American architect . . . will help him to create country places which bear the imprint at once of the local conditions, of the practical requirements, and of a high and appropriate tradition of style." Furthermore, to counter the negative connotation of "formal," Croly argues that, of course, Platt's designs are "formal" not "in the sense . . . of being stiff, rigid, and unnatural" but rather, "all that should be meant by a 'formal' garden is a garden that is really *formed*—a garden whose appearance has been considered in relation to all the conditions which may enhance or diminish its beauty." Croly reasons that "such a garden will be artificial, but it will not be unnatural; because the artificial arrangement of the surroundings of a house, so as to adapt it to human habitation, is the most natural thing in the world."[16] These remarks echo earlier ones in the *Architectural Record* in which Croly is discussing specifically the work Platt did in Cornish. The parallel Croly draws between the reason why both Renaissance Italians and turn-of-the-century Americans built their houses in the country is instructive. The villas Platt saw in Italy,

> like the American country house, were intended as the occasional country habitat of highly-civilized gentry, who in income and tastes, were the products of city life. When [the Italians] go to the country, they carry with them their civilization, their artificial and artistic demands; they do not go to the country to return, so far as decency permits, to a state of nature; and they do not feel any incompatibility, when in the country, between the formal treatment of the immediate surroundings of the house and the informal beauties of the natural landscape. What they do demand is that their country residence should give them the finest and fullest opportunities to enjoy the various pleasures of country life, and that their houses and grounds should be frankly expressive of this demand.[17]

Platt mixed his professional and social pursuits carefully. In New York, he was an early member of the New York Etching Club and the Society of American Etchers as well as the fashionable, elite Century Club and Players Club; Thomas Dewing proposed him for membership in the latter club and Stanford White seconded it. His social life among his friends in the Cornish Colony was an active one. Apparently, he was a competitive croquet player and he enjoyed golf and backgammon. He delighted in the many charade parties that were so popular among the Colonists. Among his closest friends was Barry Faulkner, who has left us an informative account of his friendship and, in particular, an explanation of a bronze relief, a caricature that Saint-Gaudens did of Platt in 1904. In Faulkner's description, it shows "Platt's head with wavy eyebrows and flowing mustache stand[ing] on the top of a post which tapers at its base in the manner of a garden herme . . . beside [the inscription] stands a small iron stove, tightly closed. The iron stove was a dig at Platt's sometimes aloof manner and his habitual economy of speech, characteristics which became known as the Platt Reserve. The Reserve existed, but was more a myth than a reality and his family and friends were conscious of it only in an amused kind of way. Certainly Platt chattered less than most men, but chatter has little inherent warmth, while Platt's silences were eminently warm and comfortable." As for the reason why Saint-Gaudens "symbolized his friend as a garden-herme, it was probably because Platt's early reputation as an architect rested on his ability to unite a house and garden in a well-considered design, located in happy relation to its landscape."[18] And the quasi-Latin-Italian inscription that Saint-Gaudens wrote on the plaque is further proof that his friends regarded him warmly. In translation it reads, "let us rejoice, people of the Cornish Colony, for the return of Charles Adams Platt and his most beautiful wife by presenting this medal in the spring of 1904."[19]

Certainly this is a fitting tribute to a man who died September 12, 1933, who became in 1919 the first president of the Board of Trustees of the Saint-Gaudens Memorial, who gave so much to both his country and his home town, and who told his students, "your mind must be so filled with beauty that you think of nothing else."[20] It is tempting to believe that Platt was thinking as much of himself as of his friend Herbert Croly when he commented that Croly: "was . . . a reasoned traditionalist, persuaded both by instinct and by study that our evolution needs to be steadied by careful consideration of the precedent . . . he never forgot the lesson of the past . . . this made him a sound educational influence."[21] When an exclusive concern with Beauty is wedded to "a reasoned traditionalist," there results an excellent definition of the power the cultural movement known as the American Renaissance had on one of its most significant exemplars.[22]

ENDNOTES

1. "Charles A. Platt, F.A.I.A. Etcher, Landscape Painter, Landscape Architect, Mural Painter, and Architect," *Pencil Points* 14, November 1933, p. 481, as quoted in Keith N. Morgan, *Charles A. Platt: The Artist as Architect* (New York: The Architectural History Foundation/New York and Cambridge, MA: The MIT Press, 1985), p. 1.

2. Sylvia Rosa Koehler, "The Works of American Etchers. XXV. Charles A. Platt," *American Art Review* 2, pt. 2, 1881, p. 156, as quoted in Morgan, *Charles A. Platt*, p. 11. The year 1881 was also the year in which Platt did two touching *hommages* to his etching teacher, Stephen Parrish: he added the initials "S.P." to his etching *Old Boat House* (Rice #12) as the identification on the stern of a sailboat docked in Gloucester, Massachusetts and he put "S. Parrish, Rockport" on the stern of a two-masted boat in his etching *High and Dry* (Rice #20).

3. Morgan, *Charles A. Platt*, p. 12. For a more detailed study of Platt's etchings, see the chapter by Maureen C. O'Brien in Keith N. Morgan, *Shaping an American Landscape: The Art and Architecture of Charles A. Platt* (Hanover, NH: The Hood Museum of Art, Dartmouth College, 1995), pp. 24-49.

4. Ibid. An equally interesting estimate by a foreign admirer of etching concerns one of Platt's early etchings: "Once in a European capital this etching was received with

incredulity by a company of eminent connoisseurs. And when convinced of its American origin, an Italian collector said: 'I knew that pork and petroleum came from America. I did not know that America produced works of art like this,'" as quoted in J. R. W. Hitchcock, *Etching in America* (New York: White, Stokes, & Allen, 1886), p. 81. The etching discussed is Rice #26 done in 1881, correctly titled *The Market Slip, St. John, N[ew]. B[runswick]., at Ebb Tide.*

5. Samuel Colman, letter to Louis A. Holman (1906), as quoted in Rona Schneider, *American Painter Etchings: 1853-1908* (New York: The Grolier Club, 1989), p. 43. A further note on Platt's etchings: as did his friend Stephen Parrish, Platt contributed some four etchings as illustrations for Dean Sage, *The Restigouche and Its Salmon Fishing* (Edinburgh: David Douglas, 1888), reprinted in 1923 by The Angler's and Shooter's Press, Goshen, CT; the Restigouche River is in northwest New Brunswick, west of Dalhousie.

6. As quoted in Morgan, *Charles A. Platt*, p. 18; for further commentary on this point, see Erica E. Hirshler's chapter on Platt's paintings in Morgan, *Shaping*, p. 58.

7. *Monograph of the Works of Charles A. Platt, With An Introduction by Royal Cortissoz* (New York: Architectural Book Publishing Co., 1913), pp. iii-iv.

8. Keith N. Morgan, "Charles A. Platt's Houses and Gardens in Cornish, New Hampshire," *The Magazine Antiques* 122:1, July 1982, p. 117. The reference to "small estates" is from Platt's friend and Cornish neighbor Herbert Croly, "The Architectural Works of Charles A. Platt," *Architectural Record* 15:3, March 1904, pp. 184-185.

9. The descriptions in this paragraph are from Platt's friend Herbert D. Croly, "The House and Garden of Mr. Charles A. Platt," *House and Garden* 1, December 1901, pp. 10-17.

10. Letter dated August 28, 1890, Stanford White Papers, Platt letter file, New York Historical Society, as quoted in Keith N. Morgan, *The Magazine Antiques*, p. 120; see also the illustration on p. 123. On the question of training and schooling, Morgan quotes a letter Platt wrote Royal Cortissoz, "I never, however, had any formal training in architecture. What I know I have learned in actual practice. In the early years, I picked something off every one I could talk to on the practical side—architects, contractors, draughtsmen, etc. I learned to do a lot of things that I am not particularly fitted to do. . . . You must know, however, that I am at bottom a practical man." (p. 121).

11. Letter to Royal Cortissoz, June 30, 1913, as quoted in Morgan, *Charles A. Platt*, p. 37.

12. See *Harper's New Monthly Magazine* 87:518, July 1893, pp. 164-180, and #519, August 1893, pp. 393-406, and the recent reprint of Charles A. Platt, *Italian Gardens*, with an overview by Keith N. Morgan (Portland, OR: Sagapress/Timber Press, 1993).

13. Morgan, *The Magazine Antiques*, pp. 126, 129; more specific comments on some of Platt's local commissions can be found on pp. 124-26. See Morgan, *Charles A. Platt*, pp. 239-262, for Morgan's "List of Buildings, Gardens, and Projects."

14. Philip Zea and Nancy Norwalk, eds., *Choice White Pines and Good Land, A History of Plainfield and Meriden, New Hampshire* (Portsmouth, NH: Peter E. Randall, 1991), pp. 136-137, 352, 396, 488.

15. Morgan, *Charles A Platt*, p. 74; see also p. 223, nn. 45, 47. Illustrations of the work Lewis did can be seen in Morgan, *Charles A. Platt*, pp. 164, 190, and *Shaping*, pp. 12, 14, 128 and 164.

16. Herbert Croly, "An American Landscape Architect: An Explanation of the Work of Mr. Charles A. Platt," *The House Beautiful* 20:5, October 1906, pp. 11-12. Platt, too, believed, as he put it, "that the term 'Italian Garden' is being too liberally applied to

the formal garden in this country, and while I am guided mainly by principles of design derived from the Italian examples, I should not call the Anderson garden [the residence of Mr. and Mrs. Larz Anderson, "Weld," Brookline, Massachusetts, 1901] an Italian garden any more than I should call one of my houses an Italian house," as quoted in Morgan, *Shaping*, p. 177, n. 18.

17. Croly, *Architectural Record*, pp. 184-185, as quoted in Morgan, *The Magazine Antiques*, p. 127.

18. The information in this paragraph comes from a "Memoir" written by Geoffrey Platt and appended to Morgan, *Charles A. Platt*, pp. 199-209, and a recollection of "Charles Adams Platt," Barry Faulkner papers, Library of Congress, Washington, DC, and the Dartmouth College Library, Hanover, NH.

19. John H. Dryfhout, *The Work of Augustus Saint-Gaudens* (Hanover, NH: University Press of New England, 1982), p. 267.

20. As quoted in Morgan, *Charles A. Platt*, p. 70.

21. As quoted in Morgan, *Shaping*, p. 23.

22. Morgan's idea that Croly's notion of the "promise of American Life" centered on artists of Platt's mold is convincingly argued; see pp. 19-23. In summarizing the significance of Platt and his commissions, Morgan links it with Croly in this way: "Platt provided the guiding hand for everything from the selection of the site to the large-scale development of the property, the general configuration of the gardens, the design of the house, and the choice of furnishing and art works (which frequently included paintings, etchings, watercolors, and photographs by Platt, or work by the circle of friends with whom he surrounded himself in New York City and in Cornish, New Hampshire). Platt could thus shape intellectual and visual landscapes of power and sophistication that he and his patrons intended to serve as models for American society at large—the work of 'constructive individuals' [Croly's phrase] informing the promise of American art." (Morgan, *Shaping*, p. 23).

Figure 130. *Charles A. Platt's home,*
originally constructed from 1890-1892.

ARTHUR HENRY PRELLWITZ
1865 – 1940

and

EDITH MITCHELL PRELLWITZ
1865 – 1944

HENRY PRELLWITZ grew up in New York, studied art with Thomas Dewing at the Art Students League from 1882 to 1887, and then went to the Académie Julian in Paris until 1890. He came to Cornish for several summers at the behest of Thomas Dewing and "that was the beginning of perfect wonders. A New York kid to be thrown into that wonderland . . . it was the first introduction of this boy into real wild country." Later he notes that he "went to Cornish for the summer boarding with George Ruggles, who had built a studio on his farm. How the place had grown! H. O. Walker was there, Saint-Gaudens had built a very fine studio and was doing work there."[1]

Meanwhile, he renewed his acquaintance with Edith Mitchell, whom he had known not only at the Art Students League, where she had studied with George de Forest Brush and Kenyon Cox, but also in Paris, where she too had been at the Académie Julian, studying with Bouguereau, Robert-Fleury, and Courtois. Edith noted in an entry to her diary in 1883 that "I am a woman of 'aspiration,' with . . . strong intentions to . . . become an artist, a great artist."[2] The two of them had even been in some of the same exhibitions. They were married in October of 1894. She received the Dodge Prize from the National Academy of Design in 1895; she later noted that "with the proceeds of that prize we built a very modest cottage on a hilltop at Cornish. It only cost about $250—being of boards and paper with no cellar—running water from a spring with pipes to the kitchen. This was the beginning of many pleasant summers at Cornish, which at that time had grown into a very fascinating place."[3] The land was purchased earlier; records indicate that Prellwitz bought land north of the Whiting-Littell home in 1897, though he started to pay taxes on seven acres, part of the Bryant farm, in 1893.[4] Several years later, "Kenyon Cox and his wife had come to board at the Tracy farmhouse and when they saw how easily the Prellwitzes got along with their little shack, they said, 'Why can't we build?' and so they purchased a little piece of land adjoining the dam by the millpond and so they built a dam site."[5] There were those, however, who were less charmed, or intrigued, by what one Colony member referred to as Prellwitz's "shanty."[6]

Although Henry painted primarily landscapes and Edith was admired for her paintings of children, during the summers they were in Cornish, the couple painted locally inspired subjects. Edith Prellwitz painted *Saint-Gaudens's Garden, Summer,* and Henry produced several paintings of Mount Ascutney as it was seen under various atmospheric conditions. (A view of the mountain was a prime requisite when most Colonists chose the site for their houses.) But there was another side to the Colonists' appreciation of the mountain, and Prellwitz's description is worthy of note. "There was a mountain at Windsor which we used to climb. It was very difficult. It was Mount Ascutney, 3,300 feet high, which had a magnificent view because it stands alone. In making a special expedition to climb this mountain, it was necessary to drive to the foot of the mountain beyond Windsor, climbing up a steep trail about two and a half miles. On several occasions, we spent the night. Saint-Gaudens, Dewing, Platt, and myself have done this several times. There were always two schools of [thought about what] shoes to be worn. I always wore sneakers. On one trip, returning, we came to a smooth ledge which we had to get across and I crept across it watching how the other would negotiate it.... Louis Saint-Gaudens coming over very cautiously... and when each one got there, he watched the others get across, but they did it very slowly."[7]

It is clear that the summers the couple spent in Cornish were of great personal significance to them. The following ecstatic description, almost in the form of a free verse poem, is an invitation to Philip L. Hale, a Boston artist who was then teaching at the Museum School. Because Hale had been at Giverny with Monet in the mid-1880s, he must have been someone well acquainted with the atmosphere of an art colony.

> The Neo-Hellenic movement flourishes—Epicureans, we of Cornish—Come up—do—Come!
>
> To our hills and dale—fragrant with airs from pines and high hills—musical with streams and fountains—with the song of birds—To our sunny fields—and shade of forests—Come, oh come!
>
> To the links where we Olympians pursue the bounding golf-ball—
>
> To the swift Connecticut where lurk the bass and the many colored perch—and by night the oozy-eel and the horned-pout.
>
> To our blue skies and floating, clear-white clouds—and glorious evening time—Come—
>
> Come and be one of us—Feast with us—Gaze on our mountain—proud and blue, with mile-wide shadows—the color of the deep sea, moving solemnly across.
>
> Feast with us!
>
> Our fields yield succulent corn and beans—and the meal of oats and wheat. Our neat-handed Phylis dresses herb and other country messes thrice daily—
>
> Lobsters and fish have we—iced out [from] the far off city by the sea where the gilded dome of the State House pales the jealous sky.
>
> And toothsome cuts of the stalled ox—"better a dinner of the stalled ox where love is"—Have not the wise said so?[8]—And but come and you have both. And we will sacrifice the lamb, too—with smoke ascending to the sky from our fire of coals and fine odor of burnt fat! Come to Olympus! Oh Phil—and bring your nostril fine and eager palate.
>
> And quaff the sour cider pressed from the wild apple of our hills—A delicious drink to true sons of Cornish. Let us test you!
>
> We can paint by day—by morn. Bring your [palette] and your prism and your

335

multi-colored pigments, and brushes long and round—and transform our green trees!—

And play golf afternoons—and hear music evenings—or watch the mountain and valley bathed in moonlight (if you come the night time)—as we smoke on our piazza. Apollo Whiting dwells at our feet with his piano and magic fingers. And the beautiful Miss Houston plays violin charmingly—

And Dewing dwells here.[9]

The departure of the Prellwitzes from Cornish was a dramatic one, again, best told in his own words: "In 1898, our little place at Cornish was struck by lightning. . . . When the lightning struck, it started a fire around the desk where a curtain wire had been fused. It felt like a hot wire up my leg—a hot, tingling sensation. I rushed to the kitchen and found the cook (a fine, Irish woman) unconscious and, having put out the fire we revived her and her first words were, Oh, Mr. Prellwitz, was it my fault?" The cook was badly burned under the corset stays and they said if she had not been such a strong healthy woman, it would have killed her. That evening, Stephen Parrish brought us a bottle of champagne."[10]

The couple never returned. For a while they rented the "shanty" in Cornish and eventually sold it to Philip Littell and his wife, Fanny. In 1899 they began frequenting Peconic, Long Island, where they became members of an art colony that included Edward Moran, Edward Bell, and Irving Wiles.[11]

ENDNOTES

1. Interview with Henry Prellwitz, DeWitt McClellan Lochman Papers, Archives of American Art, Smithsonian Institution, Film #504, frames 325-374.

2. As quoted in Rhoda Jaffin Murphy, "Where the Past Feels Like the Day Before Yesterday," *Victoria* 10:9, September 1996, p. 56.

3. Interview with Henry Prellwitz.

4. Hugh Mason Wade, *A Brief History of Cornish: 1763-1974* (Hanover, NH: University Press of New England, 1976), p. 71; Cornish Tax Records, Cornish, NH.

5. Interview with Henry Prellwitz.

6. Stephen Parrish, diary, entry for September 7, 1905, Special Collections, Baker Library, Dartmouth College, gift of Marian and Roy Garrand.

7. Interview with Henry Prellwitz.

8. An allusion to Proverbs 15, 17, "He that is of a merry heart hath a continual feast. . . . Better is a dinner of herbs where love is, than a stalled ox and hatred therewith."

9. Letter dated August 20, 1895, from Windsor, VT; Virginia Colby, Cornish Colony files. The composer and conductor Arthur Whiting lived down the road from the Prellwitzes and Miss Houston is Charlotte, the daughter of Frances and William Houston. Henry once answered questions about influence on his art: "I suppose most of my life I have really been influenced more by Thomas Dewing than anyone else . . . I think more about Abbott Thayer and [Augustus] Saint-Gaudens than any Frenchman I know." Ronald G. Pisano, *Henry and Edith Prellwitz and the Peconic Art Colony* (Stony Brook, NY: The Museums at Stony Brook, 1995), p. 11.

10. Interview with Henry Prellwitz.

11. For more on this topic, see Pisano.

Figure 1c. Sign for the Tea Tray, *by Maxfield Parrish, c. 1915.*

Figure 2c. Saint-Gaudens's Garden, *by Edith Prellwitz, 1898.*

Figure 3c. Sanctuary: A Bird Masque, *by Arnold Genthe*

ALLYN COX

LECTIO CERTA

Figure 5c. Dutch Landscape, *oil on canvas by Charles A. Platt, c. 1890.*

Figure 4c. *Mural at the Windsor, Vermont Library by Allyn Cox, 1916, based upon the motto "Accurate reading profits, varied reading delights."*

Figure 6c. Late Afternoon, *by Willard Metcalf. On the reverse he has written "Plymouth, Vermont showing Killington Peak in the distance and the upper Plymouth lake. Painted from Nature by W. R. Metcalf August 1878."*

Figure 7c. Gloucester Harbor, *etching by Stephen Parrish, after a painting by William M. Hunt (1882, S.P. #74).*

Figure 8c. Pastel Portrait *by Frances C. Lyons Houston. It may be her daughter, Charlotte Houston Fairchild, posing as Diana.*

Figure 9c. *Garden walk of Stephen Parrish's home, "Northcote,"*
by B. Martin Justice, Autochrome, c. 1913.

Figure 10c. Augusta Saint-Gaudens
by Thomas Wilmer Dewing.

FREDERIC REMINGTON

1861 – 1909

Figure 131.

FREDERIC REMINGTON'S ART, be it in the form of painting, sculpture, or illustration, is generally familiar to most Americans. His friend and admirer Owen Wister—the author of a novel mythologizing the West and cowboys, *The Virginian* (1902)— believed that Remington was "one of the kind that makes us aware of things we could not have seen for ourselves. We have been scarce enough in native material for Art to let go what the soil provides us. . . . If Remington did nothing further, already he has achieved: he has made a page of American history his own.[1] His action-filled depictions of the western plains—complete with cowboys, ranchers, Native Americans, horses, cattle, and cavalry—evoke standard images of the West that many contemporary cultural critics are attempting to revise. In fact, "he was so prolific that there are those who would argue that much of our conception of the Old West is the result of his interpretation of it. His photographic mind, enhanced by the many artifacts in his Western collection made time stand still long enough for him to reproduce it for us."[2] This extensive collection of historical and ethnographic artifacts was fundamental to his ability to achieve the direct, reportorial realism for which he is so famous. One of his contemporaries described it: "The trophies of his many visits . . . to the West hang all about the walls and litter the floors delightfully. Axes, clubs, spears, bows and arrows, shields, queer water-tight baskets, quaint rude rugs, chaparrajos, moccasins, head-dresses, miniature canoes, gorgeous examples of beadwork, lariats, and a hundred other sorts of curios from the desert and the wilderness . . . [were scattered about]."[3]

Upon his graduation from Yale at the age of nineteen, Remington headed west to Montana where he acquired first-hand experience with the lives of cowboys and cavalrymen. He soon discovered that he had a talent for drawing and sketching. Returning to New Rochelle, New York, with a portfolio of western material, he gradually began to earn a living publishing them in *Harper's Weekly* and *Outing Magazine*. He soon obtained commissions to illustrate books, too, most notably Theodore Roosevelt's *Ranch Life* and *The Hunting Trail*, which was initially serialized in *The Century Magazine* in 1888, and Longfellow's "Song of Hiawatha" for Houghton Mifflin. After study at the Art Students League, he confidently branched out to wash drawings and oil painting.

Much of his art was reproduced in the form of prints widely available in magazines and print shops. At the turn of the century, he was considered America's most famous artist. In an effort to adapt to the period's taste for impressionism, he began to introduce effects of light into his paintings. Toward the end of his life he increasingly took his painting seriously: "if Remington was not satisfied with a work he was apt to get rid of it, commonly by burning it. Diary entries for February 8, 1907, and December 1908 record that he burned seventy-five paintings on the earlier date and another twenty-three on the latter." The year after his death Royal Cortissoz, a frequent commentator on the artists of the Cornish Colony, noted that his painting once was "hard as nails. But then came a change . . . his canvasses began to take on more of the aspect of nature. Incidentally, the mark of the illustrator disappeared and that of the painter took its place."[4]

But Remington's greatest success came with his sculpture: "I was impelled to try my hand at sculpture by a natural desire to say something in the round as well as in the flat. Sculpture is the most perfect expression of action. You can say it all in clay."[5] Many people believe he did precisely that in his first and very popular sculpture, *The Bronco Buster* (1895). Subsequently he did *The Wounded Bunkie, The Fallen Rider,* and *Off the Range*—more commonly known as *Comin' Through the Rye*—showing four shouting, galloping cowboys with their six-shooters aimed in the air. It graphically illustrates one of his most famous traits: the suggestion of motion and action in the horses by having only a few hooves on the ground. In this sculpture, done in 1902, only five hooves touch the earth; in *Trooper of the Plains, 1868,* finished in the year of his death, none of the horse's hooves is on the ground. Just as his pride in his workmanship was clear in his painting, so was it in his sculpture. Experts agree that bronze casts to which he made the finishing touches are vastly superior to posthumous casts.[6]

Less well known, however, is Remington the author, yet that is how his connection with the Cornish Colony was established. In 1902 Macmillan published his novel, *John Ermine of Yellowstone.* Louis Evan Shipman, who had just finished dramatizing Winston Churchill's novel *The Crisis,* thought Remington's novel would also do well on the stage and offered to dramatize it. But no such offer could be made without much correspondence and Remington's presence in New Hampshire. Several of Remington's letters during the summer of 1903 indicate his concern about dialogue and costuming details—the proper attire for a Civil War cavalry officer, for example. Remington hoped to be able to stay at his summer place "Ingleneuk" on the Saint Lawrence River in New York and take care of the details by mail. He writes Shipman, "Say—you Indian—I am working like hell here on stuff which I cannot neglect so don't get me down to New York before August unless you have to. Of course, if it is a real necessity—I come—understand that, but don't send until you are sure the thing can't be done by correspondence. I am sorry you and Madam can't come here. But the railroad management seems never to have thought that a man would want to go from Ogdensburg to Windsor and visa-versa.

POST OFFICE,
TELEGRAMS,
TELEPHONE:
WINDSOR, VERMONT.

POINS HOUSE,
CORNISH,
NEW HAMPSHIRE.

Frederic Remington

Figure 132. *A drawing that Frederic Remington made on "Poins House" stationery. Note that the stationery says Cornish although the Shipman's house was actually in Plainfield Village.*

I would have had to spend a day and a half; have gone to Montreal and have been dumped out at Bellows Falls at 3 a.m. and there was no information as to how I would reach Windsor."[7]

Despite the travails of travel, Remington did come to visit the Shipmans at "Poins House," the brick building on the corner of Route 12A and Westgate Road in Plainfield Village. On one visit he did a signed drawing of an old man on "Poins House" stationery; on the reverse side of the paper is a drawing of a chair with a drawer in it. Ellen Shipman believed that "this particular drawing was done to represent a character in a play that my husband was doing from [Remington's] book 'John Ermine.' Also, perhaps the chair was what he thought might be a property for the performance."[8] Shipman's adaptation was chosen to be the first production at the new Globe Theater in Boston; opening night was September 14, 1903. Although the reviews were favorable, it only lasted a month; then it opened in New York in November.[9]

But disappointment at the play's outcome did not immediately sour Remington's attraction to the Cornish Colony. On the contrary, he was charmed with its ambiance. Maxfield Parrish noted that "Remington and Louis Evan Shipman were very good friends ... I remember Remington's visit very well indeed: he stayed at Herbert Croly's, but no doubt at Shipmans' frequently."[10] And Winston Churchill recalled that he "went with Remington 'for a day, over the hills.'"[11] Remington, in fact, was delighted enough with the area and the people he met to want to purchase some land.

He wrote Shipman: "I haven't yet recovered my senses after what you did to me up there. I don't really need an unknown mountain in my business but by God there is no use of my having money—when I do some guy always sells me something I don't want. Anything from a jigging house to a naphtha launch will do—I used to be content with such things, but now it's mountains. If a man is organized to be a d_____ fool, he is bound to be Cornished sooner or later."[12]

At first, Remington's excitement about being "Cornished" was great. "He told Shipman that he would 'run up' with his attorney 'and get deed for Lizard Hill.'"[13] Preoccupied with a rapid increase in commissions to fulfill, he let the project lapse; he took it up again, however, in 1905 because "the town of New Rochelle is encroaching on the view from his studio windows, and a millionaire has erected a palace on the very next island" on the Saint Lawrence River in Chippewa Bay. "He is going to a big place of his own, where the commuters will not crowd him by winter or the millionaires by summer." Remington wrote Shipman to see "'if you can find a good place for me within four miles of Windsor, closer to the train than Cornish." What he wanted was "an old farm house that I could fix over." But it soon occurred to him that Windsor/Cornish was the center of academic artists, some of the ones who were keeping him out of the National Academy, and for that reason he again decided not to be "Cornished."[14]

After an operation for acute appendicitis, Remington died several years later in 1909 at the age of forty-eight.

ENDNOTES

1. Owen Wister, "Concerning the Contents," *Drawings by Frederic Remington* (New York: R. H. Russell, 1900), unpaginated.

2. Allen P. Splete and Marilyn D. Splete, *Frederic Remington—Selected Letters* (New York: Abbeville Press, 1988), p. xv.

3. An article in *Harper's Weekly,* January 17, 1891, as quoted in Wayne Craven, *Sculpture in America* (New York: Crowell, 1968), p. 533; see also Peter H. Hassrick, *The Frederic Remington Studio* (Seattle: University of Washington Press, 1995).

4. Splete, p. 366. For more on Remington's desire to be recognized as a painter rather than an illustrator, see the remarks by Peter H. Hassrick in the exhibition catalogue *Frederic Remington: The Late Years* (Denver, CO: Denver Art Museum, 1981), pp. 7-15.

5. Ibid., as found in *Pearson's Magazine* 18, October 1907, p. 407; the magazine ran an article on Remington by Perriton Maxwell, "Frederic Remington: Most Typical of American Artists," and a letter from President Theodore Roosevelt under that title "An Appreciation of the Art of Frederic Remington."

6. Marvin D. Schwartz, "Remington and Connoisseurship," *Antiques and the Arts Weekly,* February 24, 1989, p. 82.

7. Splete, p. 340.

8. Letter from Ellen Shipman to Lawrence W. Rittenoure dated June 15, 1944; Virginia Colby files. The Remington drawing is owned by Charlene Brotman of Newton, MA.

9. Splete, p. 308.

10. Letter to Lawrence W. Rittenoure dated February 29, 1944; Virginia Colby, Cornish Colony files.

11. Peggy and Harold Samuels, *Frederic Remington* (Garden City, NY: Doubleday, 1982), p. 339.

12. Ibid.

13. Ibid. The tract of land was actually on Prospect Hill in Plainfield. Word of mouth was so strong that many people were convinced that Remington had really signed on the dotted line. Hugh Mason Wade told the Samuelses about a "local legend" that Remington "acquired a lot of land" locally, "but Remington did not buy the Cornish mountain, not even in its diminished height as Lizard Hill," Samuels, p. 339. There is also a clipping in a scrapbook on the Cornish Colony in the Windsor Public Library that reads: "Frederic Remington has purchased a large farm and extensive forest land on Prospect Mountain, now familiarly known as Remington Hill"; Virginia Colby, Cornish Colony files.

14. The quotation in this paragraph comes from Samuels, p. 360. Membership in the National Academy of Design, an association devoted to the fine arts, was restricted to 125 painters, 25 sculptors, and 25 architects and engravers.

Figure 133. *Left to right: Edward B. Burling, Juliet Rublee, George Rublee.*

GEORGE RUBLEE
1868 – 1957

and

JULIET BARRETT RUBLEE
1875 – 1966

GEORGE RUBLEE

ALTHOUGH GEORGE RUBLEE had an extremely active career in national as well as international politics, he and his spirited wife Juliet Barrett Rublee were devoted to Cornish. Despite the excitement and dazzle of life in Washington, New York, and various international centers, they considered Cornish to be the focus of their private lives. They retreated here often from the bustle of their public commitments. Homer Saint-Gaudens, in attempting to define what set Cornish apart from other summer colonies, called attention to the number of "City Folks" who remained in Cornish for most of the year.[1] George Rublee was such a person. Perhaps the repose he and his wife felt nestled in these hills is the reason why they chose to be buried here.

Rublee was born in Madison, Wisconsin, and spent his early years in Switzerland where his father, a founding member of the Republican party, was President Ulysses S. Grant's diplomatic representative. After attending the Groton School, where he was its first—and only—graduate in 1886, then Harvard University, and finally Harvard Law School, he established a law firm in Chicago with Edward Burling and soon moved on to New York and joined a law firm specializing in corporation law and railroad reorganization. Through the connections he made in the organization, he "became a canny appraiser of the possibilities of railroad bonds and made enough money to enable him to retire at the age of 32."[2]

But his retirement was short-lived; 1900 marked the beginning of years of public service. He belonged to the Progressive party and was an early supporter of Theodore Roosevelt when the latter bolted from the Republican party in 1912. In New Hampshire, Rublee helped Robert P. Bass, who was elected governor in 1910, break the power of the Boston and Maine Railroad. Rublee's efforts attracted the attention of Raymond Stevens, a Democratic member of the House of Representatives. As a member of the House Interstate Commerce Committee, Stevens got Rublee involved in legislation concerning the

Federal Trade Commission. In 1914, Rublee was responsible for putting teeth in the Commission's power by drafting Article 5 of the Federal Trade Commission Act. It declared unfair competitive methods in commerce unlawful and empowered the Commission to issue cease and desist orders. (Many people considered Rublee's contribution a major factor in the development of the policies practiced by Franklin Delano Roosevelt's New Deal because Article 5 of the FTC Act became the model for the Federal Power Commission, the Securities and Exchange Commission, and the National Labor Relations Board.[3]) President Wilson sought to make Rublee a member of the FTC, but in a fiery struggle between Wilson and the Senate, the latter twice rejected the nomination, largely due to the efforts of New Hampshire's Republican Senator Jacob Gallinger, who considered Rublee "personally obnoxious." During the First World War, however, Rublee received several important appointments: he was a special counsel to the Treasury Department and a member of the Allied Maritime Transport Council, which had the delicate job of dividing the shipping tonnage among the allies and the United States. Furthermore, he was an advisor to the U.S. delegation during the negotiations of the Treaty of Versailles. Rublee's resourcefulness and persuasive abilities were frequently called upon in this capacity; they won him the admiration of Dwight Morrow.

In 1921, Rublee became a partner in what was to be the important law firm of Covington, Burling, Rublee, Acheson, and Shorb and his Washington activities increased. Toward the end of the twenties, from 1928 to 1930, Morrow, then ambassador to Mexico, saw to it that Rublee became the embassy's legal adviser to deal with the difficult problems concerning labor and religious issues.[4] In 1930, the government of Columbia was in a dispute with businessmen from the United States and Europe over foreign oil holdings. Rublee again stepped in and refereed this tangle to everyone's satisfaction. Throughout the thirties, Rublee resisted enticements from his friend Franklin Roosevelt to become active in his administration.

In 1938, however, at the age of seventy and when he was most anticipating a quiet life in Cornish, he made what perhaps was his most significant contribution to his country. He served for two years as the United States High Commissioner to the Intergovernmental Committee on Political Refugees at Evian, France. He was responsible for negotiating with Hermann Goering an agreement that would have provided for an orderly resettlement of some 650,000 political outcasts from Nazi Germany. Upon his arrival in New York on the liner *Queen Mary* in 1939, fresh from the deliberations, he said that the "confidential" document would be "a great alleviation of the condition of Jews in Germany, and make possible orderly emigration." He added that British and Dutch Guiana, the Dominican Republic, Northern Rhodesia, and the Philippine Islands were "among the countries being considered as havens for Jewish refugees."[5] The outbreak of hostilities in Europe, of course, prevented the program from being carried out.

Given this record, it is easy to understand why Rublee considered Cornish a haven. The Rublees bought "Crossways" from the Houston family in 1907[6] and soon became involved in Cornish affairs. They both signed "An Endorsement of Birth Control," a cause for which Juliet was an ardent supporter, and they both were members of the Cornish Equal Suffrage League in 1911—Juliet was its president. She played a major role in *Sanctuary: A Bird Masque*, but George was not to be outdone. He was the Great

Heron in the accompanying pantomime. George also took part in the 1905 production of *A Masque of "Ours": The Gods and the Golden Bowl*.

It was on the tennis court, however, that he made his mark in Cornish society. First of all, he was an excellent player. At one point, he was a regular tennis partner for Crown Prince Gustav of Sweden for almost a year. So, in Cornish, he revamped the tennis court at "Crossways" and for several summers employed a professional tennis player from Europe, Mr. George Agutter.[7] In addition, he got Maxfield Parrish, another avid player, to make him a handsome cast-bronze ratchet wheel and handle for adjusting the net. One player on that court was delighted with it and describes Rublee's obsession with his game: "It became the most perfect court on which I have ever played. . . . Mr. Rublee secured the polished green granite posts from the famous quarry on the northwest side of Mount Ascutney. There never was a crooked bounce from the hard smooth surface of the dark purple sand. . . . No dogs and no children were allowed, and almost no spectators. The few that turned up knew well that they might be seen but not heard. So sensitive was Mr. Rublee's game to noise that he could not permit the distant mooing of a cow. Cows in a neighboring pasture a considerable distance away were removed. As Mr. Rublee explained: 'It is not so much the mooing of the cow that bothers my game as the thought that the cow might be going to moo.'"[8]

JULIET BARRETT RUBLEE

BECAUSE JULIET BARRETT RUBLEE was a woman so clearly ahead of her time, she ought to be an easy person to discuss. In fact, it is hard to describe her adequately. Many of the facts available cause her to seem to have been a shallow, flighty person. On the other hand, there is obvious proof that she was a woman of character, someone true to her commitments. She showed these traits primarily through her friendship with Margaret Sanger, the champion of the birth control movement in the United States. It has been said of Juliet Rublee that "through her association with [Sanger], this eccentric, if well-intentioned, woman would experience political engagement and personal adventure for which she was more than happy to exchange her money and contacts. More than any other figure in the country's social establishment, she would be responsible for subsequent changes in the orientation of

Figure 134. *Juliet Rublee as Terpsichore in* A Masque of "Ours."

the birth control movement."[9] Hence, Juliet Rublee's contributions to society are of no small order.

One reason she wanted to settle in Cornish was to be near her brother, Robert L. Barrett (see above pp. 130-134). Juliet received a proper education and studied dance while still a young girl. She appeared "as a lunar moth in a fairylike pantomime written by Mr. Joseph Lindon Smith, and incidentally she will perform a most charming dance, for which she has been trained by Mrs. Lilla Viles Wyman. The pantomime will be given in Boston and Chicago . . . with music by an orchestra."[10] In 1913, as part of her interest in Cornish, she served on the committee established to put on Percy MacKaye's production of *Sanctuary: A Bird Masque* as well as dancing the role of Tacita when the play was performed. Her interest in dance and the avant-garde naturally led her to Isadora Duncan, a friend of hers and a visitor at "Crossways." Earlier during her time in Cornish, she played, appropriately enough, the part of Terpsichore, the Greek muse of dance, in the production of *A Masque of "Ours": The Gods and the Golden Bowl.*

Presumably she met George Rublee when he was involved in the legal changing of the name of the Barrett Roofing Company to the Allied Chemical and Die Company in 1900. "The marriage apparently did not satisfy the full extent of Juliet's energies or passions, and there were no children, because she was infertile as the result of overzealous surgery for pelvic complaints when she was young."[11] Their marriage did permit her an independent life amid the fashionable, arty, and intellectual circles of New York—especially in the New York salon of Mabel Dodge. It was under such circumstances, but not necessarily under Mabel Dodge's auspices, that she met Margaret Sanger, who launched the *Woman Rebel* in 1914. It was a magazine that discussed contraceptive means and described the dangers of self-induced abortions. Because it was mailed to subscribers, it ran afoul of the 1873 Comstock laws that prohibited sending obscene material through the mails because among such items were considered "every article or thing designed, adapted, or intended for preventing conception or producing abortion."

A major step in promoting the American birth control movement was the establishment of the first clinic in Brooklyn, New York, on October 16, 1916, by Margaret Sanger. Her action was in part a challenge to those same Comstock laws. The New York police stepped in and arrested Sanger and her sister, Mrs. Ethel Higgins Byrne, who immediately went on a hunger strike. In support of these two was a subgroup of the National Birth Control League known as the Committee of 100. Its "official credo was drafted by the prepossessing Juliet Barrett Rublee. . . . The document . . . emphatically announced [the committee's] purpose: We maintain that it is no more indecent to discuss sexual anatomy, physiology, and hygiene in a scientific spirit than it is to discuss the function of the stomach, the heart, and the liver. We believe that the question as to whether or not, and when a woman should have a child, is not a question for the doctors to decide, except in cases where the woman's life in endangered, or for the state legislators to decide, but a question for the woman herself to decide."[12]

Juliet did more than go to bat for her friend; she also went to jail for her. In 1920, Sanger devised a plan to set up a network of clinics designed along the lines of a medical model then used in the Netherlands. In November of the following year, Sanger organized the First American Birth Control Conference to get support behind her clinic plan. "She then put Juliet Rublee to work on her impeccable personal contacts among the clubwomen and other potential supporters of a birth control organization Margaret might unilaterally control."[13] The conference was to have concluded with a huge rally at New York City's Town Hall. It was, however, broken up "by a band of New York City policemen, who claimed to be acting at the behest of the redoubtable Archbishop Patrick Hayes of nearby St. Patrick's Cathedral. Margaret, remaining serene and composed, and carrying a bouquet of long-stemmed red roses was hauled away."[14] During the subsequent trial, Juliet Rublee went to jail when she attempted to protest Sanger's arrest. Soon, George Rublee got into the fray. He cleverly backed the police commissioner into a corner by demanding to know who actually authorized the raid and by insisting that an investigating commission be appointed.[15] Sanger's attempt to organize the network of clinics was part of a long-range plan to quell opposition within the American Birth Control League, which was incorporated in 1922. Its board consisted of Sanger as president and Juliet Rublee as vice-president. Finally, in 1928, after they restricted Margaret's power, both she and Juliet resigned their positions.

What may have been Juliet Rublee's final contribution to the birth control movement remains supposition. It is hard to keep from wondering, however, whether she had any influence on her Cornish neighbor Learned Hand. This conjecture is especially relevant to the 1936 decision handed down in the Second Circuit Court of Appeals in New York by a three-judge panel, two of whose members were Augustus Hand and his cousin Learned. The case, *United States v. One Package Containing 120, more or less, Rubber Pessaries to Prevent Contraception,* was another challenge to the remaining vestiges of the Comstock laws. The package in question had been mailed from Japan to one of Sanger's partisans, Dr. Hannah Stone, and had been intercepted by Customs authorities under the provision of the Comstock laws. The court upheld the claim of Sanger and her associates that these items should be released to them because the laws were not designed "to prevent the importation, sale, or carriage by mail of things which might intelligently be employed by conscientious and competent physicians for the purpose of saving life or promoting the well-being of their patients."[16]

Whatever role Juliet Rublee may have had behind the scenes did not prevent her from cementing her long-standing friendship with Margaret Sanger during the twenties. Their interests ranged widely from psychic phenomena, to spiritualism, religious concerns, free love, and feminism. They traveled to Europe and visited a host of intellectuals, in particular Harold Child, who worked as an editorial writer and critic for The *Times* of London, and the novelists Hugh de Sellincourt and H. G. Wells. Some critics even believe that certain facts from Juliet's life are attributed to a character in the latter's *The Secret Places of the Heart* (1922).[17] Sanger stepped in to try and cheer Juliet up after the failure of a movie that Rublee "personally supervised." While she was in Mexico with her husband in 1928, she devoted her energies to *Flame of Mexico* described as the first feature-length movie made entirely in Mexico, "a romantic love story, human in its appeal, delightfully told. Teeming with thrills—lavishly produced—and magnificently acted by Alicia Ortiz and Donald Reed, the screen's most appealing lovers. It is amazing—amusing—audacious and authentic!"[18] Closer to Cornish, there is documentary evidence that Sanger visited the Rublees often—at least during the summers of 1921 and 1925 and as late as 1949 and 1953.[19]

During these visits to Cornish, Sanger could not help but have been aware that "Juliet had thyroid eyes, a fluttery manner, and the annoying habit of always dressing in flaming red or pink."[20] She was also famous locally for her large, colorful hats atop dresses of gay, flashing colors. Because she was color blind, she usually had someone help her select her clothes for special occasions. But these features did not blind Margaret Sanger to her friend's contributions to the birth control movement: "Juliet Rublee had been one of the pioneers, a member of the original Committee of One Hundred, and all the way through the years, she has never wavered from my side. No more inspired idealist was ever initiated into a movement. The imagination of this picturesque, romantic wife of a conservative lawyer had been so fired that she dedicated her devotion, loyalty, partisanship."[21]

ENDNOTES

1. See his chapter on the Cornish Colony in William H. Child, *History of the Town of Cornish with Genealogical Record: 1763-1910* (Concord, NH: The Rumford Press, 1911?), Vol. 1, p. 220.

2. Blair Bolles, "Rublee's Talents Re-enlisted," unidentified newspaper clipping, 1938; Virginia Colby, Cornish Colony files.

3. Ibid.

4. It was during this period that Morrow's daughter, Anne Morrow Lindberg, wrote in her diary: "I love Mr. Rublee. He is one of the kindest and gentlest men I have ever known— gentle and patient and a little somber, yet always that sense of the ridiculous. . . . And quite humble! He is the kind of man I feel I can sit with for hours and not have to say a word and yet will feel in perfect sympathy . . . he is the kind of man who, if you were sitting next to him at the theater, would let you have both arms of your chair!"; Anne Morrow Lindberg, *Bring Me a Unicorn: Diaries and Letters of Anne Morrow Lindberg, 1922-1928* (New York: Harcourt Brace Jovanovich, 1971), p. 126. Another outcome of this period, important for the history of the cinema is that "Mrs. Rublee commissioned Sergei Eisenstein to make the notable film *[Que] Viva Mexico!* and also strove unsuccessfully to enlist the Mexican peasants in the birth control movement," Hugh Mason Wade, *A Brief History of Cornish: 1763-1974* (Hanover, NH: University Press of New England, 1976), p. 84. Eisenstein was the celebrated Russian director of *Strike, Potemkin, October, Alexander Nevsky,* and *Ivan the Terrible.* One cannot help wondering whether Witter Bynner crossed the Rublees path in Mexico. In February of 1932 Bynner wrote his mother, "I have seen a good deal of Serge Eisenstein, the Russian movie director about whom you must have read in *The New Republic* and elsewhere. He has been thirteen months making a picture of Mexican Life. . . . I have . . . several times . . . spent hours talking with him. He seems to me to have something of the rare quality called genius. He has an extraordinary staff. He takes his pictures in the actual street and landscape of Mexico, picking his actors spontaneously from the watching crowd," James Kraft, *Who Is Witter Bynner?* (Albuquerque, NM: University of New Mexico Press, 1995), p. 85.

5. Unidentified newspaper clipping, Daniels scrapbook; Virginia Colby, Cornish Colony files.

6. Edward F. O'Brien (1880-1955) left Ireland in his youth and worked as a caretaker for the Houstons. He stayed on in that capacity with the Rublees for forty-five years until

his death in 1955. Virginia Colby, Cornish Colony files.

7. George Agutter (1888-1968) was brought into this country from England in 1905 by George Rublee. In 1913 he began his career as the resident tennis pro at the famed West Side Tennis Club in Forest Hills, Queens, New York. Among the tennis players whom he coached were Frank Hunter, Helen Jacobs, Bill Tilden, and Helen Wills Moody. In 1959 he figured in a scandal at the tennis club that led to his resignation. One of his pupils was the son of Ralph Bunche, who won the Nobel Peace Prize in 1950 for his efforts as the United Nations' principle representative bringing peace in the Middle East. Agutter unwittingly asked the boy to join the club, unaware that he was an African-American and unaware that the club denied African-Americans membership at that point.

8. Margaret Homer Shurcliff, *Lively Days: Some Memoirs of Margaret Homer Shurcliff* (Taipei: Literature House, Ltd., 1965), pp. 35-36.

9. Ellen Chesler, *Woman of Valor: Margaret Sanger and the Birth Control Movement in America* (New York: Simon and Schuster, 1992), p. 167.

10. Unidentified newspaper clipping, Virginia Colby, Cornish Colony files. The pantomime's author, Joseph Lindon Smith, was an artist who devoted his life to painting ancient monuments, especially those of Egypt, and played the important role of Quercus the Faun in *Sanctuary: A Bird Masque*; see below pp. 502-503.

11. Chesler, p. 167.

12. Ibid., p. 154.

13. Ibid., p. 202.

14. Ibid., p. 203.

15. Madeline Gray, *Margaret Sanger* (New York: Marek, 1979), pp. 176-177.

16. As quoted in Chesler, p. 373. It should be noted that Learned Hand, in a concurring opinion, did voice some doubts about the reasoning his cousin used in the majority opinion. His point was one that Sanger also made, namely that it is better for legislators to draft laws than for judges to do so from the bench; see Chesler, pp. 375-376.

17. Chesler, p. 188.

18. Virginia Colby, Cornish Colony files.

19. See Gray, pp. 170, 240, and Chesler, pp. 412-413, 434.

20. Gray, p. 224. It is not surprising that such flamboyancy would attract Annetta St. Gaudens, who did a sculpture of her.

21. Margaret Sanger, *An Autobiography* (New York: Norton, 1938), p. 300.

GEORGE
SYDNEY
RUGGLES
1859 – 1931

Figure 135.

THE CONNECTIONS OF GEORGE RUGGLES with the Cornish Colony were many and intimate. He and his wife took in quite a few of the earliest arrivals as boarders. Later, he constructed a studio that many of them used; they affectionately dubbed it "The Wood-chuck Hole." It is with Maxfield Parrish, however, that his name is most closely linked.

Descriptions of Ruggles are intriguing. He was a man of medium build with a thick, bushy mustache. His tenor voice was much in demand. For years he sang in the Baptist Church in Plainfield and with a quartet along with Albert K. Read II, Orlo Kenyon, and Elwin Quimby.[1] An incessant reader, he kept a memorandum book in which he would jot down "quotations from any author which had pleased him in his wide range of read-ing . . . the majority, were upon the joy of life, and the privilege of its opportunities for service . . . [also he was a] cheerful neighbor and staunch friend. He possessed a certain buoyancy of spirit that is seldom equalled."[2] Homer Saint-Gaudens, finally, thought of him as an "entertaining old carpenter, noted for his talkativeness, his Bible learning, his agnosticism, his taste for ice cream, and his habit of going barefoot in summer to save shoe-leather."[3]

A local paper noted on May 15, 1891, that "George Ruggles is building a studio for the accommodation of the New York artists who will spend the summer there."[4] He used lumber from an abandoned school house on Freeman Road, and he was careful to give the artists a large window with a northern exposure as well as three rooms and a veranda surrounding two sides of the structure. Artists known to have used "The Woodchuck Hole" were Thomas Dewing, Kenyon Cox, and two men who moved on to the artist colony in Dublin, New Hampshire: George de Forest Brush and Abbott Thayer. It was in this studio that Percy MacKaye wrote *The Canterbury Pilgrims—A Comedy* and *Jeanne d'Arc—A Tragedy.* In addition to building the studio, Mrs. Ruggles had a number of artists as boarders: Barry Faulkner, Henry and Lucia Fuller, William

Figure 136. *"The Woodchuck Hole," the studio built by George Ruggles*
for the use of visiting artists.

and Frances Houston and their daughter Charlotte, Paul Manship, Henry and Edith Prellwitz, and Henry and Laura Walker.[5] How important to the local economy this kind of activity was can be seen from the following observation in the Windsor, Vermont, newspaper: "The farmer and his wife who know how can give a bounteous table for $7 a week . . . the summer boarder at $7 a week will pay better than boarding the school marm at $1.75 per week, or raising beef at 3½ cents or wool at 27 cents."[6]

The rapport Ruggles developed with Maxfield Parrish began when the former supervised the twenty-five workmen building "The Oaks." Ruggles lived "about one-half mile from" Parrish's house "as the crow flies; going around by the road, it is nearly two miles." Lucy Ruggles Bishop, his daughter, continues: "So my father, who wished to take the shortest possible route to his work, laid out a path across our fields, through the woods, and up a very steep cliff, almost impossible to climb. Father made a winding road up the cliff and with a strong rope railing, this was the way he went to his daily work."[7] Thus, it was that Ruggles soon became Parrish's chief carpenter. Furthermore, "for 24 years Maxfield Parrish and Mr. Ruggles have been side partners in the machinist's trade. They have been working away with the carpenter's tools and machinery together up here on a New Hampshire hillside for a quarter of a century, and they both say they like each other better every day." This same account also described an incident "when Maxfield Parrish absolutely and flat-footedly refused to break his one inflexible rule and pose for a photographer, he suggested the photographer snap Ruggles. 'I tell you . . . you make a picture of Mr. Ruggles and call it me. We've been living together so long we've grown to look like each other, anyway.'"[8] A final example indicates that the two men enjoyed one another's company as well as working together: "Every fall the high point of my father's year came when Mr. Parrish took him to the big football game of the year at Dartmouth College in Hanover. Mr. Parrish would arrive about half-past eleven in his big Cadillac and the two would start off happily like a couple of school boys. I believe they went to the Hanover Inn for a big luncheon before going to the game. They both loved every bit of it, I know."[9] It is not surprising then that Parrish would turn to Ruggles as a model. He did so for the cover of *Life*, the July 20, 1922, issue with the title *Tea? Guess Again*; it may have been used later as an advertisement for Baker's Cocoa.[10]

Although it is quite personal, a measure of George S. Ruggles can be gathered from the tribute Maxfield Parrish wrote Mrs. Ruggles at his dear friend's death: "I feel almost that people should extend sympathy to me, for Mr. Ruggles was so much a part of our existence here for over thirty years, so much bound up in the growth of this place, that I cannot but feel that his passing is nearly as great a loss to me as to you. His enjoyment of life was so unusual, with his never failing spirit of eternal youth, that I cannot realize he is gone. Everything here is so intimately associated with him, and will make me miss him for many years to come."[11]

ENDNOTES

1. The group sang for the Old Home Day festivities in Meriden, NH, in August of 1901.

2. Obituary, September 17, 1931; Virginia Colby, Cornish Colony files.

3. "Maxfield Parrish," *The Critic* 46:6, June 1905, pp. 515, 517.

4. Virginia Colby, Cornish Colony files.

5. Interview: Virginia Colby with George Ruggles's granddaughters Beatrice Bishop Clark, June 24, 1982, and Anne Ruggles Curfman, August 25, 1982. At a later time, Ruggles's daughter Lucy Ruggles Bishop took in guests who included Cliff Young and Frances Grimes. Cliff Young was an assistant to Allyn Cox, son of Kenyon Cox. When Allyn Cox retired in 1981 from working on the murals for the US Capitol building, Young was assigned the task of completing them. For Grimes, see above pp. 220-223; for Cox and Young, see p. 160.

6. Quoted from a report in September of 1891 in the context of the boarders taken in by the Frank Johnsons, the Stephen A. Tracys, and the Ruggleses by Hugh Mason Wade, *A Brief History of Cornish: 1763-1974* (Hanover, NH: University Press of New England, 1976), p. 51.

7. Lucy F. R. Bishop, "My Neighbor, Maxfield Parrish," typescript dated February 7, 1974, p. 1; Virginia Colby, Cornish Colony files. Mrs. Bishop tutored "Dillwyn (or John as he later called himself) and Max, Jr." (p. 2).

8. *The Literary Digest*, May 12, 1923, picked up from an article by Charles A. Merrill in the *Boston Globe*, Sunday, April 15, 1923.

9. Bishop, p. 1.

10. Interview: Virginia Colby with Maxfield Parrish, Jr., Lexington, MA, March 26, 1979.

11. Letter dated September 7, 1931, collection of Anne Ruggles Curfman, Hampton, VA; copy in Virginia Colby, Cornish Colony files.

AUGUSTUS
SAINT-GAUDENS
1848 – 1907

and

AUGUSTA
FISHER HOMER
SAINT-GAUDENS
1848 – 1926

Figure 137.   AUGUSTUS SAINT-GAUDENS

FOR ALL HIS FAME AS A SCULPTOR, Augustus Saint-Gaudens remains an enigma. There is an air of mystery about the man and his career. There is good reason for the cover of his most recent biography to depict the head of the *Adams Memorial*. His niece, Rose Standish Nichols, who knew him both in Cornish and elsewhere, acknowledges in her diary that, "the nearer one approached my uncle, the better one knew him, the more one realized that intimacy with him was almost an impossibility. His shyness, self-consciousness, sensitiveness to other people's personalities—call it whatever you like—acted like a wall between him and even those who might be called his best friends."[1] His career was puzzling, too. Even in 1897, ten years before he died, it was remarked that "perhaps no living artist has so high a reputation as Saint-Gaudens and so strong an artistic influence with so little of his work familiar to the general public."[2] Although the man and his career have been compared to Michelangelo, people have to scrutinize his comments for any satisfactory definition of his aesthetics. There is no definitive statement similar to Michelangelo's sonnet in which he says that a sculptor's task is to reveal the idea or conception already present in a block of marble before the work begins.[3] This is not the place to examine the corners of his biography, to trace his career, to highlight his achievements, or to solve the puzzle of the man and artist. Rather, the focus will be on Cornish, its importance to and influence on Saint-Gaudens, and what his legacy to Cornish is. Using as many contemporary documents as possible, the emphasis will be both on how he reacted to his immediate environment and on how he appeared to those in it.

He first came to Cornish, as the often-repeated story has it, because his friend Charles Cotesworth Beaman not only promised him "plenty of Lincoln-shaped men,"

352

but also fulfilled it in the person of Langdon Morse, so that Saint-Gaudens could complete the statue *Abraham Lincoln: The Man*, also known as *Standing Lincoln* (1884-1887), now in Chicago's Lincoln Park.[4] Beaman cherished a vision of an artist colony sprouting up in the Cornish hills; eventually, he would control an area of a thousand acres and twenty-three houses. But early in his plan, he proposed a former inn, "Huggin's Folly," for Saint-Gaudens. However, it was far from a charming villa in the country that Saint-Gaudens and his wife may have had in mind. On the contrary, "I first caught sight of the building on a dark, rainy day in April . . . it appeared so forbidding and relentless that one might have imagined a skeleton half-hanging out of the window, shrieking and dangling in the gale, with the sound of clanking bones. I was for fleeing at once and returning to my beloved sidewalks of New York. . . . My dwelling first looked more as if it had been abandoned for the murders and other crimes therein committed than as a home wherein to live, move, and have one's being. For it stood out bleak, gaunt, austere, and forbidding, without a trace of charm. And the longer I stayed in it, the more its Puritanical austerity irritated me."[5]

But stay he did. As for Beaman's "colony," with a backward glance to the differences between when he came in 1885 and when he was composing his memoirs, Saint-Gaudens notes, a bit wryly, that "now there are many families. The circle has extended beyond the range even of my acquaintance, to say nothing of friendship. The country still retains its beauty, though its secluded charm is being swept away before the rushing automobile, the uniformed flunky, the butler, and the accompanying dress-coat."[6]

His return to Cornish in 1900 coincided with his urgent desire to get back to America. A triumphant three-year stay in Europe resulted in his sculpture projects being highly lauded, especially at the Exposition Universelle in Paris in the spring of that year. He soon learned, however, that he needed an operation for an intestinal tumor, the initial stages of a cancer that would kill him in seven years. Despite the praise he received in France, his letters bear sharp witness to his depression and desire to be home among his American friends. Cornish, then, represented a welcome relief to this strain. The tone of his letters during this Cornish period is radically different from those letters written in Europe.[7] His responses to the change of seasons are a good measure of this change in spirit; his love for Cornish is apparent throughout them.

A 1901 letter to Alfred Garnier, a French friend from his student days in Paris who became a ceramist and enamelist, elicits his pleasure in autumn. He begins with a characteristic statement about his inability to express himself in writing or public speaking. He was all too willing to let his sculpture speak for him: "as I look out of the window on the hills opposite, I wish I had your power of description, for the whole burst of autumn glory is at its full now, only more beautiful than ever, for some reason or other. There is more harmony in it than usual. It's perfectly glorious, and the weather is, too." He continues by relating the external world to his internal sense of good health and good spirits: "I stop work at one o'clock and I devote the rest of the day to out-of-door things, golf, walking, driving, cutting trees, and all that makes one see there is something else in life besides the four walls of an ill-ventilated studio—not that I renounce for a moment my love of the charm of that life too—I speak of this because I see so many of the *'confrérie'* [colleagues] living the life I led for thirty years, and I wish to drag them by the hair to where they would find other *'jouissances'*

353

[enjoyments] that would not undermine their health.—*Health*—is the thing! That's my conclusion."[8] Perhaps his joy at being alive and his expectation that his disease was under control heightened his appreciation of the beauty and harmony of the "autumn glory" and of outdoor activity.

Spring, however, was another matter. Going one better the analogy other Colonists made between Cornish and the Valley of the Arno, Saint-Gaudens gently points out that "Cornish is not perfect any more than Mount Olympus, and the Cornish imperfection comes with a vengeance in the spring. Then there is the mischief to pay. The river breaks up and floods the roads, the snow melts, and mud is everywhere. So, notwithstanding an occasional divine day, the desire at this time to escape, and to escape south, develops into an obsession."[9]

Another reference to the joys of mud season involves several important side issues of Saint-Gaudens's life and career. It exists in a letter written to Stanford White on May 7, 1906. White was a close friend and collaborator, but the *Diana* caused a major controversy. The statue was to serve as a weathervane on top of the Madison Square Tower, thus making it New York City's highest point. The installation of the slim, nude statue, poised with her bow and arrow high above the city and with her exquisite proportions shimmering in the sun, caused a furor. Traffic in the area increased; Anthony Comstock, secretary and special agent of the New York Society for the Suppression of Vice called out his cohorts in outrage; children either were not allowed to enter a nearby park or were rushed through it by a nurse or a concerned adult. Although the storm of protest had abated by 1906, the name of Saint-Gaudens was forever linked in the minds of many with the *Diana* scandal.

Thus, it was in this context that he wrote White on May 7, 1906. This was six weeks before Saint-Gaudens learned that Harry Thaw (whose name sounds odd in this context), jealous over White's relationship with Evelyn Nesbit, had murdered White while he was attending a production at Madison Square Garden's roof garden stage. Saint-Gaudens playfully chastises his dear friend and collaborator: "as to your visit here, I have been trying to get you up here for twenty years and no signs of you and Charles [McKim]. Yet now when we are having the worst spring that ever occurred (the roads are in awful condition) you want to come up in five minutes. You hold off a little while and I will let you know, perhaps in a couple of weeks from now."[10]

This letter also raises another issue in the life of Saint-Gaudens because it offers an interesting example of the frequently mentioned fiddling with his *Reminiscences*. When he was editing his father's memoirs, Homer Saint-Gaudens, perhaps in the interest of decorum, omitted a sentence that he saw fit to include when, at a later date, he also edited Stanford White's letters. Augustus Saint-Gaudens continues his letter of May 7, "But come to think of it, our friend Ethel Barrymore is coming up here. Perhaps that's the reason you old suckers want to come."[11]

Winter in Cornish, on the other hand, evokes genuine pleasure—even the exuberance of childhood. Experiencing his first full winter in Cornish, Saint-Gaudens on January 19, 1901, writes Will Low, his friend, the painter and naturalist, "I would never have believed it nor do I suppose you will believe me now, but I am enjoying the rigorous young winter up here keenly, snow all over, sun brilliant and supreme, sleighs, sleigh bells galore, and a cheerfulness that brings back visions of the halcyon winter days of my boyhood. Last night, the thermometer was fourteen degrees below zero and I slept with my windows open, and now at noon it has grown colder. But withal one suffers infinitely less from cold than in hellish, torn-up but dear old New York, or in slush-ridden Paris."[12] Later, recalling that same winter, he writes:

> I soon learned that this season in the North Country, instead of being one of gloom and slush so dreaded by the inhabitants of large cities, was one of cheerfulness and lightness of spirit. . . . But for my first winter in Cornish I was deeply impressed and delighted by its exhilaration and brilliancy, its unexpected joyousness, the sleigh-riding, the skating, and what not. I was as happy as a child. I threw myself into the northern life and reveled in it as keenly as I did in the dancing in the moonlight in Lispenard Street[13] when I was a boy; especially when, skating once more after thirty-five years and playing hockey like a boy, I was knocked down twice, receiving a magnificent black eye the first time and swelled and cut forehead the second. In these I took great pride. But without my work, assistants and congenial neighbors I could not have borne a winter in the cold country. To me, after all, Nature no matter how superb, when it lacks the human element lacks the vital thing.[14]

This last sentence, although not written as a statement of his aesthetics, certainly says pithily what he sought to achieve—an imitation of nature—and how he chose to have it measured—by the vitality of the human element.

Hockey and ice skating also figure large in his letters about the delights of winter. In one to Homer while his son was at Harvard College, Saint-Gaudens writes "Apropos of sport, I had a surprise the other day while playing hockey, with G. F. on the opposite side. I was skating in front of him without touching him in order to prevent his getting at the puck when he deliberately bucked me and knocked me down, which created mixed feelings of anger and pleasure, pleasure at being considered youthful enough to be handled in that way, and anger at the absence of proper respect shown for maturer years! He said he had a right to do that when a person interfered. Fraser and Jaegers say he doesn't know that what I was doing was all right, but that he would have been put out of a regular game for such a proceeding. Rather a complimentary shock on the whole."[15] And in December of 1903, he emphasizes his enjoyment of winter sports to Alfred Garnier: "We skate and I play games upon the ice as I played them thirty-seven years ago, a little more stiffly, but that does not make any difference since I am still feeling young." With only four years to live, he appreciates that "Now, above all, the clear and joyous weather gives a gaiety of a singular fashion, a fashion of which those who have not experienced the cold dryness of the North can have no idea. It is far from the terrible, black, sad days of the winters of London, and Paris, and even New York, where rain and clouds are dominant. Although it is very cold here, I invariably suffer a great deal more from cold on my journeys to New York."[16]

His enthusiasm for winter sports was so great that Saint-Gaudens had a long toboggan slide built at "Aspet." He writes Homer, "The toboggan will soon be forthcoming, I hope. The slide is erected about ten feet higher than the other, and has an alarming look."[17] Later, after his father's death, Homer wrote an article for *Country Life in America* in which he describes how a slide could be constructed and simultaneously gives us a clue to understanding how much it must have meant to his father. He begins quite factually: "A toboggan slide, perhaps 2,000 feet long, down a hill with a moderate fall of 100 feet, and with a moderate chute of 135 feet long with a drop of 40 feet, needs some snow, much cold weather, a good scow, the services of one man and part services of a horse, about $200 outlay at the start, and about $150 a year for maintenance." After a page of nuts-and-bolts details, he comments that "since all people enjoy the mysterious, the slide should not be too obvious in its course." Furthermore, once the toboggan is on the slide, "there is

Figure 138.

no absolute method of guiding a toboggan. Every man must use his own ingenuity . . . every man will find that his own individuality must come into play in reaching the bottom of the slide." The implied test here is emphasized in the assertion that the trip should not be a "placid" one; "the toboggan slide should never be too accurate." Now, in a vein similar to his father's penchant for roughing it up on the ice, we get a better sense of the thrills and chills: "Half of the fun lies in the knowledge that if the man on the rear does not mind his business, the other passengers will never reach the foot of the slide right side up. Therefore, it should be seen to that the course is such as to give an occasional spill, but care should also be taken that nothing but soft snow stretches for some distance on either side of the track." Then, with perhaps a touch of his father's droll humor, he closes by

Figure 139.

commenting, "though it is desirable for the owner of the slide to tumble his guests about a bit, he will find that if he cuts their lips or damages their eyes, his supply of visitors will soon give out."[18] It is his father's newly found enjoyment of the outdoors, especially in wintertime, that causes Homer to quote his father as saying, "'Play, play! . . . I wish I'd played more when I was young. I took

Figure 140. *The workshop of Augustus Saint-Gaudens in 1901 showing a group of people in front of the Sher-man Monument, unveiled in 1903. Among those pictured are: James Earle Fraser, second from the left; Saint-Gaudens, third from the left; Henry Hering, fifth from the left; Harry Thrasher, sixth from the left; and Elsie Ward, the woman on the right.*

things too seriously.' Whereupon, if some one asked him if he was not satisfied with the result of taking things seriously, he would say half in fun: 'No. Look at these awful bronzes all over the country. The thing to do is to play more and to flirt more.' "[19]

During these final years of Saint-Gaudens at Cornish, two significant events occurred; only at one of them could he have been able to "play more" and "flirt more." The first one admitted of no enjoyment whatsoever: the fire in his larger studio in October of 1904. There are two existing newspaper accounts of the disaster; both of them are interesting for their local perspective on the disaster. The longer of the two articles leads off with a damage estimate and the insurance value of the fire and then refers to some of the irreplaceable items lost, "nearly all of Mr. St. Gaudens' drawings, carbon reprints, etchings and paintings, representing the artistic work and conception of years, were in the studio and were burned, with the clay models of the Lincoln and Parnell statues, bas reliefs of noted personages, medallions, plaster casts and work in all stages of progress." A later paragraph reads in its entirety: "A valuable horse, Admi-

Figure 141. *The* Shaw Memorial, *begun in 1884 and unveiled in 1897.*

ral, cow and some hens perished in the flames, and about 20 cords of wood and several tons of coal were burned. The models of an equestrian statue of Gen. W. T. Sherman was in the barn, beside a valuable lot of antique furniture." The reporter notes of the Lincoln lost, the one "to be set up on the steps of a library building in Chicago," that "only the head and hands" were saved; "the legs were destroyed and these will be extremely difficult to reproduce because the best model of the long and lank Lincoln, Amos Bixby of this town, is dead." The briefer account also has its local perspective. Referring to "one of the most disastrous fires in recent years in this vicinity," it begins with an allusion to the loss of "many valuable pieces of work"; it immediately continues with "A barn and other outbuildings with their contents were also burned. The fire was first discovered in the barn about 8 p.m. by a neighbor, and was then under such headway that it was found impossible to save a horse and cow stabled there, and a number of hens in a building attached thereto." It is only at this point that the article specifies some of the valuable statues lost as well as "models, medallions, designs and plans, the work of a lifetime."[20]

The second significant event in Cornish was a considerably happier occasion: the presentation on June 22, 1905, of *A Masque of "Ours": The Gods and the Golden Bowl* to commemorate the twentieth anniversary of the couple's presence in Cornish. There are many valuable contemporary accounts of this exciting evening, from the *Reminiscences,* Frances Grimes, Percy MacKaye, Marion MacKaye, and Kenyon Cox, but the one in the local newspaper is significant for its tone of pride as well as wonder. The article leads off by asserting that "probably one of the most uniquely beautiful and artistic events of the kind ever planned and carried out in this country took place in Cornish." The invitations, issued after "recent rains compelled several postponements," enjoined all to bring their own hitch ropes with them. "The guests began to assemble toward the lower end of the long, sweeping lawn that slopes gently to the westward from the Saint-Gaudens home." The couple, though hosts to the event, "were the guests of honor and were ignorant both of the plot and details of the play," written by Louis Evan Shipman. The reporter, H. L. Canfield, then summarizes the plot, although he was apparently unimpressed with Maxfield Parrish's mechanical wizardry as Chiron:

> Soon music was heard for an orchestra [led by Arthur Whiting] hid from view by the foliage. The curtains parted sufficiently to admit the form of a young woman [Frances Grimes, as Iris] clad in Grecian robes, who recited the prologue [written by Percy MacKaye]. Then the curtains were thrown back and presented to view a most entrancing scene,—tall Greek columns on either side, and between them at the back of the stage-space an altar. Jupiter [John Blair, a famous Broadway actor] enters, who summons Mercury [Percy MacKaye] to notify the gods to assemble. He goes and brings one after another, each one being announced by the messenger and each advancing as from the clouds and vapor. The gods, the fates, the muses assembled, in rush troupes of satyrs, fauns, dryads, bacchantes and nymphs. Then Jupiter astonishes all by resigning his place among the gods, and a contest at once ensues between Pluto [Kenyon Cox] and Neptune [Frances Slade], who aspire to his place. Jupiter, unable to settle the quarrel, requests Minerva [Ellen Shipman] to decide the case. She declares her inability to reach a decision without first having looked into the golden bowl. Advancing to the altar, many-colored vapors surrounding it and the capitals of the columns, she received from Fame [Miss Kennedy] the golden bowl. Looking into its depths, her face lightens. With slow, majestic tread, she returns from the altar, but instead of taking her former position proceeds toward the audience and places the bowl in the hands of the astonished guest of honor, declaring him to be the worthy successor of Jove. Thereupon players and audiences set up a tumultuous shout. A chariot is brought forth, the guest of honor placed in it, and drawn at the head of a long procession of picturesque citizens of the mythological world, all wend their way to the great sculptor's studio.

The final paragraph of the article attempts to put the event into both a local and national perspective:

> Probably nothing of the sort ever attempted in this country has approached this little drama in respect of its historical and mythological accuracy, the beauty and artistic correctness of its costuming and the pervasive and irresistible charm of its sylvan setting. The tall, over-arching trees, the splashing of the brook in the ravine below, old Ascutney, mantled in imperishable blue, keeping watch and ward over all, and just at the climax of the play and casting a glory upon the retreating procession, the burst of golden light from the sun sinking behind the western hills, made a picture never to be forgotten. And when one adds to all this beauty of scene, the admiration and love for

the great man and artist that prompted all these plans and the supreme kindliness and good will that pervaded the execution of them all, the glory is intensified and the heart is thrilled.[21]

Clearly the sculptor's heart was "thrilled" too. It is interesting that as he summarizes the event, he draws on ideas that have been already noticed in his Cornish-based correspondence: Greece, nature, and neighbors. At the end of the *Reminiscences,* he remarks, "As the play ended and the performers followed the chariot up to the house in their classic dresses, all bathed in a wonderful sunset, it was a spectacle and a recall of Greece of which I have dreamed, but have never thought actually to see in Nature. It closed with a ball which marked the opening of the new studio built to replace the one destroyed by fire, and if anything can console me for the destruction that happened then, it was the beauty of the day and occurrence, and the great-hearted friendliness of the neighbors."[22]

Slightly more than two years after this consoling spectacle, Saint-Gaudens was dead. "In his life in Cornish, Saint-Gaudens drew around him many friends of artistic and literary repute, and his beautiful home, 'Aspet,' with his numerous little studios has for many years been the Mecca of the world of sculpture in America, and that it should be *there* that the hand which touched the clay and marble into life became still, was the wish of Augustus Saint-Gaudens."[23] Another poignant account will also touch all who know Cornish. On stationery belonging to Saint-Gaudens, Witter Bynner wrote a letter to Barry Faulkner a week before Saint-Gaudens died. At the end of it he says, "The last talk I had with him was while we watched a great stormy surge of clouds over Ascutney give way at their base to a low level opening of orange light,—chaos pacified. He was saying that if he were able, he would move again, away from the city-people invading Cornish and find another remote country place. After my exclamations on the sunset, that was his quiet comment. . . . He would not have died, I am convinced, so long as any of the great ideas had been reasonably near completion and not to his satisfaction."[24]

It is true that even this localized examination of the career of Augustus Saint-Gaudens has not clarified all that remains enigmatic about the man and his career. But it ought to deal with what, in Witter Bynner's words, "his satisfaction" might mean. What were his standards for assessing artistic achievement? Rose Nichols, who spent the summer of 1889 in "Aspet" while her uncle and aunt were in Europe, took it upon herself both to urge her uncle to begin his *Reminiscences* in 1900, while he was recuperating in a Boston hospital, and to edit some of her uncle's "familiar letters." Sometimes she comes to grips overtly with his aesthetics, as when she states that "the motto which he wished to place in his studio, will be seen to express the spirit of his life": "Le Coeur au Métier," the devotion of "the Heart to the Craft."[25] Sometimes she approaches the question covertly through passages in the letters. For example, she cites two occasions on which he writes about reading Leo Tolstoy's *What is Art?*, written in 1896: "I am in for reading it. You read it too, please, and tell me what you think of it, then I'll sign it and send it as my opinion! For I have no opinion, or so many that trying to put them into shape would result in driving me into the madhouse sooner than I am naturally destined to be there. . . . After all, we are like lots of microscopical microbes on this infinitesimal ball in space, and all these dis-

Figure 142. *Studio of the Caryatids, which burned down in 1944.*

cussions seem humorous at times. I suppose that every earnest effort toward great sincerity or honesty or beauty in one's production is a drop added to the ocean of evolution, to the Something higher that I suppose we are rising slowly (d___d slowly) to, and all the other discussions upon the subject seem simply one way of helping the seriousness of it all."[26] On another occasion Tolstoy elicited this characteristic outburst: "Lately I have been finishing Tolstoi's Art book to see if I should reply. I will not. He goes too far. It would take too much time and I would say some damphool thing. It has given me, however, a great admiration for Tolstoi's character, his sincerity and kindness of heart, but there are things in heaven and earth not dreamed of in his or anybody's philosophy, and the meaning of art is one of them."[27]

Rose Nichols comes closer to providing us with a brief statement of his aesthetics when she quotes him in a letter written from the Players Club on January 26, 1897. He is discussing reactions to the "symbolic figure hovering above Colonel Shaw and his men." Saint-Gaudens writes, "I still think that a figure, if well done in that relation to the rest of the scheme, is a fine thing to do. The Greeks and Romans did it finely in their sculpture. After all it's the *way* the thing's done that makes it right or wrong, that's about the only creed I have in art."[28] The similarity of this remark to one found in a note on his desk after he died gives it the stamp of being his final word. "You can do anything you please, it's the way it's done that makes the difference."[29]

Would it not be safe to say that Cornish provided Augustus Saint-Gaudens with relief from the tense, competitive world of landing commissions and then executing them? With a glance at one of his letters about a winter in Cornish, would it not be safe to say that its nature, plus the vital addition of the human element of his neighbors, helped him to arrive at the proper *way* to make his art right, to reveal the idea or conception already present in the material and thus fulfill his role as an artist?

AUGUSTA FISHER HOMER SAINT-GAUDENS, CORNISH,
AND THE LEGACY OF AUGUSTUS SAINT-GAUDENS

The legacy of Saint-Gaudens to Cornish, and to America, for that matter, is in large part a result of his wife, Augusta Fisher Homer Saint-Gaudens. Nevertheless, fewer lines in the *Reminiscences* are devoted to her than to descriptions of Cornish. Several of those that do exist suggest her husband's love and admiration for her. During the last two years of his life, he was at work on a bronze relief medallion of her. "My father worked last with his own hands at a time when he could no longer stand, nor, indeed, labor for many consecutive minutes."[30] She was not, however, everyone's favorite person. There is no question that hers was a prickly personality. But for all her private and public humiliations, she remained dedicatedly loyal to her husband. One quick snatch of conversation is telling. At the high point in *A Masque of "Ours": The Gods and the Golden Bowl,* just as the triumphant couple is about to be carried off to the ball in the chariot, she was heard to say, "Mind the paint, Gus, it's fresh."[31] It sounds as though a mother were talking to a child. For all our awareness of the power and importance of maternal love, the object of such concern is bound to chafe at it. And such was the relationship of the two.

Born to a prominent Boston family, Augusta was in Rome perfecting her drawing and painting skills when she first met Saint-Gaudens. Their courtship lasted four years because her family wanted her husband to have the security of a major commission before they settled on a wedding date. The awarding of the *Farragut Monument* in late 1876 resulted in a June wedding in 1877. Throughout her life, however, Augusta was plagued with severe deafness and a tendency to hypochondria. She was fond of hibernating for her conditions, so the pair gradually developed the habit of living separate lives, especially after 1883 when their son Homer was three years old and could accompany his mother on jaunts in both summer and winter. Augusta, unlike her husband, saw much more promise in "Huggin's Folly." It no doubt offered her a respite from their hectic life. She oversaw its refurbishing and was its skillful manager when the couple was in residence there. As far as she was concerned, it was an ideal place for Augustus to be during the final years of his long illness. Barry Faulkner and Frances Grimes, who knew her at the Cornish studios, both testify to the difficulty of dealing with her. Yet, after "the Saint's" death, Grimes indicated a change of heart in a letter to Faulkner: "You would be interested in what a personage Mrs. SG has become—a huge sombre figure—she looms up in front of the artistic world . . . black and potent . . . she is like some fate Mr. SG himself might have set in motion striding along carrying his laurels—it is terrific."[32]

Augusta took immediate steps to preserve her husband's memory. First, she arranged for the altar and columns used in *A Masque of "Ours": The Gods and the Golden Bowl* to be refashioned in marble. McKim, Mead, and White designed these into the Greek Temple, to enclose his funeral urn, on the grounds on what was to become the Saint-Gaudens National Historic Site. That was her second project, although it had its beginnings as the Saint-Gaudens Memorial. She and Homer deeded "Aspet" to a board of trustees which in turn persuaded the New Hampshire legislature

Figure 143. *Augusta Saint-Gaudens in the garden at Aspet.*

to establish the memorial in 1919. At her death in July of 1926, Royal Cortissoz, who was the art critic for the *New York Herald Tribune* and the author of a monograph about her husband, wrote that Augusta Saint-Gaudens "leaves a work of art behind her . . . the memorial to him which she and her son created out of his Cornish house and studi[o]s . . . it is given to few women to do what [she] did—to build a monument enshrining the very atmosphere in which an artist lived and breathed and had his being."[33] Soon after her death, there was a nationwide subscription to raise an endowment of $100,000 to provide for the memorial's maintenance. The *Manchester Union* could lament that, by the end of July 1926, "only $30,000 has thus far been subscribed and all of this except $125 by non-residents of New Hampshire." A final appeal was issued in November, at which point New Hampshire had contributed but 8 percent of the total "sum that has come from the country as a whole."[34] Fortunately, the full sum was raised by 1933 and the corporation governing the memorial was able to continue its work. Thirty years later, in 1964, Congress authorized the National Park Service to accept the property as a gift and it was designated a National Historic Site in 1965. Thus, Augusta's legacy is preserved for a grateful town and nation to cherish.

VIRGINIA COLBY'S PERSONAL RECOLLECTION

In 1985, Stan Colby and I answered the call for extras by New York film maker Ted Timreck who was in Cornish filming the masque, *The Gods and The Golden Bowl* for a television production.

We responded to the call mainly because I had a collection of gay nineties clothes which had belonged to my grandparents. I wore a long black taffeta skirt, black blouse, pink shawl with very long fringe, and carried a fan made of pink ostrich plumes. My black velvet hat had a wide brim which was trimmed with large black ostrich plumes. (Ernest Harold Baynes would not have approved.) Stan, on the other hand, was nattily attired in a black derby. When the costume director looked him over, he was told to remove his belt and add suspenders. Stan was issued a wide green striped tie and a beige jacket two sizes too large. He really looked like a carnival huckster.

We were told to wear *exactly* the same outfit each time we came and to be available for filming all during the week. Once we were requested to come in full costume at 9:00 in the evening to do a scene on the porch of the studio with the Japanese lanterns. The setting was beautiful. However, we felt sorry for the nymphs who were in bare feet and scanty costumes as the temperature dropped into the 40s.

There were many sessions of "hurry up and wait." Wait while everyone got properly costumed—some of the ladies had to have their hair done—and everyone had to be approved by the costume director. The costume tent was very well equipped—wooden platform to stand on while having a skirt hung, sewing machine, mirrors, clothes racks full of period dresses and jackets, hat boxes galore, ironing boards, hair dressing section—as well as helpful people to do the necessary tasks. The second tent was full of the camera crew's equipment: flood lights, extension cords, ladders—all kinds of paraphernalia. The third tent was the food tent. Fresh coffee or cold soda was always available along with assorted snacks and fruit. At meal times the caterer's truck would arrive with a wide selection of hot and cold dishes, salads, breads, and desserts. The fourth tent was where we did our "hurry up and waiting." As John Dryfhout, the director of the Saint-Gaudens National Historic Site, commented, "Welcome to tent city."

It was fun to watch the crew work, and we had plenty of time for that. I soon discovered I could tuck my little Instamatic camera under my shawl and during "waiting" times I was able to get some good pictures of the crew in action.

ENDNOTES

1. As quoted in Burke Wilkinson, *Uncommon Clay: The Life and Works of Augustus Saint-Gaudens* (New York: Harcourt Brace Jovanovich, 1985), p. 359.

2. Editorial, *Century Illustrated Monthly* Magazine, June 1897; quoted in John H. Dryfhout, *The Work of Augustus Saint-Gaudens* (Hanover, NH: University Press of New England, 1982), p. 35.

3. Michelangelo's sonnet, poem #151, in the annotated translation of James M. Saslow, *The Poetry of Michelangelo* (New Haven: Yale University Press, 1991), p. 302.

4. Another local model was Lyndon S. Smith. He is identified as being born on August 8, 1872, "a veterinary surgeon and lives in West Virginia," William H. Child, *A History of the Town of Cornish with Genealogical Record: 1763-1910* (Concord, NH: The Rumford Press, 1911?), Vol. 2, p. 333. An undated and unidentified local newspaper clipping proudly notes that "Lyndon Smith of Cornish posed for the modelling of Col. Shaw, as he appears in marble in the [Boston] common. We continue to absorb all the noted artists and sculptors of America. After traveling the world over, they know a good thing when they see it—and naturally this locality is the finest," Albert K. Read, III's scrapbook, Virginia Colby, Cornish Colony files.

5. *The Reminiscences of Augustus Saint-Gaudens,* edited and amplified by Homer Saint-Gaudens (New York: Century Company, 1913), Vol. 1, pp. 312, 316. For more on Saint-Gaudens locally, see Jerold Wikoff, *The Upper Valley: An Illustrated Tour Along the Connecticut River Before the Twentieth Century* (Chelsea, VT: Chelsea Green Publishing Company, 1985), pp. 160-167, 177-180.

6. Ibid, Vol. 1, p. 318.

7. A good comparison can be made between the letters from Cornish, about to be quoted, and the "familiar letters" his niece Rose Standish Nichols edited in *McClures Magazine* 31:6, October 1908, pp. 603-615, and 32:1, November 1908, pp. 1-16, especially pages 7-9.

8. *Reminiscences,* vol. 2, p. 237.

9. Ibid., Vol. 2, pp. 227-228.

10. Ibid., Vol. 2, p. 251.

11. Wilkinson, p. 361, based on Homer Saint-Gaudens, ed., "Intimate Letters of Stanford White," Third Installment, *The Architectural Record,* October 1911, p. 404. Wilkinson comments, "The slight testiness here may be accounted for by a feeling on Saint-Gaudens's part that the two boon companions suspected how sick he really was and were coming to say goodbye."

12. *Reminiscences,* Vol. 2, pp. 233-234.

13. In the early 1850s his father, Bernard Saint-Gaudens, owned a building on this street in New York City, where the family lived and he had a cobbler's shop.

14. *Reminiscences,* Vol. 2, pp. 227-228.

15. Ibid., vol. 2, pp. 238-239. Fraser and Jaegers were two of his assistants; see above pp. 200-202 for Fraser and p. 222 for Jaegers. "G. F." is unidentified; he may be a studio assistant or a local person who enjoyed hockey.

16. Ibid., Vol. 2, p. 235; Saint-Gaudens is going to New York for cancer treatments.

17. Ibid., Vol. 2, p. 238.

18. Homer Saint-Gaudens, "A Private Toboggan Slide," *Country Life in America* 13, Janu-

ary 1908, pp. 312-313.

19. *Reminiscences,* Vol. 2, p. 231.

20. Unidentified newspaper clippings, Virginia Colby, Cornish Colony files.

21. Unidentified newspaper clipping, Virginia Colby, Cornish Colony files; for Marion MacKaye's version of this event, see above pp. 262-263.

22. *Reminiscences,* Vol. 2, p. 352.

23. William H. Child, *History of Cornish,* Vol. 1, p. 334. For how photography helped Saint-Gaudens touch "the clay and marble into life," see below p. 478.

24. Saint-Gaudens Collections, Baker Library, Dartmouth College, Hanover, NH; see also Wilkinson, p. 369, based on an unpublished letter, courtesy of the Witter Bynner Foundation for Poetry.

25. *McClures Magazine* 31:6, October 1908, p. 603.

26. Ibid., p. 615.

27. *McClures Magazine,* 32:1, November 1908, p. 5, with an allusion to Hamlet's remark to Horatio, *Hamlet,* I, v, 166.

28. *McClures Magazine* 31:6, October 1908, p. 605. For William Vaughn Moody's thoughts on the Shaw Memorial, see above pp. 281-282.

29. As quoted in Wilkinson, p. xvi.

30. *Reminiscences,* Vol. 2, p. 353.

31. Wilkinson, p. 337, based on "Cornish lore from several sources" (p. 409).

32. Ibid., p. 374; Wilkinson also notes that Maxfield Parrish's wife Lydia was a supporter of Augusta and thought she "put up with a good deal," p. 330.

33. *New York Herald Tribune,* June 8, 1926; Virginia Colby, Cornish Colony files.

34. Newspaper clippings, July 23 and November 8, 1926; Virginia Colby, Cornish Colony files.

HOMER SAINT-GAUDENS
1880 – 1958

and

CARLOTA DOLLEY SAINT-GAUDENS
1884 – 1927

HOMER SAINT-GAUDENS

BORN SEPTEMBER 29, 1880, HOMER SCHIFF SAINT-GAUDENS was the only child of Augustus and Augusta Homer Saint-Gaudens. His middle name was in honor of Dr. Henry Shiff, an influential friend and companion during Augustus Saint-Gaudens's early days in Rome. The child was christened Homer in honor of Augusta's father Thomas J. Homer, but his name has a ring of familiarity to it: first because of its association with Winslow Homer, a cousin of Augusta's,[1] and second because of its link to Louise Homer, the famous turn-of-the-century contralto, who married Augusta's first cousin, the composer Sidney Homer. For all the dither surrounding his name, Homer Saint-Gaudens made a name for himself as an author and museum director. He became assistant director of the Carnegie Institute's Gallery of Art in Pittsburgh in 1922 and its director from 1923 to 1950.[2] He was also important to the history of Cornish art because he was a founder and a director of the Saint-Gaudens Memorial, now the Saint-Gaudens National Historic Site.

As a child, he would accompany his mother on her frequent summer trips to Nova Scotia—and elsewhere—when she would try to regain her health. Both parents regarded him as a difficult child. But "because of the many trips away from his father, he was very much of a mother's boy. Robust and headstrong, he was already becoming what he would be all his life, 'difficult but never quite impossible.'"[3] Consequently, his relationship with his father was a strained one. It is clear, however, that later in his life Homer and his father had a reconciliation. Homer's description of Augustus's reaction to Bernard Saint-Gaudens's death—Augustus's father died in 1893—tells us a great deal about how Homer came to feel about his own father: "I was too young to notice the extent of this love during Bernard Saint-Gaudens' life-time, but I have a most vivid recollection of the blow that fell upon Augustus Saint-Gaudens when his father died. For he took me that night to the barnlike Thirty-sixth Street studio and there, lighting one feeble gas-jet, walked sobbing back and forth, in and out of the black shadows, telling to my young, uncomprehending ears all that his father had meant to him."[4] Visible evidence of Homer's father's love for him can be seen in the bronze relief, done in 1882, and a plaster bust, also a relief, done three years later when Homer was five years old.[5]

One person who may have played a part in effecting this reconciliation between father and son was Barry Faulkner. He and Homer entered Harvard College in 1899, "the beginning of our long and troubled association."[6] Eventually Augustus hired Faulkner on as an assistant, more for his ability and less because he was Homer's friend, so Faulkner came to know the entire family—and the "extended" family of the studio.[7] Whether or not the "family" connection helped to bring the two together, Faulkner continued his friendship with Homer. Later, during World War I. Homer commanded the camouflage corps of the 40th Engineers. He rose to the rank of lieutenant colonel, was awarded a Bronze Star, and was hailed for his ability to arrange daubs of color on military equipment so that they were concealed from the enemy. Faulkner served under him. But even given their friendship, Faulkner was obliged to note that Homer was "intensely disliked by the men."[8] On the other hand, Homer Saint-Gaudens's address to the Cornish Memorial Day celebration in 1919 frequently referred to the bravery of the men in his unit, especially Lieutenant Harry Thrasher (see below pp. 413-417) and other men from New Hampshire: "every man wearing the khaki had a share in winning the war whether in the front lines pulling the trigger of a gun, or a clerk in a camp."[9]

In his youth, Homer worked in New York on several periodicals and later served as the assistant stage manager for the actress Maude Adams,[10] but in 1906 he returned to Cornish to help manage his father's studio. His writing experience, however, proved very useful to him—and to the world. In 1943, he brought out *The American Artist and His Times*. He was proud of this study because he believed he succeeded in writing a no-nonsense history of American art and in removing that history "from the mouths of professionals" with their "art-pregnant language."[11] But two of his other writings are significant from a Cornish point of view. The first was the major task of his early life: editing and amplifying the two volumes of his father's *Reminiscences*. Knowing full well that he was dying, Augustus had begun them during the last years of his life. It took Homer six years to do the job properly; they were published in 1913.[12]

During this same period, while Homer was still in his late twenties, he wrote a chapter on "'City Folks' in Cornish" for Child's *History of Cornish* published probably in 1911. Thus he fulfilled his second commitment to Cornish with his writing. Because it is a summary by a contemporary not only of what motivated people to come to Cornish in the first place but also of the gradual shift in the type of person who did come, it is an important document for us today. His description of the countryside is one about which we need constant reminders. Who would not be attracted by the following account? And who could not but second its implied warning? A nine-hour trip by train from New York City would have discouraged most potential visitors "had not the peace and dreamlike ripeness of the hills, with their dark clumps of trees and the river winding south before the mountain, called strongly to these artists who desired a simple living . . . Yet sadly enough through their very coming, the beauty of out-rolling pasture slopes, dotted with round-topped maples and quartz outcrops, is beginning to lose its charm. For as the 'City Folks' have bought the mowings and the pastures and have no longer tilled them or allowed stock to graze upon them, the land which they admired, through their own neglect, is rapidly reverting to that unshorn appearance from which they fled."[13]

The other important feature of this essay is his discussion of the differences in the types of people who came. The original "city folks" of "little New York" were artists who came because they "desired a simple living" and were "simple in their tastes." "From 1895 on, however, the Cornish 'Little New York' began to assume a more fashionable atmosphere, with somewhat pretentious elements creeping in . . . the newcomers have given the region a literary turn which is supplanting the artistic one."[14]

In the last two paragraphs of his chapter in Child's *History*, Homer touches on a significant issue. One can hear its delicacy in his treatment of it. He acknowledges that there has been some tension in the community: "For though, since the beginning, a desire to be friendly has lain dormant in farmers and 'City Folks,' yet the difference of inherited ideas has made it hard for the two groups to recognize the good qualities in one another and to tolerate their quite unconscious stepping on one another's toes." The fact that an increasing number among the "little New York" population choose to stay in Cornish most of the year is an optimistic sign because they "are vitally anxious for the good of the community. The remaining shyness which exists in both groups will surely wear away in the near future. Many of the 'City Folks' would be only too glad to lend their best efforts in town and school meetings or in the Grange, if they had the chance which they are somewhat too diffident to ask for. Many of those who have always been here, while glad to welcome the 'City Folks' into their circles, dread risking the snub which they feel might follow the offer. And year by year the barriers are falling."[15] Happily, Homer Saint-Gaudens has been proven accurate in his prophecy.

Nevertheless, he was rarely in Cornish to see its fulfillment. While still in Pittsburgh at the Carnegie Institute's Gallery of Art, his first wife, Carlota, died in 1927. In 1929, he married Mary McBride. The couple moved to Cutler, Florida, in 1950 where Homer Saint-Gaudens died on December 8, 1958, of an apparent heart attack.

CARLOTA DOLLEY SAINT-GAUDENS

CARLOTA DOLLEY SAINT-GAUDENS made her mark in the art world as a painter of miniatures and watercolors.[16] She was a member of the American Society of Miniature Painters, one of whose founding members was Lucia Fairchild Fuller. Later, once Carlota came to Cornish, Lucia Fuller became Carlota's instructor in miniatures. As a young woman, Carlota studied painting at the Pennsylvania Academy of the Fine Arts in Philadelphia and the Art Students League in New York.

Again, Barry Faulkner is a valuable source of information about this side of the family. "Homer Saint-Gaudens, Witter Bynner and other friends were often at my family's summer place at Silver Lake near Chesham [New Hampshire], and it was here that Homer met Carlota Dolley. In June 1905, they were married. Carlota's father, Dr. Charles Dolley of Swarthmore College, and his family spent the summer nearby at Nelson on a hillside overlooking the lake. Carlota, blonde, handsome and Junoesque, had attracted scores of eager young admirers before Homer triumphed."[17] Furthermore, Faulkner painted a tempera painting, *The Boat*, as a tribute to his two friends.[18]

As for the newly married couple's life in Cornish, Carlota joined the Cornish Equal Suffrage League. Although neither she nor her husband was that fond of living in the country, while in Cornish "she continued to attract a good deal of admiration for her high spirits and her somewhat rebellious nature."[19] At any rate, she was not "rebellious" about her career because, although she originally wanted to paint frescoes, her

Figure 144. Street Scene in Aspet, France *drawn by Carlota Saint-Gaudens, c. 1909.*

father-in-law persuaded her to stick with miniatures. Among those people associated with the Cornish Colony, Carlota painted portraits of Augustus Saint-Gaudens, Percy MacKaye, Witter Bynner, Mary Shipman, the daughter of Louis and Ellen Shipman, and Lewis Johnson, Annetta St. Gaudens's brother.

In Cornish, she lived with her husband and three children—Augustus, Carlota, and Harold, who died in infancy[20]—in "Barberry House," a place that Mrs. Augusta Saint-Gaudens bought for them and that their friend Witter Bynner named for them.[21] The daughter, Carlota, also a painter, married John E. Dodge of Stonington, Connecticut, in 1938; Augustus lived in and near Miami, Florida.

ENDNOTES

1. "I must admit my family rarely saw 'Cousin Winslow.' In those horse-and-buggy days when I was a youngster and he a mature man, his shingled house on the New England coast we regarded as very distant from our New York habitat," Homer Saint-Gaudens, *The American Artist and His Times* (New York: Dodd, Mead, 1941), p. 173.

2. "He is recognized for his special contribution to modern art in his development of the annual international exhibition sponsored by the Carnegie Institute," John H. Dryfhout, *The Work of Augustus Saint-Gaudens* (Hanover, NH: University Press of New England, 1982), p. 126.

3. Burke Wilkinson, *Uncommon Clay: The Life and Works of Augustus Saint-Gaudens* (New York: Harcourt Brace Jovanovich, 1985), p. 166; in his note to this sentence, Wilkinson adds that "this was the consensus" of the "many Cornish residents" he interviewed when researching his biography (p. 396, n. 4).

4. *The Reminiscences of Augustus Saint-Gaudens*, edited and amplified by Homer Saint-Gaudens (New York: Century Company, 1913), Vol. 1, p. 285.

5. Homer and his mother are subjects of a portrait done in 1890 by John Singer Sargent and now in the Museum of Art at Carnegie Institute, Pittsburgh, Pennsylvania.

6. Barry Faulkner, *Barry Faulkner: Sketches from an Artist's Life* (Dublin, NH: William L. Bauhan, 1973), p. 31.

7. On one occasion, Saint-Gaudens told him, "Barry, don't mind what Gussie says, I want you here"; ibid., p. 34.

8. Ibid., p. 110; see below pp. 504-505 for how a friend of his father, Abbott Thayer, relates to the camouflage issue.

9. Scrapbook, George Stowell Library, Cornish, NH; Virginia Colby, Cornish Colony files.

10. Louise Hall Tharp, *Saint-Gaudens and the Gilded Age* (Boston: Little, Brown, and Co., 1969), p. 369.

11. Saint-Gaudens, *The American Artist and His Times*, p. 1.

12. Some critics, however, have reservations about the results: "The son's interpolations are bland and affectionate, and the narrative moves competently until the white-washed, almost wartless figure is done," Wilkinson, p. xii.

13. William H. Child, *History of the Town of Cornish with Genealogical Record: 1763-1910* (Concord, NH: The Rumford Press, 1911?), Vol. 1, p. 220-221.

14. Ibid., pp. 224-225. This description of the type of people who came has been slightly modified by James L. Farley, "The Cornish Colony," *Dartmouth College Library Bulletin*, 14:1, n.s., November 1973, pp. 6-17. His variation on Saint-Gaudens's categories would distinguish the literary figures from the rich professional class; he believed, as did Saint-Gaudens, that the former came in the late 1890s but that the latter's arrival dates from roughly 1905 on.

15. Child, pp. 230-232.

16. There is some question about the spelling of her name; it appears as "Carlota" and "Carlotta." Barry Faulkner spells her name "Carlota" and that is how it appears when she is listed as a member of the Pennsylvania Society of Miniature Painters in 1915; Virginia Colby, Cornish Colony files, which also substantiate this spelling on a signed, hand-painted Christmas card.

17. Faulkner, p. 59. She was descended from Dr. Sarah R. A. Dolley of Rochester, NY, the second woman physician in the United States.

18. It is reproduced in *A Circle of Friends: Art Colonies of Cornish and Dublin,* exhibition catalogue (Durham, NH: University Art Galleries, University of New Hampshire, 1985), p. xi.

19. Wilkinson, p. 338; he also cites "local Cornish lore from various sources" that Carlota was later described as a "bluestocking that had run a little," pp. 338; 409.

20. Harold, whose nickname was Hal, was named after Homer's good friend Witter Bynner, who was affectionately known as "Hal." The child got into some poison in a medicine cabinet. His remains are buried in the "Temple" at the Saint-Gaudens National Historic Site. Witter Bynner, inspired by the boy's death, wrote a play, *The Little King* (1914) and dedicated it to Homer and Carlota Saint-Gaudens.

21. *A Circle of Friends,* p. 136. "The house once belonged to Frank Johnson, a local farmer, who rented the house to the Frenches, the Adamses, the Crolys, and the Shipmans before selling it in 1903 to Augusta Saint-Gaudens."

LOUIS ST. GAUDENS
1854 – 1913

ANNETTA JOHNSON ST. GAUDENS
1869 – 1943

PAUL ST. GAUDENS
1900 – 1954

LOUIS ST. GAUDENS

THIS PARTICULAR FAMILY OF TWO SCULPTORS and a ceramist also offers a few spelling peculiarities to those who seek to learn more about them, but these minor difficulties should not stand in the way of understanding and appreciating their important contributions to American art. Louis preferred that his name be spelled St. Gaudens, not Saint-Gaudens, and Annetta is sometimes identified as "Annette."[1] Both Louis and his wife were very important to Augustus Saint-Gaudens. Louis was "the gifted, erratic brother whom Augustus would love and shepherd all his life," yet "Louis's creative gifts with clay were almost as great as [his brother's], and markedly similar."[2] Annetta, on the other hand, was Augustus's trusted assistant. On March 16, 1901, when he was ill with intestinal cancer and required extra help to complete a mounting number of commissions, he wrote Louis, who was then in Ohio with his wife's family "to come and assist, or even send 'Nettie' alone 'for I believe she could be of serious help.'"[3] A diffident lack of ambition haunted Louis; thus, he spent most of his life in his brother's shadow. Paul, who was proud of his parents' achievements yet intent on proving his own worth, defines the relationship between the two brothers this way: "The brothers were extremely close all their lives. The dynamic, ambitious, red-headed Augustus led the way and the dark, quiet introspective Louis followed."[4]

Louis was born in New York City January 1, 1853, six years after Augustus. In addition to giving some idea of his personality, Marion MacKaye also gives us a thumb-nail sketch of Louis's early biography: "He is extremely modest—tall, quiet, reticent. He told us at length about his life, of how he and his brother had been together for forty years . . . Finally, the two brothers went to Rome where there is much demand for cameo cutting, got a studio, and in their spare time devoted all their energies to sculpture."[5]

A fuller version of that biography would point out that Louis arrived in Rome in 1873, where he worked with his brother; five years later he left for Paris and the Ecole des Beaux-Arts, where he joined his brother and his new bride. While in Paris, Louis married Louisa Lapierre who died in childbirth. Work with his brother in the latter's studios

Figure 145. Agriculture *from Union Station, by Louis St. Gaudens.*

in Paris, New York, and Cornish kept him busy until his marriage to a fellow studio assistant, Annetta Johnson, October 7, 1897. The more important commissions with which Louis assisted include: the idealized bas-reliefs of *Courage* and *Loyalty* on the pedestal of the monument to Admiral Farragut, while it was still in Paris; the decorations for the houses of Cornelius Vanderbilt II and Henry Villard in New York City in 1881; and the *Diana* weathervane for Madison Square Garden.

Louis's most important personal commissions before he came to Cornish were the marble recumbent stone lions in the hall of the main staircase of the Boston Public Library, 1889-1890, an early version of *Piping Pan*, done in 1895, and the figure of *Homer*, the Greek epic poet, in the rotunda of the Library of Congress.[6] The *Piping Pan* was greatly admired by that authoritative critic of many of the Colony's artists, Royal Cortissoz. Its beauty, he writes, "lies partly in its sweetness and grace as an interpretation of the spirit of blithe childhood, and it lies even more in the profound sculptural feeling which went to the making of the statue, in the modelling which is so full of knowledge and strength and is at the same time so subtle, so fine, so instinct with style. It is a little piece, yet the man who made it unmistakably approached sculpture with a certain largeness of view.... On this occasion, if ever in his life, the sculptor was both master and poet. Here he had his one unmistakable gust of creative genius."[7]

Once Louis came to Cornish, he worked on various versions of his brother's *Robert Louis Stevenson* memorial portrait plaque and on the angelic figures on the *George F. Baker Tomb,* a commission to his brother but finished after Augustus's death in 1907 by his atelier. But Louis also received a number of his own commissions to complete while he was living in Cornish. Notable among them was a *Faun,* which he exhibited at the Pan-American Exposition held in Buffalo, New York, in 1901, and for which he received a silver medal. For the Louisiana Purchase Exposition held in Saint Louis in 1904, he was asked to do a statue of *Painting* to complement Daniel Chester French's *Sculpture;* they were to stand on either side of the entrance. The final version was finished by his wife

Annetta and now stands in front of the city's art museum. He also completed a gold medal commemorating the bicentennial of Benjamin Franklin's birth in 1906.

His most ambitious project, however, led indirectly to his death. He was commissioned to sculpt six huge statues seventeen feet high to decorate the facade of the Union Station in Washington, DC, as well as representations of the states of the union as Roman soldiers for the interior waiting room. This enormous task excited considerable local interest, as this newspaper article indicates:

> Louis St. Gaudens was in Northfield [Vermont] last week to superintend the beginning of the work on the heroic statues, which are to surmount the central pavilion of the new Union Station at Washington, DC. They will be six in number, and will be carved from Bethel [Vermont] white granite. The six blocks are the largest of their kind ever quarried in this country. When finished, each statue, cut from the solid stone, will be sixteen feet in height, and will weigh upwards of forty tons. In their rough state, each stone is said to weigh at least eighty tons. The statues will be the largest ever cut in granite, and it will require at least a year to complete them. They are to be representations of Agriculture, Imagination, Mechanics, Freedom, Electricity, and Fire, typifying the elements that have inspired the development of the great modern railways.[8]

The *Boston Globe* added that "models are sent up from Cornish, and when a sufficiently large block is taken from the quarry, workmen knock off two or three tons from it and ship it down to the sculptor."[9] During the preparation for these statues, Augustus wrote Louis a letter that shows his admiration: "the figures carried together harmoniously and yet were diversified. They made a bully impression on me, sick as I was, and those you had modified since you sent me the larger drawings were a distinct improvement . . . the 'Fire' was changed and a great deal better. The 'Electricity' struck me as a fine idea, with the electricity at his feet and behind his head; all over, as it were. . . . There is no doubt that the work cannot be too direct, that the large simple lines and planes with strong, dark shadows are the essentials."[10]

Interest in Louis St. Gaudens was high locally as the following bemused "glimpse into the workroom of the sculptor [in] the Cornish hills" indicates: "The walls and floor were of rough, unpainted boards; the windows, on a northern slope of the roof, were without shade or drapery; there was not a chair in the room. It was clearly a place where real work was done. Tools, easels, canvas frameworks, kegs of material unknown to the uninitiated, and figures in wax and plaster were everywhere. In front of a white canvas background stood a colossal figure in wax of the Roman soldier. Mr. St. Gaudens spent nearly a year on it."[11]

But Louis and his wife did not spend all their time in the studio; they were quite active locally, too. They were members of the Cornish Equal Suffrage League, and she was an active member of the Women's Christian Temperance Union.[12] Appropriately enough, Louis was Phidias, a Greek sculptor, in the 1905 production of *A Masque of "Ours": The Gods and the Golden Bowl*.

After visiting Union Station so that he might fulfill a desire to see his statues in the flesh, so to speak, Louis returned to Cornish during a blizzard, caught pneumonia, and died March 8, 1913. Reflecting on Louis's career, Frances Grimes, who collaborated often both with Louis and his brother, wrote that "Augustus sometimes said he thought Louis was more truly an artist than himself and most of us who worked in his studio agreed with this opinion. . . . He felt no necessity to create what he was capable of imagining . . . I think all of us who worked with Louis felt there was lodged in him a knowledge of what was completely right, completely beautiful."[13] Proof that opinion of Louis was high in Cornish can also be seen from these comments in his locally written obituary: "it may fairly be said that, had his brother Augustus been less famous as a sculptor, he himself would probably have been more so. Only since the death of his brother—which also occurred in Cornish, a few years ago—had Louis St. Gaudens won independent recognition of a general character; he having previously worked almost altogether for and under the direction of Augustus. As a worker in marble, however, he was peer of the ablest, and it is no disparagement of his brother's genius to say that Louis must have contributed considerably to the renown of Augustus."[14]

ANNETTA JOHNSON ST. GAUDENS

JUST AS MARION MACKAYE PROVIDED us with a good introduction to Louis St. Gaudens, so she presents a sympathetic picture of an evening with the couple, but with the spotlight on Annetta.

Figure 146. *Louis, Annetta, and Paul at their home in Cornish. Louis preferred to spell his name "St. Gaudens."*

They are very shy people and we are the first of the Colony (some of whom have been here for years) to be asked over . . . we arrived at a veritable frontiersman's hearth. As we went in, there before the huge open fireplace, with its blackened crane and huge black kettle, with the steam sizzling from it, was our dinner—sitting in the ashes—while on the crane with its many hooks hung some more steaming viands. In the ashes and on the crane, it had all been cooked. They live in a very primitive way. Mrs. Louis doing all the work herself . . . Mrs. Louis served the dinner from the hearth. She is very diminutive, so the low serving table was not uncomfortable for her and in fact very becoming to the little nut-like quality of her reticent grace. . . . We found them rare and attractive, and she—who is always so shy and retiring out in company, sitting by herself and never saying a word—was gay and entertaining—telling stories of old southern life.[15]

Annetta was born near Columbus, Ohio, in 1869. She came to New York to study from 1892 until 1894 at the Art Students League under John Twachtman and Augustus Saint-Gaudens. The latter was so impressed with her that he asked her to be his assistant and his brother was charmed enough by her to ask her to marry him. The couple lived in Ohio until 1901 when Augustus required their help in Cornish.

The following year Annetta became interested in the nearby Shaker community of Enfield, New Hampshire. As her brother noted, "at one time there were 500 people in this settlement but she found there were only four men left, and they were all over eighty, and twenty-five women and children."[16] She visited in the community for several days and noticed a meetinghouse built in 1793. "The distinctive lines of its gambrel roof and its purposeful symmetry appealed to her; the outline of the rich blue trim against the flat white paint and plaster captivated her. Annetta and Louis had been looking for a house, and now she had found it."[17] She purchased the building for $150 and decided to dismantle it board by board and to transport the timbers and handmade nails by flatcar from the depot in Enfield to the new site on Dingleton Hill in Cornish—up the hill from "Aspet." "The lumber took two cars piled as high as we were allowed and the granite underpinning which Augustus St. Gaudens used to build the steps from the road up to his yard took another car. The building site was 4 miles and 700 feet higher than Windsor, Vermont. It took us 4 days with two wagons and 4 strong horses to get the lumber up there and the last ½ miles was so steep it took 4 horses to pull one ton."[18] Now the reconstruction job could begin. "With just three men to help, we got the building up and enclosed by Dec. 1st. We finished the roof in a snow storm. The entire cost for moving and reconstructing the building was just $600. Augustus St. Gaudens was so impressed he offered me a good job working for him but no one could get along with his wife and I was told not to try it."[19] The lamentable end to this spirited adventure was a fire that destroyed the building in 1980.

For Annetta, however, the new home and studio were revitalizing; they represented a better opportunity to work on some of Louis's projects and, soon, on her own. One of her earliest tasks in Cornish was work on her husband's commission to create the six monumental statues for the Union Station facade. As a contemporary account noted, she "is of great assistance to her husband in his work. She gets material for her husband by making sketches and studies from which he takes his subjects. In the work for the Washington station, she used college people exclusively for models. She thinks they are much finer than the professional model, and approach very clearly the classic in proportions. For the granite statues outside the building, the figure of Freedom was posed by a New England school teacher. A New England boy, a Dartmouth quarter-miler, now attending the Yale School of Forestry, posed for the figure of Inventive Imagination, while a Princeton student, an all-round athlete, was the model for the Roman soldier."[20]

What interested her most, however, were works she did in relief and in terra cotta miniatures. One work she was proud of was *Salvation*, a relief that Frances Duncan much admired because in it Annetta showed herself to be "one of the first women to express in sculpture what is essentially the woman's attitude toward the great public questions." Proving that Frances Duncan could write about material other than gardens, her interpretive description shows why she believed it to be significant:

Figure 147. Ornis, *polychrome bas-relief by Annetta St. Gaudens, depicting Miss Eleanor Wilson as the Bird Spirit Ornis in Percy Mackay's* Sanctuary: A Bird Masque *(1913).*

"Salvation" is a lunette in bold relief, dominated by the central figure, the Christ, the personification of Love. It is not the Christ most frequently represented in Art—the Christ of infinite patience, of endurance, of meekness, of pitying love for humanity. Instead this relief shows the young, victorious Christ whose wonderful energy and force drove the money changers from the temple. . . . Below it are the two groups, epitomizing the two great evils with which our modern world is grappling. Annetta Saint-Gaudens is, I think, the first to link them, and yet one has probably ruined as many lives and devastated as many homes as the other. In the left-hand group—Militarism—is the mother supporting the body of her wounded or dying soldier-son, and the young wife, or sweetheart, leaning over her shoulder. The mother, the dominating figure of this group, is fine in her dumb acquiescence to sorrow, the strong endurance in which women have for centuries faced this grief. As this group is the mother's, the tragedy in the right-hand group is peculiarly the wife's—the husband shattered and helpless, not by an enemy's bullet, but by drink. Her attitude is pitying and protecting toward the man, but with something also it of passionate revolt against his condition. From over her shoulder, half hiding behind their mother, peer the children, half frightened, half fascinated. Below these groups, like an evil root, is the heavy, sinister, crouching figure Domination by Force, and with it Inherited Privilege, producing on the one hand militarism, and the other the parasitic woman, the mere plaything and idler. . . . This idea of a state and nation freed from the age-old weight of evils, a state in which every citizen's wellbeing is a matter of mutual interest and concern, the idea expressed in Mrs. Saint-Gaudens's sculpture, is held by many a woman citizen.[21]

Annetta's own thoughts on the subject can be read in an article she wrote in the late twenties for the *Claremont Advocate*; it begins, "The world is dying of fear and hate because of the confusion following the World War and the advent of the machine age. This is not the fault of any one person or race, but a huge revolution is in progress, which through tragedy or a change in the world's psychology means a tremendous evolution toward life on a higher plane."[22]

In addition to being involved on a national and international level, she was also concerned with local affairs. This commitment began in 1905 when she played Clotho, the Fate who spins out the thread of life, in the production of *A Masque of "Ours": The Gods and the Golden Bowl*. Perhaps her most important local contribution was the bronze birdbath, in the Meriden Bird Sanctuary, cast to commemorate the production of Percy MacKaye's *Sanctuary, a Bird Masque* in 1913. She also did some bas-reliefs of scenes and of costumed individuals involved in the production as well as portraying Love Bird in the accompanying pantomime.

In 1921, she and her son Paul set up the Orchard Kiln Pottery on their property so that they could fire their works in their own kiln. For her terra cotta miniatures, Annetta used local models Bernice Fitch Johnson and her sister, Laura Fitch Woodward; they often modeled so that their graceful bodies could serve as the handles on pitchers and vases.

Toward the end of her life Annetta moved to Pomona, California, to be with her mother. While there, she taught sculpture at the Chaffey Union High School in nearby Ontario, California. Although she was modest about her level of success, she was convinced that, "if there is ever to be a real American school of sculpture, I believe it will arise in southern California. We have here the people of southern Europe, whose temperament is more suited to creative art than is the average American. Here we have physical freedom. Moreover, many people have or take more leisure here than elsewhere. Art requires leisure."[23] She died in California in 1943 at the age of seventy-three.

PAUL ST. GAUDENS

PAUL ST. GAUDENS was born in Flint, Ohio, in 1900. He attended local schools in Cornish, New Hampshire, and Windsor, Vermont. He first studied at the Museum School of Boston's Museum of Fine Arts and later studied ceramics at three places: with Frank Applegate at the School of Industrial Art at Trenton, New Jersey, with Oscar Lewis Bachelder, whose father had worked in the Bennington potteries,[24] at Omar Khayyam Pottery at Chandler, North Carolina, and with Charles Binns, director of the State School of Ceramics at Alfred, New York.

A master potter, who was admired for his beautiful glazes, Paul's life was governed by his passion for ceramics. He especially wanted to avoid pottery that had a predetermined, commercial quality. When asked by an interviewer why he did not choose sculpture as a profession, following in the footsteps of his father and mother, he said, "I don't think I have just that kind of talent. I've always loved to draw, but I think I should choose pottery because it gives you both form and color to experiment with. And, besides, the mechanical and chemical processes are infinitely fascinating."[25]

Before the Orchard Kiln Pottery was established in Cornish in 1921, he made "pottery in a crude 'ground-lay' kiln under the orchard behind his parents' studio."[26] After

Figure 148. *Vase by Paul St. Gaudens, with relief decoration possibly done by his mother, Annetta.*

1921, he was very proud of his new kiln where "he fired his pieces in a wood-burning kiln, sometimes referred to as a bee-hive kiln."[27] Describing his work in this kiln, he pointed out that there, "I try to make a distinctive sort of pottery. I prepare the clay (from New Jersey, the glaciers ground up and ruined all the Cornish clay ages ago), turn the shapes by hand on an old kick wheel, finish them and fire them in a kiln I designed myself and helped build. I formulate and mix my own glazes and colors, with two or three exceptions, apply them, decorate the things that seem to need decoration, and fire them again . . . I am also doing terra cotta statuary. The bust or figure is modeled up, dried, and fired in the kiln like a pot. This is about the only way of making sculpture direct. Marble and bronze are transitions from the original, passing through three stages."[28]

His career was hampered by a nervous condition and sickness. Nevertheless, he exhibited his work regularly in Boston and New York. In 1924 he held a one-man show at the Newark Museum, which then purchased three pieces. His studies in the history of pottery put him onto the "ancient pottery of the Yucatan, and throughout his life he made many tiles, plates, and other pottery items based on Mayan motifs." This interest also yielded a terra cotta panel, *The Plumed Serpent,* fired in Denver, Colorado, and, measuring 50" by 17"; it was described as "one of the largest pieces ever burnt."[29]

In 1938 he married a former student, Margaret Parry of Miami, Florida. They set up a studio in Panther Hammock, south of Coconut Grove, Florida, where she was particularly interested in designing and making ceramic jewelry.[30] They had no children. Paul died of Hodgkin's disease in 1954.

ENDNOTES

1. Her birth certificate gives her name as "Nettie," but in the early 1890s she started using the name "Annetta." Although Augustus Saint-Gaudens and her friends often referred to her as "Annette," she consistently used "Annetta" in official documents. This information is courtesy of Gregory C. Schwarz, Chief of Interpretation and Visitors Services as the Saint-Gaudens National Historic Site.

2. Burke Wilkinson, *Uncommon Clay: The Life and Works of Augustus Saint-Gaudens* (New York: Harcourt Brace Jovanovich, 1985), pp. 9, 170.

3. As quoted in Wilkinson, p. 313.

4. Letter, October 8, 1952, as quoted in Beatrice Gilman Proske, *Brookgreen Gardens: Sculpture* (Brookgreen Gardens, SC: Trustees of Brookgreen Gardens, 1968), p. 12.

5. Arvia MacKaye Ege, *The Power of the Impossible: The Life Story of Percy and Marion MacKaye* (Falmouth, ME: The Kennebec River Press, 1992), p. 127, diary entry for late March 1905.

6. See Appendix C of John H. Dryfhout, *The Work of Augustus Saint-Gaudens* (Hanover, NH: University Press of New England, 1982), p. 317, for a list of Louis's known works.

7. *American Artists*, pp. 277-278, as quoted in Proske, pp. 16-17. The statue is forty-three and a half inches high.

8. From a 1907 clipping in a scrapbook in the Windsor, VT, library; Virginia Colby, Cornish Colony files.

9. The *Boston Sunday Globe*, July 9, 1911; Virginia Colby, Cornish Colony files.

10. *The Reminiscences of Augustus Saint-Gaudens*, edited and amplified by Homer Saint-Gaudens (New York: Century Company, 1913), Vol. 2, p. 211-212.

11. Undated newspaper clipping; Virginia Colby, Cornish Colony files.

12. Her membership may have been prompted by her husband's drinking problem, see Wilkinson, pp. 224-225.

13. Dryfhout, *The Work*, p. 31.

14. Unidentified clipping, Daniels scrapbook; Virginia Colby, Cornish Colony files.

15. Ege, pp. 123-133, diary entry for November 22, 1905.

16. Lewis Johnson, "Early History of the Home and Studio of Louis and Annetta St. Gaudens," a typescript dated June 16, 1964, p. 1; Augustus Saint-Gaudens Papers, Dartmouth College Library, #1, Box 4.

17. Robert P. Emlen, "Raised, Razed, and Raised Again: The Shaker Meetinghouse at Enfield, New Hampshire, 1793-1902," *Historical New Hampshire*, 30:3, Fall 1975, p. 135.

18. Johnson, p. 1.

19. Ibid., p. 2. The inside of the house and its furnishings are lovingly and extensively described in Alice Van Leer Carrick, "The Orchard Potteries," *Country Life*, January 1926, pp. 48-50.

20. The *Boston Sunday Globe*, July 9, 1911; Virginia Colby, Cornish Colony files.

21. Unidentified newspaper clipping that Frances Duncan wrote for *The Tribune Institute— The New Citizen* at some point after she married John Manning in 1914 because the article is given the by-line "Frances Duncan Manning." This sculpture was exhibited at the Society of Independent Artists and at the main office building of the Women's International League for Peace and Freedom in Washington, DC; information from unidentified newspaper clippings, Virginia Colby, Cornish Colony files.

22. Undated New Hampshire newspaper clipping, with the by-line "Annette Johnson Saint-Gaudens"; Virginia Colby, Cornish Colony files.

23. As quoted in *The Gazette*, Hanover, NH, November 27, 1930, Daniels scrapbook; Virginia Colby, Cornish Colony files.

24. John H. Dryfhout, "Paul St. Gaudens and the Orchard Kiln Pottery," *Pottery Collectors' Newsletter* 3:12, September 1974, p. 172. See Dryfhout, pp. 172-173 for a preliminary bibliography of works by and about Paul St. Gaudens, which includes *How to Mend China* (Boston: Branford, 1953); an unpublished manuscript written in 1948 entitled "Craft Pottery and Its Methods" (Special Collections, Baker Library, Dartmouth College); and various articles in *Craft Horizons* from 1949 to 1952. For more on Frank Applegate, see below p. 449.

25. As quoted in Alice Van Leer Carrick, "The Orchard Potteries," *Country Life,* January 1926, p. 50.

26. Dryfhout, "Paul St. Gaudens and the Orchard Kiln Pottery," p. 171.

27. Ibid., p. 172; there is a picture of this kiln on p. 174.

28. As quoted in *The Gazette*, Hanover, NH, November 27, 1930, Daniels Scrapbook; Virginia Colby, Cornish Colony files.

29. Chester Davis, "The Orchard Kilns of Paul St. Gaudens," *The Spinning Wheel,* 30:2, March 1974, p. 55. This is the source of Paul's interest in Mayan art; the panel is illustrated on p. 56 and the description comes from the *Rocky Mountain News,* April 24, 1927. The title is a tribute to D.H. Lawrence's 1925 novel.

30. *The Miami Daily News Rotomagazine*, March 16, 1941; Virginia Colby, Cornish Colony files.

EVERETT SHINN
1876 – 1953

and

FLORENCE SCOVEL SHINN
1869 – 1940

EVERETT SHINN

EVERETT SHINN's art was unlike that of the prevailing style in the Cornish Colony because he was a member of the "Eight" or the "Ashcan School" of American Artists, a group of realistic painters bent on establishing new definitions of what was an acceptable subject of "fine art."[1] Shinn, however, denied that there was any "social significance to this movement. We simply were sick of the old National Academy output, such as idealized cherubic-looking bootblacks. We went out and painted bootblacks as they are. We weren't conscious of 'lifting up the poor.'"[2] None of his associates in that group "could hold a candle to him for the diverse, protean, mercurial character of his talent," yet early in his life he was "dazzled by the glamour of the footlights and a showy fashionableness."[3] His attraction to the theater, and later Hollywood, naturally grew out of his early fascination with the circus. Realistic pictures of the urban, usually New York, scene and sprightly depictions of circus material were certainly the subjects that were in the forefront while he was in Cornish. Shinn missed out on the formation in 1911 of the Association of American Painters and Sculptors, the future sponsors of the ground-breaking Armory Show in 1913. He was too involved with interior designs, sponsored by his patron Elsie de Wolfe—an actress, fashionable hostess, and Manhattan interior decorator—and a mural for the City Hall in Trenton, New Jersey, to become involved with the new group. Hence, he began to be edged out of the avant-garde scene. Critics generally agree that as his interests shifted to these other areas, his significance as a painter declined.

Shinn was born in 1876 in Woodstown, New Jersey, a quiet southern New Jersey town with a strong Quaker background. In 1888 his parents sent him to the Spring Garden Institute in Philadelphia where they hoped he would develop his talent for mechanics and drawing by enrolling in classes in engineering and industrial design. In 1893 he began a four-year period of study at the Pennsylvania Academy of the Fine Arts, where he studied under Thomas Anshutz, who in turn had studied under Thomas Eakins (Anshutz was also Maxfield Parrish's teacher during some of the time Shinn was a student). Shinn soon went to work as a staff artist for the *Philadelphia Press:* "they paid me $15 a week, a princely sum . . . I worked on all the papers in Philadelphia. When one would fire me, I'd go back to one of the others. They'd always take me back."[4] His job

Figure 149. *Mrs. Louise Birt Baynes with the Baynes family dogs Polaris and Heatherbloom, on the porch of Everett and Florence Shinn's house.*

introduced him to four other artists who were then working for Philadelphia newspapers, artists who were to become future members of the "Eight": Robert Henri, George Luks, John Sloan, and William Glackens. As Shinn describes it, newspaper work was a hard but swift teacher: "on wobbling ink-stained drawing boards . . . [we] . . . went to school, a school now lamentably extinct . . . a school that trained memory and quick perception. For in those days, there was not on any newspaper the handy use of the camera, that dependable box of mechanical memory which needed only the prodding of a finger to record all and sundry of the editor's wish. Rigid requirements compelled [artists] to observe, select, and get the job done."[5]

In 1897, he moved on to New York as an artist-reporter for the *New York World* and began to work part-time for various newspapers and magazines. A year later he married Florence Scovel, who was also born in southern New Jersey and was distantly connected to the prominent Biddle family of Philadelphia. During the first decade of this century, the couple was on the cutting edge of artistic and social circles in New York. They were also featured in a newspaper story written to call attention to "happily married professionals." According to the headline, "these two young artists are married, happy and proud of it." What was special, and apparently newsworthy, about the couple was that they furnished "an example of husband and wife working in the greatest harmony and contentment along lines that are radically different in many respects." The article emphasizes that what was distinctive about their relationship was that harmony prevailed despite the fact that he "is what might be called a 'legitimate artist'— that is, he paints things to be framed and hung in people's homes . . . while Mrs. Shinn confines her artistic endeavor solely to illustration, in which field she has few rivals in her own particular style."[6]

In New York, they eventually settled at 112 Waverly Place, where they built a small theater in a court behind his studio for an audience limited to fifty-five. There the couple established the Waverly Players, a group producing plays, often comic melodramatic spoofs, that Everett wrote. Some of these early "off-Broadway" shows ended up on

Broadway as elaborate vaudeville skits to the delight of huge audiences. In addition to the theater, the interior of the house was described as having Mrs. Shinn's "precious heritage of Biddle silver, furniture, pictures, and . . . letters framed for preservation, written by Hamilton, Burr, Robert Morris, Daniel Webster, and Washington [which] have come down to Mrs. Shinn from her great-great-grandfather, Francis Hopkinson. On a beautiful old sideboard of mahogany . . . are quantities of old silver of the choicest designs, brought over from England by some luxury-loving Biddle in the time of George III. An article might be written on this silver alone—the graceful pattern, which is the king's, and the splendid proportions, weight, and workmanship of the pieces."[7]

The interior and exterior design of houses was important to Shinn. Locally, the couple's life centered on Plainfield and a house they began building in 1902; Shinn himself was involved in its design. Because of the style of interior decoration Shinn used, Stanford White had become interested in Shinn's work and hired him to do ceiling murals in his own house during 1899 and 1900 as well as others that he designed. White also urged him to spend some time in Europe. Shinn willingly obliged and, after a tour to London and Paris in 1900, White sponsored a one-man show in New York early in 1901. This visit may account for the flavor of Toulouse-Lautrec, Honoré Daumier, Jean Louis Forain—even Edgar Degas—about Shinn's early style.

A decade later, however, when Shinn was in the process of severing his connections with the Cornish Colony, his style for interiors was sometimes known as "rococo revivalism." A student of Henri, and an artist associate of Shinn's, the art critic Guy Pène du Bois, defined Shinn's style this way: "Shinn may be said to be the first American interior painter of the new era. His inspiration dates back to the eighteenth century and particularly to Fragonard . . . To meet contemporaneous requirements he modified the old style but very little. It is just as frivolous, and amiable and graceful. In Shinn, there is perhaps a little less seriousness than in Fragonard, for behind Fragonard was a world of study and belief that the temper of the period fathered. Shinn is more consciously light for he cuts a laughing hole in a volume of serious art . . . He is a romanticist, one with a satirical vein, for he has a laugh ready to direct at himself and the world."[8] This florid style was quite in vogue among White's rich clientele, though it was a far cry from the realistic scenes of urban life typical of the painting done by the "Eight."

The house in Plainfield, though, smacks of neither "rococo revivalism" nor "Ashcan" realism. "Knebolo Hill," from the Indian word for "rocky ribs," referring to the rocky ledge 600 feet above sea level upon which the house was built, "is a good example of the Colonial Revival style, with its pillared covered portico, a main entry door flanked by sidelights with tracery, wide entablature beneath the roof lines, fan vents at and a one-hundred paned, north-facing Palladian window measuring 9'x13' in the main hall where Shinn sometimes painted." There is a "double open stairway in the main hall" leading to "a gallery or mezzanine floor"; on this floor are two interestingly shaped rooms: "the southwest corner room is an octagon" and "the center room on the west side is an irregular hexagon. Eight of the nine fireplaces have antique decorative mantles, the most ornate of which stand in the main hall and library; the pair, in the Adams style, is believed to have been carved in the mid-eighteenth century."[9] Some of these architectural features found their way into Shinn's decorative pastel drawings done during this period of his life. They are also present in photographs taken at a later date by another Colony resident, Ernest Harold Baynes. He captured the doorway at the front of Shinn's house in his photographs of his dogs Polaris and Heatherbloom in the illustrations for a book he did about some of his favorite dogs.[10]

It should be said, however, that Shinn drew fairly little on his experience in Cornish for his art, although there is a record of a painting, now lost, entitled *Mt. Scutney,* which once belonged to Henry C. Daniels of Plainfield, a sketch of *Christmas Eve, Windsor, Vermont,* and a caricature of Louis Evan Shipman.

It is clear, however, from entries in the diaries of Stephen Parrish and Lucia Fairchild Fuller, that he and his wife participated in the Colony's social life. Stephen Parrish noted that the Shinns are building their house (October 22, 1902), that Everett called on him (June 19, 1903), that on the same day he had a telephone installed the couple came to dinner along with Margaret Nichols and Otto Roth (June 26, 1903), that he called on the Shinns (August 2, 1903), and that on at least two occasions he dined at Mrs. Clara Potter Davidge's house with the Shinns as guests, too (June 27 and August 18, 1903).[11] Lydia Parrish jotted down in her diary the fact that on August 3, 1904, "Called on Mrs. MacKaye—Had the Shinns & Helen Henderson to dinner—glorious day & a marvelous evening glow in the east." Helen Henderson visited Cornish the previous year to gather information for an article entitled "An Impression of Cornish"; in the context of someone who relied chiefly on the natural setting of the area to provide beauty, it included the following description of Shinn's new house: "The natural beauties of the ground are great. Six huge maple sugar trees screen the house on the east side, and the ledges of granite exposed about the summit of the hill, upon which the house stands, are in themselves immensely decorative."[12] Lucia Fuller's diary entries during the summer of 1903 indicate that Shinn was an avid and frequent tennis player on the Fullers's court, especially with John Blair, the actor; Joseph De Camp, the painter; and Herbert Croly, the editor of the *New Republic.* Shinn had a more active role in the life of Lucia's husband, Henry Brown Fuller. Shinn helped him with his mural painting, *Triumph of Truth Over Error* (1906-1907), which won for Fuller the Carnegie prize for the meritorious painting submitted at the winter exhibition in 1908 of the National Academy of Design.[13]

At a much later date, probably in the 1920s when Shinn was living in Connecticut, his local newspaper there carried an interview with him under the headline "Shinn Likes Movies But Hates Artistic Colonies." One paragraph reads: "The type of Mr. Shinn's homes has been as varied as his work. Some years ago, he bought a place in Cornish, New Hampshire, in order to be one of a colony of artists. Mr. Shinn established himself in Cornish, prepared to enjoy the benefits of common interests. He left New Hampshire utterly disillusioned and disgusted with artistic colonies. Having lived in too close touch with his own kind, his reaction carried him up into the Catskill Mountains. Here he lived in such isolation that he says he wore out a car every time he had to go after a loaf of bread."[14]

Shinn's good friend William Glackens also had none too complimentary comments on the Cornish Colony. On his way to Newfoundland for a month in 1903, Glackens stopped by to visit with the Shinns, staying at the nearby Kingsbury Tavern with Mrs. Clara Potter Davidge. He wrote: "I am in a dismal spot. We have a burial ground to the right and a fifth rate mountain to the left and it has been raining ever since I arrived.

I have to take the mountain on faith as it is wiped out with rain clouds. There is a devil of an artistic set here, it would make you weep. The Davidge and Shinn factions are sort of outcasts. Mrs. D. says she is afraid they are too tough for the elite. . . . Nothing but serious-minded aesthetes here. Pleasant jocularities not allowed. As far as I can make out, everyone passes the time in running the other one down. But enough of this, I still have faith in life, and these poor beggars up here couldn't survive art. Shinn's house looks very well and is quite a size." Upon his return to New York, he added that "not much of the milk of human kindness in Cornish. Everyone roasts the other, garden, house, and family. New York is a blissful abode of angels in comparison."[15]

Although Shinn may have shared Glackens's dim view of the local scene and left New Hampshire fed up with the life of a Colonist, to a certain extent he exchanged one colony for another. For all his being unafraid "to paint with vigor the fun and drama of life," Homer Saint-Gaudens, who must have encountered Shinn on a social occasion or two, was right that "Shinn . . . left his old playgrounds, for that is what they were, to work as a scenic designer, as a motion-picture art director, and as a playwright."[16] He seemed to spend the rest of his life on the periphery of the fine arts. For example, Theodore Dreiser was alleged to have used him as the prototype for the protagonist, Eugene Witla, of his unsuccessful novel *The Genius* published in 1915. Shinn acknowledged that he and Dreiser had known one another in their early days working on *Ainslee's Magazine,* but he denied he bore any resemblance to Witla. Dreiser had the milieu down pat, with fairly exact depictions of a typical "Ashcan School" studio.

FLORENCE SCOVEL SHINN

Florence Scovel Shinn's early education was also in Philadelphia: at both the Friends Central School and the Philadelphia Academy of the Fine Arts during the 1890s. At the Academy "she struggled through dreary mornings in an effort to cramp her thought into the routine of the school curriculum, and dismally failed; but she succeeded during the noon hour, in the informal sketch-class which filled the interim between classes. The unwieldy charcoal and the pretentious paraphernalia of the painter had cramped her, suppressed her expression, but here she was always a success, because her untrammeled work contained the vital thing. So the wisest of Academy instructors, recognizing a force that needed no guiding hand to work out victory, took Florence Scovel from the class and told her to 'draw anything you choose.'"[17] This same critic, who believed that "we all profit by his wisdom," praised her for "the charm, the view-point, the essentially human element, and the humorous insight into the very root of life. . . . It is by these qualities that her illustrations are so distinguishable from the mass of pen-drawings, rather than by the tricks of a carefully acquired technique. The fact is that Mrs. Shinn, more than any other present day illustrator, has little need of technical cleverness. It is the sincerity of her work—the direct putting down of what she knows . . . and the frankness with which she states her very faults, which make her place unique."[18]

These characteristics are certainly true of *Morning, Dudley,* or *Then they trooped sadly on to school,* two of the thirty drawings she did for her fellow Cornish Colonist Winston Churchill's novel *Coniston,* which he finished at "Harlakenden House," May 7, 1906. A novel full of local New Hampshire color requires such accuracy. Churchill

Figure 150. *Pen and ink drawing by Florence Scovel Shinn.*

fictionalized the life of Ruel Durkee in his protagonist Jethro Bass, who was depicted as a political boss whose rapid rise to power in New Hampshire politics began with an iron fisted power grab of the local town meeting. In *Coniston*'s illustrations, Florence Scovel Shinn indeed bears out the assertion that "it is the keen perception of character, the clear evasion of caricature, while giving full rein to an unfailing sense of humor, the deduction from a squalid environment of the one healthy, happy note, the one wholesome human feature in a situation palpably hopeless, that gives her work its touch of truth."[19] Perhaps that is also the reason why her illustration for Alice Rice's *Mrs. Wiggs of the Cabbage Patch* (1901) and its sequel *Lovey Mary* (1903) have delighted readers for generations.

In the spring of the same year she did her illustrations for *Coniston*, she had an exhibition in New York at the Kraushaar Gallery. There, several other examples of her time in the Cornish Colony were shown: portraits of her husband, Everett Shinn, as well as of Miss Frances Davidge, and Miss [Mary?] Smoot.[20] Her life with Everett Shinn ended with their divorce in 1912. She went on to write several commercially successful books *The Game of Life and How to Play It* in 1925 followed in 1928 by *Your Word Is Your Wand*, and a sequel in 1940, *The Secret Door to Success*. She and Everett saw one another periodically, even on the three occasions that he decided to remarry. "Flossie would bless the marriage and say, 'Now this is the real one!'"[21] In the end, she died alone in 1940; he died, divorced and alone, thirteen years later.

ENDNOTES

1. For the members of the "Eight," see above p. 119, n. 4. The revolt of the "Ashcan School" from the acceptable artistic forms dictated by European academies frequently led to their replacing shards of Greek temples or Roman statuary in the background or foreground of their works with objects from everyday American urban life: a clothesline

here, an elevated train there—or even an ashcan. About the "School," it should be pointed out that "they were never a formal school, and their title was applied only in retrospect. Nevertheless, their work presents a distinctive vision of urban life that was concerned with the people of the city and inspired by its commercial energy." Rebecca Zurier, Robert W. Snyder, and Virginia M. Mecklenburg, *Metropolitan Lives: The Ashcan Artists and Their New York* (New York: W.W. Norton, 1995, for the National Museum of American Art of the Smithsonian Institution), p. 13; see also Bernard B. Perlman, *The Immortal Eight: American Painting from Eakins to the Armory Show, 1870-1913* (Cincinnati, OH: North Light Publishers, 1979), p. 196, n.

2. As quoted in an undated newspaper clipping from the *New York World Telegram;* Daniels scrapbook; Virginia Colby, Cornish Colony files.

3. Ira Glackens, the son of another member of the Ashcan School, William Glackens, in his introduction to Edith DeShazo, *Everett Shinn, 1876-1953: A Figure in His Time* (New York: Potter, 1974), p. xv.

4. As quoted in an undated newspaper clipping from the *New York World Telegram;* Daniels scrapbook; Virginia Colby, Cornish Colony files.

5. As quoted in DeShazo, p. 24.

6. Undated newspaper clipping from the Baltimore, MD, *News,* Everett Shinn Papers, Archives of American Art, Washington, DC, Roll 953, frame 195; Virginia Colby, Cornish Colony files, courtesy of John and Carolyn McNellis.

7. Charlotte Moffitt, "An Artist's House in New York," *House Beautiful,* Christmas 1902, pp. 19-20; courtesy of John and Carolyn McNellis. For more on the theatrical side of the Shinns' life in Greenwich Village, see Sylvia Yount, "Consuming Drama: Everett Shinn and the Spectacular City," *American Art 6,* Fall 1992, p. 102.

8. "An Eighteenth-Century Revival: The Work of Everett Shinn, Revivalist," *Arts and Decoration,* December 1915, p. 79.

9. The information in this paragraph comes from "Notes" for the Cornish Colony House Tour, June 21, 1985, prepared by John C. McNellis. The Shinns sold it in 1907 to Mary Trueblood Paine, the wife of the sculptor Robert Treat Paine, an assistant to Augustus Saint-Gaudens (see below pp. 490-491). The land belonged to the Daniels family. According to the Shinn papers, the painting Shinn did of Mount Ascutney mentioned in the next paragraph may have been traded to Henry Daniels (1848-1923) for additional acreage because both transfers occurred at about the same time. As for the question of who designed the house, it is clear from Shinn's letters in the Archives of American Art that Shinn and Stanford White were close friends. Although an article in *The Lamp 27,* October 1903, pp. 186-196 credits Shinn with the design of the house and Harrie T. Lindeberg, "a young architect of New York," with carrying out the plan, it should be noted that Lindeberg was just beginning to launch his career at that point in the firm of McKim, Mead, and White. Based on this information and the fact that Shinn's house is not listed among those recorded as actually having been designed by Lindeberg, Mrs. McNellis's research has led her to conclude that either Stanford White designed the house as a favor to his friend Everett Shinn or White was quite influential in the design of the house—in collaboration with Shinn—and thus White had Lindeberg merely draw up the plans for the completed design.

10. Macmillan published *Polaris: The Story of an Eskimo Dog* in 1922; Heatherbloom, to be sure, was a Scottish Terrier. The dogs are pictured in front of Shinn's house on pages 57, 85, 125, and 137. Even though it is clearly the Shinn house in Plainfield, the usual mixing of the two towns exists in the caption for the picture on p. 57: "Polaris

and Heatherbloom in Cornish." The frontispiece also shows "Polaris Fishing in Blow-Me-Down Brook."

11. Stephen Parrish, diary; Special Collections, Baker Library, Dartmouth College, Hanover, NH, gift of Marian and Roy Garrand.

12. *The Lamp* 27, October 1903, pp. 186-96; the description of Shinn's site is on p. 195.

13. Undated newspaper clipping, "Had Help on Prize Painting—Henry B. Fuller Cheerfully Admits His Indebtedness," Fuller Papers, Baker Library, Dartmouth College, Hanover, NH. For more on Shinn's role and the mural's relationship to Christian Science, see above pp. 208-209.

14. As quoted in an undated newspaper clipping from a Bridgeport, CT, newspaper, Everett Shinn Papers, Archives of American Art, Washington, DC, Roll D179, frame 98. Again, the house is in Plainfield, not Cornish.

15. As quoted in Ira Glackens, *William Glackens and the Ashcan Group: The Emergence of Realism in American Art* (New York: Crown, 1957), p. 44.

16. Homer Saint-Gaudens, *The American Artist and His Times* (New York: Dodd, Mead, 1941), p. 203.

17. Anonymous author, *The Lamp* 27, September 1903, pp. 149-150. As an earlier critic has observed, Florence Scovel Shinn's publishers typically believed "that she naturally would do children better than anything else." Nevertheless, she possesses a "real intellectual appreciation of her types; she sees them from within, and has a genial tolerance for the mischief and the mood that distinguish them. The droll and the human are never absent from her view." Regina Armstrong, "Representative American Women Illustrators," *The Critic,* 1900, pp. 417-430.

18. Ibid., p. 148.

19. Ibid., pp. 148-149. Among her friends she was known as "Flossie." A good example of her wit and sense of humor can be seen from the anecdote told about her preparation for a game of charades, perhaps at one of the many charade parties given by the Cornish Colonists. The participants had to come in the guise of a book title. She calmly and quickly drew a picture of a mill and pinned it to her dress front. Instantly she was transformed into George Eliot's *Mill on the Floss;* see Glackens, p. 186.

20. Of the latter portraits, a review noted that they were not "those dreary sights—large formal canvases repeating both pose and expression—but dainty, personal little pictures of her friends and acquaintances in their hats and coats just as they may have come into her dining-room for five o'clock tea,"; "A Portrait Painter of Intimate Subjects," *Town and Country,* May 19, 1906.

21. Glackens, p. 146.

LOUIS EVAN SHIPMAN
1869 – 1933

and

ELLEN MCGOWAN BIDDLE SHIPMAN
1869 – 1950

LOUIS EVAN SHIPMAN

THE WIDE WORLD REMEMBERS LOUIS EVAN SHIPMAN for his association with *Life Magazine* as a contributor and, from 1922 to 1924, as its editor. The Cornish Colony, however, remembers him as the author of *A Masque of "Ours," The Gods and the Golden Bowl.* Although he was very involved with the New York and national literary scene, he was deeply committed to local activities. In fact, upon returning from a six-week trip to France in 1910, he is quoted as saying. "New Hampshire is good enough for [me]."[1]

Louis and his wife Ellen Biddle first came to Cornish in 1893 as part of the literary set that followed the artists. For two summers with Herbert Croly and his wife, they shared the Frank Johnson farmhouse, the place that became the "Barberry House," the home of Homer and Carlota Saint-Gaudens. Then they took a ten-year lease and paid for "Poins House," the old brick tavern-house originally known as the Hall house on the corner of Route 12A and Westgate Road in Plainfield Village, with "the money which Mr. Shipman received for his story, *The Curious Courtship of Kate Poins.*"[2] So anxious was Ellen Shipman to stake out her claim to a Cornish address that on the reverse of one of her calling cards, she wrote "Geographically in Plainfield, Socially in Cornish."

Whatever their thoughts on the desirability of Cornish, the couple eventually settled even geographically farther from the social center. An early newspaper column, referring to land currently on the Meriden Stage Road, notes, "rumor has it that Mr. Shipman, one of the city colonists, who leased the Hall place for a term of years, is to buy land and build a house the coming year. We are glad to hear this, as Mr. Shipman and family keep their house open the whole year spending their winter with us and have always shown courtesy and consideration for all with whom they had business dealings."[3] At a later date, a newspaper item remarked that "Louis Shipman, the noted playwright, has bought the larger part of John Gilkey's place at $30 per acre. Mr. Shipman will build in the near future."[4] The Plainfield Property Tax Records first indicate the Shipmans as being charged for owning one horse in 1903. The next year the same records show that they owned one horse and 182 acres of the Gilkey Farm.[5] The Shipmans called their home "Brook Place" and in 1911 asked their friend and neighbor Charles A. Platt to help

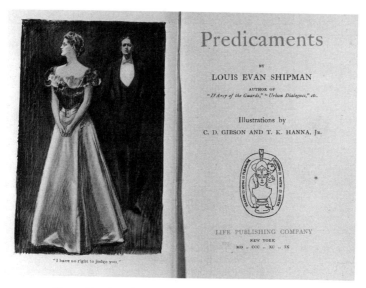

Figure 151. *Frontispiece and title page from* Predicaments,
by Louis Evan Shipman.

them with their extensive remodeling, part of which involved using some raised paneled walls salvaged from a church in nearby Brownsville, Vermont, in the living room.

Shipman by now had established himself as a permanent fixture among American men of letters and playwrights. He was an editorial writer for *Leslie's Weekly* from 1895 to 1896 and a contributor to *Life* and *Collier's.* Given the latter association, it is not surprising that one of his earliest books, *Predicaments,* published in 1899 by Life Publishing Company, is dedicated "To My Friend, Herbert David Croly." It is handsomely illustrated with Charles Dana Gibson drawings personifying what is meant by a "Gibson Girl." It is a series of five short stories with predicaments as their main plot element. Earlier that same year, he brought out the successful *D'Arcy of the Guards* that he turned into a play in 1901. His Cornish associations led him to dramatizations of the highly popular novelist Winston Churchill's *The Crisis,* published in 1901, and *The Crossing,* published in 1905. In 1914, he wrote *Adventures of a Play,* in which he describes the seesaw progress of the successes and failures during the production of a play. He is also well-known for *Fools Errant,* published in 1921, and *Poor Richard,* published in 1924.

Louis Shipman, for all his literary activities, thoroughly immersed himself in local affairs. In addition to entertaining, he had a tennis court built amid Ellen's gardens; he was a frequent tennis player there and elsewhere on one of the sixteen local courts. Margaret Homer Shurcliff described him as "the fat, roly-poly author and playwright, [who] was always on hand, dripping with perspiration from the start and pouring forth a continuous line of boasting and teasing."[6] But he was also very much committed to public service. As a 1904 newspaper report notes, "a branch of the United Irish League of America was formed when Hon. John E. Redmond, M.P., and Mrs. Redmond were in Windsor [Vermont] Friday afternoon to inspect the statue of Charles Steward Parnell, which Augustus Saint-Gaudens, the sculptor, is working on at his studio in Cornish. H[enry] B[rown] Fuller was named president of the newly formed organization. L[ouis] E[van] Shipman and A[ugustus] Saint-Gaudens were appointed chairmen of the committee to secure new members. Redmond was the noted Irish leader from Ireland."[7] Shipman was secretary and treasurer of the Plainfield Progressive League, a discussion group organized by the "chick-a-dees," those Colonists who remained in the area the entire year, the winter that the group was organized, 1908-1909. He was a featured speaker at the sixth annual Labor Day picnic held at the Summit House of Mount Ascutney in 1909. In 1913, he was part of the organizing committee for the production of Percy MacKaye's *Sanctuary: A Bird Masque* performed for the benefit of the Meriden Bird Club. During the First World War, he was a member of the New Hampshire State Committee of 100 of Public Safety, the state director of the so-called "Four Minute Men," and a local food administrator.

His marriage ended in divorce. After World War I, Shipman went to Paris, remarried, was named Chevalier of the Legion of Honor in 1930, and died three years later in Boury-en-Vexin (Oise), not far from either Giverny or Paris.

ELLEN BIDDLE SHIPMAN

Figure 152.

ALTHOUGH SHE RECEIVED no formal training as a landscape architect or designer, Ellen Shipman was a careful observer and an inherently talented woman. She steadfastly pursued her goals through one important commission after another until *House and Garden* selected her in 1933 for its Hall of Fame—"for being the dean of American women landscape architects, in a manner of speaking; for adding immeasurably to garden beauty in many states; and for having been so long a sane, understanding leader in her profession."[8] The pride she took in that profession can be seen in these notable remarks: "Before women took hold of the profession, landscape architects were doing what I call cemetery work. Until women took up landscaping, gardening in this country was at its lowest ebb. The renaissance of the art was due largely to the fact that women, instead of working over their boards, used plants as if they were painting pictures and as an artist would. Today women are at the top of the profession."[9] All the while, the same article could not refrain from pointing out that "on summer holidays she finds recreation in becoming a 'dirt gardener' at her farmhouse in Cornish, N.H."

A measure of the difficulty surrounding her entry into the field can be gathered from the remark made by the noted architect Frederick Law Olmsted, the designer of New York's Central Park, about Beatrix Jones Farrand, the only woman among the eleven founding members of the American Society of Landscape Architects (ASLA) in 1899: she was "inclined in some way to dabble in landscape architecture."[10] Even in 1908, the distinguished city planner, John Nolen, pointed out that, "in justice to women it should be remembered that they are little likely to get the chance to show what they might do in a public way . . . in landscape architecture success waits on invitation. A woman might map out the most ambitious plans for an imaginary park. But even supposing she could get anyone to look at them, they would be valueless. For the essence of success in such designing is that the plans shall fit specific conditions. Public prejudice would operate against a woman's being trusted with public work, and she would rarely be asked to submit plans for specific projects."[11]

But Ellen Shipman was undaunted; perhaps such "prejudice" is why she devoted her career primarily to residential and large private estates in the country. Born to the important Biddle family of Philadelphia, she attended Radcliffe College for three years, met Louis Shipman, married and bore him three children (Ellen Shipman Angell, Evan Biddle Shipman, Mary Shipman Jackson Barbin), came to Cornish, and put off commitment to her future profession until the children were on their way to adulthood. Her divorce led her to developing a self-supporting career. Through her connection in Cornish with Charles A. Platt, who recognized her flair for garden design, she was able to begin this career. He was drawing on her skills by 1900 and urging her to branch out on her own. Starting at home with "Brook Place" and its lovely site, "Mrs. Shipman, a landscape architect of national reputation . . . designed . . . a garden that in its charm, seclusion, and informality, harmonizes entirely with the dwelling . . . everything has the air of privacy and of almost haphazard informality which conceals the exquisite artistry that produced it"; in its "charm, simplicity, and honesty," it stands out as "the perfect expression of the New England country garden."[12] Platt's tutelage was a significant spur in the early stages of her career and he continued to draw on her knowledge and ability in a number of his projects.[13] Among the Cornish Colonists, she also had the advantage of sharing her gardening interests with Rose Nichols.[14] But not the least important of the spurs to her career was the cluster of serious, fervent gardeners among the Cornish Colonists. Referring to them, she was quick to point out that "here was the renaissance of gardening in America."[15]

Defying convention and advice from family and friends, she opened her landscape architecture office around 1912[16] in Plainfield, attached to "Brook Place," where, according to Frances Grimes's "Reminiscences," Ellen Shipman insisted that a large window be added to the south room, facing the garden, so that she could enjoy it better. In Plainfield, "she and her assistants executed garden plans for clients across the country, including a few in New Hampshire. In 1941, she was asked to restore the gardens of Augustus Saint-Gaudens's home, a memorial site in Cornish. She worked to preserve the intimate relationship of the house and the garden; and the house and view originally created by Saint-Gaudens." As for other of her local projects, it is possible that she collaborated with Charles Platt on plans for "High Court." There exists a "Planting Plan of Flower Garden for Mrs. Conger Goodyear, Cornish, N.H.: Ellen Shipman, Cornish, N.H., Landscape

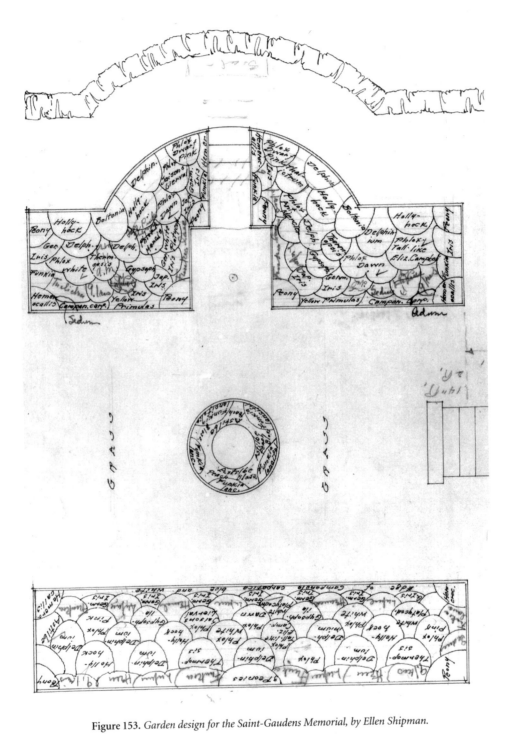

Figure 153. *Garden design for the Saint-Gaudens Memorial, by Ellen Shipman.*

Architect, September 1914," but it has not been ascertained whether or not this plan was ever carried out. (Annie Lazarus's "High Court," a beautiful Platt house, was subsequently owned by Norman Hapgood and the Goodyears.) In the 1920s, she advised the Slade sisters to simplify their Platt garden by removing the flowers from the center of some of the beds and replacing them with grass plots.[17] Although neither of the following two projects was carried out, Ellen Shipman drew up plans for the Plainfield Town Hall and school and a memorial to Ernest Harold Baynes. Finally, there is also reason to believe that she helped Herbert Croly design his gardens.[18] In the immediate vicinity, she fulfilled commissions for Elizabeth Billings in Woodstock, Vermont; Horace Brown in Springfield, Vermont; and Mr. and Mrs. Taylor Mead in Windsor, Vermont.

Although she continued to use her Plainfield office during the summers, eventually she opened a New York office at 21 Beekman Place. Interestingly enough, the walls there were hung with some of the art done by her Cornish Colony neighbors: "one of Maxfield Parrish's individual drawings . . . [and] a hillside pasture of Willard Metcalf's."[19] As was the case in the offices of the other women landscape architects, Shipman employed only female assistants. From her Beekman Place office, she collaborated with Platt, specifically on the gardens for Mary and Nellie Pruyn, East Hampton, Long Island, and later with his sons, "on commissions carried out in New York, Maine, Pennsylvania, Washington, DC, and Michigan."[20] She was also simultaneously a lecturer at the Lowthorpe School of Landscape Architecture, Gardening, and Horticulture for Women in Groton, Massachusetts; it eventually became a division of the Rhode Island School of Design, Providence, Rhode Island. When asked to describe her most important commissions, she named those for the six-mile Lake Shore Boulevard at Grosse Pointe, Michigan, and Duke Memorial Garden.[21] Other significant commissions she executed include: "Fynmere," the James Fenimore Cooper Garden, Cooperstown, New York—done in conjunction with Charles A. Platt; "Longue Vue Gardens," the estate of Edgar Stern, Jr., and Edith Rosenwald Stern, heiress of the Sears, Roebuck fortune, New Orleans, Louisiana; and the Sarah P. Duke Memorial Garden at Duke University in Durham, North Carolina—Mrs. Sarah Duke was the wife of one of the founders of the university and her daughter Mary Duke Biddle was related by marriage to Ellen Shipman. Some of her more famous clients include Henry Ford and E. F. Hutton.

Without an elaborate series of illustrations, it is hard to give an adequate sense of her "touch." It is clear, however, that it was distinctive because new clients always begged to have her plan a garden just like the one they had seen elsewhere. She followed her own precept of creating aesthetically pleasing pictures with plants so that natural placement and her sensitivity to color composition were always visible. For example, she wrote, "it will be seen, in going over the shrubs and flowers, that certain shades, such as orange or any of the red yellows, reds, or red purples, are seldom, if ever, listed. It is because they draw too much attention to themselves. However, if one desires them, a shrub planting, such as azaleas, or a flower border in which you use these tones as high notes, can be gradually built up to their level of color. It will be found best to introduce some pale yellows and use trees or shrubs to tone down their blatant notes. Many colors that are harsh and discordant out of doors are beautiful when picked and arranged in the house. The blue shadows give them what they need to be harmonious."[22] Generally speaking, she preferred an English-style garden. Thus, she advocated compartmentalizing several smaller gardens with great masses of flowers near the house balanced by a large lawn area planted with large flowering trees for a spatial accent. She sought to create a sense of intimacy through narrow walks, with low hedges between or along them and higher hedges on the outside. Contrary to Gertrude Jekyll's recommendation for a deep border of herbaceous perennials, she preferred a narrow one. She also liked to see vines espaliered on houses. A trademark of her more formal gardens was locating a bench in a wall niche and arranging for the paths in her planting beds, full of luxuriant perennials, to terminate in statuary. Declaring in 1932 that the essentials for a well-defined garden plan were paper, pencil, and an eraser, with the latter the most essential of all utensils, she wanted "to eliminate promiscuous and haphazard planting as the garden progresses . . . I stress simplicity of design, with privacy to be secured, as a garden is intended to be a place of beauty where one can go to rest and meditate—provided in these stressful days one can find the time to meditate."[23]

To close this account of Ellen Shipman's career, it should be pointed out that she used a Mr. Hathaway, an Englishman, as an assistant in Plainfield; upon his death Charles Meyette took over. She was also especially fond of the work of Wilmer Spalding, a Plainfield blacksmith. For her clients, she used to order fancy iron gates from him, which he would make to order.[24] In the thirties, when the Depression caused landscaping commissions to slacken, Ellen Shipman took up interior decorating. At one point, she asked Sylvia Gray of Plainfield to make some lampshades to match a wallpaper she was using. Ellen was so pleased with Sylvia's workmanship that she paid her twice what Sylvia had originally asked.[25] Ellen Shipman died in her winter home in Bermuda, March 27, 1950. She is buried in Gilkey Cemetery, Plainfield, New Hampshire.[26]

ENDNOTES

1. *Weekly Enterprise*, Meriden, NH, March 3, 1910; Virginia Colby, Cornish Colony files.

2. Letter from Ellen Shipman to Lawrence W. Rittenoure, dated June 15, 1944; Virginia Colby, Cornish Colony files. This point is confirmed in a letter from Allyn Cox to Virginia Colby, September 4, 1982; Virginia Colby, Cornish Colony files.

3. Undated newspaper clipping, Daniels scrapbook; Virginia Colby, Cornish Colony files.

4. Undated newspaper clipping; Virginia Colby, Cornish Colony files. From a later perspective, Geoffrey Platt in his "Memoir," appended to Keith N. Morgan, *Charles A. Platt: The Artist as Architect* (New York: The Architectural History Foundation/Cambridge, MA: The MIT Press, 1985), p. 203, calls Shipman "an unsuccessful playwright."

5. It was originally built in the 1790s by Sample Gilkey, the son-in-law of Thomas Gallup, one of the few proprietors to come to Plainfield; both men fought in the Revolutionary War—Thomas Gallup was a constable in 1776 and Sample Gilkey was one in 1789.

6. Margaret Homer Shurcliff, *Lively Days: Some Memoirs of Margaret Homer Shurcliff* (Taipei: Literature House Ltd., 1965), p. 35.

7. "Noted Irish Leader in Windsor," unidentified newspaper clipping, Windsor, VT, Public Library scrapbook; Virginia Colby, Cornish Colony files.

8. *House and Garden* 63, June 1933, p. 50. See also Dan Krall, "Early Women Designers and Their Work in Public Places," *Proceedings for Landscapes and Gardens: Women Who Made a Difference*, ed. Miriam Eston Rutz (East Lansing, MI: Michigan State University, 1987), unpaginated; and Deborah Nevins, "The Triumph of Flora: Women and the

American Landscape 1890-1935," *The Magazine Antiques* 127, April 1985, p. 913.

9. As quoted in the *New York Times,* March 13, 1938, a feature also on Mrs. Beatrix Farrand, Mrs. Annette Hoyt Flanders, Miss Helen Bullard, and Miss Helen Swift Jones.

10. As quoted in Leslie Rose Close, "Ellen Biddle Shipman," *American Landscape Architecture: Designers and Places* (Preservation Press, 1989), p. 90. Neither Shipman nor Rose Nichols was a member of ASLA.

11. Mary Bronson Hartt, "Women and the Art of Landscape Gardening," *The Outlook,* March 28, 1908, p. 695.

12. G. H. Edgell, *The American Architecture of Today* (New York: Scribner, 1928), pp. 125-126; note that his description is of her garden in the mid-1920s.

13. See the index of Morgan, *Charles A. Platt,* supplemented by Keith N. Morgan, *Shaping an American Landscape: The Art and Architecture of Charles A. Platt* (Hanover, NH: The Hood Museum of Art, Dartmouth College, 1995), p. 179, n. 40, where he indicates that there were "fourteen Shipman/Platt collaborations" plus Gwinn and Longue Vue.

14. See Deborah E. Van Buren, "Landscape Architecture and Gardens in the Cornish Colony: the Careers of Rose Nichols, Ellen Shipman, and Frances Duncan," *Women's Studies* 14, 1988, p. 378 and notes 18 and 19.

15. From Shipman's "Garden Note Book," as quoted in Rebecca Warren Davidson's chapter, "Charles A. Platt and the Fine Art of Landscape Design," in Morgan, *Shaping,* p. 80.

16. The date is based on a letter Lucia Fuller wrote dated September 19, 1912, in which she described her friend Ellen as being "very happy about having a profession"; Fuller Papers, Box 4, Baker Library, Dartmouth College, Hanover, NH; Van Buren, p. 386, n. 19.

17. Patricia Thorpe, "Down the Garden Path: A Dream of the Turn-of-the-Century Summer Life Is Still in Bloom in New Hampshire," *House and Garden,* 160:7, July, 1988, p. 118.

18. The information in this paragraph comes from Van Buren, p. 378 and notes 21, 23, 25. In note 26, she notes that the plans for the Saint-Gaudens gardens are described in Shipman's article, "The Saint-Gaudens Memorial Gardens," *Bulletin of the Garden Club of America* 8, May 1948, pp. 61-65; the actual plans are in the Cornell University Library's collection of Shipman's papers.

19. Elizabeth H. Russell, "A House on Beekman Place, New York," *House Beautiful* 62, November 1927, p. 569.

20. Van Buren, p. 386, n. 23. A more detailed account of Shipman's collaboration with Platt will be found in Judith B. Tankard, *The Gardens of Ellen Shipman,* to be published by the Sagapress, Sagaponack, NY in the fall of 1996.

21. Krall, "Early Women Designers."

22. Ellen Shipman, "Garden Note Book," unpublished, courtesy of Ann Bloom.

23. Interview in the Winston Salem, NC, *Journal,* October 8, 1932; courtesy of Ann Bloom. Catherine R. Brown was also helpful in summarizing Shipman's garden style.

24. Interview: Virginia Colby with Ellen Maylin, January 1, 1982.

25. Interview: Virginia Colby with Sylvia Gray, June 1981.

26. The Shipman's son Evan, one of Ernest Hemingway's cronies, is buried next to her.

Figure 154. *Entryway and staircase at Dingleton House, with column, newel post, and stair railing carved by Emily Slade.*

AUGUSTA and EMILY SLADE

IN 1903, FOUR WOMEN NAMED SLADE, reportedly of the Slade spice family, built summer places in Cornish. Frances and Elizabeth Slade bought pasture land from William E. Westgate on the crest of Saint-Gaudens's Hill. Their cousins, Augusta and Emily Slade, in whom we are interested, purchased from Lyman Bartlett 130 acres of land on the west side of Dingleton Hill.[1] They turned to their friend and neighbor Charles A. Platt and asked him to design them a home they called "Dingleton House," which is perched high on the hill and overlooks the Con-

necticut River and the Cornish-Windsor Covered Bridge; his designs date from 1904 and 1905. (At the same time, Platt began a design for their brother Marshall Slade, "Woodston" in Mt. Kisco, New York.) The local newspaper was quite in awe of the house while it was being built: "The large house of the Miss Slades of Cornish well up on the western slope of 'Dingleton' among the woods as seen from Windsor Village reminds one of a castle on the hills. Several of Windsor's carpenters are busy on the building which has a rocky foundation and required much blasting of rocks for its site and the road there to."[2] Stephen Parrish, on the other hand, however much he might marvel at the view, noted in his diary that he thought it "beautiful land but rather inaccessible."[3] Ellen Wilson, too, was somewhat ambivalent about the place. She wrote Woodrow Wilson at the White House that "it is on such a mountain that I was nervous going up to it in the car, for the car distinctly balked at it."[4] Needless to say, the Slades were not among the "chick-a-dees"; the same Vermont newspaper reported, let us hope belatedly, on January 29, 1906, that "Miss Emily A. Slade has closed her house in Cornish for the season, and has gone to New York to spend the winter."[5]

Be that as it may, their house was like Churchill's Harlakenden House in that "it was the kind of large-scale country estate for which Platt had then achieved a national reputation. It was built of stucco over hollow tile, which allowed Platt to return to his Italian villa model. An entrance court is formed by a projecting service wing on the right and a studio wing on the left. A loggia extends the full length of the back of the house, commanding a splendid view of the Connecticut River Valley and Mount Ascutney. The unique imprint of the sculptress owner is found in the entrance-hall stairs, which she herself carved."[6]

Emily Slade, as well as other Colony members Louise Cox and Rose Standish Nichols, were among a number of women at the turn of the century to take up the art of wood carving. Even though *The House Beautiful* could report this development with interest, noting that it was a way for "many women . . . to earn money" and that "the demand for fine hand-carved articles always remain[s] the same, and there is never any difficulty in disposing of them," the reporter could not avoid some condescension. "Trousseau chests . . . wood-boxes . . . tables, chairs, cabinets, and even wainscoting and dadoes, wooden friezes and doors are being executed by women who probably never before did anything more difficult with their hands than to wield the mashie and racquet." Furthermore, wood carving "can never become a fad, say its devotees, one reason being that women who have not a real love for it are wholly unwilling to expend the time and physical strength it takes to become moderately proficient." Emily Slade, however, was held up as a someone of a different stripe. The article quotes the opinion of Professor Karl von Rydingsvaard that "by far the largest piece of work done by a woman is that which Miss Emily Slade, a sister of William Gerry Slade, did for her country home in Vermont. She copies, in her own handiwork, the winding stairs which are preserved at the Cluny Museum. The work of Miss Slade is in a measure superior to that at Cluny, for the reason that while visiting Paris last summer I discovered that in many places the ornament was applied, while Miss Slade has carved the entire design out of solid wood. It is looked upon not only by her friends, but also by others, as a noteworthy piece of work, and people come from far and near to see it. It is done in mahogany, and will last for centuries."[7]

Because "the gardens of Cornish" were written about in national magazines, they were a major concern to anyone planning a house. The Slade sisters were no excep-

Figure 155. *Detail of newel post carved by Emily Slade.*

tion. Platt, of course, was equally committed to planning and landscaping a house to accentuate its site. The site for Dingleton House "was somewhat similar to the one at High Court, [and] Platt did not want to interrupt the view with gardens, so he placed them on the left side of the house, rising in three tiers. Adjacent to the house is a formal flower garden composed of large rectangular beds around a circular fountain. There is a woodland garden separated from the flower garden by a pergola with latticework walls. Beyond the woodland garden is a lattice arch which marks the entrance to the circular rose garden."[8]

As if in justification of the Italian Renaissance element in Platt's houses and gardens, Rose Standish Nichols begins her description of the Slades' gardens by reiterating a belief held by many members of the Cornish Colony, "few parts of New England bear so strong a resemblance to an Italian landscape as the hills rising above the banks of the Connecticut River opposite the peaks of Mount Ascutney."[9] Moreover, the combination of site, Platt's landscaping plan as well as his architectural skill, and the Slade sisters' taste result in "Dingleton House" being "unquestionably the most beautiful and complete pleasure grounds in Cornish today." Platt is credited with "various architectural accessories" that "show his mastery of detail and understanding of how to produce bold and interesting out-of-door effects in harmony with the largeness and simplicity of the landscape. . . . Even such minor details as the covered doorway leading through the high cement wall on the west side into the attractive forecourt, and the circular pool, with pond lilies and goldfish, in the midst of the flower beds, are treated in a distinctive way." Emily Slade began the arrangement of the plants, which, "since her death, [have] been exquisitely kept up by her sister." The area above an Italian garden "was designed by Miss Emily Slade and carried out under her supervision."[10] Luckily, "seven gardeners labored in the garden under the direction of the formidable Miss Slade."[11] Some of them were Scottish gardeners, "who thought nothing of turning hemlocks into peacocks, to the consternation of the natives."[12]

Sixty-four years later the house and gardens, now owned by Grace Bulkeley, were revisited in a *House and Garden* article. "Mrs. Bulkeley has cheerfully refused to be haunted by the Slades, but there is a wonderful continuity about the garden from Platt's time to the present. The plantings have been simplified a bit—grass plots, designed by Ellen Shipman in the 1920s, fill some areas that were once all flowers—but an amazing amount of the original plant material still flourishes: great old lilacs, ancient spirea, turn-of-the-century roses and peonies—none originally red because of Miss Slade. The Bulkeleys have added their own reds—and formal hedges of barberry, a Platt signature."[13]

The Slades were active in the Colony's social functions; there are numerous references to their attendance at these affairs in Stephen Parrish's diary. Grace Bulkeley tells the following anecdote that links Emily Slade's concern for garden symmetry with her social activities. One fine summer's day she invited one of her Colony neighbors to tea. Her friend replied that she would be delighted to accept but that she had a guest—would she too be welcome? Emily Slade is said to have sighed, "Oh, well, I suppose so, but I do hope she will wear a frock that will harmonize with the garden!" Locally Emily was a member of the Cornish Discussion Club and the Plainfield Progressive League. She also played Urania in *A Masque of "Ours": The Gods and the Golden Bowl*. An interesting fact about the sisters can be deduced from the 1910 Cornish tax records. Their delight in the summer activities of the Cornish Colony were not limited solely to entertaining. They took an active interest in farming, too, because they were taxed on five horses, nine cows, one neat stock, six sheep, five hogs, and a hundred fowl.

A final note concerns the settlement of the Slade estate. The house and property were sold at auction in July of 1934 by James A. Hall of Keene, New Hampshire. The forty-seven-page auction catalogue lists a huge number of artifacts and treasures brought back from Persia, Egypt, Greece, France, Italy, and Spain.[14]

ENDNOTES

1. These land purchases are detailed in William H. Child, *History of the Town of Cornish with Genealogical Record: 1763-1910* (Concord, NH: The Rumford Press, 1911?), Vol. 1, p. 230, and Hugh Mason Wade, *A Brief History of Cornish: 1763-1974* (Hanover, NH: University Press of New England, 1976), p. 49.

2. A 1904 Windsor, VT, newspaper clipping, Windsor Library scrapbook; Virginia Colby, Cornish Colony files. Their cousins, Elizabeth and Frances Slade of Boston, built a house on the crest of the neighboring Saint-Gaudens's Hill.

3. Stephen Parrish, diary, entry for September 8, 1903; Special Collections, Baker Library, Dartmouth College, gift of Marian and Roy Garrand.

4. Letter dated August 5, 1913; Arthur S. Link, ed., *The Papers of Woodrow Wilson*, (Princeton, NJ: Princeton University Press, 1976), Vol. 28, p. 120; see below p. 433.

5. Unidentified newspaper clipping, Windsor Library scrapbook; Virginia Colby, Cornish Colony files.

6. Keith N. Morgan, "Charles A. Platt's Houses and Gardens in Cornish, New Hampshire," *The Magazine Antiques* 122:1, July 1982, p. 125.

7. "Women Take Up Wood-carving: A New Element Introduced Into Country Homes," *The House Beautiful* 24, July 1908, p. 47. As Mrs. Grace Bulkeley gently points out, the wood is not mahogany but quartered oak, a wood that might even be denser and hence more of a challenge to carve.

8. Morgan, pp. 125-26.

9. Rose Standish Nichols, "A Hilltop Garden in New Hampshire: A Garden Whose Boundary Planting Frames a View of Distant Mount Ascutney," *The House Beautiful*, March 1924, p. 237. John and Maud Elliott thought their house "looked out upon a scene [John] called the Val d'Arno—it was so like the Valley of the Arno near Florence," see above p. 192.

10. Ibid., pp. 238-239. Nichols closes her comment on the Slade sisters with the following remark: "The artist [Emily] who consecrated the last years of her life to the creation of both house and grounds has given untold pleasure to many, many people who have rejoiced in their beauty. Her sister [Augusta] carries on the work thus begun with intelligent and painstaking devotion." (p. 290).

11. Patricia Thorpe, "Down the Garden Path: A Dream of the Turn-of-the-Century Summer Life is Still in Bloom in New Hampshire," *House and Garden* 160:7, July 1988, p. 118. In the early thirties, the superintendent of the Slade estate was Charles E. Bryant. His obituary notes that he was suddenly stricken after returning from the Slades because he could not get up the icy hill; Virginia Colby, Cornish Colony files.

12. Wade, p. 83.

13. Thorpe. See above p. 395 for Ellen Shipman's negative opinion of red.

14. Courtesy of Mrs. Grace Bulkeley; interview with Virginia Colby, March 9, 1990.

HENRY FITCH TAYLOR
1853 – 1925

HENRY FITCH TAYLOR is a shadowy figure in the history of American art during the early decades of this century. It is remarkable that we know so little about someone who was instrumental in organizing the celebrated Armory Show in 1913. That was the same year that he married the former Clara Potter Davidge (see above pp. 172-174), and that he established his connection with the Cornish Colony. The couple lived in Plainfield at the old Kingsbury Tavern, which Mrs. Davidge had acquired some years earlier.

Taylor was born in Cincinnati, Ohio, on September 15, 1853. In his mid-twenties, he was part of a theatrical troupe run by Joe Jefferson, a well-known actor and amateur painter. In the early 1880s, he went to Paris and enrolled at the Académie Julian, studying under Jules-Joseph Lefebvre and Gustave Rodolphe Boulanger. He came under the influence first of the Barbizon masters and later spent some time with Monet at Giverny. Once he returned to New York in 1888, he exhibited his Impressionist canvases at the National Academy of Design in 1889. He and Theodore Robinson were among the first Americans to expose New York to this style of painting. Soon, however, he transferred his allegiance to the Society of American Artists, to which he was elected a member in 1891 primarily because its more liberal jury policy suited his temperament. In fact, he chafed at the rigid rules of the New York art establishment and seems to have exhibited very little until he was inspired by a group of artists including Arthur B. Davies, William Glackens, Childe Hassam, Walt Kuhn, George Luks, Elmer MacRae, Theodore Robinson, and John Twachtman—as well as Lincoln Steffens and Willa Cather—who formed a congenial group centered in Cos Cob, Connecticut. Taylor actually bought land there in 1898, though he did not seriously take up painting again until about 1908. "The prevailing spirit at Cos Cob was one of bold independence and experimentation, which created a common bond among these diverse talents. It was probably through his new acquaintances that Taylor met Clara Potter Davidge, daughter of a prominent New York family and an energetic supporter of the arts. Together, they took over the management of the Madison Gallery in New York about 1908."[1]

This marriage was to be a turning point in his career. Not only did Mrs. Davidge enlarge his social sphere by introducing him to her friends among the Cornish Colony, but she encouraged him to expand his artistic horizons through their involvement with the Madison Gallery. In his mid-fifties, Taylor began to exhibit his art again. The gallery's purpose, at least as far as Davidge and Taylor were concerned, was to show "promising

Figure 156. Figure with Guitar I
by Henry Fitch Taylor, 1914.

artists" who were unable to find a place in established galleries; in other words, it restricted itself to the avant-garde. In fact, it was in a 1911 meeting at the Madison Gallery that Taylor, along with Kuhn, MacRae, and Jerome Myers, laid the foundations for a group called the Association of American Painters and Sculptors. Taylor, elected the group's temporary president, drafted its statement of purpose. These were the same people, though Arthur B. Davies was now president, that in 1913 organized an exhibition at the Sixty-Ninth Regiment Armory in New York, known officially at the "International Exhibition of Modern Art," or more familiarly as "The Armory Show." With its European and American artists showing Post-Impressionist, Cubist, and other styles that the public considered radical, art in America was never to be the same.

And Taylor's art was never to be the same either. "Shortly after the Armory Show, he began to immerse himself in the premises of modern art. Starting with the broad color planes of Cézanne and early cubism, he systematically explored . . . the multiple complexities and progressive stages of modernism until he arrived at his own personal expression."[2] He gradually realized that the new directions in art required new ideas about color. "Of particular interest aesthetically was his treatise entitled *The Taylor System of Organized Color*, in which he explored the physical and psychological aspects of color."[3] This brief, privately printed treatise set forth a theory of color based on a color organ, an instrument he invented both to test the effects of various combinations of hues on subjects and to measure their reactions to these, sometimes unusual, juxtapositions of color.

Taylor sought to unite theory and practice throughout the remainder of his career. He did so in part because, as did so many of his generation, he came under the influence of Henri Bergson. His book, *Creative Evolution*, published in 1907, significantly affected esthetic theory because of his poetically articulated notions about time and change. Bergson challenged the Darwinian assertion that "the reality of life and evolution was contingent on . . . a series of . . . mutations." Rather, Bergson thought it was contingent on "a movement through what he called 'cinematographically perceptible stages of change' in which past merges with present. Life was a constantly redefined process of change, evolution, and metamorphosis in which each stage was directly modified by the preceding stage."[4] After the Armory Show, Taylor turned to abstraction because he wanted to illustrate art's link to the profound changes occurring in the modern world. His decision mirrored that of many of his contemporaries—just as the hostilities that would result in World War I were breaking out. Little did any of them know how profound would be the changes in their world. For example, Taylor's painting "Figure with Guitar," done in 1914, dissects an ordinary portrait subject into its component parts in order to remind the viewer of a Bergsonian kind of contingency and modification. Taylor designs the structure of his geometrical arrangement to force the observer to see how one plane alters its neighbor as the eye gradually moves from plane to plane. With this realization comes a simultaneous awareness that each plane is contingent on its neighbor and modified by it; subtle shifts in color only serve to emphasize this point.

There is little evidence that Taylor's summer visits to the Cornish Colony had any visible effect on his painting. That he was considered beyond the pale may safely be deduced from his failure to be included among the Cornish artists shown in the 1916 exhibition at Dartmouth College. In fact, the New York avant-garde scene determined his style. The death of Clara Davidge in 1921 virtually brought an end to his active painting career, although he did show *Abstraction* and *Ave Maria* in the 1921 "Exhibition of Paintings and Drawings Showing the Later Tendencies in Art" at the Pennsylvania Academy of the Fine Arts. However, he pursued the purposes of the Madison Gallery by supporting two transient groups: the Modern Artists of America in 1922 and the Salons of America in 1923. "The exhibitions of both groups provided a forum for younger artists such as Stuart Davis, Gaston Lachaise, Joseph Stella, Thomas Benton, Andrew Dasburg, Ben Benn, William Zorach, James Daugherty, Abraham Walkowitz, and Max Weber, whose access to exhibitions was still limited."[5] It is possible that the Cornish Colony influenced Taylor's connection with William Zorach because it was Clara Davidge who rented her Echo Farm, north of Plainfield Village on the Old County Road, to Zorach and his wife Marguerite in 1917. Nevertheless, Taylor's "last years were silent ones, spent in retirement in Cornish, New Hampshire, where he died on September 10, 1925. In retrospect, it seems implausible that he should have been so totally unrecognized then and forgotten now."[6]

ENDNOTES

1. William C. Agee, "Rediscovery: Henry Fitch Taylor," *Art in America* 54, November 1966, p. 41. Agee's article is the source for most of the material in this paragraph. One of the artists they hoped to exhibit was Stephen Parrish. On September 25, 1909 he jotted down in his diary that among his callers were "Mrs. Davidge with Mr. Taylor. (Proposed an exhibition of my pictures in N.Y. in a gallery she has rented.)" This show never took place. Among the Cornish Colony artists who were shown at the Madison Gallery were the sculptors James Earle Fraser, Frances Grimes and Harry Thrasher.

2. Ibid.

3. Melvin P. Lader, "Henry Fitch Taylor (1853-1925)," *Avant-Garde Painting and Sculpture in America 1910-1925*, Delaware Art Museum Catalogue, April 4-May 19, 1975, p. 138.

4. Agee, p. 42.

5. Ibid., p. 43.

6. Ibid.; another existence of the word "Cornish" used for "Plainfield."

WILLIAM LADD TAYLOR
1854 – 1926

THE PAINTER AND WELL-KNOWN, popular illustrator William Ladd Taylor was born in Grafton, Massachusetts, in 1854. He began his study of art in Boston and went to the Art Students League in New York for a season; then in 1884 he went to Paris where he studied at the Académie Julian under Gustave Rodolphe Boulanger and Jules-Joseph Lefebvre for several years. He returned to the United States and in 1888 married Mary Alice Fitts in Norfolk, Virginia. His career as an illustrator resulted in his nationwide popularity, perhaps because his audience recognized in him the proof of what he once told a group of art students: "get the truth of what you have to represent regardless of the rules of composition."[1] A 1907 catalogue accompanying one of his exhibitions commented that "his art is of great technical excellence. His drawing and color show a rare fidelity to fact and in themselves arrest attention. But his sympathy for the quiet sentiment and romance of everyday life is the source of his appeal to the thousands who love his pictures"; it closes by noting that the "combined truth to fact and to sentiment . . . has made Mr. Taylor's pictures so popular that their reproductions are eagerly sought by magazine readers, as well as by those who like to have them as household companions."[2]

This appeal was largely due to the fact that between 1888 and 1927, *The Ladies' Home Journal* published over one hundred of Taylor's illustrations either on the front cover or inside the magazine. As far as the editors of that magazine were concerned, Taylor's "canvases are bone and sinew of the *Journal's* thriving. And in forty years his appeal has not shrunken. From the shore of the Seven Seas come repeated requests for prints. No clime seems too remote."[3] Some of these illustrations were taken from special series that he did; they include *The People of Longfellow*, *The Last Hundred Years in New England*, *The Pioneer West*, *The World's Time-Honored Songs*, *American Literature Subjects*, *Those Days in Old Virginia*, *Scenes from the Old Testament*, and a series of six pictures illustrating the Psalms. The 1907 catalogue eloquently proclaimed his success with these illustrations. Of his Biblical scenes, it somewhat enigmatically noted that they "are conceived in a reverent spirit which does not omit a frank statement of facts as he has found them through loving research." His scenes of the American West have an immediacy based on his own experience. To cure tuberculosis, he went to Colorado as a young man and spent a year in the vicinity of Long's Peak. The catalogue, however, was silent about such a dark fact. It discreetly noted that "for the series of western scenes he traveled to the spots he has drawn,

Figure 157. A Rocky Mountain Mining Camp
by *William Ladd Taylor, c. 1907.*

and his detail, landscapes and character will serve hereafter as faithful testimony to the facts." The catalogue asserted that those scenes depicting New England and the South are "an historical record of the vanishing manners and customs of the past century." There was also a note of nationalistic pride in these two series. Because his pictures were such faithful reproductions, they both conserved and reminded his audience of the glorious origins of American culture: "With a keen and loving eye for the essentials of that period, he found specimens of character and time-worn objects, which he has drawn with unerring fidelity. He has brought into these pictures the old-fashioned flavor of an age we shall soon be calling our American antiquity."[4]

Reviews of his 1908 publication *Our Home and Country,* with an introduction by William Downes Howe, continued in this nationalistic vein. They are interesting for what they say not only about his art but also about the place of that art in American culture. One reviewer found that Taylor's "pictures of American life have the true ring of nationality" about them. In fact, "one can hardly conceive of a more artistic gift book for one who enjoys the beauty of the old-fashioned days, the sweet sentiments of the home, the clear, strong call of patriotism, so gloriously answered by our fathers." Another reviewer believed that the book was "to be prized not only for its intrinsic value, but also as a desirable chronicle of the nation's progression." Clara E. Laughlin was more precise about America's shifting cultural scene:

> Painting has been the last of the fine arts to reflect American life. . . . Perhaps it wasn't always because [painters] could not recognize the pictorial quality of American life, but sometimes because they couldn't make those Americans who could afford to buy pictures, see it. And a painter must sell a picture once in a while, or stop painting. Let us grant that it may have been the tastes of our newly-rich Americans that drove our painters to the canals of Venice, the windmills and tulip-fields of Holland, the lakes and

chalets of Switzerland, to paint marketable canvases; that filled American homes with Gretchens instead of Priscillas; with French chateau scenes instead of colonial mansion scenes; with pictures of Napoleon on the Bellerophon instead of pictures of Perry on the Niagara.

The reviewer obviously believed that Taylor was good precisely because of his skillful reflection of American life.[5]

None of the nationalistic fervor touched Taylor's time in Cornish. Although there was only one of his works that had immediate Cornish connections, his life here was important to him. Taylor and his wife summered in Cornish from 1902 or 1903[6] until 1910, or shortly thereafter; by 1916, they had built a house in Maine to which they frequently returned. In Cornish they built a cottage on the southeast corner of William Westgate's orchard, near the junction of the present-day Saint-Gaudens Road and the Dingleton Hill Road. They bought a five to seven-acre property and maintained very friendly relations with the Westgates—frequently taking their meals with them. During their summers in Cornish, they were known to be involved with people other than Colonists. For example, Mrs. Taylor, a concert pianist, gave lessons to Arthur Westgate Quimby. Also, a local resident, Insley Spalding, posed for Elijah in the painting *The Parting of Elijah and Elisha*, which appeared in *The Ladies Home Journal* in October of 1915.[7] Among his correspondents are two people with connections to the Cornish Colony: Hamlin Garland and Willard Metcalf, a good friend of his while they both were students in Paris. Finally, there is a story that tells us as much about the work habits of Augustus Saint-Gaudens as it does those of Taylor:

> Harrison Smith Morris, art editor of *The Ladies' Home Journal*, tells of a time when W. L. Taylor, the illustrator, sat for a portrait bust by St. Gaudens . . . sat and sat and sat, long and often, day after day. St. Gaudens would touch the clay here and there, step back to survey the general effect, move forward or to one side, silent and apprehensive. Taylor, patient and uncomplaining, himself a slow and painstaking workman, made no comment. Then, of a sudden, after many days, St. Gaudens looked towards Taylor with surprise. "Why," he said, pointing to the bust, "it is finished." Taylor got down from the model's chair. He crossed the studio to St. Gaudens's side: "Why—so it is." And indeed it was.[8]

William Ladd Taylor died in Wellesley, Massachusetts, on December 26, 1926. His wife died May 27, 1935. They had no children.

ENDNOTES

1. Virginia Colby, Cornish Colony files; based on the William Ladd Taylor Papers, courtesy of the Archives of American Art, The Smithsonian Institution, Washington, DC. Early in his career he did the frontispiece for Harriet Beecher Stowe's novel *The Pearl of Orrs's Island: A Story of the Coast of Maine*, Vol. 6 of the sixteen-volume Riverside Edition of Stowe's writings published by Houghton Mifflin, 1896.

2. *Exhibition of Paintings by W. L. Taylor Which Have Been Reproduced in The Ladies' Home Journal*, unpaginated, a catalogue published for an exhibition at the Boston Art Club, opening April 15, 1907.

3. "Our Family Album," *The Ladies' Home Journal,* August 1926, p. 28.

4. *Exhibition of Paintings.*

5. The reviews come from the Boston *Budget,* Saturday, December 12, 1908, and the Buffalo *Courier,* Sunday, November 1908. Clara E. Laughlin's review is from the *Chicago Daily Journal,* Thursday, December 10, 1908. All the clippings are in the Virginia Colby, Cornish Colony files, based on the William Ladd Taylor Papers, courtesy of the Archives of American Art, the Smithsonian Institution, Washington, DC. The allusions pit the heroine of Goethe's *Faust,* Margaret, whose pet diminutive form is Gretchen, against the heroine of Longfellow's narrative poem "The Courtship of Miles Standish" and the image of Napoleon on the British ship, the *Bellerophon,* to which he had surrendered after the disastrous defeat at Waterloo in 1815 in hopes that England would offer him asylum, against Oliver Hazard Perry, who fought the battle of Lake Erie on September 10, 1818, and issued the famous dispatch, "We have met the enemy and they are ours," from his flagship *Niagra* after the British destroyed his first flagship, the *Lawrence.*

6. The earliest documented mention of the Taylors is in Stephen Parrish's diary. He called on them at the Westgates' on June 22, 1903; diary, Special Collections, Baker Library, Dartmouth College, gift of Marian and Roy Garrand.

7. As the magazine put it, "the problem of models is not an easy one. Apart from professionals, both family and neighbors have been glad to lend themselves to Mr. Taylor's purposes, or even now and then a stranger, as happened when he met his Elijah . . . upon a country road among the New Hampshire hills."; "The Personal Side of Mr. Taylor, Told by a Lifelong Friend," *The Ladies' Home Journal,* March 1916, p. 15.

8. Charles C. Baldwin, *Stanford White* (New York: Dodd, Mead, 1931), p. 57. It should be noted, however, that there is absolutely no evidence among the records at the Saint-Gaudens National Historic Site that Saint-Gaudens ever did a bust of Taylor.

Figure 158. *Sign for the "Tea Tray," painted by Maxfield Parrish.*
See color plate Figure 1c for the reverse side of the sign.

THE "TEA TRAY" was a landmark during the heyday of the Cornish Colony. It was a tea house on Route 12A, the first house north of the Cornish-Windsor Covered Bridge. The shop was operated by Marie Parker, of Orange, New Jersey, who also shared her house with her sister, Mrs. Anna Parker Morris, her niece Mariamne (later Mrs. Clement Newbold), and her brother, the surgeon, Dr. John Parker.

Admirers of Maxfield Parrish will always remember the "Tea Tray" for its beautiful, double-sided sign that he painted. Sue Lewin, Maxfield Parrish's favorite model, posed for three of the four characters on the sign. The tea house itself was open afternoons and many members of the Cornish Colony, along with their guests and other people from the area, enjoyed a pleasant afternoon of sociability there. President Wilson's family were delighted patrons during their stay in the summers of 1913, 1914, and 1915. And in her diaries, Lydia Parrish noted visits from Marie Parker, whose full name was Mariamne Meade Parker.

During the winter months, Marie Parker and her sister operated another "Tea Tray" in Aiken, South Carolina. The Cornish "Tea Tray," however, was sold to Elizabeth Perkins in 1922. Because the "Tea Tray" was such a favorite spot among the Colonists, here are some of its most popular recipes.[1]

Brown Sugar Cookies

Use sugar so dark as to be almost the color of molasses. This can be found in the large grocery shops. One and one-half cups of dark brown sugar; one-half cup of butter and the same of water, one-fourth teaspoonful of ground nutmeg, one-half teaspoon of soda and two teaspoons of baking powder. Flour sufficient to roll. Cream butter and sugar; add water with soda dissolved in it; then nutmeg, flour, baking powder and pinch of salt sifted together. Roll as thin as possible; sprinkle with granulated sugar, pressing grains slightly into dough with tips of fingers. Bake in hot oven for about five minutes. These are crisp and delicious.

Little Nut Cakes

Take the weight of 2 eggs in flour, about 5 oz. and the weight of 2 eggs in sugar (about 5½ heaping tablespoons); weight of one egg in butter (about 2½ oz.); 1 teaspoon baking powder. Beat the butter to a cream; add sugar gradually and mix well; then add the 2 eggs, previously beaten until very light, and fold in the flour little by little. When the mixture is quite smooth, drop it by teaspoons on a well-buttered baking sheet and put ½ of a walnut on each cake and be sure to put the cakes far apart as they spread. Cook in moderate oven 8 to 10 minutes.

Gingerbread

4 cups flour	1 cup molasses
1 cup butter	1 cup coffee
4 eggs	1 teaspoon soda
2 teaspoons cinnamon	salt
1 tablespoon ginger	1 cup sugar

Cream butter and sugar together; add spices, then eggs, salt, molasses, flour; lastly, cup of hot black coffee with teaspoon of soda dissolved in it. Bake either in roasting pan or muffin pans; serve hot.

Fruit Cookies

½ cup butter	1 teaspoon cinnamon
1 cup sugar	1 teaspoon nutmeg
1 egg	¼ teaspoon cloves
⅔ cup milk	1 cup chopped nuts
1 iron spoon molasses	1 cup sultana raisins
1 teaspoon cream of tartar	1½ cups of sifted flour
½ teaspoon soda	

Cream butter and sugar; add spices, molasses, egg, milk, and flour with cream and butter sifted in; dissolve soda in very little boiling water. Lastly, nuts and raisins; drop on buttered tin.

Cream Cake

1 cup sugar
3 egg yolks
2 egg whites
butter size of walnut
1 cup flour mixed with baking powder
½ cup water

Bake in four jelly tins (layer cake tins).

Filling

1 tablespoon corn starch
2 tablespoons sugar flavored with vanilla or fresh lemon.

Beef Sandwich

Beef should be rare. Chop it fine with a little celery and a very thin slice of onion. Add a little tomato catsup. Beat in sufficient melted butter to hold mixture together. Spread on thin slices of white bread.

For a delicious sandwich, take equal parts of chopped walnut meats, olives, and celery. Moisten with mayonnaise, and use either white or brown bread.

Chicken and Mushroom Sandwich

Chop cooked chicken finely; and add to each cupful of the meat one tablespoonful of minced mushrooms (bottled), a light sprinkling of salt and paprika, half a cupful of shredded lettuce, one tablespoonful of chopped and peeled radishes and sufficient mayonnaise or boiled dressing to moisten. Mix the ingredients well and fill between pointed dinner rolls that have been split lengthwise and buttered.

Cream Cheese Sandwiches

Mince one small white onion and mix with a small cream cheese that has been rubbed to a paste. Run two sweet cucumber pickles through the meat grinder and add them to the cheese and onion, with two tablespoonfuls of chopped pimentos. Spread between buttered slices of Boston brown bread. These furnish a very delectable supper sandwich.

Lydia Parrish's Brown Bread

2 teaspoons salt
¾ cup molasses
1 yeast cake
2 cups oatmeal
4 cups boiling water
enough flour to make stiff batter

Mix the boiled water, the salt and oatmeal; let stand until lukewarm; add the ¾ cup molasses; then the yeast cake, which has been dissolved in ½ cup warm water; add enough white flour to make a stiff batter; let rise as usual. Cook in slow oven for 1¾ hours.

Parrish's Sponge Cakes

1 lb. sugar	½ lb. flour
1 lb. eggs (8 eggs)	½ lemon

Beat yolks and sugar and lemon together until white. Beat the whites stiff; pour off any liquid; add sifted flour very gently; fold in whites.

Jellied Oranges

12 oranges	1 lb. sugar

Cut the oranges and take out the seeds as for tea. Put 1 pint of water on half box of gelatine and let it boil up twice. Then pour over the oranges and add ½ tumbler of wine. Pour in molds and serve when cold.

Puffs

1 tablespoons wheat flour
1 pint milk
2 eggs

1 pint milk well beaten into a batter; a little salt; bake in small pans.

Tea Cakes

1 cup sugar	1 quart flour
1 cup butter	1 teaspoon baking powder
3 eggs	nutmeg and lemon to taste.

Cut with a tin cutter and bake in quick oven.

Frosting

Boil 1 cup sugar and ¼ cup boiling water, leaving at boil 3 or 4 minutes. Add speck of cream of tartar and boil 3 or 4 more minutes; pour on beaten white of egg; flavor with vanilla. Continue to beat with dover egg beater; add 2 or 3 marshmallows, beating in hot syrup.

Rich Fruit Cake

2 lbs. seeded raisins	1 large tablespoon allspice
2 lbs. currants	1 large tablespoon cinnamon
1 lb. citron	½ tablespoon cloves
1 lb. butter	1 grated nutmeg
1 lb. brown sugar	1 teacup brandy
1 lb flour	1 teacup wine

Put all the spices in the liquor. Beat butter and sugar together; add 12 eggs beaten together; then fruit and liquor alternately. (The fruit must be chopped in some of the flour.) 1 teaspoon soda dissolved in liquor makes it lighter. Bake in a slow oven 5 hours. When done, cover with a heavy cover.

ENDNOTE

1. The recipes are from Marie Parker's cookbook, courtesy of its owners, Cheston and Nancy Newbold, Cornish, NH.

HARRY DICKINSON THRASHER
1883 – 1918

HARRY DICKINSON THRASHER's life and career have all the elements of a good novel; some aspects might even remind you of an Horatio Alger story or *A Farewell to Arms*. He was born in Plainfield, New Hampshire, on May 24, 1883, the son of Wallace and Eliza (Dickinson) Thrasher. His family ran mills on Blow-Me-Down Brook for several generations; his father was a respected carpenter and maker of cabinets and coffins. The family lived just over the Cornish line in Plainfield on what is now known as Thrasher Road—the house was torn down in 1964.[1] The marker for the town line was in the Thrasher's dooryard and the story goes that, as a boy, Harry thought it great sport to stand with one foot in Cornish and the other in Plainfield. Later, he attended Kimball Union Academy in Meriden, New Hampshire.

When his father died in 1902, Harry began work as a "studio boy" in the atelier of Augustus Saint-Gaudens, replacing Frederick MacMonnies. Years later, his sister recalled: "my brother Harry went to work at the age of eighteen to help our mother who was left with two small girls to bring up, the last of a family of nine. This led to a very wonderful career for him and our pride in him was great. He used to walk the two miles or more to and from his work at the Saint-Gaudens studio. He had the benefit of Saint-Gaudens's personal instruction for five wonderful years. He and Homer Saint-Gaudens became the best of friends and I can see Homer riding into our yard on his beautiful horse to spend time with Harry. Homer was a very likable and fine young man and to the last was a loyal friend to Harry."[2] With this friendship and loyalty to Saint-Gaudens himself, it is not surprising that he played the role of a faun or satyr in the 1905 production of *A Masque of "Ours": The Gods and the Golden Bowl.* In 1907, Harry moved on to New York City to work in the studio of Adolph Weinmann, a former student of Saint-Gaudens at the Art Students League and later one of his assistants. At night, Thrasher, too, attended sculpture classes at the Art Students League under James Earle Fraser (see above pp. 200-202).[3] One year later his talent was recognized when, appropriately enough, he received the Saint-Gaudens Prize.

Another prize in 1911, the coveted Prix de Rome of the American Academy, launched Thrasher's career. A local newspaper provided the details with pride: "The prize Thrasher has won carries with it a three-year scholarship abroad, one year of which the sculptor will spend visiting the great galleries of Europe and the other two pursuing his studies in a studio in Rome. There were nearly one hundred entries in the competi-

Figure 159. Salome Dancing Before Herod, *by Harry Thrasher, done in 1913 for Norman Hapgood, who then owned "High Court." The bas-relief is in the garden.*

tion. These finally were eliminated to three, one from a Boston sculptor, another from a Philadelphian, with Thrasher representing New York. His subject was 'Memory.' It is a small group of three figures, a man, woman, and child."[4]

Progress toward his goals as a sculptor was cut short by the outbreak of hostilities in Europe. And now comes the Hemingway resemblance. On a visit to London in 1913, with a touch reminiscent of Frederic Henry, Harry Thrasher married Carlotta Davis of San Francisco—his Catherine Barkley. By the time the United States entered World War I in 1917, Harry Thrasher had returned to this country and enlisted as a private in the newly formed Camouflage Corps of the Army Engineers. His wife, instead of being with him in an Italian field hospital as Catherine was with Frederic, followed Harry to the battlefields of France as a nurse in the Red Cross. He, meanwhile, was promoted to a sergeant; he won his officer's commission as a second lieutenant because of the work of his unit, the 103rd Engineers, at the front in July of 1918. Largely a result of the theories of protective coloration, or obliterative gradation, of Abbott Thayer (see below pp. 504-505), camouflage units were obliged to prove their usefulness; many old-guard officers regarded the theory behind camouflage with suspicion. These units were assigned to mask "the American batteries to the 'eyes' of the enemy . . . the 103rd Engineers [were] engaged in camouflage work assigned to painters and sculptors. This task calls the artists right up to the front, for the guns must be concealed, and many ingenious schemes are employed to carry out certain illusions to thwart the plans of the enemy. Therefore the work of the Camouflage Corps is fraught with many dangers, and frequently the members of this section of the army are under fire."[5]

414

Such proved to be the tragic case for Harry Thrasher. The best person to narrate the events is his close friend and former assistant to Augustus Saint-Gaudens in Cornish, Barry Faulkner. As members of the American Expeditionary Force, these two comrades were encamped at Dravegny, a village halfway between the Marne and the Vesle Rivers, about 25 miles west of Reims. The Germans were along the Vesle, near Fismes. "Between the two towns a wide shallow valley branched off to the west, its north side just high enough to give shelter to the dugouts of officers and company clerks. The naked valley itself gave no possible opportunity for concealment, yet almost an entire artillery brigade took up positions in it, followed by their horses, trucks and field kitchens. The valley was lively and crowded as a country fair; long lines of horses tethered or being led to water, fat bunches of puptents, men bathing in the brook, convoys of ammunition coming and going and the field kitchens smoking merrily." Needless to say, this sprightly scene was soon to be interrupted because Faulkner's and Thrasher's camouflage unit was ordered to conceal the very positions which lay exposed in the open valley. "The Camouflage section protested strongly against this willful madness, and then camouflaged the guns as well as they could. Several days passed without incident and the officers cheerfully reminded me that the Germans had not spotted the position. But the enemy found it between four and five in the afternoon of the 11th of August, and shelled and gassed 'Death Valley' heavily for two hours. Two hundred horses were killed, about fifty men, and direct hits were made on the guns. Harry Thrasher was among those killed."[6]

The rest of the sad tale comes from a letter Faulkner wrote to Frances Grimes, dated August 15, 1918:

> When I saw him he was lying on his side and looked almost alive and had that happy humorous expression he had when he'd made one of those humorous comments we used to love so well. He must have been killed instantly and had no fear at all—just amused and interested. You can imagine the anguish and fear with which I lifted the blanket—and then such reassurement. . . . He was a brave soul and did a good job. . . . Perhaps Harry's look was his amusement and interest in the next phase. It apparently wasn't any more comprehensible than this. I had him buried out in the country where he'd given his life. I'm sure he didn't want a French cemetery, though the officers offered to take him to one. The isolated graves saying "Tué pour la France" (killed for France) lying out on the great moors are always sweet and peaceful. This country is beautiful and severe and the great heave of the hills reminds me of Cornish. One of the first things I said to myself when coming here was—"What a country to be buried in!" It reminds me too of Hal's "Grenstone." Dear Frances, we are sadly bereaved. . . . Homer said he'd lost his best friend.[7]

Faulkner's opportunity to pay visible tribute to his friend came four years later in 1922 when the architect Eric Gugler organized a competition among Fellows of the American Academy in Rome to erect a memorial to two Fellows who had died in the War: Walter Ward, an architect, and Harry Thrasher. Gugler worked on a team with a sculptor with Cornish connections, Paul Manship, and Faulkner, whose talents were those of a muralist; they won the competition and their tribute was "put up in the courtyard of the new Academy building on the Janiculum" hill in Rome in 1923.[8] Faulkner designed a fresco and beneath it Manship designed a bench of red marble with the figures of two soldiers kneeling on either side of it and a frieze of soldiers in combat. Gugler designed the inscriptions, using the first verse of John Masefield's poem "Truth."[9]

Although he lived only thirty-five years, Harry Thrasher produced a significant number of pieces of sculpture. Some of them are interestingly described in a newspaper account after his death. Referring to his output while in Rome between 1913 and 1916, it commented that "a distinctive example of his work . . . was the design for the 'Spirit of America,' which represented an imaginary city beautified, with America the central figure in a court of honor. This work was accomplished by the sculptor in cooperation with a painter and an architect, and it received high praise indeed from his fellow artists." A piece that was displayed in New York, "which attracted considerable attention was the figure of a boy holding a pair of horns on his head, faun-like in effect and fraught with imagination." Another work exhibited at New York's Gorham Gallery also "attracted considerable attention [it] is entitled 'America Embattled' . . . it typifies young American manhood in a stalwart figure sturdy of limb, and as an emblem the eagle is introduced with outstretched limbs." The account noted "a portrait of Master John Goodwin, and a portrait of a woman." Finally, "Lieutenant Thrasher's last sculptural work was the modelling of the Prentiss Memorial for Lakeview Cemetery, Cleveland, Ohio, which was designed by Kenyon Cox [see above pp. 162-165]. This memorial represents two standing female figures clad in flowing robes, and is characterized by simplicity in treatment and feeling. The work was displayed at the last annual exhibition of the Architectural League of New York and was reproduced in the league catalog. The memorial was unveiled in Cleveland about the time the sculptor departed for France."[10] After his death, some of his works were exhibited in New York at a show in the Madison Art Gallery along with those of Frances Grimes and James Earle Fraser, April 22 to May 4, 1918.

Several of Thrasher's other works include the bronze sculpture *Young Duck*, done perhaps in 1914 and owned by the Metropolitan Museum of Art in New York. It was included in the exhibition "A Circle of Friends: Art Colonies of Cornish and Dublin" in 1985. Those of his works with a local connection include a 10' x 6' rectangular bas-relief commissioned by Norman Hapgood for his garden at "High Court" that Thrasher did in Rome in 1913, *Salome Dancing Before Herod*; a *Portrait Head of Frances Grimes*; and a portrait head of his mother, Eliza Ellen (Dickinson) Thrasher. Locally, two of his works were shown at Dartmouth College's exhibition of works from the Cornish Colony in 1916.

It is only fitting that Barry Faulkner should have the closing words on Harry Thrasher:

> [he] made no great stir in the world, but those who knew him will remember him long and tenderly for his character was truly distinguished and noble. His nature was harmonious and well-balanced. He loved beauty in any form; he had humor, a shrewd wisdom and a fine intolerance. Among his outstanding qualities were integrity and imaginative thoroughness. Where others procrastinated, he accomplished. He had no sentimentalities, and called all spades by their names. He had had too much hard experience to be a gay optimist, but he never dimmed his courage and his cheerfulness. He was a New Englander to the core and of that rare type which New England too seldom produces.[11]

ENDNOTES

1. In 1958, the selectmen of Plainfield decided to call the road "Thrasher Road" in lieu of "Ruggles Road." Although the Ruggles family had lived along the road for a long time, the town wanted to honor the memory of Harry Thrasher, who was killed in action while serving in the US Army in France.

2. Letter from Mrs. Jay Harold Russell (Nina "Dolly" Thrasher), spring 1970; Virginia Colby, Cornish Colony files.

3. The model for Fraser's *Head of a Young Artist* (1921-1922) is believed to be Harry Thrasher.

4. Unidentified newspaper clipping, Daniels scrapbook, Virginia Colby, Cornish Colony files.

5. Unidentified newspaper clipping, Clara Westgate's scrapbook, Virginia Colby, Cornish Colony files.

6. Barry Faulkner, *Barry Faulkner: Sketches from an Artist's Life* (Dublin, NH: William L. Bauhan, 1973), pp. 98-99.

7. Virginia Colby, Cornish Colony files. The allusions are to "Hal," or Witter Bynner, *Grenstone Poems: A Sequence* (New York: Frederick A. Stokes, 1917) and to Homer Saint-Gaudens.

8. Faulkner, p. 112.

9. Notes written by Ann Faulkner Jacobs for an exhibition of works by Barry Faulkner and Harry Thrasher, The Historical Society of Cheshire County, Keene, NH, November 23, 1987.

10. Clipping, headed "N.H. Gold Star Mothers," Manchester, NH, *The Union*, c. July 30, 1931; Virginia Colby, Cornish Colony files. The reference is to the *Year Book of the Architectural League of New York and Catalogue of the Thirtieth Annual Exhibition* (New York: Architectural League, 1915). It reproduced pictures of the following works by Harry Thrasher: a sculpture for the "Collaborative Problem, American Academy in Rome" and *Boy Pretending He Is A Faun* as well as early pieces of sculpture by Paul Manship and a pavilion Charles A. Platt designed for William Fahnestock.

11. Faulkner, p. 101.

Figure 160. Boy and Donkey *by Henry Walker.*

HENRY OLIVER WALKER
1843 – 1920

and

LAURA MARQUAND WALKER
1883 – 1938

HENRY OLIVER WALKER belonged to the tradition of the Ecole des Beaux-Arts which he absorbed in the Parisian atelier of Léon Bonnat. His stay in Paris during the late 1870s resulted in his making fast friends with people whose acquaintance he would eventually renew in Cornish: Augustus Saint-Gaudens, Thomas Dewing, Willard Metcalf, and Charles Platt. In fact, Walker was later responsible for bringing Platt to Cornish in 1889. During his time in Paris, however, Platt penned this description of Walker to his parents: "the kind of man that Henry James writes about as peculiar to Boston."[1] A mutual friend of this group, the American Impressionist Dennis Bunker, remarked that Walker was "about the only man in Boston to whom it is possible to talk about pictures and things . . . and the only one of my Boston acquaintances who has 'worn well.'"[2]

Upon his return to the United States in November of 1882, Walker, first in Boston and later in New York, became a champion of the aesthetic movement, with its emphasis on art for art's sake. The aim of these artists was, in their commitment to principles of harmony and beauty, "to infuse their work with idealism and sensuous virtue."[3] In fact, Walker is best known for his rendering of the beautiful and the ideal in the form of both portraits and murals of allegorical figures.

In 1888, partly as a result of Walker's dedication to these principles, Thomas Dewing, Walker's good friend from their days in Paris, decided to invite Walker and his bride, Laura Marquand, who were married in April, to spend the summer in Cornish. Because Augustus Saint-Gaudens and his wife were in Europe, the Walkers were able to rent "Aspet." In her *Memories*, Laura Walker recalled that "there was a barn up there on the place that Henry could paint in. The place was a hilltop with a beautiful view of the Ascutney and our nearest neighbors lived a quarter of a mile away. No houses in sight. It was lonely but very beautiful up there—lovely woods with great pines by the sides of a mountain brook and beyond the brook a mile away through the woods lived the Dewings."[4]

Incidentally, today's visitors to the Saint-Gaudens National Historic Site owe Henry Walker a debt of gratitude. It is evident that the Walkers genuinely enjoyed their summer in Cornish. As Laura Walker put it, "Henry loved it there and always for years after we felt we had a share in the place because of that summer. Some little white birches had been set

Figure 161. *Henry Walker painting* Boy and Donkey.

out by the pool which a statue of Pan guarded, and it is said that if Henry had not watered those little birches assiduously through their first summer, they would never have been what they are now, and many a time we have sat with the St. Gaudenses beside that pool and under the birches."[5] Walker's sense of stewardship both for the area and for the particular garden spot has provided successive generations with a cherished corner from which to contemplate Mount Ascutney and to enjoy the Sunday concerts on summer afternoons.

So great was the pleasure the Walkers took in Cornish that the following summer they purchased land from Major Chester Pike on what is now known as Platt Road. Again, Mrs. Walker provides the details, reminding us that theirs was the first house in Cornish that Charles A. Platt designed; they finally moved into it during the summer of 1890:

Charles Platt built our house and soon after built one near us. . . . Our second summer was spent with the Tracy family and not far from them farther down the hill we broke ground for our own house and had bought about fifteen acres of pasture and woodland and part of a brook. Later we added four or five more acres and so owned a beautiful part of a rushing brook with huge pines on its banks and rocks over which it dashed (in those days) with little waterfalls and pools. Later water was brought up to our two houses from our part of the brook. A ram, so-called, was set to work near a little waterfall and a reservoir was built near the Platts' on our land. At last we had water enough for all purposes but drinking—for that, we had a lovely spring on the Austin land piped into our kitchen and always good. We were the first ones, we and the Platts, to have real plumbing and a good water supply.[6]

Her descriptions of how they scheduled their daily activities provide us with a fascinating glimpse into the daily lives of the Colonists. Clearly they loved their house. "Henry had his studio in the house at first and work to do; his big murals came later." It was then that he added an adjacent studio. "He enjoyed the life . . . there and his own land and brook. The men came at 12:00 for a bath and we all kept away and let them have all the little waterfalls and pool to themselves. Sometimes the women and girls had their hour—Truly, it was the most sylvan glade and brook with tall trees on the bank." The land, too, also was a great attraction: "tall pines against the sky and one slope of the beautiful mountain [Ascutney] and pines, old and very high near the brook. And in the spring, linnea, that beautiful little pink flower, grew near the pathway by the brook and many of the blue blind gentians. Partridges and rabbits and squirrels were plenty in those days and strange little red lizards near the roots of the trees—pretty and decorative little things."[7]

Drawing his inspiration from his surroundings, Walker painted portraits of such local personalities as Charles Alden Tracy and Charles A. Platt. He incorporated the local landscape into *Morning Vision* (1895) and probably painted *Wood Nymph* (1901) and *Musa Regina* (1904) while he was in Cornish. One of his contemporaries, the critic W. Lewis Fraser, thought that "Mr. Walker's pictures are the work of a conscientious and talented workman. They are careful in drawing, pure in color, and excellently made; and they show an artist of much intellectuality and of a poetic temperament. Henry Walker is one of those artists (by no means uncommon in our studios) who, regardless of those who cry aloud in the market-place, quietly follow in the path marked out by Perugino, and beaten by the footsteps of Del Sarto and Raphael."[8] More typical of his work are the murals *John Eliot Preaching to the Indians*,[9] *The Pilgrims on the Mayflower* for the Massachusetts State House, *Yesterday, Today, and Tomorrow* in the Minnesota state capitol building over the Senate Chamber door, and *The Wisdom of the Law* in the Appellate Court House in New York City.

His most famous murals, however, were those he did for the Library of Congress building, erected in 1897. These were created to illustrate *Poetry* and included *The Muse of Lyric Poetry* (attended by Passion, Beauty, Mirth, Pathos, Truth, and Devotion), *Shakespeare's Adonis* (slain by the wild boar), *Tennyson's Ganymede* (borne to Olympus by Jove in the form of an eagle), *Keats' Endymion* (the shepherd boy asleep on Mount Latmus), *Emerson's Uriel* ("Gave his sentiment divine/Against the being of a line"), *Wordsworth's Boy of Winander* (at evening by the Glimmering Lake), and *Milton's Comus* (listening to the Lady's song). Samuel Isham, a visitor in Cornish, enthused in 1905 that, "the New Library of Congress [building] at Washington . . . was epoch-making in a way, for it was the first governmental building to be erected in the country where the architect had planned a complete artistic adornment as an integral part of the structure. . . . Walker's decorations were charming both in execution and sentiment, breathing the very spirit of the lyric poetry that they illustrated."[10] *Harper's Weekly* was equally glowing: "He has added to the library perhaps the most thoroughly exquisite paintings there. No one certainly, whether in the Washington edifice or in our local exhibitions, has ever quite touched the point of refinement and sweetness at which he finds his most characteristic effects. The fibre of his art is of the purest. That he has strength, spiritual strength, is shown by the mild and elevating beauty of his art. That he has the strength, the executive strength, of an accomplished painter, is made plain by the sound composition and noble handling of masses in these poetic decorations."[11] To capitalize on the excitement the building caused and to edify its public, a publisher brought out a book reproducing "the

Library Mural Paintings in the colors of the originals, with the fidelity made possible by the most perfect color process of the day, and with the softness and delicacy of the actual paintings." Furthermore, to facilitate understanding Walker's contribution to the murals, the book included "the poems of the Poetry Series [which] will add to the appreciation of the artist[']s work; and there are also given the Library Quotations, which constitute such a pleasing element of the decorations."[12] Nevertheless, the "Cornish Library Notes" were not so unequivocal in its opinion: Walker's "paintings are very lovely in coloring and are hopelessly maligned by the reproductions which one sees of them."[13]

While Henry and Laura Walker were in Cornish, they were quite active in community affairs. They both participated in the presentation on June 22, 1905, of *A Masque*

Figure 162. Delphiniums *by Laura Walker.*

of "Ours": The Gods and the Golden Bowl. While he played the part of Priam, King of Troy, Laura was Atropos, one of the three fates, the goddess responsible for cutting the web of life that Clotho spun and Lachesis measured. In September of the following year, they opened up their property to the children of the Cornish Colony for their charming production of Thackeray's comedy *The Rose and the Ring.* By acting as the children's coach, Ethel Barrymore focused her dramatic expertise on the production and participated in what was to become a traditional kind of entertainment done by the Colony's children for everyone's amusement. The Walkers served the guests and the entire company tea after the performance.[14]

Laura Walker will also be remembered for starting the Mothers' and Daughters' Club in August of 1897 with Frances Houston, Eleanor Platt, and Grace Arnold (see above pp. 286–289). Mrs. Walker was the organization's first president, serving for several years, and then held the position of honorary president for many years. Her artistic contributions included a painting entitled *Delphiniums,* designs for the rugs made by the women of the Mothers' and Daughters' Club, and a book of poems she published privately in 1914 at her Lakewood home, *Quatrains,* a collection of twenty-four four-line poems illustrated by Katharine Lewis Hinsdale.

ENDNOTES

1. In a letter dated November 4, 1882, as quoted in Erica E. Hirshler, *Dennis Miller Bunker: American Impressionist* (Boston: Museum of Fine Arts, 1994), p. 26. A thoroughly un-Jamesian fact about Walker's life in Boston: he played the kazoo in an orchestra composed of members of the Tavern Club for a New Year's celebration in December of 1885; Hirshler, p. 50.

2. As quoted in R. H. Ives Gammel, *Dennis Miller Bunker* (New York: Coward-McCann, 1953), p. 19.

3. Hirshler, pp. 74-75. When Walker left Paris, Charles A. Platt took over his studio; Ibid., p. 169.

4. Unpublished manuscript, p. 1; Virginia Colby, Cornish Colony files, courtesy of Mrs. A. Ledyard Smith, Jr.

5. Laura Walker, *Memories*, unpublished manuscript, pp. 3-4; Virginia Colby, Cornish Colony files.

6. Walker, p. 5. The "Austin land" was across the road from the Walkers' house.

7. Ibid., pp. 20, 22.

8. *The Century Magazine* 50:5, September 1895, p. 798.

9. A local newspaper proudly reprinted the following tribute from the *Boston Sunday Herald*: "Mr. Henry O. Walker, whose mural painting of 'John Eliot Preaching to the Indians,' has just been unveiled in Memorial Hall of the Massachusetts State House, was a Boston boy . . . who for many years kept the circulating library in Montgomery Place, and he received his early instruction in art in Boston. Some years ago, he was married to Miss Marquand of New York, and resided there during the winter. He now has a studio in Lakewood [New Jersey] and with Mrs. Walker spends his summers near Windsor, VT, where he has a cottage, and where a large number of artists and literary persons meet every season." Undated and unidentified entry in the Windsor, VT, Library scrapbook; Virginia Colby, Cornish Colony files.

10. Samuel Isham, *The History of American Painting* (New York: Macmillan, 1936), p. 554.

11. The issue of February 27, 1897, as quoted in a local paper; Windsor, VT, Library scrapbook; Virginia Colby, Cornish Colony files.

12. *The Library of Congress Mural Paintings* (New York and Washington: Foster and Reynolds, 1902), preface. Other artists of the Cornish Colony represented in these murals were John White Alexander, who did a series of six murals entitled *The Evolution of the Book*, and Kenyon Cox, who did two murals for the series *The Arts and the Sciences*. Philip Martiny did "the two torch-bearing, robed maidens on the newel posts of the staircase, the twenty-six fanciful pastoral reliefs with their *putti* and festoons for the balustrade, and several figures around the base of the great dome."; Walter Craven, *Sculpture in America* (New York: Thomas Y. Crowell, 1968), pp. 474-475.

13. Unidentified clipping, Cornish Library scrapbook, Virginia Colby, Cornish Colony files.

14. Unidentified clipping, September 1906, Cornish Colony file, Baker Library, Dartmouth College, Hanover, NH.

ARTHUR BATTELLE WHITING
1861 – 1936

ARTHUR WHITING was a concert pianist and composer, primarily of chamber music although he did compose a few orchestral pieces, songs, and piano pieces. He grew up in Cambridge, Massachusetts, part of a musical family, and received his early training at the New England Conservatory. From 1883 to 1885, he studied in Munich, Germany, and became strongly influenced by the music of Johannes Brahms. "Even on the personal level he regarded himself as part of a 'cult of friendship,' very much the way Schumann, Brahms, Joachim, and others thought of themselves as part of a league."[1] Later, he moved to New York and organized "an annual series called 'Chamber Music Expositions' at Harvard, Yale, Princeton, and Columbia."[2] One of his contemporaries provided the following summary judgment of Whiting and his career: "In spite of his small output, he has shown a genuine talent, which has its native characteristics. He is either a severe self-critic, or he writes only when he feels that he has something definite to say. . . . All his life Whiting has been a man of wit and humor, the coiner of epigrams that have become traditions among musicians. . . . It may be that this keen, acrid sense of humor has kept him from taking anything too seriously, including himself, and that this is responsible for his comparatively small list of compositions."[3]

Whiting first appeared on the Cornish tax lists in 1893 when he purchased eight acres of the Edward Bryant farm in the northwestern section of Cornish. The property remained in the Whiting family until 1918 when the Littell family bought it. His associations with Cornish were numerous. In 1893, he composed "A Cornish Bridal Song" as a wedding gift for the marriage of Charles and Eleanor Platt on July 18, 1893. In 1901, with a playful nod to Shakespeare's play *The Merry Wives of Windsor* and to the fact that Windsor, Vermont, was the postal address for the members of the Cornish Colony, he composed a "Merry Wives of Cornish" waltz.[4] In 1905 he brought members of the Boston Symphony Orchestra to Cornish so that they could play the incidental music he composed for the presentation on June 22 of *A Masque of "Ours": The Gods and the Golden Bowl.*[5] Finally, in 1907 Frances Grimes, a loyal assistant to Saint-Gaudens whom he greatly admired, modeled a bas-relief of Whiting.

Whiting and his wife played an important role in the social and cultural life of the Cornish Colony. Margaret Homer Nichols Shurcliff, a niece of the Saint-Gaudenses whose recollections of Colonists generally center on their abilities on the tennis court, remembered Whiting as being "small, frail and with powerful glasses, quick at the net with a most whimsical type of wit."[6] More importantly, Whiting, along with his friend, the violinist Otto Roth,[7] frequently entertained small audiences at musicals organized in his own home as well as at those of Dr. Arthur Nichols and Grace Arnold. There are entries in Stephen Parrish's diary for every year from 1899 to 1910, except for 1904 and 1909, that indicate social and musical occasions at which both he and Whiting were present. The following entries are typical: "P.M. with Anne to concert at Arthur Whiting's (Kneisel, violin); very enjoyable; large audience: Walker, Cox, St. Gaudens, Dewing, Fred, &c, &c"; "Evening to Nichols' to musical (Whiting-Roth); all of Cornish there nearly"; "Evening after supper walked over to Whiting's to meet and hear Mr. Dolmetsch, maker of clavichord, harpsichord & lute. He played all three instruments. Very enjoyable evening (the Coxes, Rublees, Mrs. Littell, Frances Grimes & ourselves)"; "P.M. to Whiting-Roth recital at Mrs. Graydon's. Most of the Colony there."[8] Others who entertained the Whitings, on evenings when Stephen Parrish was there, were the Houstons, the Rublees, the Hydes, and the Fullers.

ENDNOTES

1. "Notes for a Concert of Works by Sidney Homer and Arthur Whiting," Saint-Gaudens National Historic Site, Cornish, NH, June 24, 1984. Joseph Joachim was a Hungarian violinist and composer for whom Brahms composed his violin concerto in 1879.

2. "Notes" and John Tasker Howard, *Our American Music: Three Hundred Years of It* (New York: Crowell, 1931), p. 342.

3. Howard, pp. 342-343.

4. "Notes." As these notes point out, the "Cornish" waltz was part of a longer composition, "The Merry Wives Waltzes."

5. Some of the fragments played at the concert mentioned in the note above are: "Dance of the Armadryad," "Dance of Ceres," and "Dionysius Scene."

6. Margaret Homer Shurcliff, *Lively Days: Some Memoirs of Margaret Homer Shurcliff* (Taipei: Literature House, Ltd., 1965), p. 35.

7. For more on Otto Roth and the Kneisel Quartet, see below pp. 500-501.

8. Stephen Parrish, diary, entries for September 20, 1900; September 25, 1901; August 20, 1907; and August 3, 1910; Special Collections, Baker Library, Dartmouth College, gift of Marian and Roy Garrand. Mrs. [Clendenen] Graydon is Fannie Arnold. With sisters Charlotte and Grace Arnold, Mrs. Graydon rented the William Mercer farmhouse that Charles Beaman remodeled and called "The Butternuts." Arnold Dolmetsch (1858-1940) was famous for making early instruments and pioneering the revival of interest in performing early music on period instruments. He lived in Boston where he also made virginals and lutes.

PRESIDENT WOODROW WILSON'S
SUMMER WHITE HOUSE
IN CORNISH AND WINDSOR (1913-1915)

PRESIDENT WOODROW WILSON spent part of the summers of 1913, 1914, and 1915 in Cornish. The executive offices were established in the court house above the post office in Windsor.[1] Cables for the press lines, and a direct line to Washington, were installed so that the President was able to keep in constant touch with each government department. The clerks and other members of the executive office force lived at the Windsor Hotel. Other members of the executive staff lived at the Churchill Inn at Cornish, a farmhouse opposite Winston Churchill's summer cottage, "Harlakenden House," the actual residence of the President and his family.

President Wilson enjoyed the company of the Cornish Colony neighbors and often dined with Mr. and Mrs. Maxfield Parrish and with Parrish's father, Stephen. He also appreciated Dr. Albert Parker Fitch, a prominent minister and educator who was at that time president of Andover Theological Seminary, and later pastor of Park Avenue Presbyterian Church in New York. Fitch had a summer home on Dingleton Hill in Cornish and frequently was guest preacher at the Congregational Church, now the United Church of Cornish, where Arthur Quimby was organist.[2] President Wilson often attended church services followed by a car full of Secret Service agents.

Other outings were of a more social nature. On the one hand, in 1913, Percy MacKaye's *Sanctuary: A Bird Masque* was performed at the Meriden Bird Club in Meriden with both of the President's daughters taking part. On the other hand, guests at the President's home enjoyed taking long walks in the country and often stopped at Marie Parker's "Tea Tray" for refreshments. Recalling his 1913 vacation in Cornish, President Wilson enjoyed "the limericks from Mrs. [Adeline Pond] Adams." But he was especially nostalgic about the area: "how shall I tell you what those eight days at Cornish meant to me! They were like a new honeymoon! All the days were days of contentment, renewal, and delight. I begin to think that I am just learning what a holiday means. Perhaps when we were college people we were a bit spoiled. We had so much liberty that we did not realize how precious it was. Now I know. And it pleases me to learn of the friendships you are making, about the new experiences you are having. Bully for Mr. Vonneh! I hope the picture will be a success, even if it must be 'impressionistic.' Is he up to a really good thing?"[3]

During the last summer, 1915, the President was courting Mrs. Edith Bolling Galt;

Figure 163. *Woodrow Wilson and Homer Saint-Gaudens in France, World War I, c. 1918.*

his first wife, Ellen Axson Wilson, had died in August of 1914. The President was called back to Washington leaving Mrs. Galt and friends in Cornish. The following account of a walk across the covered toll bridge is recalled in her book entitled *My Memoir.*

The nearest village was Windsor, Vermont, to enter whose sacred precincts it was necessary to cross a toll bridge. There was a special arrangement whereby cars from the "President's Cottage," as it was called, paid the toll by the month. One day we were walking. We wanted to go into the village and had no money with us. We borrowed a dollar from one of the Secret Service men, as the old woman who kept the tollgate was a dragon, and we did not want to ask favours of her. So, we approached her and tendered our silver cartwheel. Without so much as looking at us she handed back ninety-five cents. Helen said: "What is the charge for crossing the bridge on foot?" She snapped back: "Two cents." Following this lead, Helen said: "Well, you gave me only ninety-five cents when it should have been ninety-six." "No," said the dragon, "it is two cents for one person to cross, but five cents for two together." This illuminating information explained much to me then and since concerning Vermont thrift!

The old woman was a character. People who had been there for years told us she had never been seen even to nod her head to anyone crossing the bridge, and for her to speak was unknown. So we decided to play a game and see who could break down her defense and make her acknowledge a presence. As we passed, we would all say "Good morning" or "Good afternoon," but never a sound came from those hard old lips. At last, just a few days before my visit was to end, the President, Helen, and I drove in to Windsor. We halted on the bridge and he leaned out and lifted the Scotch cap he always wore when driving in the open car and said in that delightful voice that never failed to thrill me: "I am afraid we give you a great deal of trouble going back and forth so much." "Naw," she said "it's my job." And for the first time she turned and looked at him, and, something in her responding to what he gave out, she smiled! When we drove on, Helen and I exclaimed, and the President said: "Poor old woman. Her smile reminded me of what some fellow said about another's face, that it was like 'the breaking up of a hard winter.' I think I understand how grim you must be if 'it is only your job' you are doing and you see nothing bigger ahead."[4]

In Edith Bolling Galt's private letters to Woodrow Wilson, there are several interesting remarks about her time in Cornish: a visit with the Shipmans and a dinner with Maxfield and Lydia Parrish, "they are charming people, and I am sure you would like them" (July 18, 1915); a reference to the "Discussion Club," a comment that she "walked nearly to the Windsor Bridge yesterday afternoon and went to the 'Tea Tray' for tea," another comment that "the dinner party last night was *very* nice. I was interested to meet Mr. Churchill," and finally, "tonight the elder Mr. Parrish (Stephen) comes to dinner, and tomorrow five ladies to lunch. Then, as you remember, we go to dinner with Mr. & Mrs. Fitch, and Thursday Miss Parker has asked . . . me to lunch" (July 20, 1915); her last letter from Cornish alludes to a picnic "up the River Road toward Hanover" and a drive on "that good road toward Lake Sunapee" as well as to a "Discussion Club" meeting that "was about the most amusing thing I have heard in a long time, and no one knew a bit more when we left than when we arived. But lots of the women had talked a great deal."[5]

ENDNOTES

1. The building known as the courthouse and post office in Windsor, VT, was one of the final major commissions carried out from 1856 to 1859 by the distinguished architect Ammi B. Young, who was born in Lebanon, NH, in 1798. His most nortworthy buildings include: the Congregational Church in Norwich, VT (1817); the buildings on "Dartmouth Row"—Wentworth and Thornton Halls (1827-1828) and Reed Hall (1830) as well as the Shattuck Observatory at Dartmouth (1854); the Vermont State House in Montpelier (1836-1838); and the Customs House in Boston (1837-1847). For more information on Young, see Osmund R. Overby, "Ammi B. Young: An Architectural Sketch," *The Magazine Antiques* 81:5, May 1962, pp. 529-533.

2. Virginia Colby, Cornish Colony files; on Dr. Fitch, see above pp. 14-16.

3. Letter from the White House, July 20, 1913; Arthur S. Link, ed., *The Papers of Woodrow Wilson* (Princeton, NJ: Princeton University Press, 1978), Vol. 28, p. 45. For more on Wilson's attendance at the performance of *Sanctuary,* see below pp. 502-503, n. 3.

4. Edith Bolling Wilson, *My Memoir* (Indianapolis, IN: The Bobbs-Merrill Company, 1939), p. 72.

5. *The Papers of Woodrow Wilson,* Vol. 33 (1915), pp. 525-526, 543; Vol. 34 (1915), pp. 7-8.

ELLEN AXSON WILSON:

A First Lady's Perspective on Cornish (1913)

ELLEN AXSON WILSON (1860-1914) came to Cornish with her three daughters Eleanor, Margaret, and Jessie during the summer of 1913 to escape the heat of the District of Columbia on the advice of the presidential physician, Dr. Cory Travers Grayson. They ensconced themselves comfortably in Winston Churchill's "cottage" known as "Harlakenden House." A faithful correspondent, Mrs. Wilson wrote often to President Wilson, who was obliged to remain there because of pressing political pressure surrounding tariff legislation and, especially, the Federal Reserve bill. An artist of some repute, who had studied in the Art Students League (1884-1885) and had been involved

Figure 164. *Robert Vonnoh's painting of Ellen Axson Wilson and her daughters. Photographed by Arnold Genthe, 1913.*

with the artist colony in Old Lyme, Connecticut (1908-1911), Mrs. Wilson was anticipating an exciting summer in Cornish. While in Cornish she painted five paintings that were exhibited at the Arlington Gallery in New York City in November of 1913 and sponsored by the Association of Women Painters and Sculptors. One, in particular, was called *The Terrace*. It appears to be painted from the terrace of "Harlakenden House." There were two notices of it in *The New York Times*. One described it as "a terrace from which one looks over a bank of flowers and over a stretch of table land toward the distant hills" (November 15, 1913). The other report thought it "a charming picture, the most attractive of the five" and added that "Mrs. Wilson considered [it] too intimate a picture of the Presidential summer home at Cornish to be sold."[1] Excerpts from her letters follow. They provide one of the most revealing descriptions of the summer's social life in Cornish that we have.[2]

Friday morning, July 18, 1913—

Our days keep rather full in one way or another for, of course, I paint every morning. Yesterday I had my first little tea and it was very pleasant—such nice people! I had half the Cornish crowd yesterday and shall have the other half today—about 25 each day. On Monday, I shall have all the Windsor people who have called—about 35. I am sorry to say that several of the interesting men of the Colony are not here now—among them Platt, the architect & Kenyon Cox. Mrs. Platt is charming—also a Mrs. Hand, wife of a distinguished New York lawyer, Judge Hand. He, too, is away. She presided at the little Club[3] this week with a charming mixture of real ability, modesty and a quiet, soft, feminine charm. It seems she was a classmate and friend at Bryn Mawr of Florence Hoyt.

Mr. Vonnoh[4] has begun his group of the four of us. We are "composed" in his studio window with the grape vines and columns outside. I am pouring tea at a tiny table. It bids fair to be a nice thing of the sunny impressionist sort. It is going to take a lot of our time I fear, but fortunately we do not all have to pose at once.

Sunday, July 20, 1913—

We have had a Sunday in some respects a repetition of the last "but oh!—the difference is to me!"[5] We went to the little Cornish church again and had another nobly simple sermon from Dr. Fitch.[6] Of course, we were in time today and so found as we expected that he is (to use the old phrase) "as much gifted in prayer" as in preaching. He and Mrs. Fitch were at our second little tea on Friday and he is delightfully human and simple. We are planning to see something of them alone.

Our tea was really very interesting. There were a large number of men, some of whom possibly take themselves too seriously. These were mainly the "literary fellows." The artists were, as usual, of an engaging simplicity. Mr. Stephen Parrish is an old dear. Maxfield Parrish is such a shy bird that he never goes into a crowd[.] His wife begged that he and she might come alone someday. Our nearest neighbour, Miss King (at "The Inn"[7] you know), said something that not only pleased me in itself but made me like *her* because it showed sympathetic observation. She said it was a pleasure to watch you pass every day because you had such an unusually *happy* expression—"like a boy out of school" and something more.

Monday, July 21, 1913—

We had the last of our three teas this afternoon, the Windsor people—chiefly an assorted lot of Evarts of all ages and conditions.[8] With them were three Conovers from Princeton, including Mrs. Bradford.[9]

The house is full of the most beautiful flowers sent by various people. One of today's guests brought a magnificent basket with her. . . .

I don't like to allude to politics in my letters when you are so surfeited by it all the time; but I *must* speak of the increased duty on books and pictures! I saw in a paper that you yourself had not known that it was being done and were shocked at it. Is that so? It seems to me quite dreadful that they should during *your* administration raise the duties on those things on the ground of their being luxuries! It is so incongruous. I hope and pray it is not too late to change it. It is so different from anything else because the supposed beneficiaries, the native authors and artists are of all men most opposed to it. John Alexander[10] had a long letter about it in today's paper. He is president of the Academy.

We are all perfectly well and are still having perfect weather. I paint every morning, though thanks to the mail and Mrs. Jaffrey's flow of language, I do not get at it until late—ten or after. I have engagements for every afternoon this week—to see gardens, to go to the club, to pose for Mr. Vonnoh, etc.

Tuesday, July 22, 1913—

I have just come back from the club. It was much more interesting because the subject was one about which we would all naturally know something, viz. the education of girls. There really are a number of very attractive and interesting women among them. It was at Mrs. Hand's—Florence Hoyt's old classmate; and that clever interesting Miss Goldmark[11] was there on a visit. She was on her way to the old cottage on the side of "Noonmark."

I was interrupted by the arrival of the five girls from Hanover. I am finishing this while they dress for dinner. . . .

I "laid in" today my first large Cornish canvass. It is rather promising—if I can keep the present freshness and vigour. It is rather stunning colour—deep blues and strong sunlight and shadow. I rather like it now, but I may be utterly disgusted tomorrow night. But I must stop at *once*! With devoted love,

Your little Wife, Nell.

Wednesday, July 23, 1913—

I am just back from a visit to the Maxfield Parrishes and from posing afterwards for Mr. Vonnoh. The posing was interrupted by a storm, leaving, while it lasted, no light to paint by.

The Maxfield Parrish menage is *charming* in every respect. In the first place they are all so good-looking! He is really a beautiful young man and charming, too, and she is *lovely*, with deep dark eyes, and a sweet, rather worn look like a young madonna. She has four beautiful young children, and is evidently a devoted mother. She was an artist her-self[.] The house is set high on a hill and is altogether fascinating—very artistic and at the same time unpretentious. The garden is a delightful tangle like the Boxwood garden. The[y] have a few magnificent trees—and a really stupendous view—too panoramic to paint, of course, but a glorious scene. Altogether it is an ideal artist home. And they live there all the year round. It must be very wonderful in winter.

The girls go to a little dance there next week.

They go tonight—all five of them—to one of the Evarts's houses for impromptu charades. The charades ought to be good with Nell, Ruth, and Mary Scott, besides the lively Evarts girls.

I see from other letters that Mr. Alexander rather exaggerated as regards the duty on pictures—that they are not actually *raising* the duty but only restoring it in part—when the house had made them free. Still the papers are full of protests about it—and I do hope they can be made really free. Everyone who knows anything about the subject wants them free.

I have just escaped—I hope—a visitation from the suffragists—those who are on their way to Washington. I heard rumours that they were coming to Windsor and would ask me to receive them; but they did not write me. They simply *came*, and called up on the telephone to know if I would see them. Helen told them I was just leaving the house to meet an important engagement, which was literally true—it was this after-noon. They were extremely disappointed, of course, saying that they did not expect me to put myself on record as for them, but it would "help them greatly for me just to receive them." Doubtless it *would*, for it would be considered putting myself on record!

I also had a letter on the subject from an anti-suffragist.[12]

Wednesday, July 30, 1913—

The girls all went to a dance at Maxfield Parrish's—"a small and early." This morning they took the Scotts as far as White Plains [River] Junction and put them on the train.

It is now the middle of the afternoon. I have been resting after my morning in the studio and reading the papers. When I finish this I shall dress and go to visit *Mr.!* Stephen Parrish and Mrs. Louis St. Gaudens. Mr. Stephen is "the original democrat," the father of Maxfield, and he has a lovely garden and view. Mrs. St. Gaudens is a sculptor and wants me to see her latest picture—just finished. She is the widow of Augustus St. Gaudens's brother, but looks young enough to have been his daughter, such a quaint little thing, at once fearless and very shy—like a bird . . . .

I was interrupted here and am finishing after my return from my visits. Both were unusually interesting. Mrs. St. Gaudens was the assistant of Augustus for some years before she married his brother Louis (who died last winter). He, of course, was a distinguished sculptor, too—only overshadowed by his greater brother. He did all the great figures for the station in Washington and she worked with him. It gives one quite an insight into the ways of sculptors to see their studio and its contents. She does charming bas-reliefs, all her own, and very much in St. Gaudens style.

But the Stephen Parrish house and garden is a perfect idyll, and he is the *dearest* old man—so mellow and wholesome & interested in what is worth while, *you* for instance! He & his daughter[13] live there most of the year. We took tea with them & had a beautiful time.

Friday, August 1, 1913—

I have been out to luncheon with Miss [Mary] Evarts (daughter of Wm. M.), at the old home. It was all very interesting and patriarchal, for W. M. had a *very* beautiful estate in Windsor of many hundred acres and all his sons still live on it, in separate houses, of course. There is a large pond—(really a beautiful lake), with splendid *clean* woodland on one side and the houses and gardens on the other—also a large farm. After luncheon we took a ride in their automobile, saw their estate first and then a new and very pretty road called "the brook road." Then they brought us home—Jessie and I— and took tea with us. So it practically took the day. When they left I had to rest off a headache which I had picked up on the way and then dress for dinner; for Helen and I dine at the Platts' tonight.

We are just back from the Platts where we had a delightful time. I had not met Mr. Platt before and I like him exceedingly. Of course, you remember that he is the artist-architect—of this house among others. I saw there a large and *very* beautiful picture by him of the mountain—(Ascutney) in winter—a most noble composition and so poetical![14] I knew nothing of his work as a painter. The other guests were the H. O. Walkers and Mr. Stephen Parrish and his niece, a delightfully congenial little party for me and for Helen, too.

Saturday, August 2, 1913—

I am just back from a tea at Miss Steeles' in Windsor. She has a pretty place on the Evarts estate—I don't know whether she is related or not; but she belongs to their set and is very nice—kindly and rather humorous. She is a pillar of the "old church." The Evarts are all Episcopalians. I met piles of New England spinsters—and I must say I like them, Mrs. Peck notwithstanding! They are all friendly and kindly, if one is cordial with them—just as the Middletown people used to be. And so unaffected. It was a hot day so we rode afterwards, with the result that I shall have to finish this after dinner.

Monday, August 4, 1913—

The three girls are all out to dinner. I had mine quite alone—it consisted of a glass of milk, some biscuit and a peach—and now I am very comfortably disposed in a wrapper sitting by a fire in my room. Too comfortably indeed, for I went to sleep over the paper before I had even begun the various letters I was planning to write. I have had an active day and this is the result. I painted all morning, standing of course—posed early in the afternoon—came home and had some out-of-town people who wanted to call to tea—then went myself to tea at the Goodyears'.[15] They are the rubber tire people who have bought the beautiful Norman Hapgood place. It is an *enchantment*. It is a Platt house in Italian villa style, with an adorable garden, of course, and perhaps the greatest view of all. It has the great swinging lines of the Platt view with the curving river in the centre. The house you may remember as it is set high on a hill. It adjoins the Platt place—and personally I still like the latter best. But it is great fun to go around and compare the various places. . . . My neighbours here are most considerate and have not said a word to me about that duty on art—but I am getting letters; and now I [am] being annoyed by the "bird-lovers."[16] I have *had* to consent to bring the latter matter to your attention—chiefly because Jessie herself is rather excited about it. So I just want some secretary to write me a plain statement of how matters stand on those two points so that I can know what to say to people.

Tuesday, August 5, 1913—

They are to have here a little "masque" written by the playwright Percy MacKaye in the interests of some society for bird conservation. It is to be given in the forest, no one present but invited guests, and to be a very "high-class" thing altogether. There are to be only some six actors besides a band of children and they came today to ask Nell to be the "bird spirit." I do not see the least objection but to make sure I told them I would ask you before committing myself. So please drop me a line about it as soon as you read this. It is really to be very idyllic and classic. You know, of course, that this colony is rather famous for its ["]high class" pageants and such things. But this is quite a simple little affair—not like its elaborate pageants.

I went to the Club today & they discussed the duty on pictures, and decided to follow the example of many other artist organizations and send a petition to the Senate. It seems to me that this duty is really ridiculous in view of the fact that the very persons to be supposedly benefitted by in[it] are to a man opposed to it, and that the revenue derived from it is *admitted* to be so small as to be almost negligible. Can't something be done about it? It is actually *worse* than the one it replaces, for that admitted pictures free if they were 20 years old and this requires that they shall be 50 years old. It is well known that the persons back of this change in the bill since it went to the Senate are certain rich art dealers in N. Y. who do a thriving trade in "antiques" largely faked. Really, dear, it is the sort of job that ought to be looked into. You know the regular House bill admitted all art *free*. This trouble only began in the Senate. I think the artists in working so hard for free art are really giving the country a wonderful & beautiful example of real patriotism and of unselfish devotion to the ideal. For it would, of course, be to their *personal* advantage to have the foreign stuff kept out. So they are setting a great example. . . .

Today Helen and I lunched at the Crolys' and went straight from there to the club. I really had a delightful time.—such a charming little group of women. The club met at Miss Elizabeth Slade's[17]—still another beautiful place with a charming garden and a glorious view. It is the most extensive view of all—is on such a mountain that I was nervous going up to it in the car, for the car distinctly *balked* at it. It was a gorgeous violet and green and gold day, with splendid clouds. It fairly took one's breath away. Ah, but the world is a beautiful place in spite of all drawbacks.

August 6, 1913—

I am just starting to receive at the reception given to the Farmers' wives by the women of the Colony. The latter started a Club and arranged a simple Club-house for these meetings years ago. But this is a special annual affair given at one of the charming places, Mrs. Louis Shipman's. I shall have to finish this on my return. Am waiting now for the girls.

Just back from the tea which was a great success. Mrs. Shipman's garden is one of the most beautiful in its solid masses of bloom—like the "Prospect" garden. The house was equally full of flowers, and the affair was quite a love feast. Mrs. Walker was much amused over one difficult old person who had quarreled with most of the others, would not speak to her or them on the street. But she made it all up in order to be at this tea, and meet me and the girls!

I was at the Walkers this morning to see the place, Mr. Walker's work in the studio, and Miss Schauffler, our doctor's sister[18] who is visiting them. The Walkers live at Lakewood in the winter. I had a delightful time, of course, especially seeing Mr. Walker's work, which is beautiful—ideal figures such as his fine series at the Washington library. Mrs. Walker is a very brave splendid woman. She has two children, sons, one extraordinarily tall and beautiful. He is really Jessie's type. The younger, Oliver, is no taller than a child of three & terribly twisted besides. He has a fine head & is very intelligent—is now 20 years old. He can walk a little on the level floor, but must be carried chiefly. Until a year ago, she herself carried him about in her arms and did everything for him. Then it was discovered that she had wrecked her health doing it and she had to undergo all sorts of complicated operations. Her love and devotion to him is heroic.

August 11, 1913—

I must go and pose later in the afternoon, and then go out to dine with the Kenyon Coxes. I am getting too many invitations for the evenings—three already for this week. They are all too nice and informal for me to assume the high presidential attitude and decline. Also I must give two more teas, one on Saturday and one next week;—and the "discussion club" next Tuesday! The subject is "Does Human Nature Change?" What do you think about that?

Tuesday, August 12, 1913—

This alas! is a crowded day! And it is rather alarming to find my Cornish days beginning to be crowded. A pile of mail in the morning; then painting until lunch. (I *won't* let it be crowded out!) Now after luncheon I am writing to you before dressing for the club. We have supper at 5:45 and then go over to Hanover to see a sylvan pageant. This whole New England seems to have gone mad over pageants. Mrs. Hall[19] says this one is very beautiful and artistic. It is a glorious day and we will have bright moonlight, so it will be a pleasure. Oh, this perfect, perfect weather! I almost hate it because *you* can't be here to enjoy it! I don't know whether it is an ideal summer everywhere or whether we have found an ideal spot. I had a *very* pleasant evening at the Kenyon Coxes' last night. The Coxes themselves are not attractive at first sight, but improve on acquaintance. But the only other guests, Mr. & Mrs. Herbert Adams, are among the choice spirits of the Colony—both intelle[c]tually and spiritually. I could really *love* them both. He, you know, is the sculptor whom I met in Washington. They are Boston people. She also "studies art," but I do not hear of her doing anything now. It is pretty to see how much they are loved and honoured by the younger people here. . . .

But I must dress now and help the women of Cornish decide "What constitutes a good citizen"(!) The meeting is at Maxfield Parrish's.

August 13, 1913—

I shall probably finish this tonight as I must dress and go to pose for Mr. Vonnah [Vonnoh]—I hope for the last time. I have (I think) finished one of my larger pictures this morning and I think it is pretty good for me!

Who do you think is coming to luncheon tomorrow? Gov. Bullock of Bermuda![20] He telegraphed today from the Crawford House that he would like to do so. His wife and daughter are in England.

We went over to Hanover last night and saw the pageant which was really beautiful. It was given out of doors in a very romantic glade, and some of the scenes—especially scarf dances by the spirits of the winds[,] the brooks[,] and the shadows, were exquisite. They have a large summer school there in connection with the college, and the play was given by the young women who attend that—together with all the pretty little children of the place as fairies. I hope none of them have pneumonia today, for they were all bare-footed and had next to nothing on, and it was a *cold* night, though a very beautiful one with the bright moonlight. I slept under *six* blankets!

I have just returned from a little dinner at Mr. Stephen Parrish's. Helen and I were invited and we had a delightful time. There were just that perfect old dear, Stephen himself, the sweet young cousin who keeps house for him[21]—(and does it to perfection), the adorable Maxfield (Mrs. Max was not well), and Judge and Mrs. Hand. I think I have already written about her and how fine and unusual she is. He is very interesting, too; I had not met him before. He is a bull-mooser, but seems to be infatuated with you in spite of it;—he can talk of nothing else. He says he met you some years ago and you impressed him then as the most powerful personality he had ever seen.

I posed for Mr. Vonnah [Vonnoh] until it was time to start for the dinner, so the letter was delayed until late. I am eager to get the posing done with, so I stay as long as possible. He *is* almost through with mine, and it is a pretty pose and a charming bit of colour—face, hair and dress, the latter all soft silver grey and lavender. They say it looks rather like me, too. None of them are real *portraits*, you understand.

August 14, 1913—

It is 11:15 and I am just free to write to you! Alas! for those quiet first days at Cornish! But I have had a most interesting day. After painting one hour (from ten to eleven), having seen first to my mail, of course, I went to the train to get Sir George & take him for a little drive before luncheon. He came from "Crawfords'" expressly to lunch with us and went back on the four o'clock—three hours to come and three to go. He was really a delightful guest.

After leaving him at the train we all went to tea at Mrs. St. Gaudens. She is in deep mourning for her little grandson, who you know poisoned himself accidentally shortly before we came up,[22] so I had not expected to see her; but she, of course, wanted us to see her husband's work and the place; and it ended in her inviting quite a little group of her best friends to meet us. It was a pleasant intimate little party, and there are copies of most of her husband's best works in the two great studios. All *that*, together with the very beautiful garden and house and view, made it an afternoon to be remembered always. But I have raved over so many "gardens and views" in my letters, that I will spare you further details.

After getting back from that I had barely time to rest a bit and read the paper, and then dress for dinner at the Arnolds',[23] our neighbours down the road. There are only women in the family and it was exclusively a woman's dinner. We had a delightful time, for Miss Grace Arnold is one of the finest, sweetest people here—and she has a perfectly beautiful and highly trained contralto voice, and exquisite taste in music. She sings the same sort of things that Margaret does. So we have had a regular concert, and that is why I am late getting back. She had another musical friend visiting her who both sang and played. *She* had heard Margaret sing in N. Y. and greatly admired her voice.

August 15, 1913—

I have had another whirling day, not at all what should be expected of quiet Cornish, and it is now after eleven at night, alas! I lunched with Mrs. Beaman[24] who is the eldest daughter of Maxwell Evarts and one of the great ladies of the region. She is a widow of many years, and owns some 2,000 acres on the Cornish side of the river. Needless to say she has a beautiful house and a great view and a garden! Her house, you know, is the one on the heights on the left above Blow-Me-Down Pond. We saw it whenever we came from town. I had a very pleasant time; but had to leave a little early, to come home for Jessie and then go to meet the Smiths on the 3:45.

They arrived all right and it is delightful to see them again. They are very well and just as dear and funny as ever. They had expected to come one [on] the 7:45; and we had an engagement to see the Adams and Hart gardens[25] and take tea with the former; so we "called Mrs. Adams up," explained, and took the Smiths with us; and we all had a charming time. We saw another beautiful view, of course, and one of the prettiest because [it is the] simplest and most restful of the houses and gardens. Mr. Hart is a bachelor who has a tiny but adorable cottage and a very large garden to which he practically devotes *all* his time. He is really Browning's "pictor ignotus,"[26] doesn't care for fame, is a serene philosopher who doesn't even take time to paint in the gardening season. A very pleasant shy man, who I should think would be an extremely good friend and neighbour. He lives in the "back-yard" of the Adamses, but is well to do and has a motor-car; and Mr. & Mrs. Prellwitz, both of whom are well-known painters,[27] board with his chauffeur; and they are all very intimate and happy together!

But in the meantime, before we started for this tea, Cousin John [Adams Wilson] had telephoned that they were motoring over from—somewhere with two friends and they were all invited to dinner. They reached here sooner than was expected, so that we found them all here when we returned from the tea. We left them to amuse themselves while we all made hurried toilettes. They have just left after a very pleasant evening. But, of course, my back is the worse for wear after all this, so I must say goodnight and turn in.

I really think you ought to return to Cornish to break the drought again! It is *very* bad—everyone is getting anxious about the water supply.

August 19, 1913—

It is six o'clock and my home meeting of the Club has just ended. It went off quite brilliantly. It was (of course!) a very full meeting, and the tea afterwards was unusually pleasant because everyone was still full of the subject and discussing it eagerly. The subject, which I chose, was "How can we best promote a fuller and more general appreciation of *American* art?" We had one good laugh over it. Someone had said that we must not neglect to talk about "the next generation"—no discussion was complete without *that*! Later it was said (of course) that we should have, like the French, a government bureau of art to purchase works of art, to give prizes, to encourage it in every possible way. Then I said I thought the Congressmen who would take that view were not yet born; so after all we had to drag in that next generation.

I had a very interesting evening yesterday. I dined at Miss Nichols and Mr. George Deforest Brush was there. I had not seen him since I studied under him those first two months at the League[28] before I went from the antique class to J. Alden Weir's[29] "portrait class." I broke it to him gently that I was an old pupil and he was much interested. Mr. Hart, about whom I was writing, the other day, then mentioned that he also was a pupil, and it turned out that we were there at the same time, both in the Brush and the Weir classes. I found out today that Mrs. Prellwitz was also there then.

August 20, 1913—

We have had a very interesting and full day. It was "Old Home Day" at the Cornish Centre church—a sort of grand picnic, with exercises in the afternoon, and we all went to the 12 o'clock dinner carrying a big lot of food ourselves. It was quite amusing; and fortunately we *had* to come away just after dinner because I had another engagement viz. a luncheon party with Miss Slade at 1:30. Of course, that was the extreme other end of the Cornish social scale; the most beautiful and elaborate house and garden here. The luncheon was the very perfection of elegance. Afterwards we went into the garden and there, sitting around the fountain, Miss Arnold sang to us deliciously. The whole thing was ideal. We did not get away until four o'clock. The weather is perfection again—a splendid blue day, such as we have not had since we were on our trip. It is too bad that I am never free to paint when those rare days come. I began a picture, weeks ago, on such a day, and have never touched it since. After the luncheon I went to pose for Mr. Vonnoh, I think for the last time. My picture is really very nice in the general effect of it. The other two are almost finished.

Tomorrow afternoon I have a tea from 4:30 to 5:30;—and at 6:30 I take the train for *Washington*!

September 9, 1913—

I am just back from the club. It met at Miss Slade's splendid place, and we discussed "the simple life—what is it and is it worth while?" Mary and I went alone. Lucy has a bad cold now and Helen just "cut it!"

Margaret's lovers have both gone, and she was posing. Nell & Ruth were, of course, rehearsing. Everyone is *wild* over Nell's performance—her grace, her beauty and her real gift as an actress. But oh dear me, I don't know what I will do if this cold, shivery weather lasts until Friday night; it will be so dangerous for them with those thin things on. Her costume is charming—a white shimmering silk slip and fluttering rainbow tinted gauze scarves arranged to suggest wings.

Mr. Vonnoh came around this morning to look at my work and give me a criticism. He was very encouraging. He said he "was very much surprised,["] though he had expected a good deal from the little things he had seen at the White House. He said I "was a real artist, and that if I will go on my work will be really *very* distinguished." He also thought Nell's little picture quite charming. He thought we both had any amount of individuality, and that I had with it a good deal of variety—that is that I did several sorts of things equally well—and with equal feeling. He wants to come again after I have made certain little changes in detail. He made only one general criticism and I see myself that he is right. I have been getting my tree trunks and the darkest accents in my foregrounds a little too hot—I should use more purple & less brown in them. They are not completely "enveloped!"

September 15, 1913—

Didn't we have a good time at the Fitches', and aren't they perfect dears! I hope that next summer we and they may be "intimate friends." After you left, we wandered about the place a little longer alternately praising the view and *you*. Then we came home and I got in an hour and a half of painting. I put in the sky and the distance in the little Cornish study somewhat to my satisfaction; so I think I see my way now to "the picture" proper.

Now I am writing this little note before dressing for dinner just "to tell you how I love you, dear." By the way, Margaret sang that song "Laddie" just before we left the Fitches—that and no other. She sang it beautifully and they were perfectly charmed.

This was such a happy little visit, dearest! I wish I could tell you how intensely I enjoyed every moment of it. I was distressed before you came for fear the confusion incident upon the masque would ruin it for you. In a sense of cours[e] it did mar the first 24 hours. Yet I know you were more than compensated in seeing your adorable little daughter reveal *herself* so charmingly. Please make the office collect Sunday papers telling about it. We know that a number of them were going to feature it with pictures, and we shall be sadly disappointed if we miss them all. Aren't they all *wonderful* girls— and adorable? And how intensely they all love you!

September 23, 1913—

I have been very naughty or I have put off writing until I am so sleepy and tired that I can hardly see the paper. My conscience pricks me, as it should—and I won't do it again if I can help. I painted almost all day, spent the evening with the family, and then had to attend to a lot of business after I came upstairs before I could begin writing to you.

I will not have much more time to paint now and the colour is so lovely that I could not resist doing *two* studies—morning and afternoon. Both are good—for me. The conditions were favourable for working at the house here, for everybody was away except Helen and me.

They all went at Mr. Baynes's invitation, to Corbin's Park to see the buffalos, &c. He wanted them to make it a picnic but preferred to do it all in the afternoon—and as a consequence they did not get back until eight o'clock. They had to leave the car outside and go about the park with horses. They saw some 60 buffalos and had a very interesting time. They say it is an extremely beautiful place—really park-like.

September 25, 1913—

We had a *very* good time at the Slades'[30] at luncheon—no guests but the Smiths, Margaret & myself. Their view is too wonderful for words, especially now with the colour; and the house is adorable, not big like Miss Augusta Slades' but still *perfection*. They too have lived in Italy for years so that it is almost an Italian villa in lines & furniture. The queer Miss Slade with the big man's voice is a remarkably interesting person when you get her to herself and with the most exquisite sensitiveness to *beauty* of all sorts, especially in music. It is a pathetic anomaly to have the face and the temperament match so ill. She and Mrs. Adams for instance are extreme opposites in that respect. Mrs. Adams *looks* all soul. She is doing very well indeed, by the way—is sitting up.

The above letter was her last one from Cornish; Ellen Axson Wilson and her family returned to Washington in the early fall. The following spring she came down with Bright's disease, a chronic kidney ailment, and on August 6, 1914, died in the White House.[30]

ENDNOTES

1. See the catalogue by Frank J. Aucella, Patricia A. Piorkowski Hobbs, and Frances Wright Saunders, *Ellen Axson Wilson: First Lady, Artist* (Washington, DC: Woodrow Wilson House; Staunton, VA: Woodrow Wilson Birthplace and Museum, 1993), p. 21.

2. These excerpts are quoted with permission from Arthur S. Link, ed., *The Papers of Woodrow Wilson* (Princeton, NJ: Princeton University Press, 1978), Vol. 28 (1913). Notes to these excerpts identified by "(eds.)" are herewith gratefully acknowledged.

3. The Cornish Discussion Club.

4. Robert Vonnoh; see below pp. 507-508. His portrait of mother and daughters hangs now in the Wilson House in Washington, DC. The painting was rephotographed from a color screen plate (an Autochrome) by Arnold Genthe and exhibited at the Saint-Gaudens National Historic Site; see "Photographs and Historical Processes," exhibition catalogue (Cornish, NH: Saint-Gaudens National Historic Site, 1 September-31 October 1995), unpaginated.

5. An allusion to the last two lines of Wordsworth's poem, "She Dwelt Among the Untrodden Ways" (1800).

6. The Reverend Dr. Albert Parker Fitch, who was married to Flora May Draper Fitch; see above pp. 14-16.

7. A farmhouse opposite "Harlakenden House" on the eastern side of what is now Route 12A; it was known as "Churchill Inn" because he owned it, too. Miss King is unidentified (eds.).

8. The children and grandchildren of William Maxwell Evarts (1818-1901). He was a United States senator from New York and Secretary of State (1877-1881). He lived at "Runnemede," his estate in Windsor, VT (eds.).

9. Mary Field Conover Bradford, wife of Willard Hall Bradford, Princeton 1891, proprietor of a coal brokerage firm in Philadelphia. The other two women were Mrs. Bradford's mother, Juliana Conover, and their mother, Helen Field (Mrs. Frances Stevens) Conover. The Conover ladies were old friends of the Wilsons (eds.).

10. John White Alexander; see above pp. 126-129; he was president of the National Academy of Design from 1909 to 1915.

11. Josephine Clara Goldmark, Bryn Mawr, 1898, publication secretary of the National Consumers League (eds.).

12. For more on the Suffrage issue, see below pp. 440-445.

13. Mrs. Wilson means Anne Parrish, Stephen Parrish's cousin; see below p. 492.

14. One wonders if this "picture" is *The Mountain (Mountain through the Poplars)*, a painting that Platt did in the 1890s and sold to William Gwinn Mather for his Platt-designed house on Lake Erie east of Cleveland, OH; see catalogue entry #43 and Figure 6.14 in Keith N. Morgan, *Shaping an American Landscape: The Art and Architecture of Charles A. Platt* (Hanover, NH: The Hood Museum of Art, Dartmouth College, 1995), pp. 149, 135; see also pp. 47-48 for a related image that Platt photographed and etched—other possibilities for Mrs. Wilson's "picture."

15. A. Conger Goodyear, an art collector and lumber company owner from Buffalo, NY, and his wife Mary Martha Fornan Goodyear. He was not closely related to Charles Goodyear of the famous Goodyear rubber company (eds.).

16. Led by Ernest Harold Baynes; see above pp. 138-144. The "bird-lovers" sought "a prohibitive duty on bird plumes, used in the manufacture of hats." (eds.)

17. Given Mrs. Wilson's description of the approach to the house, this is Emily, not Elizabeth, Slade's and her sister Augusta's "Dingleton House" on Dingleton Hill. Frances and Elizabeth Slade's house was on the crest of Saint-Gaudens's Hill.

18. One of several sisters of William Gray Schauffler, a physician from Lakewood, NJ (eds.). For more on the Walkers and his murals for the "Library" of Congress, see above pp. 420-421.

19. Mary Hepburn Hough (Mrs. William Richardson) Hall (eds.).

20. Lieutenant General Sir George Mackworth Bullock; his wife was Amy Isabel Thomson Bullock; their daughter is unidentified (eds.).

21. Anne Parrish.

22. Mrs. Augustus Saint-Gaudens is in mourning for the son of Homer and Carlota Saint-Gaudens; see above p. 371, n. 20.

23. Charlotte Bruce Arnold, Grace Arnold, and Frances Arnold (Mrs. Clendenen) Graydon of New York, who rented a place in Cornish known as "The Butternuts" (eds.); see below p. 460, n. 3 for more on Grace Arnold.

24. The widow of Charles Cotesworth Beaman, Hettie Sherman Evarts Beaman; see above pp. 145-146.

25. William Howard Hart; see above pp. 229-231.

26. A reference to Robert Browning's poem "Pictor Ignotus [Florence, 15___]" from his collection *Dramatic Romances and Lyrics* first published in 1845; it is a dramatic monologue of the type for which Browning was so famous.

27. See above pp. 334-336.

28. The Art Students League in New York.

29. See below p. 509.

30. This appears to be the house of Frances and Elizabeth Slade on Saint-Gaudens's Hill, not "Dingleton House."

WOMAN'S SUFFRAGE

THE PROGRESS FROM THE EARLIEST STATEMENT in American political history that women should have the right to vote to its effective realization through the ratification of the Nineteenth Amendment to the Constitution in 1920 was a long and painful one. Elizabeth Cady Stanton and Lucretia Mott organized a convention at Seneca Falls, New York; on July 19, 1848, this group issued a general declaration of the rights of women, which asserted the need for their independence with full legal equality with men, the right to equal wages, and the right to vote. The advocates of these principles were closely allied to the movements for temperance and the abolition of slavery, especially the latter. Consequently, after the Civil War, when the Fifteenth Amendment granted the franchise to the newly emancipated Negro men, the women felt betrayed. Mrs. Stanton and Miss Susan B. Anthony formed the National Woman Suffrage Association in 1869 in order to apply pressure for women's suffrage. Some local organizations worked through state legislatures; they succeeded in obtaining the franchise for women within some states and territories newly admitted to the United States—Wyoming was the first to do so in 1869. By the 1890s, the movement was gradually catching fire. By 1913, with a total of twelve new states giving women the right to vote, the "Suffragettes" could be seen everywhere, especially in Washington, DC, where women like Alice Paul and Lucy Burns and the national Woman's Party began using the pressure of these women to agitate in Congress for a suffrage amendment. It was not introduced until 1917; by 1919 it had passed both houses of Congress and was soon ratified by the necessary thirty-six states. It became a law in August of 1920.

Local residents were not immune to these issues. A dinner party given on September 7, 1910, by Judge Learned Hand and his wife, who were staying at Kenyon Cox's house, included the following people: Frances Arnold, Katreena Tiffany, Winston Churchill, William Howard Hart, and Stephen Parrish. The latter cryptically notes that there was "lively talk on Woman Suffrage & the Tariff."[1] There is a great deal of evidence that Juliet Barrett Rublee was an active participant in the suffrage parades held in New York City. Witter Bynner led "the men's section of the first parade on Fifth Avenue on May 6, 1911. . . . Ten thousand women . . . and one hundred men . . . were greeted by multitudious howls of derision and hate all along its course."[2] Frances Duncan, the horticulture and garden writer, recalled the excitement of marching in the streets, waving banners, and withstanding the verbal barrage of taunts like "who's washing the dishes?" She participated in demonstrations in both London and New York. She even recruited help from the actress Marie Dressler, who summered in Windsor, Vermont, to provide observers to help prevent mob violence.[3] Local activity is datable at least from 1911, thanks particularly to the efforts of Mabel Harlakenden Hall, Mrs. Winston Churchill.[4] There was an active meeting at the Plainfield Town Hall with Mrs. Stanley McCormack of Boston and Alice Duer Miller of New York as guest speakers. By the end of 1911, the Cornish Equal Suffrage League, including community residents as well as members of the Cornish Colony, was formed. The following newspaper article proclaimed the announcement; it is reprinted as it appeared, in its entirety:

NEW LEAGUE FORMED

Prominent Members of Famous Cornish Colony of
Artists and Writers Enroll for Equal Suffrage

In Plainfield and Cornish, New Hampshire, the home of the famous Cornish Colony of artists and writers, an equal suffrage league has just been formed auxiliary to the New Hampshire Woman Suffrage Association.

At a meeting in the Plainfield Town Hall, Miss Mary N. Chase, president of the State Association, was assisted by three other speakers: Mrs. George Rublee and Mr. Witter Bynner of Cornish, and Dr. George Clark Cox of Hanover. Rev. D. Stewart Campbell of Plainfield presided. On the platform were Mrs. Emma Daniels and Mrs. Cynthia Hadley, of Plainfield, and Mr. Fenno B. Comings, the Cornish Representative at Concord.

Mrs. Rublee, whose husband is well known in New Hampshire and New York as an able lawyer and progressive Republican, is planning to stump the state in favor of the suffrage amendment which is to be proposed at the constitutional convention next March. Eight years ago the amendment was adopted by the convention and received about a two-fifths vote in the state; and suffragists are hoping that the movement has been sufficiently advanced since then for the amendment to receive next year the necessary two-thirds vote. Mrs. Rublee laid stress on the need of suffrage as an educational influence in the home not only for mothers but for children and quoted the report of the Inter-Parliamentary Union that in Colorado, where women vote, the laws concerning children are the best to be found on any statute books in the world.

Formerly as instructor at Harvard and now lecturer on Philosophy and Economics at Dartmouth, Dr. Cox emphasized the value of equal suffrage as giving to women, in the same measure as to men, the opportunity of free individual expression and declared man's general attitude toward the question to be not one of malice but of carelessness and stupidity.

Mr. Bynner, who created a stir at Harvard last Spring by introducing the theme of woman suffrage into his Phi Beta Kappa poem on democracy, and who is to speak at the annual convention of the New Hampshire Woman Suffrage Association at Manchester on November 15, dwelt on the humanness of the movement, and maintained that it is of less urgent importance, not only for women but for men, to try the initiative, Referendum, Recall and other experimental instruments of democracy than to establish equal suffrage, which is itself democracy.

Miss Chase, stating her faith in men as "reasonable beings," who will not much longer withhold equal opportunity from women and noting the sore need in politics of the mother's vote, gave an admirable, lucid survey of the significance of suffrage and of its proven results.

At the close of the meeting twenty-seven names were pledged for the foundation of the local league, which starts with the following membership:

Mrs. Herbert Adams, Miss Grace Arnold, Mr. Witter Bynner, Rev. D. Stewart Campbell, Mr. and Mrs. Winston Churchill, Miss Mabel Churchill, Dr. George C. Cox, Mr. and Mrs. W. K. Daniels, Mr. Barry Faulkner, Mrs. Cynthia Hadley, Mrs. W. H. Hyde, Miss Martha E. Holt, Miss Harriet M. Jenney, Mrs. Albion T. Lang, Mr. and Mrs. Percy MacKaye, Miss Anne Parrish, Mrs. Maxfield Parrish, Mrs. Ida Metz Reed, Mrs. George Rublee, Mr. Deane Ruggles, Mrs. Homer Saint-Gaudens, Mr. and Mrs. Saint-Gaudens, Mrs. Kate C. Stewart.[5]

As proof that the Cornish Equal Suffrage League was to be taken seriously, they published a pamphlet, dated December 1, 1911, setting forth its officers, its objectives, its by-laws, and members. It, too, follows as it appeared, in its entirety:

Cornish Equal Suffrage League

List of Officers

President - Mrs. Juliet Barrett Rublee
First Vice-President - Mr. Witter Bynner
Second Vice-President - Rev. George Stewart Campbell
Honorary Vice-President - Mr. George De Forest Brush
Corresponding Secretary - Miss Anne B. Parrish
Recording Secretary - Miss Mabel Jordan
Treasurer - Mrs. Mabel H. Churchill
Auditor - Mr. Charles A. Tracy

OBJECT

The object of the Cornish Equal Suffrage League is to arouse a more general interest in Equal Suffrage throughout the State, with the immediate aim of carrying through an amendment to the State Constitution giving women the right to vote.

CONSTITUTIONAL CONVENTION

A Constitutional Convention will be held in this State next June. Delegates to this Convention will be elected the second Tuesday in March. It is of the greatest importance that the men sent to this Convention should vote for the Equal Suffrage amendment and each member of the Cornish League is urged to use his influence to this end.

If the Equal Suffrage Amendment is put into the new draft of the Constitution next June, the people of the state will vote upon it at the fall elections. Eight years ago it was put into the Constitution but defeated at the polls. It received about a two-fifths vote. A two-thirds vote is needed to pass each amendment.

NEW MEMBERS

The Cornish Equal Suffrage League is now the second largest in the state, having at present 68 members. Each member of the League is urgently requested to bring in as many new members as possible. The names of the new members should be sent to the Corresponding Secretary, Miss Anne B. Parrish, Windsor, Vt.

Any resident of New Hampshire may become a member by the payment of the annual dues of fifty cents. All interested in the cause of Woman Suffrage are urged to join, and to contribute toward carrying on the work. Dues, checks or money orders should be made payable to the Treasurer, Mrs. Winston Churchill, Windsor, Vt.

OFFICIAL INFORMATION

It is hoped that each member of the League will subscribe to the Woman's Journal, 585 Boylston St., Boston, Mass. This paper is the official organ of the National American Woman Suffrage Association and appears weekly. Subscription, $1.00 a year or fifty cents for six months. It contains information which can be found nowhere else about the progress of the Equal Suffrage movement not only throughout the United States but throughout the world.

NEW HAMPSHIRE'S OPPORTUNITY

New Hampshire has the opportunity to be the leader of the Eastern States in this great movement. If the cause of Equal Suffrage is won at the polls next fall, it will be a triumph for the intelligence and the progressive spirit of New Hampshire; and this State will go down in history as the first of the Eastern States to recognize the importance, the justice, and the economic and moral value to the City, the State, and the Country of giving women the vote.

EQUAL SUFFRAGE

To adopt Equal Suffrage is to apply to politics that principle which succeeds best in the home—the mutual cooperation of both men and women for the general and individual welfare.

As Wendell Phillips pointed out: If woman is like man, she should have a vote like man; if she is not like man, she cannot be represented by man.

If the foundation of government is the consent of the governed is it right that one half the people should not be represented or have a share in it?

Women vote in Australia, New Zealand, Finland, Norway, Wyoming, Colorado, Utah, Idaho, Washington, and California:

WHY NOT IN NEW HAMPSHIRE

LIST OF MEMBERS

Mrs. Herbert Adams	Professor and Mrs. Louis H. Dow
Miss Grace Arnold	Mrs. Thomas E. Dow
Miss Frances Arnold	Miss Rosamond Elliott
Mr. Witter Bynner	Mr. Barry Faulkner
Mr. and Mrs. Ernest Harold Baynes	Mrs. F. A. Graydon
Mr. and Mrs. Holmes Beckwith	Miss Evelyn Granger
Mr. George de Forest Brush	Mrs. Arthur L. Hadley
Rev. George Stewart Campbell	Mrs. Martha E. Holt
Mr. Clarence E. Clough	Mr. and Mrs. William H. Hyde
Mr. and Mrs. Winston Churchill	Miss Harriet E. Jenney
Miss Mabel Churchill	Miss Mabel Jordan
Dr. and Mrs. George Clarke Cox	Mr. and Mrs. Albion E. Lang
Mr. and Mrs. W. K. Daniels	Mr. and Mrs. Philip Littell
Miss Madge M. Daniels	Mr. and Mrs. Percy MacKaye
Mr. and Mrs. Tucker Daland	Senator R. J. Merrill
Mrs. Henry Dana	Miss Nichols
Miss Frances Duncan	Miss Rose Nichols

Miss Anne B. Parrish	Mrs. Homer Saint-Gaudens
Mr. and Mrs. Maxfield Parrish	Mr. and Mrs. Louis Saint-Gaudens
Mrs. W. R. Pearmain	Mr. Paul Saint-Gaudens
Mrs. Charles Platt	Mrs. I. W. Spalding
Mr. Robert R. Penniman	Miss Kate C. Stewart
Mr. John D. Porter	Mr. and Mrs. Charles A. Tracy
Mrs. Ida Metz Reed	Miss Emily Tracy
Mr. and Mrs. George Rublee	Professor and Mrs. George Ray Wicker
Mr. Deane Ruggles	
Mrs. George Ruggles	December 1, 1911[6]

Several years later, when Ellen Axson Wilson was in Cornish and her husband's presence was required in Washington, she wrote Woodrow Wilson about a contingent of "Suffragists" trying to visit her at "Harlakenden House." As Suffragette demonstrations multiplied in Washington, her predicament in Cornish was soon to become the President's in the White House. Mrs. Wilson commented further about the group that they "were extremely disappointed, of course, saying that they did not expect me to put myself on record as for them, but it would 'help them greatly for me just to receive them.' Doubtless it *would*, for it would be considered putting myself on record! I also had a letter on the subject from an anti-suffragist."[7]

Interest on the part of Cornish in the League and the cause of woman's suffrage was not to die down. The Meriden, New Hampshire, newspaper, The *Weekly Enterprise* for Thursday, July 8, 1915, was full of the issue as a result of the local Fourth of July celebration. In addition to printing in its entirety a speech presented by the "Honorable W. D. Lewis, president of the Texas Farmers' Union in opposition to" a bill for women's suffrage in the Texas legislature, the *Enterprise* ran a full description of "July Fourth in Cornish Flat." An excerpt from the former runs: "The primary, inherent and inseparable fitness for suffrage is supporting a family. The plow handle, the forge and the struggle for bread afford [the] experience necessary to properly mark the ballot. Government is a great big business and civilization from the very beginning assigned woman the home and man the business affairs of life. . . . We are opposed to the equal rights of woman—we want her to ever remain our superior. We consider woman's desire to seek man's level the yellow peril of Twentieth Century civilization."

As if to counterbalance these remarks, the newspaper warmly described the Cornish Flat parade:

> A very novel and striking feature of the Cornish Fourth of July celebration was the Equal Suffrage Float, which was awarded second prize in the parade which formed a large part of the day's events. The barge was brilliantly decorated with the suffrage colors, yellow and white, relieved by trimmings of evergreen. The float was divided into two sections, the first half picturing the present, showed a ballot box, where under the placard, "These can vote," were young men dressed to represent colored, half-drunk and ragged citizens, exercising their strictly masculine privilege of voting, while a group of interested and intelligent women, in white with yellow sashes, looked silently on. The second section represented another polling booth, in the Future, where men and women were voting side-by-side under the placard, "All can vote."

Suffrage songs, banners, and the distribution of suffrage literature further distinguished the barge. . . . This is the first time anything pertaining to the great Woman's suffrage movement has been done in this vicinity and the [at]tempt met with much applause and favorable comment from the open minded spectators. Women's Suffrage is recognized the world over as one of the important movements of modern times and Cornish is to be congratulated on having some wide-awake progressive young people to help swing it into line with the rest of the country.[8]

When the Nineteenth Amendment became law in 1920, there naturally was a rush to register many women voters. It is interesting to read the Cornish and Plainfield tax records for 1921 to discover the number of "Polls" added to the lists.

ENDNOTES

1. Stephen Parrish, diary; Special Collections, Baker Library, Dartmouth College, gift of Marian and Roy Garrand.

2. James Kraft, *Who Is Witter Bynner?* (Albuquerque, NM: University of New Mexico Press, 1995), p. 24. Kraft also quotes a heartfelt statement about the effect of the 1911 Equal Suffrage Parade in New York on Bynner's life and vocation as a poet; see above p. 153.

3. Fred Baumberger, "Women of Today Are Sissies, Says Suffragist," Los Angeles Times, August 26, 1956; Virginia Colby, Cornish Colony files. On Marie Dressler, see below pp. 469-470.

4. Even her obituary called attention to her activities for the right of women to vote; Virginia Colby, Cornish Colony files.

5. Daniels scrapbook; Virginia Colby, Cornish Colony files.

6. Pamphlet, gift to the Cornish Historical Society from Polly Rand.

7. Letter dated July 23, 1913; Arthur S. Link, ed., *The Papers of Woodrow Wilson* (Princeton, NJ: Princeton University Press, 1978), Vol. 28, p. 67; for the full context of these remarks see above pp. 430-431.

8. Clipping, gift to the Cornish Historical Society from Frank Ackerman.

WILLIAM ZORACH
1887 – 1966

and

MARGUERITE THOMPSON ZORACH
1887 – 1968

WILLIAM ZORACH

WILLIAM AND MARGUERITE ZORACH were part of New York's exciting avant-garde life during the years just before, and then after, the exhibition in 1913 at the Sixty-Ninth Regiment Armory known officially as the "International Exhibition of Modern Art"— "The Armory Show." They met as art students in Paris, drawn by a hope of many of their compatriots to find "fulfillment of their desire to be modern, to be a part of the new century with its promise of new freedoms and new awarenesses."[1] What they found, in fact, was twofold: "a new tradition in art based on creative spontaneity, the use of pure color, and simplification of form" and an awareness "of the fundamental change taking place in art in the early twentieth century—the change from art as a literary expression to art as the observer's subjective response to nature; the change from knowledge of the subject to the feelings of the artist."[2] Although their lives among the artistic vanguard in both New York and Paris is well-documented (for example, their designs and executions of scenery for the Provincetown Players' productions, especially Eugene O'Neill's *Bound East for Cardiff*), the primary focus here will be on their lives in New Hampshire. Their first location in the Granite State was at Randolph in 1915, thanks to the art critic and art patron Hamilton Easter Field; then, thanks to Clara Potter Davidge they returned in 1917 and 1918—to Cornish.

William was born in 1889 in the Lithuanian village of Eurburg on the Niemen River; he came to America with his family in 1893.[3] He worked from 1902 to 1908 as a commercial lithographer in Cleveland, Ohio, where he studied drawing and painting. Two years more study in New York at the National Academy of Design made his return to Cleveland intolerable and he packed himself off to Paris at the end of 1910. There he met Marguerite Thompson, a fellow art student at the Académie de la Palette, a school that provided a training distinctly different from that of the official academies. It developed "a style based on bold color and linear rhythms that paralleled French Fauvism and early works by the Blaue Reiter artists"—German Expressionist artists whom Marguerite had observed during a trip to Germany in the summer of 1910.[4] Letters back and forth from the couple indicate their growing affection. Although Marguerite returned briefly to her native California and William forsook Paris late in 1911 for the more lucrative Cleveland

Figure 165. *A graphite self-portrait by William Zorach.*

and its secure job as a lithographer, they were miserable apart from one another. They decided to forgo the lives they had unhappily established and to meet in New York on December 24, 1912. They were married the same day.

Just after they both had successfully shown works at the first exhibition of the Society of Independent Artists at Grand Central Palace, the Zorachs came to Plainfield in 1917 at the invitation of Mrs. Henry Fitch Taylor (Clara [Potter] Davidge) (see above pp. 172-174 and pp. 402-404). She owned "Echo Farm" north of Plainfield on the Old County Road and offered the use of it to the Zorachs in return for their cutting the hay, which she would then sell in order to pay the taxes. William was extremely happy there: "We had a delightful summer at "Echo Farm." . . . We had a vegetable garden, raised a pig which we sold in the fall, rented a cow for the summer for twenty-five dollars and bought a horse and buggy for another twenty-five dollars. There was only one door and it was in the kitchen, a big room with a beautiful beech floor. There was a stove but no furniture; however, we were used to that problem. We had shipped our bed and bedding by American Express. They did not arrive until fall when we were leaving. We were ingenious at making a place livable. We were living in a wilderness. I had to learn to milk the rented cow. It was a painful problem in the beginning and my hands got so numb I could hardly use them."[5] The milk from the cow, which they rented from A. K. Read of Plainfield, was necessary for the young couple's son Tessim, born March 28, 1915; furthermore, Marguerite was pregnant—their daughter Dahlov was born at the end of their stay at "Echo Farm" on November 12, 1917, in Windsor, Vermont. As William puts it, "We stayed very late at the farm until the winter shadows closed in on our valley and the sun only sat above the hills for a few hours in the middle of the day."[6]

To hear William describe that summer, however, milking was not the only problem they faced. "In return for the use of the farm, we were supposed to cut the hay. I bought a scythe and cut the whole field without sharpening it. It never occurred to me that it wasn't sharp when I bought it. We asked a farmer to help us. He looked at the field and said, 'What did you chew that off with?'" Furthermore, although "all day the country was serene and silent . . . at night, when we were securely in our beds, it was rampant with wild life. The mosquitoes roared like the sea against our window netting; heavy animals clumped and coughed and growled and bumped into the house." Deer and porcupine also plagued the family.[7]

Nevertheless, it was also a good period for them both as far as the art they were creating was concerned. The Cubism they imported from New York found few takers among the Colonists in Cornish, whom William termed "successful academic artists and writers," but Cubism was an influence basic to both his style and to his description of Marguerite's style. He describes their creations in the following terms:

> This was a transition period for us in art. We found it difficult to work. We had to dig into ourselves for material and had to build the material we found into new forms until it evolved a life of its own. I worked most of the summer on a large painting, doing it over and over, always unhappy with it, until I could no longer see it and threw it away. Marguerite felt bad about it; she liked it. I also painted a large picture of a figure with a scythe—the scythe is a beautiful form. I feel that this picture is unusual in its color and conception. Marguerite painted a lovely little picture called "Whippoorwills" . . . it was of the New Hampshire country at dusk with birds flying. She also painted a picture of a fascinating swamp we passed on the way to town, and one of a deserted mill . . . Marguerite did a series of watercolors of the woods, pictures that analyzed the colors and forms around her and built them into new combinations, yet retained the beauty of the woods.
>
> It was here at Echo Farm that I made my first carving. We found two small butternut panels, the fronts of small bureau drawers. We each started to carve a woodcut, but I got so fascinated carving that I didn't stop with a woodcut. I developed a fine and most original bas-relief . . . I don't remember what happened to Marguerite's effort.[8]

Although the decision to carve a bas-relief may have resulted from the fashion for them among artists in the Cornish Colony, Zorach in 1917 was laying the groundwork for his career in sculpture. It, too, began in Plainfield the following summer. Indicative of the couple's artistic symbiosis is the fact that one of the butternut panels was a bas-relief of a waterfall inspired by a cooperative embroidery they had completed in 1916.[9]

After a winter of activity in New York, caring both for their children and their artistic careers, Mrs. Davidge, whom William refers to as Mrs. Taylor, was instrumental in getting them the use of "a magnificent house in the village of Plainfield with so many rooms that we shut off half of them and never went into them. There was such an enormous studio that a billiard table looked like a postage stamp in it. This was the Fuller house [see above pp. 203-210] and was supposed to be in such poor condition that no one could live there, at least the kind of people that would rent a house that grand." The house that had been available to Ethel Barrymore in 1906 and later to Ernest Lawson had obviously degenerated through neglect. "Nothing was supposed to work—the plumbing, the water system, the swimming pool hadn't worked for years. We filled the swimming pool and enjoyed it all summer without a bit of algae to corrupt it. . . . This mansion, the Fuller Place, belonged to a friend of Mrs. Taylor's and had stood unoccupied for years because it was too run down to interest any possible tenant. We never used the beautiful living rooms, but we read books from the library and enjoyed the swimming pool."[10] You might think that, given these few amenities, the couple could get a lot of their own work done. Furthermore, they hired Sylvia Gray of Plainfield to take care of the children—ostensibly so that they could have uninterrupted work time.[11] However, "everything was so grandiose and luxurious that we just couldn't work. I made endless drawings but I painted only one small picture. Marguerite had an order for two embroidered bedspreads. . . . She worked on these all summer."

An important development in William's life did occur that summer of 1918: "Mrs. Taylor brought up a man named Applegate, a potter. He built a kiln out of an old stove and some fire brick, and we played with ceramics. I did my first modeling—several decorated pots and some small figures. We sat up all night firing the kiln, cooking hot dogs, singing songs, and stoking the fire. It was wild and exciting." Frank Applegate was a potter with whom Paul St. Gaudens studied; the eighteen-year-old Paul also worked with Applegate and Zorach at the Fuller place's kiln.[12] Matters were not altogether serenely academic: "Awful things happened; our work blew up from not being properly dried, bricks blew up and wrecked the kiln and everything in it. Something always went wrong. We had a lot of fun and experience but only one or two pieces survived. One of them, of Dahlov just learning to walk and balance herself before taking off, was broken but I managed to restore it and make a cast of it in bronze. 'First Steps' has all the sense of form and accomplishment that is in my later work. This was the first piece of sculpture in the round that I did."

From the reputation he built as a sculptor later in his career, the consequences of creating this piece of sculpture were major. His reflections on it are interesting, too: "I came to sculpture not as an art student, but as a mature artist. The art knowledge I had been building up, and my own natural qualities, led me into sculpture equipped with even a greater maturity than I had ever known as a painter. Sculpture, direct carving, was an expanding universe, a liberation, and a natural form of expression to me."[13]

Marguerite, in addition to her commissioned bedspreads, also seems to have had a good working summer. She "did a tapestry embroidery of our life in Plainfield. All the activities of the kitchen—all of us eating at the table, the animals, the patterns of curtains, dishes, linoleum—all interwoven, appearing and reappearing on different planes in different color patterns. A very modern and abstract work of art—with the village of Plainfield in the background; the trees and church and hills, all done in browns and blues and reds—not brilliant colors but strong. She called it 'Family Evening' and considers it her masterpiece."[14]

Before turning to her artistic achievements, especially those done while she was in Plainfield, we should let Wayne Craven remind us of the high caliber of William Zorach's sculpture. "He was one of the first American Artists to participate in the modern movement, to understand fully its aesthetics, and to break completely with the traditional art of the academies." While a student in Paris, "though [he] was developing an acute sense of abstract design, he was reluctant to give up nature, which even then—as throughout his career—was to be the original point of departure in his art." In other words, just prior to coming to Plainfield, "his aesthetic soul has been purged of academic cliches by the cauterizing modern art, and it left him and his art clean to develop a fresh and independent and meaningful art of his own. It was at that point . . . that fate turned him toward sculpture." In summarizing the effect of his sculpture, Craven notes that "when Zorach saw one or another stone he inclined toward certain subjects, such as the loving embrace of a mother and child, or the affection between a child and her pet. He had especially deep feeling for the beauty of the female nude. His work was, in fact, the result of a profound sensitivity to life—always avoiding the theatrical and sensational, but always expressive. . . . In addition to the beauty of his simplified, compact forms abstracted from nature, he infused his work with an expressive content, sometimes gentle, sometimes heroic." In a word, Zorach's "contribution to the maturity of modern art in America was an enormous one."[15]

MARGUERITE THOMPSON ZORACH

MARGUERITE was born in Fresno, California, in 1887. Her family was an odd mixture of the progressive and the conventional. She was given an excellent education and encouraged in her artistic talents. When her aunt invited her to come and visit in Paris and to continue her studies in art, her mother and father readily agreed. There she was heavily influenced by the French Fauves, renewed her childhood acquaintance with Gertrude Stein, and met Picasso.[16] When she returned home in April of 1912, she told a Fresno reporter that "the 'Post-Impressionist' type of painting" was "a bit too modern to suit California temperament." And so it was, especially for her family, "who did not appreciate her style of painting. Hoping that she would forget about being an artist, they hid her paints and tried to encourage her to become part of Fresno society. Marguerite Thompson was not temperamentally suited, however, to teas and Monday afternoon clubs, and she longed for the independence that she had experienced in Paris."[17] Letters to William in Cleveland indicate that the months alone in California were not happy ones—for either of them. They decided to meet in New York in December and marry, but before she "left California, she framed a few of her more traditional paintings for her parents, set aside a few works for herself, and then hauled all of her other paintings, prints, and drawings to the Fresno town dump."[18]

Although New York had William, the city also had its drawbacks for her. Unlike her husband, she never really felt at home in metropolitan areas. Consequently, they compromised and "agreed to 'spend the summers in nature.' Most of Marguerite's oil paintings were executed during their summer retreats."[19] And New York was not altogether receptive to her paintings either. One of them in the Armory Show earned her the following scathing review: "In the 'study,' by Marguerite Zorach, you see at once that the lady is feeling very, very bad. She is portraying her emotions after a day's shopping. The pale yellow eyes and the purple lips of the subject indicate that the digestive organs are not functioning properly. I would advise salicylate of quinine in small doses."[20]

Figure 166. *Woodcut Christmas card by Marguerite Zorach, 1915 or 1916.*

Some assessments of her career as a whole, and not merely individual items, frequently imply her deference to and sacrifices for her husband's career. Although the couple agreed to spend their summers in the country, be it New Hampshire or, later, Maine, Joan M. Marter states that after Marguerite's marriage "she was never again to find the solitude necessary for the spirited paintings of nature which had been the greatest triumph of her formative years."[21] Nevertheless, "from the time of her marriage to William Zorach in 1912 until the famous Anderson Galleries' 'Forum Show' in 1916, Marguerite and her husband were considered to be modern artists of equal merit."[22] As the above quotations from William's various autobiographic statements have already indicated, he certainly regarded her as an equal partner. He always refers to her artistic endeavors as well as his own, and without a hint of patronizing her.[23] It is hard not to see in the lives they carved out for themselves an admirable blend of artistic cooperation and mutual respect.

An example of their creative cooperation exists in a statement of artistic principles that appeared in an essay written for the catalogue accompanying the influential show, "The Forum Exhibition of Modern American Painters," held at New York's Anderson Gallery in 1916. Although the following quotation is ostensibly William's credo, it is generally thought that Marguerite helped to shape it and to write it. At any rate, its assertions are those to which they could both readily subscribe. Both of them were inspired by the mountains in New Hampshire; as for the reference to "color" on "canvas," the "organization" behind it is a principle applicable equally to any media in which either one chose to work:

It is the inner spirit of things that I seek to express, the essential relation of forms and colors to universal things. Each form and color has a spiritual significance to me, and I try to combine those forms and colors within my space to express that inner feeling which something in nature of life has given me.

The moment I place one line of color upon my canvas, that moment I feel the need of other lines and colors to express the inner rhythm. I am organizing a new world in which each form and color exists and lives only in so far as it has meaning in relation to every other form and color in that space. . . . it is the strangeness of mountains, their bigness and solemness [sic] and depth, their height, and the strange light upon them. I go into a farm house; the people sit silently around the room. . . . And in all these things there is a bigger meaning, a certain great relation to the mountains and to the primary significance of life. One feels the relation of the forms of birds, flowers, animals, trees, of everything that grows and breathes to each other and to the earth and sky.[24]

Another example of their cooperation exists in a review of their exhibition at the Daniel Gallery in 1918. It announces that there is "an exhibition of oils, watercolors, and embroideries by Marguerite and William Zorach. . . . The embroideries represent much patience and skill on the part of both artists, who have collaborated on some of the pieces. A striking example is a colorful representation of a 'Jeypur Wedding,' the central figure of the picture, an elephant, the buildings and walls of the 'pink city' forming the background."[25]

Their collaborations, which gained headway during their summers in Plainfield, attracted much interested attention. "The legend is that the Zorachs at an earlier time found they needed an embroidered pillow to complete a scheme of studio decoration. So, in a way that the Zorachs have, they sat down and made an embroidered pillow, following their artists' intuitions and inventing a technique where they did not have one to follow." As a couple, "it would seem that the Zorachs had set for themselves a high standard of achievement in a distinctly new field, an art midway between painting and tapestry. And the charm of their quaint embroideries lies not so much in their purely pictorial qualities as in their appeal through design and color to the imagination." But the artistic success of the embroidery was truly Marguerite's: "With infinite patience she stitches out in brilliantly colored wools rhapsodies on the themes of mating, motherhood, the springtime earth, the sea—the great primal subjects which engage her equally whether she works with her brush, her needle or her woodcarver's gouge." And what began as collaboration seems to have resulted in an art form uniquely hers. Marguerite Zorach has brought her handling of the medium to ever finer perfection, though it is one that seems from the very nature of things to suit her personality. Her large embroidered pieces . . . are of exactly the same seriousness as her painted work, and take rank with the best that has been produced in modern art in this country.[26]

Almost a decade later Marya Mannes was convinced not only that Marguerite was a brilliant artist, but that she stood alone in her métier. It is also worthy of note that William figured in this rapt appreciation of Marguerite Zorach's art once: as one of several subjects, along with her children and pets. Mannes provides an interesting description of Marguerite's procedure, which "is very like painting. Instead of canvas, she uses Irish linen; instead of paint, wool thread—often dyed by herself to the desired subtleties of color. The actual design she mulls over for months—develops in her mind and on scraps of paper—as any painter would. When finally she gets a clear idea of the whole, she traces it faintly on the linen; then forgets it and focuses entirely on the part. The colors of the petal or animal, the sudden, meandering tendrils of arabesque evolve at the moment of working. There is no preconception of them at all. With Marguerite Zorach the contact of the needle to the linen is the creative spark, the real beginning. A process, truly, of natural flowering." Because she chose to illustrate her article with it, Mannes seems particularly struck by *The Family Supper*, a work done in 1922 that may be related to the work William refers to as *Family Evening*, done in Plainfield in 1918.[27] Moreover, she is in awe at the apparent unity of creator and form in Zorach's work: "That she studied in Paris under various men—that she has traveled over a greater part of the world's circumference—seems to have little bearing on her embroideries. That is their remarkable quality. The just *are*. They stand alone, derive from no person or school. They are modern, perhaps, in the sense that her conventions of form—figures, etc.—suggest the conventions of the day; but they are ageless in their artistic maturity. . . . Unlike tapestries, which were done by many people, her embroideries bear the imprint of one definite personality—her own; unlike paintings, however, they have an impersonality—an abstraction—which the more fluid and indefinite science of the brush seldom achieves."[28]

Several of her works done locally deserve mention. She gave the title *A New England Family* (also called *The Father)* to both an oil painting and a linoleum block; she completed them while at "Echo Farm" in 1917. She "increased the dramatic impact of both versions . . . by distorting natural forms and by placing the towering figure of the stalwart man in juxtaposition to the small, playful children." Tarbell points out that these works were governed not by strict adherence to Cubist dicta but by principles of "design and composition, and an expression of mood through color." And her proof of this assertion tells us much about Marguerite's angle of vision. "In the painting [she] continued to use the restricted palette and consciously applied schema of the Cubist painters. When she cut the block for the print, however, she left out the faceted shapes, thereby eliminating much of the Cubist vocabulary. In the painting she added facets for their decorative value, just as in the print she added designs on the fabric of the clothing."[29]

Finally, there was an embroidered "Pegasus" on a purse, completed the following year when she was at "the Fuller Place." It shows "the rich variety of colors and the intricate stitches typical of her tapestries. Anyone familiar with the early carvings of William Zorach will recognize in this purse the composition of his walnut *Pegasus* (1925, Whitney Museum of American Art). The repetition of design emphasizes again that the art of the Zorachs is interrelated. Indeed, they often collaborated on the same work."[30]

This emphasis on the collaborative interrelatedness of the Zorachs' artistic activities is particularly characteristic of what they produced while they were in the Cornish Colony. Although it is true of Marguerite that "her later turning to the decorative arts has obscured the fact that she was once an adventurous painter—and, then, her accomplishments as an artist were overshadowed by those of her more famous husband," it is also very true that "forgotten or not . . . Marguerite Zorach made a spirited contribution to the discovery of new paths in art in America in that sensitive period before the First World War, and is worthy of much more attention than she has heretofore been accorded."[31]

ENDNOTES

1. Joshua C. Taylor, forward to Roberta K. Tarbell, *Marguerite Zorach: The Early Years, 1908-1920* (Washington, DC: National Collection of Fine Arts, The Smithsonian Institution, 1973), p. 8.

2. Tarbell, pp. 13, 19.

3. Ibid., p. 58, n. 14, provides the reason why some listings give William's birth year as 1887 and other listings as 1889: when they were married in 1912, he claimed he was born in 1887 so that he would not appear to have been younger than Marguerite, who really was born in 1887.

4. Ibid., p. 16. For more on William and Marguerite's early careers, see the exhibition catalogue by Donelson F. Hoopes, *William Zorach: Paintings, Watercolors, and Drawings, 1911-1922* (Brooklyn: The Brooklyn Museum, 1968), pp. 1-14.

5. William Zorach, *Art is My Life* (Cleveland and New York: World Publishing Company, 1967), p. 48. In the typescript draft for this autobiography, Zorach writes the following sentences, which precede the passage quoted, about living at "Echo Farm": "I might never have gone back anyway. It was in a hollow between hills, very far away without a car but very lovely"—the phrase "without a car" is deleted in pencil; from the William Zorach Papers, Manuscript Division, Library of Congress, Box 22; copy in Virginia Colby files. (They probably shipped their bedding by Railway Express, not American Express.)

6. Zorach, *Art is My Life*, pp. 49-50.

7. The quotations in this paragraph come from Zorach, *Art is My Life*, pp. 48-59.

8. Ibid., p. 49.

9. It is illustrated in Marilyn Friedman Hoffman, *Marguerite and William Zorach, The Cubist Years: 1915-1918* (Manchester, NH: The Currier Gallery of Art, 1987), p. 31.

10. This passage and all the quotations in the next two paragraphs are from Zorach, *Art is My Life*, pp. 50-51. The sentence in the typescript draft, cited above in n. 4, reads: "We never used the beautiful living rooms; we read books from the library, enjoyed the swimming pool but we were never happy in the immensity of the studio although we did play pool there."

11. Interview: Sylvia Gray with Virginia Colby, June 1981.

12. Virginia Colby, Cornish Colony files.

13. William Zorach, "The Background of an Artist," *Magazine of Art* 34, May 1941, p. 237. For a discussion primarily about Zorach's career as a sculptor, see John I. H. Baur, *William Zorach* (New York: Frederick A. Praeger, 1959); a shorter version is available as part of an exhibition catalogue, *William Zorach* (New York: Whitney Museum of American Art, 1959).

14. Zorach, *Art is My Life*, p. 57.

15. Wayne Craven, *Sculpture in America* (New York: Thomas Y. Crowell, 1968), pp. 576, 578, 580.

16. Tarbell, p. 15.

17. Ibid., p. 29.

18. Ibid., p. 35. Later, in 1920, she also destroyed many of the paintings she did between 1912 and 1920.

19. Tarbell, p. 36; the "in nature" phrase is significantly enough in a letter William wrote Marguerite from Cleveland, May 25, 1912, almost six months to the day before they were married; Tarbell, p. 60, n. 55.

20. Aloysius P. Levy, "The International Exhibition of Modern Art," *New York American*, February 22, 1913, as quoted in Tarbell, p. 36.

21. "Three Women Artists Married to Early Modernists: Sonia Delaunay-Terk, Sophie Tauber-Arp, and Marguerite Thompson Zorach," *Arts Magazine* 54, 1, September 1979, p. 95.

22. Tarbell, p. 9.

23. Marter quotes William's remark in Paris, "I just couldn't understand why such a nice girl would paint such wild pictures," *Arts Magazine*, p. 94—there is as much admiration in that statement as condescension.

24. As quoted in Hoffman, pp. 19, 22; see p. 39, n. 21, for further discussion of Marguerite's contributions to this essay. The fact that she was the only artist exhibited not to have a statement leads some critics to believe that was a mutually agreed upon philosophy of art.

25. *American Art News* 16, March 23, 1918, p. 3.

26. The quotations in this paragraph are from Jean Paul Slusser, "Modernistic Pictures Done in Wool: A Note on the Quaint Embroideries of the Zorachs," *Arts and Decoration* 18, January 1923, p. 30. It should be noted, however, that they entered separate works in the "Exposition of Paintings and Drawings Showing the Later Tendencies in Art" at the Pennsylvania Academy of the Fine Arts in the spring of 1921. Marguerite showed *Camp in the Woods, Camp at Night,* and *Yosemite Trails.* William showed *The Waterfall, Adoration, Yosemite Landscape, Mirage-Ships at Night,* and *Interior and Exterior.*

27. See n. 14 above.

28. Marya Mannes, "The Embroideries of Marguerite Zorach," *International Studio*, March 1920, pp. 29, 32.

29. Tarbell, pp. 49-50.

30. Ibid., p. 50.

31. Joshua C. Taylor, forward to Tarbell, p. 8.

THE WAY IT WAS:
LIFE IN THE CORNISH COLONY

IT IS IMPOSSIBLE TO RECREATE and recapture the flavor of the daily life members of the Cornish Colony led. Yet it might be worth while to examine some of the customs and assumptions common to life at the turn of the century. Our best source for investigating these concerns, which are not discussed directly, are the diaries surviving from this period. As we read them, we are suddenly brought up short when we encounter unfamiliar terms or realize that they accept as normal what we readily dismiss as outmoded.

For example, there was the custom of "calling," which had nothing to do with using the telephone. In fact, people dressed to make or receive "calls." "Calling" was a social occasion for which people specifically dressed so that they could receive their guests properly and those visiting, or calling on them, would be properly attired as well. To enable the artists and writers to put in a good day's work, this ritual was usually performed in the late afternoon or the early evening. Stephen Parrish, who left wonderful diaries for us to peruse, lists everyone who called on him and often includes the length of time the caller stayed. Judging from his diary, we can guess that calls were usually shorter than some of our social telephone calls. His callers usually stayed fifteen to thirty minutes, though there are those who receive the notation of staying "a whole hour." When he and his cousin Anne went calling, they often made several calls on their tour. Sometimes, they found no one home, so they would continue on to another house. When someone was absent, the caller left a "calling card." These people were not leaving something for billing their call, but a card with their names on it to let their friends know that they had dropped by.

The weather, of course, was a factor in this custom. All of their social traveling was done by horse and buggy or, in winter, by horse and sleigh. Augustus Saint-Gaudens was proud of his carriage, built by the French Company of Boston, Massachusetts, as well as of his bright red sleigh with its chorus of bells. But the weather could be a major threat to the beauty of these conveyances and their passengers. Icy roads were extremely treacherous and caused concern for the safety of travelers and sleigh. On more than one occasion, the Parrishes started out but returned home quickly because of road conditions. Then there was the in-between season, when, depending upon the location of the sun on the road, the roads were covered with mud as well as ice.

Horses figure large in these diary entries. On several occasions, Stephen Parrish refers to a horse being spooked, running away, and smashing the wagon. On June 7, 1905, he notes that their horse Betty fell, ran away, destroyed the wagon, and threw the two passengers to the ground. One evening in 1903, when the Parrishes were returning from a party at night, Henry Fuller's big dog attacked the buggy and nearly upset it, much to the occupants' consternation. In the same year, but in the diary for Louise

Cox, there is an entry that notes that Kenyon Cox and Lucia Fuller "in their two teams drove back from Windsor by way of the ferry." At another point, Louise mentions that she went to Windsor and back via the ferry and that it was quite dark in the woods near the ferry.

For any social occasion, be it a call or a dinner party or a dance, and regardless of the means of transportation, proper attire was required. The sculptor Herbert Adams once stated that women "should be careful what they wore to picnics, it made such a difference; they should wear white or bright colors." From then on, naturally enough, most of the women in the Colony adhered to that advice. There is a delightful snapshot taken at the Fuller's pool showing a woman watching children playing in the water. For this responsible task, she is wearing a big, wide-brimmed hat. Can you imagine what would have happened if she had been obliged to jump into the pool to rescue one of those children?

For us it is almost inconceivable to imagine the proper attire that required women to get in and out of a buggy with their long dresses and petticoats—and all the while, avoiding the mud, whether stepping in it or being spattered by it. Easy-care or drip-dry fabrics had never even been dreamed of then! Everything had to be ironed with a sad-iron, a heavy, metal flatiron that was heated on the top of a wood stove.

Yes, a wood stove, not a gas or an electric oven, though sometimes they used a coal stove. Dinner parties were the most common form of social interaction in the Cornish Colony. And all the cooking had to be done on a type of stove that remains in only a few houses today. There was an art to selecting the correct wood, or just the right amount of coal, so that the stove top would be hot enough for stove-top cooking or so that the oven would have a moderate, even enough temperature for baking.

Most families employed cooks to do this kind of work. When you read in the Colonists' diaries about how much entertaining actually went on, you realize how much work these cooks and household servants really did. Stephen Parrish frequently notes that Anne is going to Boston to hire a new cook. No doubt part of the hiring problem resulted from the area's isolation, but overwork may also have been a cause for her frequent trips. Anne did find one person, a Mrs. Hughes, who remained with the Parrishes for three years. In addition her daughter Gertrude was enrolled in the Tracy School. In the diary of Mrs. Maxfield Parrish, Stephen's daughter-in-law, we come across a notation that she and her husband are going out for the evening because the servants were giving a party. She also mentions several times that the maids frequently squabble among themselves.

A final assumption that would be unfamiliar to our generation is that of keeping the ice-house well-stocked. No electric refrigerators with automatic ice-making capabilities for those households. A precise notation in Stephen Parrish's diary on December 21, 1905, reads that he bought 316 cakes of ice from Harry W. Sturtevant, a local farmer, for $.02 a cake. Furthermore, he had to pay for thirty-two hours of hauling by a team of oxen at $.35 an hour and another thirty-two hours of stacking the ice-house at $.175 per hour. He predicted that this amount of ice would last him until the ice harvest in the spring of 1906. And this is ice for the winter; imagine what was involved to keep a well-stocked ice-house during the long summer entertainment season. Much of the ice, incidentally, came from the Blow-Me-Down Pond.

A SUPPLEMENTAL LIST:
PEOPLE CONNECTED WITH THE
CORNISH COLONY

FRANCES ARNOLD
1874 – 1975

FRANCES ARNOLD'S association with Cornish can be traced to her grandfather, Benjamin Green Arnold. He was a businessman from New York City involved in the coffee trade whom Augustus Saint-Gaudens met while traveling in Europe and of whom he did a portrait bust "elegant with 'Horace Greeley whiskers.'" He came to Cornish and rented a place from Charles C. Beaman; eventually Frances and her mother would purchase a farmhouse they renovated and called "Overbrook Fields."

When Frances's parents, Francis Benjamin Arnold and Augusta Foote Arnold, came to Cornish, Frances, then a young girl, delighted in playing with Margaret Nichols and using the swimming pool "at Uncle Augustus's house."[1] In 1904 after Frances had lunched with John Hay, Abraham Lincoln's private secretary and biographer, who had driven over from his country home in Newbury, New Hampshire, Saint-Gaudens sought her opinion of his recently completed bust of Hay. "On this occasion she was terrified and had no idea what to say, except that she thought the bust was a wonderful likeness. Later, she realized that Saint-Gaudens really wanted a young person's non-professional opinion."[2]

Once she was graduated from Bryn Mawr College, Frances Arnold began teaching at the eminent Brearley School in New York City. She ended her career there as headmistress. But typically, she was quick to point out, "Now, I don't want you to give me any 'airs.' . . . I was really just a school teacher at Brearley. When the headmistress died suddenly, they asked me to serve as headmistress. And I did, for three years before I retired."[3]

This no-nonsense approach also characterized her remarks about her house and members of the Cornish Colony. Among her mementos were "a plaque of her mother done by . . . Frances Grimes, a photograph of architect and landscape gardener Charles A. Platt dedicated to her Aunt Grace Arnold [and] a drawing by Maxfield Parrish ('One of those funny drawings he did that just makes you want to laugh')." She also told of a charming interchange with Maxfield Parrish: "'His mind was always active. Once, I remember, we were playing tennis on grandfather's courts. The sky was so blue. The kind of blue you only see in New Hampshire and Vermont. Well, I really hit him a tricky ball. And, don't you know, he missed it. You know what he said to me? . . . Miss Arnold laughed, 'Who could hit a ball when the sky is so blue?' And he just stood there looking up at it.'" Alluding to the woman's suffrage questions, one that greatly preoccupied her and her friends in the Cornish Equal Suffrage League, Frances Arnold was equally straightforward. She distinguished between suffragettes, which she emphatically denied ever being, and people who "believed in the suffrage movement for women. And we talked to all the men we knew until they agreed with us about the vote for women."

Once she had moved to Cornish permanently, she was also active in issues and service. During the Second World War she was the head of the Windsor County Committee of the British War Relief Society and had occasion to thank both Frances Grimes and "Mr. Maxfield Parrish for his gift of the painting 'Sunrise,' the receipts from which enabled us to finish payment on our first Mobile Kitchen and purchase the second. Also he made posters and printed notices for us and helped us constantly throughout the winter."[4]

Finally, examining the women's movement in 1975, she took a position that would surely have made her Cornish Equal Suffrage League members proud of her: "Women who want equal pay for equal work are foolish! Look for what you can do better than a man. Do that . . . Why should a woman do the same as a man, when she could probably do something better if she put her mind to it?"[5]

ENDNOTES

1. The first two quotations come from Louise Hall Tharp, *Saint-Gaudens and the Gilded Era* (Boston: Little, Brown, and Co., 1969), p. 260; see also Charlotte Pollock, "When All the Men Went 'Bull Moose,'" *Claremont Eagle-Times*, January 5, 1975, Section C, p. 1.

2. Tharp, pp. 396-397. Hay was also an ambassador to England and Theodore Roosevelt's secretary of state.

3. This quotation and those in the next paragraph come from Pollock, pp. 1, 4. It should be pointed out that the "Miss F. Arnold" who played the role of Flora in the 1905 performance of *A Masque of "Ours": The Gods and the Golden Bowl* was the aunt of the Frances Arnold of "Overbrook Fields." Her nickname was Fannie and she was the sister of the Grace Arnold mentioned in the next paragraph; information courtesy of Prue Dennis.

4. "Report of the Windsor County, Vermont, B.W.R.S., October 1, 1940-October 1, 1941"; Virginia Colby, Cornish Colony files.

5. Pollock, p. 4.

JOHN BLAIR
1875 – 1948

JOHN BLAIR was a famous actor on the New York stage. We know he was in Cornish at least on June 22, 1905, for the performance of *A Masque of "Ours": The Gods and the Golden Bowl* in which he played the part of Jupiter. Marion MacKaye noted that after the performance "we had a dance . . . in Saint-Gaudens's large and new studio with stunning music—and a gorgeous march led by John Blair and myself as Jupiter and Juno, in and out all over the building."[1] One reviewer of the Masque pointed out that the "spectacle" was enhanced "by the experienced stage-management of Mr. John Blair."[2] An article in the *Century Magazine* in 1906 also listed John Blair as a Colony member, noting that "through Arthur Whiting and John Blair, music as well as the drama are naturalized at Cornish."[3]

Those responsible for the *Masque*—Louis Evan Shipman, Percy MacKaye, and Arthur Whiting—must have felt just a little puffed up to have secured Blair's services because he had recently made quite a name for himself in theatrical circles. Blair made his New York debut in 1893, but during the 1899-1900 season he helped to launch a series of five avant-garde plays "of certain literary value, but plays which, from their originality or unconventionality, were manifestly 'unpopular,' and, therefore, never likely to be considered by the commercial theatre manager."[4] A contemporary critic deemed "the movement started by John Blair . . . was none the less grateful and scarcely the less important because it did not stir very deeply the helter-skelter theatregoing public." Each was on a "modern" theme and each had the further disadvantage of being by a European writer: the Spaniard José Eschegaray's *El Gran Galeoto*, the Frenchman Paul Hervieu's *Ties,* a version of *Les Tenailles,* the Russian Alexander Ostrovsky's *The Storm,* the Irishman Edward Martyn's *The Heather Field,* and, most notable of all, the Norwegian Henrik Ibsen's *The Master Builder*—written in 1892, but receiving its first New York performance with Blair as Halvard Solness.

Of Blair's performances, the same contemporary critic's opinion was favorable. "Mr. Blair's [character] was a well-defined creation, finely idealized, and competently resourceful. The actor was strongly dramatic, and his range of expression wide and varied. He was especially successful in reproducing the imaginative atmosphere that was so necessary to a proper understanding of the character." It seems, however, that Blair was unable to persuade the audience of Halvard Solness's "tragic power," "because the drama proved far too subtle for the casual audience, only superficially acquainted with the philosophy and method of the Norwegian dramatist." Indeed, Blair seems hardly at fault: "those that previously knew nothing about 'The Master Builder,' or about Ibsen, either . . . found the drama veritable nonsense. Giving 'The Master Builder' in this country without a preliminary course in the Ibsen drama, was not unlike plunging a child, who had just learned his ABCs, into the midst of the Greek alphabet."

After a season such as that, not only was Cornish glad to get Blair but Blair might well have been glad to get to Cornish.

ENDNOTES

1. As quoted in Arvia MacKaye Ege, *The Power of the Impossible: The Life Story of Percy and Marion MacKaye* (Falmouth, ME: The Kennebec River Press, 1992), p. 130.

2. K. K., *The Nation,* July 1, 1905, p. 519.

3. As quoted in Ege, p. 123.

4. The quotations in this paragraph and the next come from Lewis C. Strang, *Famous Actors of the Day in America,* Second Series (Boston: L. C. Page, 1902), pp. 253, 254, 261, and 270-271.

ADOLPHE BORIE
1877 – 1934

ADOLPHE BORIE was born in Philadelphia in 1877. From 1896 to 1899 he studied at the Pennsylvania Academy of the Fine Arts under William Merritt Chase and Thomas Anshutz; he was a recipient of the Carol Beck Gold Medal. He also attended the Royal Academy in Munich from 1899 to 1902. Upon his return to Philadelphia, he was instrumental in introducing modern art to his native city and in undermining the local art traditions established by Thomas Eakins. In 1915 he received a silver medal at the San Francisco Exposition, where he entered four paintings. He received numerous other awards.

Locally Borie and his family passed the summer of 1909 in Cornish when they rented Arthur Whiting's house.[1] Since the Bories were entertained frequently, it would appear that they were popular among the Colony's artists; at some of these affairs, Borie played the piano. While he was here he painted a portrait of William Henry Hyde.[2]

Most of his life was spent in Philadelphia. Its scenes and people were the focus of much of his art, which was primarily devoted to portraiture. "'His heart lay, however, in the hundreds of canvases which he did for his own pleasure and which were stacked deep in the Pine Street [Philadelphia] studio' . . . Adolphe had been conditioned to think of art as an avocation, a privilege . . . Consequently the still lifes, flower pieces, nudes, and other easel pictures became a recreation, an escape from the portraits, which were the serious business of making a living." It is on these canvases that any final judgment of his art should be based. "It is urbane, often robust, never violent. Though curious about life, it does not impose itself upon one. It is intrigued with the shades, the subtleties, the undertones of human character; yet it never indulges in satire or caricature. It is interested in the comedy of life, but content to find it in the drawing-room, the wall-enclosed garden, or the studio . . . Like any born colorist he is purely sensuous, never dogmatic in his use of color. With him it is as unconscious and intangible as a sense of humor or a smile. He will never startle the world because he has no desire to startle."[3]

ENDNOTES

1. Stephen Parrish, diary, entry for July 4, 1909; Special Collections, Baker Library, Dartmouth College, gift of Marian and Roy Garrand.

2. Ibid., August 8 and September 12, 1909.

3. The quotations in this paragraph come from George Biddle, *Adolphe Borie* (Washington, DC: The American Federation of Arts, 1937), pp. 11, 14.

DENNIS MILLER BUNKER
1861 – 1890

BUNKER, born in New York City on November 6, 1861, had a promising art career until it was nipped in the bud by cerebrospinal meningitis before his thirtieth birthday. He was a protégé of Isabella Stewart Gardner; during the roughly ten years that he painted, he played a significant role in making Americans aware of art's potential for contributing to the common weal. To be sure, he picked this notion up in France because he too learned his discipline there. It was from Paris that Charles A. Platt wrote his parents that Bunker "is small and rather handsome and is, I believe, one of the strongest draughtsmen in Gérôme's atelier. He had a studio in New York before he came here and he painted some very nice and carefully finished pictures."[1] In Paris and on trips through the French countryside with Platt, Bunker subtly shifted his style to fit in with the current French vogue of Impressionism. Furthermore, he did not hesitate to bring that style back to the United States and to assist in nurturing its growth on native ground. "Bunker's Impressionist pictures . . . were among the earliest native Impressionist works seen in Boston in the late 1880s."[2]

In June of 1890, the year of his death, Bunker came to Cornish to visit four of his old friends from Paris: Augustus Saint-Gaudens, Thomas Dewing, Charles A. Platt, and Henry O. Walker. In a letter to his fiancée, Eleanor Hardy, who would become Mrs. Charles A. Platt in 1893, Bunker unequivocally stated his position about Cornish and its artist colony: "I don't like it here at all—and I feel—I think for the first time in my life that I can remember—genuinely homesick. . . . I don't want to stay here. It is a country of great big hills and mountains and ravines perfectly impossible to paint—and I am quite out of sympathy with the people who are here; I don't think I can possibly stay—I shall be unhappy all summer and not do any work at all. Nobody here is doing at all the sort of work I care anything about and they are interested in things that bore me . . . I feel more alone here than if I were in the heart of Africa."[3] Hirshler mitigates these lugubrious remarks by noting, "it was probably not the people there who annoyed him, for they all were old friends. Instead, the easy domesticity of life in Cornish, so congenial to those who formed its art colony, doubtless grated on Bunker, who likely found it a constant reminder of his own unmarried state."[4]

ENDNOTES

1. Letter dated June 5, 1883, as quoted in David Park Curry's essay "Reconstructing Bunker" in Erica E. Hirshler, *Dennis Miller Bunker: American Impressionist* (Boston: Museum of Fine Arts, 1994), p. 94.

2. William H. Gerdts, *American Impressionism* (New York: Artabras, 1984), p. 85.

3. Letter from June of 1890, as quoted by Erica E. Hirshler in her essay "'From the School of Mud to the School of the Open Air': The Metamorphosis of Dennis Miller Bunker" in the work cited in note 1, p. 77. The quotation in her title comes from Hamlin Garland, who had his own associations with the Cornish Colony, *Roadside Meetings* (New York: Macmillan, 1930), p. 31.

4. Hirshler, p. 77; she adds: "'I had rather be entirely alone,' he confessed, later adding that 'they bore me to death with their houses and their plans and their poor little flower beds' . . . he decried [Cornish] as being 'very hot and full of mosquitoes so that one is either stewing or being eaten alive.'" Though Bunker married Eleanor Hardy on October 2, 1890, he was dead by December 28.

AUSTIN CORBIN
1827 – 1896

DESPITE THE FACT that he was not a member of the Cornish Colony, the financier and sportsman Austin Corbin had a tangential relationship to it. Because of the opulence associated with some of the Colony's estates, because of Corbin's own wealth, and because of the proximity of the two, people frequently linked them when they thought of New Hampshire.[1] And the fact that Austin Corbin, Jr. brought Ernest Harold Baynes to New Hampshire in 1904 to be a naturalist in his father's Blue Mountain Forest Park, better known as Corbin's Park, had more significant ramifications for the Colonists. Furthermore, Austin Corbin owned more land in Cornish than any single person since the eighteenth century–2800 acres.

Corbin was born in Newport, New Hampshire, on July 11, 1827. Upon earning a law degree at Harvard's law school in 1849, he went to Davenport, Iowa, in 1851 where he began his legal career. He soon became interested in banking. In 1863, once the National Banking Act was passed, the bank of which he was then president, the First National Bank of Davenport, became the first national bank in the United States. Shortly thereafter Corbin established his own banking house in New York City; its major successes came with helping railroads to get on their feet. In fact, Corbin, "a man of unusual vision and initiative,"[2] soon established his own railroad. Realizing the tremendous potential of the frontage on the Atlantic Ocean near Manhattan that we know as Coney Island, he founded the Manhattan Beach Railroad in 1878 and set up the "Manhattan Beach Improvement Co., which constructed a bulkhead along the shore and built two hotels there, and made it one of the most popular resorts in the metropolitan area." By 1881 he took over the Long Island Railroad, became its president, and built it "into a prosperous, efficient system which performed a large service in the rapid development of Long Island as a populous residential and business area." J. P. Morgan was so impressed with Corbin's results that he persuaded Corbin to do the same for the ailing Philadelphia and Reading Railroad. His success with it guaranteed him many other remunerative positions as president or director of numerous companies. Also "during the later years of his life he was projecting the development of a transatlantic steamship port at the eastern end of Long Island and . . . of a subway system for New York City." His career, truly one characteristic of America's "Gilded Age," can be briefly summed up: "he was a man of great energy, foresight and constructive ability which, coupled with his rugged independence and self-reliance, made him a natural leader among men."

His legacy to the local area, of course, is the game preserve; the Blue Mountain Forest Park Association, which once included William Evarts Beaman and the novelist Winston Churchill as members, is still an active, private hunting area. Its efforts and those of

Ernest Harold Baynes were instrumental in saving the buffalo in America. The animals preserved on "Buffalo Mountain" eventually helped to restock government herds in the West and in Canada. "A Boston & Maine freight handler at White River Junction recalled vividly, if unprintably, the reluctance of the buffalo, weighing from 1,200 to 1,500 pounds, to being loaded into the cattle cars that took them to the Wichita reservation."[3]

ENDNOTES

1. Recall the quotation from "Mr. Dooley on Vacation"; he readily associates the two: "th' poets an' thrue histhry writhers, an' sculpchoors, an' th' gr-reatest lights iv th' sinchoory—thims that inhabit stately manshuns in Cornish. . . . An' thin ye turn ye'er fataygu'd gaze on th' raysplindint Corbin Par-rk, where that gintl'man keeps his buffalos prancin' up an' down, thinkin' they ar-re not far from . . . Texas, while they're . . . in Noo-Hamsheer."—see above p. 189.

2. *The National Cyclopaedia of American Biography*, 31 (New York: James T. White, 1944), p. 279; This is the source of most of the information on Corbin and of all the quotations in the remainder of this paragraph.

3. Hugh Mason Wade, *A Brief History of Cornish: 1763-1974* (Hanover, NH: University Press of New England, 1976), p. 100.

ROYAL CORTISSOZ
1869 – 1948

ROYAL CORTISSOZ, pronounced "kor tee´ suz," was born in Brooklyn, New York, on February 10, 1869; his parents were of Spanish descent. Upon completing his education, he went to work in the office of McKim, Mead, and White. Thus began a life-long interest in architecture; it had one important ramification for the Cornish Colony: the publication in 1913 of a *Monograph of the Works of Charles A. Platt*. Although he was partial to Platt's blend of traditional styles in his buildings, what has been called an eclectic though "simplified classicism," Cortissoz asserted that "the American skyscraper is an expression of the genius of a people."[1]

Cortissoz is remembered in Cornish because he was especially helpful in the publicity that led to the establishment of the Saint-Gaudens Memorial in 1919. He was also one of its founding trustees. He is also remembered as the author of incisive appreciations of much of the art created in the Colony.

But it is as an art critic that Royal Cortissoz will be best remembered. A friend of many members of the Cornish Colony and the author of a study of Augustus Saint-Gaudens in 1907, he "became the voice of the intelligent but nonexpert Everyman who cared about art and the culture it symbolized."[2] For over fifty years he was the art critic for the *New York Herald Tribune*. An arbiter of taste who defended a classical conception of art, he said of himself: "As an art critic, I have been a 'square shooter,' knowing neither friend nor enemy. My belief, as an art critic, has been, briefly stated, that a work of art should employ an idea, that it should be beautiful, and that it should show sound craftsmanship. I have been a traditionalist, steadfastly opposed to the inadequacies and bizarre eccentricities of modernism."[3]

To be sure, there were those who chafed under these standards, especially if they believed Cortissoz's judgment was ill-advised. For example, Philip Hale, the good friend and correspondent of Henry Prellwitz, once wrote of Cortissoz, "It seems too bad, when the worthy critic was writing his good little articles, so happy, playing with pen and ink and making marks about the 'pitty picture' that one should rudely call his attention to a few fundamentals in the science of painting."[4]

Cortissoz knew how to weather such storms. He once wrote Augustus Saint-Gaudens that "I suppose the luckless art critic comes in for a good deal of wrath in this work, but just the same, he has a joy in the work he is called upon to talk about which is past all computation. Perhaps it is the constant preoccupation with artistic things that helps him; at any rate, he lives as truly among works like yours as though he were in the studio where they are produced."[5]

But such cavils should not blind us to the significance of Cortissoz's position, especially since it lies at the heart of much of the art produced by the members of the Cornish Colony. Morgan elaborates on Cortissoz's succinct self-definition, quoted above, and helps to sharpen our view of the aesthetic that governed many of the Colony's artists: "By *idea*, [Cortissoz] did not mean anecdote or incident, elements he hated in painting, but some force that viewer and creator both recognized as part of a large ongoing tradition and that provoked reflection on meaning in life. By *beauty*, he meant a surface and design that pleased the eye, intrigued the mind, and produced harmony and order, the sense of a thing well and completely done. *Sound craftsmanship* meant evidence that the artist's abilities and intentions matched within a recognizable style that moved others."[6]

Finally, Cortissoz was an excellent stylist. Perhaps that is why his writing affected so many of his contemporaries. Certainly we all have benefited from one of his quiet contributions to our culture. "His friend, Henry Bacon, the architect of the Lincoln Memorial in Washington, asked [Cortissoz] to devise an inscription for the space on the wall behind Daniel Chester French's great seated statue of the sixteenth president . . . after much thought and a moment of inspiration, he wrote out an elegant text that captured Lincoln's striking combination of simplicity and grandeur:

> IN THIS TEMPLE
> AS IN THE HEARTS OF THE PEOPLE
> FOR WHOM HE SAVED THE UNION
> THE MEMORY OF ABRAHAM LINCOLN
> IS ENSHRINED FOREVER"[7]

ENDNOTES

1. New York Times, June 3, 1923, sec. 2, p. 4; as quoted in H. Wayne Morgan, *Keepers of Culture: The Art-Thought of Kenyon Cox, Royal Cortissoz, and Frank Jewett Mather, Jr.* (Kent, OH: Kent State University Press, 1989), p. 92.

2. Morgan, p. 63.

3. As quoted from his obituary, *New York Herald Tribune*, October 18, 1948, p. 18; see Morgan, p. 99. On another occasion, Cortissoz wrote, "I believe that a work of art is the outcome of a spiritual process, involving the artist's mind and heart and imagination, all acting in the languages of proficient craftsmanship and enriched by the crowning ele-

ment of style." With a nod to Keats and to Matthew Arnold, whom he proceeds to quote, he continues: "I believe that art . . . 'keeps ever calling us nearer to the true goal of all of us, to the ideal, to perfection—to beauty, in a word, which is only truth seen from another side.' And I believe it is the duty of the critic to make what modest contribution he can to the diffusion of this philosophy, serving as an interpreter of what is right and fine." Foreward to *Loan Exhibition in Honour of Royal Cortissoz*, exhibition catalogue, (New York: Knoedler Gallery, 1941).

4. As quoted in R. H. Ives Gammell, *The Boston Painters*, Elizabeth Ives Hunter, ed. (Orleans, MA: Parnassus Imprints, 1986), p. 130.

5. Letter dated November 30, 1897, as quoted in Morgan, p. 64.

6. Morgan, p. 67.

7. Ibid., p. 98.

WALTER DAMROSCH
1862 – 1950

WALTER DAMROSCH was born in Breslau, Silesia, and came to the United States in 1871. He was most famous as a conductor and music educator, but he composed throughout his life. He urged Andrew Carnegie to construct Carnegie Hall and persuaded Tchaikovsky to come to New York for its opening in 1891. He was noted for his many important music premieres: of Wagner's *Parsifal* and of Tchaikovsky's Fourth and Sixth Symphonies as well as works of Elgar and Mahler. Among American composers he was an advocate of Charles Martin Loeffler (a good friend of Dennis Bunker), Daniel Gregory Mason, John Alden Carpenter, and Deems Taylor. "He commissioned George Gershwin's piano concerto and conducted the premiere of his *American in Paris*."[26] Later in his life he conducted the New York Symphony Orchestra in 1925 at the first symphonic program ever broadcast over the radio and relayed throughout the United States. He was involved in several musical groups and served as the director of the New York Symphony from 1903 until 1927; it was then merged with the New York Philharmonic Society.

His local connections were twofold: he rented "High Court" in the early 1920s and Philip Littell's son Robert married Walter Damrosch's daughter, Anita Blaine Damrosch, on November 8, 1924.

ENDNOTE

1. W. Wiley Hitchcock and Stanley Sadie, eds., *The New Grove Dictionary of American Music* (London and New York: Macmillan, 1986), Vol. 1, p. 565.

JOSEPH RODEFER DE CAMP
1858 – 1923

Figure 167. *Drawing of Daniel Webster by Joseph De Camp.*

JOSEPH DE CAMP was one of "The Ten American Painters" and recognized as one of the best draftsmen of his day. His exquisite color gradations—especially visible in his portraits—earned him great respect among his contemporaries. His masculine portraiture was particularly admired: his portrait of *Dr. Horace Howard Furness* is included in the collections of the Pennsylvania Academy, his portrait of *Frank Duveneck* is at the Cincinnati Museum, and his famous *Portrait of Theodore Roosevelt,* painted for his classmates at Harvard, is in the Harvard University Portrait Collection—"this formal portrait suggests Vermeer: the elegant arrangement of forms, the fine furniture, and above all the broad expanse of wall, crossed by a fine atmospheric net of light, which acts as a vast backdrop to silhouette Roosevelt."[1] Dartmouth College also owns a portrait of Daniel Webster done in charcoal and six portraits in oil.[2]

De Camp was born in Cincinnati, Ohio, in 1858. As did another member of the Cornish Colony, John Alexander, De Camp studied under Frank Duveneck at the Art Academy of Cincinnati; he also went off in 1878 with the "Duveneck Boys" to the Royal Academy in Munich—and then on to Italy with the group. He knew Whistler in Venice, where they roomed in the same *pensione.* De Camp "disliked his sharp-tongued neighbor without caring much for his pictures" since he thought "Whistler's incapacity to master chiaroscuro had forced him to create the art of crepuscular flatness which brought him fame."[3] Upon his return to America, De Camp began teaching at the Boston Museum School in 1885; indeed, a large part of his career was devoted to teaching. "De Camp . . . became far more integrated within the American Impressionism camp in the decades after The Ten was formed [1898], undoubtedly stimulated by that association."[4]

In 1903 De Camp spent the summer season in Cornish, perhaps at the invitation of Stephen Parrish, who had visited De Camp at Rocky Neck, Massachusetts, while on a trip there in 1900.[5] An interesting glimpse of De Camp's time in Cornish can be gleaned from the comments of Lucia Fuller. She enjoyed entertaining the neighborhood children, including the De Camps' four children as well as the Cox and Prellwitz children. The day's events frequently involved games and a swim in the pool; when the parents came to pick up the children, lunch was available for both children and parents. On August 26, 1903, Lucia Fuller remarked that Mrs. De Camp and her four children came for lunch; their activities included badminton, tennis, cribbage, croquet, and of course, swimming. The Kenyon Coxes, John Blair, John Elliott, the Shipmans, the Houstons, and the Hapgoods were her frequent guests.[6]

The year following De Camp's stay in Cornish was a tragic one for his art and our appreciation of it. As there was with Saint-Gaudens that year, so there was with De Camp: they both suffered a studio fire in 1904. In De Camp's case hundreds of canvases were ruined. "This event profoundly affected both his career and his posterity. Our understanding of him today has been truncated because of the paucity of works on public view."[7]

The United States government sent De Camp to Paris at the end of World War I, during the spring of 1919, to paint a picture of those involved in the Peace Conference at Versailles. He died in 1923.

ENDNOTES

1. William H. Gerdts, *American Impressionism* (New York: Artabras, 1984), p. 205.

2. Arthur R. Blumenthal, *Portraits at Dartmouth* (Hanover, NH: Dartmouth College Museum and Galleries, 1978), p. 93.

3. R. H. Gammell, *The Boston Painters: 1900-1930* (Orleans, MA: Parnassus Imprints, 1986), p. 57.

4. Gerdts, p. 178.

5. Stephen Parrish, diary, entry for September 15, 1900; Baker Library, Dartmouth College, Hanover, NH, gift of Marian and Roy Garrand.

6. Lucia Fairchild Fuller, diary for 1903; Virginia Colby, Cornish Colony files.

7. Warren Adelson in *Joseph De Camp: An American Impressionist*, exhibition catalogue, (New York: Adelson Galleries, 1995), unpaginated.

MARIE DRESSLER
1869 – 1934

ALTHOUGH MARIE DRESSLER was at one point a vaudeville performer, she is remembered primarily as an actress on the stage and screen. In her 1924 autobiography she confessed that "fate cast me to play the role of the ugly duckling with no promise of swanning"; thus she made up her mind "to play 'my life as a comedy rather than the tragedy many would have made of it.'"[1] When you think of how much the movies of the twenties and thirties depended on the fascinating allure of heroines, Dressler's career is an important anomaly. It has been said "that she was 'too homely for a prima donna and too big for a soubrette.'"[2] She won the hearts of her audiences not because of her looks but because of her technique: "she was a master of technique, improvisation, facial expressiveness, and comic timing, and she was able to adjust the broadness of her effects to the size of any theatre or medium."[3]

After her debut in New York in 1892, her first big success came the following year when she played a supporting role in *The Princess Nicotine* with Lillian Russell. The expected ups and downs in her career occurred until the play *Tillie's Nightmare* opened in 1910. Its hit, "Heaven Will Protect the Working Girl," immediately became her signature song. The character she played, "Tillie Blobbs, the boardinghouse drudge who dreams of richer worlds," led to a contract with the fledgling organization of Keystone Pictures and Max Sennett. They brought out the silent film *Tillie's Punctured Romance* in 1914 with Mabel Normand and the then unknown Charlie Chaplin, "whom Dressler is said to have selected for the film." She and the Sennett organization tried to capitalize on sequels, *Tillie's Tomato Surprise* in 1915 and *Tillie Wakes Up* in 1917, but to little avail. It was not until 1930 and the film of Eugene O'Neill's *Anna Christie* that her career in films was secure. Then she starred in two sentimental comedies with Wallace Beery, *Min and Bill* in 1930 and *Tugboat Annie* in 1933; for her performance in the former movie, she won an Oscar in 1931. One of her last successes, which came out the year before she died of cancer, was *Dinner at Eight* (1933).[4]

We know of one evening she spent with President Woodrow Wilson and his family, no doubt resulting in part from her fame in vaudeville and on Broadway. As his daughter Eleanor later recalled, "Marie Dressler, who had a summer home in Vermont across the river, asked one day if she might come and entertain us. Father was pleased, and we looked forward to an evening of laughter, but for some unexplained reason, she insisted upon singing only lugubrious ditties about little lost children, weeping mothers or blighted love. . . . Toward the end, we rebelled politely, and she swung into her Jamboree song and then told us a few amusing tales, but somehow the gloom was not dispelled."[5]

For Marie Dressler's connection with Frances Duncan and the Woman's Suffrage movement, see above pp. 440-441.

ENDNOTES

1. As quoted in Alice M. Robinson, Vera Mowry Roberts, and Milly S. Barranger, eds., *Notable Women in the American Theatre: A Biographical Dictionary* (New York and Westport, CT: Greenwood Press, 1989), pp. 226-227.
2. Ibid., p. 227.
3. Ibid., p. 229.
4. The quotations in this paragraph come from Ibid., p. 228.
5. Eleanor Wilson McAdoo, "The Wilson's White House Romance," *The Saturday Evening Post*, January 9, 1937, p. 32. The barn and outbuildings are all that remain of Dressler's place in Windsor; they can be seen on the western side of Route 5, just before climbing the hill by the golf course.

WILLIAM M. EVARTS
1818 – 1901

Figure 168. *Marble bust of William Evarts by Augustus Saint-Gaudens, 1872-1874.*

WILLIAM MAXWELL EVARTS belonged to a family with a long history of involvement with the town of Windsor, Vermont. He had an "estate consist[ing] of the old home Runnemede, in Windsor Village, six or eight residences in the neighborhood used as tenant houses for employees, the farmhouse and barns out on the meadows one-half mile from the village, 700 acres of fertile, level meadow in Windsor, 500 acres across the Connecticut on the Cornish hills, and 600 acres of wild pasturage in South Reading a few miles to the west of Windsor."[1] Through his son-in-law Charles C. Beaman, Evarts had an interest in seeing that the "Little New York" artists' colony got on its feet.

Evarts had a distinguished national and international career. In 1860 he put William H. Seward's name in nomination at the Republican National Convention as the party's presidential candidate. During the Civil War he was a legal adviser to the legation in London from the United States. Later, President Andrew Johnson selected him as his chief counsel during the lengthy impeachment proceedings; from 1868 until the end of the Johnson administration he was the attorney general. He was appointed the counsel for the United States during the arbitration of the *Alabama* claims (a suit concerned with a Confederate cruiser, built in an English shipyard, that had done considerable damage to the Union's shipping[2]). In a sensational trial in 1875 he successfully defended Harriet Beecher Stowe's brother Henry Ward Beecher, the famous clergyman and abolitionist, from charges of adultery brought by his parishioner, the noted journalist Theodore Tilton. From 1877 to 1881 he was made Secretary of State by President Rutherford B. Hayes, who was grateful to him for winning his contested election before the Electoral Commission, and, finally, a senator from New York from 1895 to 1891.

In 1920 Sherman Evarts edited the three-volume *Arguments and Speeches of William Maxwell Evarts* published by Macmillan. A reviewer ranked Evarts's legal prowess as the equal of Alexander Hamilton's and Daniel Webster's: "We have had few greater lawyers, and no lawyer since the Civil War whose professional career has made him such a commanding figure."[3]

In 1874 Augustus Saint-Gaudens did a portrait bust of him that, according to one commentator, "represents a major breakthrough in Saint-Gaudens's oeuvre . . . The sitter's powerful presence, evoked in realistically depicted features—sunken cheeks, aquiline nose, furrowed brows, and under-eye pouches—and a patrician turn of the head, infuses the piece with a vigor and authenticity that elevates it far above any other bust Saint-Gaudens executed during the early 1870s. Evarts could not have hoped for a more noble portrait."[4]

ENDNOTES

1. W. C. Belnap, "The Evarts' Rural Home/Sketch of a Remarkable Summer Colony," clipping, *Boston Transcript*, 1901(?); Cornish Historical Society, courtesy of William Platt.
2. For discussion of this case, see Henry Adams, *The Education of Henry Adams.*
3. Zechariah Chafee, Jr., *The Nation*, Vol. 111, #2893, December 15, 1920, p. 692.
4. Kathryn Greenthal, *Augustus Saint-Gaudens: Master Sculptor* (New York: Metropolitan Museum of Art, 1985), pp. 72, 74.

DANIEL CHESTER FRENCH
1850 – 1931

BORN IN EXETER, NEW HAMPSHIRE, on April 20, 1850, French later moved to Cambridge, Massachusetts, with his parents whose friends included such important representatives of American Transcendentalism as Emerson, Thoreau, and members of the Alcott family. Indeed, he did busts of Emerson and Bronson Alcott early in his career. In 1873 he won a competition, in part sponsored by Emerson, to do a statue of *The Concord Minute Man of 1775*. He finished it in time for it to be unveiled at the centennial celebration in Concord in 1875.

After a period of study in Italy, he returned to the United States with fresh ideas. One of them was for a bust of Emerson that inspired the latter's famous remark, "That is the face I shave."[1] Other impressive works French completed prior to his connection with Augustus Saint-Gaudens were a seated portrait statue *John Harvard, Dr. Gallaudet and His First Deaf-Mute Pupil*, and *The Angel of Death Staying the Hand of the Sculptor* (the Milmore Memorial).

As French's career expanded, he moved from Boston to New York, though he always kept a studio in Stockbridge, Massachusetts. In New York he mixed with social as well as artistic celebrities, including Saint-Gaudens. As one story would have it, Saint-Gaudens was responsible for there being a month's delay in French's marriage to his cousin Mary Adams French. While French was working on the Gallaudet statue in June of 1888, he wrote his bride-to-be: "What would you think if I told you that, even at the last moment I must change my statue—and I am afraid it will put off our wedding for a month? . . . Saint-Gaudens has been in and says that the legs are too short. Perhaps I should have known this without anyone telling me." Admitting that he was "diverted by prospects of approaching matrimony," he observed that "when you can pin Saint-Gaudens down and get real criticism from him, it is better than anybody's and so what can I do except give the Doctor an inch or two more of leg and meanwhile what kind of a lover will you think me, anyhow?"[2]

Perhaps Saint-Gaudens felt that he needed to atone for this affront to Cupid, although neither Daniel or Mary French ever harbored a grudge against him. At any rate, in connection with the Chicago's Columbian Exposition of 1893, Saint-Gaudens noted that he "suggested the making of the colossal statue of Liberty in the lagoon, by Mr. Daniel Chester French."[3] As it turned out, French sculpted a seventy-five-foot-high figure of the *Republic,* which stood in the lagoon in front of the peristyle at the Exposition which did so much for American sculpture.

It was in Cornish, in fact, that French did the work on the model for the *Republic;* he and his wife were both in Cornish. Mary French has left the following description of "Aspet" in 1892: "There was an elaborate fence around the top of the bank with Greek heads at regular intervals and a big, elaborate porch at the front" where, gazing at Mount Ascutney, the family had their meals "just as in Sicily they look toward Etna and in Japan toward Fujiyama." Thrall adds that "later the Frenches built a summer home in Stockbridge, Massachusetts, a huge affair of many guest rooms, and nearby a studio having a small pergola, almost a replica of the one in Cornish—facing an equally sacred view of the Berkshires."[4]

In addition to a contemporary account of "Aspet," members of the French family provide us with a glimpse into the darker side of Saint-Gaudens. Commenting upon him at the end of their second summer in Cornish in 1894, French's wife Mary felt "that there was something of a tendency toward, if not morbidness, at least toward introspection, from which he wished to escape; that he craved excitement or at least diversion." And this opinion is corroborated in part by the Frenches' daughter, Margaret, who contrasted her father's "tranquillity" with this remark: "Up in Cornish they used to tease Saint-Gaudens because he was as nervous as a prima donna when his statues were being cast. He'd strike off into the woods by himself for an entire day, or leave town altogether in an agony of apprehension."[5]

No one would deny, however, that French invariably followed in the footsteps of Saint-Gaudens. He, too, did two statues of Abraham Lincoln—a standing sculpture in Lincoln, Nebraska, in 1912 and the celebrated seated one in Washington's Lincoln Memorial, dedicated on Memorial Day, 1922.[6] French, at the end of his life, was a trustee of the Saint-Gaudens Memorial in Cornish and the Metropolitan Museum of Art in New York. It was there, as John Dryfhout points out, that French performed his final service for Saint-Gaudens and the nation: "the present role of the museum as a patron of contemporary art was almost unknown when Saint-Gaudens was working. It was not until the end of his life that the Metropolitan in New York, through the diligence of Daniel Chester French, seriously began to collect contemporary American sculpture."[7]

ENDNOTES

1. As quoted in Wayne Craven, *Sculpture in America* (New York: Thomas Y. Crowell, 1968), p. 395.

2. As quoted in Louise Hall Tharp, *Saint-Gaudens and the Gilded Era* (Boston: Little, Brown and Co., 1969), p. 251.

3. *The Reminiscences of Augustus Saint-Gaudens,* edited and amplified by Homer Saint-Gaudens (New York: Century Company, 1913), Vol. 2, p. 73.

4. Tharp, p. 252. For another comparison of Mount Fujiyama with Ascutney, see above p. 193, n. 6.

5. As quoted in Burke Wilkinson, *Uncommon Clay: The Life and Works of Augustus Saint-*

Gaudens (New York: Harcourt Brace Jovanovich, 1985), p. 265, based on Mrs. Daniel Chester French, *Memories of a Sculptor's Wife* (Boston: Houghton Mifflin, 1928), p. 187 and Margaret French Cresson, *Journey into Fame* (Cambridge, MA: Harvard University Press, 1947), p. 213.

6. Craven, pp. 404-405 presents a fascinating account of how the monumental sculpture was completed and the interesting problems with lighting it so that the face would not be "quizzically expressionless."

7. John H. Dryfhout, *The Work of Augustus Saint-Gaudens* (Hanover, NH: University Press of New England, 1982), p. 33.

HAMLIN GARLAND
1860 – 1940

HAMLIN GARLAND, a good friend of William Vaughn Moody and Percy MacKaye and a well-known novelist and writer of short stories and memoirs, was born of New England stock in West Salem, Wisconsin, in 1860. In his youth his father farmed in both Iowa and South Dakota. Hence, once he became a writer, he chose to write about the regions of America he knew from first-hand experience, the Midwest, and, later, the West. He further decided to follow the tenets of American realism as announced by Mark Twain. His commitment to truth in his writing, whether fiction or not, can be seen from the term "verist" that he devised to define his style, one devoted to fidelity to truth. Because he was especially interested in writing about the West, he was determined to avoid sentimentalizing and romanticizing descriptions, faults he found too common in most writers about that region.

Although he was a prolific writer, he is most famous for the short stories about the drudgery and solitude of rural life collected in *Main-Traveled Roads* (two volumes, 1891-1899) and *Other Main-Traveled Roads* (1913). Of *Main-Traveled Roads* the noted critic Alfred Kazin has written: "in Garland ... American farmers first talked like farmers." Kazin also pointed out that Garland was "among the very first [to dedicate] his career to realism" and that it was Garland "who, almost alone in the eighties, sat in the Boston Public Library [and wrote] out of his loneliness and poverty those first realistic stories that were to guide others to a new literature in America."[1] Garland is also famous for his autobiographical works—*A Son of the Middle Border* (1917) and *A Daughter of the Middle Border* (1921). The former is a memoir dealing primarily with his life and the latter tells of the life of his mother and wife as well as himself; it won the Pulitzer Prize for biography in 1922. He continued his family chronicle in *Trail Makers of the Middle Border* (1926) and *Back Trailers of the Middle Border* (1928). Later he turned to his diaries and based four books on them: *Roadside Meetings* (1920), *Companions on the Trail* (1921),[2] *My Friendly Contemporaries* (1932), and *Afternoon Neighbors* (1934). Many of his more well-known novels dealt with social themes. *The Captain of the Gray-Horse Troop* (1902), his most successful novel, described injustices to Native Americans and was based on his personal experiences on Sioux and Cheyenne reservations in 1897. Other novels examined political corruption, *A Spoil of Office* (1892), the single-tax notions of Henry George, *Jason Edwards: An Average Man* (1891), and railroad lobbying, *A Member of the Third House* (1892).[3]

Garland's wife Zulime was a sister of the sculptor and historian of sculpture Lorado

Taft, who worked with Augustus Saint-Gaudens on the Columbian Exposition held in Chicago in 1893. Garland's passion for and commitment to American art, be it from the Cornish Colony or not, can be seen in the Dedication of his 1894 publication *Crumbling Idols*, "To The Men and Women of America Who Have the Courage To Be Artists."

Virginia Colby always regretted that she never pressed Philip Littell or Maxfield Parrish, Jr. for more information about their memories of having met Garland in Cornish in either 1904 or 1907. Nevertheless, there exists their anecdotal evidence for his presence as a guest of one of the Colonists. Garland may even have passed through Cornish in the 1880s when he and his brother Frank tramped their way around New England trying to support themselves by means of odd jobs. In 1917 he recalled this trip in a chapter of *A Son of the Middle Border* entitled "Coasting Down Mt. Washington." Believe it or not, he and Frank did it on a plank strategically placed on the cog railroad. Tired and penniless, they eventually made their way to the Connecticut Valley. Traveling south, they found jobs hard to come by. "The haying was over, the oats mainly in shock, the people on the highway suspicious and inhospitable . . . We looked less and less like college boys and more and more like tramps, and the house-holders began to treat us with hostile contempt. No doubt these farmers, much beset with tramps, had reasonable excuse for their inhospitable ways, but to us it was all bitter and uncalled for. . . . Each day the world grew blacker, and the men of the Connecticut Valley more cruel and relentless."[4] If Garland were in Cornish then, his later visit must certainly have been more hospitable.

ENDNOTES

1. Alfred Kazin, *On Native Grounds: An Interpretation of Modern American Prose Literature* (New York: Reynal and Hitchcock, 1942), pp. 37-38.
2. This work contains a discursive appreciation of his friend and Cornish Colony member William Vaughn Moody and their trip to the Rocky Mountains in 1901 (Chapter six).
3. Henry George's notion of a single tax on land (*Progress and Poverty*, 1879) provoked quite a reaction among some members of the Cornish Colony. George de Forest Brush was his local champion, but not Thomas Dewing. The picture of Henry George which Brush had in his tepee infuriated Dewing, though he loved visiting the tepee. One afternoon, during a summer that Brush was not in Cornish, Augustus Saint-Gaudens and some cronies took it upon themselves to throw a party at the tepee, which had been left in place for the young Homer Saint-Gaudens to enjoy. It was then that "Dewing's deep design showed itself . . . As he could not in ordinary cold blood come up and annihilate this place, he reasoned, unconsciously, 'If I can get all these chaps, as well as myself, full of fire-water, nature will do the rest.' He was right, for after having eaten all that was proper and drunk much more than was necessary, we danced in glee round the tent in which blazed the bivouac fire. Presently one demon threw some object through the open flap on the fire, which increased the conflagration inside. Then another fiend added a part of the tent, and then the portrait of Henry George, and the tepee went the way of all things." For the context of this incident see *The Reminiscences of Augustus Saint-Gaudens*, edited and amplified by Homer Saint-Gaudens (New York: Century Company, 1913), Vol. 1, p. 318-322.
4. Hamlin Garland, *A Son of the Middle Border* (New York: Grosset and Dunlap, 1917), pp. 287-288.

ARNOLD GENTHE
1869 – 1942

and Photographers Associated with the Cornish Colony:

GEORGE COLLINS COX
1851 – 1902

B. MARTIN JUSTICE
1869 – 1961

and

DE WITT CLINTON WARD
1872 – 1937

ARNOLD GENTHE, a pioneer in "candid camera" images and dance photography, was a significant figure in the development of photography as an art in America. The books he wrote and illustrated with his own pictures impressed his audience with both his narrative skills and his complementary ability to produce the telling image. His 1936 autobiography, *As I Remember*, is just such a book and provides us with a good idea about his early life.

He was born in 1869 into an upper-middle-class family in Berlin, Germany. His parents valued education: his father was the founder and first president of the Wilhelm Gymnasium in Hamburg. Faithful to these roots, his son studied classical philology, archaeology, and philosophy at the universities of Berlin and Jena. In 1892 Genthe published a respected compilation, *Deutsches Slang*, the first book in German to examine seriously this aspect of language. He also edited previously unpublished letters between Goethe and Hegel. He even did what seemed to be required of every German university student at that time: he fought a duel. After he wrote his dissertation in Latin and received his Ph.D. in 1894, he went to Paris to study art history and French literature.

With this background he was well prepared to become a tutor for the son of Baron Heinrich von Schroeder, whose wife's family was well connected in San Francisco. Her father was Mervyn Donohue, a powerful banker and railroad magnate. After agreeing to serve as Heini von Schroeder's tutor for two years, Genthe arrived in the city in 1895. "The German guidebook to the United States that Genthe brought had a sentence about San Francisco that intrigued him: 'It is not advisable to visit the Chinese quarter unless one is accompanied by a guide.'"[1] Deliberately ignoring this warning, Genthe spent his leisure time during the next decade in the city's Chinese quarter, the Tangrenbu. "While rambling through its streets and alleys, he became interested in the possibilities of the camera. With a small Kodak, easily hidden, he began to make the now famous series of photographs of picturesque characters and intriguing street scenes, with which the Chinese quarter abounded, thus obtaining the now only complete pictorial record of the old Chinatown."[2]

What began as a hobby soon became his career. He opened a studio in San Francisco and gradually expanded his connections so that he knew many of the city's social élite. Little by little he secured his position in the city by doing portraits, though he always tried to follow the principle he had employed in Chinatown of being unobtrusive with his camera and not letting his subject know at what point the picture was actually shot. His chosen profession was also helped along by his wide circle of interesting and artistic friends: Gertrude Atherton, Mary Austin, Sarah Bernhardt, Ambrose Bierce, Isadora Duncan, Minnie Maddern Fiske, Will and Wallace Irwin, Sinclair Lewis, Jack London, Julia Marlowe, Frank Norris, Anna Pavlova, Edward H. Sothern, and Charles Warren Stoddard.

But more important to shaping his career were his early experiments in color photography. "He is credited with making the first satisfactory color photographs, both portraits and landscapes, which were reproduced in various magazines"[3] like *The Wave, The American Magazine, Overland Monthly,* and *Camera Craft.* His use of Autochromes, "color screen

Figure 169. *Maxfield Parrish in his studio in Plainfield, photograph by B. Martin Justice, c. 1913. The comic mask hanging on the wall is one of the original masks crafted for the outdoor set for* A Masque of "Ours."

plates, all of which are transparencies (as opposed to prints or color negatives)" is conveniently explained in "Photographs and Historical Processes."[4] Just as his career was gaining a firm foothold, however, his studio, all his photographic plates, and personal memorabilia were destroyed by the 1906 earthquake and subsequent fire that swept through San Francisco. Had it not been for his foresight to store the plates of the Chinatown series in a bank vault, this invaluable record of Tangrenbu life (with which he was so familiar, and which he made so familiar to the rest of the world) would have been obliterated. Hence, the historical importance of his photographic record.

In 1911, however, he decided to move to New York City and establish his studio there. The range of his portrait subjects was considerably increased. He photographed presidents—Theodore Roosevelt, Taft, and Wilson—financiers J. Pierpont Morgan, John D. Rockefeller, and Andrew W. Mellon—and such people in the arts as Eleanora Duse, John Galsworthy, Arturo Toscanini, and Ruth St. Denis. It was his work with dancers that led to his 1916 publication *The Book of the Dance.*

Since this book's frontispiece, a picture of Juliet Barrett Rublee as Tacita in *Sanctuary: A Bird Masque,* was on exhibit at the Saint-Gaudens National Historic Site in the fall of 1995, it might be in order to be more specific about Genthe's connection with Cornish. While Genthe was still in California, he "befriended Cornish poet and playwright Percy

MacKaye. . . . It was at this time that Genthe completed the magnificent portrait of Percy MacKaye."[5] When MacKaye was ready to produce his *Sanctuary: A Bird Masque* in September of 1913, he invited Genthe to Cornish to photograph the event. Genthe's results made an indelible impression on all those who saw the exhibitied photographs—most especially those of George Rublee as Great Heron and Juliet Rublee as Tacita.[6] The picture of Witter Bynner as Stark, a plume hunter, is complemented by a contemplative portrait of Bynner, that Genthe also did on another occasion.[7]

This same exhibition is the source of our awareness of the other photographers associated with Cornish. There is no real evidence that George Collins Cox was ever in Cornish, although Augustus Saint-Gaudens used his "photographs as preliminary visual aides or studies."[8] Rather, thanks to the fortuitous discovery by Drs. Sandy and Stephen Dorros and their generous lending of their treasures, it was the photographs of B. Martin Justice that enabled us to see a wide range of pictures of Cornish and Plainfield, especially of Maxfield Parrish calmly seated in his studio, also taken in 1913. Justice was "a photographer, illustrator, and an art editor for the *Saturday Evening Post,* where he designed the lettering for the masthead/cover of the magazine still in use today."[9] His work for that magazine and the *Century Magazine* probably put him in touch with Parrish, Leyendecker, and several Cornish Colony members who were published in the *Century*. There is contemporary evidence that Justice and his wife were involved in local affairs "during the summer and fall of 1913."[10] The final photographer, De Witt Clinton Ward, is also linked to Saint-Gaudens. In addition to his picture of the "Little Studio," there was a Saint-Gaudens portfolio "of original photographic prints" of the sculptor himself and his works that Ward "had arranged to publish . . . on high quality Japan vellum after Saint-Gaudens's death in 1907. However, the portfolio was never issued."[11]

ENDNOTES

1. *Genthe's Photographs of San Francisco's Old Chinatown*, photographs by Arnold Genthe, selection and text by John Kuo Wei Tchen (New York: Dover Publications, 1984), p. 3.

2. *The National Cyclopaedia of American Biography*, Vol. E: 1937-1938 (New York: James T. White, 1938), p. 353.

3. Ibid.

4. Exhibition catalogue (Cornish, NH: Saint-Gaudens National Historic Site, 1 September - 31 October 1995), unpaginated.

5. Ibid. It was exhibited in its original Diascope presentation box.

6. Some of Genthe's photographs can be seen in the published version of *Sanctuary* that Frederick A. Stokes published in February of 1914, "illustrated with photographs in color and monotone by Arnold Genthe."

7. It can be seen in James Kraft, *Who Is Witter Bynner?* (Albuquerque, NM: University of New Mexico Press, 1995), p. 30. Kraft believes the portrait was done while Bynner was in San Francisco in 1912 during Bynner's "first trip to the West Coast," but by then Genthe had established his studio in New York—a possible place where the portrait sitting occurred.

8. "Photographs and Historical Processes."

9. Ibid.

10. Ibid.

11. Ibid. The Saint-Gaudens National Historic Site now owns this portfolio.

HENRY HERING
1874 – 1949

ELSIE WARD HERING
1872 – 1923

HENRY HERING

HENRY HERING was born in New York City on February 15, 1874, and studied at the Art Students League from 1894 until 1898. He studied in France at the Ecole des Beaux Arts in Paris for several years. He also worked with Philip Martiny. In 1900 Augustus Saint-Gaudens took him on as an assistant and Hering remained with his mentor until 1907. Before the death of Saint-Gaudens, Hering helped to set up the pieces of Saint-Gaudens's work for the Pan-American Exposition at Buffalo and completed the "coinage designs entrusted to him.... Among the works done by 1912 is one of his finest, a serenely beautiful head of a boy, Roger Platt, the delicate contours of the face and the crisp curls ably rendered."[1]

Figure 170. *Bronze bust of Augustus Saint-Gaudens by Henry Hering, 1908.*

Saint-Gaudens cast a long shadow over Hering's career. So much so that one contemporary art critic believed that Hering "is Saint-Gaudens over again, the workman and, in many delicacies of conception, the artist." Nevertheless, "here the influence may be said to rest and through it and above it stands Hering the individual, with his own grip on thought ... Hering works quite alone and rarely exhibits ... he has made an ideal of dignity and in this he stands a little aside from modern sculptors."[2] It was this conception of dignity that he carried out in a portrait bust of John Freeman. Because du Bois admired it so, it is tempting to believe that Hering used John Freeman of Plainfield.[3] Du Bois's praise is worth noting, and not only for what it says about the bust, which du Bois had recently seen in Hering's studio.

[It] is to me the most direct expression of himself, or of his art, if you prefer, that I can call to mind. That Hering himself considered the execution of it important is certain. He spent three years getting the old farmer, who is past eighty, to pose for him. During that time he was forced to push his wit to the extreme of effort in almost every direction. Mr. Freeman, being a typical New Englander, feared the thing he could not understand, feared that possibly a fortune was to be made from him before his eyes while he, the dupe, lent time and patience to it with childlike confidence. Mr. Hering invented reasons for paying court to him, for visit-

479

ing him, for having the visits returned, and finally, with the assistance of Saint-Gaudens, did manage to get him to pose for an hour or so, during which time he worked frantically. The result, by chance, pleased the old man who sat at intervals until the completion of the bust. It is a fine sample of the power of concerted purpose . . . it is one of the most dignified portraits in American art.[4]

Du Bois also applied the same judgment to Hering's "inestimably valuable" portrait bust of Augustus Saint-Gaudens. Of them both, du Bois notes: they are "loyal to realism and loyal to an ideal—the process of selection and omission, of accentuation and subjugation carried in it with definite purpose. . . . Here are line and forms not copied from life and yet so far from ignoring life that the very spirit of it is here."[5]

Some of the numerous works of Saint-Gaudens on which Hering worked were the *Sherman Monument;* the third version of the memorial to Robert Louis Stevenson for the church of St. Giles in Edinburgh, Scotland; *The Pilgrim* in Philadelphia's Fairmount Park the plaque commemorating *A Masque of "Ours": The Gods and the Golden Bowl;* and many reliefs. Henry Hering died January 15, 1949.[6]

ELSIE WARD HERING

ELSIE WARD was born on a Missouri farm on August 29, 1872. She, too, did her stint at the Art Students League and in Paris. Although she studied with Daniel Chester French and H. Siddons Mowbray, her greatest loyalty was to Augustus Saint-Gaudens. She came to Cornish to work as his assistant in 1901. Homer Saint-Gaudens paid her high tribute for her work on the George F. Baker tomb: "with infinite care and patience, [she] developed this composition from details suggested by the Morgan Tomb figure, the 'Amor Caritas,' and the like, until, at last, she produced an astonishingly beautiful and poetic result, filled with the spirit of [my father's] work."[7] Although she and Henry Hering collaborated on many of Saint-Gaudens's works, notably the *Seated Lincoln,* they were not married until 1910. Until her death in 1923 she did "little independent work but help[ed] in her husband's studio."[8]

ENDNOTES

1. Beatrice Gilman Proske, *Brookgreen Gardens Sculpture* (Brookgreen Gardens, SC: Trustees of Brookgreen Gardens, 1968), p. 132. Roger Platt was the son of Charles A. Platt.

2. Guy Pène du Bois, "The Work of Henry Hering," *Architectural Record,* December 1912, p. 514.

3. For more on John Freeman, see the index to Philip Zea and Nancy Norwalk, eds., *Choice White Pines and Good Land: A History of Plainfield and Meriden, New Hampshire* (Portsmouth, NH: Peter E. Randall, 1991).

4. Du Bois, pp. 515, 517.

5. Ibid., p. 520.

6. See the index of John H. Dryfhout, *The Work of Augustus Saint-Gaudens* (Hanover, NH: University Press of New England, 1982) for a complete list of the works on which both Henry Hering and Elsie Ward Hering worked.

7. *The Reminiscences of Augustus Saint-Gaudens,* edited and amplified by Homer Saint-Gaudens (New York: Century Company, 1913), Vol. 2, p. 356-357.

8. Proske, p. 128.

ROBERT HERRICK
1868 – 1938

HERRICK was a popular novelist who taught English, first at the Massachusetts Institute of Technology and then, for most of his life, at the University of Chicago. He and Hamlin Garland were part of the American realists whose works had a strong sociological thrust. His academic interest in the way literature was influenced by philosophy and the social sciences found its way into his fiction. Because he wanted his novels to reflect and explain modern American life, they centered on characters whose problems are those of the man-in-the-street. Often these challenges were sparked by labor unrest, strikes, business panics, and industrial booms. His style was generally terse, unaffected, and carefully crafted; it conveyed a strong moral center that worked itself out in accurate observations and sharp perceptions of character and scene. *The Memoirs of an American Citizen* (1905) and *Waste* (1924) were two of his sharpest assessments of American life. Other popular novels include: *The Gospel of Freedom* (1898), *The Web of Life* (1900), *The Common Lot* (1904), *Together* (1908), and many others throughout the twenties and early thirties.

We know that Herrick was in Cornish from May of 1906 until March of 1907 because of the numerous references to him in the diary of Stephen Parrish.[1] Furthermore, one of William Vaughn Moody's letters to his future wife, Harriet Converse Tilden Brainerd, refers to staying up all hours of "the night at the Herrick house where I was employed until late helping Lovett get Mr. H. and young Philip settled."[2]

ENDNOTES

1. According to the entry of June 24, 1906, Stephen Parrish called on Herrick at Smoot's house; Special Collections, Baker Library, Dartmouth College, gift of Marian and Roy Garrand. It was important to be near Phillip Littell because Herrick "thought for a while of collaborating on a play" with him; Blake Nevius, *Robert Herrick: The Development of a Novelist* (Berkeley: University of California Press, 1962), p. 160.
2. William Vaughn Moody, *Letters to Harriet*, ed. Percy MacKaye (Boston and New York: Houghton Mifflin, 1935), p. 276; letter dated "Cornish, May 29 (1906)." Robert Morss Lovett was a good friend of Moody's and, like Herrick, a professor of English at the University of Chicago. He collaborated with Moody on *A History of English Literature* (1902) and *A First View of English Literature* (1905). In 1931 Lovett edited *Selected Poems of William Vaughn Moody* (Boston and New York: Houghton Mifflin).

LOUISE HOMER

1871 – 1947

SIDNEY HOMER

1864 – 1953

MADAME LOUISE (BEATTY) HOMER, the Metropolitan Opera's famous contralto and mezzo-soprano, was born in 1871 and studied both in Philadelphia and in Boston. After a period of study in Europe, she made her American debut in 1902 as Amneris in Verdi's *Aida*. In addition to roles in Italian, she was famous, especially because of her excellent diction and stage presence, for her performances of French and Wagnerian characters. She was with the Metropolitan for over twenty years and sang at the American and Metropolitan debuts of both Enrico Caruso and Arturo Toscanini. Collectors still seek her early recordings with Caruso, Martinelli, and Gigli, although they are available on remastered compact discs. Of interest to more recent music history is the fact that she was Samuel Barber's aunt.

In 1895 she married the American composer Sidney Homer, who had studied in Boston with George Whitefield Chadwick. Although his health was delicate, he accompanied her to Europe during her study abroad. Upon their return to America they settled in New York where he did most of his composing, primarily of songs. He wrote 103 of them, ranging from the lyric to the dramatic; his wife frequently sang them in recitals of his works and in her own recitals. "The piano and vocal parts [of the songs] are mostly well balanced. His most popular pieces include 'A Banjo Song' (from the *Bandanna Ballads*), 'Song of the Shirt,' 'How's My Boy?,' and *Songs from Mother Goose*; 'Dearest' is perhaps his best-known love-song."[1]

The Homers were in Cornish for the better part of the summer of 1901. Again, Stephen Parrish's invaluable diary establishes some parameters of their visit. He mentions that he and his cousin Anne Parrish called on them on June 9 and again on August 11, that he and Anne lunched with the Homers and, naturally enough, Otto Roth at the Nicholses' on July 10, and that the Homers called on them on July 2. Finally, "at noon" on August 16, "Mr. and Mrs. Homer came with Fred and Lydia and Bertha Day. Mrs. Homer sang for an hour. Then we all went to Fred's for lunch."[2]

ENDNOTES

1. W. Wiley Hitchcock and Stanley Sadie, eds., *The New Grove Dictionary of American Music* (London and New York: Macmillan, 1986), Vol. 2, p. 415.

2. Stephen Parrish, diary; Special Collections, Baker Library, Dartmouth College, gift of Marian and Roy Garrand.

SAMUEL ISHAM

1855 – 1914

ISHAM was a painter who studied with Gustave Boulanger and Jules-Joseph Lefebvre and at the Académie Julian. He received a silver medal at the Louisiana Purchase Exposition at St. Louis in 1904. Commenting on a recent exhibition, *The New York Times* critic Holland Cotter thought highly of one of his landscape drawings. He notes that Isham is "remembered as an early art historian, but forgotten as an artist. A striking charcoal drawing of pollarded trees in a winter landscape and another of two trees bending toward each other with the lithe sensuality of dancers are memorably personal images."[1] His work as an historian of American art exists in his 1905 publication, *A History of American Painting*. In 1927 Royal Cortissoz, who was alert to the trends among his contemporaries both in Cornish and throughout America, added a series of five supplemental chapters to this important study.

Isham's first visit to Cornish occurred in the summer of 1898 when he rented the house of Augustus Saint-Gaudens. During the discussions he had with Mrs. Saint-Gaudens before he arrived concerning the actual rental, matters such as the items of linens, provisions for ice, the availability of wagons, and a supply of wood were negotiated. When the final agreement was reached, Isham had to pay $1,000 rent for the season, provide his own linens, and pay extra for whatever hay, wood, and ice that he used. Although he eventually brought his own horses, harnesses, and wagon, he did get his ice from Mr. Charles C. Beaman. One result of his stay that we know about is a painting he did of their garden.[2]

To his friends Isham reported that he passed a very pleasant summer in Cornish. His wife Julia's name was listed on the medallion that Saint-Gaudens made for each participant in the 1905 production of *A Masque of "Ours": The Gods and the Golden Bowl*.[3]

Perhaps in reaction to his Cornish connection, but definitely in reaction to the under-current for realism in American art among his contemporaries, Isham believed that the personality traits of American art patrons at the turn of the century militated against the success of the painters called "the Eight": "Life in the country and in the open air is more inspiring than that penned up in city rooms and it has been more painted, but even there the tendency has been to make a thing of beauty rather than to give the 'true truth.' Not only the artists but their patrons preferred it so. The American man finds enough of prose in the day's work."[4]

ENDNOTES

1. Review of "Nature Observed, Nature Interpreted" at the National Academy Museum, *The New York Times*, June 2, 1995.

2. Saint-Gaudens papers; Special Collections, Baker Library, Dartmouth College, Hanover, NH; on the garden painting, see also *A Circle of Friends: Art Colonies of Cornish and Dublin*, exhibition catalogue (Durham, NH: University Art Galleries, University of New Hampshire, 1985), note on Edith Prellwitz, p. 136.

3. On the Saint-Gaudens medallion at the Saint-Gaudens National Historic Site, Cornish, NH.

4. Samuel Isham, *The History of American Painting* (New York: Macmillan, 1936), p. 500. Although this is the edition with the supplemented chapters by Royal Cortissoz, Isham's remark was first published in 1905. The first major exhibition of "the Eight" opened at the Macbeth Galleries in New York on February 3, 1908.

JOSEPH CHRISTIAN LEYENDECKER
1874 – 1951

FOR OVER HALF A CENTURY J. C. Leyendecker was active as a highly successful artist and illustrator. His covers for The *Saturday Evening Post* —three hundred and twenty-two of them—and *Collier's*—forty-eight—as well as advertisements for Chesterfield cigarettes, Hart, Schaffner & Marx clothes, and especially those designating the "Arrow Collar Man" for the advertising agency Cluett, Peabody and Company commanded instant recognition among his contemporaries. Indeed, they still do for us. His images sum up a particular generation. Leyendecker, for his part, delighted in the poster art of Jules Chéret, Henri de Toulouse-Lautrec, and Alphonse Mucha (artists whose work he saw first-hand). Their designs are synonymous with what we think of as Paris in the 1890s. Correspondingly, Leyendecker belongs to that select group including Howard Chandler Christie, James Montgomery Flagg, Charles Dana Gibson, John Held, Jr., Howard Pyle, N. C. Wyeth—and, of course, Maxfield Parrish—whose images typify the people of the first three decades of this century. Many people visualize the typical turn-of-the-century woman in Gibson's images, the typical early twentieth-century man in J. C. Leyendecker's images, and the youth of the Twenties in John Held, Jr.'s images.

Born in Germany of Dutch parents, Leyendecker came to America in 1882 at the age of seven with his brother, three years his junior, Frank Xavier, another famous illustrator whose career was to parallel his older brother's, though they eventually had a falling out over J. C.'s commitment to commercial art. The latter attended the Art Institute in Chicago under John H. Vanderpoel and later the Académie Julian in Paris under the aegis of Adolphe Bouguereau; he was specifically taught by Benjamin Constant and Jean-Paul Laurens. The story goes that he entered a design to appear in the August 1896 midsummer holiday issue of the *Century Magazine* for which he received the first prize—money enough to go to Paris, though perhaps not enough to pay for his and his brother's stay there. The runner up was another familiar Cornish name: Maxfield Parrish.[1] But the first major exhibition of J. C.'s paintings was a one-man show in Paris at the Champs de Mars Salon in 1897.

Joseph and Frank returned to Chicago in September of 1897 and opened a successful studio. By 1900 they felt secure enough to move to New York because their commissions were so numerous. Nevertheless, "throughout his life J. C. refused commissions that would have given his work a permanent audience. He was asked to do murals for the Boston Public Library, the ceiling of the main reading room at the New York Public Library, and many similar works. He declined them all."[2] Rather, he steadily and purposefully pursued his career. He consistently painted his commissions in oil so that his work is characterized by "crisp, angular brush strokes"[3] that helped to define "the

J. C. Leyendecker style—the very wide, deliberate stroke done with authority and control."[4] Charles Beach was his main male model. When Leyendecker and his brother moved to their comfortable estate in New Rochelle, New York, Beach went with them eventually becoming J. C.'s "closest companion, assistant, and business manager."[5]

We know very little about Joseph C. Leyendecker's connection with the Cornish Colony and its members. Our strongest—perhaps our only—piece of evidence is a picture entitled "Joseph C. Leyendecker at the Rev. Albert P. Fitch's 'Home Acre,' Cornish, New Hampshire." This image was a rephotograph from a color screen plate (an Autochrome) by B. Martin Justice belonging to Drs. Sandy and Stephen Dorros and on exhibition in Cornish in the fall of 1995.[6]

ENDNOTES

1. Michael Schau, *J. C. Leyendecker* (New York: Watson-Guptil, 1974), pp. 16-17.
2. Ibid., p. 27.
3. Obituary, *New York Times*, July 26, 1951, p. 21.
4. Schau, p. 34.
5. Ibid., p. 30.
6. See "Photographs and Historical Processes," exhibition catalogue, (Cornish, NH: Saint-Gaudens National Historic Site, 1 September - 31 October 1995), unpaginated.

JONAS LIE
1880 – 1940

JONAS LIE was a Norwegian-born artist who came to America at the time of the World's Colombian Exposition in Chicago in 1893. An Impressionist painter who achieved fame for his paintings of the Panama Canal while it was being constructed, he also painted numerous harbor scenes and winter landscapes.[1] Lie was in Cornish in 1912.[2] Done locally was a painting of the Cornish-Windsor Covered Bridge; a landscape entitled *White Birches* may have been done here, too. We also know that there was "an exhibition of paintings by Jonas Lie . . . shown in the new barn ball-room of Kingsbury Old Tavern at Plainfield Plain, New Hampshire (Province of Cornish) from August twenty-fourth to September seventh—accommodations for man and motor, luncheons, dinners, and rooms at Mrs. Lewin's, opposite tavern."[3]

ENDNOTES

1. William H. Gerdts, *American Impressionism* (New York: Artabras, 1984), p. 290.
2. Interview: Maxfield Parrish, Jr., with Virginia Colby.
3. Announcement, undated, collection of Saint-Gaudens National Historic Site.

WALTER LIPPMANN
1889 – 1974

WALTER LIPPMANN was one of America's most influential journalists and political thinkers in the twentieth century. When he was only twenty-five, Theodore Roosevelt claimed that he was "the most brilliant young man of his age in all the United States."[1] His stands on specific issues could often strike both his supporters and his detractors as inconsistent, but he steadfastly sought to bring the dispassionate light of human reason to the thorny problems of human existence. His career was a persistent exercise first in dispelling the veil of perplexity hanging over the problems of his day. He would then proceed to reveal and define their basic paradigms. In fact, Lippmann devoted his life to the "long and troubled search to define the role of the intellectual in the polity of a free society. . . . The office of the intellectual, Lippmann has generally proposed, is to articulate the guiding faith which will enable society so to discipline itself and focus its purposes that its members can live effective, coherent, fulfilled lives. To give the intellectual this function is to imply, of course, that such a central faith exists—that there is some ultimate perspective in terms of which everything else will fall into its proper place."[2]

A person who could both articulate the role of an intellectual and profess the faith in a shaping vision for the intellectual was precisely the kind of individual who would attract Herbert Croly. It did not take long for him to decide to hire Lippmann for the editorial board of *The New Republic*. On January 5, 1914, while he was gathering together his cohorts to form *The New Republic*, Croly wrote a letter to his Cornish friend and neighbor Learned Hand that is instructive about what Croly admired in Lippmann: "he knows a lot and his general sense of values is excellent. He has enough real feeling, conviction, and knowledge to give a certain assurance, almost a dignity to his impertinence, and, of course, the ability to get away with impertinence is almost the best quality a political journalist can have. . . . I consider him as a gift from Heaven. . . . I don't know where I could find a substitute with so much innocence of conviction united with so much critical versatility."[3] By the fall of 1914, Lippmann, Croly, and *The New Republic* were up and running—practically the same day as World War I broke out in Europe.

Lippmann's early education at a New York City private school, Dr. Julius Sach's School for Boys, plus summer vacations in France and Germany with his family, and, finally, Harvard University—finishing the required courses in three years—prepared him well for the life of the mind he chose to lead. But there was an interlude before this life took hold. He rejected practical politics after a brief, disillusioning experience as an assistant to the Socialist mayor of Schenectady, New York, in 1912. Though he attended Mabel Dodge Luhan's bohemian salon on Fifth Avenue in Greenwich Village, he was not always the life of the party. He "was so offended by the conduct of the dancer Isadora Duncan that he left the party early and wrote to his hostess from the more proper surroundings of his quarters at the Harvard Club: 'If this is Greece and Joy and the Aegean Isles and the Influence of Music, I don't want anything to do with it.'"[4] Instead, he turned to writing; he quickly produced two books that greatly impressed his generation. The first was *A Preface to Politics* in 1913, "a bold attempt to force reformers to acknowledge the dark elements of human irrationality—will, impulse, drive, taboo—before they announced grand schemes for the betterment of the world." The second was *Drift and*

Mastery in 1914 in which he pressed an argument that was music to Herbert Croly's ears, largely because it was akin to that of Croly's *The Promise of American Life*, published in 1909. Lippmann believed that "modern man had to chose between 'drift,' mindless trust in the huge forces of the world, the fatalist's confidence that everything would, somehow, end well, and 'mastery,' the 'substitution of conscious intention,' the brave and willful effort to think and plan and act upon society's problems. . . . Lippmann now insisted that the scientific method, the patient pursuit of facts coupled with a willingness to experiment, offered mankind limitless promise for a better future."[5]

The evidence for Lippmann's actual presence in Cornish, even as a visitor, is primarily hearsay. But because of his close friendship with both Croly and Learned Hand, rooted in their mutual connections with Harvard University—one that also existed with numerous Colonists—there is every reason to believe that Lippmann was exposed to the social and geographical landscape of the Upper Valley.

ENDNOTES

1. As quoted in David W. Levy, *Herbert Croly of "The New Republic,"* (Princeton, NJ: Princeton University Press, 1985), p. 192.

2. Arthur M. Schlesinger, Jr., "Walter Lippmann: The Intellectual v. Politics," in *Walter Lippmann and His Times*, eds. Marquis Childs and James Reston (New York: Harcourt, Brace, 1959), p. 190.

3. Levy, p. 196

4. Larry L. Adams, *Walter Lippmann* (Boston: Twayne Publishers, 1977), p. 15.

5. The two quotations commenting on the theses of Lippmann's two books come from Levy, p. 194.

PHILIP MARTINY
1858 – 1927

PHILIP MARTINY and Augustus Saint-Gaudens came to Cornish together. Saint-Gaudens brought Martiny as an assistant during his first summer in New Hampshire—the summer of 1885. The two were also in Chicago in the winter of 1892-1893 during preparations for the Columbian Exposition. Martiny was a native of Strasbourg, France; yet he attracted the attention of Saint-Gaudens in New York where Martiny worked on the wood carvings for the Vanderbilt mansion; Saint-Gaudens shared the commission for the Vanderbilt interior with John La Farge; the former was in charge of decorating the dining and watercolor rooms and the latter was responsible for the sculptural decorations.[1] Before long Martiny, under the supervision of Saint-Gaudens, was hard at work on *The Puritan.* Eventually, Saint-Gaudens, once he had completed a work's design, would turn many projects over to Martiny. The latter's contributions were important to *The George Washington Inaugural Centennial Medal* (1880) and to the *Henry W. Bellows Memorial* (1885).[2] Martiny was also useful in helping Saint-Gaudens to develop a cheaper and effective form of plastoline, a substance used for modeling that did not need the constant, time-consuming process of watering down that ordinary clay required.[3]

Martiny, however, went off in his own direction, partly influenced by his early exposure to highly ornamental and decorative sculpture in the Parisian Beaux-Arts tradition. His difference from Saint-Gaudens can be seen on two counts. First, it was clear to many that "Saint-Gaudens's sense of design was more delicate and refined than was Martiny's and Saint-Gaudens's sculpture demanded far more in the way of structural form."[4] This distinction came to a head when—partly as a result of Martiny's connection with Saint-Gaudens—Martiny met McKim, Meade, and White, the leading American architects at the end of the nineteenth century, and landed a commission from them to sculpt the decorations for their ornate Agricultural Building at Chicago's Columbian Exposition. Martiny was able to go his own way even though Saint-Gaudens was an adviser for all the fountains, statuary, and more to the point, for all the sculptural embellishments to the fair's architecture. His respect for Martiny outweighed his differences with him in terms of taste in sculpture. The fact that Martiny worked much faster on a project than Saint-Gaudens marks a second difference between the two men: "In less than a year's time [Martiny] was able to cover the long-stretching cornices and facades . . . with the richest ornamentation ever seen in America."[5]

ENDNOTES

1. John H. Dryfhout, *The Work of Augustus Saint-Gaudens* (Hanover, NH: University Press of New England, 1982), p. 131.
2. Ibid., pp. 150, 177.
3. Burke Wilkinson, *Uncommon Clay: The Life and Works of Augustus Saint-Gaudens* (New York: Harcourt Brace Jovanovich, 1985), pp. 265-266.
4. Wayne Craven, *Sculpture in America* (New York: Thomas Y. Crowell, 1968), p. 473.
5. As quoted from "one of the illustrated art handbooks of the exposition," *The Dream City* (1893) in Craven, p. 474.

HELEN FARNSWORTH MEARS
1872 – 1916

HELEN MEARS was born in Oshkosh, Wisconsin, on December 21, 1872. After study locally, she went to New York City and, at the Art Students League, attracted the attention of Augustus Saint-Gaudens, who took her on as one of his assistants. Later, when she was studying in Paris in 1898, she met Saint-Gaudens; at that point she worked on the Sherman Monument. This was the period when she modeled a bas-relief of the sculptor from life; the original is in Baltimore's Peabody Institute of Art—the Saint-Gaudens National Historic Site has a copy.

Helen Mear's sister Mary was also in Paris. Wilkinson comments that she was gathering "material for her novel *The Breath of the Runners.* Published in 1906 by Frederick A. Stokes, it tells the story of two sculptresses whose rivalry bears a striking resemblance to the love-hate relationship of Saint-Gaudens and MacMonnies. Since Mary was also doing some work for the latter, she had a good chance to observe both sculptors in action."[1]

In 1905, having returned to America, Mears executed a portrait statue of Frances E. Willard, the American educator who devoted her efforts to the temperance movement and was president of the Women's Christian Temperance Union. While Mears was working on this statue, Saint-Gaudens wrote her the following interesting piece of advice that typifies his principles: "I don't think I would put a shawl on Miss Willard unless she wore one. If she did, I should do it by all means, or something of the kind thrown over her shoulder, as a wrap would be good and justifiable. Women frequently do that to keep off the chill in a lecture room or a public hall. You know I don't despise the making of modern dress. Something can be done I'm sure."[2] He also is quoted as saying of this statue, "that only a woman could have made it, that it was as strong as a man's work and had in addition a subtle, intangible quality, exceeding rare and spiritual."[3]

Finally it should be mentioned that the Mears sisters are counted as the first colonists of what was to become the MacDowall Colony in Peterborough, New Hampshire.

ENDNOTES

1. Burke Wilkinson, *Uncommon Clay: The Life and Works of Augustus Saint-Gaudens* (New York: Harcourt Brace Jovanovich, 1985), p. 300.

2. *The Reminiscences of Augustus Saint-Gaudens,* edited and amplified by Homer Saint-Gaudens (New York: Century Company, 1913), Vol. 2, p. 30.

3. *The National Cyclopaedia of American Biography,* 35 (New York: James T. White, 1936), p. 287.

LANGDON MITCHELL
1862 – 1925

IN ADDITION TO BEING A MEMBER of the New York bar, Langdon Mitchell was a successful author, playwright, and poet. He is generally considered important for adding "sophistication" and "lightness of touch" to American drama, characteristics that had previously been lacking. For example, in his *The New York Idea* (1906), "the kaleidoscopic divorces and remarriages among a group of well-bred but bored social leaders afford the dramatist an opportunity to reveal his delight in the human comedy. In all of his plays Mitchell proved his ability to portray convincing characters amid the artificialities of social life."[1] This same delight and ability was also apparent in his adaptation of two of Thackary's novels—*Becky Sharp* (1899), taken from *Vanity Fair*, and *Major Pendennis* (1916).

During his visits to Cornish he stayed in "The Snuff Box," once Percy MacKaye moved on to Read's Hill,[2] and in 1907 he was living in Mrs. Lewin's house.[3] He also rented the Quimby house for one season. In 1909 he appeared on the Cornish tax records; he was taxed for two horses.

ENDNOTES

1. Sculley Bradley, "The Emergence of the Modern Drama" in Spiller, et al., *Literary History of the United States* (New York: Macmillan, 1959), p. 1013; see also Joseph Wood Krutch's article on "Eugene O'Neill": "Langdon Mitchell [was] a popular playwright whose work exhibited some increase in literary sophistication," p. 1237.

2. Hugh Mason Wade, *A Brief History of Cornish: 1763-1974* (Hanover, NH: University Press of New England, 1976), p. 73.

3. Stephen Parrish, diary, May 25, 1907; Special Collections, Baker Library, Dartmouth College, gift of Marian and Roy Garrand. Parrish's diaries also contain many other references to Mitchell.

ROBERT TREAT PAINE
1870 – 1946

ROBERT TREAT PAINE was born in Valparaiso, Indiana, in 1870 and attended the Chicago School of Art before coming east to study sculpture with Augustus Saint-Gaudens at the Art Students League in New York. From 1893 until 1914 he maintained studios both in New York and across the Hudson River in West Hoboken, New Jersey. His strong Socialist views led him to speak frequently at their gatherings and to run as the Socialist Party's candidate for mayor of Weehawken, New Jersey, in 1911. In 1913 he designed a model, displayed at an Architectural League exhibition, for a floating civic arts building that was to have been moored off New York's Battery Park.

Paine was a particularly helpful assistant to Saint-Gaudens because he devised an accurate system of enlarging the scale of a sculptor's model by using an "enlarging or pointing machine . . . [it] is simply a device for giving in exact proportions the different dimensions of the model, point by point, as desired by the operators of the machine. . . . Hitherto, the work of 'pointing up,' being done by the primitive method of measurements and cross measurements by hand-compasses from point to point, was . . . elaborate and expensive."[1] Paine worked with Louis St. Gaudens, presumably in 1912 and 1913 when Louis was finishing the figures for the Union Station building in Washington, DC, on developing a "cubical pantograph,"[2] which permitted up to 400 points to be plotted mechanically. "Previous to this, all sculpture had to be enlarged from the working model to the final size by a series of 'points' taken by hand . . . my father had an especially rough experience with the standing 'Lincoln,' the 'Peter Cooper,' and the horse for the 'Logan.' After they had been laboriously enlarged by the old system, he was forced to remodel them entirely free-hand in order to bring back the effect he desired . . . Mr. Paine solved the problem of mechanical enlargement, and before long" the procedure was applied first to the horse on the *Sherman Monument,* unveiled at the Grand Army Plaza adjacent to New York City's Central Park in 1903.[3]

In 1907 Paine's wife, Mary Trueblood Paine, bought the Everett Shinn house, which had originally been part of the Westgate farm, on what is now Daniels Road in Plainfield.[4] In 1944 Mrs. Paine, who was then of Carmel, California, sold the property to Bruce Beals, Jr.; it is now occupied by John and Carolyn McNellis.[5]

ENDNOTES

1. Robert T. Paine, "How the Sculptor's Model is Enlarged," *Brush and Pencil* 13, December 1903, pp. 184-185, 188-189. One of the illustrations in this article, p. 187, is of a sculpture, *Shield Holders,* by Adolph Alexander Weinman, another assistant to Saint-Gaudens.

2. Burke Wilkinson, *Uncommon Clay: The Life and Works of Augustus Saint-Gaudens* (New York: Harcourt Brace Jovanovich, 1985), p. 266.

3. *The Reminiscences of Augustus Saint-Gaudens,* edited and amplified by Homer Saint-Gaudens (New York: Century Company, 1913), vol. 2, p. 97-98; see also John H. Dryfhout, *The Work of Augustus Saint-Gaudens* (Hanover, NH: University Press of New England, 1982), pp. 253-254.

4. William H. Child, *History of the Town of Cornish with Genealogical Record: 1763-1910.* (Concord, NH: Rumford Press, 1911?) Vol. 1, p. 230, in Homer Saint-Gaudens's chapter " 'City Folks' in Cornish."

5. Plainfield, NH town tax records.

ANNE BOGARDUS PARRISH
1878 – 1966

STEPHEN PARRISH'S SECOND COUSIN ANNE first came to Cornish to be his hostess and companion when his wife, Elizabeth Bancroft Parrish, departed for California to join a religious community.

She became quite active in the Colony's social, artistic, and intellectual life. In the 1905 production of *A Masque of "Ours": The Gods and the Golden Bowl,* she played the role of "Venus" and the role of "Bluebird" in the 1913 production of *Sanctuary: A Bird Masque* done on behalf of the Meriden Bird Club. During the winter months she frequently joined friends ice skating on the pond at the Beaman's place or at Admiral Folger's. Given the local interest in sculpture, it did not take her long to follow suit. She constructed her own studio next to Stephen's on the west side of the property, overlooking Mount Ascutney. She sculpted a bust of Priscilla Tracy Hodgeman; Frances Grimes, in turn, did a bas-relief of Anne that is now at the Saint-Gaudens National Historic Site. When the Colony got behind the women's right-to-vote issue and the Cornish Equal Suffrage League was formed in 1911, Anne immediately became its corresponding secretary.

Her duties at "Northcote," however, kept her very busy. When help was scarce, Anne pitched in with the household chores, the gardening, and the outdoor painting.[1] Because cooks seemed consistently to have a short tenure with Stephen Parrish, Anne frequently went to Boston in search of new ones. It would appear, too, that her life with a horse and buggy was fraught with danger. On several occasions the horse reared and ran off; the buggy was smashed and its passengers were thrown onto the road.[2]

In her later years Anne would spend her winters as resident of the Hanover Inn and return to "Northcote" for the summers. She died in 1966 and is buried in the Chase Cemetery.

ENDNOTES

1. For a photograph of Anne in Stephen Parrish's garden, see Figure 84 above p. 217.
2. Stephen Parrish, diary; Special Collections, Baker Library, Dartmouth College, gift of Marian and Roy Garrand.

ERNEST CLIFFORD PEIXOTTO
1869 – 1940

ERNEST PEIXOTTO was a noted author and illustrator. He and his wife were in Cornish in 1906 when they may have stayed with the Crolys.[1] That was the same year that Charles Scribner brought out his *By Italian Seas*, for which he did all the illustrations. He was born in San Francisco and studied in Paris with Constant, Lefevre, and Doucet.

His usual practice was to visit interesting and historic places, write engagingly about them, and illustrate them with his own brush and pencil drawings to draw attention to their attractions. This is the procedure he followed in *Romantic California, Through the French Provinces*, and the *Pacific Shores from Panama*, published in 1913 as well as in *Our Hispanic Southwest* published in 1916. And because "a new wave of patriotism has swept over the land and cre-

Figure 171. Concord Bridge *by Ernest Peixotto, 1917.*

ated a revival of the 'American Spirit,'" he brought out *A Revolutionary Pilgrimage* in 1917 that he wrote and then illustrated with over seventy-five drawings.[2] He would also follow the same pattern for magazine articles. One of the earliest was a piece on the Château of Chinon in the December 1899 issue of *Scribner's Magazine* that weaves delicately between reminiscences of Jeanne d'Arc and a current market day; both topics are suggested in a full-page drawing he did for that issue.

Of more immediate local interest was the article "A Saint-Gaudens Pilgrimage" illustrated with four of his drawings. Written during World War I, "Aspet" is termed "a peaceful place consecrated to the memory of some great worker in the arts." He goes on to describe the conditions under which it was bought and quotes from the *Reminiscences* about the improvements, namely the long veranda with a classic balustrade and fluted Ionic columns. One person said that "it looks like an austere, upright New England farmer with a new set of false teeth" and it prompted some Cornish wag to liken the house to "some austere and recalcitrant New England old maid struggling in the arms of a Greek faun." Inside the "small studio" Peixotto notes there is the desk of Saint-Gau-dens, "built by the country carpenter, tucked away in one corner, just as he left it. The calendar is torn off at September 21, 1906—perhaps the last time that he sat at it, as Mrs. Saint-Gaudens told me." He also recounts the conversation that took place in Rock Creek Cemetery in Washington, DC, between John Hay and Saint-Gaudens, which Mrs. Barrett Wendell repeats, when she asked the sculptor what he called the figure of the Adams Memorial. "He hesitated a moment and then replied: 'I call it the Mystery of the Hereafter.' 'Is it not happiness?' she asked again. 'No,' was the reply; 'it is beyond pain, and beyond joy.'" Peixotto closes the account of his pilgrimage with a plea that "Aspet" can become a home for young sculptors and a memorial to him, as Mrs. Saint-Gaudens intends, and with these words: "there comes over you a sense of utter quiet as you allow your gaze to wander over the fair landscape round about. The wooded Cornish hills unmarred by any habitation, the stillness broken only by the tinkling of sheep-bells or the hoot of an owl, the fine and familiar Italianesque silhouette of Mount Ascutney brooding against the glowing western sky create an atmosphere peculiarly conducive to meditation."[3]

During World War I he was able to put his artistic ability in the service of his country. "In 1918 Ernest Peixotto became Captain Peixotto of the Engineers, being recently one of the artists selected to join General Pershing's forces to make historic records of scenes where the American army is fighting. He will leave for France shortly."[4]

ENDNOTES

1. Stephen Parrish, diary, entry for December 25, 1906; Special Collections, Baker Library, Dartmouth College, gift of Marian and Roy Garrand.

2. Ernest Peixotto, *A Revolutionary Pilgrimage* (New York: Scribner's Sons, 1917), p. viii.

3. *Scribner's Magazine* 63, April 1918, pp. 424-431. The sections in the *Reminiscences* can be found in Vol. 1, pp. 316, 362.

4. "Book Notes," *Scribner's Magazine* 63, April 1918, p. 8.

MAXWELL EVARTS PERKINS
1884 – 1947

MAXWELL PERKINS was un-
questionably the most influential
book editor of his time. Most of
the significant authors that
Charles Scribner's Sons published
in the first half of this century
came under his guidance and
tutelage. As his daughter, Bertha
Perkins Frothingham, recently
wrote, quoting from a letter
Perkins wrote to Thomas Wolfe,
Perkins's "life came to be dedicated to [the] precept that 'nothing is as important as a book can
be.'"[1] Thomas Wolfe, for example, brought him sprawling,
chaotic manuscripts which he
painstakingly and patiently ca-
joled Wolfe into reducing and rewriting: *Look Homeward, Angel*
(1929) and *Of Time and the River*
(1935), with its touching dedica-

Figure 172. *Sketch from one of Maxwell Perkins's letters to his daughters.*

tion to Perkins. F. Scott Fitzgerald and Ernest Hemingway were also grateful for his meticulous attention and advice. He encouraged the former to rewrite *This Side of Paradise*
(1920) and upon receiving the final version he wrote Fitzgerald: "I think that you have
improved it enormously. As the first manuscript did, it abounds in energy and life and it
seems to me to be in much better proportion. I was afraid that when we declined the first
manuscript, you might be done with us conservatives. I am glad you are not. The book is
so different that it is hard to prophesy how it will sell, but we are all for taking a chance
and supporting it with vigor."[2] Perkins greatly admired Hemingway, especially *For Whom
the Bell Tolls* (1940), about which he wrote Hemingway, "I cabled you the morning after I
read what you sent of the ms. The impressions made by it are even stronger after the lapse
of time. The scenes are more vivid and real than in the reading. This has always happened
to me after reading your novels, and it is true of mighty few writers."[3] Other famous writers whose works Perkins helped to mold were Marcia Davenport, Will James, Ring Lard-
ner, Marjorie Kinnan Rawlings, S. S. Van Dine, and Stark Young.

Perkins was born in New York City in 1884. His maternal grandfather, for whom he
was named, was William Maxwell Evarts (see above pp. 471-472). His paternal grandfather, a friend of Robert Browning's, was a noted art critic from Boston, Charles Callahan
Perkins. Maxwell Perkins attended St. Paul's School in Concord, New Hampshire, and
was graduated from Harvard in 1907. After three years at the *New York Times*, he went to
work for Scribner's where he spent all his working life. He sought this new job because

he believed his impending marriage required more substantial employment. On December 31, 1910, he married Louise Saunders, who wrote *The Knave of Hearts*, which Maxfield Parrish illustrated and Scribner's published in 1925. Their eldest daughter, Bertha, married John Gerrish Frothingham and lives in Windsor, Vermont (1996).

Marcia Davenport, who was indebted to him for his interest in her biography of *Mozart* (1932) and *The Valley of Decision* (1942), has written a perfect tribute to Maxwell Perkins: he "possessed the ability to evoke from people of talent the best that they had in them; the ability to get out of them better work than they ever otherwise did; the mysterious spell of personality which gave . . . writers . . . confidence, and encouraged them to do what, they often said, they did not know they had it in them to do."[4]

ENDNOTES

1. Bertha Perkins Frothingham, Louise Perkins King, and Ruth King Porter, eds. *Father to Daughter: The Family Letters of Maxwell Perkins,* (Kansas City: Andrews and McMeel, 1995), p. xii.

2. John Hall Wheelock, ed., Marcia Davenport, Preface, *Editor to Author: The Letters of Maxwell E. Perkins* (New York: Scribner's Sons, 1987), p. 20.

3. Ibid., p. 152.

4. Ibid., p. xv.

MAURICE PRENDERGAST
1858 – 1924

MAURICE PRENDERGAST, as they say, needs no introduction. Most commentators would agree with author William Gerdts that he was "the most original among the Impressionist-related artists of the Eight."[1] He was born in Saint John's Newfoundland, studied in Boston, and left for the Académie Julian in Paris in 1890. Five years later he was back in the Boston area painting—particularly watercolors of beach scenes that soon became the "rage of the town . . . unable to keep pace with the demand." This success enabled him to return to Europe and especially Venice, where he did a series of famous watercolors. He "returned from Europe in late 1899 and transferred the scintillating qualities of his Venetian pictures to American beaches and park scenes."

It was at this point that he secured his ties with future members of the Eight and that we find him in Cornish. Entries in the diary of Stephen Parrish indicate that he and his wife were here at the end of June and early July of 1901 staying with the Prellwitzes.[2]

ENDNOTES

1. William H. Gerdts, *American Impressionism* (New York: Artabras, 1984), p. 282; for the other two quotations in this paragraph, see Ibid., pp. 285, 286.

2. Stephen Parrish, diary, entry for June 21, 1907; Special Collections, Baker Library, Dartmouth College, gift of Marian and Roy Garrand. The last reference to a call from them is in the entry for July 7.

ALEXANDER PHIMISTER PROCTOR
1862 – 1950

ALTHOUGH PROCTOR was born in the province of Ontario, Canada, he spent most of his youth in Denver, Colorado. Throughout his life his sculptural ideal was influenced by the cowboys, the pioneers, the Native Americans, and the wild animals, especially horses, with which he grew up. In 1888, because he yearned to learn how to sculpt, he reluctantly went to New York City and enrolled in classes at both the Art Students League and the National Academy of Design. "But there were, of course, at that time no teachers at either institution who offered instruction in the modeling of such subjects as cowboys, Indians, and wild animals."[1] His big break, however, came later when he was commissioned to create some decorative sculpture for the 1893 Columbian Exposition in Chicago. "There can be no doubt that Proctor added a new ingredient to American sculpture, for while others in his profession were creating robed maidens and assorted neoclassical personifications, Proctor brought to the attention of the world the strength and beauty of the wild animals of America. Moreover, his cowboy on his pony and his Indian scout scanning the horizon were among the first monumental equestrian statues to give dignity to those subjects from the American West."[2]

It was precisely this ability to sculpt horses so realistically that attracted the eye of Augustus Saint-Gaudens. He asked that Proctor return from his Parisian studies to work on two equestrian statues: the one of General John A. Logan in Chicago's Grant Park and the other of General Sherman in New York's Central Park. The former monument "was the first use of Robert Treat Paine's device for mechanical enlargement of sculpture."[3] In his autobiography Proctor described how he returned to New York with his wife Margaret to work on the Logan because no one could seem to satisfy Saint-Gaudens. It seemed Logan's son "had a stallion that he thought would be suitable for a model, and since he was indeed a beautiful animal, I decided to use him. Saint-Gaudens had a studio near Windsor, Vermont, which he agreed to lend me, while he remained in New York. The stallion was shipped there, and Margaret and I arranged to stay at a farmhouse a mile from the studio. . . . Every few weeks Saint-Gaudens came up from New York to check on my progress . . . Saint-Gaudens often criticized my work, and I learned a good deal during that period."[4]

Although he never achieved the popularity of Frederick Remington, Proctor's career continued until almost the middle of this century. Admiration for his ability to portray both wild animals and people remained consistent from the early days of Saint-Gaudens and Theodore Roosevelt until J. Frank Dobie said of Proctor's *Monument to the Mustangs* in 1948: "As I behold these glorious plunging creatures that Phimister Proctor has arrested in enduring bronze, they inspire in me a kind of release and elation. I am free with them and with the wind, in spaces without confines. . . . Like the longhorn, the mustang . . . has been bred out of existence. But here, beautiful and free, he lives for centuries to come."[5]

ENDNOTES

1. Wayne Craven, *Sculpture in America* (New York: Crowell, 1968), p. 521.

2. Ibid.

3. John H. Dryfhout, *The Work of Augustus Saint-Gaudens* (Hanover, NH: University Press of New England, 1982), p. 253; for more on Paine's device, see above pp. 490-491.

4. Alexander Phimister Proctor, *Sculptor in Buckskin: An Autobiography*, ed. by Hester Elizabeth Proctor (Norman, OK: University of Oklahoma Press), pp. 128-129. Proctor also tells how the thirteen-year-old Homer Saint-Gaudens, "a more mischievous youngster never tormented a neighborhood," disturbed "a fine herd of twenty blooded milch cows" by losing control of a kite in the pasture of their neighbor, William M. Evarts; loc. cit.

5. As quoted in Craven, p. 524.

EDWIN ARLINGTON ROBINSON
1869 – 1935

OF ALL THE POETS connected to the Cornish Colony, Edwin Arlington Robinson was certainly the most well-known and well-recognized by his contemporaries, and—for better or worse—the most well-remembered. Few poets have the honor of receiving the Pulitzer Prize three times, though he refused to attend the ceremonies for any of them.[1] Reuben Bright, Miniver Cheevy, Richard Cory, and residents of Tilbury Town are indelibly printed in the American imagination. It should not be surprising, then, that among Percy MacKaye, William Vaughn Moody, Robinson, and Ridgely Torrence there should be much evidence of interaction both beyond the confines of a place where they spent their summer holidays and within it. Robinson even dedicated some of his works to people associated with the Colony: *The Man Who Died Twice* (1924) was dedicated to James Earle Fraser and Laura Gardin Fraser; *Cavender's House* (1929) was dedicated to the memory of William Vaughn Moody;[2] and *Matthias as the Door* (1931) was dedicated to Ridgely Torrence. Torrence, in turn, edited Robinson's *Selected Letters* in 1940 and Percy MacKaye is the source for our knowledge of Robinson's visit to Cornish in 1907. There is reason to believe, too, that Robinson loved Olivia Howard Dunbar, who rejected him and married Torrence in 1914. Percy and Marion MacKaye "believed that [Robinson's] whole life and the character of his work would have been different had she married him."[3]

Robinson was born in Maine and spent most of his youth in Gardiner, the prototype of Tilbury Town and a typical New England village, with all of the social and human undercurrents that Robinson delighted in exploring. This was not, however, a task he could immediately accomplish. After several years at Harvard, he returned to Gardiner determined to get his poetry published. He printed many poems privately "and mailed copies to a selected list of literary critics. Most of those who deigned to review it, while acknowledging its originality, pronounced the poetry mystic and obscure." Encouraged by a minority of responses that discovered in it "emotional" and "intellectual content" with a "vital relation to everyday life," he added sixteen more poems. A Boston publisher brought it out in 1897, *The Children of the Night*, to cries that here was "a new poet of an individual cast of thought."[4]

The bright lights of New York City soon outshone those of Gardiner, Maine. It was there that Robinson met the other three members of Cornish's quartet of poets. (Moody is even the subject of a Robinson poem, "Broadway Lights," published by Macmillan in their 1927 edition of Robinson's *Collected Poems*.) The bond that linked them was an interest in bringing poetry to drama, in becoming what MacKaye would call "America's first group of theatre poets."[5]

One of Robinson's big breaks came in 1905 when President Theodore Roosevelt enthusiastically praised Robinson's 1902 book *Captain Craig* in *The Outlook* for August 12, 1905. William Vaughn Moody informed Robinson "that you have been discovered by the national administration. Roosevelt is said to stop cabinet discussion to ask Hay, 'Do you know Robinson?' and upon receiving a negative reply, to spend the rest of the session reading *Captain Craig* aloud." Moody thought Robinson should get "a nice lazy berth in the consular service in England."[6] Instead, as did Nathaniel Hawthorne before him, Robinson was given a job with the Customs Office.

But, because it was a lazy enough "berth," he was able to get away and visit Cornish two years later. Marion MacKaye describes the reason for his visit in March of 1907 as a desire to read a recently finished play personally to Percy and Marion: "we heard [it] last night: a distinctive, finely-drawn, light colored glass of liqueur—very much like the man himself, with rare and unexpected touches of thought and individuality. Somewhat meager, bloodless, lacking in the suggestion of abounding life or passion, and winding by slender paths of individuality where the flavors are of spices, rather than flowers, and where a whimsicality all his own edges the pathway."[7] Marion's description of Robinson manifests her own powers of observation: "I think a great deal of attitude on his part has been caused by a cramped life and that underneath it is a sweet and loveable personality. In appearance as in personality, nature has withheld herself, as he lacks the usual length of little finger, giving his hand a pinched look as he only half extends it in salutation.— His ears and chin have the same attenuated appearance and his near-sighted, bending carriage shows the reticence to which his voice, never quite reaching the open air, attests."

Because of its perceptive, though mysterious, psychological acuity, Robinson would have admired this "portrait" of him. In the final analysis, "Robinson has been perhaps the only American poet—certainly the only one of major status—interested *exclusively* in human beings as subject matter for poetry—in the psychological, motivational aspects of living, in the inner life as it is projected upon the outer. His work is one vast attempt to tell the stories that no man can really tell, for no man can know their real meaning, their real intention or even whether such exists, though it persistently appears to do so."[8]

ENDNOTES

1. He won the Pulitzer Prize in 1922 for his *Collected Poems*, in 1925 for *The Man Who Died Twice*, published in 1924, and in 1928 for *Tristram*.
2. In his notes to *Letters to Harriet*, p. 428, n. xxv, Percy MacKaye says that "another poem about Moody, by E. A. Robinson, is 'Broadway Lights,' published in Robinson's *Collected Poems* (Macmillan, 1927)." A search of the five-volume edition published in 1927 turned up no such poem. Perhaps MacKaye meant "The White Lights (Broadway, 1906)," first published in Robinson's *The Town Down the River* (Macmillan, 1910); it reads:

When in from Delos came the gold
That held the dream of Pericles,
When first Athenian ears were told
The tumult of Euripides,
When men met Aristophanes,
Who fledged them with immortal quills—
Here, where the time knew none of these,
There was some islands and some hills.

When Rome went ravening to see
The sons of mothers end their days.
When Flaccus bade Leuconoë
To banish her Chaldean ways,
When first the pearled, alembic phrase
Of Maro into music ran—
Here there was neither blame or praise
For Rome, or for the Mantuan.

When Avon, like a faery floor,
Lay freighted, for the eyes of One,
With galleons laden long before
By moonlit wharves in Avalon—
Here, where the white lights have begun
To seethe a way for something fair,
No phrophet knew, from what was done,
That there was triumph in the air.

3. Arvia MacKaye Ege, *The Power of the Impossible: The Life Story of Percy and Marion MacKaye* (Famouth, ME: The Kennebec River Press, 1992), p. 148, n.

4. The quotations in this paragraph come from *The National Cyclopaedia of American Biography* (New York: James T. White, 1947), Vol. 33, p. 145.

5. William Vaughn Moody, *Letters to Harriet*, edited, with introduction and conclusion, by Percy MacKaye (Boston and New York: Houghton Mifflin, 1935), p. 22.

6. Ibid., p. 28.

7. This quotation and the next are from Ege, p. 148. Robinson's play was probably *The Porcupine*, which Percy MacKaye notes was written in 1907, though published in 1915; see *Letters to Harriet*, p. 418, n. ix.

8. James Dickey, introduction to Morton Dauwen Zabel, ed., *Selected Poems of Edwin Arlington Robinson* (New York: Collier Books, 1966), p. xvi.

OTTO ROTH (1866 – 1954) and the Kneisel Quartet

OTTO ROTH and the members of the Kneisel Quartet are mentioned rather often in the diaries of Lucia Fairchild Fuller and Stephen Parrish—usually in the context of Arthur Whiting. Margaret Homer Nichols Shurcliff also alludes to him in the same sentence as Arthur Whiting, but she adds an interesting sidelight about Roth the tennis player: "good old Otto Roth, the violinist who spent a month with us every summer and who adored tennis. All the way over to [the Houstons'] court he would ask me what was wrong with his stroke. He never allowed himself more than two sets a day for fear he might injure his violin wrist. He began tennis late in life and was a hopeless player, and what a lot of teasing he had to put up with."[1]

Roth was the second violinist with the quartet, which was formed in 1885 by the concertmaster of the Boston Symphony Orchestra, Franz Kneisel; its members were principal players with the orchestra. In 1903 they left the orchestra to devote their energies exclusively to chamber music, performing in Boston, New York, and throughout the country. They are credited with "setting new standards of performance in the USA . . . [they] set out to educate their audiences by performing complete quartets of Haydn, Mozart, or Beethoven."[2] In addition to championing American composers such as Whiting, Amy Beach, George Whitefield Chadwick, Arthur Foote, and Charles Martin Loeffler, they were the first to perform Schoenberg's *Verklarte Nacht* and compositions by Brahms, Debussy, Franck, Ravel, and Kodaly in America.

ENDNOTES

1. Margaret Homer Shurcliff, *Lively Days: Some Memoirs of Margaret Homer Shurcliff* (Taipei: Literature House Ltd., 1965), p. 35.
2. W. Wiley Hitchcock and Stanley Sadie, eds., *The New Grove Dictionary of American Music* (London and New York: Macmillan, 1986), Vol. 2, p. 645.

JOSEPH LINDON SMITH
1863 – 1950

JOSEPH LINDON SMITH, painter, muralist, and teacher, was born in Pawtucket, Rhode Island, in 1863. He studied at the Museum School of Boston's Museum of Fine Arts and at the Académie Julian in Paris. He served for a while as a representative in Europe for the Boston patron of the arts, Isabella Stewart Gardner. In the Isabella Stewart Gardner Museum today can be seen *The Adoration of the Kings,* an example of his passionate interest in archaeology. He was present at the excavation when the parents of Queen Tiy were discovered in 1904, and he is credited with the actual discovery of the tomb of Queen Tiy herself in 1907. His journals, notes, and letters were edited by his wife in 1956 and published by the University of Oklahoma Press as Joseph Lindon Smith, *Tombs, Temples, and Ancient Art.* A reviewer of this memoir notes that Smith was "a man of outstanding ability as a painter, of great sensitivity and of unusual charm, he was for over fifty years associated with most of the great archaeologists of his day."[1] In summarizing his career, with its dual focus on studying the art of the past and creating art in the present, Smith wrote, "The great single fact of art in its historical perspective is the steady continuity, age in and age out, of man's drive toward durable and striking artistic expression. . . . The power of laughter, like that of grief, has survived in every age."[2]

In Cornish he is remembered for being on the committee that organized the production of Percy MacKaye's *Sanctuary: A Bird Masque* in September of 1913; he was also on the Masque's costume committee and played the important role of Quercus the Faun.[3] A year later he was the stage producer of MacKaye's *Pageant and Masque of St. Louis,* which commemorated the sesquicentennial of the city's founding and was performed before 500,000 people (see above p. 263).

He and his wife, Corinna Putnam, the daughter of the New York publisher George Putnam, settled at a house on Dublin Pond in southern New Hampshire during the early 1900s and are more commonly associated with the activities and personalities of the Dublin Colony. There he continued his interest in theatricals, which he began in Cornish, by organizing frequent *tableaux vivants,* one of which was of "Mother and Child," based on a painting by George de Forest Brush, a friend whom Smith knew in Cornish and whom he invited to Dublin, setting Brush up in a studio in Smith's own barn.[4]

ENDNOTES

1. Dows Dunham, *New York Times Book Review,* July 7, 1956, p. 5.
2. As quoted in the review cited in the above note.
3. Ernest Henderson, in his book *The World of "Mr. Sheraton"* (New York: David McKay, 1960), describes a vivid memory that indicates the interaction of the art colonies of Dublin, New Hampshire, and Cornish:

   > Dublin's leading summer resident, and impresario, officially Joseph Lindon Smith, was known to all of Dublin as just Uncle Joe. He was asked to stage one of the magnificent outdoor pageants for which he was justly famous, in Cornish, some seventy miles away. Many of Dublin's summer colony, children and grown-ups alike, were given on such occasions frocks or tunics from Uncle Joe's reservoir of medieval costumes so they might be transformed into elves, fairies, sprites, and other characters in his spectacular extravaganzas.

The scene of the pageant was an outdoor theater with a stage all of grass. Pines, spruces, balsams, and other evergreens provided the rustic backdrop. The seats, in amphitheater style, could take care of an audience of several hundred, and many came from Dublin for this special occasion. The size of the Dublin contingent was an added mark of devotion to Uncle Joe, partly because at the time motor cars were primitive, but especially because New Hampshire dirt roads were even more so (pp. 105-106).

Mr. Henderson continues by remembering that "the breakdowns and tire changes so common in the era made us arrive late in the outskirts of Cornish, but we were not the last. A car with District of Columbia number plates was just ahead, and another, similarly equipped, followed close behind. Little did we dream that one held men of the White house Secret Service; the other the President of the United States" (p. 106). You can imagine the immediate consternation, especially because "the late arrival of Woodrow Wilson meant the performance was delayed" (ibid). The bemused family, "unaware of the presence of the famous visitor, were surprised to be virtually lifted from our car, rushed through an arch of roses, and assigned flag-bedecked chairs in the pit just in front of the stage. The curtain, rising at that moment, cut off all possible retreat" (ibid). The Henderson family was right there in the center of the presidential party. "I suspect the faces of the Secret Service, if recorded on some color chart, would appear somewhere in the region between scarlet and vermilion." (ibid).

4. Nancy Douglas Bowditch, *George de Forest Brush: Recollections of a Joyous Painter* (Peterborough, NH: William L. Bauhan, 1970), p. 200.

ABBOTT HANDERSON THAYER
1849 – 1921

Figure 173. *Drawing of Gerald Thayer by his father, Abbott Handerson Thayer.*

THAYER quite properly belongs to the art colony established at Dublin, New Hampshire, but his friendship with George de Forest Brush, Thomas Dewing, and Augustus Saint-Gaudens, merits Thayer's mention in this Supplement about people associated with the Cornish Colony. Not all his connections to it, however, are limited to artists; he helped to stage Percy MacKaye's play *Jeanne D'Arc.* William Vaughn Moody, in a letter to Harriet Converse Tilden Brainerd, dated Cornish, June 1, 1906, remarked that "Percy has not been here for some time; he is in New York getting the elaborate stage-arrangements for his *Joan of Arc* ready, stained glass windows that come to life, and brushes that turn into fairy Ladies of Lorraine, and what-not."[1] In a note to this passage MacKaye himself added that this stage set "included new experiments in stage lighting and mechanics conducted by Abbott H. Thayer, assisted by Rockwell Kent and Barry Faulkner, based on Thayer's discoveries in protective coloration."

Barry Faulkner, who so gracefully straddled the two art colonies at Dublin and Cornish, has given us a succinct explanation of what these "discoveries" entailed. Faulkner describes how "Thayer had arrived at this part of his theory of protective coloration by his observation that birds and animals average darker on the back and lighter on the belly. The light from the sky lessens the darkness of their backs and throws the lighter tint of the belly into shadow, thus lessening their appearance of solidity." Furthermore, "Thayer's perception that many birds and some animals carry on [both] their plumage and [their] hides a stylized picture of their most frequent habitats"[2] laid the groundwork for the theory behind camouflage units' activities in World War I.

Although it was Faulkner's connection with Homer Saint-Gaudens and the camouflage unit the latter command during World War I, it was really Homer's father who provided a close link with Abbott Thayer. Both Thayer and Augustus Saint-Gaudens were great admirers of Robert Louis Stevenson; each artist paid the writer tribute in their respective disciplines. Of Thayer's Stevenson Memorial, Saint-Gaudens had this to say in a letter to Thayer: "I wish I could tell you how I feel about your Vailima figure. It is a glorious inspiration, and when I came upon it unexpectedly at Albright's Gallery it took my breath away. It was inspiring when I saw it before, but your changes had sent it flying heavenward."[3] For Thayer this was important praise. Thayer's daughter Gladys observed that her father numbered Saint-Gaudens among his "dearest friends" and "in the matter of using wings in so many of his figures, which was frequently condemned, his motive was somewhat abstruse. The decorative element entered in[;] also, no doubt, the influence of Saint-Gaudens whom he revered as an artist and dearly loved as a man. He explained the wings as partly an urge to endow the individual depicted with a quality beyond the casual, the momentary aspect, but rather make her a creature of all time."[4]

A final quotation will indicate the bond between the other artistic bulwarks of the Cornish Colony. George de Forest Brush said that Thayer "talked about [Thomas Dewing] constantly from the time he first met him, worshipping always his exquisite delicacy and fineness of form." Furthermore, Thayer had "the greatest reverence for Augustus Saint-Gaudens and cherished for years the large photograph of the 'Sherman' which Saint-Gaudens had sent him. He admired Brush's work, and although they did not always agree upon minor points of technique their aims were essentially similar. It might be fairly said that Brush was closer to Thayer, both as artist and friend, than to any other of his contemporaries."[5]

ENDNOTES

1. William Vaughn Moody, *Letters to Harriet*, ed. with introduction and conclusion by Percy MacKaye (Boston and New York: Houghton Mifflin, 1935), p. 277.

2. For these two quotations see Barry Faulkner, *Barry Faulkner: Sketches from an Artist's Life* (Dublin, NH: William L. Bauhan, 1973), pp. 18-19.

3. *The Reminiscences of Augustus Saint-Gaudens*, edited and amplified by Homer Saint-Gaudens (New York: Century Company, 1913), Vol. 2, p. 57. "Vailima" was the name of Stevenson's estate in Samoa where he died. He insisted upon being buried "under the wide and starry sky" on top of Mt. Vaea, as he described in the famous poem "Requiem." Thayer includes a reference to "Vaea" on the angel's left in his Memorial.

4. As quoted in Nelson C. White, *Abbott H. Thayer: Painter and Naturalist* (Hartford, CT: Connecticut Printers, Inc. 1951), pp. 191, 219.

5. Ibid., p. 222.

(FREDERIC) RIDGELY TORRENCE
1875 – 1950

The dramatist and poet Ridgely Torrence spent part of three seasons in Cornish. He served as managing editor of *The Critic*, an editor at *Cosmopolitan* from 1905 to 1907, and poetry editor of *The New Republic* from 1920 to 1934. He came to Cornish as a guest of his poet and dramatist friend William Vaughn Moody, who had rented the "Snuff Box House"; at that time, it still belonged to Admiral Folger.

We have the memories of two wintry descriptions of Torrence's time in Cornish. First, Stephen Parrish noted in his diary on February 12, 1906, that he attended a dinner party at "Fred's" (Maxfield's) that included Percy MacKaye, Moody, Torrence, Louis Shipman, and Miss Marie Parker. He wrote that they had a very jolly evening; he did not leave until midnight and then he returned home through the snow in the company of the three poets.[1] Second, Henry Hering, an assistant to Augustus Saint-Gaudens, recalled seeing Moody and Torrence on the road late one dark night doubled over beside a one-horse sleigh with an oil lantern. Using only their fingers, they were desperately trying to dislodge the icy balls of snow that were densely packed in the horse's hooves.[2]

Torrence published several books during his years of association with the Cornish Colony: *The House of a Hundred Lights* in 1900 and *El Dorado, A Tragedy* in 1903. His most important contribution to the theater was to be the first American to write a collection of three *Plays for a Negro Theatre* (1917) at a time when it was difficult to assemble an acting troupe to stage them. He published later editions of his poetry in 1941; a posthumous edition appeared in 1952. A brief appreciation of him by the eminent translator and poet Rolfe Humphries asserted that Torrence was "a fine poet and a spirit at once perceptive, humane, and reconciled."[3]

ENDNOTES

1. Stephen Parrish, diary; Special Collections, Baker Library, Dartmouth College, gift of Marian and Roy Garrand. For Moody's description of that evening during a wintry visit to Cornish, when "Torrence and I were given a royal welcome," see the letter cited on p. 281.

2. William Vaughn Moody, *Letters to Harriet* (Boston and New York: Houghton Mifflin, 1935), pp. 66-67; the incident occurred in January of 1908. In the notes to *Letters to Harriet*, p. 428, n. xxv, Percy MacKaye mentions that Ridgely Torrence's poem, "Santa Barbara Beach" is a tribute to Moody, who, shortly before his death, had moved to California for his health. As printed in Ridgely Torrence, *Poems* (New York: Macmillan, 1952), pp. 63-64, the poem reads:

Now while the sunset offers,
   Shall we not take our own:
The gems, the blazing coffers,
   The seas, the shores, the thrones?

The sky-ships, radiant masted
   Move out, bear low our way.
Oh, Life was dark while it lasted,
   Now for enduring day.

Now with the world far under,
To draw up drowning men
And show they lands of wonder
Where they may build again.

There earthly sorrow falters,
There longing has its wage;
There gleam the ivory altars
Of our lost pilgrimage.

—Swift flame—then shipwrecks only
 Beach in the ruined light;
Above them reach up lonely
 The headlands of the night.

A hurt bird dries and flutters
 Her dabbled breast of brown;
The western wall unshutters
 To fling one last rose down.

A rose, wild light after—
 and life calls through the years,
"Who dreams my fountain's laughter
 Shall feed my wells with tears."

3. Stanley J. Kuntiz, ed., *Twentieth-Century Authors: A Biographical Dictionary of Modern Literature* (New York: H. W. Wilson, 1955), p. 1413.

ROBERT WILLIAM VONNOH
1858 – 1933)

BESSIE POTTER VONNOH
1872 – 1955

THE IMPRESSIONIST PAINTER ROBERT VONNOH was an instructor in composition and the painting of portraits, the figure, and plein-air scenes at the Pennsylvania Academy of the Fine Arts in Philadelphia where among his students were Maxfield Parrish, Robert Henri, and William Glackens. Not one of the many Americans who studied with Monet at Giverny, Vonnoh was more attracted to the art colony at Grez-sur-Loing near Fontainebleau, dominated by the influence of Jules Bastien-Lepage (1848-1884) and Alfred Sisley (1839-1899). After a stint at the Académie Julian in Paris from 1881 to 1883, Vonnoh spent most of the years between 1887 and 1891 in the Fontainebleau region. He is quoted as saying of his conversion to Impressionism that "I gradually came to realize the value of first impression and the necessity of correct value, pure color and higher key, resulting in my soon becoming a devoted disciple of the new movement in painting."[1] Earlier in his career, before his training in France, he taught in Boston at the Cowles Art School and the Museum of Fine Arts. Later he was associated with the art colonies in America at Cos Cob and Old Lyme in Connecticut.

He was in Cornish during the summer of 1913 because both Lydia Parrish and Ellen Axson Wilson took lessons from him then. Mrs. Wilson wrote Woodrow Wilson that "Mr. Vonnoh came around this morning to look at my work and give me a criticism. He was very encouraging. He said he 'was very much surprised,['] though he had expected a good deal from the little things he had seen at the White House. He said I 'was a real artist, and that if I will go on my work will be really very distinguished.' "[2] Mrs. Wilson was staying at Winston Churchill's "Harlakenden House"; she and her three daughters Jessie, Eleanor, and Margaret sat as Vonnoh did their portrait, which is currently in the Wilson House in Washington, DC. Mrs. Wilson says of this portrait that "we are 'composed' in his studio window with the grape vines and columns outside. I am pouring tea at a tiny table. It bids fair to be a nice thing of the sunny impressionist sort. It is going to take a lot of our time I fear, but fortunately we do not all have to pose at once."[3] One of Vonnoh's contemporaries echoes Mrs. Wilson's beliefs: "[Vonnoh] argues that, for instance, a face, however well it may be reproduced by a painter's technique, looks dead in comparison to the tremulous vitality of colour in a living head . . . Vonnoh endeavors to preserve this vibration of nature by painting his portraits and landscapes entirely in dots, pure bright color dots of the Impressionist's palette."[4]

His second marriage occurred in 1899; it was to Bessie Potter, a sculptor of note, who entered three pieces of sculpture in the 1916 Dartmouth College Cornish Colony exhibit.[5] Characteristic of her early sculpture was "the fragile charm of girls and the tender sentiment of mothers and children. . . . In the gentle spirit which animates her work there is some kinship to Herbert Adams, though the daintiness of treatment and lightness of touch are peculiarly her own. . . . She was a fellow of the National Sculpture Society, and a member of the National Academy of Design and the National Institute of Arts and Letters."[6]

ENDNOTES

1. *National Cyclopedia of American Biography*, Vol. 7, 1897, p. 462, as quoted in William H. Gerdts, *American Impressionism* (New York: Artabras, 1984), p. 121.

2. Letter dated September 9, 1913, Arthur S. Link, ed., *The Papers of Woodrow Wilson* (Princeton, NJ: Princeton University Press, 1978), vol. 28, p. 269. For the context of this letter, see above pp. 436-437.

3. Ed. cit., letter dated July 18, 1913; see above p. 429. For President Wilson's trepidations about this portrait, see above p. 425. This painting was rephotographed from a color screen plate (an Autochrome) by Arnold Genthe and exhibited recently; see "Photographs and Historical Processes," exhibition catalogue (Cornish, NH: Saint-Gaudens National Historic Site, 1 September - 31 October 1995), unpaginated.

4. Carl Sadakichi Hartmann, *A History of American Art*, Vol. 2, p. 245, as quoted in May Brawley Hill, "The Early Career of Robert William Vonnoh," *The Magazine Antiques*, vol. 126, November 1986, p. 1022.

5. George Breed Zug, "Exhibition of Cornish Artists," *Art and Archaeology*, April 1916, pp. 207-211.

6. Beatrice Gilman Proske, *Brookgreen Gardens Sculpture* (Brookgreen Gardens, SC: Trustees of Brookgreen Gardens, 1968), pp. 82-83.

JULIAN ALDEN WEIR
1852 – 1919

IN THE EARLY PART OF THIS CENTURY J. Alden Weir was a major force in American art. An early follower of Impressionism, he was a founding member of "The Ten," the group of American Impressionists that included three other members of the Cornish Colony: Joseph De Camp, Thomas Dewing, and Willard Metcalf. Although he was born in West Point, New York, where his father was a drawing instructor at the United States Military Academy, he is not a Hudson River painter. He is best known as a Connecticut painter, primarily because he spent most of his later years in Branchville, Connecticut, near Wilton, at the Weir Farm, which in the spring of 1992 became a National Historic Site under the supervision of the National Park Service. Weir's purchase of the farm in 1882 is analogous to Augustus Saint-Gaudens's purchase of "Huggin's Folly." Weir bought it from an art collector, Erwin Davis, for $10 and a painting—both purchasers were certain they got the better deal.

Weir studied with his father and then in Paris at the Ecole des Beaux-Arts with Jean-Léon Gérôme. In Paris he opted for academic training and was revolted at the formlessness and inept drawing of the Impressionists. In the mid-1880s, after his return to America and upon viewing an exhibition of their works in New York, he began gradually to incorporate their techniques and stylistic devices into his own works. Before long he was considered a stalwart of their style. At the same time as his painting was shifting in style, roughly from 1887 to 1894, he also started to do a number of etchings and drypoints. Their content reflects many themes similar to those in his Impressionist paintings. During his lifetime he completed over 140 plates, which he generally printed himself.[1]

We know Weir was in Cornish during the summer of 1905 because of a terse entry in Stephen Parrish's diary: "called on J. Alden Weir who has the Prellwitz shanty (first time). To dinner at Mrs. Graydon's. The Weirs (Mr., Mrs., & Miss) & the Whitings."[2]

ENDNOTES

1. Robert Spence, *The Etchings of J. Alden Weir*, exhibition catalogue (Lincoln, NB: University of Nebraska Art Galleries, 1967).
2. Stephen Parrish, diary, entry for September 7, 1905; Special Collections, Dartmouth College, gift of Marian and Roy Garrand. The same trio returned the call on September 9 when Miss Weir drove "over with Anne to lunch at Lawrences."

ILLUSTRATION CREDITS

Frontispiece: Courtesy of U.S. Department of the Interior, National Park Service, Saint-Gaudens National Historic Site, Cornish, NH.

Map of Cornish, New Hampshire taken from the *Town and City Atlas of New Hampshire* (Boston: D.H. Hurd, 1872), p. 147; modern copy courtesy of Teenie Rock. The approximate designations of some of the houses of Cornish Colony members are added. They are based on a map Stephen P. Tracy of Cornish drew in 1985 as published in *A Circle of Friends: Art Colonies of Cornish and Dublin,* exhibition catalogue, (Durham, NH: University Art Galleries, University of New Hampshire, 1985), p. 57.

Figure 1. Courtesy of Virginia Colby, the Cornish files, Cornish Historical Society.

Figure 2. Courtesy of the Cornish Historical Society.

Figure 3. Courtesy of Virginia Colby, the Cornish files, Cornish Historical Society.

Figure 4. Courtesy of the Cornish Historical Society, gift of Miss L.C. Dodge, Washington, DC.

Figure 5. Courtesy of the Cornish Historical Society, gift of Miss L.C. Dodge, Washington, DC.

Figure 6. Reprinted from Laura Chase Smith, *The Life of Philander Chase* (NY: Dutton, 1903), frontispiece.

Figure 7. Photograph by Stan Colby.

Figure 8. Courtesy of the Hood Museum of Art, Dartmouth College, Hanover, New Hampshire, gift of George S. Edgell, Class of 1870.

Figure 9. Courtesy of Virginia Colby, the Cornish files, Cornish Historical Society.

Figure 10. Courtesy of George Stowell Memorial Library, Cornish, New Hampshire. Photograph by Stan Colby.

Figure 11. Courtesy of Virginia Colby, the Cornish files, Cornish Historical Society.

Figure 12. Courtesy of Virginia Colby, the Cornish files, Cornish Historical Society.

Figure 13. Courtesy of the Abby Aldrich Rockefeller Folk Art Center, Williamsburg, Virginia.

Figure 14. Courtesy of the Abby Aldrich Rockefeller Folk Art Center, Williamsburg, Virginia.

Figure 15. Courtesy of Virginia Colby, the Cornish files, Cornish Historical Society.

Figure 16. Courtesy of the Cornish Historical Society.

Figure 17. Hilliard Patent, # 1858, copy in Virginia Colby, the Cornish files, Cornish Historical Society.

Figure 18. Courtesy of the Cornish Historical Society. Gift of James B. Rogers.

Figure 19. A. A. Parker, *Recollections of General Lafayette on his visit to the United States, in 1824 and 1825* (Keene, NH: Sentinel Printing Company, 1879) frontispiece.

Figure 20. Courtesy of The Museums at Stony Brook. Gift of William Jarvis, Jr., in memory of Lucretia Jarvis, 1957.

Figure 21. Samuel F. B. Morse (1791-1872), Self Portrait, 1812-13, oil on canvas, 30 x 25 in., 1930.13. Gift of anonymous donor, © Addison Gallery of American Art, Phillips Academy, Andover, Massachusetts. All Rights Reserved.

Figure 22. William H. Child, *History of the Town of Cornish, New Hampshire, with Genealogical Record, 1763-1910* (Concord: New Hampshire Rumford Press, [1911?]; rpt. edition, Spartenburg, S.C.: the Reprint Co., 1975), Vol. 2, p. 286. Photograph by Frank J. Lather.

Figure 23. Courtesy of The New Hampshire Historical Society, accession number 1945.14.

Figure 24. Courtesy of Old Constitution House, Windsor, Vermont.

Figure 25. Photograph by Virginia Colby.

Figure 26. Courtesy of Yale University Art Gallery; gift of the Medical Class of 1826 to the School of Medicine.

Figure 27. Courtesy of Dartmouth College Library.

Figure 28. Courtesy of Virginia Colby, the Cornish files, Cornish Historical Society.

Figure 29. Courtesy of The Connecticut Historical Society, Hartford, Connecticut.

Figure 30. Commissioned by the Trustees of Dartmouth College, Hanover, New Hampshire; courtesy of The Hood Museum of Art.

Figure 31. Photograph Courtesy of the Plainfield Historical Society.

Figure 32. Courtesy of The Hood Museum of Art, Dartmouth College, Hanover, New Hampshire, gift of Ellen Cabot Torrey.

Figure 33. Child, *History of Cornish*, II, 402.

Figure 34. Courtesy of U.S. Department of the Interior, National Park Service, Saint-Gaudens National Historic Site, Cornish, NH

Figure 35. Collection Eugene B. Sydnor, Richmond, Virginia; photograph courtesy of Hirschl & Adler Galleries, Inc. New York.

Figure 36. Photograph by Virginia Colby.

Figure 37. Photograph by Virginia Colby.

Figure 38. Photograph by Virginia Colby.

Figure 39. Courtesy of Virginia Colby, the Cornish files, Cornish Historical Society.

Figure 40. Photograph by Stan Colby.

Figure 41. Child, *History of Cornish,* I, facing p. 107. Photograph by Frank J. Lather.

Figure 42. Courtesy of The Cornish Historical Society. Photograph by Frank J. Lather.

Figure 43. Courtesy of the Estate of Percy MacKaye.

Figure 44. Courtesy of Virginia Colby.

Figure 45. Courtesy of Albert K. III and Kathleen Phillbrick Read.

Figure 46. Private collection. Photograph courtesy of Richard York Gallery, New York.

Figure 47. Courtesy of Virginia Colby, the Cornish Colony files, Cornish Historical Society. Photograph by Frank J. Lather.

Figure 48. Courtesy of Albert and Kathleen Phillbrick Read.

Figure 49. Courtesy of Dartmouth College Library.

Figure 50. Photograph by Mrs. Louise Birt Baynes. Courtesy of the Cornish Historical Society.

Figure 51. Photograph by Ernest H. Baynes, courtesy of the Cornish Historical Society.

Figure 52. Courtesy of Virginia Colby, the Cornish Colony files, Cornish Historical Society.

Figure 53. Courtesy of the Family of Mary Stacy Borie.

Figure 54. Courtesy of a Cornish Collection. Photograph by Frank J. Lather.

Figure 55. Modern Print from Arnold Genthe negative no. LC-G 39-418-G, Prints & Photographs Division, Library of Congress.

Figure 56. Courtesy of the Cornish Historical Society. Photograph by Frank J. Lather.

Figure 57. Courtesy of U.S. Department of the Interior, National Park Service, Saint-Gaudens National Historic Site, Cornish, NH. Courtesy of Allyn Cox.

Figure 58. Courtesy of a Cornish Collection. Photograph by Frank J. Lather.

Figure 59. Photograph by Virginia Colby.

Figure 60. Courtesy of Virginia Colby, the Cornish Colony files, Cornish Historical Society.

Figure 61. U.S. Department of the Interior, National Park Service, Saint-Gaudens National Historic Site, Cornish, NH. Courtesy of Allyn Cox.

Figure 62. Courtesy of Christy MacKaye Barnes and the Estate of Percy MacKaye.

Figure 63. *American Gardens,* ed. Guy Lowell (Boston: Bates & Guild, 1902), plate 24 no. 2.

Figure 64. Courtesy of the Yale University Art Gallery. Gift from the estate of Mrs. Francis L. Howland.

Figure 65. Maria Oakey Dewing (1845-1927), A Bed of Poppies, 1909, Oil on canvas, 25⅛ x 30⅛, 1931.2, Gift of anonymous donor, © Addison Gallery of American Art, Phillips Academy, Andover, Massachusetts. All Rights Reserved.

Figure 66. Photograph from *The Century Illustrated Monthly Magazine,* 72 (May 1906), p. 10.

Figure 67. Courtesy of U.S. Department of the Interior, National Park Service, Saint-Gaudens National Historic Site, Cornish, NH. Gift of George and Ellen Rublee.

Figure 68. Courtesy of a Cornish Collection. Photo-

graph by Frank J. Lather.

Figure 69. Illustration by W. E. Kemble for Finley Peter Dunne, *Mr. Dooley's Philosophy* (New York: Harper & Brothers, 1906), frontispiece.

Figure 70. Frontispiece, Maud Howe Elliott, *John Elliott: The Story of an Artist* (Boston, MA: The Riverside Press, 1939). Courtsey of a Cornish Collection.

Figure 71. Illustration by John Elliot for Isabel Anderson, *The Great Sea Horse* (Boston: Little, Brown, 1909), facing p. 80. A Cornish Collection. Photograph by Frank J. Lather.

Figure 72. Photograph by Virginia Colby.

Figure 73. Photographer unknown. Photograph courtesy of Virginia Colby, the Cornish Colony files, Cornish Historical Society.

Figure 74. Photograph by Virginia Colby.

Figure 75. Courtesy of Virginia Colby, the Cornish Colony files, Cornish Historical Society.

Figure 76. Courtesy of C. A. Russi, Enfield, NH.

Figure 77. Photograph © 1996 The Detroit Institute of Arts, Gift of George G. Booth.

Figure 78. U.S. Department of the Interior, National Park Service, Saint-Gaudens National Historic Site, Cornish, N.H. Courtesy of Allyn Cox.

Figure 79. Courtesy of Mr. and Mrs. William White Howells.

Figure 80. Courtesy of Dartmouth College Library.

Figure 81. Photograph by Jeffrey Nintzel.

Figure 82. Courtesy of Virginia Colby, the Cornish Colony files, Cornish Historical Society. Photograph by Frank J. Lather.

Figure 83. Courtesy of Virginia Colby, the Cornish Colony files, Cornish Historical Society.

Figure 84. Herbert Croly's garden, designed by Charles A. Platt, photograph from *American Gardens,* plate 24, no. 1.

Figure 85. Photograph from *American Gardens,* plate 79.

Figure 86. U.S. Department of the Interior, National Park Service, Saint-Gaudens National Historic Site, Cornish, NH. Courtesy of Frances Ferguson.

Figure 87. Courtesy of U.S. Department of the Interior, National Park Service, Saint-Gaudens National Historic Site, Cornish, NH. Collection of Walter Jenckes.

Figure 88. Norman Hapgood's masthead "Seen from the Study Window," *Collier's Weekly,* Feb. 28, 1903, p. 32. Courtesy of Virginia Colby, the Cornish Colony files, Cornish Historical Society.

Figure 89. Courtesy of Donald G. M. Hart.

Figure 90. Photograph by Jeffrey Nintzel.

Figure 91. Illustration from *The Century Illustrated Monthly Magazine,* 75:6 (April 1908), p. 957.

Figure 92. Courtesy of the Cornish Historical Society. Gift of Virginia Colby.

Figure 93. Courtesy of Virginia Colby, the Cornish Colony files, Cornish Historical Society.

Figure 94. Courtesy of a Cornish Collection.

Figure 95. Courtesy of Helen Taylor Davidson.

Figure 96. Courtesy of Helen Taylor Davidson.

Figure 97. Courtesy of the Hood Museum of Art, Dartmouth College, Hanover, NH; gift of Mrs. Daisy V. Shapiro in memory of her son, Richard David Shapiro, class of 1943.

Figure 98. Photograph from *Monograph of the Works of Charles A. Platt,* with an Introduction by Royal Cortissoz (New York: Architectural Book Publishing Co., 1913), plate 11. Courtesy of a Cornish Collection. Photograph by Frank J. Lather.

Figure 99. Courtesy of the Cornish Historical Society. Photograph by Frank J. Lather.

Figure 100. Reprinted, by permission of the author, from Les Allen Ferry, *The Make Believe World of Sue Lewin* (1978), p. 19.

Figure 101. Courtesy of Virginia Colby, the Cornish Colony files, Cornish Historical Society.

Figure 102. U.S. Department of the Interior, National Park Service, Saint-Gaudens National Historic Site, Cornish, NH. Courtesy of Allyn Cox.

Figure 103. Courtesy of Virginia Colby, the Cornish Colony files, Cornish Historical Society.

Figure 104. Courtesy of the Estate of Percy MacKaye.

Figure 105. Courtesy of The Bennington Museum, Bennington, Vermont.

Figure 106. Courtesy of John Manship.

Figure 107. Courtesy of John Manship.

Figure 108. Courtesy of the Minnesota Museum of Art.

Figure 109. Collection of Mrs. Nancy Streeter; photograph by Jeffrey Nintzel; courtesy of U.S. Department of the Interior, National Park Service, Saint-Gaudens National Historic Site, Cornish, NH.

Figure 110. Photograph Courtesy of Berry-Hill Galleries, New York.

Figure 111. Reprinted from *Poems and Plays of William Vaughn Moody,* vol. 2 (Boston: Houghton Mifflin, 1910), frontispiece. Courtesy of a Cornish Collection.

Figure 112. Reprinted from *Selected Poems of William Vaughn Moody,* ed. Robert Morss Lovett (Boston: Houghton Mifflin, 1931), frontispiece. Courtesy of a Cornish Collection.

Figure 113. Courtesy of The Plainfield Historical Society.

Figure 114. Courtesy of Virginia Colby, the Cornish Colony files, Cornish Historical Society.

Figure 115. Courtesy of The Dorros Collection.

Figure 116. Courtesy of The Cornish Historical Society. Photograph by Frank J. Lather.

Figure 117. Courtesy of Virginia Colby, the Cornish Colony files, Cornish Historical Society.

Figure 118. Courtesy of The American Precision Museum, Windsor, Vermont.

Figure 119. Courtesy of The American Precision Museum, Windsor, Vermont.

Figure 120. Courtesy of The American Precision Museum, Windsor, Vermont. Photograph by Frank J. Lather.

Figure 121. Courtesy of The American Precision Museum, Windsor, Vermont. Photograph by Frank J. Lather.

Figure 122. Courtesy of the Town of Plainfield, photograph by Jeffrey Nintzel.

Figure 123. Courtesy of Dartmouth College Library.

Figure 124. Courtesy of a Cornish Collection. Photograph by Frank J. Lather.

Figure 125. Courtesy of The Cornish Historical Society. Gift of Virginia Colby. Photograph by Frank J. Lather.

Figure 126. Courtesy of a Cornish Collection. Photograph by Frank J. Lather.

Figure 127. Courtesy of a Cornish Collection. Photograph by Frank J. Lather.

Figure 128. Courtesy of a Cornish Collection. Photograph by Frank J. Lather.

Figure 129. *Platt monograph,* p. 179. Photograph by Frank J. Lather.

Figure 130. *American Gardens,* plate 62, no. 1.

Figure 131. Reprinted from *Done in the Open,* Drawings by Frederick Remington, with an Introduction and verses by Owen Wister and Others (New York: P. F. Collier & Son, 1903), cover. Courtesy of a Cornish Collection. Photograph by Frank J. Lather.

Figure 132. Courtesy of Charlotte Brotman.

Figure 133. Courtesy of U.S. Department of the Interior, National Park Service, Saint-Gaudens National Historic Site, Cornish, N.H.

Figure 134. U.S. Department of the Interior, National Park Service, Saint-Gaudens National Historic Site, Cornish, NH. Courtesy of Allyn Cox.

Figure 135. Photographer unknown; copy in Virginia Colby, the Cornish Colony files, Cornish Historical Society.

Figure 136. Photograph by Virginia Colby, the Cornish Colony files, Cornish Historical Society.

Figure 137. Augustus Saint-Gaudens by Dorothy R. Perloff. Courtesy of The Cornish Historical Society. Gift of Virginia Colby.

Figure 138. Illustration from Homer Saint-Gaudens, "A Private Toboggan Slide," *Country Life in America,* 13 January 1908, pp. 312-313.

Figure 139. Illustration from Homer Saint-Gaudens, "A Private Toboggan Slide," *Country Life in America,* 13 January 1908, pp. 312-313.

Figure 140. Courtesy of U.S. Department of the Interior, National Park Service, Saint-Gaudens National Historic Site, Cornish, NH.

Figure 141. Courtesy of U.S. Department of the Interior, National Park Service, Saint-Gaudens

National Historic Site, Cornish, NH.

Figure 142. Courtesy of Virginia Colby, the Cornish Colony files, Cornish Historical Society.

Figure 143. Courtesy of U.S. Department of the Interior, National Park Service, Saint-Gaudens National Historic Site, Cornish, NH.

Figure 144. Courtesy of a Cornish Collection. Photograph by Frank J. Lather.

Figure 145. Courtesy of U.S. Department of the Interior, National Park Service, Saint-Gaudens National Historic Site, Cornish, NH.

Figure 146. Courtesy of U.S. Department of the Interior, National Park Service, Saint-Gaudens National Historic Site, Cornish, NH.

Figure 147. Courtesy of a Cornish Collection. Photograph by Frank J. Lather.

Figure 148. Courtesy of a Cornish Collection. Photograph by Frank J. Lather.

Figure 149. Reprinted from Ernest Harold Baynes, *Polaris: The Story of an Eskimo Dog* (New York: Macmillan, 1922), p. 85. Courtesy of a Cornish Collection.

Figure 150. Courtesy of a Cornish Collection. Photograph by Frank J. Lather.

Figure 151. Louis Evan Shipman, *Predicaments,* illustrated by C. D. Gibson and T. K. Hanna, Jr. (New York: Life Publishing Company, 1899). Courtesy of a Cornish Collection. Photograph by Frank J. Lather.

Figure 152. Courtesy of Dartmouth College Library.

Figure 153. Courtesy of Division of Rare and Manuscript Collections, Cornell University Library.

Figure 154. Photograph by Frank J. Lather.

Figure 155. Photograph by Frank J. Lather.

Figure 156. Courtesy of the Hirshhorn Museum and Sculpture Garden, Smithsonian Institution, gift of Joseph H. Hirshhorn, 1972.

Figure 157. Courtesy of a Cornish Collection. Photograph by Frank J. Lather.

Figure 158. Courtesy of a private collection. Photograph by Frank J. Lather.

Figure 159. Courtesy of Mrs. Jay Russell and U.S. Department of the Interior, National Park Service, Saint-Gaudens National Historic Site, Cornish, NH.

Figure 160. Courtesy of William Postar.

Figure 161. Courtesy of Jacqueline Walker Smith.

Figure 162. Courtesy of Mrs. Stephen Tracy.

Figure 163. Courtesy of U.S. Department of the Interior, National Park Service, Saint-Gaudens National Historic Site, Cornish, NH.

Figure 164. Courtesy of Woodrow Wilson House/National Trust, Washington, DC.

Figure 165. Courtesy of a Cornish Collection. Photograph by Frank J. Lather.

Figure 166. Courtesy of a Cornish Collection. Photograph by Frank J. Lather.

Figure 167. Courtesy of Dartmouth College Library.

Figure 168. Courtesy of U.S. Department of the Interior, National Park Service, Saint-Gaudens National Historic Site, Cornish, NH.

Figure 169. Courtesy of The Dorros Collection.

Figure 170. Courtesy of U.S. Department of the Interior, National Park Service, Saint-Gaudens National Historic Site, Cornish, NH. photograph by Jeffrey Nintzel.

Figure 171. Illustration from Ernest Peixotto, *A Revolutionary Pilgrimage* (New York: Scribner's, 1917), p. 29. Courtesy of a Cornish Collection. Photograph by Frank J. Lather.

Figure 172. Courtesy of Bertha Perkins Frothingham and Louise Perkins King.

Figure 173. Courtesy of a Cornish Collection. Photograph by Frank J. Lather.

Color insert

Figure 1c. Courtesy of a private collection. Photograph by Frank J. Lather.

Figure 2c. Courtesy of U.S. Department of the Interior, National Park Service, Saint-Gaudens National Historic Site, Cornish, NH.

Figure 3c. Courtesy of Woodrow Wilson House/National Trust, Washington, DC.

Figure 4c. Courtesy of the Windsor Public Library, Windsor, Vermont. Photograph by Frank J. Lather.

Figure 5c. Courtesy of Virginia Colby.

Figure 6c. Courtesy of a Cornish Collection. Photograph by Frank J. Lather.

Figure 7c. Courtesy of a Cornish Collection. Photograph by Frank J. Lather.

Figure 8c. Courtesy of a Cornish Collection. Photograph by Frank J. Lather.

Figure 9c. Courtesy of the Dorros Collection.

Figure 10c. Courtesy of U.S. Department of the Interior, National Park Service, Saint-Gaudens National Historic Site, Cornish, NH.

INDEX

(Bold page numbers keynote illustration.)

FOOTPRINTS OF THE PAST

Dust jacket and text designed by Barbara Homeyer

Text composed by Barbara Homeyer in Minion

Index prepared by Nancy Norwalk

Illustrations researched and edited by Carrie Brown, PhD

Production:

Matt Bucy

Marge Grace

Barbara Homeyer

Nancy Norwalk

Gay Palazzo

Virginia Reed Colby was born in Chattanooga, Tennessee, in 1921 and grew up in Connecticut. In 1948 she married Herbert P. Reed of Milford, Connecticut. The couple purchased "White Swan Farm" on Saint-Gaudens Road in Cornish in 1958. After her first husband died in 1976, she married Stanley W. Colby, who died in 1986.

Virginia Colby's love of Cornish and its past led to her being the first president of the Cornish Historical Society. The fledgling organization was brought into existence by her ceaseless activities that ranged from unearthing the town's official faded and mildewed records, then making sure they were indexed and microfilmed; to disseminating inventories and indices of the town's vital statistics; to supervising the republication of several town histories and historical documents; to acquiring memorabilia for the Society's collection and displaying them for all to see; to seeking support to repair, preserve, and maintain the town's four covered bridges; to clipping indefatigably, and then storing, anything pertaining to Cornish so that future historians would have documentary evidence with which to work; and finally to responding eagerly to any request to learn more about Cornish's past. Her efforts were rewarded in part by a national award to the Cornish Historical Society from the American Association for State and Local History.

Her devotion to Cornish was matched by her admiration of Maxfield Parrish. From her research and publication of *In the Beginning* and an article in *The Magazine Antiques,* we have a better idea of how Parrish saw the human form and how he and his father Stephen Parrish were interconnected. She constantly received requests for information and assistance about Maxfield Parrish—and, needless to say, she responded with gracious and informed replies.

Virginia Colby died in 1995. Publication of *Footprints of the Past* will be a reminder not only of her accomplishments as an historian but also of her unforgettable presence. It will evoke the spirit of someone whose personal warmth, demonstrated in her concern for each person as an individual, guided her every act. Never a mere dispenser of fact, Virginia Colby's humility, even self-effacement, in the midst of all her achievements is a model to all who knew her.

James B. Atkinson was born in Honolulu, Hawaii, in 1934. He came to Cornish, New Hampshire, in 1989 where he transferred his interest in the literature of the European Renaissance to the art of the American Renaissance.

He has taught English and Comparative Literature at Dartmouth College, Earlham College, and Rutgers University. He has translated Machiavelli's *The Prince* and was the translator and co-author of both *The Comedies of Machiavelli* and *Machiavelli and His Friends: Their Personal Correspondence.* He has also translated several books from the French and written on Montaigne and French Renaissance poetry.

Following in the footprints of Virginia Colby as president of the Cornish Historical Society, he continues to nurture his love for Cornish and his admiration of its contributions both to New Hampshire and to the nation.